AF361506

THE PEDAGOGY OF IMAGES

THE PEDAGOGY OF IMAGES

DEPICTING COMMUNISM FOR CHILDREN

Edited by Marina Balina and Serguei Alex. Oushakine

UNIVERSITY OF TORONTO PRESS
Toronto Buffalo London

ISBN 978-1-4875-0668-1 (cloth)   ISBN 978-1-4875-3466-0 (EPUB)
ISBN 978-1-4875-3465-3 (PDF)

Studies in Book and Print Culture

Library and Archives Canada Cataloguing in Publication

Title: The pedagogy of images : depicting communism for children / edited by
Marina Balina and Serguei Alex. Oushakine.
Names: Balina, Marina, editor. | Ushakin, S. (Sergeĭ), 1966– editor.
Description: Includes bibliographical references and index.
Identifiers: Canadiana (print) 20210139285 | Canadiana (ebook) 20210139331 |
ISBN 9781487506681 (cloth) | ISBN 9781487534660 (EPUB) | ISBN 9781487534653 (PDF)
Subjects: LCSH: Children's literature, Soviet – History and criticism. | LCSH: Illustrated children's
books – Soviet Union. | LCSH: Literacy – Political aspects – Soviet Union. | LCSH:
Education – Political aspects – Soviet Union. | LCSH: Avant-garde (Aesthetics) –
Soviet Union. | LCSH: Communism in literature. | LCSH: Propaganda, Soviet.
Classification: LCC PG3190.P43 2021 | DDC 891.709/9282–dc23

Page ii illustration: Sasha Hedges Steinberg

The book has been published with the assistance of the Program in Russian, East European and
Eurasian Studies of the Princeton Institute for International and Regional Studies at Princeton
University, The Cotsen Children's Library at Princeton University Library, and the Artistic/
Scholarly Development grant provided by the Illinois Wesleyan University.

University of Toronto Press acknowledges the financial assistance to its publishing
program of the Canada Council for the Arts and the Ontario Arts Council, an agency
of the Government of Ontario.

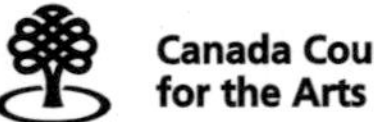

CONTENTS

ILLUSTRATIONS

Illustrations

ACKNOWLEDGMENTS

This edited volume is a result of a lengthy and complex collaboration aimed at exploring the proliferation of new visual media in early Soviet Russia. The Cotsen Children's Library at Princeton University, a host of an incredible collection of illustrated children's books from the Soviet Union, became the foundational resource for our attempts to understand how writers and artists of the 1920s and 1930s translated Communism into idioms and images accessible to children. Andrea Immel, the curator of the Cotsen Library, and Thomas Keenan, the Slavic East European and Eurasian Studies Librarian at Princeton, were highly instrumental in making these books digitally available, first to the research group, and later to the world. Without their support and contribution, the project would have never taken off the ground.

In 2015–17, Thomas Keenan, Serguei Oushakine, as director of the Program in Russian, East European, and Eurasian Studies at Princeton's Institute for International and Regional Studies, and Katherine M.H. Reischl, assistant professor at the Department of Slavic Languages and Literatures organized a series of seminars on the pedagogy of images. Eventually, these seminars found their presence online: the web-resource "The Pedagogy of Images: Depicting Communism for Children" (https://PedagogyOfImages.princeton.edu) served as a springboard for this volume.

This series has evolved over the course of its development. Starting as an experimental attempt to navigate the process of amalgamation of text and image within the boundaries of illustrated books for Soviet children, it quickly grew into a much larger investigation of the role of optics in the production of the first Soviet generation of readers, writers, artists, publishers, and pedagogues. We are thankful to the participants of the workshops, who were brave enough to embrace the unknown and to play along. We are grateful to Robert Bird, Christina Kiaer, Nariman Skakov, Maria Starkova-Vindman, Dmitry Bykov, Elena Fratto, Molly Brunson, and Eugene Ostashevsky, who all helped us navigate this path by sharing their expertise, by questioning our frameworks, and by suggesting alternatives.

From its beginning, *The Pedagogy of Images* was envisioned as an intergenerational and interdisciplinary project. The participation of Tyler Adkins, Massimo Balloni, Siarhei Biareishyk, Irina Denischenko Marlow Davis, Gabriella A. Ferrari, Philip Gleissner, Bradley Gorski, Pavel Khazanov, Natalia Klimova, Abigail Kret, Ksenia Nouril, Maya Vinokour, Emily Wang, and Susanna Weygandt in the initial symposium in 2015 helped to turn a rather amorphous intellectual endeavour into a vibrant and robust scholarly exchange. Without their inquisitive minds, fresh eyes, and boundless energy, this project would not have moved beyond the symposium stage.

We also want to thank the participants of the 2017 symposium: Marina Alexandrova, Meghanne Barker, Carlotta Chenoweth, Polina Dimova, Cécile Pichon-Bonin, Silja Pitkänen, Zdenko Mandušić, and Laura Todd. Their enthusiasm and passion for Soviet children's literature helped us see a bigger and brighter future for the pedagogy of images.

All these exchanges and debates were possible because of generous support from a network of institutions at Princeton University: the Institute for International and Regional Studies; the Program in Russian, East European, and Eurasian Studies; the Council of the Humanities; the Princeton University Library; the Cotsen Children's Library; the Department of Slavic Languages and Literatures; the Center for Collaborative History; and the University Center for Human Values. Carole Frantzen, with her amazing administrative skills, brought all these institutional contributions and support together. She was the true engine of this project.

Avram Brown and Tomi Haxhi were tremendous help for us in preparing this volume for publication with dedication and skill. We have also benefited greatly from the encouraging comments and useful suggestions of the two anonymous peer reviewers.

We are grateful to Sasha Hedges Steinberg for unorthodox visual ideas and suggestions: the cover of the book is based on the poster that Sasha created for one of our workshops.

Working with images might be exciting; but this excitement has its own price. We are lucky to have had the support of Princeton's Program in Russian, East European, and Eurasian Studies at the Institute for International and Regional Studies and the Cotsen Children's Library, which covered most of the costs associated with the reproduction of images in this book. We are also deeply thankful to the Illinois Wesleyan University, which covered the costs of editing. Finally, we would like to thank Mark Thompson from the University of Toronto Press for shepherding this project through its various stages. We are very grateful to Christine Robertson, our University of Toronto Press managing editor, for her careful and thorough work on this volume.

Ultimately, we are indebted to the early Soviet artists, writers, and designers of the 1920s and 1930s; the outburst of their immense creativity continues to fascinate, motivate, and inspire. This collection is a scholarly tribute to their talent, and a sign of remembrance of their – often tragic – lives.

THE PEDAGOGY OF IMAGES

introduction

PRIMERS IN SOVIET MODERNITY: DEPICTING COMMUNISM FOR CHILDREN IN EARLY SOVIET RUSSIA

SERGUEI ALEX. OUSHAKINE AND MARINA BALINA

The October Revolution of 1917 was many things. It radically altered the former Russian Empire's political, legal, and social landscape; it precipitated the nationalization of the economy; and it triggered fundamental cultural shifts. To an extent perhaps unmatched by any other revolt in history, the revolution was staged and carried out "in the name of the masses," eventually generating a variety of mass phenomena of unprecedented scale and breadth: from mass employment (*massovaia zaniatost'*) to the mass consolidation of resources by the state; from a mass health care system (*massovoe zdravookhranenie*) to mass housing (*massovoe zhilishche*); from mass education (*massovoe obrazovanie*) to mass enthusiasm – and mass terror.

A striving for mass – or universal – literacy was also a major feature of the revolution. In 1921, Lenin succinctly summarized the role and importance of literacy in the Soviet state, coining a phrase that would become a popular slogan for the next seventy years: "An illiterate person stands outside politics." Speaking to the Congress of Departments of Political Enlightenment (*politicheskoe prosveshchenie*), Lenin expanded his thought: the illiterate person, he insisted, "must first learn his ABCs. There can be no politics without that; otherwise, there are just rumors, gossip, fairy-tales and prejudices."[1] Literacy, then, was politicized, and elevated to the status of a major tool for creating a new communist state and a new, Soviet person (*chelovek*).

Lenin's talk was aimed at practitioners of "mass agitational work," but his main message – *there is no enlightenment without politics, nor politics without enlightenment* – could easily have been applied to the instructional work conducted by Soviet Departments of Enlightenment.[2] In 1924, *Igra i trud* (*Play and Work*), a reading manual for pre-school and elementary-school children, graphically emphasized the enduring sociopolitical importance of literacy, suggesting an aspirational model for those who could not yet read. Two pictures present the living conditions of workers' families before and after the revolution (fig. 0.1). A dark, cramped basement is contrasted with

0.1. "Workers' living conditions before and after," in K. Sokolov, ed., *Igra i trud*, 10th ed. (Moscow: Gosizdat, 1930), 18.

a brightly lit (enlightened?) room where a family is seated around the dinner table. In the latter, the room is lit with an electric bulb rather than a candle; instead of a disconsolate peasant mother with a child, a modern woman is listening to the radio on her headphones. Amid radical transformations, one thing alone has remained constant: as before, the father is still reading his newspaper – the main source, presumably, of all these changes.

Naturally, this broad understanding of literacy and reading as key institutions of sociopolitical transformation brought with it a heightened emphasis on the importance of literature. Nikolai Chuzhak, one of the leading voices of the *Proletkult* (proletarian culture) movement, proposed in 1928 that literature be approached from the standpoint of its "'methods of treatment' [*priemy obrabotki*] of human and social material."[3] Blurring the distinction between the organization of literary material and the social organization of people, Chuzhak saw mass literature and art as not just tools for building a new life, but also as a process of "life-building" (*zhiznestroenie*) itself.[4]

In the light of Lenin's dictum on the political significance of literacy, Chuzhak's purposeful conflation of literature and life and his emphasis on the active and activating impact of literature help clarify why the Soviet state, even in its impoverished and parlous condition after the First World War, revolution, and civil war, would invest so much energy and so many resources in creating, cultivating, shaping, and, of course, controlling the field of literary production. Within two decades, proper Soviet writers and readers were shaped by newly created institutions.[5] Mass newspapers and magazines were launched.[6] Libraries and reading clubs for workers and peasants were built, and a system of criticism, oversight, and censorship was in place.[7]

It would be easy to read these efforts solely as elements of a wide-scale campaign to create what Peter Kenez a few decades ago termed a "propaganda state."[8] But reducing the Soviet version of "political enlightenment" to strategically exercised brainwashing would be to endow early Soviet culture practitioners with an utterly anachronistic organizational capability and political foresight. Available public documents from the period convincingly demonstrate that, until the mid-1930s, the only thing certain about Soviet culture was the profound lack of certainty as to what it was and what it should be. Like the communist state itself, the state ideological apparatuses had to be created from scratch, without any templates or guidelines to rely on.

The chapters in this volume seek to move beyond the traditional analytical and ethnographic privileging of institutions of power so glaring in Cold War–era studies of early Soviet society and culture. Instead, this volume contributes to the growing body of scholarship that approaches Soviet history as an example of a competing, alternative, or communist modernity.[9] Without neglecting the brutality and militancy with which communist ideas and projects were often implemented in post-revolutionary Russia, this collection analyses how a historically specific – Soviet – context shaped the vision of practices and trends that were themselves not specifically Soviet, whether mass electrification, the popularization of cinema, or industrialization. By somewhat "provincializing" the epistemological function of power, the contributors shift their focus from examples of direct repression and violence to the capillary presence of power in various practices of expression and narration. This methodological shift is instrumental for exposing the persistent and laborious work of translation – the "methods of treatment," indeed – that transformed abstract communist ideas into institutions and manuals, narrative clichés and visual formulas, ritualized acts and behavioural patterns.[10]

The viewpoint from which this collection approaches Soviet modernity is decidedly non-canonical. Its main sources are illustrated books produced for the first Soviet generation of children in the 1920s and 1930s. Scholars of modernity tend to ignore these books, even as this literature offers a unique and, we argue, crucially important venue for understanding how early Soviet society gradually came to terms with itself and learned to tell its own, Soviet, story. In a sense, early Soviet books for children were the ABCs of the Soviet enlightenment. They were manuals for reading, primers on writing and guides for storytelling that helped the young reader enter the field of politics by entering the field of literature. Children's literature provided the basic vocabulary and grammar for understanding new, post-revolutionary realities;

but it also taught young readers how to perceive modern things, events, and processes as communist. Simply put, this volume traces the formation of a mass modern readership just as much as it tracks the creation of the communist-inflected visual and narrative conventions that these readers were supposed to appropriate.

Primers of Soviet modernity did not appear overnight; their creation was neither quick nor easy. A social institution and an artistic object at the same time, the Soviet children's book found itself at the crossroads of multiple trends and fields in the 1920s. In 1928, Iakov Meksin, an important popularizer of children's literature (and the founder of the first Museum of Children's Literature in Moscow in 1934), observed that Soviet children's literature was under a permanent stress-test of "friendly fire" coming from experts in "the arts, ideology, pedagogy, education [*pedologiia*], publishing, and commerce."[11] The main reasons for such constant evaluations from different areas were simple. Most fundamentally, affordable children's literature for a mass readership did not exist before the revolution, and the criteria for its success (or failure) were yet to be articulated and agreed upon.[12] Institutionally, the increased visibility (and vulnerability) of children's literature went hand in hand with the growing number of educational and ideological organizations eager to ensure that "children's literature would reach every school, and every worker's and peasant's family," as Zlata Lilina, a leading expert on children's literature at the time, put it.[13] By 1928, this literature's potential consumers numbered thirty-two million – the USSR had more children than, for instance, the *total* populations of Spain and Portugal combined – and the sheer size of the target audience made children's literature a major cultural and political phenomenon.[14]

Without established standards and traditions, the new type of literature developed initially through trial and error. Undoubtedly, post-revolutionary children's literature was supposed to act as "a counterbalance to the old, pre-revolutionary literature."[15] It was just as obvious that the new genre should provide working-class youngsters with "clearly narrated, emotional, artistic, and literary" books.[16] It was the actual *content* of these categories that remained obscure. It took almost two decades of heated debates among educators, publishers, writers, and artists to decide what precisely should count as "outdated" and "pre-revolutionary," or what "clearly narrated" meant. In a 1931 article revealingly titled "What Should We Aim Our Fire At?" ("Kuda napravit' ogon'"), Izrail Razin, the chair of the children's literature section of the Association of State Book and Magazine Publishers (OGIZ), complained that, when it came to books for children, "we are groping along, feeling our way [*rabotaem naoshchup'*] ... We still have no Marxist theory of children's literature."[17] Two years later, in 1933, Maxim Gorky, at the time the Soviet Union's most influential writer, lamented in *Pravda*:

> We teach children to read when they are seven or eight years old ... Every year, we see the arrival of hundreds of thousands of new readers, but there are no books for them ... "No books." These words mean that there are not enough copies of those two dozen genuinely

successful books that we've managed to produce during the last fifteen years [since the revolution]. But also, this means that we have not created, we have not written children's books that could facilitate young readers' interest in and taste for learning … It is critical and necessary to create for our children a new, Soviet, socialist, scientific and popular, and artistically attractive book.[18]

Quite a few publishers and writers opted to "feel their way" by resorting to artistic recycling. The results were often abysmal. In some cases, old novels for and about children were "updated," with stories about pre-revolutionary life mechanically transposed into new, post-revolutionary settings.[19] Other forms of "modernization" were cruder still. For instance, one post-revolutionary version of Charles Dickens's *Oliver Twist* drastically shortened the novel: paying no heed to the composition's internal coherence, the publisher cut everything but the episodes depicting the horrors of orphanages and the exploitation of children.[20] Yet many more authors, artists, and publishers preferred to experiment with new formats, plots, iconography, and even fonts. This segment of children's literature in general, and children's *illustrated* literature in particular, quickly evolved into what Meksin called "a laboratory for experiments that many might deem too risky."[21] The lack of any tradition to build on was treated as a productive challenge. It unleashed artistic creativity and typographic imagination, producing what would later be known as the "golden age" of Soviet children's books.[22]

It is precisely this dynamic state of children's literature in the 1920s and 1930s that makes it so valuable and interesting for scholars of Soviet culture and Soviet modernity. Oscillating between the retrospective "modernization" of old plots and traditions and the avant-garde commitment to creating a truly new, *modern*, book, this form of literature engendered a vibrant field with competing and contradictory intentions, assumptions, and outcomes. Children's literature became a primary outlet for both artistic innovation and stale propaganda, for imaginative design and opportunistic hackwork.[23] Contemporary scholarship on Soviet children's literature, however, tends to homogenize this field of artistic and literary production by foregrounding and isolating its most creative aspects. For example, Marietta Chudakova, a vocal and opinionated scholar of Soviet literature, describes – not without a certain sentimentalization – the early stages of children's literature as a "gulp of freedom."[24] Other scholars have gone so far as to present children's literature as a "safe heaven" for creators,[25] a space in which a writer or illustrator could shut themselves away from revolutionary dictates. For Irina Arzamastseva, another literary scholar from Russia, early Soviet children's literature was a refuge for supporters of the less radical *February* Revolution of 1917: "Having retreated into children's libraries and publishing houses as if into a new underground, [liberals] worked in Soviet institutions. While fulfilling the state's ideological demand [*zakaz*], they managed, to the extent possible, to insert their personal thoughts and moods into their work."[26]

Appealing as this "view from the underground" might be, it is rather one-sided and romantic. As this volume shows, from its originary stage, Soviet children's literature was conceived as an ideological apparatus (among several) of the state.[27] In many respects, children's literature introduced the rules and modes of literary production that would later constitute the organizational basis of "grown-up" literature. By 1934, the year when Soviet literature was finally consolidated institutionally (under the auspices of the Union of Soviet Writers) and ideologically (within the framework of socialist realism),[28] literature for children had already established the aesthetic principles and institutional formats that enabled (and, to some extent, secured) its existence under conditions of increasing ideological pressure. In the remainder of this introduction, we will sketch the two main trends of this process, demonstrating how Soviet children's literature emerged as a distinct literary institution and as a set of coherent aesthetic principles.

Weaponizing Children's Literature

On 17 January 1918, *Pravda*, the main newspaper of the Bolsheviks, ran an article titled "Zabytoe oruzhie" ("A Forgotten Weapon") by L. Kormchii.[29] The article was symptomatic on many accounts. It was the first-known Soviet statement to call for the creation of a new – proletarian – literature for children. More crucially, the call was articulated by a representative of "old" – that is, pre-revolutionary – children's literature. Before the revolution, Kormchii, a writer of liberal orientation, had been a contributor to the magazine *Krasnye zori* (*Red Dawn*, 1904–12), becoming its last editor in 1912.

That *Pravda* would provide a platform for an author of less than revolutionary pedigree was hardly surprising: *new*, revolutionary, children's writers had yet to be discovered and cultivated. So, how did Kormchii envision the new literature for children? First and foremost, he assigned far more importance to the educational function than to artistry: books were expected to shape young readers' political views and ideological values. Kormchii was the first to insist on a class approach to children's literature. To avoid unwelcome influences, the pre-revolutionary heritage had to be meticulously reviewed and, if need be, purged. Developing the theme declared in the title of his article, Kormchii envisioned the new children's literature in military terms, as "a powerful weapon that must not be ceded to enemies," but seized from them and used to advance the cause of communism. "A Forgotten Weapon" was one of the earliest public documents to highlight the organizing role of the state in the process of supplying proper reading material. "It is the duty of the state," insisted the author, "to provide its children with a spiritual food that is not contaminated by harmful additives." Denouncing "bourgeois" children's literature as a tool for "bringing up slaves," Kormchii demanded that new literature be "freed" from the "poison, filth, and garbage" that the bourgeoisie supplied for its own children.[30]

0.2. Vera Ermolaeva, cover for Natan Vengrov's *Myshata* (Petrograd: Segodnia, 1918).

Kormchii's views were largely in tune with the policy being implemented at the time. On 27 October 1917, two days after the Bolshevik takeover, the new government issued its Decree on the Press, which significantly restricted the activity of "class-alien" (*klassovo chuzhdye*) publishers, newspapers, and magazines.[31] There was, however, still some room to manoeuvre. For example, in early 1918, the artist and writer Vera Ermolaeva (1893–1937) organized a private art cooperative called Segodnia (Today), which included iconic artists of the Russian avant-garde such as Natan Altman, Iurii Annenkov, and Nadezhda Liubavina. Together with writers such as Natan Vengrov, Mikhail Kuzmin, and Ivan Sokolov-Mikitov, they produced small-run editions of children's books, using a cheap linocut technique. In a situation where the art market was virtually non-existent, such cooperatives helped artists and writers survive in post-revolutionary Russia (fig. 0.2). Ermolaeva's cooperative lasted only until the fall of 1919, but her subsequent career revealed a pattern that would become characteristic for many artists. In the 1920s, she started working for prominent children's magazines such as *Chizh* (*The Siskin*) and *Ezh* (*The Hedgehog*), and later authored several publications for Detgiz, a state publishing house specializing exclusively in children's literature.[32]

In 1919, upon the establishment of Gosizdat, the state publishing house with oversight of the output of every publisher in the country, the Soviet government began a gradual consolidation of book production. Private presses continued to exist until the late 1920s, but they functioned within tightening ideological and institutional limits.[33] Gosizdat had the authority to register and issue permits for the publication of books and magazines (including those for children). More significantly, however – especially in a country ravaged by civil war and isolated internationally – this state agency also controlled the distribution of paper and printing facilities.

Among the most successful and important projects set up by Gosizdat was its special children's division (*detskaia sektsiia*) in Leningrad. This was headed by Samuil Marshak (1887–1964). Unlike Kormchii, Marshak was a "new man" in children's literature. A successful author of poems for children, he was also a talented organizer and editor. Projects headed by Marshak managed to bring together diverse authors of children's literature, including Boris Zhitkov, Evgenii Shvarts, Leonid Panteleev, Vitalii Bianki, and Evgenii Charushin. His publishing program focused primarily on popular-science literature for young readers. As he explained, "children expect help from their literature, they expect encouragement and scientific and everyday facts that would affirm in them a new, still-forming worldview."[34]

Along with popular-science works, Marshak introduced a series of "cheerful" (*veselye*) books, a modern analogue of playful folk poetry and ludic folklore. Such publications hardly meant the rejection of the didactic goals of children's literature so emphasized in Kormchii's article. Literature for young readers should be educational, Marshak maintained, but its didactic function was no excuse for inferior aesthetic or entertainment quality. Describing Marshak's publishing projects, the Russian literary scholar Mikhail Gasparov emphasizes the emergence of a new type of reader, the target audience of these primers for a new life:

> Marshak addressed a young reader that Russian children's literature had never seen before: the "child with no room of its own" [*deti bez detskoi* – lit., "children without a nursery"]. These readers were not children from rich families, taught how to live by a nanny or governess – there were none of those left after the revolution. Nor were they proletarian children, schooled in life by life itself – those would not be able to afford the colourful little books of the publishing house Raduga that brought out Marshak's works.
>
> This was a middle social stratum. There were many such children, and during the years of revolution and civil war their numbers grew. They had been cast into a very complex and turbulent life without any preparation for it. These books were supposed to help them get oriented in this life.[35]

Another canonical figure of Soviet children's literature who significantly influenced its institutional development from its very inception was Marshak's close

0.3. A spread by Alexei Radakov in *Elka* portrays "Animals for good kids" and "Animals for bad kids." *Elka*, edited by Alexander Benois and Kornei Chukovsky (Petrograd: Parus 1918).

colleague Kornei Chukovsky (1882–1969). A folklore enthusiast, Chukovsky was also an expert in foreign, primarily English, children's poetry. Before the revolution, he had authored a few publications on child psychology and language acquisition. He had some publishing experience as well, having run the children's department of the private publishing house Parus (the Sail) from 1916 until its closure in 1918. For this press, Chukovsky edited a collection of stories titled *Elka* (*The Fir Tree*), said to be the first significant publication for children after the October Revolution (fig. 0.3).[36]

In addition to being a prolific writer, translator, and editor, Chukovsky also ran a children's literature studio and a fiction-translation workshop in Petrograd in the 1920s. He would eventually summarize his conception of and experience writing for children in a 1929 article called "Trinadtsat' zapovedei dlia detskikh poetov" (Thirteen Commandments for Children's Poets).[37] These "commandments" championed the traditions of the Russian avant-garde, privileging the formal aspects of poetry. In verses for children, explains Chukovsky, melodic quality and rhythm should generate the effect of a quick dance tune, a "jig" (*pliaska*), while the graphic aspect of the verses should appeal to the imagistic tendencies of children's perception.

Together with Marshak, in 1921 Chukovsky initiated the creation of Raduga (Rainbow), a private publishing house in Petrograd specializing in children's literature. By far the most innovative producer of children's literature to appear in the whole Soviet period, Raduga experimented with formats and typography, seeking to create, or synthesize, the sort of book that could productively engage both textual and visual components. Headed by Lev Kliachko, over the course of its existence Raduga put out about 400 titles with illustrations that became iconic representations of early Soviet book design.[38] Raduga did not survive the gradual nationalization of the publishing industry, and was closed in 1930. Adding insult to injury, the People's Commissariat of Enlightenment specified in its shutdown decision that the apolitical books published by Raduga were "too removed from the pressing issues of contemporary life."[39]

By 1933, the children's literature publishing infrastructure had acquired the administrative outline that would largely remain in place until the end of the Soviet period. From that time on, the two major state presses – Molodaia gvardiia (Young Guard) and Detgiz (the children's literature state publisher) – basically monopolized the production of all children's literature in the country. The following figures express well the rapid growth of the children's publishing sector. In 1921, at the end of the civil war, the book industry hit its lowest point, releasing a paltry 33 book titles for children. But the following year, the number of titles published in this category reached 200. A crucial breakthrough came in 1924: with 558 titles, the industry finally superseded pre-revolutionary levels (approximately 400 titles), entering a period of mass production of cheap books with a standard circulation of 5,000–10,000 copies. In 1926, there were 936 titles; in 1929, over 1,500.[40] By 1936, Detgiz produced 40 million copies of books and magazines for children annually.[41]

The reorganization of the publishing industry was accompanied by a series of institutional and administrative decisions aimed at establishing children's literature as a distinctive *literary* field. In the first post-revolutionary decades, the development of children's literature was controlled primarily by the People's Commissariat of Enlightenment (headed by Anatoly Lunacharsky), which in the 1920s held a series of conferences and meetings to identify and consolidate the work of experts on children's literature. The first Conference of Children's Librarians took place in Moscow in March 1925; a year later, in May 1926, came the All-Russian Conference on Educational and Children's Books.

In 1928, with the beginning of the first Five-Year Plan, the Communist Party issued a pivotal resolution on improving young-adult and children's media.[42] Initially, party documents approached the new literature for youth from workers' and peasant families as a prophylactic tool, as a shield called upon to distance and protect. In "promoting the communist education of the young masses," the new literature was "to withstand the growing influence of tabloid publications."[43] Gradually, documents became more and more antagonistic, sketching elaborate action plans for a major assault on the old literature, just as Kormchii had envisioned in 1918. In a string of decisions adopted throughout the 1920s, the party's Central Committee outlined a set of measures meant to finally generate a children's literature ("under the close control and guidance of the party") capable of closely attending to the issues of "class, internationalist, and labor education."[44]

"Cleansing Libraries of Worthless Trash"

Until children's literature was transferred in 1931 to the jurisdiction of the Central Committee of the League of Young Communists (Komsomol), the field was closely supervised by the Commissariat of Enlightenment, which oversaw publishing houses, libraries, museums, and theatres, along with children's literature. Paradoxically, this extensive scope of the commissariat's controlling function helped situate children's literature at the productive intersection of multiple administrative and creative networks. Nadezhda Krupskaia (1869–1939), Lenin's wife and later widow, was a crucial figure in this regard, being second-in-command at the commissariat and simultaneously in charge of the Main State Committee for Political Enlightenment (Glavpolitprosvet).

As with publishing, most of the initial work on the institutionalization of children's literature was inspired by a determination to "counteract pre-revolutionary literature."[45] In practical terms, this often meant purging library collections of books deemed no longer acceptable, or, as Krupskaia herself put it, "cleansing libraries of worthless trash."[46] Whole categories and genres were removed from library shelves and schools. Beginning in 1924, the fairy tale disappeared from children's reading material, adventure and historical literature was reduced to a minimum, and the list of "acceptable" foreign authors was significantly curtailed.[47] The flipside of this purging and censorship was that the state had to supply *new* books for reading, and vocal demands for a new kind of literature generated a network of academic institutions tasked with setting policy guidelines for producing new, politically acceptable, publications.

The first generation of Soviet children's literature specialists consisted mainly of party functionaries and educators interested in very particular aspects of literature. In their criticism, party officials usually prioritized the class approach: children's literature as a whole was supposed to reflect the interests of working-class children.[48] For their part, Soviet educators perceived children's books primarily as textbooks, emphasizing developmental value and social usefulness.[49] Marshak complained to Maxim Gorky about this didactic pragmatism: "Our work is greatly hindered by the attitude of pedagogues (and these, unfortunately, are virtually the only critics and reviewers of children's literature we have). They almost always evaluate a work solely from a thematic standpoint: what was the author trying to say?"[50] In the 1920s, GUS, the State Academic Council, a special section of the Commissariat of Enlightenment, brought together experts in the field of children's reading who finally issued a set of criteria for evaluating children's publications.[51] According to these "Basic Requirements for Children's Books," the new children's book had to demonstrate "political significance, some artistic elements, and pedagogical value."[52]

Along with policy institutions, the state set up new think tanks and research units. In 1920, the Commissariat of Enlightenment founded the Institute for Children's Reading (Institut detskogo chteniia), headed by Anna Pokrovskaia. This institute's goal was to assemble a specialized library for children and adults; it was also expected to

0.4. "The best gift," an illustration from *Zadushevnoe slovo*, no. 9 (1885).

conduct ethnographic and sociological studies of children's reading practices (mostly focusing on groups with low literacy levels). Working closely with teachers, the institute held conferences, conducted regular surveys of young readers, and organized discussions of new publications for children. In particular, it explored the role and importance of the visual dimension of children's literature, its aesthetic and affective impact on the young reader. The results of the institute's research proved controversial. Despite the preferences of Soviet pedagogues, the Soviet child still preferred sentimental stories and fairy tales to informative but boring books about the people's economy.

The Institute for Children's Reading lasted until 1923; it was then reorganized as a department of the Institute for Methods of Extracurricular Work, and was finally shut down in 1930 as superfluous (its staff was accused of focusing on research "of little relevance to the practice of communist upbringing").[53] In its place, the Central Committee of the Komsomol in 1932 established the critical-bibliographic journal *Detskaia literatura* (*Children's Literature*), whose mission was to "assist the implementation of the party's program in the field of literature."[54] The journal gathered leading critics and scholars of children's literature, offering a platform for multiple discussions and debates. Published (with some breaks) throughout the Soviet period, *Detskaia literatura* gradually faded away in the 1990s, after the disappearance of the USSR itself.

Workable Models

Publishing houses, libraries, and research and policy institutions provided the field of children's literature with crucial material, political, and scientific support. In turn, magazines and journals offered mobile and interactive platforms for communication between children, writers, politicians, publishers, and educators. These included, for a time, a few holdovers from the pre-revolutionary period. The venerable children's magazine *Zadushevnoe slovo* (*A Heartfelt Word*), which was started in 1876 (fig. 0.4), did not suvived the changes: it was closed in 1917. Yet some pre-revolutionary magazines, such as *Zhavoronok* (*The Lark*, 1913–22) (fig. 0.5), *Iunaia Rossiia* (*Young Russia*, 1906–18), and *Maiak* (*The Lighthouse*, 1909–18) (fig. 0.6) continued to exist for some time. Alexander Fedorov-Davydov – famous

0.5. M. Grinbal's illustration for the cover of *Zhavoronok*, no. 5 (1916). The caption under the image says, "And they say that school years are the happiest years ever!"

for his pre-revolutionary translations of collections of fairy tales by the Grimm brothers and Hans Christian Andersen – managed to edit until 1920 his *Svetliachok* (*The Firefly*), a magazine for younger children that was founded in 1902 (fig. 0.7).[55]

Gradually, these survivors were ousted by magazines of a new type. The history of Soviet-era children's periodicals begins in 1919 with the establishment of *Severnoe siianie* (*Northern Lights*), a children's magazine sponsored by the People's Commissariat of Enlightenment. The journal appeared to follow the general trajectory of the program outlined in Kormchii's *Pravda* article, although not without some modification. Maxim Gorky, the most influential and authoritative voice in the creation of the new Soviet literature, was one of the magazine's founders. In his preface to the first issue, Gorky wrote: "Through this periodical, we attempt to inculcate in our children the spirit of activity; we will foster their interest and respect for the power of the mind, for the curiosity of science, as well as for the great educational task of the arts – for all those aspects of human activity that strengthen and ennoble a person."[56] Prioritizing the educational agenda, Gorky aimed at a new reader, the proletarian child, who also became the main character of stories published in this journal. The fiction in *Northern Lights* focused on the hard living conditions of working-class children in Imperial Russia (fig. 0.8). Essays on political education

0.6. Cover of *Maiak*, no.16 (1916). The magazine existed from 1909 to 1918 and was aimed at secondary school–aged children. Published by Ivan Gorbunov-Posadov, a follower of Leo Tolstoy, it was famous for its democratic orientation.

0.7. Cover of *Svetliachok* no. 9 (1911). The caption is "A shipwreck." Designed for small children, this magazine was published from 1902 to 1918 by a prolific children's writer, Alexander Fedorod-Davydov.

0.8. In an illustration by M. Severnyi for V. Mai's poem "Captured Castles," a father draws the attention of his son to the Winter Palace in pre-revolutionary St. Petersburg, the residence of the tsar's family. An image on the next page depicts the prison "for the common people," which is located across the river from the Winter Palace. *Severnoe siianie*, nos. 10–12 (1919): 5.

(e.g., "What the Revolutionary Masses Can Do") were interspersed with texts offering diverse information on science and history in a section appropriately titled "The Curious Readers' Club" (Klub liuboznatel'nykh). Anti-religious education was also quite prominent: Gorky himself contributed to this trend with the first Soviet-era proletarian fairy tale "Iashka," which resolutely denied the existence of God. *Northern Lights* offered a basic organizational structure that subsequent Soviet children's periodicals would tweak in various ways. Some would foreground literary texts (e.g., *Novyi Robinzon* [*The New Robinson*]); others would prioritize political education (e.g., *Baraban* [*The Drum*] and *Pioner* [*Pioneer*].)

Iunye tovarishchi (*Young Comrades*, 1922), and *Baraban* (1923–6) (fig. 0.9) were among the first periodicals to be directly associated with the development of the Pioneer organization. Established in 1922 in Moscow, the first Pioneer troop was initially seen as an updated version of the Scout movement. Interestingly enough, the Soviet authorities seemed to have no particular concerns about this "bourgeois" form of organizing children. Instead, closely replicating the logic of Kormchii, Krupskaia suggested repurposing this useful bourgeois weapon: "Even as the goals of the Boy Scouts are inimical to us, their methods could be highly, highly suitable [*ves'ma i ves'ma priemlemye*], and may be duly made use of."[57]

Like new books for children, new Pioneer magazines followed the same path of trial and error. Mikhail Stremiakov, the editor-in-chief of *The Drum* and the first leader of the first Pioneer troop in Soviet Russia, recalled that the editorial board of his magazine included "kids who did not have the slightest inkling of how to publish such magazines."[58] An amateur publication with low production values, *The Drum* nonetheless managed to offer a crucial basis for what would later develop into the movement of school-aged "Pioneer correspondents" (*PiKory*) – that is, young journalists writing for their own magazine. The magazine's accessibility, coupled with the state's patronage of children's literary groups, generated an army of young correspondents, even producing along the way its own celebrity writers, who publicly enjoyed their fifteen minutes of fame.[59]

Baraban, however, fell victim to its own popularity: "The number of children who wrote had multiplied to such a degree that the low quality of the literary 'product' and the dubious moral state of the authors themselves were finally publicly condemned."[60] Nevertheless, *Baraban*'s organizational model flourished: its methods of treating literary materials were emulated and multiplied throughout the country. Using *Baraban* as their matrix, new magazines for children would similarly center on a core "sociopolitical" section, orbited by popular-science items, fiction, do-it-yourself instructions, charts, and templates.

Pioner, the main ideological magazine for Soviet children, exemplified the success of this publication model. Along with expected ideological essays and articles, it prominently featured the constructivist photography of Aleksandr Rodchenko, factographic essays by Sergei Tret'iakov, and high-quality fiction from leading Soviet

0.9. Cover of *Baraban*, no. 8 (1923). One of the very first politically oriented magazines for the Young Pioneers, *Baraban* was established in 1922 and absorbed by *Pioner* in 1926.

authors. For instance, Lev Kassil's *Konduit* (*The Conduct Book*), a novel popular with several generations of Soviet children, was initially published in *Pioneer* in 1926. (Its sequel, *Shvambraniia*, was also serialized in *Pioner* in 1931.) Founded in 1924, the magazine still exists today, albeit in a radically different form – as a non-political media outlet for young adults (figs. 0.10 and 0.11).

Two illustrated magazines specifically targeted younger children from two different class milieux. *Murzilka* (1924–present), named after a cute puppy, had a structure that was similar to *Baraban,* but it aimed at pre-school and elementary school children of workers (figs. 0.12 and 0.13). Published by the Rabochaia Gazeta press (the Workers' Newspaper publishing house), the magazine was focused on political socialization of children, yet it was saturated with games, do-it-yourself projects, poems, and short stories. *Druzhnye rebiata* (*Friendly Kids*, 1927–53), a magazine for peasant children, was another publication that emulated the organizational template of *Baraban,* in this case however targeting children from the countryside: it tailored its DIY section to the needs of villages, offering regular rubrics on "experimenting in the vegetable garden," and so on.

The Soviet authorities actively supported children's magazines and newspapers by initiating official policies formulated in multiple decrees and decisions and by publishing their own articles in the these outlets. While ideological to the core, children's magazines did manage to preserve some diversity. They combined memoirs about childhood written by major Soviet functionaries with works by prominent children's writers (e.g., Marshak, Kassil'). Agniia Barto (1906–1981), a poet who would later significantly influence Soviet children's literature, published her first poem in 1924 in *Pioner* – a story about the life and struggle of Van Li, a young Chinese boy.[61] At the same time, pre-revolutionary writers also found in *Pioner* an outlet for their work. During Russia's civil war, Sergei Auslender (1886–1937), a literary critic and symbolist writer, was closely associated with Admiral Kolchak, the leader of the White Movement, acting as the admiral's speechwriter and biographer. But, by the mid-1920s, Auslender would publish his historical novels in *Pioner.*[62] With time, this relative diversity would radically diminish, and, in 1931, the First All-Union Conference on Children's Literature would finally come up with a binary classification template that would divide all children's writers into "fellow travellers," whose literary work "lacked social acuity," and "proletarian writers," to be actively promoted by the authorities.[63]

Novyi Robinzon, which was inspired and conceived by Marshak,[64] offered a somewhat different set of methods for treating literary and social materials for children (fig. 0.14). The magazine was published from 1923 to 1925, following Marshak's general interest in making scientific information accessible for young readers. Natal'ia Volotova, Marshak's assistant, would later recall that *Novyi Robinzon* "offered 'first-hand' accounts of archeologists' excavations in Crimea, … pieces on the first flight from Moscow to Peking, on sanitation, on salt mines, and on revolutionary

0.11. Cover of *Pioner*, no. 1 (1967).

0.10. Cover of *Pioner*, no. 22 (1926). From 1924, *Pioner* was the main outlet of the All-Union Pioneer Organization named after *Vladimir Lenin*. The organization was dissolved in 1991. However, the journal, reformatted and re-branded, is still in print.

0.13. Cover of *Murzilka*, no. 12 (1926).

0.12. The cover of the first issue of *Murzilka*, no. 1 (1924). Established in 1924, *Murzilka* is the oldest illustrated children's magazine in today's Russia. It is designed for preschool and elementary school children.

0.14. Cover of *Novyi Robinzon*, no. 7 (1925). Although this illustrated magazine was only published for two years in Leningrad (1924–5), it was instrumental in creating a working model for other Soviet periodicals for children.

0.15. The cover of the first issue of *Ezh*, no. 1 (1928). An illustrated magazine for middle school-aged children, *Ezh* was published by the Leningrad section of Detgiz, the main Soviet publisher of books for children of all ages. Relying on its innovative poetry and illustrations, *Ezh* actively promoted the best examples of children's literature.

0.16. Cover of *Ezh*, no. 5 (1929).

events in Russia and abroad."[65] In addition to writers and poets, the magazine's contributors included doctors and engineers, astronomers and chemists. They brought in their own points of view and approaches: the astronomer Vsevolod Sharonov ran a special section called "Look to the Skies" (Pogliadi na nebo), while the professional chemist Mikhail Il'in (Marshak's brother) contributed to the magazine's science section.

After *Novyi Robinzon* was closed, Marshak and his team created *Ezh*, the most popular children's periodical of the late 1920s. Literally translated as "The Hedgehog," the title was conceived also as an abbreviation for *Ezhemesiachnyi zhurnal* (i.e., *Monthly Magazine*) – with playfulness characteristic of this monthly publication that lasted from 1928 to 1935. *Ezh* in Leningrad, just like *Murzilka* in Moscow, was driven by a conscious attempt to merge political and educational goals, promoting children's activism and engagement in the life of the country. At the same time, it actively sought new verbal and visual methods of interacting with its young readers born after the 1917 Revolution (figs. 0.15 and 0.16).

Ezh and its equally famous counterpart *Chizh* (1930–41)[66] were designed for children aged ten to twelve.[67] With their innovative styles and literary professionalism, both magazines epitomized children's writers' reluctance to completely surrender in the face of political and pedagogical pressure to conform. Continuing the tradition of *Novyi Robinzon*, they materialized Marshak's overall aspiration to combine edification and entertainment, despite the pedagogical demand that youngsters be spoken to "seriously."

By 1928, Lenin's earlier insistence on merging enlightenment with politics was firmly established in literature for children. In *Ezh*, the literary component remained strong, even as the political content grew ever more prominent. Every issue included the section "Here Speaks Ezh," which conveyed dispatches from Soviet construction sites, factories, oil fields, and kolkhozes (figs. 0.17 and 0.18). These news items were presented in a new way: political information was delivered in the form of "field reports" from *Ezh*'s "special correspondents" Sergei Bochkov (for domestic news) and John Marlay (for foreign news). The reporters were fictitious, but their bylines personalized political news reports, providing them with a sense of trustworthiness. Expanding their readers' educational horizons and shaping their political awareness, the invented "special correspondents" also infused their young readers with the feeling of belonging to a larger Soviet collective.

The legacy of the first Soviet children's journal, *Severnoe siianie*, was evident in *Ezh*. Not only was the old way of life condemned, but so too was its analogue, as found abroad. Against the backdrop of happy Soviet childhood, full of joy and creativity, stories of the hard life of foreign children resembled earlier tales about the gloomy fate of proletarian children in tsarist Russia. Entertainment and puzzles remained an integral part of the journal, stimulating its readers' active exchange of correspondence. *Ezh* also distinguished itself by introducing its readers to classical texts of Russian and Western writers such as Vasilii Zhukovskii, Anton Chekhov, Leo Tolstoy, Charles Dickens, and François Rabelais. Richly illustrated, this periodical became a real laboratory for experiments in various genres in children's literature – political sketches, humorous poetry, and new literary fairy tales.

This brief outline of the history of Soviet periodicals for children illustrates the overall institutional trajectory of children's literature in the Soviet Union. Constructed to administer and control literary production for young readers, this literary genre (and literary institution) was constantly in search of new organizational forms and innovative literary approaches. The state-sponsored infrastructure constrained but also enabled several generations of authors, artists, critics, and publishers.

Built from scratch and envisioned as an opposition to available – "old" – literary and publishing traditions, the field of Soviet children's literature was fully institutionalized in less than fifteen years. By the time Soviet writers assembled in Moscow on 17 August 1934 for their first congress, children's literature already had a constitutive framework necessary for its institutional existence: a network of specially designated presses, libraries, and research units; a roster of trade journals, youth magazines, and newspapers; and a set of official "requirements" and unofficial "commandments." Established during the first two decades after the revolution, this infrastructure sustained the "great literature for the little ones" – to use Marshak's description – until the disappearance of the very state that had birthed this institution in the first place.

Generative Schemes

The consolidation of aesthetic principles, narrative tasks, and pedagogical methods of Soviet children's literature more or less matched the trajectory of the field's infrastructural consolidation. No plots came ready-made. No artistic principles could be easily adapted. No methods could be borrowed. Basic categories had to be identified, elaborated, tested, and popularized.

Among critics and authors of children's books, it was the *Soviet* part of "*Soviet* literature for children" that was most actively discussed. Debates were driven in part by a basic discrepancy between experience and expression perceptively formulated by Anatoly Lunacharsky, the unorthodox Marxist in charge of the Commissariat of Enlightenment. As the commissar saw it, the proletariat had the greatest number of individuals capable of truly understanding "the gigantic spread of vital forces" in the Soviet Union. At the same time, however, this population suffered from a glaring lack of "proletarian writers whose skills would allow them to speak about themselves in their own words."[68] In 1925, a party resolution situated this idea of the proletariat's representational deficiency in terms of political domination: "Proletarian writers have not yet established their hegemony, and the [Communist] party should help

0.17–0.18. One issue of *Ezh* from 1930 introduced its readers to new urbanist projects around the country. Under its modernist cover (fig. 0.17), the issue explained the principles of skyscraper constructions and even published a plan of a "city of the future," which included, among others the House of Culture, the Kitchen-Factory, residential Commune Houses for the workers of a Metal Plant, and a School Town for their children (fig. 0.18). *Ezh*, no. 21 (1930).

them earn their historical right to this hegemony."[69] Meanwhile, children's literature was being created mostly by "cadres of writers … of petty-bourgeois background," as one newspaper put it.[70]

In the absence of "hegemony," how could "actually Soviet" children's books be distinguished from "pseudo-Soviet" ones?[71] Moreover, was "Soviet" meant to describe a particular *set* of issues, things, or events? Or did it indicate the *way* in which any such issue, thing, or event should be perceived and narrated? By the mid-1930s, the general position on new books for Soviet children had begun taking visible shape. In 1931, a volume of essays titled *Children's Literature: A Critical Collection*, edited and prefaced by Lunacharsky, usefully crystallized the core views.[72]

To characterize the major approaches to children's literature at the time, one of the contributors, Boris Bukhshtab, a literary scholar and younger member of the Russian formalist group, proposed the binary of "theme vs. method." According to Bukhshtab, merely expanding the range of themes and topics would not suffice to create truly revolutionary literature. Taken by itself, no theme is inherently "revolutionary or non-revolutionary." Any major revolutionary holiday, for instance, could easily be presented in the most "boring, gray, and bureaucratic" manner.[73] "The *specificum*," as Bukhshtab calls it, of Soviet literature for children must be sought in the specificity of the methods of artistic expression: "If the chosen method makes a particular theme incomprehensible for the child …, if this method makes the theme uninteresting, if the book … evokes a feeling of boredom or even repulsion, then the book is socially dangerous, regardless of its theme."[74]

In his analysis of the latest poetry for children, Bukhshtab singles out two important features that clearly distinguish successful examples of the new Soviet literature from "opportunistic literary hackwork."[75] One is that *fabula* – that is, the overarching framework within which the literary composition (the plot) unfolds – should be palpably present and dynamic.[76] In the *fabula*, "lyrical" fragments and isolated vignettes that are otherwise frequently disjointed find a structure that is neither mechanical nor static. Bukhshtab's second *specificum* is the close-up and highly realistic depiction of ordinary things: in the new literature, fantastic or distorted representations give way to the almost documentary – "factographic" – portrayal of real-life objects.[77] Bukhshtab's attempt to link the genre of the children's book with clearly defined macro- *and* micro-levels of narration (structure versus element; general framework versus concrete objects) is further developed by other contributors to the *Critical Collection*, who channel Bukhshtab's *specifica* into the two basic "methodological" principles of *schematism* and *gaze-appeal*. We will discuss the former principle here, and take up *gaze-appeal* in the next section.

In a survey of historical novels for children, Bukhshtab's fellow formalist Lidiya Ginzburg warns Soviet writers against uncritical fascination with the factographic method of narration. As Ginzburg emphasizes, the unconditional privileging of the historical document – "documentalism," as she calls it – may be useful during the research stage but, as a guiding principle, is detrimental to the process of constructing the actual story.[78] The narrative poverty of documentalism, she maintains, is especially obvious in children's historical novels, in which an excess of "archeological" facts cannot make up for an "insufficiently eventful" *fabula*."[79] Certainly, the historical novel ought to be factually "adequate," Ginzburg concludes, but it is just as important that it be ideologically and socially "grounded" and emotionally "sound."[80] To retain a successful balance between "the number of words and the quantity of action," she suggests, children's literature "must be based on *obvious schemes*" of perception and interpretation.[81]

Ginzburg's appeal to lay bare the motivational structure, the narrative message, and the affective valence of the material, her enthusiastic endorsement of literary schematism (for the sake of narrative accessibility), went beyond the borders of the historical novel. A few years before the appearance of her article, a group of education specialists working with preschool children had come to a similar conclusion. After reading various stories to children, the educators asked them to recall the content or to restore it, using the illustrations in the relevant book. As the scholars observed, the children had difficulty reconstructing texts that lacked obvious story structures; in such cases, all they could produce was a random list of disconnected details and objects. They showed a marked preference for books with "a distinctive, accelerating *fabula* with a clear narrative turning point that leads to the resolution of the story," and ignored those books that tried to compensate for a weak *fabula* with an easy language of narration or multiple illustrations.[82]

The method of narrative, pictorial, and social schematization would become one of the major constructive devices of Soviet children's literature. Countless books published in the 1920s and 1930s would organize diverse social material and complex political ideas into lucid binaries and unambiguously polarized narrative schemes, often succinctly captured by their titles: *Vchera i segodnia* (*Yesterday and Today*); *Geroi i zhertvy revoliutsii* (*Heroes and Victims of the Revolution*); *Chto takoe khorosho i chto takoe plokho* (*What Is Good and What Is Bad?*); and *Nashi vragi i druz'ia* (*Our Enemies and Friends*) (figs. 0.19 and 0.20a–b).[83] The boilerplate quality of such books did cause some anxiety among experts on children's literature. Yet story templates – *shablony* (from the German *Schablone*, "template"), as they were often called by Soviet critics[84] – were seen as problematic not because of their schematism per se,[85] but rather because authors frequently animated their schemes with inferior, incorrect, or even improbable material.[86]

That Soviet literature in general and Soviet literature for children in particular would rely on repetitive schemes and formulas is not surprising. In her seminal study of the Soviet novel, Katerina Clark conclusively established that socialist-realist fiction was based on what she calls "the prototypical plot." As a coherent genre, the Soviet novel was a collection of variations of the same tale about "a questing hero who sets out in search of 'consciousness.'"[87] Cultural production was thus doomed to be a form of enforced cultural recycling. As Clark puts it, "all Soviet novels … repeat the

0.19. A spread from Vladimir Mayakovsky's book *Chto takoe khorosho i chto takoe plokho?* (Moscow: Priboi, 1925). The poem provides a basic ethical and optic lesson:

If a nasty brawler
harasses a weak kid,
I would not even put him in this book.

But a boy who shouts loudly:
"Do not even think of touching
those who are smaller than you"
is simply a pleasure to look at.

master plot, which is itself a codification of major cultural categories."[88] Clark's model directly links the process of literature's ritualization to political control over the reproduction of the master plot. Presumably, the absence of direct state pressure would correspond with a greater variety of narrative structures and plot configurations. Yet the existing scholarship on English-language children's books adds a dimension that significantly complicates Clark's view.

Describing the apparent sameness of children's novels, Perry Nodelman has convincingly argued that children's literature challenges the foundational assumption by which "distinctive details" foreground a "distinct personal vision."[89] The remarkable

0.20a–0.20b. Aminadav Kanevskii, illustrations for Nikolai Studenetskii, *Nashi vragi i druz'ia* (Moscow: Krest'ianskaia gazeta, 1930). Ill. 12. This spread describes one enemy in the rhyme "A Never-Ending Story": "The League of Nation keeps 'disarming' itself. But instead of real actions, there are only talks, as usual." In contrast, fig. 0.20b highlights a friend in the rhyme "Colonized Nations Are Militant Reserves of the Proletariat." The rhyme encouraged such friends:

Keep up your march

And raise the flame

Of the struggle.

The country of the Soviets

Is your beacon.

And Lenin

is your banner.

fact about children's literature, Nodelman observes, is that the "unique surface details that create [the] tone and atmosphere" of individual books point to "the same basic set of opposite ideas, and a propensity for bringing them into balance."[90] Distinctive literary "surfaces" in this case are nothing but examples of ornamentalism, with no significant value of their own. However, these unique details do not simply mask the sameness beneath. Their main function is to individualize access to the same basic set of ideas, images, and affects that are constitutive of the genre.

In her study of the aesthetics of children's books, Maria Nikolajeva extends Nodelman's point by drawing attention to the developmental task of this literature. Confronting the core story again and again, young readers are forced to compare and contrast it with what they have read earlier. By reading similar books in a row, a reader constructs, from below, a "memory of the genre,"[91] as well as a set of expectations associated with this genre. In this context, then, the goal of ritualized, schematized, and repetitive literature is to reveal to the reader the principles of its own organization, "to make the structure of the myth apparent," as Claude Lévi-Strauss puts it in a different context.[92] The main message of this literature is not in its predictable content, but in its overall frame: "In canonical texts structure is the very essence of information."[93] Constant recitations of the Soviet "prototypical plot" were a historically specific way of uncovering what Jacques Derrida would later describe as the generic law of the plot, its internal code.[94]

The large-scale research conducted in the 1920s by Pavla Rubtsova on children's reading practices provides interesting support for this conclusion vis-à-vis the early Soviet milieu. Asked about their reading preferences, 23 per cent of the children surveyed described the book they were then reading or planning to read next as "like" what they had just finished (*vrode etoi*). In some cases, "likeness" became literal sameness: one of the children, a ten-year-old son of a low-ranking state official, explained his request to the librarian this way: "How many *Robinson Crusoes* do you have? A lot? Give me all of them, every one you have." In others, the repetition was seen as repetition with a difference: a thirteen-year-old boy, having read a book about American Indians, asked "for something similar," clarifying that in the book "there should be a leader, and that he should be in charge of Indians."[95] Thus, a clear scheme helped young readers to recognize the key elements of "the story of stories,"[96] but also to organize the knowledge already accumulated by turning individual characters into types, distinctive situations into generic scenarios, and diverse narratives into identifiable frameworks. Prototypical plots and story templates performed the flipside of the technique of estrangement or "defamiliarization" (*ostranenie*) elaborated by the Russian formalist Viktor Shklovsky. If, for Shklovsky, to "defamiliarize" objects (primarily through striking metaphors) meant releasing them from the sensorial dullness of routinized perception, then for the practitioners of early Soviet literature for children, the purpose of literary schematism was to routinize the narrative organization of unknown or emerging cultural experience. At stake here was the construction of the very "sphere of automatized perception"[97] – of such "systems of generative schemes"[98] that would ensure the continuous reproduction of narrative solutions, stylistic preferences, and, eventually, behavioural choices.

Gaze-Appeal: Making the Eye Work

The growing narrative schematism of early Soviet children's literature was a major method of presenting communist ideas and concepts for children. But it was not the only one. The second crucial methodological requirement was the principle of "gaze-appeal" (*nagliadnost'*), which emphasized the semantic and affective potential of the image.[99] By the mid-1920s, Soviet children's books had significantly altered the visual conventions of book publishing: picture books had become the main literary medium for illiterate or semi-literate children.[100] The ready-made illustrations so prevalent in pre-revolutionary publishing gave way to highly individualized pictorial narratives designed specifically for each book (fig. 0.21).

Increasingly, the book artist was understood as "an author in their own right, not just a mere illustrator."[101] Covers of many publications listed both the writer and the artist as equal contributors. Yet it was not immediately clear what exactly the increasingly prominent artist should produce. Two contributors to the 1931 volume of critical essays on children's literature tried to develop the idea of co-authorship by proposing that the traditional ancillary function of book illustrations – "supporting" and/or "clarifying" the textual material – be replaced with their conception as autonomous or even self-sufficient visual configurations with their own, independent, semantic value.[102] Nikolai Kovarskii, yet another formalist, stressed that "the drawing must be just as efficient (semantically speaking) as the text," and proposed to ensure "the systemic equivalence between the graphic and the textual elements of the book" by strictly implementing "the principle of gaze-appeal" in books for children.[103] Elena Dan'ko, an artist and an author, underscored the educational function of the image in her analysis of the artistic design of children's books: "To develop, the eye must work; it must overcome some difficulty."[104] Hence, every new book should constitute "an independent solution for new artistic puzzles," "new work for the reader's eye to perform" (*novaia rabota dlia glaza chitatelia*). This is an educational task: the mission of book illustration is "to train the eye [to be] unbiased and free of routinized viewing; to be capable of working through a piece of art independently and actively."[105]

This ongoing recognition of the semantic and structural independence of the pictorial component of the children's book was precipitated at least in part by the influx of professional artists into the publishing business after the revolution, when the shrivelled art market forced many to change their medium. There were other, aesthetic and ideological, reasons as well. Since the early 1920s, Russian theoreticians of revolutionary art had been elaborating the concept of "productivist art" (*proizvodstvennoe iskusstvo*).[106] The "old visual art," with its mimetic painting, was proclaimed dead.

0.21. An advertising spread from the book publisher Priboi (1925) emphasized the trend towards visual individualization of books by presenting graphic covers of its book series for children. The left side depicted the book *Pioneers* (by R. Volzhenin), stating "All kids are reading this now." The right side promised even a more exciting diversity that includes such books as *Pioneers around the World*; *About Old Man's Superstitions*; *Witches, and a Pioneer*; *Bulldog and Cat*, and *Petia's Tricks*.

Instead of the "pictorial illusionism" (*illiuzionizm izobrazitel'nosti*) practised by the artists of the past, new artists were to construct self-sufficient, "genuinely real things" that would not merely "copy the objects of the actual world," as Nikolai Tarabukin, a leading theorist of productivism, explained.[107] Productivist art was supposed to be fully integrated with life, providing practical guidance to the world of knowledge and objects, not an escape from it. A catalyst and organizer of its audience's activity, productivist art was to be a scientific alternative to the illusionistic art of the past – as chemistry was to alchemy, or astronomy to astrology.[108]

The illustrated book was ground zero for this active, organizing, productive understanding of artistic "things" that were to challenge and educate their audience. El Lissitzky, a professional printmaker and graphic artist (and designer of the first red Communist Party banner with sickle and hammer), was one of the most vocal proponents of the conception of the book as a site of "creative sign-formation."[109] Foregrounding the scopic aspect of reading, Lissitzky insisted that words on the page are learned "by sight, not by hearing"; therefore "the book space" should embody a new economy of expressive means, privileging "optics instead of phonetics."[110]

Lissitzky's own *Suprematicheskii skaz pro dva kvadrata v shesti postroeniiakh* (*Suprematist Tale about Two Squares in Six Constructions*), designed during his collaboration with Kasimir Malevich in Vitebsk in 1920, is exemplary of this new approach.[111] In the *Tale*, "a particular condensation of thought" (as Lissitzky termed it) is successfully accomplished through a creative combination of narrative schematism and basic optical solutions.[112] The education of the reader is inextricably linked in the *Tale* with the education of the "mental eye" of the viewer: the epistemic and the optic are purposefully inseparable.[113] As a result of this "education through optics," the reading process goes far beyond the simple operation of following the lines of the text.[114] Instead, the page bombards the reader with different visual stimuli; it pulls them in different directions and trajectories, forcing them to create their own idiosyncratic method of perceiving the page.

Relying on the visual vocabulary developed in Malevich's suprematist art, Lissitzky constructs in his *Tale* a minimalist yet intricate assemblage of text, lines, and coloured geometric objects (figs. 0.22–0.24). The visual language is not mimetic, and the text's syntax is deliberately non-linear. The hybrid language of Lissitzky's tale begins on the book's cover, which combines a word ("About"), a number ("2"), and a coloured square (red). Instead of an introduction to the story, a page offers instructions for the reader. The sentence "Don't read" at the top of the page is followed by a zigzag line that crosses the whole page, leading, at its bottom, to the next directive: "Take [it]." The directive then indicates three equally plausible choices of objects and forms of activity: "*paper (fold), columns (colour), woodblocks (build)*" (fig. 0.22).

The rest of the book constitutes a sequence of diagrams that outline a story frame (*fabula*) for unpacking basic actions (take, fold, colour, build) into a meaningful narrative. Six minimally coloured plates tell a tale about a journey of two squares, one red, the other black. The squares fly from afar to a red globe (Earth?), upon which they witness alarming disarray. The black-and-white illustration of disorder on the globe is followed by a plate depicting a "blow" (*udar*) and further "scattering" (fig. 0.23).

The final two plates establish some balance. One shows the black square as the basis supporting an orderly arrangement of several three-dimensional red structures. In the other, the *Tale* concludes with a view from above showing a flat black circle (Earth again?) with vertical three-dimensional red structures (columns? towers?) *semi-covered* (protected?) by the red square, while a diminished black square is located in (has been relegated to) the top right corner of the page. The text at the bottom reads: "Here it is all over." Yet this would-be closure is immediately disavowed by a final, diagonally placed, word: "Dal'she" (And then) (fig. 0.24).

It is tempting to interpret this condensed story about chaos, a violent "blow," and eventual stabilization as an "iconotext" abstracting the alarming havoc of the First World War, the turmoil of revolution and civil war, and Russia's gradual reconstruction.[115] Lissitzky's own political activism certainly points in this direction. What is, perhaps, more interesting about this tale is not its actual meaning, but rather Lissitzky's general desire "to formulate an elementary idea using elementary means."[116] As

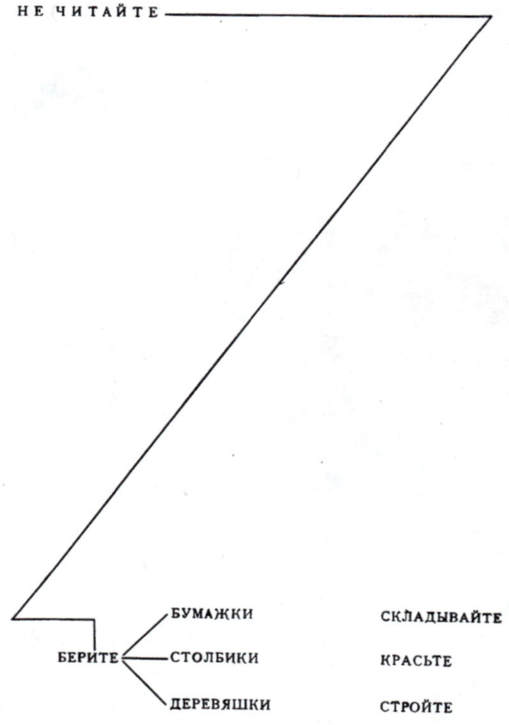

0.22. Opening images of El Lissitzky, *Pro dva kvadrata* (Berlin: Skify, 1922).

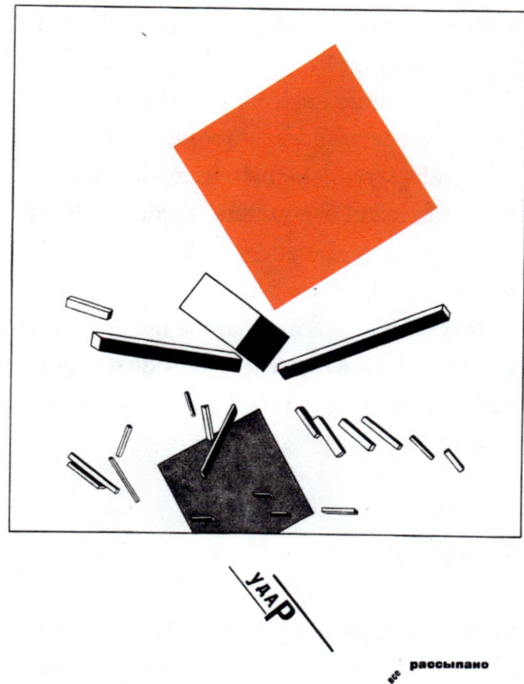

0.23. Image from Lissitzky, *Pro dva kvadrata*.

0.24. Final plate, Lissitzky, *Pro dva kvadrata*.

his *Tale* compellingly shows, vivid narrative or condensed visual schemes do not have to be one-dimensional or limiting. In fact, elementary means, elementary building blocks, can create a highly dynamic environment that activates readers' creative potential.[117] Like many other Soviet children's books, Lissitzky's *Tale* presents a world of polarity – before/after, black/red, enemies/friends, chaos/peace – demonstrating the transformative power of violent encounters. Through his imaginative typography and topography of the book space, he encourages the reader to oscillate constantly between the image and the word, between an abstract idea and a concrete form, between a picture and a real object. Reading here is not the passive consumption of a text or an image; nor is the book's iconotext a reproduction of reality. Instead, it is a self-sufficient construct that offers both a model of the world and a scenario for active and playful engagement with it.

The Pedagogy of Images

Lissitzky's vision of the new book functions as a paradigmatic framework for the chapters collected in this volume. Inspired by early Soviet avant-garde artists, the contributors trace, in the transition from pre-revolutionary to early Soviet children's literature, a radical shift, from the primacy of phonetics and orality to that of optics and visuality. The contributions explore how books visualized ideological norms and goals, translating communism into idioms and images accessible to children. A new – *Soviet* – pedagogy of images demanded from artists and writers a visual language that could combine easy legibility and direct appeal without sacrificing the political dimension of the overall message.

Relying on a process of dual-media rendering, illustrated books presented propagandistic content as a simple, repeatable narrative or verse, while also casting it in easily recognizable graphic images. A vehicle of ideology, an object of affection, and a product of labour, the illustrated book for the young Soviet reader emerged as an important cultural phenomenon. Communist in its content, it was often visually complex and avant-gardist in its form (fig. 0.25).

The contributors take care not to overdraw the avant-garde dimension of the early Soviet book. While Vladimir Mayakovsky, Vladimir Tatlin, and a few other avant-garde artists did contribute to the formation of the genre of the new children's book, the field was shaped mainly by authors aiming to "harmoniously combine children's interests with the tasks of the class struggle" in a far less artistically radical manner.[118] The visual dynamism, narrative fragmentation, and hybridity of expressive means that were typical of avant-gardist attempts to push the limits of the "book space" in translating communism for children existed side by side with a more traditional striving to impose visual predictability and narrative coherence. And yet, in both cases, avant-garde and otherwise, one is struck by the same basic trend, the same dominant determination to rely on schematism and gaze-appeal in organizing visual and textual stories.

This volume presents a coherent set of interdisciplinary approaches (literary criticism, film studies, historical analysis, studies of material culture, and so on) to studying the verbal/visual representation of communist pedagogical ambitions. It offers a variety of scholarly views on new forms of the social imaginary that took shape within the bounds of Soviet children's literature, forms that would later become a visual lingua franca in Soviet culture generally. While offering a diversity of methods for studying illustrated literature for children, the collection spotlights three thematic threads: to be implemented, communist goals (*utopia*) had to be closely linked with practices of enlightenment (*pedagogy*) and techniques of persuasion (*propaganda*).

Each section of this collection highlights a particular constellation of these three themes. Part I, "Mediation," outlines the transition from pre-revolutionary methods and media to specifically Soviet institutions and mechanisms for visualizing and disseminating communist ideas. In part II, "Technology," the contributors explore multiple links between communist imagination and industrialization. Part III, "Power," analyses the ideological work of early Soviet visual regimes. Media, technology, and power are approached here through a lens that is still quite uncommon in studies of children's literature. Focusing on major aspects of the early Soviet period (from mass electrification and industrialization to the proliferation of new tools of cinematic and

0.25. A 1931 poster *Books – to Children* by the artist V.P. Akhmet′ev (Molodaia Gvardiia Press). The rhyme at the top says, "Be prepared to learn communism by working at the floor-bench and by reading books."

photographic expression), the volume aims to move beyond reductionist approaches to studying ideological phenomena. Following the growing field of research on Communist aesthetics, the volume insists on the need to take seriously the specificity of the visual language of Soviet propaganda for children in general, and of the process of translating communist discourses into pictorial analogues in particular.[119] While inspired by communist ideas and beliefs, these visual languages and pictorial strategies are not equivalent to these ideas and beliefs; they have a life of their own, above and beyond the period that made them possible. Building on recent scholarship on Soviet children's literature, this collection expands its scope by documenting the centrality of visual media for educating the first communist generation.

Communism always had major pedagogical ambitions: building a new society was tightly linked with creating new forms of social imagination and new vocabularies of shared images. Lenin's plan of monumental propaganda is well known and well researched. The artifacts of visual culture developed by major artists and writers in Soviet-era illustrated books for children that this volume explores are, while certainly less monumental, no less significant. In fact, as this volume demonstrates, primers in Soviet modernity may be providing us with a much more insightful path for understanding the ways through which this society emerged, existed, and vanished.

NOTES

1 Lenin, "The New Economic Policy," 78.
2 For more detail, see Fitzpatrick, *The Commissariat of Enlightenment.*
3 Chuzhak, *Literatura zhiznestroeniia*, 2. Unless otherwise indicated, all translations of Russian sources are by the contributors.
4 Chuzhak, "Under the Banner of Life-Building," 119.
5 Dobrenko, *The Making of the State Writer*; Dobrenko, *The Making of the State Reader.*
6 Lenoe, *Closer to the Masses.*
7 Siegelbaum, "The Shaping of Soviet Workers' Leisure"; Ermolaev, *Censorship in Soviet Literature*; Hoffmann, *Cultivating the Masses.*
8 Kenez, *The Birth of the Propaganda State.*
9 Kotkin, *Magnetic Mountain*; Steinberg, *Proletarian Imagination*; David-Fox, *Crossing Borders*; Kachurin, *Making Modernism Soviet.*
10 Oushakine, "Translating Communism for Children."
11 Meksin, "Illiustratsiia v sovetskoi detskoi knige," 39.
12 For more discussion, see Lilina, "O deshevoi detskoi literature," 21.
13 Ibid.
14 Ibid.
15 Pokrovskaia, *Osnovnye techeniia*, 7.
16 Lilina, "O deshevoi detskoi literature," 21.
17 Razin, "Kuda napravit' ogon'."
18 Gor'kii, "Literaturu – detiam."
19 See Kon, *Sovetskaia detskaia literatura*, 21.

20 Pokrovskaia, *Osnovnye techeniia*, 9–10.

21 Meksin, "Illiustratsiia v sovetskoi detskoi knige," 44.

22 Blinov, *Russkaia detskaia knizhka-kartinka*, 89–184. For useful surveys, see Karasik, *Udarnaia kniga sovetskoi detvory*; Steiner, *Stories for Little Comrades*; Compton, *Russian Avant-Garde Books*.

23 For historical studies of early Soviet children's literature, see Arzamastseva, *Vek rebenka*; Balina, "Creativity through Restraint"; Fateev, *Stalinism i detskaia literatura*; Olich, *Competing Ideologies*; Hellman, *Fairy Tales and True Stories*.

24 Chudakova, "Skvoz' zvezdy k terniiam," 347. For more critique of this approach, see Weld, *An Ecology of the Russian Avant-Garde Picturebook*, 28.

25 Kondakov, "Detstvo kak ubezhishche."

26 Arzamastseva, *Vek rebenka*, 81.

27 For more detail on the state-sponsored development of Soviet literature for children, see Kon, *Sovetskaia detskaia literatura*; Putilova, *Ocherki po istorii*; Lupanova, *Polveka*.

28 See Dobrenko, *Political Economy of Socialist Realism* for a useful overview of the consolidation of Soviet literature in the mid-1930s.

29 Kormchii (Leonard Piragis), "Zabytoe oruzhie"; for more detail on Kormchii, see Khellman, "Detskaia literatura kak oruzhie."

30 Kormchii, "Zabytoe oruzhie," 3.

31 Govorov and Kupriianova, eds., *Istoriia knigi*, 257.

32 Ermolaeva was arrested and later executed in the Karaganda "corrective labour" camp during the Great Terror; see Gerasimova, "Ermolaeva, Vera Mikhailovna."

33 Govorov and Kupriianova, eds., *Istoriia knigi*, 263.

34 Marshak, "O bol'shoi literature dlia malen'kikh," 215.

35 Gasparov, "Marshak i vremia," 415.

36 Luk'ianova, *Kornei Chukovskii*, 288.

37 Chukovsky, "Trinadtsat' zapovedei,"

38 *Raduga*'s books were awarded a special medal for innovative design at the International Exhibition of Modern Decorative and Industrial Arts in Paris in 1925. For more detail, see Rothenstein and Budashevskaya, *Inside the Rainbow*.

39 Olich, *Competing Ideologies*, 98.

40 Kon, *Sovetskaia detskaia literatura*, 63–5; Rubtsova, "Produktsiia detskoi knigi."

41 N.A., "Za bol'shuiu detskuiu literaturu."

42 *O partiinoi i sovetskoi pechati*, 217.

43 Ibid., 218.

44 Ibid., 251.

45 Pokrovskaia, *Osnovnye techeniia*, 7.

46 Cited in Dobrenko, *The Making of the State Reader*, 203.

47 Ibid.

48 See Olich, *Competing Ideologies*, 163–74.

49 See Putilova, *Ocherki po istorii*.

50 Marshak, *Pis'mo Maksimu Gor'komu*, 95.

51 Krupskaia was the chair of the council's research and pedagogy section. Prior to publication, children's books had to be cleared by a State Academic Council commission (see Arzamastseva, *Vek rebenka*, 97).

52 Putilova, *Ocherki po istorii*, 10.

53 Kaluzhskaia, *Stanovlenie i razvitie otechestvennoi pedagogiki*, 62.

54 Putilova, *Ocherki po istorii*, 33.

55 Kolesova, *Detskie zhurnaly Rossii.*

56 Gorky, "Slovo k vzroslym."

57 Krupskaia, *Pedagogicheskie sochineniia*, 37.

58 For more detail on *The Drum*, see D'Arkandzhelo, "Baraban." On Pioneer literature, see Le-ont'eva, "Deti i ideologiia"; Kolesova, *Detskie zhurnaly Rossii.*

59 Kolesova, *Detskie zhurnaly Rossii*, 123.

60 Arzamastseva, *Vek rebenka*, 92.

61 See Barto, "Van Li."

62 See Auslender, "Pugachionok," 6–9.

63 Putilova, *Ocherki po istorii*, 33.

64 Technically, Zlata Lilina, the head of the Children's Books Department at Gosizdat, was the magazine's editor-in-chief. However, Marshak was effectively in charge of the magazine (see Kolesova, *Detskie zhurnaly Rossii*, 193–205).

65 Volotova, "Kak sozdavalsia 'Robinzon,'" 144.

66 The magazine's title is likewise ludic, simultaneously having a literal meaning ("siskin") and deriving from an abbreviation: *Chrezvychaino interesnyi zhurnal* – "A Highly Interesting Magazine."

67 Alekseeva, "O publitsistike detskikh zhurnalov."

68 Lunacharsky, "Puti detskoi knigi," 163.

69 "O politike partii v oblasti khudozhetsvennoi literatury," in *O partiinoi i sovetskoi pechati*, 345.

70 Kal'm, "Protiv khaltury."

71 "Za deistvitel'no sovetskuiu detskuiu knigu"; on "pseudo-Soviet" books, see Kal'm, "Protiv khaltury."

72 Lunacharsky, *Detskaia literatura.*

73 Bukhshtab, "Stikhi dlia detei," 105.

74 Ibid., 105.

75 Ibid., 127.

76 The pedagogical guide *What and How to Narrate for Pioneers*, composed by Glagoleva in 1927 for leaders of children's teams at schools and camps, defined *fabula* as "the main thread of a story" that "brings all the collected materials together." In turn, *suzhet* is a particular "account" that composes events, following the author's plan (Glagoleva, *Kak i chto*, 25). For Tzvetan Todorov, *fabula* (the story) is the chronological sequence of events, while *suzhet* (the plot) "personalizes" this sequence as a distinctive arrangement (*The Poetics of Prose*, 26).

77 Bukhshtab, "Stikhi dlia detei," 111, 118.

78 Ginzburg, "Puti istoricheskoi detskoi povesti," 162.

79 Ibid., 166.

80 Ibid., 177.

81 Ibid., 161; our emphasis.

82 Rubtsova, "Eksperimental'naia retsenziia," 12–13.

83 Works or subtitles of works by Marshak and Lebedev, Mayakovskii (two works), and Studen-etskii and Konevskii, respectively.

84 Anna Pokrovskaia defined such literature as having *shablonnaia fabula,* a "template narrative," in her *Osnovnye techeniia* (25).

85 In a 1929 address to educators and children's writers, Lunacharsky put it plainly: "Taken by itself, scheme is not a disaster [*beda*]. Scheme is something that can be filled with animating content" ("Puti detskoi knigi," 175).

86 Ibid., 176; Pokrovskaia, *Osnovnye techeniia*, 26; Margolina, "Proizvodstvennaia detskaia literatura," 109.

87 Clark, *The Soviet Novel*, 162.

88 Ibid., 9.

89 Nodelman, "Interpretation and the Apparent Sameness," 19.

90 Ibid., 20.

91 Bakhtin, *Problems of Dostoevsky's Poetics*, 121.

92 Lévi-Strauss, The Structural Study of Myth," 105.

93 Nikolajeva, *Children's Literature Comes of Age*, 55.

94 Derrida, "Living On / Border Lines," 86.

95 Rubtsova, "Chto vliiaet na detskie knizhnye zaprosy," 28.

96 Derrida, "Living On / Border Lines," 100.

97 Shklovsky, "Art as Device," 6. See also the forum "Estrangement Revisited" for a detailed discussion of the concept.

98 Bourdieu, *Distinction*, 166.

99 For more detail, see Oushakine, "Realism with Gaze-Appeal."

100 Pokrovskaia, *Osnovnye techeniia*, 43; Petrov, "Iz istorii detskoi illiustrirovannoi knigi."

101 Pokrovskaia, "Novye puti detskoi knigi." For an informative and detailed discussion, see Fomin, *Iskusstvo knigi*, 435–61. See also a biographic directory of writers and artists of early Soviet books for children, Semenova, *Tvortsy sovetskoi detskoi knigi*.

102 Kovarskii, "Delovaia knizhka," 155.

103 Ibid., 157.

104 Dan'ko, "Zadachi khudozhestvennogo oformleniia knigi," 227.

105 Ibid., 229. Nikolajeva and Scott usefully operationalize these debates, suggesting a typology of relations between the image and the text created in children's books: from symmetry, enhancement, or extension to alternation, deviation, or counterpoint (*How Picturebooks Work*, 6–27).

106 For more detail, see Lodder, "Constructivism and Productivism."

107 Tarabukin, *Ot mol'berta*, 8.

108 Ibid., 42.

109 Khardzhiev, "El' Lisitskii," 147; Lisitskii, "Primechaniia ne k etoi knige," 24.

110 Lissitzky, "Topography of Typography," 359.

111 There is a recent English translation by Christina Lodder: Lissitzky, *About Two Squares*.

112 Cited in Khardzhiev, "El' Lisitskii," 154.

113 For more discussion about this process, see Oushakine, "Machines, Nations, and Faciality."

114 For an extensive discussion on education through optics, see Leving, *Vospitanie optikoi*.

115 The concept of iconotext as "an inseparable entity of word and image" is discussed by Nikolajeva and Scott (*How Picturebooks Work*, 6–7). For perceptive historical and pictorial interpretations of the *Tale*, see Victor Margolin, *The Struggle for Utopia*, 37–42.

116 Lissitzky, "Typographical Facts," 80.

117 Social content is similarly translated into abstract elementary shapes in Leo Lionni's popular book *Little Blue and Little Yellow*; for a discussion, see Nikolajeva and Scott, *How Picturebooks Work*, 88–9.

118 Razin, "Kuda napravit' ogon."

119 See, in particular, two major recent publications: *Comintern Aesthetics*, edited by Glaser and Lee, and *The Oxford Handbook of Communist Visual Cultures*, edited by Skrodzka, Lu, and Marciniak.

BIBLIOGRAPHY

Alekseeva, M. "O publitsistike detskikh zhurnalov vtoroi poloviny 1920-kh godov." *Vestnik Moskovskogo universiteta*, no. 2 (1979): 11–18.

Arzamastseva, Irina. *Vek rebenka v russkoi literature 1900–1930 godov*. Moscow: Prometei, 2003.

Auslender, Sergei. "Pugachionok." *Pioner*, no. 3 (1926): 6–9.

Bakhtin, Mikhail. *Problems of Dostoevsky's Poetics*. Edited and translated by Caryl Emerson. Minneapolis: University of Minnesota Press, 1984.

Balina, Marina. "Creativity through Restraint: The Beginnings of Soviet Children's Literature." In *Russian Children's Literature*, edited by Marina Balina and Larissa Rudova, 1–19. New York: Routledge, 2008.

Barto, Agniia. "Van Li." *Pioner*, no. 2 (1924): 12–13.

Blinov, Valerii. *Russkaia detskaia knizhka-kartinka, 1900–1941*. Moscow: Iskusstvo XXI vek, 2005.

Bourdieu, Pierre. *Distinction: A Social Critique of the Judgment of Taste*. Translated by Richard Nice. Cambridge, MA: Harvard University Press, 1984.

Bukhshtab, Boris. "Stikhi dlia detei." In *Detskaia literatura: kriticheskii sbornik*, edited by Anatolii Lunacharsky, 103–30. Moscow: Khudozhestvennaia literatura, 1931.

Chudakova, Marietta. "Skvoz' zvezdy k terniiam." In *Izbrannye raboty v 2-kh tomakh*, 339–67. Moscow: Iazyki russkoi kul'tury, 2001.

Chukovsky, Kornei. "Trinadtsat' zapovedei dlia detskikh poetov." *Kniga detiam*, no. 1 (1929): 13–19.

Chuzhak, Nikolai. "Literatura zhiznestroeniia (Teoriia v praktike)." *Novyi LEF*, no. 10 (1929).

– "Under the Banner of Life-Building (An Attempt to Understand the Art of Today)." Translated by Christina Lodder. *Art in Translation* 1 (2009): 119–51.

Clark, Katerina. *The Soviet Novel: History as Ritual*. Bloomington: Indiana University Press, 2000.

Compton, Susan. *Russian Avant-Garde Books, 1917–1934*. Cambridge, MA: MIT Press, 1992.

Dan'ko, Elena. "Zadachi khudozhestvennogo oformleniia knigi." In *Detskaia literatura: kriticheskii sbornik*, edited by Anatolii Lunacharsky, 209–31. Moscow: Khudozhestvennaia literatura, 1931.

D'Arkandzhelo, Roza. "Baraban: shagaem s pionerami." In *"Ubit' Charskuiu": paradoksy sovetskoi literatury dlia detei, 1920-e–1930-e gg.*, edited by Marina Balina and Valerii V'iugin, 96–109. St. Petersburg: Aleteia, 2013.

David-Fox, Michael. *Crossing Borders: Modernity, Ideology, and Culture in Russia and the Soviet Union*. Pittsburgh: University of Pittsburgh Press, 2015.

Derrida, Jacques. "Living On / Border Lines." Translated by James Hulbert. In Harold Bloom et al., *Deconstruction and Criticism*, 75–176. New York: Continuum, 1979.

Dobrenko, Evgenii. *The Making of the State Reader: Social and Aesthetic Contexts of the Reception of Soviet Literature*. Trans. by Jesse M. Savage. Stanford, CA: Stanford University Press, 1997.

– *The Making of the State Writer: Social and Aesthetic Origins of Soviet Literary Culture*. Trans. by Jesse M. Savage. Stanford, CA: Stanford University Press, 2001.

– *Political Economy of Socialist Realism*. Trans. by Jesse M. Savage. New Haven, CT: Yale University Press, 2007.

Ermolaev, Herman. *Censorship in Soviet Literature, 1917–1991*. Lanham, MD: Rowman & Littlefield, 1997.

"Estrangement Revisited: A Forum." *Poetics Today* 26, no. 4 (2005) and 27, no. 1 (2006). https://www.dukeupress.edu/estrangement-revisited

Fateev, Andrei. *Stalinism i detskaia literatura v politike nomenklatury SSSR (1930-e–1950-e gg.)*. Moscow: Maks Press, 2007.

Fitzpatrick, Sheila. *The Commissariat of Enlightenment: Soviet Organization of Education and the Arts under Lunacharsky, October 1917–1921*. Cambridge: Cambridge University Press, 2002.

Fomin, Dmitrii. *Iskusstvo knigi v kontekste kul'tury 1920-kh godov*. Moscow: Pashkov dom, 2015.

Gasparov, Mikhail. "Marshak i vremia." In *O russkoi poezii*. St. Petersburg: Azbuka, 2001.

Gerasimova, Dar'ia. "Ermolaeva, Vera Mikhailovna. Nepokorennaia stikhiia." http://bibliogid.ru /khudozhnik/764-ermolaeva-vera-miklajlovna

Ginzburg, Lidiia. "Puti istoricheskoi detskoi povesti." In *Detskaia literatura: kriticheskii sbornik*, edited by Anatoly Lunacharsky, 159–81. Moscow: Khudozhestvennaia literatura, 1931.

Glagoleva, N. *Kak i chto rasskazyvat' pioneram*. Moscow: GIZ, 1927.

Glaser, Amelia M. and Steven S. Lee, eds. *Comintern Aesthetics*. Toronto: University of Toronto Press, 2020.

Gorky, Maxim. "Literaturu – detiam." *Pravda*, no. 159 (1933).

– "Slovo k vzroslym." In *M. Gorky o detskoi literature*, edited by N. Medvedeva, 75–7. Moscow: Detskaia literatura, 1968.

Govorov, Aleksandr, and Tat'iana Kupriianova, eds. *Istoriia knigi*. Moscow: Svetoton, 2001.

Hellman, Ben. *Fairy Tales and True Stories: The History of Russian Literature for Children and Young People (1574–2010)*. Leiden: Brill, 2013.

Hoffmann, David. *Cultivating the Masses: Modern State Practices and Soviet Socialism, 1914–1939*. Ithaca, NY: Cornell University Press, 2011.

Kachurin, Pamela. *Making Modernism Soviet: The Russian Avant-Garde in the Early Soviet Era, 1918–1928*. Evanston, IL: Northwestern University Press, 2013.

Kal'm, D. "Protiv khaltury v detskoi literature." *Literaturnaia gazeta*, 16 December 1929.

Kaluzhskaia, Iuliia. "Stanovlenie i razvitie otechestvennoi pedagogiki detskogo chteniia v pervoi treti XX veka." PhD diss., Moscow State Art and Cultural University, 2003.

Karasik, Mikhail. *Udarnaia kniga sovetskoi detvory: fotoilliustratsii i fotomontazh v knige dlia detei i iunoshestva 1920–1930-kh godov*. Moscow: Kontakt-Kul'tura, 2010.

Kenez, Peter. *The Birth of the Propaganda State: Soviet Methods of Mass Mobilization, 1917–1929*. Cambridge: Cambridge University Press, 1985.

Khardzhiev, Nikolai. "El' Lisitskii – konstruktor knigi." In *Iskusstvo knigi 1958–1960*, 3: 145–68. Moscow: Iskusstvo, 1962.

Khellman, Ben. "Detskaia literatura kak oruzhie: tvorcheskii put' L. Kormchego." In *"Ubit' Charskuiu": paradoksy sovetskoi literatury dlia detei, 1920-e–1930-e gg.*, edited by Marina Balina and Valerii V'iugin, 20–6. St. Petersburg: Aleteia, 2013.

Kolesova. Larisa. *Detskie zhurnaly Rossii: XX vek*. Petrozavodsk: Izd. PetrGU, 2009.

Kon, Lidiia. *Sovetskaia detskaia literatura, 1917–1929*. Moscow: Detskaia literatura, 1960.

Kondakov, Igor'. "Detstvo kak ubezhishche ili 'Detskii diskurs' sovetskoi literatury." In *Kakoreia: iz istorii detstva v Rossii i drugikh stranakh*, edited by Galina Makarevich, 138–67. Moscow: Nauchnaia kniga, 2008.

Kormchii, L. (Leonard Piragis). "Zabytoe oruzhie. O detskoi knige." *Pravda*, 17 February 1918.

Kotkin, Stephen. *Magnetic Mountain: Stalinism as Civilization*. Berkeley: University of California Press, 1995.

Kovarskii, Nikolai. "Delovaia knizhka." In *Detskaia literatura: kriticheskii sbornik*, edited by Anatolii Lunacharsky, 131–58. Moscow: Khudozhestvennaia literatura, 1931.

Krupskaia, Nadezhda. *Pedagogicheskie sochineniia*. Moscow: Akademiia pedagogicheskikh nauk, 1959.

Lenin, Vladimir. "The New Economic Policy and the Tasks of the Political Education Departments." In *Collected Works*, 33: 60–80. Moscow: Progress Publishers, 1973.

Lenoe, Matthew. *Closer to the Masses: Stalinist Culture, Social Revolution, and Soviet Newspapers.* Cambridge, MA: Harvard University Press, 2004.

Leont'eva, Svetlana. "Deti i ideologiia." In *Kakoreia: iz istorii detstva v Rossii i drugikh stranakh,* edited by Galina Makarevich, 124–36. Moscow: Nauchnaia kniga, 2008.

Lévi-Strauss, Claude. "The Structural Study of Myth." In *Myth: A Symposium,* edited by Thomas A. Sebeok, 81–106. Bloomington: Indiana University Press, 1972.

Leving, Yuri. *Vospitanie optikoi.* Moscow: NLO, 2010.

Lilina, Zlata. "O deshevoi detskoi literature." *Kniga detiam,* no. 1 (1928): 21–30.

Lionni, Leo. *Little Blue and Little Yellow.* New York: Harper Collins, 1959.

Lissitzky, El. *About Two Squares: A Suprematist Tale of Two Squares in Six Constructions.* Translated by Christina Lodder. London: Tate, 2014.

– "Primechaniia ne k etoi knige." In *Fil'm zhizni, 1890–1941,* 7: 24. Moscow: Novyi ermitazh, 2004.

– *Suprematicheskii skaz pro dva kvadrata v shesti postroeniiakh.* Berlin: Skify, 1922.

– "Topography of Typography." In *El Lissitzky: Life, Letters, Texts,* edited by Sophie Lissitzky-Küppers, 359. New York: Thames and Hudson, 1992.

– "Typographical Facts." In *El Lissitzky: Life, Letters, Texts,* edited by Sophie Lissitzky-Küppers, 359–60. New York: Thames and Hudson, 1992.

Lodder, Christina. "Constructivism and Productivism in the 1920s." In *Art into Life: Russian Constructivism, 1914–1932,* edited by Henry Art Gallery, Richard Adams, and Milena Kalinovska, 118–68. New York: Rizzoli, 1990.

Luk'ianova, Irina. *Kornei Chukovskii.* Moscow: Molodaia gvardiia, 2007.

Lunacharsky, Anatoly, ed. *Detskaia literatura: kriticheskii sbornik.* Moscow: Khudozhestvennaia literatura, 1931.

– "Puti detskoi knigi." In *Anatoly Lunacharsky. O detskoi literature, detskom i iunosheskom chtenii,* edited by N. Medvedeva, 158–80. Moscow: Detskaia literatura, 1985.

Lupanova, Irina. *Polveka: Sovetskaia detskaia literatura, 1917–1967.* Moscow: Detskaia literatura, 1969.

Margolin, Victor. *The Struggle for Utopia: Rodchenko, Lissitzky, Moholy-Nagy, 1917–1946.* Chicago: University of Chicago Press, 1997.

Margolina, S. "Proizvodstvennaia detskaia literatura." *Pechat' i revoliutsiia,* no. 5 (1926): 107–16.

Marshak, Samuil. "O bol'shoi literature dlia malen'kikh." In *Sobranie sochinenii v 8 tomakh,* 7: 195–243. Moscow: Khudozhestvennaia literatura, 1971.

– "Pis'mo Maksimu Gor'komu. 9 marta 1927 goda." In *Sobranie sochinenii v 8 tomakh,* 8: 95. Moscow: Khudozhestvennaia literatura, 1972.

Marshak, Samuil, and Vladimir Lebedev. *Vchera i segodnia.* Moscow: Raduga, 1925.

Mayakovsky, Vladimir. *Chto takoe khorosho i chto takoe plokho.* Moscow: Priboi, 1925.

– *Oktiabr' 1917–1918: Geroi i zhertvy revoliuitsii.* Petrograd: Izdanie Komissariata narodnogo prosveshcheniia, 1918.

Meksin, Iakov. "Illiustratsiia v sovetskoi detskoi knige." *Kniga detiam* nos. 5–6 (1928): 39–45.

N.A. "Za bol'shuiu detskuiu literaturu." *Literaturnaia gazeta,* 26 January 1936.

Nikolajeva, Maria. *Children's Literature Comes of Age: Toward a New Aesthetic.* New York: Garland Publishing, 1996.

Nikolajeva, Maria, and Carole Scott. *How Picturebooks Work.* New York: Garland, 2001.

Nodelman, Perry. "Interpretation and the Apparent Sameness of Children's Literature." *Studies in the Literary Imagination* 18, no. 2 (1985): 5–20.

O partiinoi i sovetskoi pechati. Sbornik dokumentov. Moscow: Pravda, 1954.

Olich, Jacqueline. *Competing Ideologies and Children's Literature in Russia, 1918–1935.* Saarbrücken, DE: VDM Verlag, Dr. Müller, 2009.

Oushakine, Serguei Alex. "Machines, Nations, and Faciality: Cultivating Mental Eyes in Soviet
    Books for Children," 157–96. In *The Oxford Handbook of Communist Visual Cultures*, edited
    by Aga Skrodzka, Xiaoning Lu, and Katarzyna Marciniak. Oxford: Oxford University Press,
    2019.
– "Realism with Gaze-Appeal: On Lenin, Children, and Photomontage." In *Jahrbücher für
    Geschichte Osteuropas* 1 (2019): 11–64.
– "Translating Communism for Children: Fables and Posters of the Revolution." *Boundary* 243,
    no. 3 (2016): 159–219.
Petrov, V. "Iz istorii detskoi illiustrirovannoi knigi 1920-kh godov." In *Iskusstvo knigi 1958–1960*. 3:
    349–64. Moscow: Iskusstvo, 1962.
Petrovskii, Miron. *Knigi nashego detstva*. St. Peterburg: izdatel'stvo Ivana Limbakha, 2006.
Pokrovskaia, Anna. "Novye puti detskoi knigi." *Literaturnaia gazeta*, 8 July 1929.
– *Osnovnye techeniia v sovremennoi detskoi literature*. Moscow: Rabotnik proshveshcheniia, 1927.
Putilova, Evgeniia. *Istoriia kritiki sovetskoi detskoi literatury*. Leningrad: Prosveshchenie, 1975.
– *Ocherki po istorii kritiki sovetskoi detskoi literatury, 1917–1941*. Moscow: Detskaia literatura,
    1982.
Razin, Izrail. "Kuda napravit' ogon': Zametki o detskoi literature." *Literaturnaia gazeta*, 14 January
    1931.
Rothenstein, Julian, and Olga Budashevskaya, eds. *Inside the Rainbow: Russian Children's
    Literature, 1920–35 – Beautiful Books, Terrible Times*. London: Redstone Press, 2013.
Rubtsova, Pavla "Chto vliiaet na detskie knizhnye zaprosy." *Kniga detiam*, no. 2 (1928): 17–28.
– "Eksperimental'naia retsenziia detskoi knigi." *Novye detskie knigi*, no. 4 (1926): 12–13.
– "Produktsiia detskoi knigi." *Novye detskie knigi*, no. 4 (1926): 69–70.
Semenova V.G., ed. *Tvortsy sovetskoi detskoi knigi. Prozaiki, poety, khudozhniki. Spravochnik. 1917–
    1932*. Moscow: Rossiiskaia gosudartsvennaia detskaia biblioteka, 2017.
Shklovsky, Viktor. "Art as Device." In *Theory of Prose*, 1–14. Translated by Benjamin Sher. Normal,
    IL: Dalkey Archive Press, 1990.
Siegelbaum, Lewis H. "The Shaping of Soviet Workers' Leisure: Workers' Clubs and Palaces of
    Culture in the 1930s." *International Labor and Working-Class History*, no. 56, *Gendered Labor*
    (1999): 78–92.
Skrodzka, Aga, Xiaoning Lu, and Katarzyna Marciniak, eds. *The Oxford Handbook of Communist
    Visual Cultures*. Oxford: Oxford University Press, 2019.
Steinberg, Mark. *Proletarian Imagination: Self, Modernity, and the Sacred in Russia, 1910–1925*.
    Ithaca, NY: Cornell University Press, 2002.
Steiner, Evgenii. *Stories for Little Comrades: Revolutionary Artists and the Making of Early Soviet
    Children Books*. Translated by Jane Anna Miller. Seattle: University of Washington Press, 1999.
Studenetskii, N., and A. Konevskii. *Nashi vragi i druz'ia*. Moscow: Krest'ianskaia gazeta, 1930.
Tarabukin, Nikolai. *Ot mol'berta – k mashine*. Moscow: Rabotnik prosveshcheniia, 1923.
Todorov, Tzvetan. *The Poetics of Prose*. Translated by Richard Howard. Ithaca, NY: Cornell
    University Press, 1977.
Volotova, Natal'ia. "Kak sozdavalsia 'Robinzon.'" In *Zhizn' i tvorchestvo Marshaka*, edited by Boris
    Galanov, I. Marshak, and M. Petrovskii, 141–50. Moscow: Detskaia literatura, 1975.
Weld, Sara Pankenier. *An Ecology of the Russian Avant-Garde Picturebook*. Amsterdam: John
    Benjamin Publishing, 2018.
"Za deistvitel'no sovetskuiu detskuiu knigu." *Literaturnaia gazeta*, 30 December 1929.

 Tatiana Pravosudovich, spread for Valentin Kataev's *Radio-zhiraf* (*Radio-Giraffe*) (Leningrad, Moscow: Raduga, 1926). The spread presents a visual dialogue between visitors in a zoo and animals equipped with new media. A poem from the book clarifies the scenario:

> People are stunned: Instead of wild animals,
> There are radio-lovers in the zoo now.
> A grey hare contacts a seller regarding her carrots:
> Madam, how much is a kilogram?
> If it's not too expensive, can I get two hundred grams?

PART I

MEDIATION

Early Soviet literature for children performed many functions, but it would be no exaggeration to say that the most crucial of these was *mediation*. The format of the illustrated book served as an institutional framework that allowed pre-revolutionary and non-revolutionary authors and artists to transition to the new publishing realities. The Soviet children's book also helped to build bridges between traditional print media and relatively new forms of education and entertainment such as cinema, photography, and radio. As a tool of mediation, the children's book encouraged the reader to explore different modalities of interacting with the book itself. Reading was not the only option: the book could also be a material resource for producing something new – from cut-out toys to film-on-paper ("flipbook") devices.

Part I focuses precisely on the emergence of the early Soviet children's book as a dynamic interface and a versatile platform for various experiments with book formats in post-revolutionary Russia. Helena Goscilo opens the collection with a study that reconstructs the awkward conversion of a major pre-revolutionary realist artist, Boris Kustodiev, into an illustrator of communist books. In Kustodiev's picture books, all-American boys turned into Soviet Pioneers, effecting, both visually and narratively, a fundamental social and political alteration. A story of adaption and adoption, Goscilo's contribution highlights a critical dimension of the Soviet book: its revolutionary iconography was deeply rooted in non-revolutionary visual tradition. Yuri Leving offers an exploration of a more organic artistic project. Focusing on a single book illustrated by Alisa Poret, Leving demonstrates the emergence of a visual vocabulary that successfully blended cinema, photography, graphic art, and book illustrations. Presenting two different strategies of artistic development, these two case studies usefully point to two poles that defined the limits of the possible in the Soviet Union: even as it promoted communist ideas, Kustodiev's iconography remained markedly pre-revolutionary, whereas Poret's creative illustrations used dynamic visual language to amplify a story of political upheaval.

Erika Wolf expands the study of the early Soviet visual turn in a different direction by exploring the emergence of the first Soviet photo-magazines for children. Significantly, creating a readership in this case meant the transformative creation of persons capable of visually documenting the country's ongoing changes: readers of Pioneer magazines were actively encouraged to become amateur photographers. In this case, optics triumphed not only over phonetics but also over writing. Readers became active producers of socialist narratives, visual and otherwise.

This part's final two contributions explore in detail the activating power of the early Soviet children's book. Using *Samozveri* (*Autoanimals*), illustrated by Aleksandr Rodchenko and Varvara Stepanova as his main example, Aleksandar Bošković demonstrates how the book was turned into a cut-out toy, demanding from its reader, or rather user, a close engagement and constructive input. Didactic yet stimulating, such book-toys, Bošković argues, occupied a transitional position. They unleashed readers' creativity, encouraging them to perform the "deformation" of cardboard figures so as later to design their own three-dimensional paper toys. Perhaps even more significantly, these books taught readers to discern volume and depth beyond flat outlines and templates.

Birgitte Beck Pristed takes this theme to the next level of abstraction by approaching the early Soviet children's book not only as a vehicle for content but also as a material substance. New books, she argues, brought with them a new paper regime that involved children in multiple networks of material exchange and circulation.

When read together, the essays in part I conceptualize the early Soviet children's book as an inter-media genre that encouraged modifications not only of visual and textual languages but also of practices of interaction with books themselves. No longer a static object, the children's book re-emerged in early Soviet Russia as an institution that could effectively mediate between different traditions and generations of book publishing; as a tool for expanding children's visual aptitude and disseminating new ways of seeing; and as a source for developing creative skills and constructing new objects.

chapter one

THREE DEGREES OF EXEMPLARY BOYHOOD IN BORIS KUSTODIEV'S SOVIET PARADISE

HELENA GOSCILO

Boyhood is the longest time in life for a boy.

Booth Tarkington

For to a boy it can seem that he shall never
have what he alone has never had.

Pier Paolo Pasolini

The function of book illustrations, and those in publications targeting children *a fortiori*, is a highly polemical issue, though consensus exists to the extent that no commentator deems illustrations superfluous. Among numerous theorists, Joanne Golden posits five different types of verbal-visual relationships in picture storybooks: "text and picture are symmetrical; text depends on picture for clarification; illustration enhances, elaborates text; text carries primary narrative, illustration is selective; and illustration carries primary narrative, text is selective."[1] For Jane Doonan, the possible goals of visuals vis-à-vis the verbal text are to elaborate, amplify, extend, complement, contradict, and deviate.[2] In a kindred if somewhat profligate vein, Joseph Schwarcz identifies congruency, elaboration, specification, amplification, extension, complementation, alternation, deviation, and counterpoint as the possible interactions between text and pictures.[3] W.J.T. Mitchell, however, famously and programmatically eliminates the longstanding binarism in this multimodal representation to explore what he calls the "imagetext," and, to some extent, Lawrence Sipe follows his example by citing "synergy" as the key element uniting verbal text and image.[4] As evidenced below, of all these categories, I have found Golden's and Doonan's most apposite for my analysis of Boris Kustodiev's (1878–1927) illustrations of three children's books in the 1920s, inasmuch as several coincide with the roles fulfilled by the graphics I examine.

Entering a Brave New World

Renowned primarily for his numerous self-portraits and memorable portraits of notable contemporary *Kulturarbeiter* (Alexander Benois, Ivan Bilibin, Feodor Chaliapin, Aleksander Golovin, Evgenii Lansere, Aleksei Remizov, Ilia Repin, Nikolai Rerikh, Nikolai Sapunov, Konstantin Somov, Maximilian Voloshin, Evgenii Zamiatin), his gallery of "Russian types,"[5] colourful paintings of lush female bodies, affluent merchants' lives and wives, and provincial rituals of boisterous seasonal festivities, Astrakhan-born Kustodiev also designed costumes and sets for the theatre as well as illustrating both adult and children's books.[6] As a member of Mir Iskusstva (World of Art) from 1910 onward,[7] Kustodiev generally favoured figuration, decorativeness, and a broad, vivid palette, while avoiding the technological and scientific themes so popular among the early Soviet avant-garde.[8] Yet he not only supported the revolutionary takeover, as evidenced in his renowned painting *Bolshevik* (1920), which depicts the eponymous figure in strikingly mythic proportions, but also joined the Association of the Artists of Revolutionary Russia (AARR) and participated in its exhibitions in 1925 and 1926 – the only member of Mir Iskusstva to do so.[9] His last decade showcased his skill in adjusting not only to the new Soviet regime, but also to the period's literature for children that his graphics accompanied. Perhaps the championship of his highly placed admirer Anatoly Lunacharsky, the unpredictable, film-obsessed people's Commissar for Enlightenment, accounted for the artist's numerous commissions. In any event, Kustodiev gave every evidence of unproblematically accepting the new order. Multifaceted and eloquent, his visuals in children's books range from a modified minimalism unambiguously indebted to Vladimir Mayakovsky to painterly pastel-lyricism, depending on the subject and ideological orientation of the given written text. In this genre, Kustodiev's stylistic diversity translated authors' political orientation into images that buttress the specifics of each author's "program," whether it be to educate or indoctrinate. My analysis of his visuals rests on three children's books positing increasingly praiseworthy boyhoods: *Bol'shevik Tom* (*Bol'shevik Tom*), *Dzhimmi Dzhoi v gosti k pioneram* (*Jimmi Joy Visits the Pioneers*), both published in 1925, and *Detiam o Lenine* (*For Children about Lenin*), which appeared a year later.

After a drastic decline in the production of books for children immediately following the October Revolution,[10] the genre effloresced in the mid-1920s, stimulated partly by the 1921 establishment by the Commissariat of Education (Narkompros) of the Institute of Children's Reading and the announcement by the party's Central Committee in 1924 of the need for a special kind of literature for children.[11] Responding to this imperative, both state and private publishing houses such as Ivan Sytin, Raduga (Rainbow), and Siniaia Ptitsa (Blue Bird) proliferated children's books intended to shape the "New Soviet Child" as an enlightened little citizen of the new order.[12] While the main issue for authors may have been the degree of adherence to party ideology, aesthetics is what tended to divide illustrators into two diametrically contrasting groups: those working in a figurative mode versus proponents of modernist abstraction exemplified by cubism and suprematism, of which El Lissitzky (1890–1941) was the chief, most extreme, exponent. It is impossible to determine whether his geometry-inspired illustrations engaged children or paralleled the fate of the avant-garde's artistic overall efforts, which remained incomprehensible to the masses. Many illustrators occupied an intermediate position, such as Vladimir Lebedev (1891–1967), art editor of Detgiz publishing house (State Publishing House for Children's Literature) in Leningrad (1924–33), whose volume-based figures, frequently suspended in two-dimensional space, surely appealed to its small readers. Yet when Socialist Realism became obligatory in 1932–4, it was Lebedev who fell afoul of authorities for his highly individual avant-gardism, whereas the more radical Lissitzky fared better, possibly because of his international status and the tuberculosis that augured his early death (1941). Despite his accommodation to the new sociopolitical structures and the expectations they imposed upon artists, Kustodiev never abandoned the figurative mode for the abstractionism that was so alien to his lifelong aesthetics, though the influence of the latter modified his palette and his representational mode. Like Sergei Mikhalkov in his prodigious output within children's verbal culture, Kustodiev in many ways was "a traditionalist in the land of innovators,"[13] and, had he lived into the 1930s, his fundamental aesthetic would have found favour with official cadres monitoring artistic production.

Reoriented Co-optation in *Bol'shevik Tom*

Among the many presses publishing children's literature during the creatively and chaotically prolific twenties, Leningrad's Brokgauz-Efron publishing house printed a series of children's poems by such authors as Samuil Marshak and Aleksei N. Tolstoi, illustrated by Kustodiev, Vladimir Konashevich, Mstislav Dobuzhinskii, and other notable graphic artists.[14] *Bol'shevik Tom,* a ten-page booklet of children's verses by Nadezhda Pavlovich, with seventeen black-and-white drawings by Kustodiev, had a print run of 10,000 copies.[15] As most adult Soviet readers doubtless realized, Pavlovich without acknowledgment had pilfered Tom's escapades from Mark Twain's *Adventures of Tom Sawyer* (1876) but inflected them ideologically in addition to dramatically altering Twain's ending.[16] Her manifest goal was to deliver a political salvo against the deleterious effects on children's upbringing of an affluently indolent United States while promoting the Soviet Union as a haven for youth and, more broadly, as a land of happy, bustling unanimity.

Belonging to the popular genre of bad boy literature, Twain's internationally renowned novel, published in a variety of illustrated editions, narrates in an ironic key the hooliganish activities of its juvenile protagonist, eventually transforming the inventive, irrepressible ne'er-do-well into a more sober near-adult suddenly in possession of capital. Resurfacing in several sequels, Tom radiates the traditional appeal of the rebellious adolescent endowed with spunk and imagination who skillfully outwits adults, including the seemingly strict but affectionate aunt who rears him.[17]

Pavlovich's verses recast Twain's tale into a propagandistic tract that decries Western bourgeois values and rescues Tom from the moneyed, self-indulgent household of his purportedly repressive Aunt Polly. Instead of abruptly acquiring wealth, Pavlovich's incorrigible and bored Tom flees to the Soviet Union, where he joins the gratified beneficiaries of Soviet power and thrives among the joyous, purposeful collective allegedly indifferent to material wealth. This drastic change aside, Pavlovich preserves several highlights of Twain's plot but interprets their significance, and Tom's environment, through Soviet values. At the same time, Kustodiev materialized the text's transparent message in arresting images.

Though his canvases typically teemed with vivid hues, Kustodiev here adjusted his aesthetic to the minimalism associated above all with Mayakovsky's illustrations and posters, which favoured the ideologically infused red of the Soviet army. Iurii Molok astutely noted the impact of posters on book illustrations in general during this decade.[18] Kustodiev used colour only for the cover, where the red in the title and of the Soviet star on Tom's checkered cap reinforces Tom's identity, at tale's end, as a Soviet protagonist (fig. 1.1). The boy's headgear, lively face, merry smile, and missing tooth anticipated above all the ebullient image of Ostap Bender in *Dvenadtsat' stul'ev* (*Twelve Chairs*, 1928), an older but similarly anti-establishment, roguish manipulator of the 1920s who captured adult Soviet readers' imagination.[19]

Inside the booklet, the first illustration depicts Aunt Polly as a representative of greed and punitive capriciousness: a mountainous woman with a moon-shaped face, pince-nez, and frown, she recalls the representation of bloated Yankee capitalists in early Soviet posters (e.g., Viktor Deni's *Kapital* [1920]) as well as Kustodiev's own caricatures, such as that of Graf Ignat'ev (Count Ignatiev) for the issue titled *Olimp* in the satirical journal *Adskaia pochta* (*The Mail of Hell*) [1906] (fig. 1.2).[20] Her subsequent image – sprawled limply on a couch, shown from the rear as she bends over Tom to whip him, or sobbing melodramatically before three stone-faced American elders – captures her as the pumped-up, ill-tempered capitalist given to wielding the rod and adopting emotional stances (fig. 1.3). Clearly, she has no understanding of her nephew and his needs, and Kustodiev's caricatures of her, comic and alienating for the young reader, visually convey her incomprehension of and remoteness from ebullient young life. In short, unlike the young Soviet state, America, as represented by Aunt Polly, cannot or will not allow young talent and energy to flourish and cannot direct it to worthwhile social goals. Hence the flight to the land of the newly established Soviets – a popular scenario in the propagandistic orientation of children's literature during this and later decades.

1.2. This early instance of Boris Kustodiev's skill at caricature confirms that, two decades later, he had retained his talent for pointed satirical depictions of individuals and groups. Kustodiev, caricature of Graf Ignat'ev, cover of *Olimp* issue of *Adskaia pochta*, no. 3 (1906).

1.1. Boris Kustodiev, cover of *Bol'shevik Tom* by Nadezhda Pavlovich (Leningrad: Brokgauz-Efron, 1925).

1.3. The hyperbolic technique of caricature, which Kustodiev uses to highlight Aunt Polly's undesirable character traits – histrionic emotionalism and obese self-indulgence – likewise applied in the treatment of desiccated, senescent American officialdom. Boris Kustodiev, illustration for *Bol'shevik Tom*, unpaginated.

Throughout the text, Tom appears younger than on the cover, partly because, without his peaked cap, we see his dishevelled hair and his knee-length black pants, as well as his white shirt and a loose black tie that in shape conjures up the red kerchief of the Pioneers.[21] Kustodiev illustrates Tom's solitary antics – stealing candy from a jar, cutting off the luxurious fur of his aunt's Siberian cat, appropriating her makeup, and painting an insulting image of her, infested with rats, on the wall of a room – in the cartoonish style popularized by posters, comics, and his own earlier satirical visuals (fig. 1.4).

Once Tom sees an atlas and learns where the "country of Bolsheviks" is located, the visuals gain amplitude and complexity, primarily to reflect the wealth of experience available in the Soviet Union but presumably lacking in the United States. Images, in other words, bolster the concept of Soviet plenitude, one that forges meaningful socialist connections, in contrast to its American egotistical counterpart, which breeds isolation and alienation among the young. Accordingly, Kustodiev's visual of Tom's dream, which adumbrates his auspicious destiny, shows various boys waving welcomingly; huge banners with the Soviet star and the hammer and sickle; a speeding steamboat in the Finnish Gulf; and crowds of young people brandishing pennants, projected against a partial map of Leningrad (fig. 1.5). This vision of large-scale celebrative hospitality and vigorous activity causes Tom to smile in his sleep and subsequently to flee from the benighted United States. The final image of Tom in the USSR, standing – outsized,

1.4. Boris Kustodiev, illustration for *Bol'shevik Tom*, unpaginated.

triumphant, legs astride, and hands on hips – against the background of a thriving factory, is of a contented adolescent, wearing a peaked cap and a Komsomol kerchief, "free as a bird," as the text phrases it. He finally has discovered liberty, education, and purpose, as suggested by his stance (fig. 1.6). That he was "made to be a Soviet citizen" is implied throughout by the repeated phrase, "You've become a real Bolshevik, Tom," as when he stoically endures his aunt's whipping without uttering a sound.

In short, Kustodiev's images, rendered in a graphic style indebted to Mir Iskusstva, yet simplified under avant-gardist and revolutionary influences, support and enhance or elaborate (according to Golden's and Doonan's categories) the message of the text, which equates American life with wanton excess and idleness, self-indulgence, and pointless mischief, contrasting it to the teleological discipline of Soviet communal existence. Children reading the booklet and perusing its images are meant to learn the inestimable value of education and work, while also appreciating the superiority of their country's way of life to that in the financially successful but misguided United States. The visuals reinforce the propaganda through satire and hyperbole in the American segment and, by contrast, through the appealing aura of focused vigour and maturity that Tom emanates once he becomes assimilated into the Bolshevik paradise. Boyhood in America corrupts, whereas the Soviet Union facilitates a meaningful life for the adolescent. Banalized in the quagmire of America's superfluous wealth and leisure, Tom belatedly finds a true calling by flight to the land of work, community, and self-fulfillment, all conveyed in the final image of him as a goal-oriented, self-confident young man projected against the industrial background of the utopian future to which his formerly undirected energy is now consecrated.

1.5. Tom's dream constitutes a prophetic vision of the bliss and plenitude to be discovered only in the Soviet Union. Boris Kustodiev, illustration for *Bol'shevik Tom*, unpaginated.

1.6. Joining the vibrant society of the Soviets and its Komsomol, Tom lands in Eden, where he succeeds in attaining the ego fulfillment unavailable to him in the degenerate United States. Boris Kustodiev, illustration for *Bol'shevik Tom*, unpaginated.

Turning Fairy Tales into Reality: *Dzhimmi Dzhoi*

A similar aesthetic informs Kustodiev's seven illustrations for Lidiia Lesnaia's seven-page fairy tale in verse titled *Dzhimmi Dzhoi v gosti k pioneram* (*Jimmy Joy Visits the Pioneers*), published by Dom knigi, with a print run of 10,000 copies, but with a more muted political message than that in *Bol'shevik Tom*.[22] What links the two works are the young male protagonists, their voyages to the terrestrial Eden that is the USSR, and their blissful arrival in the land of untold joys for adolescents. The name in the booklet's title, clearly not of Russian origin, also references an American persona: the musician Jimmy Joy (1902–1962), a big-band leader, singer, saxophonist, and clarinetist especially popular in the 1920s.[23] Indeed, what particularly seems to stimulate Lesnaia's Dzhimmi is Soviet Pioneers' drumming, which prompts the boy to hide in his father's suitcase when the man refuses to take Dzhimmi along on his voyage to Leningrad, the cradle of the 1917 revolution. Once the ship carrying father and son encounters turbulence, Dzhimmi tumbles overboard (fig. 1.7). His subsequent adventures showcase his fortitude and determination to join the Pioneers, whatever the trials or temptations en route, including an island populated exclusively by simians and peacocks (fig. 1.8). Unlike Tom, Dzhimmi shows his superiority by realizing early, with no history of nefarious or foolish antics, that the

1.7. Dzhimmi goes overboard. Boris Kustodiev, illustration for Lidiia Lesnaia, *Dzhimmi Dzhoi v gosti k pioneram* (Leningrad: GIZ, 1925), unpaginated.

country in which a boy can realize his potential is the Soviet Union. More serious and organized than Tom, he yearns for adventure and, above all, a locus worthy of his abilities.

Eager and resourceful, Dzhimmi jettisons possessions (a bourgeois burden, after all) and transforms his (significantly) red kerchief into a flag on his suitcase, which serves as a boat when opened and emptied (*chelnok*). Offered humorously useless advice by avian and piscine sages in the role of fairy-tale magic helpers, he finally is rescued by a Soviet hydroplane, which transports him to hospitable Leningrad. As a bona fide magic helper descending from the sky, Russia's modern aeronautical technology prevails over nature, and, true to the era's touted spirit of internationalism, Leningrad's residents hail Dzhimmi enthusiastically, tolerating his peculiar American tastes: he neither eats seeds nor drinks tap water (*ne p'et syroi vody*), and he washes his hands before eating.

Embracing the trajectory of many fairy tales, but with a new state message, the text is somewhat predictable and hackneyed. Admittedly, the narrative follows the structure and motifs of countless fairy tales: the young hero in search of a goal, the teleological journey, obstacles that cause delays throughout the journey, unexpected encounters

1.8. In the spirit of children's adventure narratives, Kustodiev creates in *Dzhimmi Dzhoi* an image of an island teeming with exoticism and possibilities that Dzhimmi nevertheless bypasses in his eagerness to experience Soviet bliss. Kustodiev, illustration for *Dzhimmi Dzhoi*, unpaginated.

1.9. Happy at last to reach the land of the Soviets, Dzhimmi is greeted by a hospitable and egalitarian population. The habits distinguishing Dzhimmi from his Soviet counterparts are inscribed on the hangar: Dzhimmi does not eat sunflower seeds; he washes his hands before every meal; and he does not drink water that has not been boiled. Kustodiev, illustration for *Dzhimmi Dzhoi*, unpaginated.

en route, anthropomorphized beings, magic helpers, the final attainment of the goal, and the happy ending. Whereas most fairy tales require decoding, however, Lesnaia unambiguously spells out the meaning of her verses and their protagonist's desire to bond with lucky Soviet children. The text "redeems" the then-contentious genre of the fairy tale by sovietizing it.

Kustodiev manages to inject originality into his visuals: combining black, red, bronze, and blue, he uses red sparingly, so that it stands out in the flag/Pioneer kerchief and in the Soviet pentagram on the hydroplane, though the cover and concluding image exploit red's national associations more profusely. As in *Bol'shevik Tom*, the West is portrayed as a site of helter-skelter immoderation and luxury, whereas the Soviet Union is a Shangri-la of disciplined communal merrymaking. The last image, which incorporates red in symmetrical rhythm, shows festive Pioneers rejoicing in their "happy childhood," while the three habits distinguishing Dzhimmi from his Soviet counterparts are inscribed on the roof of the hangar over which the boy, standing on top of the hydroplane, flourishes what now has become his red Pioneer/Komsomol kerchief. The USSR and its youth generously accept such outlandish preferences as washing hands before meals because the country purportedly welcomes diversity and acknowledges differences (though apparently scorns hygiene) (fig. 1.9).

Like Bol'shevik Tom, through fortitude Dzhimmi attains his commendable *telos*, and visuals in both narratives spotlight the young heroes' integration into a broad social group basking in self-fulfillment. Both texts contrast adolescents' economically privileged but socially isolated and aimless existence in the United States to the fruitful promise of an exuberant collective that is the USSR. And unlike in many children's texts of the era, international traffic here flows in one direction – to the Soviet Union as the New Eden – a *telos* likewise popularized in films of the 1920s such as Lev Kuleshov's *Neobychainye prikliucheniia Mistera Vesta v strane bol'shevikov* (*The Extraordinary Adventures of Mr. West in the Land of the Soviets*, 1924), which illustrates just how much the new USSR has to teach the misguided West and above all the United States as the bastion of capitalism. Dzhimmi's boyhood surpasses Tom's because he needs no prompting to choose the Soviet Union as his preferred destiny. Unlike Tom, he ignores his father's wishes because his ideals trump parental caveats, for he realizes precisely which country can accommodate his dreams and enable him to realize his full potential. Spotlighting his journey rather than what prompts it makes for greater diversity in both verbal and visual texts.

Selection of what precisely should be illustrated suggests several emphases on Kustodiev's part: if *Bol'shevik Tom* contrasts rebellious mischief and an overly pampered life to a buoyant, educated, and useful one, *Dzhimmi Dzhoi* portrays a disorientingly frenetic America, but focuses on youthful adventure, with one of the seven illustrations devoted to a beguiling image of playful monkeys encountered by the boy en route to the USSR – a touch of exoticism in a *Treasure Island* key at odds with the new values of industrial advancement, but bound to appeal to children, with their addiction to narratives of adventure (fig. 1.8).[24] In both instances, Kustodiev's visuals equate the United States with distracting, dead-end superfluity and culminate in images projecting the fruitfully harnessed energy of the utopia finally attained. Children perusing both of these "political indoctrination" texts encounter edifying images that cast the Soviet Union as the ultimate dream of all children wishing to escape the pernicious forces of capitalism and reassure them that they live in Leibnitz's "best of all possible worlds."

The *Lenineid* as the Nation's History

Whereas the two publications discussed so far proselytize about dissatisfied American boys' *Sehnsucht* – their estimable yearning to join their purportedly more fortunate counterparts in the Soviet Union – *Detiam o Lenine* (*For Children about Lenin*, 1926) offers a hagiography of the major Soviet icon of the 1920s, merely two years after his death. Lenin's was the exemplary boyhood par excellence because it prepared him for the adult role of proclaimed international saviour and icon. Whereas Tom's narrative pivots on personal/political conversion and Dzhimmi's partly on the seduction of adventure, Lenin's provides the very foundation for the nation's history, and American boys prove the beneficiaries of his supreme achievements. The Soviet Union, after all, was his brainchild, guaranteeing the meaningful boyhood to which American youth reportedly aspired.

Created by Anna Kravchenko for the Institute of Children's Reading and published in a run of 15,000 copies, the book follows the conventional structure of hagiography, tracing the various stages of Lenin's life virtually from womb to tomb.[25] Here the biography of the Soviet Union's supreme ideologue supplies the text's doctrine, for that life is sutured to key moments in the nation's history and therefore charts the progress of the Bolshevik cause and triumph. And the uninspired pudgy face on the cover likely gratified children, for it confirmed that the incomparable Lenin once was also an unprepossessing-looking child, if a peerless, unique one fated for greatness.[26] In fact, *For Children about Lenin* leaves no doubt that Lenin's boyhood surpasses those of Dzhimmi and Tom, for it readies him for political sainthood.

Each of the thirty-four narrative paragraphs in prose (one per page) has its own illustration. As befits a genre different from the stories of Tom and Dzhimmi, the aesthetic mutes contours, with a pencil for outlines, and offers a colour scheme distinct from that in the narratives of the two American boys' flight from the jaded West. Kustodiev lyricizes Lenin in a painterly idiom that, moreover, favours pastels, rendering in pencil and watercolor the illustrations that accord with the more leisurely narrative of a historicized, highly condensed, consummate Soviet life unfolded as a story of national origins, not unlike Virgil's *Aeneid*.[27] Since that life is framed in the politics of class struggle, Kravchenko launches it with a denunciation of lamentable inequities during the tsarist era, contrasting the shiftless exploiters with the oppressed toilers in both city and countryside, in the timeworn

1.10. Boris Kustodiev, illustration in Anna Kravchenko, *Detiam o Lenine: Sbornik rasskazov* (Moscow & Leningrad: GIZ, 1926), 9.

juxtaposition of "then and now," "before and after," popularized by Mayakovsky and flourishing nowadays in ads for diets and cosmetic makeovers: "That's how bad life for peasants was under stardom" ("Tak plokho zhilos' pri tsare krest'ianam," 4), "All workers in the factories lived just as badly" ("Tak zhe plokho zhili vse rabochie … na fabrike," 8).

Such reductive polarities preponderate throughout: the privileged predators benefit from the oppressed workers, who suffer unjust punishment and incarceration (fig. 1.10); whereas the text presents the assassination of Alexander II as condign ("He owned a lot of estates and money" ["Mnogo bylo u nego imenii i deneg"], 16),[28] it registers admiringly the courage of Sof'ia Perovskaia and Andrei Zheliabov, the two major Narodnaia Volia (People's Will, the Populists' political organization) orchestrators of his violent demise. Their efforts anticipate what the next section casts as the Ul'ianov pantheon – "A family of great revolutionaries" ("Sem'ia velikikh revoliutsionerov," 18) – in preparation for the early political exploits of the narrative's focal hero: Volodia Ul'ianov (20), a well-rounded *otlichnik* (star pupil) with a passion for books, chess, and skating: in sum, a young Soviet "Renaissance man" (fig. 1.11).

1.11. Boris Kustodiev, illustration in *Detiam o Lenine*, 21.

The subsequent pages compress the revolutionary and military activities of the early twentieth century, including the Bloody Sunday Massacre of 1905 and the horrors of the First World War. They spotlight Lenin's extraordinary intelligence and vision, commitment, self-sacrifice, oratorical skills, and inspirational capacities as he oversees ameliorative measures from abroad, foments anti-governmental action once he returns to Petrograd, writes inflammatory articles, and finally masterminds the 1917 October Revolution (though earlier he is cited as declaring, "We'll stop killing one another" ["Perestanem ubivat' drug druga," 42]). Like the saints of hagiographies, he distinguishes himself from the common run by virtue of his miraculous vision, exceptional talents, and charisma – all of which dramatically ameliorate the lives of those around him and, by extension, of the country's entire population. After Lenin's sickness and death, which the narrative bathetically ascribes to self-sacrificing overwork ("Vladimir Il'ich overtaxed himself working … He became exhausted and fell ill" ["Rabotal Vladimir Il'ich sverkh sil … On ochen' utomilsia i zabolel,"

[62]), his supporters attract peasants and workers "from all over the world" (though only China, Japan, and India are explicitly mentioned and feature in Kustodiev's illustration, 61).[29] They struggle for their rights according to the principles codified by Lenin. Among his grateful legatees number not only the two classes that Lenin supposedly championed, but also members of the Komsomol, as well as Pioneers and their younger cohort of Octobrites – all of them Leninites in the making. They, too, presumably had older members of their families perish in the noble fight against tsarism.

Since Kustodiev's illustrations correspond to paragraphs that often contain reports of several developments, the drawings are necessarily selective, although, in some cases, they amplify the text. Once Lenin enters the story (21), he appears in only eight of the subsequent twenty-five visuals (often interacting with sizable audiences), while the remainder focus primarily on peasants, urban workers, or masses embroiled in war or revolution. Kustodiev relies on the familiar, depicting Lenin in his trademark flat cap (63) and in poses that duplicate iconic paintings and posters[30] – Lenin as the central element in the image, addressing rapt crowds, his arm extended (47, 53) or hand outstretched (55), as in Adol'f Strakhov-Braslavskii's *V. Ul'ianov (Lenin),*

1.12. Boris Kustodiev, illustration for *Detiam o Lenine*, 47.

1870–1924 (1924), Valentin Shcherbakov's *Prizrak brodit po Evrope, prizrak kommu-nizma* (*A Spectre Is Haunting Europe, the Spectre of Communism*, 1920s), countless monuments, and paintings by Valentin Serov, Isaak Brodskii, and many other artists (fig. 1.12).[31]

To ensure Lenin's instant identifiability, Kustodiev consistently colours his clothing a dark grey or black, with a light tinge of blue or green (27). According to Erikh Goller-bakh, who worked in publishing and collaborated with Kustodiev, the artist, despite his many illustrations of Lenin, complained about having to rely on photographs of the leader instead of drawing him from life.[32] An outstanding and prolific portraitist, Kustodiev argued that the static nature of photography and the ephemerality of the photographic moment militated against an authentic representation of a human be-ing, for it could not render movement, shifts in expression, and gestures intrinsic to a given individual.[33] Film, he maintained, made for a more reliable source[34] – a view widespread among artists of the 1920s, including Alisa Poret (1902–1984), whose *sui generis* images of revolution recall Eisenstein's shots of the masses, favouring a cine-matic high angle perspective and split-screen effects (see Yuri Leving's chapter in this volume).

As in other genres of Soviet culture, so in Kustodiev's illustrations, Lenin's continu-ing presence following his death manifests itself symbolically in legends and banners

1.13. Boris Kustodiev, illustration of a procession to Lenin's tomb, in *Detiam o Lenine*, 65.

bearing his name (71). The closing visual evoking his "spirit" presents marching Pioneers/Komsomolites, followed by small children, most clad in red, who model for the book's readers what ideally awaits them as little Soviet citizens – mass processions commemorating Lenin's legacy as they pass by the sacred altar: the mausoleum containing his chemically preserved corpse (fig. 1.13).[35] Intriguingly, Kustodiev's depiction of the population's outpouring of emotion at Lenin's death in the form of crowds snaking in a long, sinuous line to Lenin's coffin (65) would be reprised two decades later in Sergei Eisenstein's *Ivan Groznyi* (*Ivan the Terrible*, 1944), as hordes of Russians approach Ivan's retreat in a cave, imploring his return to the capital as the country's ruler (fig. 1.14). Thus, one may conclude that a lively symbiosis existed among book illustrations, film, and posters in the early Soviet period.

A chief goal of Kustodiev's illustrations in *Detiam o Lenine* is to initiate children into the iconography of Soviet power. For instance, to situate Lenin in a context of revolutionary activists, Kustodiev flanks his image with those of the two Krzhizhanovskiis (Gleb and his spouse, Zinaida)[36] to the left and his wife, Nadezhda Krupskaia, and Vasilii Shelgunov to the right (23).[37] Encircling their portraits are the politically loaded visual emblems of the new Soviet regime: the jettisoned shackles of capitalism beside a toppled crown and sceptre; books that educate the population according to Lenin's reading of Marxism; smoke-belching factories as guarantors of industrial

1.14. Still from Sergei Eisenstein's *Ivan the Terrible*, Part 1 (1944). Camera work by Eduard Tisse and Andrei Moskvin, Central Cinema Studio.

progress; and the hammer and sickle that signalled the twenties' *smychka* and would become the ubiquitous emblem of Sovietism, likewise highlighted in Iakov Protazanov's *Aelita: Queen of Mars* (1924) of those years (fig. 1.15).[38]

Here the "pedagogy of images," with their capacity for simultaneity, deftly conflates fundamental principles that would be difficult to enumerate concisely through the medium of words. Similarly, the many depictions of the populace's deplorable living and working conditions (25), the smug indifference of the portly affluent (49), and the violence of war and revolution (35, 37, 41, 43) are all communicated in compressed, eloquent images (e.g., 39) that arguably could have served as preliminary sketches for posters and paintings of the sort produced by Iurii Pimenov and Kuz'ma Petrov-Vodkin during the late 1920s, but, like ABC texts, are simplified for the child reader. By learning about Lenin's life, children would be able grasp their nation's history and its remarkable progress in the first decades of the twentieth century, which triumphed over the inequities of the tsarist era, creating the quintessential egalitarian society that is the Soviet Union. And Kustodiev's illustrations cement the official symbols of Sovietdom into young readers' memory.

1.15. Just as icons and religious paintings show Jesus Christ with his disciples, so Lenin appears flanked by his disciples – canonical Soviet saints – and framed by the symbols of Sovietdom as well as symbols of defeated tsardom. Boris Kustodiev, illustration in *Detiam o Lenine*, 23.

Troping Progress/ion

Maria Nikolajeva, an opinionated scholar of children's picture books, has argued that journeys in children's books may follow a linear or, more often, circular pattern: "home – departure from home – adventure – return home," with the last functioning as security, and the journey itself undertaken for the purpose of maturation.[39] Rather dogmatically extolling the linear mode, Nikolajeva associates it in Russia with the twentieth century and specifically Kornei Chukovsky's pioneering *Krokodil* (*Crocodile,* wr. 1916; pd. 1917), while in a sweeping Mayakovsksian gesture carelessly and unjustly dismissing children's books of the tsarist era as "trash" and "safe" stories with "a pretty kitten or bunny as protagonist" and transpiring in a closed space.[40] She ignores the fact that the circular journey draws on oral narratives (including Homer's *Odyssey*) and may serve as an aesthetic/conceptual structural device, not merely symptomatize a conservative ideological stance. Journeys, after all, are not confined to the geographical, as Laurence Sterne's *Sentimental Journey* (1768) whimsically established. And the ideal journey of the young Volodia Ul'ianov – exiled in 1897 to Siberia and then abroad, only to return home in 1917 as Vladimir Lenin – was both geographically circular and ideologically linear, as the historian Edward Crankshaw has insisted.[41] Perhaps Lenin's most significant journey, however, was vertical, for the small, unprepossessing boy from a provincial bourgeois family eventually was elevated to the status of a national (arguably, international) icon.[42]

Moreover, as Ella Gankina amply demonstrates, pre-Soviet offerings for children encompassed a wide variety of topics and genres: illustrated alphabet books such as Ivan Terebenev's *Podarok detiam …* (*A Gift for Children,* 1814), with images of various social types and professions that anticipate Mayakovsky's children's books a century later; an intriguing volume by Leontii Magnitskii, *Arifmetika* (*Arithmetic,* 1703); and both literary and folkloric fairy tales, such as Vladimir Odoevskii's *Pestrye skazki* (*Motley Folktales,* 1833) and Petr Ershov's *Konek-Gorbunok* (*Hunchback Horsey,* 1856). The didacticism of many pre-Soviet publications – from which the second half of the nineteenth century distanced itself to a degree – presaged the often ponderous propagandistic nature of Soviet children's books, where the journey proved both circular and linear, depending on the author. In most cases and periods, what mattered most was the centrality of the exemplar-protagonist's journey, for it conveyed dynamism and, in the context of the early twentieth century, readiness to change – a requisite for the new Soviet man, woman, and child.

The road in Soviet children's books structured and troped a clutch of concepts fundamental to the ideology of the new state: internationalism, progress, production, collectivity, and historical inevitability – all phenomena inseparable from labour and Lenin. The concepts operated most frequently in the form of heavily freighted binaries, articulated most simply and forcefully in Mayakovsky's influential, militantly politicized verses and visuals as bad/good, then/now, old/new, victims and enemies/

victors and allies, white or black/red, with the October Revolution as the watershed episode. Such binaries are rhetorically instanced in his publication with the nakedly moralistic title of *Chto takoe khorosho i chto takoe plokho?* (*What's Good and What's Bad?* 1925. Indeed, Mayakovsky's works established the aesthetic of the "imagetext" theorized by W.J.T. Mitchell in *Picture Theory* (1994) or "iconotext" by Kristin Hallberg (1982) and "picturebook" by Nikolajeva that few subsequently essayed with comparable success.[43] Mayakovsky's *Oktiabr' 1917–18: geroi i zhertvy revoliutsii* (*October 1917–18: Heroes and Victims of the Revolution*, 1918) in both title and contents adheres to the reductive binary model akin to mathematical formulae that he made his own. Lissitzky materialized the most radical version of the imagebook in his innovative and unrepeatable "children's" *Pro dva kvadrata: Suprematicheskii skaz* (*About Two Squares: A Suprematist Tale*, 1922), which leaned on Kazimir Malevich's black and red squares.[44] Children's ability to understand, let alone enjoy, such an intellectualized rendition of revolutionary victory, which may delight specialists and academics, seems dubious at best.

Though Kustodiev's modified palette took the Mayakovsky trend into account, he had little in common with Lissitzky. Moreover, his visuals in *For Children about Lenin* seem downright retrograde by comparison with his illustrations of Tom's and Dzhimmi's flights to the USSR. And his images accord with Kravchenko's text, for, *pace* Nikolajeva, the iconic boyhood of Volodia Ul'ianov soft pedals his actual sojourn abroad as an adult and presents his early years within the geographical frame of pre-revolutionary Russia. Significantly, his journey, unlike Tom's and Dzhimmi's, is not spatial, but temporal, echoing Peter the Great's renowned historical leap forward to create a politically modern, changed world, one in tune with technological and political progress. In fact, Kustodiev's illustrations, and especially those in *For Children about Lenin*, suggest the compatibility of graphics and the new, revolutionary media of film. Lissitzky astutely declared, "We're moving to structuring the book like a film: beginning, plot development, major moments, and dénouement" ("My idem k knige, kotoruiu stroim kak fil'm: zaviazka, razvitie deistviia, udarnye momenty, razviazka").[45] While Lissitzky focused on montage, many children's books borrowed from photography and various aspects of film, under the influence of original theorists and directors such as Dziga Vertov, Lev Kuleshev, Vsevolod Pudovkin, and Sergei Eisenstein. Not unlike the preceding era, when Mir iskusstva crossed traditional boundaries of genre to forge a new aesthetic, so the twenties and early thirties experimented with multiple genres in their struggle to devise an expressive form for the new world of the Soviets as the *telos* of the revolution. And the concept of the route from the egregious pre-revolutionary past to the auspicious present and envisioned radiant future dominated not only children's books but also adult literature and film for decades. It also informed the discourse of literary criticism and biography, prompting countless titles of *Tvorchestii put'* (*Creative Trajectory*) along with the subject's name: *Pushkina, Lermontova, Turgeneva, Bloka,* and so forth.

The narrative of American boys' flight to the USSR paralleled three of the most famous and implausible films of the Soviet imaginary: Kuleshov's *The Extraordinary Adventures of Mr. West in the Land of the Bolsheviks* (1924), where the signally named condescending Mr. West visits the Soviet Union, only to be humbled by realizing its superiority; Grigorii Aleksandrov's *Tsirk* (*Circus*, 1936), in which the USSR provides the heroine with a democratic refuge from the racism of the United States; and Aleksandrov's post-Ezhov-era *Svetlyi put'* (*The Radiant Path*, 1940), which overtly engages the fantasy of fairy tales as it celebrates a female worker's heady ascent (quite literally, in a heaven-bound car) from the provinces to the symbolic centre of Stalin's Moscow, with Stalin as the sovereign-spouse.[46] The two American-boyhood publications illustrated by Kustodiev fully accord with the three films targeting Soviet adults. And, of course, Lenin's boyhood led to the maturation of a political genius who enabled the creation of a world-changing modern utopia.

Paradigmatic Boyhoods and Kustodiev's Modulations

The three texts illustrated by Kustodiev belong to the rich fund of highly politicized materials for children's edification proclaiming that they dwell in an unequalled Eden, one masterminded by the singular genius and unremitting efforts of the supreme Soviet leader, Lenin – the unsurpassed icon of Soviet boyhood. Stalinism would revise that narrative, substituting Stalin (devoid of boyhood and adolescence in official propaganda) as the ultimate architect of children's happiness, for which they ritualistically thanked him, frequently in posters that paired him with groups of breathlessly adulatory "little citizens" whose gratitude purportedly knew no bounds.[47] What might astound those specialists in Kustodiev's art who are accustomed to his chromatic palette on canvas and in stage designs is the colourist-artist's transition to standard black-and white-graphics coupled with tendentious texts, so at odds with his role as the foremost visual chronicler of the merchant and entrepreneurial class, religious rituals and personae, and provincial beauties and bounties.[48]

Mark Etkind justly emphasizes Kustodiev's versatility, his fertile exploration of virtually every genre available to the artist – painting, graphics, engraving, stage design, and sculpture – and his receptivity to myriad forms and influences. Within genres, Kustodiev also embraced diversity, as attested by his satirical graphics and illustrations of children's books. Whether in his visuals for Russian classics by Pushkin, Tolstoy, Korolenko, Uspenskii, and many others, or for the overtly propagandistic narratives that touted Soviet ascendancy, Kustodiev shifted to a medial style that was responsive to avant-gardism yet was basically figurative, and doubtless would have proved acceptable during the increasingly repressive 1930s, had Kustodiev lived to experience that decade's draconian proclamations and prohibitions. Given his early death from the spinal tuberculosis that had left him a paraplegic in 1916, Kustodiev cannot be called fortunate as regards health. Yet that death allowed him to escape the tragic fate of talented artists whom Stalinism eradicated, such as Lebedev. Kustodiev's striking receptivity to numerous, diverse stimuli as well as his embrace of the young Soviet regime doubtless accounted for his popularity and the support of such establishment figures as Lunacharsky, resulting in a sizable and varied body of memorable works.

For today's readers, Kustodiev's illustrations of the three volumes discussed in this chapter have the appeal of the Aristotelian Golden Mean, inasmuch as they wed a modified version of the bare-bones simplicity promoted by avant-garde aesthetics – clean, almost geometric lines and an elegant minimalism – with the pleasurable recognizability that figuration vouchsafes. Neither so abstract as to puzzle young readers nor so fussily detailed as to hinder the quick-paced narrative, they convey the emotions and atmosphere of the written texts they accompany with an economy of means and an expressiveness that surely would appeal to contemporary young readers, and not only in Russia. It is no accident that the Greeks linked the Golden Mean to beauty and viewed it as a means of circumventing both excess and dearth. Within that context and in light of the polemics dividing traditionalists and avant-gardists in Russia's 1920s, Kustodiev occupied the happy and productive position of a creative mediator, an artist who still speaks to us today as more than just a historical figure.

NOTES

1 Golden, *The Narrative Symbol in Childhood Literature*, 104.
2 Doonan, *Looking at Pictures in Picture* Books, 18.
3 Schwarcz, *Ways of the Illustrator.*
4 Mitchell, *Picture Theory,* 9; Sipe, "How Picture Books Work," 98.
5 Genre paintings to which his scenes of village festivities also belong.
6 His work as a book illustrator dates from 1905, and the many adult literary works he illustrated encompass Pushkin's fairy tales (1919), Gogol, "Shinel'," Ostrovskii's *Groza* (1920), poems by Nekrasov (1922), Leskov's *Shtopal'shchik* (1922) and *Ledi Makbet …* (1923), Gor'kii's *Suprugi Orlovy* (1926), Tolstoi's *Posle bala* (1926), and many others. Through this category of work, Kustodiev contributed in the early 1920s to "the revival of the neglected art of lithography," which artists belonging to Mir Iskusstva explored widely. Etkind, *Boris Kostudiev*, 30.
7 Kustodiev collaborated with various established contemporaries, such as Dobuzhinskii, Lansere, Serov, and so on.
8 Evgenii Steiner's fine study *Stories for Little Comrades* focuses on the avant-garde's preoccupation with technology in children's books.
9 As Mark Etkind notes, Anatoly Lunacharsky, the people's commissar for education, singled him out as the greatest painter in contemporary Russia. Etkind, *Boris Kustodiev*, 23.
10 For a Soviet survey of Russian children's literature of the tsarist era, see Setin, *Russkaia detskaia literatura.*
11 Rosenfeld, *Defining Russian Graphic Arts*, 168.
12 The State Publishing House Detgiz, founded by party decree in 1933, was renamed first into Detizdat (1936) and finally into Detskaia literatura (1963). The most innovative part of Detgiz,

its Leningrad section, was led by Samuil Marshak. Officially serving as a consultant, Marshak, a renowned children's writer, was its *de facto* editor-in-chief. During its first year, Detgiz released 7,744,000 copies of 168 book titles; see "'Children's Literature' Publishing House Established." *Detskaia literatura*, a biweekly literary-critical magazine, pioneered in 1932 under the supervision of the Central Committee of the Young Communist League (TsK VLKSM). It was published until the beginning of the Great Patriotic War, 1941. Its circulation was renewed in 1965 under the auspices of the Union of Soviet Writers. For a very brief overview of the genre and the vagaries of governmental control of it during the Soviet era, see Balina, "Creativity through Restraint."

13 This is the title of Elena Prokhorova's excellent chapter on Mikhalkov Sr. in Balina and Rudova, *Russian Children's Literature and* Culture.

14 In addition, the press produced colouring books, in which Kustodiev played a major part. Leningrad section of OGIZ likewise issued numerous illustrated books of children's verses and stories by Evgenii Shvarts, Kornei Chukovsky, Vitalii Bianki, and Marshak, with visuals by Natan Al'tman, Vladimir Lebedev, Aleksandr Samokhvalov, and many others.

15 That same year, critics trounced Pavlovich for her romantic verse tale *Paravoz-guliaka* and Kustodiev's concomitant drawings, which, in their detractors' eyes, were "murky …; detail is heaped upon detail, but the main problem lies in its absolutely unnecessary anthropomorphism." "The book," they declared, "in light of both its plot and its drawings, should not be made available to children, inasmuch as it muddies the preschooler's experience." Steiner, *Stories for Little Comrades*, 124.

16 Twain's works enjoyed adaptive popularity in the USSR. For instance, Sergei Mikhalkov's first play, *Tom Kenti* (1938), dramatized Twain's *Prince and the Pauper*. See Prokhorova, "A Traditionalist in the Land of Innovators," 300.

17 Tom subsequently reappeared in *The Adventures of Huckleberry Finn* (1884), *Tom Sawyer Abroad* (1894), and *Tom Sawyer, Detective* (1896).

18 Molok, "Nachala moskovskoi knigi," 45.

19 On the appeal of Il'f and Petrov's trickster protagonist, see Lipovetsky, *Charms of the Cynical Reason*, 89–124.

20 The satirical publication was edited by Petr Troianskii and published by Evgenii Lansere.

21 Established in 1918, the Komsomol (short for Kommunisticheskii soiuz molodezhi – Youth Communist League) was the youth division of the Communist Party, comprising members ranging from fourteen to twenty-eight years in age. The Pioneer organization, which materialized in 1922, enrolled children aged ten to fifteen. These political organizations, intended to "forge" suitable little Soviet citizens, figure prominently in the two poems illustrated by Kustodiev. In addition to the red kerchief, a badge with Lenin's portrait in profile certified members as Pioneers and Komsomolites.

22 Lesnaia, *Dzhimmi Dzhoi v gosti k pioneram*. Though the traditional fairy tale fell on hard times during the early Soviet era, with time the genre modulated to a form that absorbed the miraculous transformation achieved by Soviet forces as an equivalent for the supernatural forces featured in its folkloric heyday, and developed into a major ideological genre. See Balina, Goscilo, and Lipovetsky, eds., *Politicizing Magic*.

23 Born in Texas, Jimmy, aka Jimmie Joy (real name James Monte Maloney), helmed the Jimmy Joy Orchestra, which enjoyed enormous popularity, especially in the American Midwest. For a history of jazz in the Soviet Union, see Starr, *Red and Hot*. Pioneered by African Americans, jazz in the USSR was subject to the vagaries of state ideology.

24 As Marina Balina notes, research by the Institute of the Study for Children's Reading and Maksim Gorky's later survey of children's tastes (1933) revealed, unsurprisingly, their love of adventure. Balina, "Creativity through Restraint," 8, 12.

25 Kravchenko, *Detiam o Lenine.*

26 Apparently, the publisher was dissatisfied with Kustodiev's original portrayal of Lenin as a child, which he modelled on a photograph, and requested that the artist revise it. See Gollerbakh, *Grafika B.M. Kustodieva*, 37–8.

27 According to one critic, Kustodiev's illustrations for books on the Lenin theme "marked the first attempt in Soviet art to create the image of Lenin in book illustrations." Etkind, *Boris Kustodiev*, 29.

28 For the sake of simplicity, the date of 1881 is omitted in Kravchenko's text, as, for different reasons, are all references to Alexander's reforms.

29 Here the engagement is with the East, not the West.

30 Kustodiev's own posters, however, were supremely painterly, unlike those of the avant-gardists.

31 Sergei Eisenstein's *October* (1928) likewise relies on the iconic image of Lenin with arm flung forward.

32 "s natury" in the Russian; Gollerbakh, *Grafika B.M. Kustodieva*, 37.

33 For more details of Kustodiev's ideas on the topic, see Gollerbakh, *Grafika B. M. Kustodieva*, 37–8.

34 Ibid., 38.

35 Intriguingly, in an earlier visual in the book (65), Kustodiev portrays a kindred outpouring of emotion in the crowds snaking in a long, sinuous line to Lenin's coffin – a visual that surfaced later in Sergei Eisenstein's *Ivan Groznyi* (*Ivan the Terrible*, 1944), as hordes of common Russian people approach Ivan's retreat in a cave to implore his return as ruler of the country.

36 An early Communist ally of Lenin, the economist Gleb Krzhizhanovskii (1872–1959) twice headed Gosplan and served the state in multiple capacities.

37 Shelgunov (1867–1939) was a committed revolutionary who lost his vision while incarcerated in the early 1900s, yet served as the official editor of the Bolshevik newspaper *Zvezda* and helped to found *Pravda* in 1912.

38 The policy of *smychka* urged upon the population entailed the union or at least symbiosis of urban (hammer) and country (sickle) forces in the interests of a progressive labour that would enable the country to achieve its ambitious economic goals.

39 Nikolajeva, "Children's Literature as a Cultural Code," 46.

40 Ibid., 42. Ella Gankina's *Dlia serdtsa i razuma* (1998) would appear only three years after Nikolajeva's article, but, even in 2001, Nikolajeva completely ignored Gankina's substantial scholarship, including the 1998 study of pre-revolutionary illustrated children's books, which shows all too clearly the reductive inaccuracy of Nikolajeva's condescending rejection in a quintessentially Soviet vein.

41 Crankshaw, "When Lenin Returned."

42 Even in the United States statues of Lenin were erected in New York, Seattle, and other cities, preserved until today.

43 Nikolajeva, "Children's Literature as a Cultural Code," 43; Nikolajeva and Scott, *How Picture Books Work*, 6–16. A prolific and well-informed scholar of children's illustrated books, Nikolajeva dogmatically propounds a hierarchy of relationships between image and text that reflects her own priorities.

44 For an enthusiastic and complex analysis of Lissitzky's contribution, see Oushakine, "Translating Communism for Children," 191–5. It is difficult to imagine that children could "correctly" interpret Lissitzky's daring experiment in pure visual images.

45 *Brigada khudozhnika* 4 (1931): 23, as cited in Molok, "Nachala moskovskoi knigi," 59.

46 Elena Stishova astutely noted the underlying fairy-tale structure and mode of many films during the Soviet period. See Stishova, "Prikliucheniia Zolushki v strane bol'shevikov." These, of course, include Vladimir Men'shov's Oscar-winning *Moskva slezam ne verit* (*Moscow Does Not Believe in*

Tears, 1979), which casts Aleksei Batalov as Gosha, the fairy-tale prince whom Aleksandra (Natal'ia Vavilova) "earns" through years of deprivation and work dedicated to the Soviet Union.

47 See the works by V. Efanov, V.I. Govorkov, D. Grinets, and B. Vladimirskii, among a large cohort of sycophants.

48 Erikh Gollerbakh's bald, unexplained claim that these affectionate works are ironic (12) strikes me as groundless and dictated by his determination to ally Kustodiev exclusively with the new Soviet regime. As Ivan Lazarevskii notes in his short introduction to Gollerbakh's volume, the commentator focused on Kustodiev's responsiveness to the times ("chetkuiu otzyvchivost' khudozhnika na zhizn' nashego vremeni"), unpaginated.

BIBLIOGRAPHY

Balina, Marina. "Creativity through Restraint: The Beginnings of Soviet Children's Literature." In *Russian Children's Literature and Culture*, edited by Marina Balina and Larissa Rudova, 3–17. London: Routledge, 2008.

Balina, Marina, Helena Goscilo, and Mark Lipovetsky, eds. *Politicizing Magic: An Anthology of Russian and Soviet Fairy Tales*. Evanston, IL: Northwestern University Press, 2005.

Balina, Marina, and Larissa Rudova, eds. *Russian Children's Literature and Culture*. London: Routledge, 2008.

Bogdanov, Konstantin A. "Volodia Ul'ianov: 'Samyi chelovechnyi chelovek.'" In *Veselye chelovechki: kul'turnye geroi sovetskogo detstva*, edited by Il'ia Kukulin, Mark Lipovetsky, and Maria Maiofis, 61–100. Moscow: Novoe literaturnoe obozrenie, 2008.

"'Children's Literature' Publishing House Established." Presidential Library (named after Boris Yeltsin). www.prlib.ru/en-us/History/Pages/Item.aspx?itemid=66

Colomer, Teresa, Bettina Kümmerling-Meibauer, and Cecilia Silva-Díaz, eds. *New Directions in Picturebook Research*. London: Routledge, 2012.

Crankshaw, Edward. "When Lenin Returned." *Atlantic*, October 1954. www.theatlantic.com /magazine/archive/1954/10/when-lenin-returned/303867/.

"Detskaia literatura Rossii kak kanal vosproizvodstva dukhovnykh tsennostei naroda." *Refsru*, 8 September 2012. www.refsru.com/referat-7326–10.html.

Doonan, Jane. *Looking at Pictures in Picture Books*. Stroud: Thimble Press, 1992.

Etkind, Mark. *Boris Kustodiev*. Leningrad: Aurora Art Publishers, 1983.

Gankina, Ella. *Dlia serdtsa i razuma: Detskaia illiustrirovannaia kniga v Rossii konets 17 – pervaia polovina 19 vv*. Jerusalem: Jerusalem Publishing Center, 1998.

– *Khudozhniki v sovremennoi detskoi knige*. Moscow: Sovetskii khudozhnik, 1977.

– *Russkie khudozhniki detskoi knigi*. Moscow: Sovetskii khudozhnik, 1963.

Golden, Joanne M. *The Narrative Symbol in Childhood Literature: Explorations in the Construction of Text*. Berlin: Mouton de Gruyter, 1990.

Gollerbakh, E. *Grafika B.M. Kustodieva*. Moscow: Gosudarstvennoe izdatel'stvo, 1929.

Kravchenko, Anna, ed. *Detiam o Lenine*. Moscow: Gosizdat, 1927.

Lesnaya, Lydia. *Dzhimmi Dzhoi v gosti k Pioneram*. Moscow: Gosizdat, 1925.

Lewycka, Marina. "Inside the Rainbow: How Soviet Russia Tried to Reinvent Fairytales." *Financial Times*, 27 September 2013. www.ft.com/content/fdaa6fc4-2523-11e3-9dcc-00144feab7de.

Lipovetsky, Mark. *Charms of the Cynical Reason: The Trickster's Transformation in Soviet and Post-Soviet Culture*. Boston: Academic Studies Press, 2011.

Mitchell, W.J.T. *Picture Theory: Essays on Verbal and Visual Representations*. Chicago: University of Chicago Press, 1994.

Molok, Iu. "Nachala moskovskoi knigi: 20-e gody." *Iskusstvo knigi* 7 (1967–71): 35–62.

Neumann, Matthias. *The Communist Youth League and the Transformation of the Soviet Union, 1917–1932*. London: Routledge, 2013.

Nières, Isabelle. "Writers Writing a Short History of Children's Literature within Their Texts." In *Aspects and Issues in the History of Children's Literature*, edited by Maria Nikolajeva, 49–56. Westport, CT: Greenwood Press, 1995.

Nikolajeva, Maria, ed. *Aspects and Issues in the History of Children's Literature*. Westport, CT: Greenwood Press, 1995.

– "Children's Literature as a Cultural Code: A Semiotic Approach to History." In *Aspects and Issues in the History of Children's Literature*, 39–48. Westport, CT: Greenwood Press, 1995.

– *Children's Literature Comes of Age: Toward a New Aesthetic*. New York: Garland Publishing, 1996.

Nikolajeva, Maria, and Carole Scott. *How Picturebooks Work*. New York: Garland Publishing, 2001.

Oushakine, Serguei. "'My v gorod izumrudnyi idem dorogoi trudnoi': Malen'kie radosti veselykh chelovechkov." In *Veselye chelovechki: kul'turnye geroi sovetskogo detstva*, edited by I. Kukulin, M. Lipovetskii, and M. Maiofis, 9–60. Moscow: Novoe literaturnoe obozrenie, 2008.

– "Translating Communism for Children: Fables and Posters of the Revolution." *Boundary* 243, no. 3 (2016): 159–219. https://doi.org/10.1215/01903659-3572478.

Pantaleo, Sylvia. "'Reading' Young Children's Visual Texts." *Early Childhood Research and Practice* 7, no. 1 (2007). ecrp.uiuc.edu/v7n1/pantaleo.html.

Pavlov, Mikhail. *Sel'skii trud: Kartinki dlia raskrashivaniia*. Leningrad: Brokgauz-Efron, 1925.

Pavlovich, Nadezhda. *Bol'shevik Tom*. Leningrad: Brokgauz-Efron, 1925.

Prokhorova, Elena. "A Traditionalist in the Land of Innovators." In *Russian Children's Literature and Culture*, edited by Marina Balina and Larissa Rudova, 285–306. London: Routledge, 2008.

Rosenfeld, Alla, editor. *Defining Russian Graphic Arts: From Diaghilev to Stalin, 1898–1934*. New Brunswick, NJ: Rutgers University Press, 1999.

– "Figuration versus Abstraction in Soviet Illustrated Children's Books, 1920–1930." In *Defining Russian Graphic Arts*, edited by Alla Rosenfeld, 166–98. New Brunswick, NJ: Rutgers University Press, 1999.

Saarinen, Tatiana. "Constructivism and Children's Books in Soviet Avant-Garde Propaganda Art." *Scandinavian Journal of Design History* 11 (2001): 120–37.

Schwarcz, Joseph H. *Ways of the Illustrator: Visual Communication in Children's Literature*. Chicago: American Library Association, 1982.

Setin, F.I., ed. *Russkaia detskaia literatura*. Moscow: Prosveshchenie, 1972.

Shirshova, Liubov'. *Boris Mikhailovich Kustodiev*. St. Petersburg: Khudozhnik Rossii and Zolotoi vek, 1997.

Sipe, Lawrence R. "How Picture Books Work: A Semiotically Framed Theory of Text-Picture Relationships." *Children's Literature in Education* 29, no. 1 (1998): 97–108.

Starr, S. Frederick. *Red and Hot: The Fate of Jazz in the Soviet Union, 1917–1991*. Oxford: Oxford University Press, 1983.

Steiner, Evgenii. *Stories for Little Comrades: Revolutionary Artists and the Making of Early Soviet Children's Books*. Seattle: University of Washington Press, 1999.

Steiner, Wendy. *The Colors of Rhetoric*. Chicago: University of Chicago Press, 1982.

Stishova, Elena. "Prikliucheniia Zolushki v strane bol'shevikov." *Iskusstvo kino*, no. 5 (1997): 98–107.

Youngblood, Denise J. *Movies for the Masses: Popular Cinema and Soviet Society in the 1920s*. Cambridge: Cambridge University Press, 1992.

chapter two

HOW THE REVOLUTION TRIUMPHED: ALISA PORET'S TEXTBOOK OF CULTURAL ICONOGRAPHY

YURI LEVING

When Cinema Did Not Yet Know How to Talk

Most early Soviet illustrators, apart from being professional artists, were also attentive and eager moviegoers. This statement needs no special proof: their work bears testimony to the fact that particular cinematic devices and even broader cinematic aesthetics migrated from a highly fashionable new medium to the pages of books designated for an emerging generation of communist children. While the discussion of how literature has influenced film has become cliché, in this chapter I will reconstruct the "shot/reverse shot" paradigm, in the process, examining an immediate effect of early Soviet film on the concurrent art of Soviet children's book illustration. As a case study, I will use the book *How the Revolution Triumphed* (*Kak pobedila revoliutsiia*), illustrated by Alisa Poret.[1] The book, published in 1930, thirteen years after the October Revolution, offered a visual-verbal narrative that served, in effect, as a primer for teaching communism to Soviet children. Its key didactic goal was to introduce the newest generation of Soviet readership to the sequence of historical calamities that led to the Bolshevik seizure of power and, even more importantly, to ensure that their interpretation of the anti-imperial coup was correct.[2] The book relies on both the clear visual expressionism of Poret's imagery and the accompanying text. Yet the primacy of pictures over text is implied by the omission of the author's name, especially because the writer was not merely *someone* in the editorial staff of the State Publishing Company (Gosudarstvennoe Izdatel'stvo), but the poet Nikolai Zabolotsky.[3] (Visuality also dominated text in Soviet children's books for the practical reason that often neither kids nor their peasant or proletarian parents had yet mastered the basics of literacy.) With *How the Revolution Triumphed*, Poret invented a didactic "cinebook" (or a "knino"), a hybrid work conceptually blending a totalitarian optics with a print medium.

Parallel approaches to representing traumatic historical events (the Bolshevik Revolution, in this instance) raise issues of *cultural iconography*, rather than of a direct borrowing from one medium (cinema or photography) by another (graphic art or book illustration). The methodological question to be resolved, therefore, is not how artists utilized cinema but, rather, how the same archetypical plots have been tackled by different branches of the visual arts, and what kind of dramatic tensions ensue as a result of either unexpected creative convergences or conscious reminiscences in the context of literature, pedagogy, and propaganda.

Alisa Poret was born in 1902, just seven years after the invention of modern cinema by the Lumière brothers, and, like most contemporary artists, she owed much to the new medium. It comes as no surprise that Poret tried her hand at amateur photographic sketches modelled after films, much like some of her fellow artists. According to Poret's memoirs, she and her friends shot "films [i.e., took photographs] and used props from any epoch."[4] Symptomatically, her own unpublished diaries, which have only recently appeared in print, have been analysed using cinematographic language: in her attempt to define the genre of Poret's memoirist stories, a reviewer resorts to a comparison with Charlie Chaplin's and Buster Keaton's silent films and their eccentric use of montage.[5]

The Soviet period saw the rise of a pronounced emphasis on the didactic potential of film, whereas, as Denise Youngblood writes, before the revolution this kind of rhetoric was half-hearted: "If the [pre-revolutionary] cinema community really had believed in the primacy of film's didactic function, then studios and distributors should have been concerned with taking cinema to the countryside, which they were not. Nor did studios evince interest in making films for children. They didn't even tone down the sensationalism of their often-salacious adult fare. Sometimes on holidays, theatres devoted an early evening program to children's fare, but managers were hard-put to obtain suitable films."[6]

Cinema evolved rapidly from a form of entertainment to a distinct art form. Following their Italian counterparts, futurists in Russia embraced cinema "precisely because it was associated with the music-hall, the cabaret, the fairground and the other popular forms of 'low' art which they were using to attack the hegemony of 'high' art. After all, by the outbreak of the First World War, the audience for cinema outnumbered the total audience for all other forms of entertainment in both the towns and cities of the Russian Empire."[7] Although Alisa Poret's true passion turned out to be not moving but still images, she often frequented public screening venues, a fact to which her diary testifies.[8] Poret's second husband, Petr Snopkov (1900–1942), in addition to being a painter and a book illustrator, also worked for the theatre and film industry: in 1934, he took part in the production of a film, *Poruchik Kizhe* (*Lieutenant Kijé*), based on Iurii Tynianov's script.

From 1925, Poret worked for children's magazines while taking an active part in the avant-garde art scene. She was a close friend of the Russian absurdist poet Daniil Kharms: they became romantically infatuated with one another until Poret terminated their relationship in 1932.[9] Kharms's peculiar understanding of children's literature can be seen in Poret's graphic art, in which she combined stylized naïveté and genuine avant-garde techniques, which at least partially compensated for the state-approved ideological message.[10] Poret also had ties to the artist Pavel Filonov (1883–1941). In 1925, some of Filonov's students – dubbed the *Filonovtsy* (Filonovites) – came together to form what would be known as the Collective of Masters of Analytical Art (MAI). Tatiana Glebova and Alisa Poret joined the group in 1926. In spite of some critics' suggestion that Glebova and Poret were Filonov's closest collaborators,[11] Filonov apparently suspected Poret of undesirable bohemian habits and amorous behaviours.[12] Poret was also a former pupil of Kuz'ma Petrov-Vodkin at VKhUTEIN (Higher Institute of Arts and Technology, Moscow), where she had studied and applied analytical art in her paintings. The influence of both mentors on the young artist should not be underestimated: it can be seen in traces of avant-garde practice that are easily recognizable in her illustrations for *How the Revolution Triumphed*. Rather than presenting a direct visual connection to the written text, Poret artistically interprets it by offering choreographically arranged objects and human subjects in intricate graphic relationships. She schematically collapses big historical events into a series of carefully orchestrated graphic vignettes within her characteristically busy images. While Soviet art was increasingly expected to promote "proletarian art" and "new realism," Filonov's students sought to depict the inner essence of human social existence, which often led to a representation of Soviet reality with a surrealistic touch (or even with an element of "alienation," as some hostile critics would characterize their unorthodox approach).

Pavel Filonov expanded upon his theory of analytical art and propagated it among his group of devoted students, both in the Art Academy of Petrograd and then independently (he was forced out in 1927), but the paths of Poret and her mentor soon diverged. While Poret tried to apply creatively what she had learned, first from Petrov-Vodkin and later from Filonov, in her 1930 propagandistic work, by the time *Kalevala* (a Finnish folklore epic) was published in December 1933, Filonov had become a persona non grata in the Soviet Union. Moreover, Kharms and Vvedensky were arrested by the secret police in December 1931 (then freed and exiled to the small town of Kursk in the summer of 1932, returning to Leningrad in October 1932). Considering the time and place of its creation, Poret's illustrated book served as more than a poetic reconstruction of the emerging Soviet ethos: *How the Revolution Triumphed* provided her with safe conduct when so many of her contemporaries were falling under suspicion – that said, the book did not prevent Zabolotsky from being arrested eight years later.[13]

Books Forced to Be Silent: Moving Away from Filonov towards *Sotsrealizm*

How the Revolution Triumphed presents an intriguing case of negotiation between what was still permissible in 1929–30, with its remnants of the Russian avant-garde legacy, and the impending victory of what would soon become the only officially recognized artistic style in children's literature under Soviet totalitarian optics.[14] Poret's choice of palette and her representation of human figures approximate abstract patterns: individuals are indiscernible and arranged in large groups based on artistic compositional principles. The central subject of the drawing in figure 2.1 is Vladimir Lenin's return to Russia from his forced exile. Enthusiastic crowds greet the leader at the train station in Petrograd. In Poret's illustration, Lenin's energetic posture may be seen as a reductionist evocation of Aleksandr Samokhvalov's painting *Speech Atop an Armoured Vehicle* (*Rech' s bronevika*; fig. 2.2), completed in 1930, the same year as Poret's book – or even of Pavel Filonov's painting *The Narva Gate* (1929).

Poret's illustration and Samokhvalov's painting nonetheless differ in several aspects, most notably in their treatment of the background (staffage). Moreover, it is likely that both artists drew on an earlier prototype of clear cinematic origin: the depiction of Lenin's impassioned speech in front of the revolutionary soldiers and workers in Sergei Eisenstein's *October*, released only three years earlier. Poret's illustration in figure 2.1 is *compositionally* modelled after this scene in the film. As in the film (figs. 2.3 and 2.4), Poret retains the arched façade of the train station in the background, and preserves the prominence of the waving flag – to maximize the visual effect, she paints the banner in red. That said, the Bolshevik leader's gesture, the overall composition, and the banner against the chaotic crowd was already a predictable iconographic set by the early 1930s, and Poret might have seen it elsewhere: even such an emotionally charged artistic creation as Eisenstein's film cannot claim monopoly over the visualization of this canonical scene.

Poret explores the symbolism of gates – whether of the train station as an entry point to a city or within the semantics of the decorative arcs – echoing Eisenstein's preoccupation with the depiction of thresholds being breached. We see this in a number of his films. For example, the masses break through the blocked factory gates in *Strike*; soldiers storm the Winter Palace's majestic fenced entrance in *October* – in both instances, protesters/attackers gain access to the symbolic seats of power and decision making. Poret, Filonov, and Eisenstein metaphorically interpret gates as thresholds of a new and infinitely better life.

Poret's approach to illustration is consistent with the role that visual imagery plays in cinema, which incorporates a "figurative and semantic spiral of artistic ideas, with their interactions and interconnections" that constitute the larger circle of culture. This approach refers to various means by which "film reflects the cinematic production of previous cultural periods and assumes a systematic unfolding of its potential symbolic essence."[15] More specifically, Poret domesticates Eisenstein's montage of attractions for the needs of her younger audience by breaking down his mobile cultural iconography into a series of static scenes. Methodologically, this approach trained Soviet children in a pedagogically accessible way to read visual narratives in an ideologically correct manner.

2.1. Alisa Poret's artistic interpretation of history through choreographically arranged objects and people forming intricate graphic relationships in abstract patterns. In Nikolai Zabolotsky, *Kak pobedila revoliutsiia* (Moscow: GIZ, 1930), 6.

2.2. A. Samokhvalov, *Rech's bronevika (Speech Atop an Armoured Vehicle)* (1930), oil on canvas, 77 x 112.

2.3–2.4. Stills from the film *October* (1927), directed by Sergei Eisenstein.

Without Verbal Aids: Painting and Early Films

Nikolai Zabolotsky's plain descriptive text in *How the Revolution Triumphed* does not reveal any of the poet's typical idiosyncrasies; the writer evidently did not relish this commission, and, ultimately, the end result could easily have been produced by any anonymous state publishing supervisor. Another reason, perhaps, for this uncharacteristic lack of imagination was the literary scandal instigated by *Stolbtsy* (1929), the young absurdist's debut collection of poems, forcing its author to lie low in 1930. Alisa Poret's imagery in the book, in contrast, was confident and daring: the illustrator's visual story aimed precisely at the non-verbal qualities of graphic art, as if she were trying to adapt the aesthetics of silent cinema to the practical needs of illustrative art. John MacKay hypothesizes that film-maker Dziga Vertov "conceived of documentary photographic registrations as having the ability, if properly executed and displayed, to make the specific, salient features of a given phenomenon (a place, an action, a process) actually legible to an audience *without verbal aids*."[16] In a similar vein, Poret regarded the print text as something on the margins of the page and, therefore, as more or less an unavoidable – but literally marginal – nuisance. Significantly, while the text simplifies the chain of historical events leading to the revolution, the illustrations undermine this teleological order by representing the uprising in a fragmented visual narrative with the inevitably chaotic participation of a faceless armed mob.

The title of Poret's book, *How the Revolution Triumphed* (*Kak pobedila revoliutsiia*), besides falling into the stock pattern of artistic works commemorating the tenth anniversary of the revolution, quotes almost verbatim from the repeated sets of intertitles in Vertov's film *The Eleventh Year* (1928): "K pobede sotsializma v nashei strane" (Toward the victory of socialism in our country).[17] Likewise, the political theme of Vertov's film is "as orthodox and plain as its photography and editing are daring and complex … for in the eyes of a left-wing artist of the 1920s, ten years of Socialism (well, eleven) was a radical social experiment, and as such deserved, nay required, presentation in a radically experimental way."[18] Poret might have intuitively followed the same artistic logic when she counterbalanced Zabolotsky's dull text with highly conceptual illustrative material.

Early theorists of cinema embraced the conceptual apparatus and terminology of the visual arts; paradoxically, they also seriously strove to separate the new medium from its older visual cousins. Lev Kuleshov, for example, proclaimed that, in creating film sets, the artist must forget and renounce oil painting and pencil or charcoal drawing. He immediately went on to add that the film artist "paints with *objects*, flats (walls) and *light* (collaboration with the cameraman)," but their canvas is "the film camera's 35 degree angle of perception, like a triangle on a plane. On the screen what is important is not what is in the frame but how the objects are distributed, how they are composed on the plane."[19] In her illustrations for *How the Revolution Triumphed*,

Poret relies on pure colours, by and large preferring a monochromatic palette while adding a striking red banner to several of the book's illustrations.[20] I will discuss the cinematic origins of this particular colourization device below, but for now I wish to note the added semantic significance of a small detail in Poret's illustrations that draws the reader's attention: the ideological prominence of the object that embodies Bolshevism's imminent domination over the gloomy tsarist regime on the brink of collapse: the flag. Poret's high angles and flat perspectives were most probably inspired by the paintings of her teacher Petrov-Vodkin, whose treatment of vast landscapes, with dynamic internal movement of groups from left to right, and use of pure colours she must have found admirable.

But, whereas Petrov-Vodkin explores the pain of the individual and motifs of poeticized martyrdom (for example, in *At the Firing Line*, 1916, and *The Commissar's Death*, 1928), Poret is more concerned with making history accessible to children. The tale of the revolution ultimately relays the turbulent story of the birth of the new Soviet species: according to Poret, this story is about "the nation in the making." The means that she uses to depict this violent narrative are analogous to a 1915 American silent epic directed by D.W. Griffith. The dozens of soldiers on the cover of *How the Revolution Triumphed*, armed with bayonet and enshrouded in clouds (fig. 2.5), recall similar imagery that Griffith employed in his characteristic panoramic long shots, pioneering carefully staged battle sequences with hundreds of extras and added colour tinting for dramatic purposes (fig. 2.6).[21] For Poret, obviously, red is the colour of bloody sacrifice and the victory of communism (figs 2.7 and 2.8).

Alongside the sparse use of colours, which evokes early woodcut print techniques, some of Poret's "flat" illustrations clearly utilize the lack of visual perspective in the *lubok*, the traditional Russian woodcut, in an attempt to synchronize multiple incidents of the revolution and to present them as the sweeping but unified outburst of the people's will, an outburst of nearly cosmic proportions. Poret's visual style in *How the Revolution Triumphed* may be indebted to the mass-circulated and mechanically reproduced *lubok*, but it also reinforces the poster-like accessibility of the images, making them deceptively comprehensible (as with Eisenstein's or Vertov's intellectual montage). For instance, the well-known *lubok* plot "How the mice buried the cat" also combines intricate visual composition with the function of a social-political pamphlet.

Yet what Poret seems to borrow most importantly from the *lubok* is its playfully interactive nature: to "read" the *lubok*'s visual contents correctly, one is often required to toy with it, to turn it around in one's hands. I would suggest that, for Poret, the *lubok* mechanism of the book actualizes the principle of dynamic construction in an otherwise static object, in comparison with the cinematic flow of images that one is, in principle, unable to stop (at least before the invention of a video player). Another aspect of popular art that Poret employs in some illustrations is the conjunction of

2.5. In Poret's treatment, the turbulent story of the birth of a new Soviet species is analogous to the violent narrative in D.W. Griffith's 1915 silent epic *The Birth of a Nation*. Front cover of *Kak pobedila revoliutsiia*.

temporally different scenes – a device rooted in the art of icon painting. Poret's ingenuity lies in her combination of devices belonging to folklore and the religious sphere along with specifically cinematic devices, while balancing and carefully preserving her own idiosyncratic style.

Although early film-makers insisted on their virtual independence from the visual arts, Walter Benjamin finds a comparison of cinema with painting especially fruitful. According to Benjamin's classical treatise, a painting may be viewed by, at most, only a few people at once.[22] Therefore, he claims, painting is in no position to present an object for simultaneous collective experience, as it was possible for architecture or the epic poem, or for cinema today. The fact that cinema directly confronts the masses encapsulates its social role, and Poret, so it seems, found a golden mean in her creative work for the children's book industry – actively promoting the ideological cause and channeling her artistic vision into mechanically reprinted images for multiple young consumers while, at the same time, relying on the latest cinematic accomplishments of her time.

2.6. Still from Griffith's *The Birth of a Nation*.

2.7. Poret, illustration from *Kak pobedila revoliutsiia*, 5.

2.8. Poret, illustration from *Kak pobedila revoliutsiia*, 11.

Static Illustrations and Moving Images

Early film-makers embraced literature as one of its natural allies – unlike theatre, for example, which they considered a competitor. Vsevolod Pudovkin stated in his programmatic book *Film Technique and Film Acting* that cinematography has advanced with rapid strides and "its possibilities are inexhaustible … Cinematography stands now upon the threshold of its own methods."[23] At the same time, practitioners and theorists alike claimed cinema as an art form, if one deeply rooted in forms such as painting and photography. Yet, as I demonstrate below, the artists themselves saw more similarities than distinctions between the two mediums.

As early as 1935, Leonid Sabaneev claimed that "it has to be realized that cinema is *fundamentally photography*, endowed with movement" and that "both movement and sound are essentially photographic."[24] The same is true for abstract, expressionistic art forms such as music and painting (especially modern visual art). However, cinema's fundamental function of storytelling translated from the verbal into the visual had not changed; therefore, looking back at the early years of the new medium, Sabaneev suggests that silent cinema "was simply an animated illustration of the captions which represented the *rudiments of literature*, the text, as it were, of the romance unfolded on the screen. When the film began to talk, its nature was not thereby altered: the only difference was that the literary element of the captions was converted into the dramatic element of dialogue; the illustrative nature persisted."[25]

Poret, like other artists of her generation, endowed the illustrated book form with an intrinsic and self-explanatory visual quality – enabling her visual narrative to "speak" in a manner analogous to what had been achieved in films through the use of intertitles. In order to adapt their centuries-old craft of printing and graphic art in response to the influence of the emerging medium of motion pictures, illustrators and other artists occasionally resorted to complex aesthetics paralleling cinematic language. Among the first to take advantage of the eclectic avant-garde nature of the book as a hybrid literary-visual product in Russia were the proponents of the linguistic experiments of *zaum*. In Kruchonykh's radical examples, the book is "little more than an assemblage of miscellaneous pages, each self-sufficient" and the sequence is not important – not unlike the cinematic montage.[26] "Text" no longer requires sequential reading in linear time: it can be "taken in at a glance and absorbed by the same process of free visual exploration used in studying a painting."[27] The same kind of simultaneity occurs in Poret's illustrations, successfully exploding any idea of sequentiality in *How the Revolution Triumphed*. The artist merges fragmented story-units into a coherent "big picture," essentially editing these units as would a film editor splicing segments of a film to achieve the desired effect. Short paragraphs on the margins supply conventional linearity to the developing story, but, as I suggested earlier, Poret's book could easily do without any textual interpolation altogether. Instead of a horizontal montage projected onto the silver screen, a vertical montage of micro-drawings drives the compound visual narrative within the framework of the static page. Thus, each illustration in *How the Revolution Triumphed* – with a painted plot occupying between 90 to 100 per cent of the print sheet – serves as the equivalent of a cinematic sequence or scene (with several shots edited into a single "page-frame").

Poret's depiction of a strike at the Putilov factory (fig. 2.9) can be broken down into a series of distinct images, most probably drawn from a similar episode in Eisenstein's *Strike* (fig. 2.10).[28] The artist allows for an observer's view that is endowed with a keen investigative power to examine not only multiple objects at once, but also their intense interrelationships. Cinema theorists have long been fascinated with the psychology of human perception and have explored the consequences of the intentional preservation of specific details on screen: Pudovkin, for instance, maintained that "when we wish to apprehend anything, we always begin with the general outlines, and then, intensifying our examination to the highest degree, enrich our apprehension by an ever-increasing number of details."[29] Therefore, according to Pudovkin, the particular, the detail, will "always be a synonym of intensification. It is upon this that the strength of the film depends, that its characteristic specialty is the possibility of giving

2.9. Poret illustrates the Putilov Ironworks strike, which led to the events of "Bloody Sunday" and helped ignite the 1905 Revolution. The strike served as a source for Sergei Eisenstein's montage in *The Strike. Kak pobedila revoliutsiia*, 3.

a clear, especially vivid representation of detail."[30] Poret, it seems, experiments with similar effects produced on the page of the book. The number of vignettes occupying each drawing in *How the Revolution Triumphed* is astonishing. Considering the usual size of a printed book page, Poret invests a great deal of attention into small details, making her drawings appear dizzyingly busy.

To make her illustrations stand out on the basis of their own aesthetic merit (rather than serving a subsidiary function of illustrating prose), Poret applies unconventional means of artistic refraction: scaling objects up and down; using particular colours to emphasize or de-emphasize certain action; and distorting natural proportions, as mentioned in the above discussion of the *lubok*. An unusual choice for children's illustrations, Poret's artistic treatment is in line with Pudovkin's belief that "to show something as everyone sees it is to have accomplished *nothing*."[31] Pudovkin's philosophy of film technique as a tool for visual de-familiarization had to do with his general understanding of the mechanics of spectatorship; he thought that the spectators' attention was entirely in the hands of the film technician equipped with a camera: "The lens of the camera is the eye of the spectator. He sees and remarks only that which the

2.10. Still from *Stachka* (*The Strike*, 1925), directed by Sergei Eisenstein.

director desires to show him, or, more correctly put, that which the director himself sees in the action concerned."[32]

Poret dwells on the Putilov Ironworks incident, aggregating the optico-ontological (un)certainty from the early pages of her book (fig. 2.9).[33] The Putilov strike, and "Bloody Sunday," which followed it, ignited the February Revolution, the first Russian Revolution. Like Sergei Eisenstein's montage of these events in *Strike*, Poret, in her illustrations, opts for a direct optical assault on her young readership/spectatorship, lingering over the images of mounted gendarmerie armed with sabres, soldiers with protruding bayonets, and victims lying in pools of blood. Such a level of intensity parallels that sought by Eisenstein and by the Italian futurist Filippo Marinetti, both of whom understood that, when they "were tapping into a source of energy" in their films or performance, they "would need focusing and intensification to fulfil its [their art's] revolutionary possibilities. Both Eisenstein and Marinetti planned to exaggerate the impact on the spectator, Marinetti proposing to literally glue them to their seats (ruined garments paid for after the performance) and Eisenstein setting off firecrackers beneath them."[34] In her sharply detailed and evocatively coloured book, Poret trusts the avant-garde's proven recipe, selecting a few traumatic moments from the short span of revolutionary and Soviet history. By eliciting horror and suspense, she manipulates the readers' reception and intensifies the psychological impact on her young audience.

2.11. Alisa Poret's panoramic representations of proletarian masses with barely discernable faces evoke long shots in cinematic practice and adapt Sergei Eisenstein's brand of heroic realism to print media. *Kak pobedila revoliutsiia,* 4.

A Symphony of the Revolution

Russian intellectual filmmakers of the 1920s, first and foremost the masterminds Dziga Vertov and Sergei Eisenstein, pushed moviemaking forward while also using the art of motion pictures as a propagandistic tool in work ranging from experimental newsreels to revolutionary agitation. Eisenstein's films, in particular *Battleship Potemkin* (1925), *Strike* (1925), and *October* (1927), sought to shape Russia's recent history and contribute to the creation of a communist identity, marked by the triumph of the formerly downtrodden masses over their past.[35] The paradox of the cinema of that period lies in its combination of sheer propaganda and genuine formal artistic innovation, a successful mix that Poret was also able to adopt in her illustrations for *How the Revolution Triumphed.* Poret's reliance on panoramic representation (fig. 2.11), which may be compared to the cinematic long shot, is consistent with Eisenstein's brand of heroic realism, which promoted the proletarian masses, their faces barely discernible, over the individual (as in *Strike*).[36] Similar scenes of demonstrators and their subsequent brutal shooting by the tsarist army were portrayed in Iakov Protazanov's *The White Eagle* (*Belyi orel*, 1928; figs. 2.12–2.14). Protazanov crosscuts the mid-range and close-up shots, shots reminiscent of those in Poret's treatment of a crowd in front

2.12–2.13. Stills from the film *Belyi orel* (*White Eagle*, 1928), directed by Yakov Protazanov.

2.14. Still from the film *Belyi orel*.

of the Tavricheskii Palace in Petrograd (anachronistically referred to as "Leningrad," saving the young reader the trouble of a historic detour).

Poret's graphic scene of protestors being shot during the October Revolution (fig. 2.15) also follows a cinematic prototype: Eisenstein's early violent sequence from *October* (1928). Within two minutes of aggressively edited screen time, an orderly procession of street protesters is dispersed and quickly disintegrates into a chaotic and disoriented crowd (figs. 2.16 and 2.17). The scenes where the police confront a peaceful mass demonstration on Petrograd's main thoroughfare, Nevsky Prospekt, is a vivid example of visual counterpoint and collision in *October*; as Tim Harte points out, Eisenstein begins with conventional transitions between shots of the crowd and portentous shots of a machine gun. As Eisenstein cuts repeatedly from a frame of the machine gun, the cross-cutting suddenly becomes rapid and fierce, producing an effect of rattling montage and double exposure.[37] Both Eisenstein and Poret had a common source for their artistic reconstruction of the episode – a photograph by Viktor Bulla (fig. 2.18) from July 1917 of government troops shooting protesters, taken from approximately the same point of view found in the film and in Poret's illustration.[38]

While thematically close in the message they communicate, once juxtaposed, Poret's illustration and both Bulla's photograph and Eisenstein's scene yield delicate differences

2.15. Poret's reconstruction of the trauma of the mass murder of protestors evokes Eisenstein's *October* (figs. 2.16 and 2.17), but the perspective of both the illustration and the related scenes in the film also reflects that in Viktor Bulla's photograph (fig. 2.18). *Kak pobedila revoliutsiia*, 8.

in form. Poret moves her "camera-eye" higher and to the left, relative to the position of Eisenstein's camera, but preserves the specific location (the recognizable semicircular façade and tramway rails on Nevsky Prospekt). To compensate for the optical absence of the machine gun images, Poret conveys a dynamic sense of rhythm by merging several temporal layers into one: the peaceful demonstration, the shooting, and, finally, its bloody aftermath. Such a compromise is obviously required by the nature of print media: in her graphic artwork, Poret has to merge and compositionally organize disparate still shots borrowed from Eisenstein's moving pictures and reinstall them back into the static space of a drawing. This process, in turn, gives birth to a remarkable blending of the Eisensteinian signature double exposure with what essentially becomes a "multiple exposure" in a one-dimensional illustration on a book page. On the one hand, Poret's illustration is still less than a moving picture; on the other hand, in terms of mechanical reproduction, it is much more than a photo by Viktor Bulla.

Poret's presentation of converging and parting tramlines (fig. 2.19) adapts shots from contemporary "city symphonies" – Walter Ruttman's *Symphony of a Great City*

2.16–2.17. Stills from Eisenstein's *October*.

2.18. Viktor Bulla's photograph of troops firing on demonstrators at the corner of Nevsky Prospekt and Sadovaya Street, 4 July 1917.

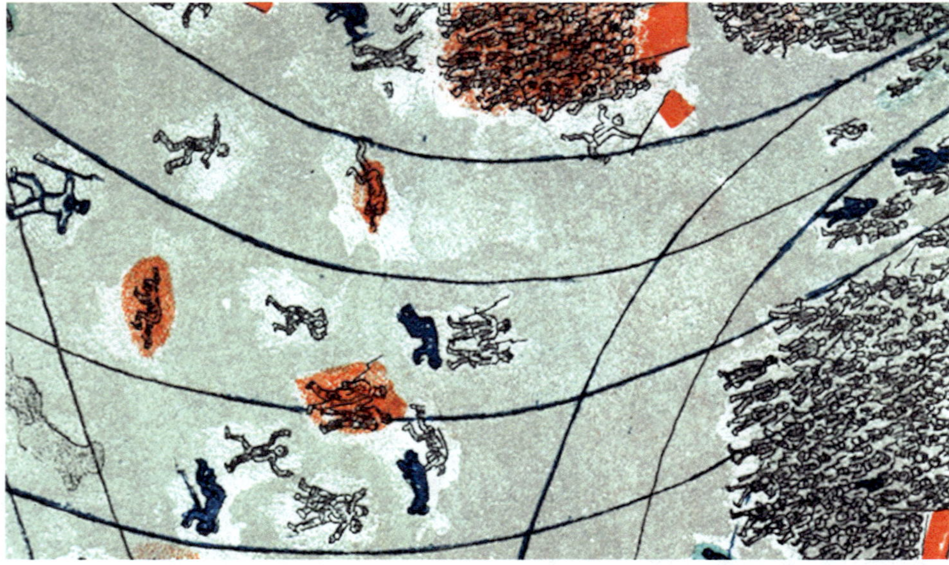

2.19. In this detail from Poret's illustration, Soviet optics poeticized martyrdom, and the scene transforms it into a vibrant composition akin to music notation. *Kak pobedila revoliutsiia*, 8.

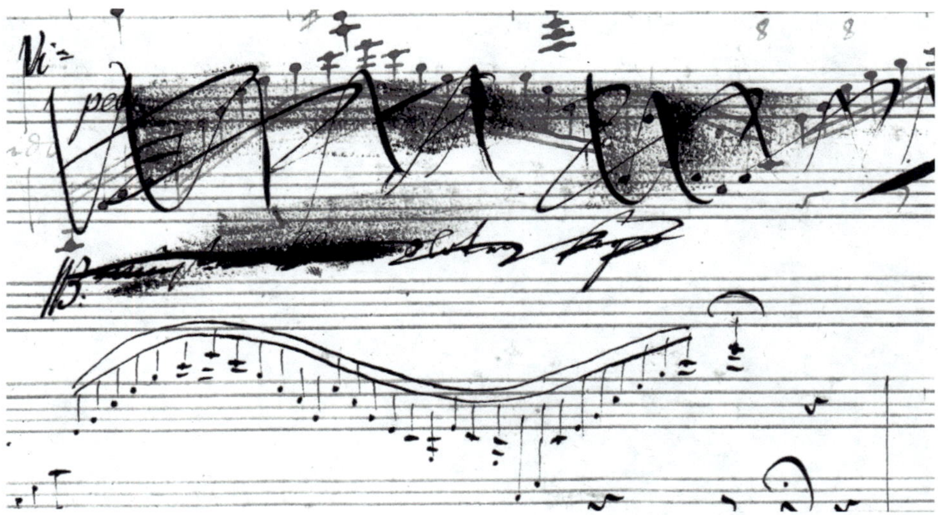

2.20. From the manuscript of Beethoven's Violin Sonata No. 9, Op. 47, in A major.

(1927) and Vertov's *The Man with the Movie Camera* (1929) – that explore the interaction between the cityscape and modern machinery. Although, in contrast to Ruttman or Vertov, Poret is not interested in either the machines per se or in transportation metaphors of connecting and disconnecting human relations. Poret's city is shown devoid of all means of transportation because the only driving force behind the uprising is the Collective (which ultimately fulfils the dictum of History). Such an ambitious concept required careful choreography of the participating masses: the illustrated personages are either running or marching in small groups or lying motionless on the ground. Despite the still-life quality of this composition (literally *nature morte*, considering that most of its elements constitute a depiction of corpses), one must commend Poret's ability to display so energetically the scattered figures across the page. The totality of these bodies makes for an extremely vibrant and animated composition akin to music notation (see, for instance, the sample of Ludwig van Beethoven's notation sheet in fig. 2.20).[39]

For the sake of example, Poret's drawing is rotated clockwise, whereby it unexpectedly acquires a musical function resembling the implied musical soundtrack in a movie. Dziga Vertov employs a similar device in his *Cine-Eye* (1924), showing in one shot a Moscow street on its side, with vertically standing pavement and tram lines. As Yuri Tsivian suggests, what could be misinterpreted as a technical "glitch" gains a subtle meaning once considered within the context of artistic avant-garde ideology: according to Viktor Shklovsky, in order to recognize an object one must turn it upside down.[40] The filmmakers of the late 1920s tried to achieve this oxymoronic effect in their *silent* "city symphonies." In *Arsenal*, for example, Dovzhenko makes people run at the tramway tracks while the camera is tilted almost 45 degrees to the right, underscoring the incessancy of the rapid downward movement (fig. 2.21).

2.21. Still from the film *Arsenal* (1929), directed by Aleksandr Dovzhenko.

Incorporating geometric patterns into graphic imagery empowers the metaphoric reading of Poret's cityscape as a space that one could "play back" like a sound recording of the revolution's ambience (in keeping with the poet Alexander Blok's famous plea "to hear the music of the Revolution" in his 1918 article "Intelligentsia and Revolution"). An attempt at translating a musical score into a depiction of modern epic (and vice versa) moves Poret's commissioned project beyond conventional book illustration. Her retrospective reflection on the nature of cataclysmic events and her multidisciplinary experiments with the poetics of speed and rhythmic combinations of line and colour produce a glossolalia effect and transgress any specific genre.

The significance Poret assigns to sporadic colours in her monochromatic visual repertoire (though partially dictated by limitations of contemporary typography) complements her use of a hidden soundtrack. Her resort to an intense red in the visual narrative can be traced back to the iconic shots of the raised banner found in *Battleship Potemkin*. To achieve the striking effect, Eisenstein manually painted the film frames so the flag was red (fig. 2.22). Poret uses the same device for the purpose of emphasis in her drawing, consciously basing it on Eisenstein's earlier shrewd decision. During the opening night screening of *Battleship Potemkin* at the Bolshoi Theatre in Moscow, the audience broke into spontaneous applause when they saw the hand-painted red flag (as well as between reels). Compare the film's climactic scene on the *Potemkin* deck with the upward movement of a soldier carrying the red flag in Poret's book (fig. 2.23).

2.22. The hand-painted red flag in Sergei Eisenstein's avant-garde *Bronenosets Potemkin* (*Battleship Potemkin*, 1925).

2.23. Adapting cinematic devices to the needs of graphics. Detail of illustration, showing a soldier carrying the red flag, in Poret, *Kak pobedila revoliutsiia*, 4.

Whether benefiting from the celebrated film-maker's accomplishments or not, Poret took a step forward in adapting the cinematic devices to the needs of graphics. Thus, the graphic sequence of figures in the "frame within the frame" (fig. 2.24), while arresting the motion, forms a micro-story that develops as a tripartite metamorphosis: a Christ-like figure (to the left); a person in a blot of blood (in the middle); and the raised banner proclaiming the victory of the Bolsheviks as a symbolic resurrection and overcoming of victimhood (to the right). The trio economically stand for Poret's manifesto of the revolution's development. It unfolds, from left to right, as (a) a ritualized sacrifice, which leads to (b) an ideological rebirth (see, for example, the embryo-like position of a wounded person), and, subsequently, boils down to (c) an idea of the inevitability of uprising personified in the image of a protester carrying the flag. The imagery itself suggests the iconography of crucifixion, with a hint of spiritual regeneration. One can easily imagine the same story in three movements told through a cross-cut sequence of several shots. Poret "shoots" her *iconotext* in a single frame. The technique itself might have been borrowed from Petrov-Vodkin (fig. 2.25), but its semantic and ideological application in the children's book is novel: Poret is turning Death into the catalyzer of a dynamic revolutionary plot.

God Is Perhaps Everywhere (Mainly in the Square)

I now turn to one of the most dramatic scenes in Poret's book, which depicts the Bolshevik attack on the Winter Palace, where the Kerensky government had locked itself prior to its surrender. The storming of the key sacralized imperial residence marked a symbolic takeover by the revolutionary forces and the de facto establishment of the new social and ideological regime in Russia.

2.24. Alisa Poret cleverly utilizes the iconography of crucifixion in this graphic rendering of a revolutionary riot. Detail from *Kak pobedila revoliutsiia*, 8.

2.25. Fragment from Kuz'ma Petrov-Vodkin, composition with figures of boys (1918). Lead pencil on paper, sepia, brush, 33 x 48.8.

Poret's use of a bird-eye perspective here has cinematic roots: it was earlier utilized by large-scale contemporary theatrical, and later filmic, productions. The most prominent example of such an elevated shift in perspective occurred in a celebrated mass performance on 25 October 1920 commemorating the third anniversary of the communist coup. An artistic reconstruction of the events of 1917, featuring the "Winter Palace seizure" as a dominant matrix behind the emerging myth of the revolution, was staged under the directorial guidance of the dramatic theorist, historian, and dramatist in his own right, Nikolai Evreinov. Iurii Annenkov was responsible for the stage decorations and costumes.[41] The spectacle was filmed, and, although the surviving footage quality is rather poor, the geometrical shapes and broad movements of people can be seen clearly. What's more, the angle and the general view of Poret's illustration is virtually identical to that of the opening credits in the visualization of Annenkov's stage props, with the Alexander Column in the middle, and the arch of the long bow-shaped façade of the General Staff Building.

Annenkov, it is worth noting, produced an *artistic* recreation of the crucial revolutionary episode without claiming any historical veracity or stating that it was an exact replica of the storming of the Winter Palace. Poret maintains this aesthetic plane in her visual narrative but enhances its pedagogical dimension (the "how" of the didactic title). Keeping the grandeur of the events intact, and in conformity with the official discourse (by all eye-witnesses' accounts, they were, in fact, much more modest in scale), the young artist – who herself was fifteen years old at the time of the event – presents the scenic dramatization through the prism of poetic and metaphoric allusions going back to Eisenstein's pseudo-documentary of the same episode, *October* (1927).

In her illustrations for *How the Revolution Triumphed*, Poret uses Eisenstein's skillful historical forgery in order to provide further legitimacy for this alternative history among the young Soviet readers, and invites them to accept her visuals as part of the official narrative. Exquisitely drawn, her pictures blur the line between high art and historical record, assuming a blatantly propagandistic role in the emerging politics of communist imagery for children. In the illustration shown in figure 2.26, Poret builds up the tension by again using a visual rhetoric enriched by subtle religious sensibilities. She tacitly activates the idea of the ritualized sacrifice of the corrupt old order in favour of the new order by alluding to comparable iconographic venues possibly familiar to her more mature viewers and, hence, extending potential appreciation of the story and its visual subtexts beyond the target young readership.

The carnivalesque bacchanalia of mass murder takes place in what is the symbolic heart of the tsars' capital and, according to Pushkin, the metaphysical epicentre of the Russian sublime, washed with the blood of innocent workers during the tragic Bloody Sunday shooting. In Poret's staging, the square once again comes to the semantic and spatial forefront of the nation-in-making, as she solemnly installs the 1917 military upheaval into a crucial niche of the modern Soviet myth.

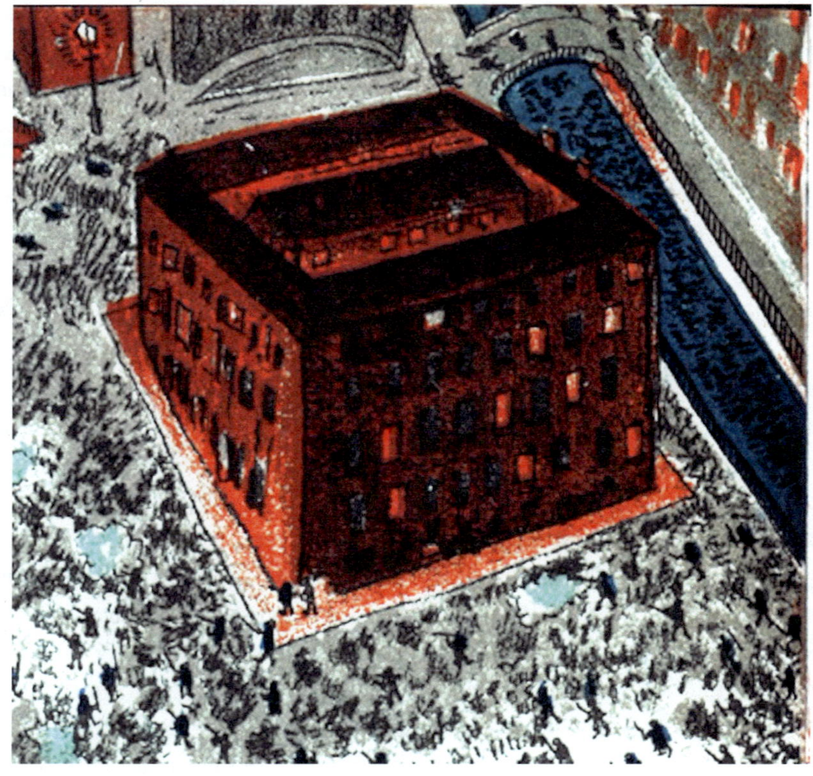

2.26. By evoking iconography of ritual sacrifice, Poret invites visual parallels between imperial Petersburg and the spiritual centres of Mecca and Jerusalem. *Kak pobedila revoliutsiia*, 12.

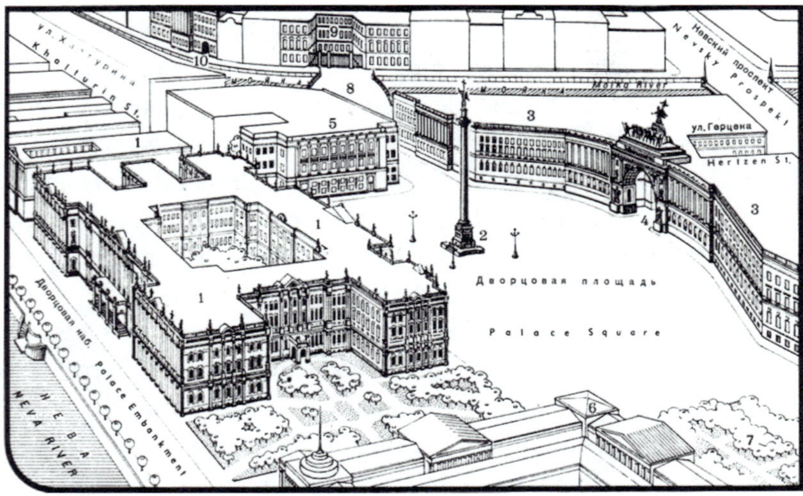

2.27. Palace Square chart, 1960.

2.28. Poret's rendition of the Palace Square, in *Kak pobedila revoliutsiia*, 8.

The presence of a cube-shaped edifice occupying the right side of Poret's picture (fig. 2.28) makes the entire image ambiguously overcharged. Judged by its topographical location and architectural shape, this darkly lit, enigmatic cube can be roughly identified as the building of the Guards Corps Headquarters, designed by Alexander Brullov and built on the eastern side of the Palace Square (see fig. 2.27). However, in Poret's rendition of the dramatic advance on Palace Square, featuring a dislocated and artificially enlarged cube of the Guards Corps Headquarters building and a singular column in its vicinity (fig. 2.28), the setting visually "rhymes" with another prominent square – namely, the one surrounding the Kaaba (Arabic: *Ka'aba*, meaning the Cube) in Mecca (fig. 2.29). Such an ostentatious comparison, as corroborated by vintage postcards, could very likely have been employed deliberately.

According to Muslim tradition, the Kaaba at the centre of Islam's most sacred mosque is believed to be one of the three stones God sent down from the Garden: "the Station of Abraham, the rock of the children of Israel, and the Black Stone, which God entrusted Abraham with as a white stone. It was whiter than paper, but became black from the sins of the children of Adam."[42] Although the Quran does not make an explicit connection between the Kaaba and Adam, structurally the myth of Mecca's miracle is oriented toward the Foundation Stone (Hebrew: *Even haShtiya*), which was located beneath the Ark of the Covenant and now sits inside the Dome of the Rock on the Temple Mount in the Old City of Jerusalem. Jewish tradition views the holiest site of Judaism as the spiritual junction of Heaven and Earth.

2.29.　Ottoman illustration depicting Mecca, 1893.

It is difficult to speculate whether Poret, as a student of Filonov and a beloved of the passionately religious Kharms,[43] was more fascinated with the mystical undertones of the revolutionary human sacrifices on the Palace Square (reverberating fundamental Judeo-Christian-Muslim archetypes from sacred texts and places) or with the visual parallels between imperial Petersburg and spiritual Mecca or Jerusalem.[44] For Poret, an eclectic web of religious connections could also be prompted by the very presence of the monumental neoclassical sculpture of Nike, the goddess of victory, on Palace Square: she paints part of the long bow-shaped façade of the Winter Palace while retaining the sculptural composition above the square filled with running combatants (in fig. 2.28). A winged silhouette of the goddess, commemorating the Patriotic War of 1812 on top of a triumphal arch, now bears witness to the triumph of the revolution.

At the same time that Poret was labouring over *How the Revolution Triumphed*, Aleksander Vvedensky, another member of the Association for Real Art (OBERIU) interested in metaphysical reality and the philosophical categories of God, death, time, and memory, had been contemplating his poem "God Is Perhaps Everywhere" ("Krugom vozmozhno Bog," 1931). Poret was present at the inaugural reading of this poem in September 1931. What Kharms and Vvedensky perceived as the increasingly absurd monstrosity of the Soviet social order, Poret tried to reconcile in her art with her less confrontational attitude toward Soviet reality. Through her mythopoetic inquiry into the violent origins of the Russian Revolution, she managed to explore its borderline phenomena. For cultural emissaries of the late 1920s, this was, perhaps, the last chance to do so – by the mid-1930s, they themselves would be turned into the sacrificial scapegoats of socialist realism.

Expressionist Distortions and Interior Spaces

Like many of her contemporaries, Alisa Poret was keenly aware of Edward Tisse's innovative photography. Eisenstein, who worked with this cameraman on all of his films, often demanded that Tisse's camera provide unusual angles, including very high ones. Impressed with *Potemkin* and *October*, Poret efficiently utilized these angles and perspectives in her graphic rendering of the revolution. One of the consequences of this cinematographic vogue for "fresh" compositions is the fact that Poret's imagined interior spaces seem extravagantly distorted. The closest natural cinematic counterpart for such imagery can be found in similar shots of Aleksandr Dovzhenko's *Arsenal* (1929). Lamps placed directly above the depicted subjects complement matching angles and dramatic lighting choices in both sources (figs. 2.30–2.32). The angles of Dovzhenko's and Eisenstein/Tisse's cameras make the spectator feel vertiginous, and Poret is captivated by the same effect.

It is also tempting to suggest that Poret's visual vocabulary extends beyond the Soviet cinematic tradition and is influenced, to some extent, by the dark and twisted visual style of German expressionism. In a letter to Poret, Kharms requested the return of a copy of Gustav Meyrink's novel *Der Golem* (1915).[45] Their correspondence does not mention a 1920 horror film by Paul Wegener of the same title, but, considering such a manifest interest on their part, it is quite possible that they saw the screen adaptation. Architect Hans Poelzig, who designed the sets for *The Golem*, did not so much reproduce the medieval Jewish ghetto of Prague as create a highly expressionistic version of it. The mystical story about the formation of a giant Golem out of clay by Rabbi Judah Loew in the sixteenth century acquires the undertones of a class battle between the persecuted Jews of Prague and their oppressors unsuccessfully seeking protection in the figure of an automaton. The mythologization of the Russian Revolution and German social debates of the time seem to converge in a melting pot of ideas that preoccupied Poret and her peers.

Another early German horror film, *The Cabinet of Dr. Caligari* (1920), had particularly influenced Soviet avant-guard film productions, including the science fiction film *Aelita* (1924). *Dr. Caligari* was available to Russian movie-goers, and Poret in her illustrations might have been toying with shapes and contours inspired by the bold German sets. Opting for unusually high angles in most of her compositions, Poret had evidently learned from the film's techniques. Where the director seems to be perfectly satisfied with a rather predictable position of his camera (for instance, Robert Wiene's

2.30. While the visual vocabulary of *How the Revolution Triumphed* was undoubtedly influenced by the Soviet cinematic tradition, it was also affected by German expressionism, with its extravagantly distorted compositions. Poret, *Kak pobedila revoliutsiia*, 9.

grotesque shots of people gathered around the table in a slanted room), Poret literally "upgrades" it. If we comparing figures 2.33 and 2.34, showing Poret's illustration of the hall of the Winter Palace and Sergei Eisenstein's similar shots in *October*, both depict small tense figures of the members of the provisional government in darker shades, one notices Poret's dramatic change in vantage point. Although the fact that she expressly alludes here to Eisenstein is beyond doubt, as both the director and the artist, for example, are drawn to the tucked curtains covering the tall windows Compared to Eisenstein's standard medium shots at eye-level, Poret lifts the entire perspective upwards. If accepted as depicted, the artist's presumed location would be directly where the wall chandelier is attached, which would be logistically impossible.

Conclusion

Alisa Poret's appropriation and reconstruction of various artistic and cinematic techniques for use in children's propaganda may, at first glance, appear to implicate her

2.31. Still from Dovzhenko's *Arsenal*.

2.32. Still from Eisenstein's *Stachka*.

2.33. Members of the provisional government in the Winter Palace as seen in Eisenstein's *October*.

2.34. Members of the provisional government in the Winter Palace as depicted in *Kak pobedila revoliutsiia*, 13.

2.35. Poret, *Kak pobedila revoliutsiia*, 15.

2.36. Still from Eisenstein's *October*.

as one of the many to support the primacy of ideology in new socialist art. The kind of counterfeit historical record of the revolution that she produced, along with the methodical substitution of documentary narrative by artistic conventions, would eventually result in the total collapse of the Soviet art model several decades later. Some of the more acute contemporary critics foresaw the dangers associated with such an approach, but they were quickly silenced.[46] Reconstructing – or, more accurately, reimagining – the historical record almost a decade and a half after the revolution had taken place accommodated nothing but a specific perspective in demand. This agitational use of such mass-produced books for Soviet children came on the heels of various cinematic portrayals of the revolution from 1926: films like *Battleship Potemkin*, *The Mother*, and their successors "conveyed a more euphoric vision of tyranny overthrown and the revolutionary transformation of both a society and its art. Now the success of the Revolution, against all odds, was being demonstrated by the sheer impact of its art. In the absence of other accessible evidence, these early films assumed a quasi-documentary status – an imaginary newsreel of the Revolution's course."[47] While Poret's visual style has proven itself formalistically innovative and bold, the content and ideological message of her work conformed to what was expected from the commissioned edition. The slogan on her illustration of a stage – "Vsia vlast' sovetam" ("All power to the soviets!") – was the same banner prominently placed above the podium in Eisenstein's reconstruction in *October*.

"The Revolution has triumphed, comrades!" announces the final page of Poret's book. The tale nears its climactic end, and so do the talented Ms Poret's[48] hunches with respect to artistic experimentation, soon to be curtailed. In the elated finale, Poret still uses economic contours and basic shapes (lines, circles, patches of colour), but she is clearly more focused on the consistency of the general ideological message. After the initial blossoming of artistic self-awareness during Soviet culture's experimental decade, art was submerged, within a couple of years, into the ideological tenets of socialist realism: "Myth-creating storytelling, simplified narrative plots, and political subtexts displaced the montage-type artistic consciousness from the horizon of Russian culture."[49] In contrast to this view, Boris Groys believes that "turning to Socialist realism was part and parcel of the development of the European avant-garde."[50] Whatever view one accepts, it is undeniable that Russian artists learned their lesson while apparently also enjoying the aesthetics of cinema, the *lubok*, and poster art. Alisa Poret's explorations in the graphic possibilities of (re)presenting motion on paper and canvas – delivered in a tight, poster-inspired artistic manner – turned out to be a true triumph of visual art's early liberating strategies of creative engagement with contemporary media.

NOTES

1   The 18.9 x 23.1 cm book is sixteen pages, including wrappers, with colour illustrations. See Zabolotsky, *Kak pobedila revoliutsiia*. Poret had collaborated with Detgiz since 1928, where,

among other projects, she contributed to the popular children's magazines *Ezh* and *Chizh*. *How the Revolution Triumphed* was her sixth or seventh illustrated edition, and some of the work was done jointly with Tatiana Glebova (who, most probably, also contributed as an uncredited co-illustrator in some pictures for this book in pictures about the revolution).

2 The target audience of Poret's book was children born soon after the events of 1917 (that is, those between seven and eleven years old by the time of its publication).

3 In Poret's own words, "I was an official author of this book, and I was asked to read the text. '– And who wrote it?' – I asked the editor. '– Some young fellow, his name is Zabolotsky, but you may omit his name on the cover.'"

4 Poret, *Zhivopis', grafika, fotoarkhiv, vospominaniia*.

5 Stepanova, "Chto tam uvidela Alisa."

6 Youngblood, *The Magic Mirror*, 69.

7 Christie and Taylor, eds., *The Film Factory*, 21.

8 On different occasions, she mentions Mikhail Romm's *Pyshka* (1934) and the foreign films *La rue sans joi* (1925) and *Die Rothausgasse* (1928).

9 Poret, "Vospominaniia o Daniile Kharmse," in *Panorama iskusstv*, 348.

10 Poret, "Vospominaniia o Daniile Kharmse," in *Daniil Kharms*, 425. Qtd. in Pankenier, "The Birth of Memory," 816.

11 Milner-Gulland, "'Masters of Analytic Art,'" 23.

12 Poret, *Zhivopis', grafika, fotoarkhiv, vospominaniia*.

13 Although, at a certain point, Poret was accused of "formalism in art" and expelled from the MAI group. See the biographical sketch in Golenkevich, *Alisa Poret*.

14 For more on the concept of educational optics, see Leving, *Vospitanie optikoi*.

15 Avrutin, "The Soldier, the Girl, and the Dragon," 74–5.

16 MacKay, "Film Energy," 49.

17 *The Eleventh Year* (1928), stills at 49:50, 50:07.

18 Yuri Tsivian's catalogue entry for the Vertov retrospective at the 2004 Giornate del Cinema Muto was "Odinnadtsatyi" ("L'Undicesimo/The Eleventh Year"). Qtd. in ibid., 41–2.

19 Kuleshov, "O zadachakh khudozhnika v kinematografe," 47.

20 See, for example, the illustration on pages 4 and 6 of *How the Revolution Triumphed*.

21 Significantly, both Vsevolod Pudovkin and Dziga Vertov admitted that Griffith's films had a profound influence in their choice of profession.

22 Benjamin, "Work of Art," 676.

23 Pudovkin, *Film Technique and Film Acting*, xviii. See also Sabaneev, "Aesthetics of the Sound Film," 213.

24 Sabaneev, "The Aesthetics of the Sound Film," 213.

25 Ibid., 214.

26 Janecek, *Look of Russian Literature*, 116.

27 Ibid., 117.

28 The artist's father, Ivan Poret (1870–1924), was a doctor and pharmacist in the Putilov factory clinic, and must have had first-hand knowledge of the events that took place there.

29 Pudovkin, *Film Technique and Film Acting*, 62–3.

30 Ibid.

31 Ibid., 63–4.

32 Ibid.

33 On 3 January 1905, the entire workforce of the Putilov Ironworks went on strike after the plant manager refused to rehire the unjustly fired workers. The number of strikers in the city quickly went up to 150,000; by 8 (21) January 1905, the city had no electricity and no

newspapers; the next day, dozens of peaceful protesters were massacred in front of the Winter Palace.

34   Gunning, "Cinema of Attraction," 68–70.

35   Taylor, *Film Propaganda*, 92–4, 101.

36   Tim Harte writes about the sequence in *Strike* where the authorities turn hoses on the protesters. In the film, only a mass of bodies and legs can be seen. Through those shots, Eisenstein "conveys more than just speed: the velocity and strength of the spraying correspond metaphorically to the film-making's visual force, specifically its capacity to influence viewers by overpowering them with a particular viewpoint." Harte, *Fast Forward*, 202.

37   See the director's own description in Eisenstein, "Dramaturgy of Film Form," 172. See also Harte, *Fast Forward*, 206.

38   Bulla's studio was located at the corner of Sadovaya and Nevsky Prospekt. I am indebted to Kat Hill Reischl for this information, provided during a discussion of the first draft of this paper presented at Princeton University in May 2015.

39   Beethoven was Vladimir Lenin's favourite "revolutionary" composer; according to M. Gorky, he proclaimed the "Appassionata" sonata to be "amazing, superhuman music."

40   See Tsivian, "Gestures of the Revolution."

41   Annenkov, *Dnevnik moikh vstrech*, 352–9.

42   Peters, *The Hajj*, 6.

43   Between 1927 and 1931, D. Kharms tried to learn the Hebrew language and was very interested in the Kabbalah and Jewish occultism. See Zinde, "Daniil Kharms."

44   Filonov visited Palestine three times in 1905–7, and D. Kharms's father was in Jerusalem shortly before him. See Iuvachev, *Palomnichestvo v Palestinu k Grobu Gospodniu*.

45   Letter qtd. in Carrick, "A Familiar Story," 7.

46   See also B.V. Alpers's sarcastic and witty review, "The New Stage in the Soviet Cinema": Alpers, "Novyi etap v sovetskom kino," 13.

47   Christie and Taylor, *The Film Factory*, 2.

48   This is what P. Sokolov and P. Snopkov jokingly called her.

49   Avrutin, "The Soldier," 75.

50   Groys, *Gesamtkunstwerk Stalin*, 28.

BIBLIOGRAPHY

Alpers, B. *Dnevnik kinokritika: 1928–1937*. Moscow: Fond "Novoe tysiacheletie," 1995.

Annenkov, Y. *Dnevnik moikh vstrech*. Moscow: Zakharov, 2001.

Avrutin, Lily. "The Soldier, the Girl, and the Dragon: Battles of Meanings in Post-Soviet Cinematic Space." *Cinema Journal* 38, no. 2 (1999): 72–97.

Benjamin, Walter. "The Work of Art in the Age of Mechanical Reproduction." In *Film Theory and Criticism: Introductory Readings*, edited by Leo Braudy and Marshall Cohen, 665–82. New York: Oxford University Press, 1999.

Carrick, Neil. "A Familiar Story: Insurgent Narratives and Generic Refugees in Daniil Kharms's 'The Old Woman.'" *Modern Language Review* 90, no. 3 (1995): 707–21.

Christie, Ian, and Richard Taylor, eds. *The Film Factory: Russian and Soviet Cinema in Documents, 1896–1939*. Translated by Richard Taylor. London: Routledge, 1988.

Eisenstein, Sergei. "Dramaturgy of Film Form." In *Selected Works*, Vol. 1, *Writings, 1922–34*, edited and translated by R. Taylor, 161–80. London: BFI Publications, 1988.

Golenkevich, N. *Alisa Poret. Zapiski, risunki, vospominaniia.* Moscow: Barbaris, 2012.

Groys, Boris. *Gesamtkunstwerk Stalin. Stat'i.* Moscow: Fond Pragmatika kul'tury, 2003.

Gunning, Tom. "The Cinema of Attraction: Early Film, Its Spectator and the Avant-Garde." *Wide Angle* 8, nos. 3–4 (1986): 63–70.

Harte, Tim. *Fast Forward: The Aesthetics and Ideology of Speed in Russian Avant-Garde Culture, 1910–1930.* Madison: University of Wisconsin Press, 2009.

Iuvachev, I.P. *Palomnichestvo v Palestinu k Grobu Gospodniu: Ocherki puteshestviia v Konstantinopol', Maluiu Aziiu, Siriiu, Palestinu, Egipet, Gretsiiu.* St. Petersburg: n.p., 1904.

Janecek, Gerald. *The Look of Russian Literature: Avant-Garde Visual Experiments, 1900–1930.* Princeton, NJ: Princeton University Press, 1984.

Kuleshov, Lev. "O zadachakh khudozhnika v kinematografe." In Kuleshov, L. V. *Kinematograficheskoe nasledie. Stat'i. Materialy,* 46–54. Moscow: Iskusstvo, 1979.

Leving, Yuri. *Vospitanie optikoi.* Moscow: Novoe literaturnoe obozrenie, 2010.

MacKay, John. "Film Energy: Process and Metanarrative in Dziga Vertov's *The Eleventh Year* (1928)." *October* 121 (Summer 2007): 41–78.

Milner-Gulland, Robin. "'Masters of Analytic Art': Filonov, His School and the 'Kalevala.'" *Leonardo* 16, no. 1 (1983): 21–7.

Pankenier, Sara. "The Birth of Memory and the Memory of Birth: Daniil Kharms and Lev Tolstoi on Infantile Amnesia." *Slavic Review* 68, no. 4 (2009): 804–24.

Peters, F.E. *The Hajj: The Muslim Pilgrimage to Mecca and the Holy Places.* Princeton, NJ: Princeton University Press, 1994.

Poret, Alisa. "Vospominaniia o Daniile Kharmse." In *Daniil Kharms. Antologiia satiry i iumora Rossii XX veka.* Moscow: Eksmo, 2003.

– "Vospominaniia o Daniile Kharmse." In *Panorama iskusstv,* vol. 3. Moscow: Sovetskii khudozhnik, 1980.

– *Zhivopis', grafika, fotoarkhiv, vospominaniia,* edited by I.I. Galeev. Moscow: Galeev-Galereia, 2013.

Protazanov, Iakov, dir. 1928. *Belyi orel.* USSR: Mezhrabpom-Russ.

Pudovkin, V. *Film Technique and Film Acting: The Cinema Writings of V.I. Pudovkin.* Translated by Ivor Montagu. New York: Bonanza Books, 1949.

Sabaneev, Leonid. "The Aesthetics of the Sound Film." In *Celluloid Symphonies: Texts and Contexts in Film Music History,* edited by Julie Hubbert, 213–21. Los Angeles: University of California Press, 2011.

Steiner, Evgenii. *Stories for Little Comrades: Revolutionary Artists and the Making of Early Soviet Children's Books.* Seattle: University of Washington Press, 1999.

Stepanova, Maria. "Chto tam uvidela Alisa." Review of *Zapiski, risunki, vospominaniia* by Alisa Poret. *Kommersant Weekend,* no. 3 (February 2013). https://www.kommersant.ru/doc/2111243.

Taylor, Richard. *Film Propaganda: Soviet Russia and Nazi Germany.* London: Croom Helm, 1979.

Tsivian, Yuri. *Na podstupakh k karpalistike: Dvizhenie i zhest v literature, iskusstve i kino.* Moscow: Novoe literaturnoe obozrenie, 2010.

Youngblood, Denise. *The Magic Mirror. Moviemaking in Russia, 1908–1918.* Madison: University of Wisconsin Press, 1999.

Zabolotsky, Nikolai. *Kak pobedila revoliutsiia.* Illustrated by Alisa Poret. 2nd ed. Moscow: GIZ, 1930.

Zinde, Elisha. "Daniil Kharms: 'Vse vse vse evrei paf.'" *Lehaim* 8, no. 232 (2011). http://www.lechaim.ru/ARHIV/232/zinde.htm.

chapter three

"FOTO-GLAZ": CHILDREN AS PHOTO-CORRESPONDENTS IN EARLY SOVIET PIONEER MAGAZINES

ERIKA WOLF

In August 1927, Arkadii Shaikhet's photograph of three children gathered around a camera on a tripod appeared on the cover of the Soviet children's magazine *Pioner* (*Pioneer*) (fig. 3.1). The trio's rapt engagement with this technological apparatus is palpable. Body tensed, the boy appears to be straining on tiptoes in order to peer through the folding plate camera's viewfinder, while the girl to the right intently gazes over his shoulder. To the left, another girl grasps the leg of the tripod and studies the hidden lens and bellows of the camera. The scarves around their necks identify them as Pioneers, members of the children's organization of the Communist Party. Consequently, there is an explicitly ideological component to their activity. Appearing on the cover of an official publication of the Pioneer movement, this image calls upon its young readers to take up photography and to master it as a *political* tool. This is no mere child's play – the cultivation of photography among children is of political significance, critical to the development of a new Soviet culture and society. Collectively engaging with the world through the camera, the children shown are part of the new social and political order taking shape in the Soviet Union.

One year earlier, this same photograph was prominently featured on the third page of the premiere issue of *Sovetskoe foto* (*Soviet Photo*). The journal's debut editorial heralded the significance of photography to the construction of socialism in the Soviet Union: "We absolutely need photography in all areas of construction ... Photography at the service of our technology, industry, education, volunteer societies, press, agitation, propaganda, study of local lore, physical culture – everywhere it takes its place as a powerful urgent necessity."[1] Dedicating itself to the broad development of Soviet photography, *Sovetskoe foto* here vows to assist both professional photo-reporters and amateur photographers. The extent to which Soviet efforts to promote grassroots photography foregrounded children is seen in the text immediately following this editorial: accompanied by Shaikhet's image of the Pioneers, it advocates the

3.1. Published on the cover of the magazine *Pioner*, Arkadii Shaikhet's image of a group of children gathered around a camera captures the children's engagement with photography. *Pioner*, no. 15 (August 1927).

incorporation of photography into the basic education of school children as a means to facilitate broad photographic literacy in the Soviet Union. In this text, Anatoly Lunacharsky, people's commissar of enlightenment, asserts the significance of this technology in developing the new Soviet culture: "Presenting itself to the pupil as an amusement, photography is indissolubly coupled with diverse learning and pedagogical tasks, providing a powerful medium in the hands of the pedagogue." He further argues that photography provides a broad foundation for engagement with the sciences, exploration of the material world, and the development of aesthetic sensibilities. The camera itself, he declares, is integral to the project of creating the new Soviet person: "It is important for us to introduce the advantages of photography into the heart of the masses [*v samuiu gushchu mass*] to put it into the hands of all workers. Just as each vanguard comrade should have a watch, they should also be able to master a photographic camera."[2] The watch was critical to the creation of the new Soviet person, who was to live according to the regulated industrial time of modernity (as opposed to the natural flow of time and seasons of a premodern agrarian economy). Like the watch, the camera functions as a technological extension of the human body, a mechanical eye for recording and enhancing vision. Lunacharsky envisions photography as part of the Bolshevik project of literacy (his responsibility as head of the Commissariat of Enlightenment): "Just as there will be general universal literacy in the USSR, there will likewise be photographic literacy in particular. And this will take place much faster than the sceptics believe."[3] After the revolution, literacy was no mere matter of developing basic reading skills; to the Bolsheviks, it was, rather, essential to the realization of a communist society, to the inculcation of Soviet ideology among the people and their participation as political actors in the new order. And *photographic* literacy was just as inherently political in the new society under construction.

Since the dawn of the snapshot era, technological developments have progressively (and drastically) simplified the capturing of images. Nowadays, anyone can be a photographer; but, as early as 1900, Kodak had already introduced the Brownie, a one-dollar film-cartridge camera marketed specifically for children – one that "any school-boy or girl can make good pictures with."[4] While the Brownie and other easy-to-operate consumer cameras made photography accessible to children, the extensive scholarship on the history of photography pays scant attention to child photographers.[5] This is due to the dominance of accounts concerning technological or aesthetic mastery of the medium, which tend to foreground the work of elite (and usually male) professional practitioners and to downplay what has been produced by ever-swelling ranks of amateurs since the introduction of the Kodak No. 1 in 1889. This pioneering consumer camera was marketed with the slogan "You press the button, we do the rest" – a denial of agency to the photographer beyond a simple mechanical task. A denial of agency is also evident in much of children's photographic activity, due to its conformity to the structures of both consumer photography and social expectations under capitalism. In 1921, a Kodak advertisement asserted that a "good Scout needs a Brownie"[6] – focusing on the camera helping the child develop skills of observation. Kodak advertisements, of course, never promised that children's photography could lead to radical social transformation, nor did they suggest that children might use the camera as a weapon of class war. But, after the October Revolution, this is exactly what the Soviet state proposed for the bourgeois Boy Scout's ideological opponent – the Soviet Pioneer.

In accord with Lunacharsky's views, several early Soviet children's magazines affiliated with the Pioneer movement encouraged their young readers to take up photography, to use the camera as a tool for reporting on their political activities and to submit their photographs for publication. This promotion of photography was an outgrowth of the worker-correspondent movement that blossomed within Soviet journalism in 1923–4. Instead of merely reporting on news affairs, the Soviet press was envisioned as a force that could intervene and determine the course of current events, and this would be achieved in part by transforming readers of newspapers and magazines into correspondents. Worker and peasant correspondents would take over the means of cultural production, reporting from factories and the countryside on both the failures and successes of Soviet modernization. Led by Mariia Ul'anova (Lenin's sister) and guided by activist journalists, the worker-correspondent movement rapidly spread within the Soviet periodical press, and from it to other modes of cultural production, such as photography and film. This radical expansion of authorship beyond the ranks of professional journalists also included children, who became active agents of sociopolitical transformation.

Pioneer Troops

The Pioneers first took shape in Moscow in early 1922. The Central Committee of the Russian Young Communist League (RKSM, known as Komsomol) directed its subordinate cells to organize children's groups. The Moscow branch of the Komsomol established a bureau to facilitate this work, leading to the formation of a number of early Pioneer groups. Mikhail Stremiakov, a nineteen-year-old Komsomol member and former Russian Scout leader, organized a troop of "young Pioneers" at the factory school of the 16th Printing House of Mospoligraf in the Krasnaia Presnia district. In Soviet histories of the Pioneers, this particular group is often identified as the first troop. In 1924, the All-Union Pioneer Organization was established, transforming the Pioneers into a significant mass political movement. Although troops were initially tied to workplaces, factory schools, and worker neighbourhoods, their number quickly proliferated. The Pioneers emulated the military-style organization and activities of the Scout movement, which had first originated in Great Britain before the First World War. Unlike the apolitical Scouts, the Pioneers were explicitly communist. From its foundation, the goal of the Pioneer Organization was the cultivation of politically literate and engaged individuals. Children successfully inculcated with communist politics via the Pioneer movement would advance into the Komsomol and then full membership in the Communist Party.

In 1923, the Komsomol adopted sets of rules and habits to be followed by Pioneers.[7] Collectively, these directives describe the character features of the new Soviet person in formation. Foremost is the requirement to be loyal to the working class, the Komsomol, the Communist Party, and other Pioneers. The Pioneer is also required to be industrious, brave, honest, healthy, and positive. Two rules are of particular relevance to the Pioneers' adoption of photography: "7. The Pioneer strives for knowledge. Knowledge and skill are a force in the struggle for the worker cause. 8. The Pioneer does their work quickly and accurately."[8] As an efficient tool for studying and accurately recording the world, the camera could no doubt embody this weaponization of knowledge on behalf of the working class. In addition to these rules, the Komsomol also mandated such good habits as getting up early in the morning, following a set routine of personal hygiene, neither smoking nor drinking, always knowing the date and hour of the day, and speaking concisely. The guidelines emphasize that Pioneers should be able to do things themselves, and should master tools and technology: "The Pioneer is able to work with a hatchet, chisel, hammer, and plane; he is able to turn on and turn off a motor." Likewise foregrounded are the Pioneer's powers of observation: "The Pioneer has a sharp-sighted eye and a quick ear. He is observant; he listens attentively and accurately records."[9] Clearly, the integration of photography into the political activities of the Pioneers was in full accord with the spirit of these rules and habits.

A number of children's magazines were soon established to assist in propaganda, agitation, and the promotion of the Pioneers. These included *Iunye tovarishchi* (*Young Comrades*, 1922), *Vorobei* (*The Sparrow*, 1923–4), *Baraban* (*The Drum*, 1923–6), *Novyi Robinzon* (*New Robinson*, 1924–5), *Iunye stroiteli* (*Young Builders*, 1923–5), *Krasnyi galstuk* (*The Red Scarf*, 1926), and *Pioner* (1924–present).[10] The establishment of these magazines coincided with the rise of the Soviet illustrated press and the emergence of Soviet press photography. The modernity of photography and its educational potential made it not just an instrument but a prominent theme of Soviet children's magazines.

In March 1924, the Leningrad magazine *Vorobei* initiated a recurring section titled "Brodiachii fotograf" ("The Strolling Photographer"). Early instalments were narrated by a child photographer named Volodia, who wanders the city with his camera (fig. 3.2). In the first instalment, he comments on his choice of instrument: "Instead of chattering, it's better to take pictures. Not with some kind of lousy little Kodak but with a genuine camera – have you seen photographers with one like this? People laugh, even comrades. They say, 'You put on a machine that weighs a thousand poods – don't bring it.' This, of course, is insulting. These idiots don't understand that my machine is top-grade."[11] Stressing his technical mastery, Volodia refers to the camera as his "machine" (*mashina*). The large-format reflex plate camera he carries (fig. 3.2) was the standard for professional photo-reportage at this time.

БРОДЯЧИЙ ФОТОГРАФ

Зовут меня Володей. Человек я рабочий и дельный, учусь в классе Д I-ой ступени, школа № 252. Я думаю, что самое интересное—фотографией заниматься.

Отец мой, Николай Николаевич, замечательные снимки делает. Вообще всяких интересных картинок и снимков у него уйма. Чем зря болтаться, лучше снимки снимать, да не каким-нибудь паршивым кодачишком, а самым настоящим аппаратом,—вот у фотографов такие видали?

Народ смеется, товарищи—тоже: — Что, говорят, ты машину нацепил в тысячу пудов, не снесешь! Это, конечно, обидно. Того глупцы не смыслят, что машина моя первый сорт.

Она показывает только правду, уж тут не соврешь, это не то, что когда художник из головы рисует. Все что есть—на земле и под землей, на воде и под водой—все покажу...

Вышел я из редакции в марте, отсюда начались и все мои приключения.

Иду по улице—по Охте, там, где Охтенские Пороховые заводы, где порох делают. Что за чудо—настоящая весна, такой ручей посреди улицы—потонуть можно!

23

3.2. The child photographer Volodia holding a bulky large-format reflex plate camera in the first instalment of "Brodiachii fotograf" ("The Strolling Photographer"), *Vorobei*, no. 3 (March 1924): 23. Photographer unknown.

It featured bellows at the front that allowed the lens to move for focusing through the folded hood at the top. A mirror that enabled the focusing through the hood had to be mechanically shifted before releasing the shutter. Volodia's defensiveness notwithstanding, this was indeed a cumbersome camera; it required skill to operate, unlike a simple Kodak that required the mere pushing of a button. This camera produced high-quality large glass negatives, which were deemed necessary for halftone reproduction in newspapers and magazines during this era.

Armed with this camera, Volodia set out from the editorial offices of *Vorobei* to record his adventures in Petrograd. The loose narratives of this column string together disparate photographs. The first instalment combines diverse images: children shovelling snow in Petrograd, a snowfall in Berlin (a photo allegedly sent to Volodia by a German friend), the Pioneer Museum, a children's theatre, children working in a nail and wire factory, and a shot of the American child movie star Baby Peggy with jam on her face. In his commentary, Volodia asserts the truthfulness of photography as opposed to painting or drawing: "[The camera] shows only the truth ... not something that the artist draws from his head. Everything that exists – on earth and underground, on water and under water – I'll show everything."[12] Despite this valorization of photography's factual nature, there is no clear articulation of a Soviet materialist politics of the photograph. In closing, the photographer promises to next take pictures at the zoo, a topic that would hardly be out of place in a bourgeois children's magazine. Similarly, the photographs are not the product of a collective group but of a single child working alone. Bundled up for cold weather and with no red scarf visible, Volodia is not dressed as a Pioneer.

While the magazine presents the photographs as the snaps of a child, it is clear that they – and the accompanying text – are the work of adult professionals.[13] After a few instalments of this column, a recurring graphic image of an adult photographer was introduced, and the pretence of a child photographer/narrator was abandoned. When *Vorobei* was renamed *Novyi Robinzon* in August 1924, the column continued as a regular feature, appearing in most issues until publication ceased the following year.[14] While it was clearly a dedicated photography feature, both format and content varied widely from issue to issue.

Pioneer "Foto-glaz"

In October 1924, the Moscow magazine *Baraban* initiated a recurring feature called "Foto-glaz" ("Photo-Eye") to showcase photographs of Pioneer activities. Its debut was announced with a close-up photograph of an eye (fig. 3.3), accompanied by a note instructing Pioneer groups to telephone the editorial offices so as to organize the shooting of "interesting moments of life and work."[15] Individual instalments of "Foto-glaz" were thematic in nature and usually consisted of roughly a dozen photographs

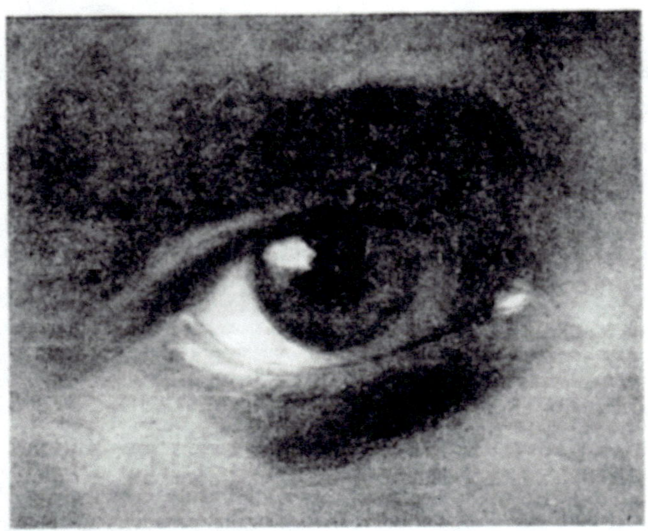

Смотри ФОТО-ГЛАЗ «Барабана» в пионер-клубе. 1-ая дюжина.
Редакция просит всех пионеров, все звенья, отряды и форпосты
сообщать в редакцию обо всех интересных моментах из жизни и
работы для зас'емки их для фото-глаза по тел. 1-18-09.

3.3. A close-up photograph of an eye announced the start of the recurring feature "Foto-glaz" ("Photo-Eye"), which showcased photographs of Pioneer activities in the magazine *Baraban*, nos. 13/14 (October 1924): 28.

appearing across several pages near the end of the magazine, alongside letters written by *pikory* (Pioneer correspondents). Like the accompanying correspondence, the photographs tell of the activities of the Pioneers. In the first instalment, readers are enjoined to "look at the *FOTO-GLAZ* of *Baraban* at the Pioneer club." In a typical spread, four photographs are interspersed with letters from Pioneers that tell of their group activities (fig. 3.4).[16] The Pioneers are shown working on their clubrooms, reading around a table, and assembling a wall newspaper (*stengazeta*). The accompanying captions comment on these activities but, unlike the signed letters, they do not identify any specific Pioneer groups, standing instead as generic exemplars for emulation by the magazine's readers. The captions assist the reader in understanding the political significance of Pioneer activities and how to correctly pursue them, as in the text accompanying the image at the lower right in figure 3.4: "The wall newspaper is a mirror of the detachment's work. It displays all of the successes and shortcomings of work. All children should participate in the wall newspaper." In the photograph, two boys and a girl are at work on creating a handmade "newspaper" to be hung on the wall of their clubroom. A key propaganda vehicle up to the end of the Soviet Union, the wall

В клубе все должны быть сделаны руками пионеров. Даже самое скверное помещение можно превратить в хороший клуб...

...ле осмотра мы пошли в сад, и стали с ними рисовать. Рисовали до чаю, после чая пошли с ребятами играть на площадку. Играли в «кошку-мышку», «змейку», в «жгуты», качались на гигантских шагах и прямо с площадки пошли на реку и стали купаться. Перед обедом мы хотели уйти в лагерь (нам в детдоме нужно было быть только до обеда), но ребята затащили нас к себе и нам пришлось остаться на обед. Когда мы уходили, они просили передать большое спасибо нашему отряду. С тех пор мы каждый день занимались в детдоме.

Пикорка Назарова.

ЖИЗНЬ ПОСЕЛКОВОГО ОТРЯДА.

В поселке Первомайском, Бежицкого уезда, 1 мая 1924 г., организовался отряд юных пионеров имени Ленина. В отряде 4 звена. Сначала в пионеры мог записаться каждый мальчик и де-...чка от 10 до 15 лет без исключения; через некоторое время оказалось, что некоторые из пионеров стали заводить бузу, т.-е. не хотели сами работать и мешали другим, кроме того, они устраивали мещанские вечера без ведома пионеров и вообще, не хотели подчиняться пионерской дисциплине. Совет отряда совместно с вожатым постановил, что таких пионеров в отряде не должно быть, и их вычистили. Теперь у нас остались хорошие пионеры в количестве 30 чел., которые хотят работать и работа у нас значительно улучшилась после чистки. Вожатый, совместно с советом отряда, стали всеми силами следить за хулиганством и искоренять его. Политзанятия бывают три раза в неделю и спорт два раза. Имеем шефа, который заботится о нас. Всего около двух недель как выпустили стенгазету «Юный Строитель».

Шлем привет всем пионерам и желаем, чтобы они писали о своей жизни и работе через журнал «Барабан».

Пикор И. Локшин.

СТРЕЛКИ.

Кружок естественников попросил денег у отряда для покупки патронов, пистонов и т. п. Отряд согласился и купил все, что им было нужно. И вот кружок стал ходить на охоту за птицами, чтобы из них наделать чучел, но так как у них все очень хорошие стрелки, то ничего не убивали. Как только кто-нибудь придет с охоты, его спросит, что убил. Отрелок же начи-нает разводить бузу: «вот попал ей в бок, а она полетела издыхать». Один из пионеров заявился хорошим стрелком, и когда ребята пришли и он узнал, что они ничего не убили, то стал ругаться: «Эх, вы, стрелки, даром заряды портите», и взяв ружье пошел сам. Когда он пришел, ребята спросили у него, что он убил. Он же ответил: «Нет, ружье неправильно бьет».

Матюхин, 4-й Сок. отр.

...не надо только бояться работы.

Книги, одни из лучших друзей пионера. В каждом клубе должна быть образцовая библиотека—читальня.

В РЕДАКЦИЮ «БАРАБАНА».

Шлем свой братский привет всем пионерам Москвы.

Наш 2-й железно-дорожный отряд при омских главных мастерских гор. Омска; живем неважно, помещение неважно, средств тоже пока нет, но «Барабан» будем выписывать. Детская неделя у нас началась 31-го. Было торжественное заседание, где секретарь райкома Мишка Горшков делал доклад. Потом была поставлена пьеса «Святой пионе-рий», коллективная декламация драмкружка нашего пионерского клуба. У нас в отряде сейчас 28 человек. Несмотря на это, отряд 2-го апреля 25-го года будет праздновать 2-летие. Отряд мал по количеству, потому что в нем были ребята из мастерских, их расформировали по месту службы их отцов. Желаем хорошего успеха в проведении 7-го Октября. Хорошо будет, если наш братишка журнал скажет одному отряду Москвы, чтобы они нам писали письма. Если плохо написано, не суди «Барабан». Другой раз лучше напишу.

Пикор А. Васюк, г. Омск.

3-й райком РЛКСМ 2-му отряду Ленинцев.

ЧЕСТНОЕ ПИОНЕРСКОЕ СЛОВО.

Раз в магазине мне дали сдачи серебром. Когда я отошла от кассы, то увидела что одна монета старинная. Я подошла к кассе и сказала кассиру:

«Что вы даете такие деньги»? А он мне сказал: «Ты врешь». Тогда я сказала' «Честное пионерское слово», и после этого он мне переменил деньги.

М. Коровкина.

Стенгаз—зеркало отрядной работы. Он выявляет все успехи и недостатки работы. В стенгазете должны принимать участие все ребята.

3.4. A spread with photographs of Pioneer activities accompanied by letters from children that tell of their collective political work. *Baraban*, nos. 13/14 (October 1924): 40–1.

newspaper, which originated as part of the worker-correspondent movement, began to flourish in this period. Produced collectively within clubs, schools, and factories, the wall newspaper encouraged individuals to actively contribute texts, drawings, and photographs, and it promoted literacy and political education generally.[17] In the "Foto-glaz" instalment in question, the children have pasted at the top of their news-paper a large photograph: a clipping from the preceding issue of *Baraban* that shows a Pioneer group performing a theatrical "living newspaper."[18] Subsequent instalments of "Foto-glaz" would move out of the clubrooms to show Pioneers in the village, at school, at the Red Army barracks, helping with work at home, and working both with smaller children and with *besprizorniki* ("unsupervised" homeless children).

"Foto-glaz" – the title of this recurring feature – evokes the writings and films of the innovative Soviet documentary film-maker Dziga Vertov, whose newsreels and ideas were being extensively discussed in the Soviet press around the time that *Baraban* initiated the column.[19] Vertov predicated his work upon the camera as a mechanical eye that could perceive the world better than the human one, a dynamic machine for exploring the material world. In his manifesto "Kinoki. Perevorot" ("Kinoks: A Revolution," 1923), Vertov hails the camera as a tool for transforming human perception of reality: "I am kino-eye [*kino-glaz*]. I am a mechanical eye. I, a machine, show you the world only as I can see it."[20] As conceived by Vertov, *kino-glaz* does not merely record reality; it rejects neutrality as a pretence. Through special filming techniques and montage editing, it persuades viewers to look at the world in a new way. Just as Soviet newspapers and magazines played a central role in ag-itation and propaganda, *kino-glaz* exerted the discursive power of film on behalf of Soviet ideology. Vertov envisioned *kino-glaz* functioning with a broad network of cinema-correspondents, analogous to the worker-correspondents of the periodical press, who are to provide the raw footage for editing into documentary films.[21] Ver-tov's neologism *kinok*, derived from the words *kino* (cinema) and *oko* (an archaic ver-sion of "eye"), refers both to his core working collective and to the mass participants in this envisioned network. When Vertov first articulated the concept of *kino-glaz*, his primary work was on the serial newsreel *Kino-Pravda* (*Cinema Truth*, 1922–5), whose title suggests its function as a cinematic supplement to *Pravda*, the official Communist Party newspaper. A critic writing in the newspaper *Pravda* observed: "*Ki-no-Pravda* is a magazine. An illustrated, living magazine. A magazine which none of the printed illustrated magazines can compete with, since no photographs can replace film stock."[22] While *kino-glaz* stressed the filmic montage of images, the compilation of still photographs on the pages of a magazine could perform an analogous function, albeit in a less dynamic manner.

Baraban likely selected the term *foto-glaz* as an overt reference to Vertov's *kino-glaz* – a concise way to endorse the mechanical camera-eye's adaptation to the political activities of the Pioneers.[23] In mid-October 1924, Vertov's film *Kino-glaz: Zhizn' vrasplokh* (*Cine-Eye: Life Caught Off-Guard*) was released. Pioneers are featured in both this six-reel film and the related newsreel, *Kino-Pravda No. 20: Pion-erskaia* (*Cine-Truth No. 20: Pioneer*), that was issued a few months later. The close-up photograph of an eye that appeared with the initial announcement of "Foto-glaz" strongly echoes the advertisements and posters designed by Aleksandr Rodchenko to promote Vertov's new feature at that time.[24] Making the film, Vertov worked closely with the 11th Krasnaia Presnia Pioneer Troop, which was affiliated with the Krasnaia Oborona textile factory. This group provided a clear connection between Vertov and *Baraban*, which from the start of its publication was the "organ of the Moscow and Krasnaia Presnia bureaus of the Young Pioneers";[25] and as mentioned, the magazine's editor, Mikhail Stremiakov, had established the first Pioneer troop in 1922 in that same working-class district of Moscow. The leader (*vozhatyi*) of the Krasnaia Ob-orona troop was Boris Kudinov, one of Stremiakov's first Pioneers, a contributor to *Baraban* from its first issue, and a member of the Krasnaia Presnia Young Pioneers' Bureau.[26] Born in 1907, Kudinov was already a Komsomol member and a worker at the textile factory when Vertov started to work with his troop.[27] The month before *Baraban* initiated the feature "Foto-glaz," it published an article by Kudinov entitled "Kino-glaz. Nash lager' na kino-lente" ("Kino-glaz: Our Camp on Cinema Film") (fig. 3.5). In this text, the troop leader provides a detailed account of the activities of the Pioneers from the Krasnaia Oborona factory at their summer camp in the coun-tryside, and then notes that these activities were all recorded on film for a movie by Goskino, the main Soviet film production organization of the time. He explains the method employed in the film:

> *Kino-glaz* ... is the first picture in the world that has not a single dressed-up actor, no fake decorations, and which is filmed without any sort of fairytale scripts [*bez vsiakikh stsenariev-skazok*]. *Kino-glaz* shows real life; it shows what really exists in the world around us. For two weeks we lived together with the comrades from Goskino, and we never noticed that we were being filmed. *Kino-glaz* caught us off-guard [*vrasplokh*].[28]

Kudinov uses the word *vrasplokh*, a term that Vertov employed often in his writings and that appears in the full title of his film *Kino-glaz*. Often translated as "unawares," this term has led the film-maker's work to sometimes be hailed as an early version of *cinema verité*, in which a hidden camera records its subjects without their knowl-edge.[29] Not playing or acting for the camera, the Pioneers simply went about their activities as the *kinoks* filmed (the photographic analogy here would be the difference between a staged photograph and a candid one). Through the editing process, the raw footage of the children's activities was transformed into a persuasive narrative detail-ing the construction of a new society in the Soviet Union.

Seeking to foment social change, *Kino-glaz* shows both the good and the bad, just like the wall newspapers composed by the Pioneers. The sections of the film that fea-ture Pioneers show the rising generation constructing a new society and culture. The

КИНО-ГЛАЗ.

Наш лагерь на кино-ленте.

11-й Красно-Пресненский отряд при фабрике «Красная Оборона» большую часть лета провел в лагере в деревне Павло-Ленинской. Неделя пошла на оборудование, после чего торжественное открытие. На открытие мы пригласили крестьян окрестных деревень, рабочих нашей ф-ки, пионеров и других. Открыв лагерь, мы запустили свои щупальцы всюду, где только могли: в 5-ти деревнях работают наши звенья с неорганизованными ребятами. Организовали один отряд при деревне, кружок пионеров и деткоров, работаем в яслях при деревне, детдоме ближайшей ф-ки, открыли паяльную мастерскую и парикмахерскую, которые бесплатно обслуживают ближайшие к лагерю деревни. Четыре часа ежедневно работаем на поле, помогая беднейшим крестьянам. В лагере выпускали свой журнал и стенную газетку, держали связь с ячейкой РЛКСМ деревни и, конечно, своей ф-ки. Частенько бывали у нас совместные собрания пионерских отрядов волости (их в ней 4) неорганизованных ребят, и в одно воскресенье устроили воскресник по заготовке дров для деревенской школы. Лагерная палатка, читальня своими интересными книгами, портретами вождей и лозунгами постоянно привлекали много крестьян и их ребятишек, которые пользовались из нее книгами и газетами. Ни одного митинга в деревне не обошлось без пионеров, а беседы с ребятами без «Барабана», из него мы читали интересные статейки, попутно говоря о значении журнала и кружка пионеров, работали на поле, доставляли в 5 деревень книги крестьянам. Не

Кино-глаз. Деревенские пионеры.

видавшие никогда даже, как растет хлеб (рожь), наши ребята теперь умеют жать, молотить, вязать снопы, косить и полоть траву, пахать, боронить и выполнять другие крестьянские работы. Немало пользы принесли мы и крестьянам, о пионерах не говорят уже плохо, пионеры сумели поставить себя хорошо.

«Госкино», жившие с нами, засняло всю нашу работу в деревне и самом лагере на кино-ленту, которая называется «кино-глаз».

«Кино-глаз» — это первая в мире картина, которую выпускает наше «Госкино» и в которой нет ни одного наряженного артиста, никаких поддельных декораций и которая заснята без всяких сценариев — сказок. «Кино-глаз» показывает настоящую жизнь, показывает то, что действительно существует в окружающем нас мире. Две недели мы жили вместе с товарищами из Госкино и никогда не замечали, что нас снимают. Кино-глаз заставал нас врасплох.

Как интересна та картина, в которой участвует наш отряд, пионеры могут увидеть в середине сентября месяца. Фотографии помещенные в этом номере, взяты из кадриков этой ленты, о которой я только что говорил.

Бор. Кудинов.

ПИОНЕРЫ НЕ ХОТЯТ ВОЙНЫ.

Это сказала конференция пионеров Красной Пресни. Это подтвердил 55-ый отряд Красной Пресни, выйдя 20-го августа со своими отцами и старшими братьями (издательством «Рабочей Москвы») на демонстрацию против новых

Кино-глаз. Паяльная мастерская в лагере 11 тр. Красной Пресни.

войн. Несмотря на жару и усталость, шагали не плохо. И около Моссовета, на призыв «К борьбе против грядущей войны будь готов», 55-ый отряд громко ответил: «Всегда готов!»

Е. Крекшин.
55 отр., 4 звено «Красн. Перец».

РАБОТА В ЛАГЕРЕ И СМЫЧКА С ДЕРЕВНЕЙ.

Работая в далекой Киргизии, мы 26 июня с. г. выехали в лагерь за пять верст от города «Пестрое». Сделав свою повседневную работу в лагере, мы двинулись в ближайшую деревню «Бишкуль». Солнце палит беспощадно. Начинает издалека показываться лесок, а за ним нам странные домики деревни, и через некоторое время мы уже в школе деревни. Школа полна крестьянской детворы, можно видеть и дряхленьких старушенок. Делаем доклад о «детском коммунистическом движении», после него целый ряд декламаций, спорт-выступлений и пьеса. Молодежь с удивлением смотрит на пионерское творчество. После всего этого мы собрали несколько кучек ребят, и в каждой пионер с номерами «Барабана», чтение которого ребята слушали с большим удовольствием и задавали много вопросов. Такова была первая попытка нашего отряда к смычке с деревней. В дальнейшем деревенские ребята просили, чтобы мы не забывали их и почаще приходили. Все были довольны и изъявляли желание вступить в нашу организацию.

Ю. Соломонов.
5 отряд Ю. П. зм. В. И. Ленина при школе «семилетка», г. Павловск, Акм. губ.

МЫ СДЕЛАЛИ СВОЕ ДЕЛО.

Наш 3—4 отряд Ю. П. расположился на дачном месте Сходне по Октябрьской ж. д. Приехавши, познакомились с местом нашего жи-

Кино-глаз. Крестьяне встречают пионеров.

тельства и принялись за работу. Первой нашей работой была работа по уборке вокруг лагеря. Кончив это, мы стали ходить работать в очередь на сенокос. Но нашей основной работой считалась работа в деревне, как работа политпросветительная, так и труд-работа. Мы выбрали село Черкизово и начали там свою работу. Мы выделили для беспрерывной работы по организации отряда Ю. П. несколько человек, которые принялись тут же за работу. Кроме этого, мы стали ходить в село Бурцево помогать крестьянам в их работах по хозяйству и по полю. Крестьяне, которые в начале относились к нам подозрительно, не обращая должного внимания, впоследствии, узнавши нас, искренно благодарили нас за проделанные работы в их селе. В результате, когда мы закрывали свой лагерь, к нам собралось много крестьян и из окружных деревень и явился результат нашей работы—новый отряд Ю. П. при селе Черкизово. Товарищи из М. Б. Ю. П. и Райбюро Ю. П., закрывая наш лагерь, утвердили новый в СССР — Черкизовский отряд Юных Пионеров под № 56-ым. Уехав в город, мы не оставляем 56-ой отряд и выделенные пионеры будут ездить к ним и проводить с ними работу.

Пикор Анатолий Алфеев.
** ** ** **

МЕЖДЕТНЕДЕЛЯ НАЧАЛАСЬ.

Вчера 31 августа в Богородске начался первый день проведения междетнедели открытием уездной конференции пионеров.

С утренним поездом прибыла делегация пионеров Бауманского района. На вокзале их встретила конференция. Пионеры Москвы и Богородска обменялись приветствиями. Быстро был организован летучий митинг при участии большой

Кино-глаз. Крестьянин отдает салют при поднятии флага.

3.5. Boris Kudinov's written account of how his Pioneer troop worked with Dziga Vertov in recording their summer camp activities for the film *Kino-glaz: Life Caught Off-Guard. Baraban*, no. 10 (September 1924): 46–7.

children appear as active agents for political change. In the city, they investigate food prices on the black market (whose sellers make personal profit at the expense of the collective), put up posters promoting state-run cooperatives, and distribute leaflets about tuberculosis at a beer hall. In the countryside, the Pioneer summer camp functions as a microcosm of the future society under construction, while also fulfilling the Bolshevik mandate to link the city and the village. The mechanical eye of the camera functions to make things clear, to explain how things have come to be. After a sequence showing smaller rural children being hosted for various activities in the Pioneer camp, the camera shows how the camp was prepared for these activities: a trench was excavated to create a cafeteria table and benches, a camp stove was built in the ground, a flagpole was raised. Thematically similar to some of the spreads in *Baraban*'s feature "Foto-glaz," this sequence stresses the organized, planned group activities that create a microcosm of the new society. The film also stresses the significance of literacy and media in creating this new society. The Pioneers are shown reading, writing, engaged in oratory, taking notes, delivering letters, posting notices, distributing pamphlets, and making active use of Pioneer magazines. The Pioneers read to the young children from *Baraban*, and a copy of the Komsomol magazine *Smena* (*The Shift*) appears in a sequence showing the work of the camp's reading tent. In a meeting to mark the organization of a new village Pioneer troop, Boris Kudinov (identified in the intertitles as "Boria") holds a copy of *Pioner* as he makes a speech (fig. 3.6). He refers to the magazine and, at the end of the speech, distributes it and other printed materials to the village children.

In two sequences of the film, the camera takes charge. Using innovative montage and backward-running, time-reversing film footage to visibilize networks of economic relations, *Kino-glaz* reveals where meat comes from, how bread is made, and how grain connects the countryside to the city. A similar strategy appears in *Baraban*. On the second anniversary of the magazine, "Foto-glaz" presented a series of twenty-five photographs in an item entitled "Kak izdaetsia 'Baraban'" ("How *Baraban* Is Published"; fig. 3.7).[30] The sequentially numbered photographs are spread across seven pages, interspersed amid a miscellany of material celebrating the anniversary, including letters from readers and reminiscences about the magazine by Stremiakov and Kudinov. This instalment of "Foto-glaz" presents a visual narrative that shows how the magazine is made, with emphasis given to how the writings of Pioneer correspondents are published in it: the arrival of letters from readers, their sorting and preparation for publication, typesetting, correction of proofs, page layout, preparation of images for reproduction via zincography, the printing and binding of issues, preparations for distribution, and the distribution of the magazine to readers via news-stands and post. As a whole, this sequence demystifies how the magazine was made in terms of both editorial and physical production processes, while also showing its readers how their written correspondence appears in print. It accomplishes this in a primarily visual manner, with sequentially numbered photographs and minimal accompanying text.

3.6. Boris Kudinov holding a copy of the magazine *Pioner* as he makes a political speech to a group of village Pioneers in Dziga Vertov's film *Kino-glaz*, 1924.

In celebration of the Krasnaia Oborona troop's first anniversary, in September 1924, the *kinoks* gave the Pioneers a present, a "genuine photographic camera with all accessories. There was no end to the joy. Now the kids publish, on their own, the weekly newspaper *Foto-glaz*, made up of their photographs (including all their photos, even spoiled ones). With this newspaper, the kids consider their achievements in photography and, in addition, illuminate all the highlights of events for that week in their lives."[31] The wall newspaper was hung in the factory yard, where it attracted the attention of the workers.[32] With the encouragement of the *kinoks*, the Pioneers of Krasnaia Oborona took up photography with great enthusiasm. Shortly after the gift of the camera, their initial foray into photography caught the attention of the Komsomol. A report on the activities of the Krasnaia Oborona troop by the Moscow Bureau of Young Pioneers from 11 October 1924 noted: "There is a circle with a purely technical bias (*uklon*), the result of Goskino's [i.e., the *kinoks'*] great enthusiasm for this detachment. The kids have a camera, make individual shots, and learn how to carry out shoots in the circle."[33] The group had only just begun work and was no doubt focused on basic technical mastery of photography. As their skill developed, they could apply this technology to various tasks. By giving the camera to the Pioneers, the *kinoks* encouraged them to develop skills that could be applied to cinema and other forms of socialist media. The children employed the camera to document their activities and to report on them in an explicitly photographic wall newspaper.

Working with Vertov on the film *Kino-glaz*, Pioneers presumably gained insight on how they might utilize the camera as a mechanical eye in their political work. Similar to the photographs featured in *Baraban*, the film documents children undertaking various group activities, such as repairing metal pots for peasants, helping a poor widow with her farm work, giving villagers haircuts, and providing first aid. Once again, this is no mere child's play; these activities contribute to the common good. The children work as a group to document social ills and take action to intervene. Working on their photographic wall newspaper, the Pioneers of Krasnaia Oborona likely produced comparable content and sequences of images. However, none of their newspapers are extant. While wall newspapers were a

Фото-глаз. Как издается «Барабан».

1. Принес заметку.

Дорогой товарищ «Барабан», в день твоего юбилея шлем тебе горячий пионерский привет и наше пионерское пожелание.

Мы хотим, чтобы ты проник во все глухие уголки нашего Союза С. С. Р., и чтобы тебя читала вся пролетарская детвора.

— «Барабан»—шире в массы!

Пионеры 60-го отряда Красной Пресни.

Читаем «Барабан».

С апреля наши звенья первой базы «Пролетарки» г. Твери читают пионерский журнал «Барабан».

Каждый пионер теперь может прочесть журнал не только в клубе, но и в семье родителям.

— «С большим интересом читаешь свой журнал, а стоит всего по 10 копеек с пионера в месяц».

Пионерское творчество не должно погибнуть.

Поддержим журнал.

Даешь 25 000 подписчиков.

Пионер 1-го отряда А. Шитов.

Спасибо «Барабану».

Во 2-ю годовщину нашего журнала «Барабан», я хочу рассказать, как я стал пионером. До того, как я не читал «Барабана», я не знал, кто такие пионеры и не интересовался ими: знал только, что это ребята с красными галстуками, ходят по улице и бьют в барабан. Когда я прочел «Барабан» (который дал мне один пионер), то я узнал, кто такие пионеры, как они живут и работают, и сам захотел стать пионером. Спасибо «Барабану» за то, что он помог мне узнать, кто такие пионеры и самому стать им.

Борис Галкин, 75-й отряд Кр.-Пр.

4. И 2.500 в месяц.

«Барабан» и наша работа.

Я думаю, что выражу мнение всех ребят, если скажу, что «Барабан» является лучшим другом и помощником в работе каждого пионера в отдельности и всей нашей организации в целом. Для нас, пионеров, он важен, как руководящий центр всей нашей работы. Указания, даваемые «Барабаном» к проведению той или иной кампании, конечно, во многом способствуют к поднятию нашей работы и направлению ее по определенному руслу Нужно еще указать на одну из важнейших работ «Барабана», это работа по укреплению связи между всей нашей Московской пионерской организацией с другими частями нашего Советского Союза и жизнью наших заграничных товарищей, давая возможность нашим московским пионерам каждый шаг своей работы связывать с жизнью своих и заграничных пионеров. Кроме того, празднуя двухлетие организации «Барабана», необходимо отметить то, что Барабан сослужил большую пользу в отношении выявления активности самих ребят, давая им возможность быть самими строителями своего пионерск. журнала. Мы, пионеры, надеемся, что и в будущем при коллективном содействии всех пионеров «Барабан» будет и в будущем вести по правильному пути нашу пионерскую работу!

Пикор 2-го отр. Баум. р. Б. Липкин.

3. И так 80 заметок в день.

БАРАБАННОЕ.

Дел не мало. Каждый час в учете,
Каждый час расписан до минут.
И се-унды в бешеной работе
С быстротою бешеной бегут.

Сколько раз, звонками телефона
От страниц оторванный, бегу
И бросаю в трубку непреклонно:
— К сожаленью, сдел-ть не могу.

— Нет, никак, простите, до свиданья!
И опять перо дрожит в руке,
И опять с усилием вниманье
Собираю в прерванной строке.

Чтоб—звонок. И в рукописи рана,
И опять встревоженный бегу
— Да! алло?.. Звонят из Барабана.
— Не могу, товарищ, не могу.

Знаю—зря. Прижмут в последнем счете,
Знаю выразят нужный им ответ,
Потому что в их живой работе
Не хотят и слышать слова—«нет»!

АНДРЕЙ ИРКУТОВ.

2. Зарегистрировали.

«БАРАБАНЩИКИ».

Январь 1924 г.

Искал долго. Нашел. В Леонтьевском, где «Молодой ленинец». Около пальто и галош. Два с половиной аршина незанятого галошами пространства. Стол. На столе клочек бумаги. На клочке бумаги надпись:

Верстаем «Барабан».

На следующий день уже не искал. Пошел прямо туда, где пальто и галоши, и нашел ту же коротенькую записку:

Верстаем «Бзрабан».

Я ходил три дня. Три дня изучал различные формы галош. Три дня любовался фасонами чужих пальто. Три дня ругался всеми нехорошими словами и три дня читал:

Верстаем «Барабан».

Времена меняются. Пальто и галоши—в области воспоминаний. Три стола. Телефон с двумя трубками. Большая Дмитровка. Кипа иностранной литературы между шкафом и печкой. На одном из столов клочек бумаги. На клочке бумаги—надпись:

«Ушли обедать».

А. Иркутов.

5. На машинку.

6. Кое-что в корзину.

ВОСПОМИНАНИЯ РЕДАКТОРА.

Два года работы в редакции. Срок пустяковый. Мы всегда «Барабан» делали сообща, каждый из сотрудников-комсомольцев выполняет свою долю работы, и я могу определенно сказать, что лучших ребят, как Федосеев Володя, Солнцев и любезный Рыжий Саша, я редко встречал в комсомольских и пионерских редакциях.

7. Остальное в наборную.

11. На оттиске исправляют ошибки.

ВОСПОМИНАНИЯ.

Этот дружно спаянный товарищеский коллектив на своих плечах вынес много «горьких» дней «Барабана», не опускал рук и шел всегда вперед, отдавая все свой силы и способности нашему общему делу, делу детской коммунистической печати.

Помню, как сейчас, 22 января 1924 года получено известие о смерти вождя и учителя В. И. Ленина. Все в редакции. Все на местах и ждут заданий на специальный ленинский номер. В те дни и часы все как-то рвалось изнутри.

Я бегаю из редакции в МК. В редакции телефонные звонки. Снарядили двух ребят-корреспондентов в Горки. Они получили задание—пробраться туда обязательно. Фотограф Зубков навострил лыжи. План готов. Всю ночь на-пролет работали. Пишем, пишем и пишем. Гигант—Малинин, художник, согнувшись в 6 раз, тушью «кроет» заставки и концовки.

Ночью по телефону т. Дмитриевский сообщает подробности покушения на тов. Ленина эсеркой Каплан. О сне никто не думает. Вся редакция завалена бумагой, сдвинуты столы, масса фотографий, слышно на всю комнату гортанный, медный голос—крик Федосеева и лязг его «ужасных» ножниц, я всегда болею душой, когда он начинает «карнать» фотографии для монтажа. Шамет, скрючившись в теплой кепке, куда он влез по уши, с'узил глаза «до отказа», правит «отдел по отрядам». Я и Солнцев кончаем биографию Ильича. Номер готов. Все свободно вздохнули.

Телефон работает без перерыва. Всю ночь пионеры забегали в редакцию с корреспонденцией, стихами. Стихи даже передавали по телефону.

7 часов утра. В 9 утра надо быть в типографии, а оттуда нет возврата до ночи. Нужен отдых. Где кто стоял и сидел, тут-же и лег, нас трое легли на мой стол и укрылись полотнищем. Невозмутимый Малинин срисовал нас и картину повесил на стенку. Спим. Сквозь сон слышишь громкий смех, поднимаю голову, у картинки стоят товарищи из издательства и заливаются. Мы были злы, но этот раз не ругались, даже благодарили за побудку «смехом», быстро вскочили и айда за работу. Номер выпущен. Этот Ленинский № 2 был одним из лучших наших номеров.

Так, не считаясь с временем мы создали «Барабан».

9. Затем составляют в гранку.

ДЕВЯТЫЙ.

Летом мне приходилось частенько работать на паровозе по Казанской железной дороге, сперва кочегаром, а потом и помощником машиниста.

Однажды мы вели паровоз резервом—без поезда по Муромской ветке.

После сделанного нами маршрута мы получили заслуженный отдых

8. Сначала набирают на верстатку.

10. Тиснают на станке.

3.7. This spread of sequentially numbered photographs with accompanying text breaks down and demystifies the publication processes of the magazine *Baraban*, no. 6 (March 1925): 12–13.

widespread phenomenon during this era, few have been preserved, even as photo-graphic reproductions.

The gift of the camera was meant to encourage the Pioneers to hone skills that would facilitate the realization of a network of cinematic correspondents – the *kinoks*. This vi-sion was realized in Boris Kudinov. In 1925, the part of the Krasnaia Oborona factory where he worked was transferred to another enterprise. With Vertov's encouragement and the endorsement of the Moscow committee of the Komsomol, he took up work at Kul'tkino, where he participated in the filming of *Shestaia chast' mira* (*A Sixth Part of the World*) and *Shagai, Sovet!* (*Forward, Soviet!*) (both 1926). The photography skills he initially honed with his Pioneer group facilitated his transition to filmmaking: "I fairly quickly understood the point of the composition of the frame and calculated the needed shots almost without error."[34] One week after starting his new work, Kudinov was sent on his first expedition as assistant to the cameraman Mikhail Kaufman (Ver-tov's brother) to shoot the mechanization of the harvest at a state farm in the Kuban. During a stop, Kudinov shot a photograph of Kaufman filming from a train window that was published on the back cover of the popular film magazine *Sovetskii ekran* (*Soviet Screen*) (fig. 3.8). Kudinov's rapid progress is evident in this photograph. A year earlier, Kaufman had filmed him as the leader of a Pioneer troop; now, an active participant in *kino-glaz*'s further deployment, Kudinov himself wielded the camera to take a striking image of the celebrated cameraman. He also attended *kinok* meetings and was part of a working group on the development of an official organization of *kinok* circles.[35] Working in film, he also continued to promote photography among Soviet youth. He was involved in Sovkino's establishment of a Komsomol photogra-phy circle, also called Foto-glaz, which made wall newspapers for display at the film organization. As he described this group's work in *Komsomol'skaia pravda* (*Komsomol Truth*) in early 1927, "The method of work is taken from the *kinoks*. The group strives to 'show life as it is.' Fact, fiction, and sharpness of material have done their work. The first two issues have revealed the liveliness and usefulness of the [wall] newspaper. 'Foto-glaz' has won the sympathy of adults and youth."[36] In line with the *kino-glaz* concept, the group rejected the staging of photographic shots. Kudinov's trajectory is evidence of the realization of Vertov's goal of developing a grassroots movement of *kinoks*. Just as Pioneers would progress into the ranks of the Komsomol and then full Communist Party membership, Kudinov progressed from a working-class child into an adult worker and organizer in Soviet mass media, using both film and photography as tools for political persuasion. His activities as both a media maker and activist ran the gamut from wall newspapers to printed magazines, photography, and films.

Pioneer Photography

While none of the Krasnaia Oborona troop's photographs are extant, images submit-ted by Pioneer groups were published in "Foto-glaz." All photographs in this feature's

3.8. With Dziga Vertov's encouragement, Pioneer troop leader Boris Kudinov took up photography and then film. He took this photograph of cameraman Mikhail Kaufman while working as his assistant on a film shoot. Back cover of *Sovetskii ekran*, no. 21 (18 August 1925).

first eight instalments were taken by *Baraban*'s staff photographer Fedor Zubkov, who was dispatched to report on various Pioneer activities, but in the ninth instalment (March 1925), "Foto-glaz" began to include photographs submitted by Pioneers (fig. 3.9). In a break with its usual format, this instalment of "Foto-glaz" was accompanied by a full-column text discussing the feature as it had run thus far and what was planned for it in the future.[37] Having reviewed the various themes covered since its debut, the text goes on to criticize the lack of Pioneer engagement: "'Foto-glaz' must note that Pioneer detachments and units have done little to help its work; they have sent few photos, and rarely called 'Foto-glaz' to 'look' at them. And as you can see, in order to see better, 'Foto-glaz' is forced to wear glasses." Quite literally, the photograph of an eye accompanying this text is wearing a corrective lens – unlike the naked eye that appeared with the first instalment of "Foto-glaz" (see fig. 3.3). To correct this situation, the magazine calls upon Pioneer troops to use photography to record their activities, just as they keep written inventories of their work in diaries. Guidance is provided on how and what to photograph:

> Learn to shoot by yourself and send photos to the editor for printing. Try to shoot a few pictures on one and the same topic (for example: the alliance [of the city] with the village) that develop this topic, indicating how to work in this area (for example: meetings with kids, assistance to the reading huts [the *izby-chital'nye*, reading-rooms used as part of the literacy campaign], assistance in carrying out the organization of a village troop, helping village kids publish a wall newspaper, etc.).

Acknowledging that not all groups would be able to make their own pictures, the column also proposes the engagement of professional photographers to record their activities. Referring to the Pioneer-submitted photographs published with this instalment, the column seeks to "teach" the reader what makes a photograph successful. Lackluster group portraits of Pioneers are dismissed as worthless: "All these groups are lifeless, they don't say anything, they don't reflect the work, they don't help it. It's not necessary to shoot like this." Other images, like the two reproduced on the page with the close-up of the eye, are praised: "These photographs are interesting; they live, they speak about the lives and work of the Pioneers." Both of these images, an intimate interior view taken at a Pioneer club and a shot looking up at a Pioneer speaking at a tribune, have the spontaneous quality of the snapshot. As with Vertov's rejection of staged film in favour of life caught off-guard, here posed images are out, captured activity is in. The column concludes with a pledge: "By May 1, all instalments of 'Foto-glaz' should consist of photographs by children themselves … Let's produce Pioneer photography." This change would represent a radical transformation of the column – a rejection of the professional photo-reportage of the staff photographer in favour of images provided by Pioneers themselves. The column promises "Pioneer photography" instead of mere photographs of Pioneers.

ПИОНЕРСКОЕ

Фото-глаз.

Ребята!

В этом № „Барабан" помещает 9-ую дюжину фото-глаза.

Начав свое существование с № 13—14 прошлого года фото-глаз проделал большую работу.

На страницах „Барабана" промелькнули фотографии, посвященные работе пионер-клуба, пионер-коммуне, деревенскому отряду, работе форпостов в школе, общественно-политической работе пионеров, работе звена, работе пионеров в Красной Армии, в семье и, наконец, в этом № фото-глаз, составленный из фотографий присланных с мест.

Каждый фото-глаз содержит от 12 до 15 фотографий.

Каждый фото-глаз наглядно показывает, как нужно работать пионеру в той или иной области.

Подводя итог работе фото-глаза нужно отметить, что пионеры очень мало помогали его работе: мало присылали фотографий, редко звали фото-глаз к себе „поглядеть". И как видите, чтобы лучше видеть, фото-глаз принужден одевать очки.

Этот недостаток нужно изжить. Необходимо сообщать в редакцию обо всем интересном в работе отрядов и звеньев для засемка.

Необходимо самим учиться запечатлевать всю работу на фотографии!

Каждый понимает необходимость учета работы в дневниках. Нужно, чтобы все поняли не меньшую важность учета работы в фотографии.

Не всякий отряд, однако, сможет приобрести фото-аппарат и снимать сами, придется прибегать к услугам фотографа - специалиста. И здесь нужно уметь указать фотографу **что снимать и как снимать.**

Посмотрите в этом № на фотографии № 7, 9, 12 и 13. Интересны он?—Нет. Все эти группы безжизненны, они ничего не говорят, они не отражают работу, не помогают ей. Так снимать не нужно!

Взгляните на фотографии № 1, 2, 3, 4, 5, 8, 15. Эти снимки интересны, они живут, говорят о жизни и работе пионеров (пионеры в клубе, на производстве, пирамида, приветствие пионеров, торжественное обещание и т. д.). Такие фотографии нужны.

Прежде чем начать снимать, надо продумать тему снимка (работа на столярном верстаке, устройство уголка, беседа с неорганизованными ребятами, на сельских работах). Фотографии на одну и ту же тему можно снять по разному. Так напр. фотографии № 6, 10, 16, имеют одну и ту же тему—стенгазета. Фотография № 10 скучна и наталкивает на шапки справа и слева газеты), фотография № 6 уже интереснее (слишком издалека снята) и фотография № 16 совсем хороша—здесь непосредственно видна вся коллегия за работой.

Итак, нужно всегда продумывать тему снимка.

Интересно обратить внимание на фотографии № 16. Там на стене нарисована обложка Барабана № 9. Размер пионера на рисунке немного больше настоящего пионера.—Интересно было бы снять 1—2 пионеров, ну хотя бы за игрой в шашки, на фоне этой картины. Здесь наглядно была бы видна работа пионеров этой картины. В следующих №№ „Барабан" будет специально беседовать на эти темы, а пока призывает все отряды: Учиться снимать самим и присылать фотографии в редакцию для напечатания. Старайтесь снимать на одну и ту же тему (например: смычка с деревней) несколько снимков, развивающих эту тему, указывающих как надо работать в этой области (напр. беседа с ребятами, помощь в избе читальне, помощь в проведении сбора пионерского отряда, помощь в издании стенгазеты деревенскими ребятами и т. д.).

Фото глаз выдвигает лозунг:—К 1 мая 1925 г. все фото-глазы должны составляться из снимков самих ребят.

Фото-глаз надеется, что многие отряды и звенья примут участие в работе фото глаза, и с его помощью он окрепнет и будет отражать все хорошие и плохие стороны работы пионерских отрядов и звеньев.

Даешь пионерскую фотографию!

Работа в детском саду.

Мы, пионеры, часто и очень много говорим о наших маленьких товарищах дошкольниках, над которым мы берем шефство. Но главное не то, чтобы взять над ними шефство и помогать их работе, а то, чтобы знать цель этой работы. И часто когда мы ходим к дошкольникам и работаем с ними, мы не знаем для чего мы это делаем: для того, чтобы показать дошкольникам, что пионеры о них заботятся или для чего другого. Так как вопрос этот является серьезным, то давайте его рассмотрим.

Первое, это давайте рассмотрим возраст дошкольников и мы увидим, что в этом возрасте из них можно воспитать какого хотите человека. А так как наша страна только что начинает проходить и устанавливать строителям ее нужна хорошая стойкая смена, которая все трудности строительства СССР могла бы легко перенести, то надо ребят с малолетства приучать к коллективному труду. И мы, пионеры, должны дать дошкольникам этот навык, чтобы они могли в будущем ко всему подойти с руками, а не только с словами. И так же, как нам пионерам нужна помощь комсомола, так и дошкольникам нужна помощь пионеров. Но тут у вас явится вопрос: для чего же эту работу возлагать на пионеров, что в детском саду есть педагог, что ли, они пионер больше педагога знает? Нет, ребята, не потому мы берем эту работу. Ведь мы, пионеры, сами только вышли из этого возраста, в котором находятся сейчас дошкольники и поэтому нам легче к ним подойти, чем взрослым, да и дошкольнику легче нас понять.

При работе в детском саду нужно пионерам правильно поставить себя с дошкольниками. При первом появлении пионеров ребята налегают на пионеров со всех сторон, обхватывают и того с ног сшибут. Конечно, нельзя показаться, что это пустяки, что дошкольники очень рады видеть пионеров. Но как раз это наоборот, потому что при таком постоянном отношении дошкольники серьезно к работе относится не будут, а на пионеров будут смотреть как на нянек или игрушек. И чтобы избежать такого явления, дошкольников нужно немного пристыдить, доказать им, что то хорошо это делать и ненужно. Не надо и свысока относиться к ребятам и разыгрывать из себя командиров, потому что ребята будут тогда бояться пионеров. Надо, чтобы были старшими товарищами дошкольников и чтобы дошкольники серьезно это понимали.

Работу нужно вести с дошкольниками такую, которая бы их интересовала и которой они добивались бы какой нибудь цели. Больше времени надо уделять играм и гимнастике, но нельзя обходится и без бесед. Играть в игры надо простые, понятные всем дошкольникам, и лучше в такие, в которые все участвуют. Гимнастика тоже должна быть легкая и короткая, потому что дошкольникам вредно заниматься много. Если ребята устанут, то надо сейчас же переменить занятие например, вместо игры беседу или рисование Беседы тоже должны быть короткие и такие, чтобы все дошкольники понимали те слова, которые будут в беседе, потому что, если дошкольники не поймут чего, то они не смогут запомнить беседу. Для того, чтобы они лучше запомнили беседы, можно рисовать рисунки к беседе или делать инсценировки во время беседы, например, проводя беседу МОПР'а, устроить инсценировку камеры в тюрьме.

Песни должны тоже быть понятными и короткими, потому что длинные песни ребятам трудно запомнить. Если песня длинная, то ее можно разучить в несколько раз. Надо также заниматься с дошкольниками чтением, рисованием, лепкой, вырезыванием из бумаги т. п.

При всей этой работе с дошкольниками пионерам нужно не только ими руководить и заниматься, но и участвовать с ними во всей жизни детского сада. Надо помочь им в работе мастерских и в комиссиях. На первое время организовать нужно хозяйственную и санитарную комиссию. Надо ходить с ними на прогулки, покупать разные вещи (напр. щетки) и т. п.

Если пионеры войдут во всю работу детсада, то дошкольники поймут лучше, зачем пионеры к ним ходят. На всю работу в детском саду нужно всегда составить план и не приходить в детский сад для занятий не зная прежде, что там делать и выдумывать из головы, уже придя в него. Каждый пионер должен заранее знать, что ему делать: проводить беседу, игру или песню и какую.

Кроме того почаще надо приглашать дошкольников в отряд на вечера и спектакли и подготовить с ними легкие выступления.

Во всей работе с дошкольниками пионеры должны иметь перед собой одну цель—сделать из них октябрят и пионеры

№ 1. Фото-глаз. В клубе 1 Сергеевского отряда на ст. Хотьково.

№ 2. Фото-глаз. Дагестан, Махач—Кале. Пионер приветствует комсомольцев в мендетнеделю.

ТВОРЧЕСТВО.

Вообще ко всей этой работе нужно как можно серьезней относится и чаще советоваться с педагогами. Они эту работу хорошо знают и за нее отвечают и часто пионеры, еще только взявшиеся за работу могут показать дошкольникам вредное для них гимнастики и игры. Поэтому пионерам нужно всегда переговариваться о своей работе с педагогами и доктором и всегда иметь подробный план работы.

Пионеры должны также наладить стенную газету у дошкольников и приносить им свою, чтобы познакомить их с пионерской работой. Кроме этого надо дошкольникам делать подарки, например, наделать чурбаков для игр, журналы и книги и т. п. Дошкольники могут тоже делать подарки пионерам, например, сделать у себя в мастерской полочки или какой ни будь портрет. Такие подарки заставят дошкольников серьезнее относиться к пионерам, так как они будут думать, что они помогают пионерам в работе.

должны с самого начала свою работу направлять к этому. Но не надо сразу их организовать в октябрят. Надо повести работу так, чтобы дошкольники стремились к этому и только, когда у них работа пойдет хорошо организовать торжественно группу октябрят.

Мы призываем все отряды взяться за работу в детских садах, так как она очень важная и пионеры должны сами подготовить себе смену.

Звено Красный тех-ин 17 Сокольнич. отряда.

№ 3. Фото-глаз. Нарофоминск. Звено со своим неразлучным другом.

«Барабан» предлагает всем отрядам поделиться своим опытом в работе в детских садах. Желательна присылка следующего материала: игр, песен, инсценировок, как проводить беседы, как организовать стенную газету.

У нас хорошо.

Форпост при школе совцхоза на ст. Льгов Дон. ж. д. охватывает до 110 чел. С организацией форпоста дисциплина в школе особенно среди пионеров сильно поднялась. Ученики не пионеры к отряду стали относится лучше и больше стало записываться в отряд, отчасти потому, что было устроено несколько бесед «Юные ленинцы и их задачи» и «Детское движение в Германии». Организована газета «Вперед», которая сильно повлияла на отношение к отряду.

Борис Якубовский.

Гражданская война.

Это происходило в 1919 году.

Я тогда жил в Москве, а мои родители работали на заводе. В один день я проснулся, уже рассветало. По комнате носился запах сырости и плач крошечной сестренки. Она просила поесть, но где взять я не знал, потому что дома никого не было. Мать ушла на работу вместе с отцом. Плач сестренки раздавался все громче и громче. Я тут-же вскочил с нар и пошел утешать ее. Я всячески старался утешить ее, но не мог, потому что у самого меня бурлило в животе от голодухи. Покинув сестру, я пошел на кухню поискать что-нибудь с'естного. Обшарил все уголки, но не мог найти даже завалявшейся корки хлеба. Вдруг я увидал на полке штук семь лепешек, приготовленных на весь день. Я с яростью накинулся на них и принялся есть, позабыв про свою маленькую голодную сестренку. В то время, пока я с аппетитом ел лепешки, сестренка заливалась слезами. На часах пробило ровно 12, на фабрике раздался гудок на обед. На дворе показались рабочие с грязными блузами в легких кепочках. Они, перегоняя друг друга, спешили разойтись по домам и отдать свободные часы отдыху. А потом снова гудки и снова адский грохот машин. Меня уже клонило ко сну и я лег на нары. Только что стал засыпать, как вдруг услышал стук в дверь, я быстро поднялся с нар и открыл дверь. В комнату ворвались клубы пара и вошли мать с отцом. Они были грязные и закоптелые от заводского дыма. Они хотели есть, но ничего не было, так и пришлось лечь голодными и в холоде Через несколько минут наступила тишина, только лишь изредка всхлипывал ребенок, но и тот через несколько минут успокоился, и наступила немая тишина. Я тоже заснул, не помня себя. Проснувшись часа в 4 утра, я уже слышу топот отца с матерью. Я прислушался к звукам—они говорили, о том, что надо уехать на Кубань, где нет голода. На другой день собрали вещи и поехали на рынок. Они продали почти все вещи, потому что нужны были деньги на поездку. Собравши немного денег, мы собрались и тронулись на санях к вокзалу. На вокзале купили билеты и проехали на. Курск по Брянской дороге. Когда приехали туда, мы все сильно заболели, а на другой день умер отец и мы остались шестеро ребят с матерью. Через неделю умерла моя маленькая сестра. Для нас наступили кошмарные дни. В это время Деникин наступал на Курск. Раздавались резкие разрывы шипящих гранатов, треск пулеметов и выстрелы из винтовок. Везде виднелись обозы, ползущие по пескам. У нас в саду рвались снаряды с адской силой. Мы от страха все попрятались в подвал и боялись выходить отгуда, потому что думали, что нас всех перебьют. Кто мог взять с собою святые книги, тот молился, но я не молился и то остался жив. Залпы раздавались все реже и реже и, наконец, все стихло. Мы понемногу стали вылезать. Город был взят Деникиным и производилась расправа с красными. На другой день опять послышались залпы орудий и треск пулемета. Деникин стал отступать, красные его окружили и стали биться в рукопашную. Везде раздавались крики „Ура красным".

М. Хитров.

№ 4. Фото-глаз. Нарофоминск. Пионер на текстильном производстве.

№ 5. Фото-глаз. г. Троцк, Самарской губ. Отрядная пирамида.

Мои воспоминания.

Дорогие товарищи. Я сама украинка и большей частью жила в деревне и была темная, необразованная, даже людей боялась, да не то что взрослых, а даже своих маленьких товарищей и всегда избегала с ними встречи. Так и была домоседкой, никогда не читала ни книжки, ни газеты, то и дело, что дома убирала да горшки мыла. Я с самого детства жила все время у чужих и работала. Это было еще до потери родителей, а когда родителей убили в 1917 г., то меня одни люди взяли к себе. В 1923 г. я уехала с ними в Москву.

Приехав в Москву, я начала интересоваться окружающей жизнью и всячески старалась поступить в школу, почитать книги и т. д. Поступила я в III школу переростков I ступени, записалась в библиотеку и начала почитывать

In May 1925, *Baraban* announced that it had fulfilled its pledge. A notice near the start of the magazine declared, "In this issue for the second time we publish a 'Foto-glaz' that consists of photographs sent in by Pioneers themselves," asserting further that, "in content and technique, this 'Foto-glaz' is executed much better than the preceding one."[38] Yet, unlike earlier instalments, it is difficult to discern which photographs the Pioneers took, as they are not clearly labelled; this was a first sign of the breakdown of the coherence of the column. Following the inaugural "Foto-glaz" in October 1924, the next ten consecutive issues of *Baraban* (until April 1925) included the feature, with a clearly structured format: each instalment was specifically labelled "Foto-glaz" and presented a particular theme explicitly related to Pioneer activities, and the photographs appeared amid related texts by Pioneers, usually at the end of the magazine. After April 1925, the feature became more sporadic and no longer followed a clear format. The brief commitment to publishing only photographs provided by Pioneers also disappeared after May 1925. Some later instalments even failed to include any photographs of Pioneers, which was ostensibly the purpose of "Foto-glaz" at the outset. These changes were likely due to the departure in April of the editor, Mikhail Stremiakov, who established the weekly newspaper *Pionerskaia pravda* (*Pioneer Truth*) in March 1925; in his absence, no further efforts were made to solicit photographs taken by Pioneers. "Foto-glaz" hobbled on as an irregular feature until *Baraban* was absorbed by the magazine *Pioner* in October 1926.

The merging of the two publications marked the ascendance of *Pioner* as the sole popular magazine for Soviet children. From the time in appeared in 1924, *Pioner* immediately stood out as the foremost popular magazine of the Pioneer movement, due to its designation as "the organ" of the Central Bureau of Young Pioneers and the Central Committee of the Komsomol. While *Baraban* and *Vorobei / Novyi Robinzon* were publications of the city bureaus of the Komsomol in Moscow and Leningrad, *Pioner* was the official publication of the entire organization – an all-union magazine that thus had a broader target readership and higher print run, and was even physically larger.[39] *Baraban* had been first established as the organ of the Krasnaia Presnia Bureau of Young Pioneers, and it stressed the involvement of local Pioneers themselves. With Pioneers like Kudinov assisting in putting together early issues, the children themselves contributed to showcasing their activities and organizational work. While *Baraban* expanded to include subscribers outside of Moscow, it continued to work closely with its base. In contrast, *Pioner* was an all-Russia publication from the first, and from 1926 on an all-union one, intended to reach Pioneers across the Soviet Union. It also had far closer ties to the upper ranks of the Soviet political leadership, as evidenced by the presence of Nadezhda Krupskaia (Lenin's wife, then widow) on the editorial board. As deputy commissar of enlightenment, Krupskaia had been involved with the establishment of the Pioneers and was a leading figure in Soviet pedagogy. Not surprisingly, compared to *Baraban*, *Pioner* was more remote from its base. Intended for all Soviet children between the ages of ten and fourteen, it provided its readers a mixture of literary and more journalistic writing that was socially and politically engaged. Combining high literary quality with coverage of contemporary events, it was hailed as a new type of children's magazine.[40] While the magazine featured leading Soviet authors and journalists, from the outset it also published the work of child correspondents (*detkory*), albeit to a much lesser extent than *Baraban*.

Pioner was an illustrated magazine that featured both drawings and photographs. In its first two years of publication, it had a dedicated photo section titled "Foto-gazeta" ("Photo-Newspaper").[41] This feature took the form of a two-page spread of press photographs showing current events and political figures; it did not, however, work to promote the activity of photography itself or the critical reading of photographs. While a graphic of a boy and girl with neck scarves and cameras appeared in several issues, there was no attempt to encourage Pioneers to take up photography themselves. During the 1920s, *Pioner*'s use of photography was visually engaging, but it is difficult to discern anything specifically socialist in the images. It was very much a modernist children's magazine, but few of its photographs would seem out of place in a bourgeois Scouting publication; the subjects in its staged photographs of Pioneers could easily be reimagined in Scout uniforms (fig. 3.10).[42] Many of the photographs published in the magazine lacked distinct socialist content. The irregular column "So vsego sveta" ("From All over the World") presented spreads with diverse images, and with no sense of specifically socialist subject matter or viewpoint. They primarily featured foreign press photographs, including of such mundane subjects as a circus horse that had been flown from London to Paris via airplane (allegedly the first flying equine).[43] In 1928, this section was renamed "Okoshko vo vse strany" ("A Little Window to All Lands"), and it continued sporadically through 1930.[44] Early instalments consisted of texts illustrated by photographs, featuring a range of topics that included natural history, geography, technology, and current affairs. The bulk of the subject matter was non-Soviet.

In 1927, *Pioner* began to encourage its readers to take up photography, in September running what was titled the "Stranichka foto-detkora No. 1" ("Little Page of the *Foto-detkor* No. 1"; fig. 3.11), and announcing plans to publish not just the written observations of child correspondents, but also photographs taken by them. Noting that thousands of children had cameras, and that many schools and Pioneer troops had photography circles, the magazine called upon its readers to send their most interesting photographs for publication: "After all, even the most experienced photographer cannot shoot such little scenes and moments from the lives of children as could easily be taken by the participants themselves."[45] The photographs published with this notice present a selection of images of children engaged in both playful and productive activities at Pioneer summer camps in Armenia, North Ossetia, and Kaluga. With snaps showing Pioneers playing croquet and board games, the images seem less overtly political than those published earlier in *Baraban*.

Despite *Pioner*'s exhortation that readers contribute their photographs for this feature, no further instalments of it appeared. Nevertheless, over the next few years,

ПИОНЕРЫ О „ПИОНЕРЕ"

Хороший ли журнал „Пионер"?

„...Я уже получил первый номер „Пионера" и был ему рад, как приезду близкого товарища. Он близок тем, что считается с мнением и строится на отзыве и самодеятельности ребят. Как заманчиво—все, что только тебя интересует, может быть напечатано на страницах „Пионера".

Из письма Вс. Бессонова—г. Кашин, Тверской губ.

„Пионер" я выписываю с 1927 года; как видите, подписчик я еще „молодой". Но за этот год я сроднился с „Пионером", привык с нетерпением ждать каждый его номер и с жадностью набрасываться на него. „Пионер" дает занимательный литературный материал и массу практического материала.

„Пионер" нравится мне еще тем, что на его страницах печатают свои стихи крупнейшие современные поэты, как например, Маяковский и Жаров. Художественное оформление журнала тоже хорошо. Ценно то, что в нем принимают участие такие известные художники, как Моор, Елисеев, Ефимов. Лучшие иллюстрации—художн. Кузнецова и Покровского".

Из письма В. Егорова—г. Кашин, Тверской губ.

„Журнал „Пионер" я выписываю с 1926 года. Он мне очень нравиться, и я его выписываю на 1928 год. Если сравнить 1926 г. и 1927 г., то 1927 г. куда лучше".

Из письма Оксаны Сапоненко—хутор Выдумка, Брянской губ.

ПОЧЕМУ ЭТИ РЕБЯТА.....

...Потому, что они...

„Журнала не выписывал никогда. Выписать журнал лично на себя нет средств, а читать—аккуратно читаю. Отряд выписывает—ношу на дом, читаю. Читаю вслух, громко маме, отцу и братишкам. Мои родители очень интересуются чтением".

Из письма Анатолия Абрамова—дер. Верхне-Семеновская, Сев.-Двинской губ.

Алло! Звену „Красный Пионер"

„Я всегда жду журнала „Пионер" с нетерпением и всегда, как только получаю, так ищу „Дневник звена".

— А, есть!—восклицаю я и

....НЕ ОТКЛИКАЮТСЯ.....

...получили новый номер „Пионера"...

начинаю с жадностью читать. Когда читаешь—прямо слюнки текут: „А, ну, что дальше будет?".

Ну, а дальше много смеха, живот поджимаешь от смехоты, да как не смешно, когда Коля Солнцев предлагает в будущий клуб пионерский впустить акул?! Смехота!

А Коля Шамет вздумал закрасить оконные стекла красной краской.

— Авось, мол, хорошо будет.

Но вышло наоборот.

— Ха-ха-ха!

Но кроме смешного есть и полезное, хорошее, как например, звено делало вещи... Мой товарищ читал „Дневник звена", и вдруг:

— Петюха! Давай и мы попробуем сделать прибор для приема сигнализации. Или мы не сумеем? Что мы хуже, что ли, их?

.....КОГДА ИХ ЗОВУТ?

...и не могут от него оторваться

— Эх, и верно, давай!—просиял я. Бросили другие дела и принялись работать. Прибор готов.

— Слушай, давай и ящик для мусора сделаем,- говорю я,—ведь его придумал Сережа Федосейчиков, младший брат, надо его удостоить, провести в жизнь его изобретение.

Скоро был и ящик готов.

Теперь весь мусор в него бросают.

Шлю благодарность звену „Красный Пионер".

Письмо Петра Толпегина—Сормово, Нижегор. губ.

Что дает „Пионер" ребятам?

„Без всяких других пособий научился играть в шахматы исключительно по журналу „Пионер". Также хорошим пособием в изучении сигнализации послужил № 21 „Пионера". Из 17-го номера журнала „Пионер" мы показали опыт с яйцом в графине на отрядовом вечере".

Из письма Льва Васильева—г. Москва, 72-й отряд.

„Выучился играть в шахматы. Сделал противогаз, который отослал на конкурс, организованный вами. Сделал действующую модель турбины".

Из письма А. Шубочкина—с. Сараи-Рязанские, Рязанской губ.

„Организовал записную книжку—она дает очень много пользы. Мои товарищи по отряду последовали моему примеру—теперь все в нашем отряде ее имеют".

Из письма Саши Теплицкого—Гайсин, Под. губ.

3.10. *Pioner's* imagery was rarely explicitly socialist. These photographs of Pioneers reading *Pioner* magazine could just as easily be imagined as Boy Scouts or Girl Scouts. Inside cover of *Pioner*, no. 5 (March 1928).

СТРАНИЧКА ФОТО - ДЕТКОРА № 1

„Пионер" решил освещать жизнь и работу пионеров, школьников и неорганизованных не только заметками деткоров, но и фотографиями ребят. Ведь у нас имеются тысячи ребят, имеющих фото-аппараты и сотни фото-кружков в отрядах и школах. Редакция „Пионера" обращается к вам с просьбой — присылайте интересные фотографии для помещения в журнале. Ведь и самый опытный фотограф не сможет заснять тех сценок и моментов из работы и жизни ребят, которые легко могут заснять сами участники. Помещая первую страничку фото-деткора, „Пионер" ждет, что хорошему примеру первых фото-деткоров последуют все пионеры, занимающиеся фотографией.

Колонка слева: 1) село Гомучкал — место лагеря отряда профсоюза печатников, Владикавказ, фотография В. Логинова, 2) на пионерской даче за игрой в крокет, Калуга, фотография—работа фото-кружка, 3) приготовляют фонари на ночь, лагерь отряда печатников, Владикавказ, фотография В. Логинова, 4) мытье посуды после обеда, лагерь отряда печатников, Владикавказ, фотография В. Логинова, 5) у мельницы на рыбной ловле, Свердловск, фотография В. Старикова. Наверху справа: 6) ловят раков, Свердловск, фотография В. Старикова. Внизу справа: 7) в час отдыха в лагере пионеров г. Эривани в с. Дараличаг, Армения.

3.11. In 1927, *Pioner* announced a new recurring column that would feature photographs by Pioneers, but just a single instalment appeared that featured the activities of Pioneers in summer camps in various parts of the USSR. Inside back cover of *Pioner*, no. 18 (September 1927).

Pioner continued to urge its readers to take up photography and use it as a tool for social transformation. Just as the magazine encouraged child correspondents, it also sought to cultivate photo-correspondents. It did this at multiple levels: by providing technical guidance for beginning photographers; calling upon readers to submit photographs for publication; and providing narratives that described the social transformation that could be achieved through active engagement with socialist media. This promotion of photography within *Pioner* reflects the general boom in amateur photography that occurred around 1926, when the magazine *Sovetskoe foto* began publication and the Society of Friends of Soviet Cinema (ODSK) organized an amateur film and photography section. In 1928, the Central Committee issued a resolution to harness amateur photography to the worker-correspondent movement.[46]

Pioner promoted photography as a modern technology integral to socialist construction. In 1928, the recurring technology column "KIP" (the acronym for *Klub inzhener-pionerov* – Club of Engineer-Pioneers) was initiated.[47] Edited by the popular technology and science writer Mikhail Il'in (pen name of Ilya Marshak, brother of the renowned Soviet children's author Samuil Marshak), this imaginative column employed visual means to educate its readers about technology.[48] In 1929, KIP initiated a new section entitled "Fabrika na stole" ("Factory on the Table"), which was presented in terms of Pioneer mobilization for the first Five-Year Plan (1928–32), when the Soviet government embarked upon an ambitious program of industrialization and the collectivization of agriculture. During this era, both the periodical press and photography were mobilized to promote active engagement with the construction of socialism. The goal of "Factory on the Table" was for Pioneers to develop mastery in an area useful to achieving the plan. The factory would consist of two workshops: photography and electrical technology. The photo workshop would train instructors, who could then share their expertise with others: "Here will be made photographers who are able to build cameras and repair them. Each will be able to build a small photography workshop. In general, each Pioneer leaving our factory will be a Pioneer-master."[49] "Factory on the Table" was open to all who wanted to train there. It instructed Pioneers to form into groups, register their participation, and send reports about their activities to the magazine. The workshops would function in the manner of correspondence courses. Upon completion of the lessons, students would complete a test, and all those who passed would receive a certificate for their work.

Written by David Bunimovich, a Soviet expert on photographic technique and processes, "Fotograficheskii tsekh" ("The Photographic Workshop") promised to provide guidance on all aspects of photography, from building a camera to organizing photo groups through a projected series of twelve instalments.[50] In the introduction to the first instalment, the wall newspaper is singled out as an important focus for Pioneer photography: "In every troop and in every school there is a wall newspaper. This newspaper will become especially interesting if there are photos that depict what is described in it. For this wall newspaper, first and foremost, it will be necessary to use knowledge of photography." While the series promised a comprehensive plan of work, only four instalments were published, the last appearing in February 1930. The early curtailment of the series could be attributed to any number of factors: a paucity of readers signing up for the workshop; the technical level of its content, too advanced for the magazine's target audience; the chronic shortage of cameras and basic photographic materials; and a failure to solicit photographs of a quality suitable for reproduction.

A 1931 story entitled "Fotokory" ("Photo-Correspondents"), credited to a child correspondent named Finogenov, tells of how the Pioneer Misha uses photography to facilitate positive social change and work toward the resolution of labour problems.[51] Across from the factory where his father works, Misha stations himself outside a beer hall and waits as it grows dark. It is payday. Some workers stumble out of the beer hall, about to get into a fight, and he shoots their photographs using magnesium flash to illuminate the darkness. After school the following day, Misha develops the photographs in an improvised darkroom at home. He must work quickly, as he has been forbidden by his parents to practise photography ever since he stained a tablecloth by accidentally spilling some solution on it. Only two of the five shots turn out; Misha prints them. The first is a shot of an evidently drunken worker hanging onto the railing and sitting on the steps in front of the beer hall. He prints the second: "A drunken worker appeared in the shot, as if in life: hands spread wide open, cap aslant. Misha peered at the photo and his mouth gaped in astonishment. 'No way, I shot dad! Eh eh! Indeed, that's him,' Misha repeated, peering at the card." Misha goes to the head of the factory's Communist Party committee, who is shouting into the phone about production breakdowns due to absenteeism. The Pioneer cuts to the front of a line of workers waiting to meet with this director and shows him the photographs. It turns out his father has been absent twice in the past ten days, presumably following payday drinking binges. The photographs are hung on the factory's "black board," a propaganda vehicle for publicly shaming bad conduct, and workers crowd around and disparage the drunken behaviour of Misha's father. When the father himself sees the photos, he demands to know who made them – and Misha steps forward to claim authorship: "Yes, I made them. And I will do it again, if you drink." After his father storms off, Misha does not go home that night, only returning the following day after school. His mother threatens that his father will thrash him, but he narrowly escapes punishment due to a guest's arrival. On the next payday, his father considers going to the beer hall, but he wonders if Misha will again be there with his camera and, for the first time on a payday, does not go in.

This story tells of Misha's mastery of photographic technique, harnessing it to effect social transformation. The *fotokor* employs magnesium flash powder to shed light on the darkness both literally and figuratively. He does so in a manner recalling the Danish-American slum reformer Jacob Riis, who employed magnesium flash powder to raid flophouses and pubs on New York's Lower East Side in the dark of night and record "how the other half lives." Riis hardly identified with his subjects. Photographs of immigrant children in his book *The Children of the Poor* (1908) are accompanied by texts that compare them to animals, as in his description of child trashpickers: "Filthy and ragged, they fitted well into their environment – even the pig I had encountered at one of the East River dumps was much the more respectable, as to appearance, of the lot – but were entirely undaunted by it. They scarcely remembered anything but the dump. Neither could read, of course."[52] This is in sharp contrast to Misha, who is engaged in working-class *self*-representation. Misha's mastery of photography is also evident in his ability to set up a temporary darkroom for use in his home. The fact that he succeeds in producing only two good shots out of five exposures means he still has some room for improvement of his technique. However, this too reflects positively on his character: he perseveres despite setbacks, his example encouraging others to accept failure and learn from their mistakes.

Misha's photographs are put to political use. Published on a board in the factory, they document and draw attention to the antisocial behaviour that erupts on paydays. Specifically, they provide proof of the cause of his father's work absenteeism and neglect of his family. As a result of the photographs, Misha's father changes his behaviour, thus effecting positive social change. While Misha is just a child, who must stand on his tiptoes to shoot the photographs, he is more politically aware than his parents. There is a clear gulf between them: Misha is a Soviet child, born into the new world after the revolution, while his parents have character flaws that mark them as the damaged remnants of the older social order. Placing more value on a tablecloth than their son's exploration of a progressive technology, they forbid him to pursue photography because of something so trivial as a stain. Beatings are clearly a feature of family life, but Misha perseveres in his photographic work and finds the courage to return home. In developing his photographs covertly, he may be disobeying his parents; but in this he is morally upright and politically conscious, and his actions are fully vindicated in the story.[53]

Credited to the child correspondent Finogenov, "Photo-Correspondents" is a fictional account presenting an ideal vision of activist Pioneer photography to be emulated by the magazine's readers. The story reveals a significant shift in the conception of Pioneer photography; so far from "Foto-glaz's" rather uncontroversial call to visually document the activities of Pioneers, the camera of the relatively militant Misha stands as a weapon for deployment in the class war that accompanied the first Five-Year Plan. Most children who took up photography were likely not interested in pursuing this type of extreme political exposure of their parents or peers. Notably, in official Pioneer magazines, scant visual evidence exists of Soviet children's political engagement with photography during this period. While *Pioner* continued to call for the submission of photos, there seems to have been little response on the part of its readers. In 1929, the magazine urged readers to submit texts, drawings, and photographs for publication: "Readers of *Pioner* in the North, South, West, and East! Send notes and photos about all interests, about what is going on in your town, village, *kishlak*, *aul*, hamlet, camp."[54] Another issue exhorted: "Child correspondents – write, draw, shoot."[55] A notice published with the final instalment of "The Photography Workshop" stated: "The administration of the Factory on the Table calls upon all workers of the photo section to send their test photos with a report about the work of the group."[56] In April 1931, an announcement for a photography contest appeared on the back cover:

> A jury is feverishly working in the editorial offices from morning to night. It is drawing up the conditions for a contest. What kind? For *fotokory*! The desks of the editorial offices are covered with folders fat with photographs submitted to the contest. Materials keep coming and coming, but we will not cut off the receipt of materials, because we await photos from you, from your detachment, your troop.[57]

Despite the claim that abundant photographs had already been submitted, this was the only announcement published about this contest – and the results were never announced.

While writings and drawings credited to child correspondents were published in the magazine, no photographs were credited to Pioneers during the first Five-Year Plan. The repeated exhortations to send photographs indicate an active commitment to the work of Pioneer *fotokory*, yet *Pioner*'s promotion of photography failed to bear fruit, at least of a quality suitable for publication. Pioneer photo circles did exist, but prints made by ill-equipped fledgling photographers were likely of inadequate quality for publication. These groups did not have access to the type of large-format professional glass-plate camera that Volodia valorized in 1924 and that remained the standard for Soviet press photography into the 1930s. While imported cameras and supplies were available earlier in the decade, the start of the first Five-Year Plan vastly restricted access to such items. These problems were acutely evident by 1930, when paper shortages affected the publication of magazines. However, the true publication of Pioneer photographs did not take place in the illustrated periodical press, but on the notice boards and wall newspapers of Pioneer clubs and workplaces. Pioneer photography languished after the end of the first Five-Year Plan, when children's politically engaged photographic self-representation was at odds with an increasingly repressive state. While the potential of Pioneer photo-correspondence was not realized due to material shortages, technical problems, and political upheaval, the legacy of the early Soviet period's stress on photographic literacy, youthful engagement with technology, and the development of socialist media would bear fruit with the revival of photo amateurism and children's photography after the end of Stalinism.

NOTES

1 Kol'tsov, "Za sovetskuiu fotografiiu," 1.
2 Lunacharsky, "Nasha kul'tura i fotografiia," 2.

 3 Ibid., 2.
 4 Kodak, "Eastman Kodak Co.'s Brownie Cameras $1.00," *Cosmopolitan* (1900), in Ellis Collection of Kodakiana (1886–1923), Duke University Library, available electronically: https://idn.duke.edu/ark:/87924/r4xg9h35n.
 5 Tinkler, "A Fragmented Picture."
 6 Kodak, "A Good Scout Needs a Brownie," 26.
 7 "Zakony iunykh pionerov," 19; "Obychai iunykh pionerov," 28.
 8 "Zakony iunykh pionerov," 19.
 9 "Obychai iunykh pionerov," 28.
10 Kravchenko, "Detskaia pechat'."
11 Nikitin, "Brodiachii fotograf."
12 Ibid., 23.
13 In the text, Volodia identifies his father as "Nikolai Nikolaevich," while the table of contents credits the text to "Nikolai Nikitin"; the author is likely Nikolai Nikolaevich Nikitin, the Soviet writer and former member of the Serapion Brothers literary group.
14 The final issue was *Novyi Robinzon* 19/20 (November 1925). While the children's writer Boris Zhitkov added some continuity to this feature through his authorship of seven of the instalments, the format and content otherwise varied widely from issue to issue.
15 "Smotri FOTO-GLAZ," 38.
16 *Baraban* 13/14 (October 1924): 40–1.
17 Kelly, "A Laboratory"; Kenez, *Birth of the Propaganda State*, 237–9.
18 "Zhivaia gazeta 55-go otriada," 16–17.
19 See the anthology of such texts in Tsivian, *Lines of Resistance*.
20 Vertov, "Kinoki. Perevorot," 141; English translation from Michelson, *Kino-Eye*, 17.
21 Hicks, *Dziga Vertov*, 16–20.
22 Cited in Tsivian, *Lines of Resistance*, 47.
23 In 1926, Osip Brik employed the term *foto-glaz* in a text published alongside a selection of Aleksandr Rodchenko's photographs ("Chego ne vidit glaz," 22–3). While Brik used the term to advocate for Rodchenko's extreme camera angles, it is clear that the term was already in circulation and with a broader Vertovian conception of the camera's role in recording and capturing the visible world. Speaking at a screening of *Kino-glaz* on 14 October 1924, Vertov stated that "people invented the cinema camera in order to more deeply penetrate into the visible world, in order to research and describe visual phenomena, in order to not forget what is taking place and what will have to be remembered in the future." Rossiiskii gosudarstvennyi arkhiv literatury i iskusstva (hereafter RGALI), fond 2091, op. 2, d. 390, l. 10.
24 See, for instance, the Rodchenko-designed advertisement run in *Kino-nedelia* 38 (21 October 1924).
25 *Baraban* 1 (April 1923): 1. My research into this troop was inspired by and is indebted to McKay, "Vertov and the Line."
26 Kudinov, "Pervyi zimnii lager' iunykh pionerov," 15.
27 Rossiiskii gosudarstvennyi arkhiv sotsial'no-politicheskoi istorii (hereafter RGASPI), fond M-1 (Tsentral'nyi komitet VLKSM, 1918–91), op. 23, d. 282, l. 23.
28 Kudinov, "Kino-glaz," 46.
29 Hicks, *Dziga Vertov*, 23–5.
30 *Baraban* 6 (March 1925): 12–15, 18–19.
31 Cited in Drobashenko, *Dziga Vertov*, 93. Kudinov was likely the author of this report. The group is also mentioned in Vertov, "Tvorcheskaia kartochka," 166, 189. John McKay dates the origins of the photo circle and a celebration that Vertov attended with the Pioneers to 1926 ("Vertov and the Line," 90), but both events took place in 1924.

32 Kudinov, "Posviashchenie v kinorazvedchiki," 115.

33 RGASPI, f. M-1, op. 23, d. 282, l. 31; McKay, "Vertov and the Line," 91.

34 Kudinov, "Posviashchenie v kinorazvedchiki," 116–20.

35 On 2 November 1925, he attended a meeting of the Commission to Organize a Circle of Kinoks along with Vertov, Kaufman, the cameraman Ilya Kopalin, and Viktor Komarov (the organizer of a kinok group at another Pioneer troop). At the meeting, it was resolved that Kaufman, Kopalin, and Kudinov would work on drafting the bylaws of the proposed organization, which would be called Kino-glaz. RGALI f. 2091, op. 2, d. 390, ll. 21–4, 26.

36 Kudinov, "Komsomol'skii foto-glaz." An anonymous and briefer version of this text was published in *Sovetskoe foto* 4 (1927): 122. McKay identifies the "Foto-glaz" circle as a children's group, yet it consisted of Komsomol members (ages fifteen to twenty-eight) who worked at Sovkino.

37 "Foto-glaz," *Baraban* 5 (March 1925): 20.

38 *Baraban* 10 (May 1925): 2.

39 *Baraban* began publication with a print run of 3,000 copies per issue, climbed as high as 20,000 copies, and ended at 15,000. In contrast, *Pioneer* began publication with 10,000 copies per issue, increased to 20,000 copies by January 1925, and 60,000 copies by January 1930.

40 Kholmov, *Stanovlenie sovetskoi zhurnalistiki*, 102–3.

41 "Foto-gazeta" appeared in fourteen of the thirty-four issues published in 1924–5.

42 See also *Pioner* 8 (April 1928): 20–1. The photos often followed the formats of popular photo magazines: trick photos, photographic "novels," and even shaming photographs that demonstrated children's bad habits.

43 Fifteen instalments appeared between 1924 and 1928.

44 Twelve instalments appeared between 1928 and 1930.

45 Inside back cover of *Pioner* 18 (September 1927). Possibly marking the new editorial emphasis on photography, Shaikhet's image of Pioneers with a camera had, as mentioned at the outset of this chapter, appeared on the magazine's cover a month earlier.

46 Wolf, "The Soviet Union."

47 "Inzhener-Pioner," 14–15.

48 The column sometimes included a "Kino-KIP" – a "cinema" that presented visual materials, including drawings, diagrams, and photographs.

49 "Fabrika na stole," 23.

50 Bunimovich, "Fotograficheskii tsekh," *Pioner*, no. 21 (November 1929): 24; *Pioner*, no. 22 (November 1929): 21; *Pioner*, no. 24 (December 1929): 23; *Pioner*, no. 4 (February 1930): 16.

51 Finogenov, "Fotokory," 9.

52 Riis, *Children of the Poor*, 29.

53 As Lisa Kirschenbaum has noted, early Soviet family conflict often approximated class warfare, with children as proletarians and adults in the role of class enemy (*Small Comrades*, 151).

54 "Okoshko vo vse strany," 16.

55 *Pioner* 15 (August 1929): 23.

56 Bunimovich, "Fotograficheskii tsekh," *Pioner* 4 (February 1930): 16.

57 Back cover of *Pioner*, no. 12 (April 1931).

BIBLIOGRAPHY

Brik, Osip. "Chego ne vidit glaz." *Sovetskoe kino* 2 (1926): 22–3.

Drobashenko, S., ed. *Dziga Vertov: Stat'i, dnevniki, zamysly*. Moscow: Iskusstvo, 1966.

"Fabrika na stole." *Pioner*, no. 21 (November 1929): 23.

Finogenov. "Fotokory." *Pioner*, no. 10 (April 1931): 9.

Hicks, Jeremy. *Dziga Vertov: Defining Documentary Film*. London: I.B. Tauris, 2007.

"Inzhener-Pioner: Izvestiia kluba inzhener-pionerov no. 1." *Pioner*, no. 20 (October 1928): 14–15.

Kelly, Catriona. "'A Laboratory for the Manufacture of Proletarian Writers': The *Stengazeta* (Wall Newspaper), *Kul'turnost'* and the Language of Politics in the Early Soviet Period." *Europe-Asia Studies* 54, no. 4 (2002): 573–602.

Kenez, Peter. *Birth of the Propaganda State: Soviet Methods of Mass Mobilization, 1917–1929*. Cambridge: Cambridge University Press, 1985.

Kholmov, M.I. *Stanovlenie sovetskoi zhurnalistiki dlia detei*. Leningrad: Izdatel'stvo Leningradskogo universitata, 1983.

Kirschenbaum, Lisa. *Small Comrades: Revolutionizing Childhood in Soviet Russia, 1917–1932*. New York: Routledge, 2000.

Kodak. "A Good Scout Needs a Brownie." *Scout Gazette* (15 July 1921): 26.

Kol'tsov, Mikhail. "Za sovetskuiu fotografiiu." *Sovetskoe foto*, no. 1 (April 1926): 1.

Kravchenko, Artem. "'Detskaia pechat' – vozhak i organizator mass': K istorii formirovaniia komosomol'skoi sistemy rukovodstva tsentral'nymi pionerskimi zhurnalami Moskvy v 1920-e gg." *Detskie cheteniia* 10, no. 2 (December 2016): 190–213.

Kudinov, Boris. "Kino-glaz. Nash lager' na kino-lente." *Baraban*, no. 10 (September 1924): 46.

– "Komsomol'skii foto-glaz." *Komsomol'skaia pravda* (9 February 1927).

– "Pervyi zimnii lager' iunykh pionerov." *Baraban*, no. 1 (April 1923): 15.

– "Posviashchenie v kinorazvedchiki." In *Dziga Vertov v vospominaniiakh sovremennikov*, edited by I.Ia. Vaisfel'd, 112–21. Moscow: Iskusstvo, 1976.

Lunacharsky, Anatoly. "Nasha kul'tura i fotografiia." *Sovetskoe foto*, no. 1 (April 1926): 2.

McKay, John. "Vertov and the Line: Art, Socialization, Collaboration." In *Film, Art, New Media: Museum without Walls?*, edited by Angela Dalle Vacche, 81–96. Houndmills, UK: Palgrave Macmillan, 2012.

Michelson, Annette, ed. *Kino-Eye: The Writings of Dziga Vertov*. Translated by Kevin O'Brien. Berkeley: University of California Press, 1984.

Nikitin, Nikolai. "Brodiachii fotograf." *Vorobei*, no. 3 (March 1924): 23–9.

"Obychai iunykh pionerov." *Baraban*, no. 3 (ca. October 1923): 28.

"Okoshko vo vse strany." *Pioner*, no. 11 (June 1929): 16–17.

Riis, Jacob. *The Children of the Poor*. New York: Charles Scribner's Sons, 1908.

"Smotri FOTO-GLAZ 'Barabana' v pioner-klube." *Baraban*, nos. 13/14 (October 1924): 38–48.

"Stranichka foto-detkora No. 1." *Pioner*, no. 18 (September 1927): inside back cover.

Tinkler, Peggy. "A Fragmented Picture: Reflections on the Photographic Practices of Young People." *Visual Studies* 23, no. 3 (December 2008): 255–66.

Tsivian, Yuri, ed. *Lines of Resistance: Dziga Vertov and the Twenties*. Pordenone, IT: Giornata del Cinema Muto, 2004.

Vertov, Dziga. "Kinoki. Perevorot." *LEF*, no. 3 (March 1923): 135–43.

– "Tvorcheskaia kartochka, 1917–1947." *Kinovedcheskie zapiski* 30 (1996): 160–92.

Wolf, Erika. "The Soviet Union: From Worker to Proletarian Photography." In *The Worker Photography Movement (1926–1939)*, edited by Jorge Ribalta, 32–46. Madrid: Museo Nacional Centro de Arta Reina Sofia, 2011.

"Zakony iunykh pionerov." *Baraban*, no. 3 (ca. October 1923): 19.

"Zhivaia gazeta 55-go otriada Krasnoi Presni." *Baraban*, no. 12 (October 1924): 16–17.

chapter four

AUTONOMOUS ANIMALS ANIMATED: *SAMOZVERI* AS A CONSTRUCTIVIST PEDAGOGICAL CINE-DISPOSITIVE

ALEKSANDAR BOŠKOVIĆ

In the inaugural issue of the journal *Novyi LEF* (*New LEF*) from January 1927, the well-known constructivist artists Aleksandr Rodchenko and Varvara Stepanova published five photographs they had created to illustrate Sergei Tret'iakov's children's book *Samozveri* (*Autoanimals*) (fig. 4.1). The black-and-white photographs, featuring three-dimensional figures of animals, humans, and objects cut from paper, are glossed as "photo-animated illustrations" (*fotomul'tiplikatsionnye illiustratsii*) on a double-page spread, and explicated further in a brief note in the back of this first issue of *Novyi LEF*. The note asserts that, in preparing these illustrations for *Autoanimals*, Rodchenko and Stepanova "are the first to use spatial [three-dimensional] photo-animation (*prostranstvennaia fotomul'tiplikatsiia*) instead of planar [two-dimensional] film animation."[1] The note further explains that the artists conceived this innovative method of representation as having a dual function:

1. In illustrating a children's book, [spatial photo-animation] gives the child a visual aid for independent work on the production and placement of figures and things constructed in the course of play. Material and techniques are simple, flexible, and accessible to the child.
2. Due to the rich lighting effects and composition possibilities, volumetric photo-animation has high mobility, and can be used for any thematic treatment.[2]

If the first aim of spatial photo-animation is to enhance the child's active relationship with the children's book as a mediator between the child and the surrounding world, the second lies in the increased mobility and adaptability of this novel representational method. It serves as "a visual aid," a model for the child to follow in constructing objects and figures for play; but it also has applications in other arts and media, especially cinema, as the note concludes: "Having advanced to the cinema, this technique will enrich the existing methods of film animation. Thus have Tret'iakov, Rodchenko, and Stepanova already arranged a series of short films for a film studio."[3]

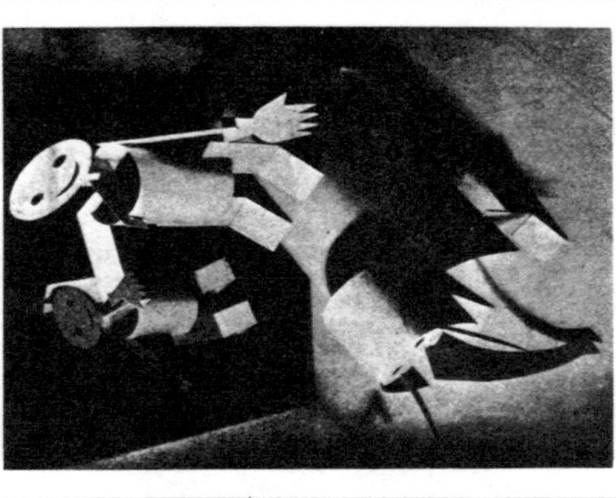
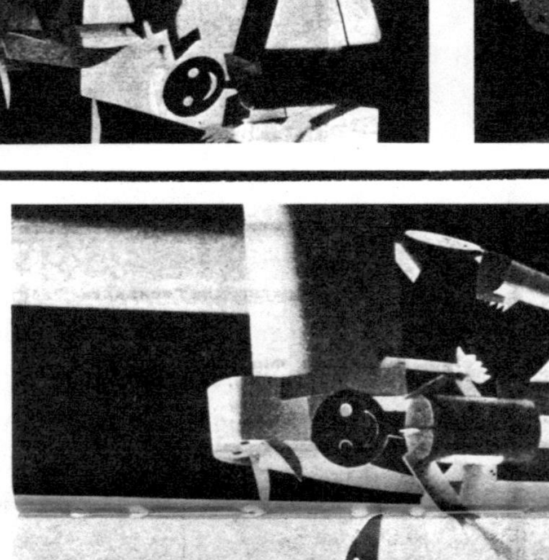

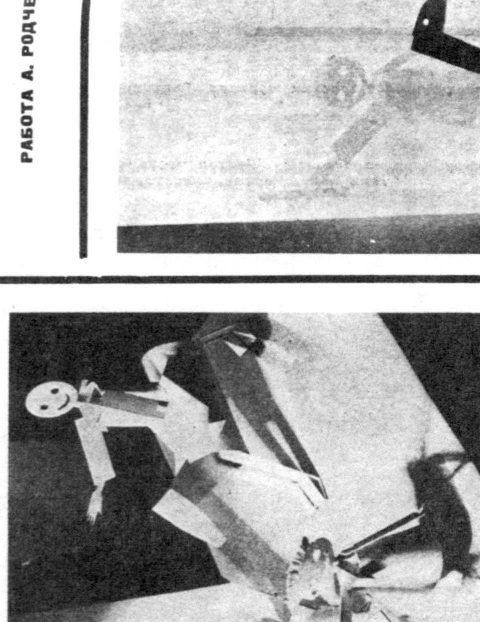

4.1. Aleksandr Rodchenko and Varvara Stepanova, paper figures, design, and photography for the unfinished children's book *Samozveri*, by Sergei Tret'iakov. These shots from *Novyi LEF*, no. 1 (1927) demonstrate how the artists applied artificial lighting and scenic arrangement of the paper figures to achieve the effect of movement and animation in their photographs.

The promise of the method's application in cinema is even more pronounced in a commentary written by Stepanova and published alongside another photo-illustration from *Autoanimals*, in this case in the section of the magazine *Sovetskoe kino* (*Soviet Cinema*) (edited by Rodchenko) on photography in cinema:

> The spatial photo-animated illustrations of A. Rodchenko and V. Stepanova for S. Tret'iakov's children's book *Autoanimals* are of particular interest for cinema. Models of animals and people are for the first time spatial as opposed to the planar … forms (dolls) of film animation as it has been done hitherto. This provides great opportunities for diversifying the use of light.
>
> The problem of light in planar animation has not been resolved; the appearance of spatial animation in cinema will thus help move film animation forward, enabling it to include a wider range of subjects; animation is so to speak cinematized [*kinofitsiruetsia*] by acquiring all the properties of the film shot. It will find a wide application in the scientific film, where its spatial character can be fully used.[4]

The project, unfortunately, was never finalized: the children's book *Autoanimals* was not published as a separate edition, and the series of short films envisioned never came to fruition.[5] The publication is no less fascinating for its non-existence, but how might we investigate it? All we are left with of this collaborative children's book is a blueprint, with a snapshot of its creators' work in progress. How to describe a blueprint that addresses the *potentialities of its use* rather than the *specifics of its design*? We might, perhaps, take a cue from that very blueprint, and address its potentialities from the perspective of their historical realizations – by contextualizing the unrealized photo-poetry book *Autoanimals* within the materialized designs of Soviet children's books of the 1920s and 1930s.[6] Taking such an approach, this chapter examines Sergei Tret'iakov's unfinished *Autoanimals*, with its Rodchenko-Stepanova photo illustrations, as an early constructivist and pedagogical alternative cine-dispositive (*dispositif, apparatus*) that combined what are today regarded as the two major types of Soviet children's books: the photo-illustrated children's book – especially the children's photo-poetry book – and the do-it-yourself book (*kniga-samodelka*).[7]

Constructing Toys: Soviet Pedagogy and Do-It-Yourself Books

Rodchenko and Stepanova conceived their photo-illustrations for *Autoanimals* as both a continuation and extension of the existing design practice of homemade cut-out toys. Even in the first publication of Tret'iakov's poem, in the children's journal *Pioner* (*Pioneer*), accompanied by Boris Pokrovskii's hand-drawn illustrations (fig. 4.2), one finds an editorial note suggesting to young readers that they could make

4.2. Drawing by B. Pokrovskii accompanying Tret'iakov's poem "Samozveri," *Pioner*, no. 22 (1926). Pokrovskii's illustrations emphasize the transformative power of imagination and encourage children to engage in make believe by deploying their bodies as the main prop – an "engine" – for dynamizing and animating the represented animals.

characters out of the most ordinary household objects: "You can invent innumerable *autoanimals*. As you can see from the drawings, it is easy to make them."[8] At the same time, Rodchenko sought a path that would diverge from traditional drawing. He was guided by a fundamentally constructivist dictum shared with Tret'iakov: to create a clear visual model that a child could emulate using simple techniques and suitable materials – flexible and functional, easy to handle and relatively sturdy at the same time. Together with Varvara Stepanova, the artist and designer with whom in 1925 he had a daughter, Rodchenko decided to illustrate Tret'iakov's book *Samozveri* with photographs of humorous figures cut out from paper.

Rodchenko and Stepanova had at their disposal numerous examples of using paper as material for constructing toys. In the course of his wide-ranging constructivist practice, Rodchenko had experimented extensively with various materials, including wood and metal (used in his spatial constructions and design, for instance, of a workers' club), newspapers and illustrated publications (used in his photomontages), and paper and cardboard (used to make the intertitles for Dziga Vertov's early films). In the *Autoanimals* project, Rodchenko and Stepanova could be said to have followed El Lissitzky's injunction in his children's book *Suprematicheskii skaz pro dva kvadrata v 6-ti postroikakh* (*A Suprematist Tale of Two Squares in Six Constructions*, 1922): "Don't read this book / Take – / paper … fold / rods … color / blocks of wood … build."[9] Stepanova, whose costume designs suggested the cut-out technique as one of the most expressive and practical models of constructing objects for everyday use, additionally informed and advanced the entire *Autoanimals* project.[10]

Paper cut-outs and cardboard toys had attracted Russian creative spirits long before the October Revolution. Recognized as a flexible and easy-to-handle material, paper was widely accepted as functional not only in constructing various toys, but also in developing children's work habits and crafts skills.[11] In a 1912 article entitled "Igrushki i nachatki ruchnogo truda" ("Toys and the Beginnings of Manual Labour"), Nikolai Bartram, an art historian, collector, and museologist, emphasized the importance of homemade toys for the child's development: "Adults see a toy as entertainment, while for children it is a joy; and the greatest joy comes from the toy made by the child himself. A homemade toy [*samodel'naia igrushka*] develops in children the main engine of life – work; and for adolescents, moreover, it can serve as a kind of introduction to a number of crafts."[12] According to Bartram, the child's interest in homemade toys goes hand in hand with interest in drawing; and it is through these media that children first become acquainted with art. Paper and cardboard play the main role in this process:

> The use of paper, and a little later of cardboard, gives even more freedom in the world of homemade toys. To cut the parts of the image from coloured paper and paste these as a mosaic on paper often yields a very interesting picture. Gluing thin cardboard to coloured paper and colouring it in, you can make simple boxes, pencil cases, and so on, but, most importantly, it is easy, with a little skill in drawing, to cut out of the cardboard

various profile figures of animals children have read about and seen, the house in which they live, the thin silhouettes of Christmas trees, and so on.[13]

The popularity of cardboard and paper toys among children and Soviet pedagogues continued after the October Revolution. Consider, for example, the 1925 publication *Iskusstvo v bytu* (*Art in Everyday Life*), for which Bartram was the editor of the pedagogy section.[14] Published as a supplement to the magazine *Krasnaia niva* (*Red Field*), *Art in Everyday Life* was a compilation of thirty-six illustrated charts (*tablitsy*) with accompanying text and colour drawings, providing practical samples illustrating various homemade facets of the new everyday life of Soviet citizens, including toys for children. As the editors put it in the foreword:

> This compilation album is a visual aid. The voluntary worker will find in it samples of different decorative elements for revolutionary celebrations, clubs, and reading rooms, whereas the theater worker will find samples of the most simplified solutions for sets, costumes, and props. The Soviet female worker will find in it models of the simplest clothes; the young reader, useful information relating to sports, as well as samples for games and activities, which are at the same time the foundations of appropriate manual labour.[15]

There are several commonalties between this illustrated album and the Rodchenko-Stepanova spatial photo-animations. First, both offer their illustrations as a visual aid for independent work on the production of useful everyday objects, whether paper figures, costumes, or toys. Second, both works recommend the production of objects simple enough to be homemade; in the case of the album, moreover, the design for each object is accompanied by a clear explanation of how that object is to be made. Third, both works encourage the reader/viewer to actively participate in the making process. As we read in the foreword of *Art in Everyday Life*:

> [This] does not mean that the publication should be treated as a collection of immutable samples and finished molds, like a "fashion" album – its task is only to give the reader's artistic thought a boost, to awaken in him a kind of initiative (*samodeiatel'nost*, lit., do-it-yourself-ness) and imagination (*izobretatel'nost'*). As a first attempt in this regard, our collection does not claim to be infallible, and the sooner its readers, influenced by it, create something better and simpler, the more pleased the editors will be.[16]

Fourth, they both propose the cut-out technique as a requisite step in the process of object making. This is evident in: (1) the sheets depicting the Pioneer and athletic suits (charts 11 and 20, respectively; see figs. 4.3 and 4.4), both featuring drawings by Vera Mukhina, based on models by N. Lamanova; (2) the sheet depicting Red Cavalry toy figures (chart 30), with drawings by M. Ezuchevsky; and (3)

4.3. This Pioneer costume (*pionerskii kostium*) design is one in the series of costume designs Vera Mukhina created for *Art in Everyday Life*. Her pattern includes a unisex blouse, short pants for boys, and a skirt for girls. *Iskusstvo v bytu* (1925), chart 11.

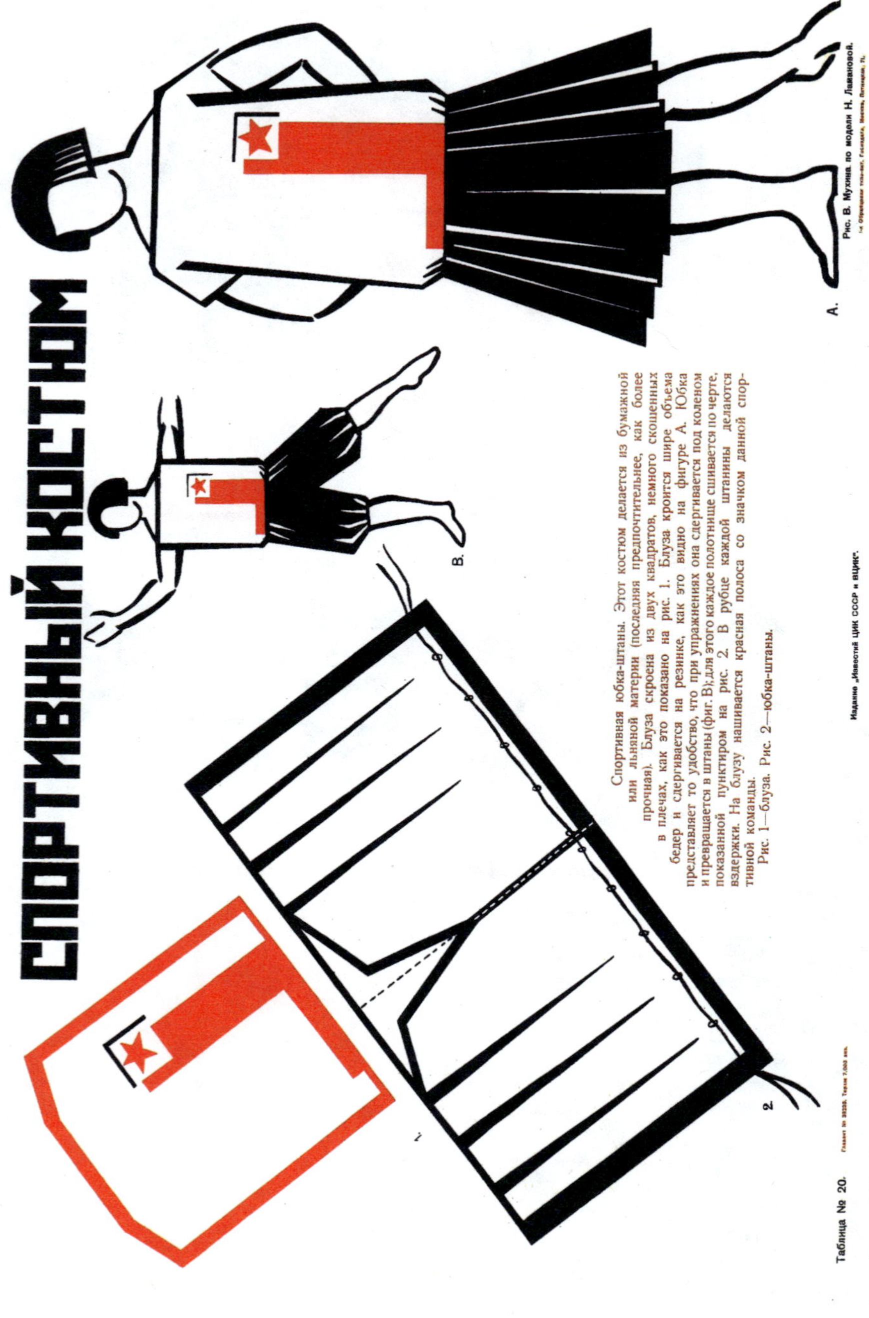

4.4. Vera Mukhina's sport costume (*sportivnyi kostium*) draws on earlier unisex designs by V. Stepanova, published in *LEF* (1923). Mukhina's boxy forms are made to be wider than usual, thus evoking human bodies conforming to a geometric order. Her inventive *iubka-shtany* (skirt-pants) – a skirt which is designed to transform into short pants during exercise, a more appropriate outfit for the proletarian *fizkultura's* (physical culture) body in action – echoes Stepanova's androgynous vision, most evident in an evocative photograph of male and female students of the Academy of Social Education in Moscow, all dressed in the same sports costume of her design. *Iskusstvo v bytu*, chart 20.

the sheet depicting figures for a homemade shadow puppet theatre (chart 36), with drawings by N. Simonovich-Efimova. Finally, both works recommend making toys from paper or cardboard. Not coincidentally, several sheets in the album that pertain to the production of toys feature drawings by Bartram. Aside from designs of paper toys – such as the sheets showing how to make masks to play the characters from the folktale "Kurochka-riabka" ("The Speckled Hen") (chart 31) or to build a factory out of cardboard (chart 35; see fig. 4.5) – one finds sheets depicting a wood-carved toy (chart 33) and a plush doll made by sewing (chart 34; see fig. 4.6), all with Bartram's drawings.

Both *Autoanimals* and *Art in Everyday Life* expressed the agenda shared by the constructivist artists around the Left Front of Art and the People's Commissariat of Enlightenment. Acknowledging the still materially humble Soviet Union's inability, in the mid-1920s, to radically transform all previous bourgeois culture, this program thus stood for simple and functional forms of domestic and public apparel that would correspond to the lifestyle of workers and the new everyday life (*novyi byt*).[17] Simplicity, hygiene, and expediency were the main Soviet slogans for improving living conditions in the New Economic Policy (NEP) era. Around the same time, Walter Benjamin was detecting, in "the false simplicity of the modern toy," a sort of "authentic longing to rediscover the relationship with the primitive, to recuperate the style of a home-based industry."[18] But in the simplicity of *socialist* homemade toys and everyday objects, the editors of *Art in Everyday Life* saw, instead, the "need to save power and resources," and a way to implement improvements that would distinguish Soviet revolutionary culture "from the rest of Europe, which, for all its enormous technical progress, still feeds on the unhealthy fashions of degenerate bourgeois culture."[19]

Homemade cardboard toys fully embodied these aspirations in the field of Soviet pedagogy.[20] As the 1927 instruction book *Kartonazhnaia igrushka* (*Cardboard Toys*) by E. and M. Bykovskii explains, the production of toys "can serve as a good method for the training and development of technical skills and knowledge."[21] Furthermore, cardboard and paper are "materials you can find everywhere" and are "easy to work with, needing no physical force or preliminary knowledge or preparation"; all they require is "great attention and precision."[22] The book proposes a number of samples, which are arranged in order of difficulty, explaining to the reader, "Once you get the hang of them, it is easy to make new models of your own."[23] Such injunctions to "do it yourself" are repeatedly put before the young Soviet reader in all the sources discussed above, from Tret'iakov's advice to the young reader in *Pioner*, to the Rodchenko-Stepanova note in *Novyi LEF*, and to the editors' foreword in the *Art in Everyday Life* album.

In order to enable and inspire such self-engaged activity among readers, these publications lay out the details of the crafting process. They not only address the instruments and materials needed, but also list the consecutive steps of the process, explaining them carefully. The materials included pencils and soft erasers; various knives and scissors; a ruler and try square; a compass; pins and needles;

ФАБРИКА

Фабрика, общий вид которой представлен на рисунке А, выпиливается лобзиком из клееной фанеры или из тонких дощечек. Отдельные части соединяют при помощи маленьких и очень тоненьких гвоздиков, покрывая дерево в частях соединений столярным клеем. Б—передняя часть здания. В—задняя сторона. Отмеченное буквой Г является боковой стороной фабрики, которая помещается между частями также помеченными буквами Г. Д и Д—две части скатной крыши, на самую высокую часть фабрики. Е—боковая стенка, помещающаяся между боковой частью главного здания, на местах указанных таковыми же буквами. Отмеченное буквой Ж—прорезывается насквозь и служит отверстием для продвижения туда подвесной дороги; указанные же на этой части пунктиром места служат для укрепления на них навеса, буква—З (делать в двух экземплярах). И—является крышкой, соединяющей эти бока. К—две части скатной крыши на правую, самую низкую, часть здания. Буквой Л—указан бок низкой части здания, помещающийся между такими же буквами. О—две фабричных трубы, одна из которых ставится с левой стороны главного здания, а другая—позади здания под прямым углом; трубы устанавливаются в особые устои, отмеченные буквой—П. Для каждой трубы нужно по два устоя, между которыми она укрепляется. В целях устойчивости как устои, так и трубы, размещается на особой подножке—Р. С—покрытия устоев трубы, соединяющие эти устои сверху. Т—боковая часть вышки для подвесной дороги; количество вышек делается по желанию, в зависимости от длины дороги. Каждая вышка состоит из двух боковин, по образцу, указанному на рисунке, которые укрепляются на подножке—У. Буквой Ф—указана одна боковая часть крыши этой вышки, под которой помещается маленькая арочка Х—соединяющая сбоку верхние части вышки между собой. Таких арочек нужно по две на каждую вышку. Буквой Ц отмечено изображение вагонетки, которую лучше делать из тонкого картона, так как она слишком мала по размеру. Вагонетка снабжается двумя проволочными крючками, для подвешивания на нитку.

Сделанную фабрику следует поставить на толстый картон или кусок фанеры, так же, как и вышки. В крайней вышке и в главном здании помещается по круглому, неподвижному валику, через которые протягивается связанная нитка, образующая замкнутый круг, с подвешенными на ней вагонетками.

В виду того, что фанера или дощечки, из которых делаются части фабрики, могут быть различной толщины, их следует каждый раз проверить и плотно пригнать к нужному месту.

Вырезанное и склеенное здание, хорошо просушивается, покрывается в виде грунта тонким слоем клея, чтобы не давать краске впитываться в дерево и и прокрашивается клеевой и масляной краской, согласно изображению.

4.5. N.D. Bartram's drawing includes his design of different construction components accompanied by instructions of how to build a toy factory out of laminated plywood and thick cardboard. *Iskusstvo v bytu*, chart 35.

4.6. Bartram's sewing design for a Red Army soldier doll includes a detailed explanation of how to make each of its parts by using a string for shaping the two-dimensional textile into voluminous three-dimensional form – a pouch, which is to be filled with cotton wool. *Iskusstvo v bytu*, chart 34.

a pot, jar, cup, or other small container; bristle brushes of various sizes for wood and paper glues; cardboard, as the main material; all different kinds of paper; and various sorts of glue. The steps included drawing (which should be clear, simple, and done with lines), cutting out the paper, and gluing its parts together. The vocabulary and method of these instructions is quintessentially constructivist. Aside from the importance of the line, the manuals emphasize the use of the grid, as in this advice from *Cardboard Toys*: "If you need to increase or decrease the pattern, usually use a grid. For this, the figure is divided into equal square cells."[24] The technical drawing accompanying this instruction and Bartram's drawing of "Speckled Hen" masks in *Art in Everyday Life* (chart 31) are as akin visually as they are pedagogically/methodologically.

The transparent nature of the manufacturing process in *Cardboard Toys* aims to turn constructing toys into an easy, playful, and rewarding activity.[25] Children are encouraged to make various paper toys – a planar toy (*ploskaia igrushka*), toys made of several joined planes, and boards of simple geometric shapes – as well as cardboard toys made by using different methods and devices: a Komsomol doll, a little dog, a little boat, a mill, a steam locomotive, and screens and lampshades. As the authors state in the conclusion, their book is meant to encourage children to master the materials and tools involved, and to apply acquired knowledge. Moreover, it is claimed, the book provides "plenty of room for children's flights of fancy," should little ones make use of its "method of various layouts [*maketi*], that is, little models of individual objects, and entire scenes enclosed in walls, like a room or theatre, or simply placed on a board."[26] The authors could almost be referring to the Rodchenko-Stepanova photographic illustrations, which similarly represent a kind of pocket-theatre of stylized cardboard animals that seem to come alive and invite children to construct them and invent their own stories.

There was, however, a key difference between the Rodchenko-Stepanova blueprint for *Autoanimals* and these instruction books: not the proposed layouts of the cardboard toys, but rather the design of the book itself proposing these layouts. The *Autoanimals* project was intended to be something more than a toy-making manual. It was one of the early attempts to turn a book *itself* into a constructivist toy, thus pointing the way for the emergence of what in the late 1920s became known as the Soviet "homemade book" or "do-it-yourself book" (*kniga-samodelka*). The Rodchenko-Stepanova project suggested that visual appeal and graphic design were crucial if the heavily text-based and relatively "dry" instructions of pedagogical editions were to be turned into something truly engaging for children.

As an interactive medium, the Soviet do-it-yourself book invited children not only to learn and reflect, but also "to develop practical skills needed for the construction of a Communist society."[27] In these books, children were encouraged to design and construct toys from different materials, such as paper, bottle caps, carrots, potatoes, matchboxes, wood, metal, and so on. Like the pedagogical editions mentioned above, these books included instructions, a list of the required materials and tools, an explanation of the process, and recommendations to young readers for expanding on what they had learned. Unlike the dry pedagogical instruction books, however, they were full of hand-drawn illustrations, multicoloured and engaging, sometimes with "a simple plot with characters that walk the reader through the steps of assembling an object."[28]

The heyday of the children's do-it-yourself book genre was the late 1920s and early 1930s, when the Soviet Union entered the reconstructive period and began to rapidly develop its domestic industry. "During the First Five-Year Plan (1928–32)," writes the artist, collector, and art historian Mikhail Karasik, "about a hundred of these books were published, not counting special columns in periodicals for children."[29] The rising generation of the builders of socialism – Soviet youth – was to join in the great common cause, but still in a playful way. Publishers of children's books faced new objectives: to acquaint young readers with the latest technology, production, and professions. Not only did children listen to various tales about production, they were also encouraged to assemble their own machinery (toy factories, etc.) and objects.[30] The utilitarian approach to the new book, which offered children an "education in production," demanded a rational relationship to the material.

Similarly to the Rodchenko-Stepanova paper figures for *Autoanimals*, a number of early Soviet do-it-yourself books proposed that children construct various cardboard and paper toys.[31] Along with the numerous cut-out books (*knigi-vyrezalki*), colouring books with tales of colour and optics (*knizhki-raskraski*), engraving and screen-printing instructional booklets (*knizhki-instruktsii*), and series of books of illustrated jigsaw puzzles (*risovannye golovolomki*, in which children themselves cut out the pieces), the Soviet do-it-yourself books employed formalized graphic language, thus often manifesting the main ideas of constructivism.[32] The use of geometrical forms for composing planar shapes, so typical for constructivism, is perhaps most obvious in the 1927 book *Figurki-golovolomki iz 7 kusochkov* (*Seven-Piece Puzzle Figures*) by the popularizer of physics, mathematics, and astronomy Iakov Perelman.[33] As Karasik aptly remarks, all these books "were a direct continuation of the unpublished do-it-yourself book *Samozveri* by Rodchenko and Stepanova. The child would himself cut out the paper parts from the drawings, and out of those he would invent a game."[34] The cut-out toys were not conceived as confining the child to a specific physical interaction with content but, on the contrary, as inviting them to create and take charge of their own visual experience – to *play*. Toys open up an imaginary world to children, invite play, stimulate imaginative activity, and engender world-making. Just like illustrated children's books, toys can be seen as children's media devices.

Children's Media Devices: Constructivist Toys and Cine-dispositives

Benjamin's claim that toys are always steeped in cultural history was borne out in the Soviet context as well.[35] In his essay "The Cultural History of Toys," Benjamin calls for doing away with the erroneous assumption "that the imaginative content of a child's toys is what determines his playing," and adds that, in reality, the opposite is true: "A child wants to pull something, and so he becomes a horse; he wants to play with sand, and so he turns into a baker; he wants to hide, and so he turns into a robber or a policeman."[36] This initial child's impetus for action and transformation through play is, indeed, what Tret'iakov's poem "Autoanimals" is all about. The poet describes how children, playing, transform into different animals: elephant, tortoise, ostrich, seal, giraffe, squid, kangaroo, and horse. These animals are highly anthropomorphized, through the attribution of emotional traits and social conventions (and values). For example, the elephant is calm ("carries a burden") and steady ("has a collected character"); the seal is "too lazy to move" but "not too lazy to eat," so "he eats the fish without even salting"; the children Lelka and Kolka, who transform into giraffes, are depicted as walking around "quite blind" (because they hold their noses so high), such that "eventually they will probably be fined," and so on.[37] The Rodchenko-Stepanova photographic illustrations lend a supplementary dimension to Tret'iakov's text, turning the initial children's impetus for transformation and play into a kind of pocket-theatre. In their version, it is *the stylized toys* of animals and humans that invite children both to construct them and play with them. But how do these stylized toys enter into dialogue with Soviet cultural history?

The case of paper and cardboard toys of animals has already been partly discussed in this essay. Animal toys have been and remain the most frequent early toys for children across cultures and historical periods. Peculiar to the cultural history of the Soviet 1920s, however, is statistical data regarding the publishing of children's books in this period. Whereas, in 1918–24, "the publication of children's books featuring pictures of the animal world [*mir zhivotnykh*] outnumbered all other children's illustrated books,"[38] by the time of Rodchenko and Stepanova's work on the *Autoanimals* project, the situation had already changed. As anthropomorphized characters, animals were connected with fables and, more importantly, with the genre of fairy tale, which "became one of the most persecuted genres in Soviet children's literature" around the same time.[39] As we read in Pavla Rubtsova's survey of children's books published in 1926, the greatest demand was for the "everyday-life book" (*bytovaia kniga*), while animal tales were in a slump:

> Modern pedagogy seeks to create realistic literature for children, to acquaint them, through books, with the life of working people, with the reality around them, using simple everyday plots to introduce children's minds to a range of ideas about the social

order – about children building a new life and fighting for a new existence, about pioneer-heroes, and so on. This special role of everyday literature [*bytovaia literatura*] as a conduit of new ideas has made it conventional and tendentious.[40]

The Rodchenko-Stepanova stylized paper toys of smiling human figures, on the other hand, are even more steeped in 1920s Soviet cultural history. They were conceived, to be sure, to represent the specific children characters from Tret'iakov's poem, but we should also keep in mind the general significance in childhood development (as recognized by psychologists) of the toy-like little humanoid figure. As the Russian and Soviet child psychologist N.A. Rybnikov writes in his 1922 essay "Detskie igrushki" ("Children's Toys"):

> The child begins with what God finished: the Mr. "Man" that often appears in early childhood drawings … Representing the father, mother, or nanny, the child often uses one and the same graphical expression; he is rarely interested in the details. In the child's speech, we observe a similar picture … This syncretism of the child's thinking, that is, the fact of perception of things as a whole, in their general terms, takes into account a number of requirements that we can recognize in one of the first children's toys – the little man. This little man must be very primitive, and it should be just a little man, not a soldier or a merchant. It should be a very simple, schematic figure, without any painted details, in a standing pose, two inches in size … The primitiveness of toys provides a greater diversity of their use; it must be more than an incentive for discovering the creative instincts of the child.[41]

Rodchenko and Stepanova's smiley little humanoids have a typically constructivist graphic identity, perfectly matching the requirements proposed by Rybnikov's text. These voluminous, three-dimensional figures are rendered via elementary geometric shapes (line, circle, rectangle) and forms (cone, cylinder). It is relatively easy to find their prototypes in the artists' earlier constructivist works, such as Rodchenko's spatial constructions and graphic designs, or Stepanova's costumes and stage sets. Notably, one finds the same graphic representation of the little figure – with the round head, banana-shaped mouth and dots for eyes, and outstretched white hands – in Rodchenko and Mayakovsky's well-known poster of 1923 advertising rubber pacifiers made by the State Rubber Trust, designed during the transitional period of NEP (fig. 4.7), and Rodchenko's graphic drawings for the promotional bookmarks (*reklamnye zakladki*) of the State Publishing House (GIZ) (fig. 4.8).[42] Rodchenko and Stepanova began working on the illustrations for *Autoanimals* at the moment when Rodchenko and Mayakovsky's collaborative Reklam Konstruktor (Advertising Constructor) design enterprise ceased to exist, which signalled the gradual dismantling of NEP and its transition toward what would soon become known as the period of the first Five-Year Plan.[43] Rodchenko and Stepanova's unpublished work in progress,

4.7. A pacifier ad created by Rodchenko and Mayakovsky's commercial design business Reklam Konstruktor (1923). Mayakovsky fashioned the clever slogan *Luchshikh sosok ne bylo i net / gotov sosat' do starykh let* (There have never been, nor are there now, better suckers. They are ready for sucking until you reach old age), while Rodchenko designed the highly dynamic poster composition featuring the stylized little humanoid with(in) geometrically divided sections of colour.

then, maintained the main constructivist principles embodied in the graphic identity and utility of represented socialist objects and toys, while simultaneously heralding the transformation by which one's relationship with these objects and toys would redefine future generations of subjects of the Soviet state.

We find, post-*Autoanimals*, the same constructivist design of the little humanoid in various artists' graphic works, especially in advertisements for children's book publishers. For example, Grigorii Miller's poster "Presses in the USSR," created for the 1927 international Art of the Book exhibition in Leipzig, features a little anthropomorphic figure in a pose enthusiastically promoting the State Publishing House (GIZ), and David Vilenskii's 1928 children's book *Kino* (*Cinema*), with colour drawings by

4.8. Rodchenko deploys stylized little humanoids in sketches for his 1924 design of promotional bookmarks. Along with the application of geometrical shapes, Rodchenko's design brings into play careful colour alternations and typographical variations, converting the promotional bookmarks into a series of the little humanoid's acrobatic performances.

Leonid Gamburger, presents the same figure in a cinematic projection of an advertisement promoting the Proletarii children's publishing house (fig. 4.9).

The stylized little humanoid functions not only as a sign for both toys and books, but also for their intermediary role. Both toys and books function as mediators between the child's internal and external world and as devices for generating narratives and developing the child's sense of self in relation to the surrounding world. The influential Italian philosopher Giorgio Agamben has reflected on the intermediary role of toys and apparatuses, suggesting that toys reveal to us the originary status of things: they demonstrate that things should not be possessed and mastered, but should rather function as mediators opening the world to us.[44] He has proposed, moreover, that the dispositive, or "apparatus" in his usage, should be given a broader significance than in Foucault's definition; dispositives could be seen, he maintains, as frames of perception, tools of interaction, or interfaces between a person and the world.[45] The transformation of the little humanoid toy into the children's book, and of the do-it-yourself books into cardboard toys – exemplifies the oft-repeated claim by media archaeologists that any pair of dispositives can translate, remediate, metamorphose, and incorporate each other, and, through this process, can redefine themselves and one another.[46]

Since the ability of a dispositive to open a space for a third, potential world between the internal and external is most immediate and effective in the case of cinema, it is no wonder that the most appropriate children's books in this regard would be those designed as *an alternative cine-dispositive.*[47] Not coincidentally, many Soviet children's books from the late 1920s and early 1930s were realized either as or in relation to different parts of the cinematic dispositive – film strip, cinema theatre, movie-going experience, film frame, and screen.[48] As the Russian art historian Dmitrii Fomin observes, "many books from the 1920s (especially for children) resembled storyboards [*raskadrovki*] of future films, with the artists sometimes consciously amplifying this resemblance by inserting drawings or photographs in rectangular frames with curved edges, as on a cinema screen, or by placing them on a narrow strip, reminiscent of a fragment of a film reel."[49] These hand-drawn illustrated books had multiple goals, but they all shared the incentive to enhance the Soviet child's active relation toward the children's book as an intermediary – that is, a dispositive/apparatus, a tool of interaction, an interface – with the changing world around.

The Rodchenko-Stepanova blueprint demonstrates that the artists intended the *Autoanimals* book to function as a *cine-dispositive* – a suggestion-apparatus meant to change the Soviet child's perception of and relation to the surrounding socialist world then under construction. Their project may be seen as a precursor of the materialistic conception of the book advanced by Soviet pedagogues of the 1930s who put a specifically Pavlovian emphasis on processes of inurement and the transformative potential of new stimuli, and proposed the more vigorous application of the method of dialectical materialism in Soviet children's books:

4.9. David Vilenskii's 1928 children's book *Kino*, with colour drawings by Leonid Gamburger, addresses the 1920s Soviet culture of cinema-going in an amusing and colourful way, presenting it as a pleasant, appealing, and entertaining experience for a young audience. Drawing and page design for *Kino* (Kharkov: Proletarii, 1928).

The book is a stimulus. The child's perception of the book, his feedback, conversation, and actions under the influence of reading it are a reaction to stimuli. The better, the more accurately we know the "stimulating" complex, the deeper and more enduringly we are able to trace the reaction of the child, the easier it will be *to direct the reaction in socially productive directions* … Not only must the whole set of artistic techniques be materialistic, *materialistic must be the very approach to the material*: each work of children's literature must expand the horizons of the child's experience, must help him understand the world … Since comprehending and changing the world are ultimately due to *the development of the productive forces of society*, it is natural that Marxist children's literature tends toward the closer intertwining of the elements of narrative art with a message of actual scientific, technical, and industrial information.[50]

Finally, the Rodchenko-Stepanova photo-animated illustrations imply that the artists envisioned designing Tret'iakov's "Autoanimals" not only as a do-it-yourself book for making cardboard toys, but also as a constructivist "philosophical toy," to use Annette Michelson's term – a mechanism for generating toys, games, and narratives;

that is, an animation apparatus, an alternative cine-dispositive.[51] Their photographic illustrations turn Tret'iakov's autoanimals into animals "acted out," and give the unusual impression of photography turned into film by presenting different projections of one and the same subject. As previously discussed, the use of photography also allows the potential child reader to immediately visualize how the animal and human figures are made of cardboard and intuitively experience animating them.

Animation: Photo-Illustrated Children's Books and the Stimulation of Play

In their photo-animated illustrations for Tret'iakov's poem, Rodchenko and Stepanova employ photography as a sign system with its own distinct grammar to *perform* the "deformation" of photographed cardboard cut-out figures. Rodchenko's photographic language derives from the Russian formalists' concept of "deformation" (*deformatsiia*).[52] For formalists, "deformation" is identical to "design" – that is, to the organization of the material according to the rules defined by the medium's grammar. Photography (de)forms its material primarily through its framing, or, in other words, via detachment from its undefined spatio-temporal scope: "Detachment [*vydelenie*] of material in a photo," proposed Iurii Tynianov in 1927, "leads to the unity of each photo, to a particular closeness [*tesnota sootnosheniia*] of all objects or elements of one object in the photo. As a result of that internal unity, the relationship between the objects, or, within the object – between its elements – is redistributed. Objects are deformed."[53] The "discrepancy" between the order of things, which the photograph refers to as its material, and the syntactic order of the photo itself, between the signified and the signifier, according to Tynianov, is the source of "deformation."

Structurally, the photographic "deformation" in *Autoanimals* functions just as Tynianov describes: it performs the discrepancy between the signifier and the signified by presenting the multiple viewpoints and heightened realism of three-dimensional figures. Pragmatically, however, it produces an effect quite opposite from the radical revaluation of photography (as espoused, for instance, by Nikolai Tarabukin in 1925), since it naturalizes the figurative representations of little animals and children.[54] In other words, the Rodchenko-Stepanova photo-illustrations introduce creative "deformation" as a tool for transformation. First, they "de-naturalize" the inanimate cardboard figures of animals and children, (de)forming them into photo-animated beings. Next, they invite children to play with the cardboard, deforming and transforming it into toys. In effect, the artists are thus transforming the children into creative, skilful, and versatile individuals, capable of "universal readiness for action."[55]

As Rodchenko and Stepanova assert in the short notes quoted at the beginning of this chapter, this "deformation" of cardboard figures into photo-animated toys is enabled by the use of sculptural angular forms and voluminous cut-out models instead of planar, two-dimensional designs; rich lighting and stark tonal effects along with shadow reflections; and compositional possibilities of stage-like space, suggesting "cinematic motion and dynamism," as "actual and silhouetted forms are relieved through tonal and dimensional contrasts with the background space."[56] The high mobility of such volumetric photo-animation is, on the one hand, reminiscent of the mobility and adaptability of the furniture in Stepanova's stage design for Aleksandr Sukhovo-Kobylin's play *Smert' Tarelkina* (*The Death of Tarlekin*, 1922). On the other hand, it acquires all the properties of a shot from a film due to its use of varied planar perspectives, unusual viewpoints, and dramatic *chiaroscuro* in presenting different projections of one and the same subject – spatial cardboard cut-out figures. The Rodchenko-Stepanova photo-animated illustrations, therefore, combine so-called scenic effects (*veshchestvennoe oformlenie*)[57] – related to the volumetric constructivist stage designs that negated the tradition of painted theatre stage sets – with the highly effective and dynamic properties of the cinematic shot.

Rodchenko and Stepanova envisioned the front cover for Tret'iakov's *Autoanimals* as a composite photograph of cardboard cutout figures (fig. 4.10).[58] Using the process of double or multiple exposure, the artists created a composite image that capitalizes on photography's inherent transparency: the layered images of children and animals appear as discrete see-through shadows while still retaining a considerable amount of detail. In this period, avant-garde artists in general were finding double exposure useful for simulating the model in motion, showing it in multiple perspectives simultaneously, as in cubist and futurist canvases; such works may at first glance appear to be montages but are the product of far more complex technologies. As in the case of Rodchenko and Stepanova, artists were no longer mechanically connecting parts of finished images, but were experimenting with lighting and ways of processing film and photo paper such that the montage was executed as if in a single frame, already at the stage of shooting or print. On the front cover of *Autoanimals*, for example, different images are specially superimposed on each other, creating the illusion of a reality of surreal hybrids.[59] Rodchenko was most likely inspired by Lissitzky's well-known self-portrait *Konstruktor* (*The Constructor*, 1924), made by using several different negatives.[60] In both cases, all elements of the composition appear at once tangible and ghostly: they merge into a single, highly complex and ambiguous image, the true meaning of which escapes any totalizing reading.[61]

Rodchenko and Stepanova's cardboard cut-out toys are animated either by the camera apparatus, lighting effects, and the composition of stage-like space, as their blueprint and writings suggest; or by children's play; or by both these apparatuses – the technological and the imaginative – in combination. On the one hand, the animating principle, that is, the "soul of the toy,"[62] is revealed as a functioning technology – the camera, the machine, an apparatus, a dispositive – which serves as a piece of "equipment set apart from the integral body,"[63] as a prosthetic of the humano-mechanical new man whom the Italian futurists famously called "the extended man."[64] For

4.10. Rodchenko and Stepanova's composite photograph of cardboard cut-out figures for the cover of *Samozveri* was most likely produced through sandwich printing, a darkroom technique wherein negatives are combined in the film carrier of the enlarger and then printed together as a single image. Distorted and exaggerated, blurred and defamiliarized, the cut-out figures appear full of fantastic kinetic energy.

Rodchenko and Stepanova, photography and cinematography animate the toy. Since both these apparatuses are contingent on light, electricity, as yet another sign of modernity, becomes the source of the animating principle.[65] And a light bulb (*lampochka*) becomes its sign (fig. 4.11).[66] On the other hand, the animating principle is embodied in *play*, which is a supreme mediator between subject and object, between the real world and an imagined one. Just like any dispositive, play is ontologically ambivalent: it characterizes the experience of becoming and/or entering into a relationship with something unknown. Play opens up a new relationship toward objects (toys, books, apparatuses); it kindles imaginative activity (*izobretatel'nost*) and stimulates "independent activity" (another possible rendering of the above-cited *samodeiatel'nost*). "Imitation," observes Benjamin, "is at home in *the playing*, not in the plaything."[67] Just like any other dispositive, play can be seen both as a liberating activity and a disciplinary mechanism. It may release us from disciplinary structures and mindsets and restore us to a more profound experience of being in the world;[68]

4.11. Rodchenko's commercial advertising for the FerroWatt lamp company's Edison-style light bulb features a stylized little humanoid with a light-bulb trunk, outstretched limbs in a pose of urgency, and widely opened mouth as if emitting Lenin's famous battle-cry for national electrification: "Communism equals Soviet power plus the electrification of the entire country." *LEF*, no. 3 (1923).

at the same time, it may function as a disciplinary mechanism based on repetition, standing thus as "the mother of every habit."[69]

In addition, Rodchenko and Stepanova conceived their cine-dispositive as a photo-series presenting different projections of spatial cardboard cutout figures, liberated from any prescriptive narrative program. In their conception, the photo-series of cardboard toys is largely static, lacking temporal, diachronic (i.e., narrative) character. Their perception is synchronic and does not consider possible historical development. In *Autoanimals*, time comes to a standstill. This is the same position we see in Rodchenko's photographs; the dynamic of his photos, in principle, is mechanical: among the elements included in his perspective, we find no qualitative differences, but only quantitative (albeit frequently grand-scale) gradations.[70] The non-prescriptive narrative program of the Tret'iakov-Rodchenko-Stepanova dispositive put forward the notion of the child's constructivist self-design as an aesthetic presentation and an ethical subject: by designing one's self and the socialist environment in a constructivist way, the Soviet child declared their faith in the collective values, attitudes, programs, and ideologies of building socialism.

The Tret'iakov-Rodchenko-Stepanova project, despite lacking any overt ideological content, essentially belonged to the left-experimental flank of children's books: it functioned as an alternative cinematic apparatus and a constructivist pedagogical dispositive, intended to inculcate in Soviet children the spirit of the playful, practical, and independent member of the nascent communist collective. The Rodchenko-Stepanova cut-out paper toys were imagined not to confine the viewer to a specific physical position in relation to their content; rather, they invited play, stimulated imaginative activity, and incited world-making. It could be argued that *Autoanimals* was conceived to function as a dispositive for the production of toys as children's media devices (or apparatuses, to use Agamben's term), the cultivation of practical technical skills, and the stimulation of play, through which the child both animated these new dispositives (toys) and developed a sense of self in relation to the surrounding socialist world under construction.

NOTES

1　"O fotomul'tiplikatsionnykh illiustratsiiakh," 48.

2　Ibid.

3　Ibid.

4　*Sovetskoe kino* 1 (1927): 15.

5　The book was later reconstructed and published with all the Rodchenko-Stepanova photographs and Tret'iakov's poem, first in a German translation, then in French, and finally in the original Russian. See Rodčenko and Tretjakov, *Samozveri*; Rodtchenko and Tretiakov, *Animaux à mimer*; Rodchenko and Tret'iakov, *Samozveri*. See also Karasik and Sgibnev, "Samozveri Rodchenko," for their animated film (created in St. Petersburg) featuring the Rodchenko-Stepanova "photo-animated illustrations."

6　For more on the notion of photo-poetry, see Toman, *Foto/Montáž tiskem*, 284–311.

7　On the concept of the cine-dispositive, see Albera and Tortajada, *Cine-Dispositives*.

8　Tret'iakov, "Samozveri."

9　Lissitzky and Railing, *About 2 Squares*. For more on the design of the book, see Wolfe, "Introduction to *About 2 Squares*"; and Oushakine, "Translating Communism for Children."

10　The recollection of Rodchenko and Stepanova's daughter, Varvara Rodchenko, as retold by her son, the art historian Aleksandr Lavrentiev, provides insight into how this collaboration transpired. See Lavrentiev, "Chto za zveri? Samozveri," 36–8.

11　Pre-revolutionary Russian children's books that encouraged the making of various figures from paper and cardboard included Solomin, *Za rabotu!* (*To Work!*); Augsburg, *Novaia shkola risovaniia* (*The New School of Drawing*); and Karavaeva and Karavaev, *Kak sdelat' zmeek?* (*How to Make Kites?*).

12　Bartram, "Igrushki i nachatki ruchnogo truda," 238.

13　Ibid., 241.

14　As head of the Committee of the Decorative Arts Museum of the People's Commissariat of Enlightenment, Bartram took an active role in the field of early Soviet pedagogy during the

1920s. He published books and scholarly articles, edited a number of children's pedagogy collections, and collaborated on various state-sponsored editions. For example, he was the main editor of the series *Svoimi rukami* (*With Your Own Hands*) of the *Novaia detskaia biblioteka* (*New Children's Library*). In 1918, Bartram initiated the opening of the Museum of Toys in Moscow and became its director. Walter Benjamin visited the Museum of Toys during his stay in the Soviet capital in December 1926 and January 1927; see Benjamin, *Moscow Diary*, 120.

15 Akhmet'ev, Lamanova, and Mukhina, *Iskusstvo v bytu*, 1.

16 Ibid.

17 Ibid. As the editors put it in the album's foreword, "These new forms, this cultivation of clothing, atmosphere, and the equipment of everyday life, are not tantamount to a luxury; they can be achieved without the help of professional specialists – with the creative force of a working family, a school, or a club collective."

18 Benjamin, "The Cultural History of Toys," 114.

19 Akhmet'ev, Lamanova, and Mukhina, *Iskusstvo v bytu*, 1.

20 Among the many NEP-era editions dealing with making cardboard and paper toys were Murzaev, *Vyrezyvanie i vyshchipyvanie iz bumagi* (*Cutting and Tweezing Paper*); Labunskaia and Eisner, *Kak sdelat' lozung* (*How to Make a Slogan-Sign*); Galkin, *Igrushki iz bumagi* (*Paper Toys*); Perel'man, *Figurki-golovolomki iz 7 kusochkov* (*Seven-Piece Puzzle Figures*); Beliakov, *Sdelai sam bumazhnyi zmei* (*Make Your Own Kite*).

21 Bykovskii and Bykovskii, *Kartonazhnaia igrushka*, 11.

22 Ibid., 11–12.

23 Ibid., 12.

24 Ibid., 27.

25 See also Mayakovsky, *Kon'-ogon'*; Mayakovsky, Mandelstam, and Kharms, *The Fire Horse*, 7–17. In this children's poem by Mayakovsky, a father satisfies his child's wish for a wooden toy horse on wheels by guiding him through the whole process, from seeking out the materials (making the acquaintance of a shop clerk) to the elaborate construction with the generous help of a "whole company" of professionals: a craftsman and worker who help with the cardboard and glue; a carpenter who helps with the horse's wheels; a bristleman (for the horsehair); and a blacksmith and painter (for nails, colouring).

26 Bykovskii and Bykovskii, *Kartonazhnaia igrushka*, 108.

27 Borislavov, "Do It Yourself."

28 Ibid.

29 Karasik, "Samozveri." Karasik's text accompanied an exhibition of children's do-it-yourself books from 1929–35, which he himself curated and titled "Samozveri" after Tret'iakov-Rodchenko-Stepanova's unpublished book.

30 See, for example, the following titles: *Detmashstroi* (*Children's Machine Construction*); *Konveier* (*The Conveyer*), *Shchepki, rezinki, zhest'* (*Scraps, Rubber Bands, Tin*); *Stroim dvigateli* (*We Build Engines*); *Nash tsekh* (*Our Workshop*; also translatable as *Our Production Department*). As Borislavov writes in his informative essay, a number of do-it-yourself books "introduce[d] children to current developments and … technological advancements" ("Do It Yourself").

31 These books include *Igrushki* (*Toys*), *Smotr igrushek samodelok* (*A Parade of Homemade Toys*), and *Vyrezai, pechatai* (*Cut Out and Print*) by Aleksandr Abramov with drawings by Konstantin Kuznetsov, as well as the following books by Vera Ermolaeva and Lev Iudin: *Bumaga i nozhnitsy* (*Paper and Scissors*); *Gore-kucher* (*The Woeful Coachman*); *Oden' menia* (*Dress Me*); *Bez bumagi, bez kleia* (*Without Paper, Without Glue*); and *Pokataemsia. Igrushki iz bumagi i bez kleia* (*Let's Take a Ride: Toys from Paper, Without Glue*). The book *Trafarety* (*Stencils*) by Aleksandr Gromov, for example, deals with the same revolutionary topic, and in the same

visual vernacular, as the sheet from *Art in Everyday Life* with drawings by Vera Mukhina (chart 25) that urges children to make a room in an orphanage more cheerful by painting it using stencils.

32 See Sher, *Vyrezalki* (*Cutouts*); Sinitsyna, *Igry so svetom i tsvetom* (*Games with Light and Colour*). "In 1929–30, there appeared a whole series of illustrated jigsaw puzzles by the quite traditional artist, Aleksandr Gromov. Stretched horizontally like little notepads were such books as *Puzzle. House* (*Golovolomka. Dom*), *Puzzle. Factory* (*Golovolomka. Zavod*), *Puzzle. Steam Locomotive* (*Golovolomka. Parovoz*), *Puzzle. American Indian* (*Golovolomka. Indeets*), etc." (Karasik, "Samozveri").

33 Perelman's book represented a Russian version of tangram, the Chinese dissection puzzle consisting of seven flat geometrical shapes; it came in the wake of the tangram craze seen on the home front and in the trenches on both sides during the First World War.

34 Karasik, "Samozveri."

35 "Children do not constitute a community cut off from everything else. They belong to the nation and the class they come from. This means that their toys cannot bear witness to any autonomous separate existence, but rather are a silent signifying dialogue between them and their nation. A signifying dialogue to the decoding." Benjamin, "The Cultural History of Toys," 116.

36 Ibid., 115.

37 Tret'iakov, "Autoanimals," 242–3.

38 Simonovich-Efimova, "Graficheskii iazyk detskikh knizhek-kartinok," 93.

39 Balina, "Creativity through Restraint," 7. See also Rosenfeld, "Does the Proletarian Child Need a Fairytale?" and Fomin, *Iskusstvo knigi*, 443–5, 447.

40 Rubtsova, "Produktsiia detskoi knigi v 1926 g.," 72. Nonetheless, some very interesting children's books focusing on the animal world were published in this period, either with hand-drawn illustrations, such as Valentin Kataev's humorous verses *Radio-Zhiraff* (*Radio Giraffe*, 1926) with drawings by T. Pravosudovich, and Vladimir Mayakovsky's *Chto ni stranitsa, to slon, to l'vitsa* (*Any Page You Look At, There's an Elephant or a Lioness*, 1926), with drawings by K. Zdanevich; or with photographic illustrations, such as *Zoosad: putevoditel' po Leningradskomu zoologicheskomu sadu* (*The Zoo: A Guide to the Leningrad Zoo*, 1928), with constructivist page layout by Dmitrii Bulanov and a front cover by Sergei Senkin.

41 Rybnikov, "Detskie igrushki," 81–2. Rybnikov goes on to say that, "with age, interests change, and the form of the toys the child is interested in changes accordingly. After the stage of syncretism, or the actual synthesis, follows a period in which analysis predominates, when the child's particular interests awaken" (82).

42 The same constructivist graphic vocabulary, visible in the use of simple geometric shapes and forms for the little figures' body parts, is also employed in the Rodchenko-Mayakovsky poster of 1923 advertising the State Department Store (GUM)'s Mozer clocks; Stepanova's costume for the Mavrushka character in the 1922 theatre play *The Death of Tarelkin*, suggesting the cone shape for the female torso instead of the cylinder shape reserved for males; or the Stepanova-Mayakovsky advertisement poster (1925) for the satirical magazine *Krasnyi perets* (*Red Pepper*).

43 Around 1926, the competition from NEP manufacturers, traders, and importers began to be eliminated, as Soviet state enterprises moved toward becoming the exclusive suppliers of everyday goods. On the Reklam-Konstruktor enterprise, see Kiaer, *Imagine No Possessions*, 143–98.

44 Agamben, *Stanzas*; Agamben, *What Is Apparatus?*

45 Agamben, *What Is Apparatus?*, 53.

46 Flusser, *Towards a Philosophy of Photography*.

47 For more on the definition of *alternative cinematographic apparatus*, see Levi, "Cinema by Other Means," 53–6; Levi, *Cinema by Other Means*, 27.

48 For example, aside from the aforementioned *Cinema* (1928) by D. Vilenskii: V. Shklovsky's *Puteshestvie v stranu kino* (*A Journey to the Land of Cinema*, 1926), with drawings by D. Mitrokhin; B. Zhitkov's *Kino v korobke. Stroboskop* (*The Cinema in a Box: The Stroboscope*, 1927, 1931), with his own drawings; G. Gaidovsky's *Sen'ka kino-akter* (*Senka the Movie Actor*, 1927), illustrated by Evgenii Belukha and with a front cover by A. Mogilovskii; the series of "cine-books" (*kinoknizhki*, what are in English called "flipbooks") by the well-known Soviet artist and animator Mikhail Tsekhanovskii, including *Miach* (*The Ball*), *Bim-Bom* (*Bim-Bom*), and *Poezd* (*The Train*) (1927); T. Shishmareva's *Kino-zagadki* (*Cine-Riddles*, 1930), with text by Evgenii Schwartz, and F. Kobrinets's *Knizhka-kino seans o tom, kak pioner Gans Stachechnyi Komitet spas* (*A Book-Film-Performance about How the Pioneer Hans Saved the Strike Committee*, 1931), with drawings by Isaak Eberil. For more on the last book from this list, which is also a do-it-yourself book, see Birgitte Beck Pristed's contribution to this volume.

49 Fomin, *Iskusstvo knigi*, 228.

50 Zhak, "Detskaia literatura," 78–9; emphasis mine.

51 Taking the cue from Baudelaire's essay on children's toys ("The Ethic of the Toy," 1859), Michelson uses the term "philosophical toy" to refer to proto-cinematic apparatuses and the birth of the cinema ("On the Eve of the Future").

52 Rodchenko saw in photography a technology of representation and a tool of interaction, and, like other constructivists, he set out to boldly and recklessly manipulate photo images. To defend the camera's right to subjectivity, Rodchenko used unusual and oblique angles, distorting optics, double exposure, shots of repetitive patterns, and repeated enlargements and reductions of the image. Rodchenko was unjustly accused of plagiarizing the works of foreign photographers, most notably Moholy-Nagy. The controversy played out in part in polemical essays and letters by Rodchenko himself and by the critic Boris Kushner on the pages of *Novyi LEF*.

53 Tynianov, "Ob osnovakh kino," 335.

54 "APART FROM PHOTOMONTAGE, PHOTOGRAPHY POSSESSES IN AND OF ITSELF CERTAIN QUALITIES THAT ENABLE IT TO ESCAPE FROM THE NARROW ORBIT OF THE NATURALISTIC PHOTOGRAPHIC IMAGE," writes Tarabukin, in capital letters ("The Art of the Day," 69).

55 Reflecting on the Soviet polytechnic education in his article "A Communist Pedagogy," Benjamin writes: "Only if man experiences changes of milieu in all their variety, and can mobilize his energies in the service of the working class again and again and in every new context, will he be capable of that *universal readiness for action* which the Communist program opposes to what Lenin called the 'most repulsive feature of the old bourgeois society': its separation of theory and practice. The bold, unpredictable personnel policy of the Russians is wholly the product of this *new, nonhumanist, and noncontemplative but active and practical universality*; it is the product of universal readiness … The immeasurable versatility of raw human manpower, which capital constantly brings to the consciousness of the exploited, returns at the highest level as the *polytechnical* – as opposed to the specialized – education of man. These are basic principles of mass education." Benjamin, "A Communist Pedagogy," 274–5; emphasis mine.

56 Summer, "Cinematic Whimsy," 245.

57 The application of scenic effects is humorously depicted in the episode of a workers' club staging of a play about pre-revolutionary life in Ilf and Petrov's *The Twelve Chairs* (*Dvenadtsat' stul'ev*).

58 The inscription on the photograph reads, "First type page of cover: Photo illustrations to children's book by S. Tret'iakov *Samozveri*, artist A.M. Rodchenko, 1927." See the J. Paul Getty Museum, object number 84.XM.844.9.

59 Rosalind Krauss sees the surrealist photomontage's ability to produce the "seamless integrity of the real" as its distinctive feature ("The Photographic Conditions of Surrealism," 23).

60 For more on this and other examples of Soviet artists' composite images created by multiple exposure, see Gough, "Lissitzky on Broadway," and Tupitsyn, "Colorless Field."

61 The technique of manipulating photo images so as to execute montage as if in a single frame would be widely employed in the 1930s photo-illustrated Soviet children books, such as Nikolai Bulatov's, Lev Kassil's, and Pavel Lopatyn's *V strane Dzin'-Dzin'* (*In the Country Jin-Jin*, 1936) with photomontages by M. Gershenzon; Aleksandr Vvedenskii's *Katina kukla* (*Kati's Doll*, 1936); Nikolai Bulatov's *Puteshestvie po elektrolampe* (*The Journey across the Light Bulb*, 1937) and Ian Larri's *Neobyknovennye prikliucheniia Karika i Vali* (*The Extraordinary Adventures of Karik and Valia*, 1937).

62 In his essay on children's toys, Baudelaire addresses the child's search for the toy's soul. Traditionally, the soul is seen as the vital principle: an inscrutable thing that gives life to all beings. The Latin word *anima*, meaning breath, is the origin of the English word *animation*; it is also the Latin translation of the Greek word *psyche*, meaning life.

63 Dickerman, "Radical Oblique," 26.

64 Marinetti, "Extended Man," 85–8.

65 This topic is highlighted in another important photo-illustrated Soviet children's book, *Egor-monter* (*Egor the Electrician*, 1928), by the constructivist artists (and pupils of Rodchenko) Ol'ga and Galina Chichagova. For more on the topic of electrification in Russian children's books, see Kirill Chunikhin's contribution to this volume.

66 As a visual symbol of electric energy, the light bulb not only brings light, but also represents the spirit of socialism (it has an almost sacred character, like the red star or sickle and hammer). The image of the light bulb is found in many Soviet illustrated children's books, such as Tatiana Tess's *Marsh molodyh* (*March of the Young*, 1931), with photomontage by S. Senkin; L. Tsinovskii's *200 000 Vol't* (*200,000 Volts*, 1931); and B. Uralskii's *Elektromonter* (*The Electrician*, 1931), with drawings by A. Deineka.

67 Benjamin, "The Cultural History of Toys," 116; emphasis mine.

68 According to Agamben, play is an organ of profanation, which he defines as a kind of deactivation that emancipates a programmed behaviour, preserving its structure, but not its function and meaning (*Profanations*, 86).

69 "We know that for a child repetition is the soul of play, that nothing gives him greater pleasure than to 'Do it again!'… Not a 'doing as if' but a 'doing the same thing over and over again,' *the transformation of a shattering experience into habit – that is the essence of play … For play and nothing else is the mother of every habit*. Eating, sleeping, getting dressed, washing have to be instilled into the struggling little brat in a playful way, following the rhythm of nursery rhymes. *Habit enters life as a game, and in habit, even in its most sclerotic forms, an element of play survives to the end.* Habits are the forms of our first happiness and our first horror that have congealed and become deformed to the point of being unrecognizable." Benjamin, "Toys and Play," 120; emphasis mine.

70 Ironically, it was Tret'iakov who would theorize the concept of the photo series as a *protracted photo-observation*. In his essay on the photo series of the Filippov family, Tret'iakov describes movement as development, as the entire dialectical process that mobilizes the individual.

The accent on the diachronic nature of the series differentiates the concept of the "protracted photo-observation" from the early photo series of Rodchenko and Boris Ignatovich. For more on how the Filippov series was discussed in *Proletarskoe foto* (*Proletarian Photo*), see Wolf, *The Worker Photography Movement*, 122–75.

BIBLIOGRAPHY

Agamben, Giorgio. *Profanations*. Translated by Jeff Fort. New York: Zone Books, 2007.
– *Stanzas: Word and Phantasm in Western Culture*. Translated by Ronald L. Martinez. Minneapolis: University of Minnesota Press, 1977.
– *What Is Apparatus? and Other Essays*. Translated by David Kishik and Stefan Pedatella. Stanford, CA: Stanford University Press, 2009.
Akhmet'ev, V P., Nadezhda Lamanova, and Vera Mukhina. *Iskusstvo v bytu: 36 tablits: Igrushka, odezhda, izba chital'nia, klub, teatr*. Moscow: Izvestiia TsIK SSSR i VTsIK, 1925.
Albera, François, and Maria Tortajada, eds. *Cine-Dispositives: Essays in Epistemology across Media*. Translated by Franck Le Gac. Amsterdam: Amsterdam University Press, 2015.
Augsburg, Zh. *Novaia shkola risovaniia: Kniga pervaia; Risovanie dlia detei mladshego i srednego vozrasta*. 2nd ed. Moscow: n.p., 1912.
Balina, Marina. "Creativity through Restraint: The Beginnings of Soviet Children's Literature." In *Russian Children's Literature and Culture*, edited by Marina Balina and Larissa Rudova, 3–17. London: Routledge, 2008.
Bartram, Nikolai Dmitrievich. "Igrushki i nachatki ruchnogo truda." In *Igrushka, ee istoriia i znachenie*, edited by N.D. Bartram, 237–45. Moscow: Sytin, 1912.
Beliakov, N. *Sdelai sam bumazhnyi zmei*. Leningrad-Moscow: Gosudarstvennoe izdatel'stvo, 1928.
Benjamin, Walter. "A Communist Pedagogy." In Benjamin, *Walter Benjamin: Selected Writings*, 273–5.
– "The Cultural History of Toys." In Benjamin, *Walter Benjamin: Selected Writings*, 113–16.
– *Moscow Diary*. Cambridge, MA: Harvard University Press, 1986.
– "Toys and Play." In Benjamin, *Walter Benjamin: Selected Writings*, 117–21.
– *Walter Benjamin: Selected Writings*, Volume 2: *Part 1: 1927–1930*, edited by Howard Eiland, Michael W. Jennings, and Gary Smith. Translated by Rodney Livingstone et al. Cambridge, MA: Harvard University Press, 2005.
Borislavov, Rad. "Do It Yourself." In *Adventures in the Soviet Imaginary: Children's Books and Graphic Art*, edited by Robert Bird, 25–31. Chicago: University of Chicago Library, 2011. www .lib.uchicago.edu/collex/exhibits/soviet-imaginary/technology/do-it-yourself/
Bošković, Aleksandar. "Agitatsionnaia fotopoema kak rukotvornyi pamiatnik." In *Fotomontazhnyi tsikl Iuriia Rozhkova k poeme Vladimira Maiakovskogo "Rabochim Kurska, dobyvshim pervuiu rudu …": Rekonstruktsiia neizdannoi knigi 1924 goda. Stat'i. Kommentarii*, edited by Andrey Rossomakhin, 27–42. St. Petersburg: Izdatel'stvo Evropeiskogo universiteta v Sankt-Peterburge, 2014.
– "Photopoetry and the Bioscopic Book: Russian and Czech Avant-Garde Experiments of the 1920s." PhD diss., University of Michigan, 2013. hdl.handle.net/2027.42/100092.
Bykovskii, E., and M. Bykovskii. *Kartonazhnaia igrushka*. Leningrad-Moscow: Gosudarstvennoe izdatel'stvo, 1927.
Dickerman, Leah. "Radical Oblique: Aleksandr Rodchenko's Camera Eye." *Documents* 3, no. 12 (1998): 23–34.
Flusser, Vilém. *Towards a Philosophy of Photography*. London: Reaktion Books, 2000.

Fomin, D.V. *Iskusstvo knigi v kontekste kul'tury 1920-kh godov*. Moscow: Pashkov dom, 2015.

Galkin, I. *Igrushki iz bumagi*. Leningrad-Moscow: Gosudarstvennoe izdatel'stvo, 1926.

Gough, Maria. "Lissitzky on Broadway." In *Object: Photo. Modern Photographs: The Thomas Walther Collection, 1909–1949. An Online Project of the Museum of Modern Art*, edited by Mitra Abbaspour, Lee Ann Daffner, and Maria Morris Hambourg. New York: Museum of Modern Art, 2014. https://www.moma.org/interactives/objectphoto/assets/essays/Gough.pdf.

Karasik, Mikhail. "Knizhka s zagadkami." *Proektor* 4 (2010). www.art1.ru/2013/05/10/knizhka -s-zagadkami-11966.

– "Samozveri." *Art1*, 14 April 2013. www.art1.ru/2013/04/14/samozveri-9045.

Karasik, Mikhail, and Taras Sgibnev. "Samozveri Rodchenko." Uploaded 24 June 2011. Video. https://vimeo.com/25579209.

Karavaeva, L., and Zh. Karavaev. *Kak sdelat' zmeek? (Ploskii, figurnyi, korobkoi i prochie)*. Seriia: Kak mne sdelat' samomu? No. 13. Moscow: Biblioteka I. Gorbunova-Posadova dlia detei i iunoshestva, 1915.

Kiaer, Christina. *Imagine No Possessions: The Socialist Objects of Russian Constructivism*. Cambridge, MA: MIT Press, 2005.

Krauss, Rosalind. "The Photographic Conditions of Surrealism." *October* 19 (1981): 3–34.

Labunskaia, G., and A. Eisner. *Kak sdelat' lozung*. Edited by L.U. Zelenko. Moscow: Rabotnik prosveshcheniia, 1927.

Lavrentiev, Aleksandr. "Chto za zveri? Samozveri." In Aleksandr Rodchenko and Sergei Tret'iakov, *Samozveri*, 39–44. Moscow: Kar'era Press, 2014.

Levi, Pavle. "Cinema by Other Means." *October* 131 (2010): 51–68.

– *Cinema by Other Means*. Oxford: Oxford University Press, 2012.

Lissitzky, El, and Patricia Railing. *About 2 Squares + More about 2 Squares*. Translated by Christiana Van Manen. Cambridge, MA: MIT Press, 1991.

Marinetti, Filippo Tomaso. "Extended Man and the Kingdom of the Machine" (1910). In *Critical Writings* by Filippo Tomaso Marinetti, 85–8. Edited by Günter Berghaus, translated by Dog Thompson. New York: Farrar, Straus, and Giroux, 2006.

Mayakovsky, Vladimir. *Kon'-ogon'*. Leningrad: Gosudarstvennoe izdatel'stvo, 1928.

Mayakovsky, Vladimir, Osip Mandelstam, and Daniil Kharms. *The Fire Horse: Children's Poems*. Translated by Eugene Ostashevsky. New York: NYRB, 2017.

Michelson, Annette. "On the Eve of the Future: The Reasonable Facsimile and the Philosophical Toy." *October* 29 (1984): 3–20.

Murzaev, V.S. *Vyrezyvanie i vyshchipyvanie iz bumagi*. Edited by G.F. Miramanova. Moscow: n.p., 1924.

"O fotomul'tiplikatsionnykh illiustratsiiakh–Rodchenko-Stepanovoi." *Novyi LEF: Zhurnal levogo fronta iskusstv*, no. 1 (1927): 48. http://www.ruthenia.ru/sovlit/j/3193.html.

Oushakine, Serguei. "Translating Communism for Children: Fables and Posters of the Revolution." *Boundary* 243, no. 3 (2016): 159–219. https://doi.org/10.1215/01903659-3572478.

Perel'man, Ia. I. *Figurki-golovolomki iz 7 kusochkov*. Leningrad-Moscow: Raduga, 1927.

Rodčenko, Alexander, and Sergej Tretjakov. *Samozveri: selbst gemachte Tiere*. Edited by Fütterer Werner and Hubertus Gaßner. Cologne: Verlag der Buchhandlung Walther König, 1980.

Rodchenko, Aleksandr, and Sergei Tret'iakov. *Samozveri*. Moscow: Kar'era Press, 2014.

Rodtchenko, Alexandre, and Serge Tretiakov. *Animaux à mimer*. Translated by Valérie Rouzeau and Odile Belkeddar. Nantes: Éditions MeMo, 2010.

Rosenfeld, Alla. "Does the Proletarian Child Need a Fairytale?" *Cabinet Magazine* (Winter 2002/3). www.cabinetmagazine.org/issues/9/rosenfeld.php.

Rubtsova, P.A. "Produktsiia detskoi knigi v 1926 g." *Novye detskie knigi* 5 (1928): 69–78.

Rybnikov, N. "Detskie igrushki." In *Detstvo i iunost', ikh psikhologiia i pedagogika: Pedologicheskii sbornik*, edited by K.N. Kornilova and N.A. Rybnikova, 79–84. Moscow: Rabotnik prosveshcheniya, 1922.

Sher, N., ed. *Vyrezalki*. Leningrad: OGIZ-Detgiz, 1934.

Simonovich-Efimova, N. "Graficheskii iazyk detskikh knizhek-kartinok." *Novye detskie knigi* 4 (1926): 93–115.

Sinitsyna, E. *Igry so svetom i tsvetom*. Leningrad: Gosudarstvennoe izdatel'stvo, 1930.

Solomin, E.K. *Za rabotu! Raboty iz papki i kartona*. Knizhka 3-ia. Moscow: n.p., 1911.

Summer, Susan Cook. "Cinematic Whimsy: Rodchenko's Photo-Illustrations for *Autoanimals*." *Art Journal* 41, no. 3 (1981): 245–7.

Tarabukin, Nikolai. "The Art of the Day" (1925). Translated by Rosamund Bartlett. *October* 93 (2000): 57–77.

Toman, Jindřich. *Foto/Montáž tiskem*. Prague: KANT, 2009.

Tret'iakov, Sergei. "Samozveri." *Pioner*, no. 22 (1926), 6–7; *Pioner*, no. 23 (1926): 6–8.

Tret'iakov, Sergei M. "Autoanimals." Translated by Susan Cook Summer and Gail Harrison Roman. *Art Journal* 41, no. 3 (1981): 242–4.

Tupitsyn, Margarita. "Colorless Field: Notes on the Paths of Modern Photography." In *Object: Photo. Modern Photographs: The Thomas Walther Collection, 1909–1949. An Online Project of the Museum of Modern Art*, edited by Mitra Abbaspour, Lee Ann Daffner, and Maria Morris Hambourg. New York: Museum of Modern Art, 2014. https://www.moma.org/interactives/objectphoto/assets/essays/Tupitsyn.pdf.

Tynianov, Iuri. "Ob osnovakh kino." *Poetika, istoriia literatury, kino*. Moscow: Nauka, 1977.

Vilenskii, David. *Kino*. Illustrated by Leonid Gamburger. Kharkov: Proletarii, 1928.

Wolf, Erika, ed. *The Worker Photography Movement (1926–1939): Essays and Documents*. Madrid: T.F. Editores, SLC, 2011.

Wolfe, Ross. "Introduction to *About 2 Squares*." *Cambridge Literary Review* 5, no. 8, (2015): 59–67.

Zhak, V. "Detskaia literatura i metod dialekticheskogo materializma." *Na literaturnom postu*, no. 19 (1930): 77–9.

chapter five

THE FRAGILE POWER OF PAPER AND PROJECTIONS

BIRGITTE BECK PRISTED

Unrefined, thin, pulp paper, with a high wood-fibre content that absorbs too much ink, and sometimes leaves print lines blurred – such is the physical texture of early Soviet children's books. A nightmare for librarians responsible for their preservation, an aesthetic-tactile pleasure to the connoisseurs curating them.[1] A challenging matter, but also a creative possibility in the hands of their Soviet readers and writers. The great fragility characteristic of these books of the 1920s seems paradoxically incompatible with the rather rough handling to be expected from their target readership – children who have not yet fully developed their fine motor skills and concentration. However, these children's books turn their lack of paper fortitude into a display of political and pedagogical power.

Bumazhnyi zmei (*The [Paper] Kite*, 1933) by Soviet Ukrainian writer Natal'ia Zabila (1903–1985), with illustrations by Iosif Daits (1897–1954), is a fine example of an early Soviet children's book that reflects its own status as paper object (fig. 5.1). Its rhymed narrative presents the double function of paper both as a toy that children play with, cut, fold, and construct models with, and as a blank screen for political projections of the Soviet child's future. Re-enacting and revoking the legend of Icarus, the boy protagonist builds a large kite out of paper that becomes a vehicle of his dreams of flying to Africa, across the oceans, and even into outer space, where he gets too close to the burning sun. He awakens safe and sound in the gentle sunlight, and soon heads out to fly his kite again, stumbling and tumbling across the muddy fields with his playmates. In parallel with the young Soviet state's failures in the fields with the first Five-Year Plan (1928–32), leading to disruption and famine in Ukraine, the misfortunes of the young Soviet boy do not lower his high-flying ambition of a great leap from the mud field into open space. The story ends with the boy's vision of becoming a Soviet airplane mechanic when he grows up. This is a promise of replacing childish paper models with real machines of solid metal, thus realizing

5.1. Cover of Natal'ia Zabila and Iosif Daits, *Bumazhnyj zmei* (Kiev: Molodoi bol'shevik, 1933), presenting the airborne child, flying toward freedom with a forward-pointing gesture, yet pulled by strings of the paper kite attached to his back.

unripe fantasies through the work of the mature Soviet man. At the same time, Zabila's verses and Daits's illustrations that unfold and launch the boy's paper fictions are themselves conveyed by the medium of a short, light, tenuous paper book. How did early Soviet writers and illustrators and their young readers perceive the status of this paper medium? How did the "pedagogy of paper" affect Soviet child readers?

Today, the spread of digital media has provoked a heightened retrospective attention to the social and cultural history of the apparently obsolescing medium of the book and to the contrastive materiality of the printed text. Informed by media and book historians' approaches to the intrinsic qualities and social functions and values of paper,[2] I wish to examine the printed, illustrated children's book, not so much as a dual visual-verbal representational mode, but rather as a tangible object. This material aspect is especially important for children's literature, because a child's experience is hands-on. Preliterate children learn by playing with toys and handling objects. When we learn to read, we slowly slide the tip of our index finger across the physical texture of the page, while hesitatingly forming the sounds of the printed signs.

An *idea* fixed to paper is *manifest*. Paper makes ideology palpable. Whichever political system it occurs in, however, this rich and diverse resource – paper – is characterized by the paradox of its simultaneous durability and fleetingness.[3] Within the Soviet cultural/political system, a glaring discrepancy developed between the utopian completeness of the communist idea and the manifestation of this idea in lower-end print products; between the high artistic ambitions and cultural symbolic value of literature and, on the other hand, its materialization on low-value pulp paper.[4]

How does the very "paperness" of the printed publication gain ideological and pedagogical significance in early Soviet children's books? Beyond the visual-verbal propaganda message at "content" level, how does the paper book in itself *work* politically? Can playing with paper be a political act? How were Soviet child readers of the 1920s and 1930s educated to act and interact politically with/through the material of paper? I will examine these questions by focusing on four aspects of Soviet paper that the illustrated children's books under discussion both physically embody and symbolically represent: first, the function and status of paper as medium in relation to other, new media; second, the political and economic issue of paper amid the severe shortage thereof in the early Soviet period; third, relations of labour and production embedded in paper; and finally, the deterioration process of paper, its abjection and destruction.

The Old Book, Mass Print, New Electronic Media, and Children's "Living News"

Early Soviet propaganda highlighted electrification and celebrated the modern media of film and radio as new vehicles of communism. Even if mass print-runs of agitation literature and classics soon became an indispensable part of the Soviet enlightenment project, the medium of the book in its traditional form was subject to a certain hostility. Such enmity was directed not only at children's literature of a potentially dubious "class orientation," as expressed most prominently by Nadezhda Krupskaia, who found the reprinting of fairy tales politically suspect,[5] but also at the passiveness of reading itself, the fact that conventional books offered children nothing in the way of interaction with the social-material environment. Hence, in his 1924 manifesto "Bor'ba s detskim chteniem" ("The Struggle against Children's Reading"), revolutionary librarian Vladimir Nevskii states that the children's book is a harmful surrogate for (adult) life, and that reading nurtures passivity and sentimentalism, especially in the weak and quiet child. Books deform children's physical development by crumbling their spine and reducing their blood circulation and eyesight, thus destroying the child's natural capacity for observation. However, if the children's library were to begin facilitating club activities for children's self-organized collective work, books could promote action by a new type of reader-creator child.[6]

Such anti-book rhetoric led to a paradoxical play with medial self-destruction in early Soviet children's books, which may be observed in the poet Nikolai Agnivtsev (1888–1932) and illustrator Ivan Maliutin's (1891–1932) de- and re-construction of the illustrated fairy-tale book, *Oktiabrenok postrelenok* (*The Little Octobrist-Scamp*, 1925). On his way through the city, the self-assured little Octobrist, who belongs to the generation of those born in the revolutionary year of 1917, happens upon a children's bookstore and is confronted by three famous characters from Russian folk tales: Ivan Tsarevich, the witch Baba Yaga, and the good fairy (fig. 5.2). Three times (in good old fairy-tale fashion), the titular "scamp" denies their false existence by pointing at their inferiority in comparison with Soviet social progress and technical innovation. Rejecting their influence, the little Octobrist distributes mass-printed Pioneer periodicals and prefers a radio receiver to the old bookstore, with its lopsidedly lettered signs hanging dilapidated over the shop window. However, beside this apparent celebration of new media and dismissal of the old, Agnivtsev and Maliutin display an artistic fascination with such traditional genres as peasant ditties, fairy tales, and *lubki* that survive as over-written palimpsests, presented to the young audience as a sort of "evidence" in what amounts to putting the medium of the children's book on trial.

Despite such competition between the old printed book and new electronic media, and despite the fact that, from an aesthetic viewpoint, film and printed arts are considered separate forms of artistic expression, the twentieth-century advent of printed and electronic mass media technologies were closely interlinked. Instead of replacing paper, the spread of electronic media in the modern age expanded the demand for it, and led to new forms of printed materials: thus did the invention of the telephone beget the phone book; the telegraph, telegram paper labels; and so on. Furthermore, electrification sparked the industrialization and rationalization of paper production, the standardization of paper sizes, and the mechanization of writing.[7] In the Soviet context, paper was integral to political agitation (pamphlets and posters) and the expansion of bureaucracy; to party decrees, files, documents, tram tickets, library

Тонок,
Звонок,
Как щегленок,
Так же весел, так же мал,
Октябренок —
Постреленок
В школу весело шагал.

Вдруг, бегом —
Кувырком,
Из витрины
Магазина
Детских книг
Вмиг, —
„Иван Царевич" прыг.

5.2a–b. Illustrations from *Oktiabr'enok postrelenok*, by Nikolai Agnivtsev and Ivan Maliutin (Moscow: Oktiabr'enok, 1925), displaying the little Octrobrist passing the old children's bookstore (left) and enjoying his new radio receiver (right).

index cards; but, most importantly, to the establishment of a state printed press and the mass publication of literature – including children's literature. The Soviet period has often been metonymized as an era of iron and steel; but it was certainly also an era of a considerably less propagandized material: paper.

One Soviet children's book that severely challenged the borders between cellulose and celluloid was *Knizhka-kino-seans o tom, kak pioner Gans stachechnyi komitet spas* (*A Book-Film-Performance about How the Pioneer Hans Saved the Strike Committee*, 1931) by the artists Fedor Kobrinets (1907–1977) and Isaak Eberil (1909–1942). Their cinema-book, which contains a strip of four picture frames on each page, a total of thirty-two "still shots," followed by a strip of intertitles, tells the story of a strike at a Berlin factory. The capitalist director flees the worksite and uses the modern medium of the telephone to alert the police and order the arrest of the strike committee. Hence, electronic communication is presented as an exclusive privilege of the exploitive ruling class, something to which the workers have no access.[8] Luckily, the young Pioneer Hans is on guard on the roof and alerts the strike committee the old-fashioned, "unplugged" way – by shouting. Eventually, he compensates for the lack of electronic devices by substituting the telephone as a "living medium," bringing a courier letter – a premodern, handwritten message on physical paper – from the strikers to the Red Front fighters, who (albeit apparently unarmed) fight off the police and save the strike committee. Proletarians thus communicate through a humble "surrogate medium," paper, which is by no means "static," but rather is set in motion and brought to life by the actions of a child who becomes, himself, the medium of the message (figs. 5.3 and 5.4).

With the use of "montage technique" and display of film motifs, Kobrinets and Eberil's book alludes, like several other early Soviet children's books, to the aesthetics of Soviet silent cinema of the 1920s.[9] However, this book goes further than merely entering an "intermedial" dialogue with the external medium of film; it downsizes the abstract form-language of Sergei Eisenstein's famous film *Stachka* (*The Strike*, 1925), not just to a comprehensible storyline, but also to an actual, tangible mini-object. The media-transgression involved is all the more radical for its taking place at a material level: on the last page, children (and the adults assisting them) receive do-it-yourself instructions on how to craft their own film spool and screen, and turn the thirty-two book illustration frames into a little 12 cm film. The user of this "manual" is literally directed to slice up the old medium of the book in order to create the new medium of cinema – a double act of destruction and construction. Of course, we cannot determine how many of the 50,000 book copies actually *were* sliced up. The collection copies that have survived until today have obviously not fulfilled their inherent, self-destructive telos. Both Agnivtsev and Maliutin's and Kobrinets and Eberil's books thematize modern electronic media and not paper itself; but, in doing so, they make use of paper as a seemingly given, unmarked medium that tends to negate itself. Avoiding its own representation, paper becomes a blank void, which at the same time lends it a flexible capacity to imitate – celebrate and subvert – other media in playful transformations.

5.3. and 5.4. Black-on-white and white-on-black details in the style of silent movies, creating a contrast between the telephone and paper letter, from Fedor Kobrinets and Isaak Eberil, *Knizhka-kino-seans o tom, kak pioner Gans stachechnyi komitet spas* (Leningrad: OGIZ-Molodaia gvardia, 1931).

Other children's books foreground their very paper materiality. One example is Nikolai Smirnov's (1890–1933) industrial non-fiction book *Detiam o gazete* (*For Children about the Newspaper*, 1924), illustrated by the sisters Ol'ga (1886–1958) and Galina (1891–1966) Chichagova with the assistance of members (Akhtyrko and Sanina) of the first working group of the constructivists (fig. 5.5). Its cover displays the title in large red capital letters against the background of a front-page fragment of the newspaper *Izvestiia*. The typographic experiments continue inside the book, which explains how news about foreign policy and production from China to Paris reach Moscow through telegraph wires. At the top of the media hierarchy, these electronic messages are transformed by the editor and his skilled typesetters, who, notably, still work with pre-mechanized hand setting.[10] While the night-shift workers are reduced to blue silhouettes seemingly serving the machinery, depicted in all detail is the huge rotary press that turns the selected news into mass information on paper, which is then distributed by trains and planes across the Soviet Union.[11] At the bottom of the media hierarchy, anonymous, faceless paperboys act as living message-carriers who, through the act of delivering newspapers, empower both the masses and the Soviet political leadership, represented by an inserted photograph of Trotsky, to properly react to the current international threats being reported. However, in the end, we are told that Trotsky's response remains a secret; apparently, the news flows only in one direction.

Soviet children's books did not only inform young readers about the political necessity of printed news and their own role of distributing it. Writing guides also

5.5. A bookspread of Nikolai Smirnov, *Detiam o gazete*, illustrated by Ol'ga and Galina Chichagova (Moscow & Petrograd: Gosizdat, 1924).

Тираж — 50 000! (Живая диаграмма.)

5.6. Illustration of children performing "living statistics," celebrating the children's journal *Leninskie iskry* reaching a print-run of 50,000 copies. A. Afanas'eva and L. Berman, *Pionerskie zhivye gazety* (Leningrad: Priboi, 1929), 21.

encouraged children to become activist editors and printers themselves by producing "wall newspapers" ("stengazety"). Beginning in the early 1920s, *detkory* and *iunkory* (child and youth correspondents), who organized local networks in parallel with the adult *rabkory* (worker correspondents) movement, imitated mass printed newspapers by creating single-copy, homemade, handwritten news sheets, placed on stands in the corridors and corners of classrooms, clubs, and other institutions.[12] As this genre of educational and simultaneously *directed/self*-publication developed,[13] Ekaterina Zonnenshtral and Konstantin Kuznetsov's do-it-yourself book *Ia pechatnik* (*I Am a Printer*, 1932) instructed children and pedagogues how to engrave stamps using sliced potatoes and, employing this primitive printing technique, to reproduce coloured, stylized patterns and Soviet emblems on old newspaper leaves. So, rather than the celebrated modern media of radio and film, it was actually the humble materials of potatoes and waste paper that were accessible to children and offered them the possibility of participation and agency within the frames of the political system.

Stengazety became an omnipresent children's medium throughout the Soviet period. Due to their ephemeral nature, statistical evidence about their exact prevalence is uncertain, but Dmitrii Safonov suggests that the genre's popularity peaked around the mid-1920s, when the early Soviet paper and press crisis reached its height.[14] Children were thus compensating for the low penetration of party-circulated mass-printed newspapers from above by creating, and even themselves acting as, periodicals from below. Unlike wall newspapers, so-called living newspapers (*zhivye gazety*) represented an exclusive children's genre, consisting of local-level pioneer agitation and live "news performances" through a mixture of poster display, song, recitation, and choreography. In figure 5.6, the pyramid-shaped "mass ornament" of the five children's bodies represents but also replaces the (absent) 50,000 copies of the child-correspondents' journal *Leninskie iskry* (*Lenin's Sparks*, founded 1924) – a seemingly impressive print-run that, however, fell well short of its ambitious declared goal: "For every Pioneer, a paper" ("Kazhdomu pioneru – nomer Leninskikh iskr"). By growing taller than their own individual heights, the Pioneers embody the print run, but also transform its mass-published message into a unique, *organic* matter.

The Shortcomings of the Early Soviet Politics of Paper

Especially in the early Soviet period, the state publishing and printing industry suffered paper shortages. Literary and public debate of this period was rife with "book hunger" and laments over print quality, and paper came to represent both a scarce resource and desired cultural object. The Russian paper industry had collapsed around the end of the First World War. In the years of civil war that followed the October Revolution of 1917, the extreme shortage of fuel, chemicals, and specialists resulted in a drop of annual paper production to less than 10 per cent of pre-revolutionary levels.[15] Since paper was still the main means of agitation, the new leadership saw its unsatisfied demand as a top priority. Already in 1917, a Main Committee on the Paper Industry and Trade, shortened Glavbum (an amalgam of the Russian words for "main" and "paper"), was established. Glavbum controlled paper production and distribution and oversaw the 1918–19 nationalization of paper mills. However, the "hunger ratio" of paper forced Glavbum to import foreign paper, which left the new Soviet state dependent on its ideological enemies.[16]

Soviet historian of children's literature Lidiia Kon attests to the dire state of post–civil war children's literature with reference to publishing data indicating that, in 1921, only thirty-three book titles were issued.[17] This coincides with the lowest point of annual paper production, of 27,000 tons nationwide. Paper shortage influenced the business practices of publishers, the artistic practices of writers, and the collecting practices of their young readers. As an example of the first: the private publisher Zinovii Grzhebin, which was supported by Maxim Gorky and, on his initiative, began publishing children's literature, "outsourced" publishing and printing from Petrograd to Berlin, where paper was more available, and from 1921 to 1923, he published several hundred book titles abroad on commission from the paper-hungry Soviet authorities.[18] However, the agreement came to an early end; the Soviet authorities refused to pay for the books received and instead accused Grzhebin of fraud. Since his products were unsellable in Berlin – they used the new post-revolutionary orthography, rejected by the traditionalist Russian émigré community – the publishing house lost its financial foundation and closed down.[19]

How the paper shortage affected writers may be exemplified by a diary entry of the popular literary critic, translator, and children's poet Kornei Chukovsky from 24 January 1926. Chukovsky had struggled for five days with the editing and direct censorship of a preface to his new feuilleton novel scheduled to begin publication the following day in the literary supplement of the revolutionary evening paper *Krasnaia gazeta* (*The Red Newspaper*). When Chukovsky called his editor, Iona Kugel, that morning, he was shocked to learn that the newspaper would not be running his novel after all, and that its own future existence was uncertain:

> It turns out that there is a paper crisis in Leningrad. There are no newspaper rolls available. A special commission to cut paper costs has been set up, and this commission, which initially decided to shut down one of the evening papers, has now ended up permitting every newspaper not six and not eight, but *four* pages! Because of this, there is no space for my novel! The novel has been postponed indefinitely.[20]

In 1925, *Krasnaia gazeta* had sided with one of Stalin's main rivals, Grigorii Zinoviev (1883–1936), who aspired to succeed to the leadership role after Lenin's death in 1924. However, in January 1926, the Stalin-supporter Ivan Skvortsov-Stepanov became editor-in-chief of the newspaper. Hence, it is a reasonable assumption that controlling the scarce resource of paper was a way of executing indirect censorship and purging a newspaper's literary section of unwanted texts. In other words, the "paper crisis" was a political crisis.[21] In 1929, the state publishing organization Gosizdat, whose approval was required at every step in the publication process, from publishing programs to print runs, ceased delivering paper entirely to private publishing houses, in effect (and quite intentionally) shutting them down, even before private publishing was declared illegal in 1930 as part of the transition to a planned economy.[22]

Art historian Erast Kuznetsov describes the experimental period of Soviet book art of the 1920s as a "paperback decade" and perceives the light-paper wrappers, which are so suitable for illustrations, as an aesthetic quality of these books.[23] When today we look at the artistic surplus and colourful cultural heritage of avant-garde books, their seemingly spontaneously created covers of wallpaper and other makeshift materials appear as a protest against the bourgeois book-object on fine printing paper. However, these books were also most assuredly products of a paper shortage, a lack of paperboard and bookbinding materials that were expensive, if not unavailable, in this period.

5.7a–b. Poor paper covers of Nikolai Shestakov and Dmitrii Moshchevitin, *Strok dvesti pro knizhkiny bolesti* (Moscow: G.F. Mirimanov, 1925).

This situation is reflected in Nikolai Shestakov's (1894–1974) rhymed story *Strok dvesti pro knizhkiny bolesti* (*Some 200 Lines on the Woes of a Book*, 1925), illustrated by Dmitrii Moshchevitin (1894–1974), about an animate but worn-out children's book who complains of an aching spine and cries because she has lost her paper cover (fig. 5.7). Luckily, she is treated by a bookbinder, this process presented as a doctor's advanced, and painful, operation of incisions, stitches, and presses. Hence, bookbinding is still represented as a pre-industrial, premodern handicraft for a select few books, but certainly not for mass-published books. Seeing her fancy post-operative look, her envious book-comrades all begin protesting: "We demand bindings!" ("Daesh pereplet!") This cry was echoed in a short 1929 thesis on book covers by G.D. Brylov (of the Graphic Arts Faculty, Art Academy of Leningrad), who lamented the technical backwardness of Soviet printing, noting that only 10 per cent of all books then being issued had a binding. In the context of state centralization of the publishing industry, Brylov called for the introduction of a single, standardized, and mass-produced publisher's binding for the whole print run of every book.[24]

Samuil Marshak's (1887–1964) *Knizhka pro knizhki* (*A Little Book about Little Books*), published in 1927, with illustrations by Sergei Chekhonin (1878–1936), likewise uses the motif of old books as animate creatures complaining of their own decrepitude. The illustrations display the destructive force of the little hooligans Mishka and his visiting friend Grishka, who, amid their reckless brawling, rip such august luminaries as the *Brother Grimms* and *Don Quixote* to shreds (fig. 5.8). However, together with their fellows classics, these books manage to escape their misgoverning young owner and are offered refuge by the Soviet public library's Great Catalogue (also an animate being).

The story may be read as an allegory of the anarchy of revolution being replaced by the control of a state institution. In the library, the book doctor repairs, binds, and glues the worn-out paper covers of the trembling books in a frightening operation. When misbehaving Mishka wants to check out one of the restored, as it were re-canonized, books, which have been catalogued by the (admirably organized, power-consolidating) state, the adult librarian authoritatively denies him access.[25]

The first Five-Year Plan gave high political priority to the expansion of the Soviet paper industry. Glavbum was reorganized and further centralized in the All-Soviet Soiuzbumaga (Paper Union). The 1930s saw the rise of new, large-scale paper mills located closer to the forest resources, but further from the printing industry in the main cities.[26] Within the planned economy, transportation, water, and energy costs were of secondary importance to the rapid growth of forced industrialization. Among several reasons for the persistent problems and lack of modernization of Soviet paper production, Elena Kochetkova observes that, "despite the fact that the Soviet Union (particularly the RSFSR) was brimming with forests, timber cutting, which was under the auspices of the Gulag system until the mid-1950s, was poorly managed."[27] Since the increase in Soviet paper production was accompanied by a corresponding decrease in foreign paper imports, paper shortage became a permanent condition of Soviet book publishing.

Дрался Мишка с Гришкой,
Замахнулся книжкой,
Дал разок по голове—
Вместо книжки стало две.

Разговаривали книжки
Про свои дела-делишки.
Было в комнатах темно,
Свежий ветер дул в окно.
Мишка спал в своей постели,
А страницы шелестели:

—Молчи ты, старый Минус,—
Сказали Братья Гримм:—
И больше не серди нас
Брюзжанием своим.
Бежим в библиотеку,
В свободный наш приют.
Там злому человеку
Трепать нас не дадут!
—Нет!—сказала Хижина
  Дяди Тома:
Мишкой я обижена,
  Но останусь дома!

—Вперед!—воскликнул Дон-Кихот,
И книжки двинулись в поход.

Несчастные калеки
Пришли к библиотеке.
Шлеп-шлеп на порог.

Там их встретил Каталог,
  Важная книжка,
  Толстая крышка,
  Медные застежки,
  Тоненькие ножки.

„Эй“,—сказал он:—„Что за хлам
Привалил сегодня к нам?
Что за куча всякой рвани
Без обложек, без названий?“

Отвечали Братья Гримм:
—За привет благодарим.
Но ошиблись вы немножко—
И у нас была обложка.
Мы клочки ее храним.
Наше имя—Братья Гримм!

Книжка в толстом переплете
Закричала:—„Нет, вы врете!“
—Нет, мы правду говорим!
Отвечали Братья Гримм.

5.8a–b. Shredded books, presented in Samuil Marshak, *Knizhka pro knizhki*, illustrated by Sergei Chekhonin (Leningrad & Moscow: Raduga, 1927).

As a result of the gradual consolidation of the state publishing industry, the mid-1930s onward saw a certain "hardening" of cover material for Soviet adult fiction, with the introduction of mass-fabricated publisher's binding, a development that ran exactly opposite to the "paperback revolution" in the West (1935–60). However, thin booklets in large format with paper covers, which were stitched in the middle and produced in cheap print-runs of several million, remained characteristic of illustrated Soviet children's literature in subsequent decades as well.[28]

In one of his many popular non-fiction books, *Chernym po belomu: Rasskazy o knigakh* (*Black on White: Stories about Books*, 1928), Mikhail Il'in (1895–1953, pseudonym of Il'ia Marshak, younger brother of Samuil Marshak) pedagogically brings the combined cultural-technical history of books alive to a young audience. Il'in titles a chapter on the history of paper manufacturing from ancient China to modern times "Bumaga-pobeditel'nitsa" ("The Paper-Victor"), thus ascribing to paper a certain agency and human status as "winner" of a cultural-evolutionary process. Almost every spread contains lithographic illustrations by the famous Leningrad artist Nikolai Lapshin (1891–1942), which are integrated in the text as small miniatures, inspired by East Asian art.[29] However, the paper of Il'in's book itself is not so much victorious as frail: this is a very modest paperback of low printing quality, with narrow page margins and fonts hardly large enough for child readers. Despite the intentions of author and illustrator, then, the book's ideological message is resisted and undermined by the shortcomings of its material. While Il'in presents paper as the prime media technology in the history of humanity and celebrates its ability to store and preserve information, the pages of his book threaten to dissolve at any moment, highlighting their own finitude and inadequacy.

Playing Production with Paper

Despite its great fragility, Soviet paper was not just a medium for reading, but also, as Aleksandar Bošković discusses in chapter 4, a flexible toy that children could use to craft, colour, and construct models. Even if paper was a scarce commodity, it still served as a cheaper surrogate for such inaccessible foreign-manufactured toys as construction sets. Catriona Kelly explains how pedagogues of the revolution considered toys frivolous consumer goods. During the New Economic Policy period, socially privileged families could still obtain manufactured toys, but, with the abolishment of private trade, the "toy famine" grew worse in the early 1930s, until the state administration began giving some priority to toy production from the mid-1930s on.[30] In the vast cultural history of homemade toys, creating and playing with paper dolls and other figures probably belong to one of the most popular activities among children in both East and West. But the Soviet "do-it-yourself" books from the period of the first Five-Year Plan stand out due to their strong emphasis on topics of industrial production, and the ambitiousness of the advanced paper constructions of grand machines, mills, factories, and other objects that they encouraged.[31] On the one hand, one may argue that such books turned children from passive to participating readers, casting them as integral co-constructors, not only of the paper model-plants presented, but also of the larger project of building up socialism. On the other hand, this ideological goal of embedding a work ethic in children's play clashes with the more general notion of play as an "unproductive" and spontaneous activity, based on free participation.

The tension inherent in Soviet paper-play is seen in a juxtaposition of two otherwise quite dissimilar children's books: Iakov Meksin's (1886–1943) *Kak Alla khvorala* (*How Alla Was Ill*, 1926), illustrated by Vladimir Konashevich (1888–1963), and Aleksandr Abramov's *Konveier* (*The Conveyor*, 1931), illustrated by Aleksei Laptev (1905–1965). In the former, Konashevich's illustrations, inspired by the World of Art (*Mir iskusstva*) movement, depict a group of kindergarteners around a table, all deeply engrossed in diverse paper projects meant to develop particular handicraft skills, the current rudimentariness of which in these children is evident from the crooked flags and figures hanging on the walls and windows above them. To cheer up the absent Alla (at home with an illness), the children dictate to the school nurse a letter for her, presented in the book as a group of unevenly handwritten sheets of lined paper.

In contrast, Abramov and Laptev's constructivist booklet, inspired by the assembly line production of the modern car industry, instructs children to organize themselves into a brigade, headed by the eldest of the group, and line up at a long table. Page by page, the book demonstrates how to produce paper figures at record speed by introducing the children to the conveyer method, with each child executing a particular step in the folding process (fig. 5.9). In *How Alla Was Ill*, paper appears to be ideally pliable to whatever form the children may impose on it. The children may express themselves through paper, and paper enables them to communicate with the person absent from their group. In *The Conveyor*, paper becomes an instrument of the children's discipline: their brigade line leaves no room for potential absence or wrong folds. Compared to the creation of a whole paper figure, the simple task of executing a single fold appears to be an activity that neither challenges skills nor stimulates the creativity of the individual child. Instead, by introducing principles of serial production into play, this paper exercise prepares the children for their future work-life on the factory floor; thus, the act of folding paper bends the children themselves.

Other Soviet children's books play with reproductions of production by introducing meta-narratives that explain the very process by which the books themselves are made. This is done, not with reference to the book's devising by some ingenious author, but rather to its own physical existence as a product of labour. This is the case for books such as Elena Afanasieva's (1900–1998) *Kak delaetsia eta kniga* (*How This Book Is Made*, 1930) and Natalia Dirsh's *Bumaga* (*Paper*; illustrated by Nikolai Popov), displaying the labour processes of book and paper production, respectively. Afanasieva

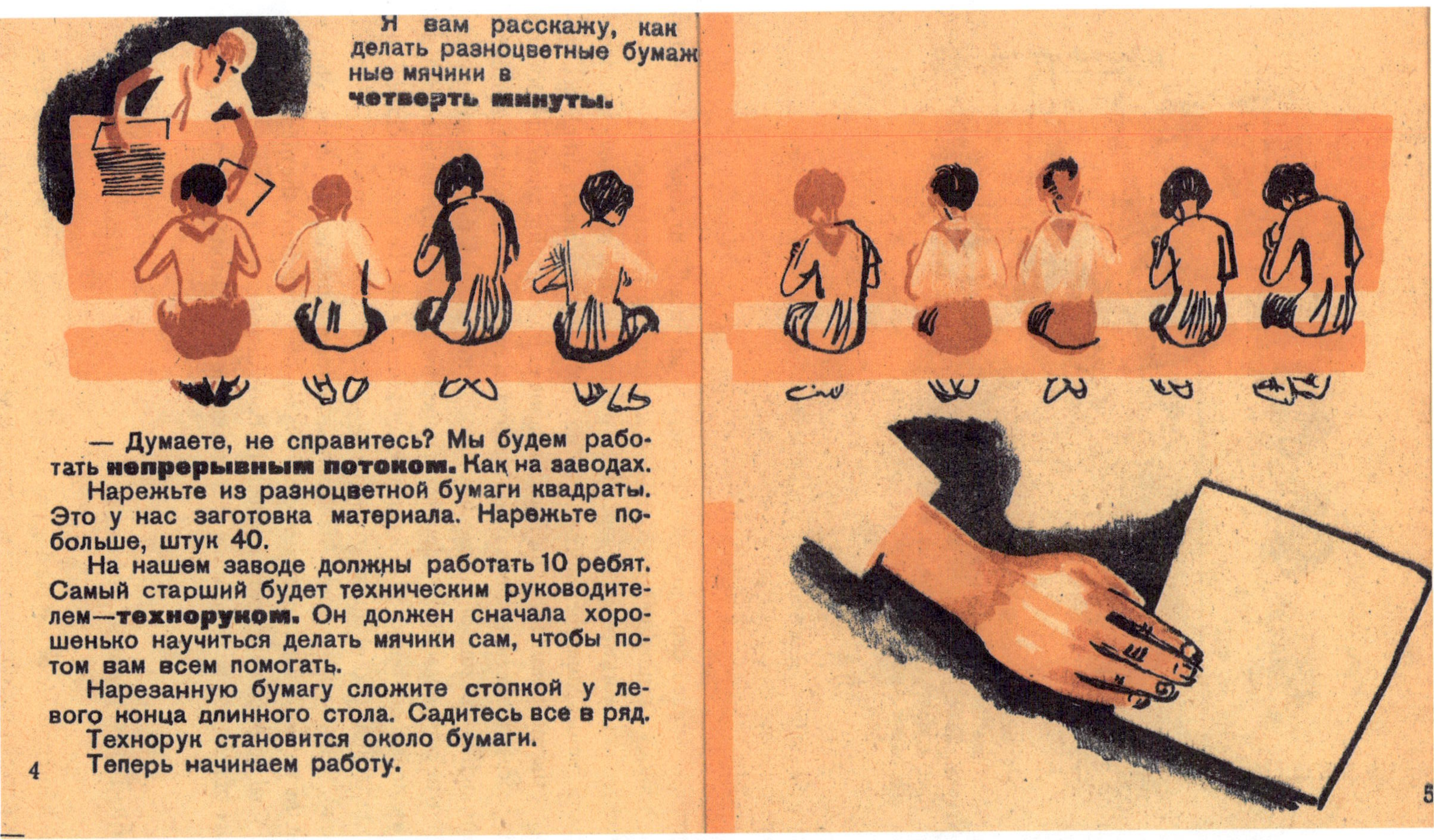

5.9. A row of children, presented with their bended backs to the viewer, begin their paper-folding work at the assembly line. At record speed, they mass produce their own paper toys. Spread from Aleksandr Abramov and Aleksei Laptev, *Konveier* (Moscow: OGIZ-Molodaia gvardia, 1931).

5.10. Illustration from Elena Afanas'eva, *Kak delaetsia eta kniga* (Moscow: Krest'ianskaia gazeta, 1930) demonstrates the manual folding of offset printsheets.

foregrounds detailed depictions of machinery – advanced four-colour offset printing technology. Occupying a more modest and somewhat blurry social position in the background, workwomen engage in the pre-mechanized, and by 1930 outdated, process of hand-folding the paper sheets (fig. 5.10). This supremely simple act, representing the most basic form one could imagine of transforming material through a labour process, tends here to betray the ideological message of empowering proletarians through the seizure of the means of production. Instead, the depicted workers appear to be compensating for a double shortage, that of raw materials and machinery, that threatens these books' grand narrative of progress and betrays "stuckness" at a pre-industrial stage. But unlike in the meta-narrative of Shestakov's old-fashioned, unbound, weeping paper book, Afanasieva introduces a moment of sentimentalism only at the very end, when an exalted child in a remote village (here the mere recipient of the final book-product) runs to greet the book distributor – the bearer of paper's message of progress, who, however, gets around the old-fashioned way: on foot.

Cleaning Out: Wasted Paper

Soviet children were not just playing but were also interacting with paper in a far more serious game of building up a new, utopian, *and* totalitarian society. As part of their political education, young Pioneers, members of the Soviet youth organization for schoolchildren age ten to fifteen, were encouraged to do their own (small-scale) part to implement the great Five-Year Plan. It was particularly in this regard that one of Mikhail Il'in's other children's books, *Rasskaz o velikom plane* (1930; published in Boston the following year in English as *New Russia's Primer: The Story of the Five-Year Plan*), with illustrations and photo layout by Mikhail Razulevich (1904–1993), grew tremendously popular and was issued in seven editions and several hundred thousand copies.[32] In the book, Il'in directly addresses his young audience with a twelve-point "to do" list to fulfil their role in the Five-Year Plan, with the overall goal of preparing new Soviet citizens for a new, utopian life. Point 2 on the list deals with collecting such waste materials as rags, bones, and scrap, with each Pioneer expected to collect twenty kilos a year. Waste, in Il'in's description, is a tragic consequence of capitalist greed: in *that* system, watermelons are discarded, milk is dumped into rivers, and corn burned, all to keep prices high for the wealthy few, while the poor children of New York go hungry.[33] However, Soviet waste reutilization was encouraged not out of environmental, but rather industrial, concerns. Hence, Soviet children took active part in paper circulation, not only as paper carriers, distributing newspapers, but also as Pioneers in paper-collecting campaigns.

Under the headline of "We'll give the country paper. We'll clean out waste paper from institutions, depots, and houses," the 5 January 1929 edition of the newspaper *Pionerskaia pravda* (*Pioneer Truth*) ran an anonymous artist's cartoon of a determined, almost angry-seeming Pioneer, Kolia. This self-assured young man's remarkably long, rebellious Pinocchio nose sweeps like a broomstick through a huge pile of chaotically disordered paper. Rather aggressively, Kolia puts his foot down on the paper stack, rolling his eyes in contempt at the ridiculous bureaucrat below him, who is being crushed and pulped himself under his mountain of superfluous protocols, circulars, and other files.

The article emphasizes that it is the duty of every Pioneer to collect paper to keep the economic "organism" of state and country healthy. The Soviet economy, it is explained, has reduced paper imports to gain independence from foreign capitalism, so now every Pioneer is needed to overcome the "current" (in reality, chronic) paper crisis: "Without paper, there can be neither books, nor newspapers, nor journals, and without this, no culture is possible."[34] Hence, old paper is presented as a dead instrument of bureaucracy that may be destroyed, refabricated, and gain a new life as a symbolic carrier of new Soviet culture, emphasized as a literary or print culture. However, this early apparition of "paper recycling" was merely rhetorical; Soviet paper plants were not yet sufficiently equipped to process fine writing paper out of waste paper. The collected paper was more likely to end up as board or pulp for industrial or export purposes than as new books for Pioneers.

Regardless, no piece of paper was too small for the cause. The editorial board cites a letter purportedly received from a boy proposing that Pioneers undertake the systematic collection of streetcar tickets from Moscow's half-million daily passengers, which would add up to a mass of paper.[35] To the economic value ascribed to a single ticket (similar to the value ascribed to paper notes within a monetary system) is added a secondary value: the total pulped mass of used tickets. The local Moscow collecting points of Utilgostorg (the State Office for the Procurement, Processing, and Supply of Utilizable Waste Material for Industry and Export) offered three kopeks per kilo of ordinary waste paper and up to twenty-five kopeks for high-quality office paper. The amount collected by the Pioneers was to be donated to orphanages.

What is not explicitly stated in the article, but evident from its historical context, is the ideological significance of *cleaning out* old waste paper from homes and institutions – an act, after all, of purging. On 20 December 1928, the People's Commissariat of the Workers' and Peasants' Inspectorate, whose task it was to monitor administration and combat inefficiency and corruption, promulgated a resolution "On procedures for removing archival and other waste paper from institutions and enterprises for the needs of the paper industry." This became the starting point of the so-called *makulaturnaia kampaniia* (waste paper campaign). During the following two months, adults and more than eight million mobilized schoolchildren collected 80,000 tons of waste paper, of which a conservatively estimated 14,069 tons represented irreplaceable archival material: approximately twenty-eight million files belonging primarily to the historical and cultural heritage of tsarist Russia. Notably, it was not archivists, but employees from the waste material agencies Utilgostorg and Bumtrest, who selected which documents were to be sent for industrial pulping. Eventually, many of the "old specialists" of the state archives would suffer a fate analogous to the documents formerly under their care, falling victim to Stalin's purges.[36]

In this act of radical modernization, archival documents were perceived not only as the old regime's preservative medium, but also as the remaining evidence of its authority and legitimacy, which children were sent out to collect and destroy once and for all. However, unlike the later, symbolically loaded book-burnings of the Nazi regime, the Stalinist waste paper campaigns did not have a primarily ritual character; rather, it was utilitarian, with the economic goal of speeding up production in the paper industry. Fine writing paper was too valuable to be simply incinerated; its destruction would go instead to yield board and pulp.[37]

The Pedagogy of Paper: Eternal/Ephemeral Books and Their Readers

The October Revolution replaced an old paper regime of hand-bound books – lofty cultural objects understood as meant for the eternal preservation of human, God-given inspiration – with a new paper regime, disenchanting the old book and instead celebrating modern, industrialized mass printing, empowering children and adults alike with the latest ephemeral news and agitation flyers. It was precisely this ephemerality, the quantitative shortcomings and physical inadequacy of Soviet paper, that lent the new children's culture a certain affinity with this "weapon of the weak": children and paper shared a fragile power. Soviet paper thus gained a political and pedagogical significance in illustrated children's books of the 1920s and 1930s, because, as compared with other mass media, paper was relatively accessible and cheap, an ersatz material easy for children to handle. Paper's blank surface would seem to constitute a neutral and transparent message-bearer, and its flexibility easily lends itself to imitation and the celebrative subversion of other media. At the same time, the lack of solidity of Soviet paper reveals the limitations of the ideological projections imposed on its blankness. The material resists its own message.

The new paper regime involved Soviet children in all stages of paper circulation, from the distribution of periodicals to the collection of waste paper. This involvement resulted in two ways of playing with paper. On the one hand, children were engaged by artists and pedagogues in an unfolding, productive ludicness: imitating the mass-printed press through one-off wall newspapers; constructing short-lived models of a utopian society, which they could crumble up and throw away again at any time; and so on. Paper became a very rich material in the hands of poor, young proletarians. On the other hand, the new paper regime also disciplined children to future industrial labour processes through the repetitive act of folding and taming paper – thus, not so much empowering children as instrumentalizing them for the sake of a modern, mechanized economy. Ultimately, the Stalinist *makulatura* campaigns abused Soviet schoolchildren in a destructive totalitarian game, casting them as an easily manipulated, pulping mob. This two-sided but coherent "pedagogy of paper" also implied a double attitude to books *qua* objects. On the one hand, the eternal book turns into self-negating, pulpy printing matter, literally giving instructions for its own mutilation; on the other, certain books are doctored, bound as doctrines, catalogued and re-canonized on the closed shelves of the children's library whose entrance is governed by an authoritative adult – the guiding, guarding librarian, on whom the little reader depends.

How did this double-folded political meaning of paper affect the imagination of the first Soviet generation that grew up under the buildup of socialism and was socialized during the Stalin years? Did the "father of Soviet *samizdat*" Nikolai Glazkov (b. 1919) and the paragon of *tamizdat* (works smuggled out to be published in the West) Andrei Siniavskii / Abram Terts (b. 1925) play "I am a printer!" and learn wall-newspaper techniques at school before declaring themselves self-publishers as adults? Was it owing to this state-sanctioned pedagogy that subsequent generations developed a talent for nonconformist paper architecture (e.g., in the alternative press of the 1980s)? The child reader became a living carrier of Soviet paper; the child was its labour force and creative force, its embodiment, legitimation, and compensation. By cutting, constructing, collecting, distributing, destroying, writing, printing, editing, and even acting as paper, the child reader was formed by and transformed its message.

NOTES

1 Ruggles, "Deterioration of Soviet Paper."
2 See, for example, Gitelman, *Paper Knowledge*, and Häkli, *Ingen Dag Utan Papper*. For a recent survey of the history of Russian book and print culture, see Remnek, *The Space of the Book*.
3 Derrida, "Le papier ou moi," 35–6.
4 Lovell, *The Russian Reading Revolution*, 25–44.
5 Balina, "Creativity through Restraint," 6. See also, in the present volume, Reischl, "Aeroplane, Aeroboat, Aerosleigh," fig. 11.1.
6 Nevskii, "Bor'ba s detskim chteniem," 21–3; see also Dobrenko on the 1920s debates on libraries and the young reader in *The Making of the State Reader*, 68–81.
7 Müller, *Weiße Magie*, 310–23.
8 For a counterexample, see Kirill Chunikin's chapter in this volume.
9 See the discussion in Yuri Leving's chapter in this volume.
10 For an interesting, detailed account of work processes and hierarchies within early Soviet newspaper print shops, see Koenker, *Republic of Labor*, 21–6.
11 For a discussion of the depiction of the human worker and their machine, see Aleksey Golubev's contribution to this volume.
12 Kelly, "A Laboratory," 579–81. Kelly focuses exclusively on wall newspapers for adults; on *stengazety* guides for children, see, for example, Shamrai and Poletaev, *Detkory i pionerskaia pechat'*, and Berman and Khalturin, *Rebiatam o gazete*.
13 In her transcriptions of issues of *stengazety*, including some housed in the personal archive of Nikolai Ognev (author of *Dnevnik Kosti Riabtseva* [*Diary of a Communist Schoolboy*] and pedagogue at the revolutionary, experimental secondary boarding school Iskra no. 3), Vinogradova gives a sense of the multiple and competing wall newspaper types of the period: "official" and typewritten versus the self-asserting, anonymous, and subversively humorous handwritten kind. Vinogradova, "Tri izmereniia," 260–71.
14 Safonov, "Stengazety kak element," 140–1.
15 Chuiko, *Istoriia tselliulozno-bumazhnoi promyshlennosti*, 8–9.
16 Ibid., 30–1.
17 Kon, *Sovetskaia detskaia literatura vosstanovitel'nogo perioda*, 14–15; see also Balina, "Creativity through Restraint," 6.
18 One of Grzhebin's adult titles, Boris Pilniak's *Golyi god* (*The Naked Year*, 1922), presents the chaos of the revolutionary and civil war period through a montage of voices and sounds in which the Soviet bureaucratic abbreviation "Glavbum" melts together with the sound of a snowstorm as a destructive natural force, the sound of shooting ("boom, boom"), and the Russian word for paper (*bumaga*): "Snowstorm. March. – Ahh, what a snowstorm, when the wind eats the snow! Shoyaa, Shoy-oyaa, Shoooyaaa! Gviiu … gu-vu-zz! Gu-vu-zz! … Gla-vbum! Gla-vbum!" (Pilnyak, *The Naked Year*, 165).
19 Nikitin, "Izdatel'stvo Z.I. Grzhebina (1919–1924)."
20 Chukovsky, *Dnevnik*, 357.
21 See Lenoe, "NEP Newspapers," 627–8, for a discussion of how newspaper print-runs affected the paper crisis, and (I would add) vice versa.
22 Becker, *Verlagspolitik und Buchmarkt*, 60–1.
23 Kuznetsov, "Sovetskoe iskusstvo knigi," 9–10.
24 Brylov, *Oblozhka knigi*, 75–6.
25 See also Dobrenko's discussion of the absence of "open shelves" in Soviet children's libraries, making the child dependent on adult guidance and approval of not only what, but also how, to read (*The Making of the State Reader*), 75.

26 Mashkina, "The Pulp and Paper Industry," 292; Chuiko, *Istoriia tselliulozno-bumazhnoi promyshlennosti*, 36–7.

27 Kochetkova, "Modernizatsiia sovetskoi," 32.

28 I have developed this thesis of a "Soviet hardback revolution" in Pristed, *The New Russian Book*, 33–59.

29 Yasen, "The Development of Children's Book Illustration," 63–4.

30 Kelly, *Children's World*, 443–5.

31 See Maria Litovskaya's contribution to this volume; for further "do-it-yourself" illustration examples, see Borislavov, "Do It Yourself," 28–30.

32 See Larissa Rudova's contribution to this volume.

33 Il'in, *Rasskaz o velikom plane*, 15–17; 168–71. On the English and American reception of this book, see Mickenberg, "The New Generation," 103–7.

34 "Dadim strane bumagu. Ochistim uchrezhdeniia, sklady i doma ot bumazhnogo khlama." *Pionerskaia pravda* 261, no. 3 (1929): 1.

35 Ibid.

36 Khorkhordina, *Istoriia i arkhivy*, 181–2, 203–4.

37 To broaden the comparative perspective, it could be noted that the Soviet campaigns of the late 1920s differed from the later "paper drives" initiated by both Allied and Axis powers during the Second World War to enhance resource mobilization on the home front. Unlike the latter, framed symbolically as the sacrifice of something *valuable*, the Soviet campaigns treated pre-revolutionary archival documents as *unwanted*—material of no or even *negative* value that could, however, be made into something useful. For a study of the British "paper drives," see Thorsheim, "Salvage and Destruction."

BIBLIOGRAPHY

Abramov, Aleksandr, and Aleksei Laptev. *Konveier*. Moscow: OGIZ-Molodaia gvardiia, 1931.

Afanas'eva, A., and L. Berman. *Pionerskie zhivye gazety*. Leningrad: Priboi, 1929.

Afanas'eva, Elena. *Kak delaetsia eta kniga*. Moscow: Krest'ianskaia gazeta, 1930.

Agnivtsev, Nikolai, and Ivan Maliutin. *Oktiabrenok postrelenok*. Moscow: Oktiabrenok, 1925.

Balina, Marina. "Creativity through Restraint: The Beginnings of Soviet Children's Literature." In *Russian Children's Literature and Culture*, edited by Marina Balina and Larissa Rudova, 3–17. London: Routledge, 2008.

Becker, Petra. *Verlagspolitik und Buchmarkt in Russland (1985 bis 2002): Prozess der Entstaatlichung des zentralistischen Buchverlagswesens*. Weisbaden: Harrasowitz, 2003.

Berman L., and Khalturin, I. *Rebiatam o gazete: Chto delat' s gazetoi shkol'niku i pioneru*. Leningrad: Leningradskaia pravda, 1927.

Borislavov, Rad. "Do It Yourself." In *Adventures in the Soviet Imaginary: Children's Books and Graphic Art*, edited by Robert Bird, 25–31. Chicago: University of Chicago Library, 2011.

Brylov, G.D. *Oblozhka knigi. Opyt istoricheskogo issledovaniia*. Leningrad: Izdanie Akademii khudozhestv, 1929.

Chuiko, Vladimir A., ed. *Istoriia tselliulozno-bumazhnoi promyshlennosti Rossii*. Arkhangelsk: RAO Bum-Prom, 2009.

Chukovsky, Kornei. *Dnevnik 1901–1929*. Moscow: Sovetskii pisatel', 1991.

Derrida, Jacques. "Le papier ou moi, vous savez … (Nouvelles spéculations sur un luxe des pauvres)." *Les cahiers de médiologie* 4 (1997): 33–57. https://www.mediologie.org/ancien-site/cahiers-de-mediologie/04_papier/derrida.pdf.

Dirsh, Natal'ia, and Nikolai Popov. *Bumaga*. Kiev: Molodoi bol'shevik, 193[?].

Dobrenko, Evgeny. *The Making of the State Reader: Social and Aesthetic Contexts of the Reception of Soviet Literature*. Translated by Jesse M. Savage. Stanford, CA: Stanford University Press, 1997.

Gitelman, Lisa. *Paper Knowledge: Toward a Media History of Documents*. Durham, NC: Duke University Press, 2014.

Häkli, Esko, ed. *Ingen Dag Utan Papper: Om papper och dess roll som kulturbärare*. Helsingfors, FI: Söderström, 2008.

Il'in, M. *Rasskaz o velikom plane*. Moscow: Gosizdat, 1930.

Il'in, M., and Nikolai Lapshin. *Chernym po belomu: Rasskazy o knigakh*. Moscow: Gosizdat, 1928.

Kelly, Catriona. *Children's World: Growing up in Russia, 1890–1991*. New Haven, CT: Yale University Press, 2007.

– "'A Laboratory for the Manufacture of Proletarian Writers': The *Stengazeta* (Wall Newspaper), Kul'turnost' and the Language of Politics in the Early Soviet Period." *Europe-Asia Studies* 54, no. 4 (2002): 573–602.

Khorkhordina, T.I. *Istoriia i arkhivy*. Moscow: Ros. gos. gumanit. un-t, 1994.

Kobrinets, Fedor, and Isaak Eberil'. *Knizhka-kino-seans o tom, kak pioner Gans stachechnyi komitet spas*. Leningrad: OGIZ-Molodaia gvardiia, 1931.

Kochetkova, Elena. "Modernizatsiia sovetskoi tselliulozno-bumazhnoi promyshlennosti i transfer tekhnologii v 1953–1964 godakh. Sluchai Ėnso-Svetogorska." *Laboratorium* 5, no. 3 (2013): 13–42. www.soclabo.org/index.php/laboratorium/article/view/100/890.

Koenker, Diane P. *Republic of Labor: Russian Printers and Soviet Socialism, 1918–1930*. Ithaca, NY: Cornell University Press, 2005.

Kon, Lidiia. *Sovetskaia detskaia literatura vosstanovitel'nogo perioda, 1921–1925*. Moscow: Gos. izd-vo detskoi literatury, 1955.

Kuznetsov, Erast. "Sovetskoe iskusstvo knigi." In *Knizhnoe iskusstvo SSSR: II: Oformlenie, konstruirovanie, shrift*, edited by Mariia Chegodaeva and Evgeniia Butorina, 7–22. Moscow: Kniga, 1990.

Lenoe, Matthew. "NEP Newspapers and the Origins of Soviet Information Rationing." *Russian Review* 62 (2003): 614–36.

Lovell, Stephen. *The Russian Reading Revolution: Print Culture in the Soviet and Post-Soviet Eras*. London: Palgrave Macmillan, 2000.

Marshak, Samuil, and Sergei Chekhonin. *Knizhka pro knizhki*. Leningrad: Raduga, 1927.

Mashkina, Olga. "The Pulp and Paper Industry Evolution in Russia: A Road of Many Transitions." In *The Evolution of Global Paper Industry 1800–2050: A Comparative Analysis*, edited by Juha-Antti Lamberg, 285–306. Dordrecht: Springer, 2012.

Meksin, Iakov, and Vladimir Konashevich. *Kak Alla khvorala*. Moscow: Gosizdat, 1926.

Mickenberg, Julia. "The New Generation and the New Russia: Modern Childhood as Collective Fantasy." *American Quarterly* 62, no. 1 (2010): 103–34.

Müller, Lothar. *Weiße Magie: Die Epoche des Papiers*. Munich: Hanser, 2012.

Nevskii, Vladimir. "Bor'ba s detskim chteniem." *Krasnyi bibliotekar'*, no. 12 (1924): 21–5.

Nikitin, Evgenii. "Izdatel'stvo Z. I. Grzhebina (1919–1924)." *Kniga. Issledovaniia i materialy* 92, nos. 1–2 (2010): 166–94.

Pilnyak, Boris. *The Naked Year*. Translated by Alexander Tulloch. Ann Arbor, MI: Ardis, 1975.

Pristed, Birgitte Beck. *The New Russian Book: A Graphic Cultural History*. London: Palgrave Macmillan, 2017.

Remnek, Miranda. *The Space of the Book: Print Culture in the Russian Social Imagination*. Toronto: University of Toronto Press, 2011.

Ruggles, Melville J. "Deterioration of Soviet Paper." *American Slavic and East European Review* 19, no. 1 (1960): 101–4.

Safonov, Dmitrii. "Stengazety kak element sovetskoi deistvitel'nosti 1920–1930-kh godov." *Vestnik Orenburgskogo gosudarstvennogo pedagogicheskogo universiteta* 13, no. 1 (2015): 136–55.

Shamrai, A., and B. Poletaev. *Detkory i pionerskaia pechat'*. Moscow: Molodaia gvardiia, 1925.

Shestakov, Nikolai, and Dmitrii Moshchevitin. *Strok dvesti pro knizhkiny bolesti*. Moscow: G.F. Mirimanov, 1925.

Smirnov, Nikolai, Ol'ga Chichagova, and Galina Chichagova. *Detiam o gazete*. Moscow-Petrograd: Gosizdat, 1924.

Thorsheim, Peter. "Salvage and Destruction: The Recycling of Books and Manuscripts in Great Britain during the Second World War." *Contemporary European History* 22 (2013): 431–52.

Vinogradova, Ol'ga. "Tri izmereniia: neskol'ko dokumentov iz arkhiva N. Ogneva: Arkhiv DCh." *Detskie chteniia* 12, no. 2 (2017): 246–79.

Yasen, Yelena. "The Development of Children's Book Illustration in Postrevolutionary Russia." *Design Issues* 8, no. 1 (1991): 57–66.

Zabila, Natal'ia, and Iosif Daits. *Bumazhnyi zmei*. Kiev: Molodoi bol'shevik, 1933.

Zonnenshtral', Ekaterina, and Konstantin Kuznetsov. *Ia pechatnik*. Leningrad: OGIZ-Molodaia gvardiia, 1932.

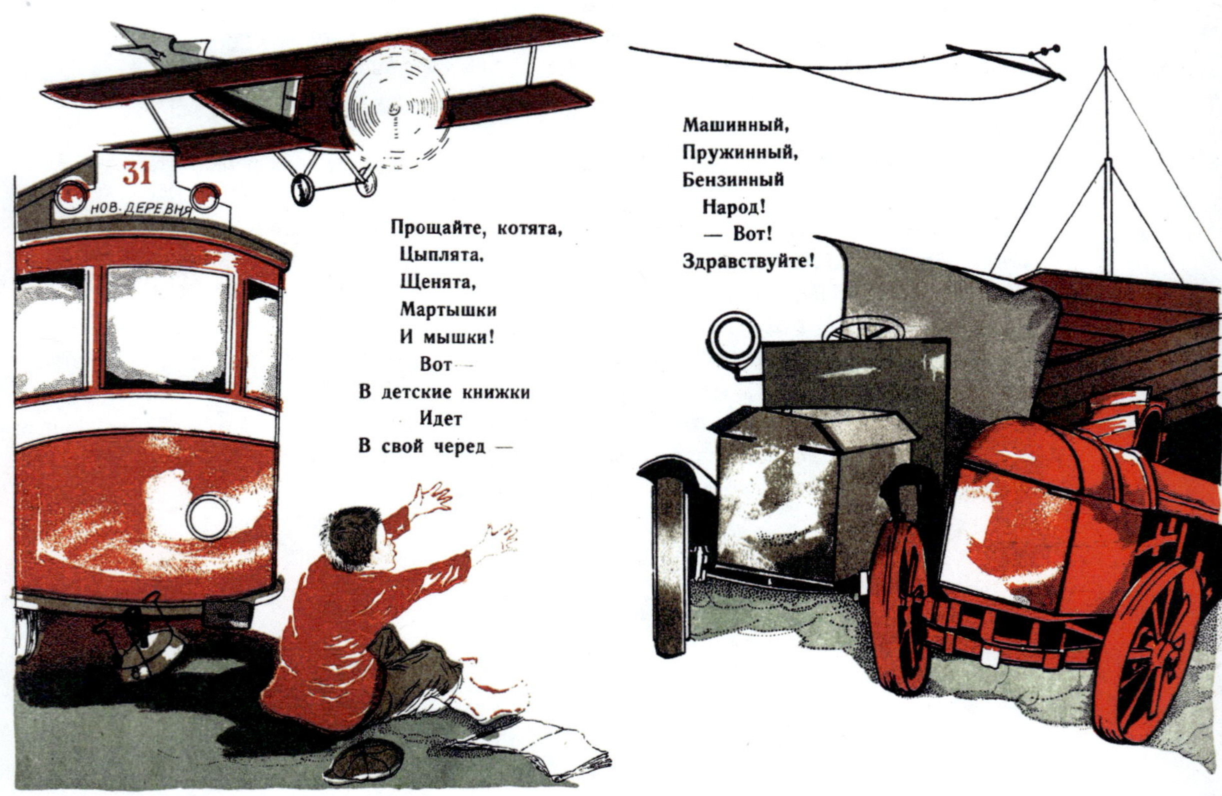

II.1. Aleksei Efimov, a spread in Nikolai Agnivtsev's *Tvoi mashinnye druzia* (*Your Mechanical Friends*) (Leningrad & Moscow: Raduga, 1926). The illustration presents a culmination of a story in which the protagonist decides to make a radical shift and replaces his old friends with new technological options:

> Farewell to you all –
> kittens, puppies, monkeys and mice!
> Children's books
> now host
> new kinds of beings:
> Mechanical,
> Spring-loaded and
> Oil-infused!
> Welcome aboard!

PART II

TECHNOLOGY

In part II, the new Soviet children's book is explored primarily from the standpoint of its representational capacity. In the 1920s and 1930s, the building of a new communist society was associated mostly with creating a new industrial backbone of Soviet life. Communism, to repeat Lenin's famous slogan, equalled "Soviet power plus the electrification of the whole country." As a primer in Soviet modernity, new books for Soviet children informed young readers about new industrial trends, processes, and projects, simultaneously shaping their grammar of perception.

In chapter 6, Larissa Rudova draws our attention to various modalities of engaging with nature as articulated in children's books. Descriptions of radical transformations of the environment – "battles" or "struggles" against nature during the first Five-Year Plan – were accompanied by a type of literature that used anthropomorphism and animation to blur the distinction between nature and culture. In her chapter, Sara Pankenier Weld looks at the other side of the same process by tracing the iconography of hybrid, post-human, and post-social human-machines, ideal biomechanical inhabitants of the coming technological future. As Kirill Chunikhin's chapter convincingly argues, electricity, a major part of this future, posed significant representational challenges. Invisible yet powerful, electricity emerged in children's books as an instance of materialist magic: a wonder and a practical tool at the same time.

In chapter 9, Maria Litovskaya continues the exploration of this dual process of demystifying and enchanting representations of daily objects in the Soviet Union. Focusing on the complementary relationships between verbal and visual elements within a do-it-yourself magazine published in Sverdlovsk, Litovskaya analyses how the magazine developed its readers' technical literacy in the hopes of spurring them to independent technological creativity. Similar concerns are at the centre of Michael Kunichika's chapter. In this case, Viktor Shklovsky's *Turksib* (1930), a story about the construction of the Turkestan-Siberian Railway, is used as an entry point into a discussion about the relationship between vision and modernity in the face of developmental unevenness in Central Asia. Shklovsky's work presents a unique case for the study of how a formalist and modernist writer could train children to envision, and take part in, the construction of the socialist future.

The dynamic imagery of Soviet industrialization is also the focus of Katherine M.H. Reischl's contribution. While her chapter shares Kunichika's thematic concern with the new roads and paths of Soviet modernity, in this case the point of view becomes highly personalized. Her investigation of the fluid sourcing of visual materials – brought to us from the driver's seat of the hydroplane or the aerosleigh – presents the reader with the framework of *vezdekhodnost'*, literally "going-everywhere-ness." Transcending elements and media, technology merges means of transportation with modes of seeing.

chapter six

FROM NATURE TO "SECOND NATURE" AND BACK

LARISSA RUDOVA

We are currently facing a most difficult question: how … to create a literature on the basis of a new world view. We have different methods of dealing with animals. We threw the rabbit across the Urals … We bred the nutria in Colchis and are bringing back the sable population and changing the color of the Arctic fox on the Commander Islands … Nature is controlled not by one person … It is controlled by an entire people.

Viktor Shklovsky

Forests adorn the earth, teach man to understand the beautiful, and instill in him a lofty attitude of mind.

Anton Chekhov

We change Nature in order that people may live better.

Mikhail Il'in

In a 1931 letter to Maxim Gorky, the celebrated author-naturalist Mikhail Prishvin complained: "Only yesterday my children's stories, 'Hedgehog,' 'Little Willow Tits,' 'Rooks,' and others were considered classics, but now nobody would publish a story like this because my animals do not act according to the general line . . . I myself have begun to think about the insignificance of hares and birds in the context of the grand construction."[1] Prishvin, who started his career before the October Revolution, held a "Romantic belief in the child's union with nature."[2] He portrayed animals "like people," with recognizable features of human behaviour and emotions, and taught the young to observe, understand, and respect them. He sought to convey "the soul of nature" in the vein of Leo Tolstoy's "Kholstomer" (1886) and Anton Chekhov's "Kashtanka" (1887), and the ideologization of the natural world in children's books was alien to him. His impassioned letter to Gorky reflects not only his personal frustration with a new direction in nature writing, but also the ideological and aesthetic zeitgeist that radically changed the nature of children's literature.

It is not that animals were no longer portrayed "like people" – they certainly were. Rather, their roles in literature were increasingly reframed to advance new social messages. Books with anthropomorphic animals, for instance, could embody a "creative reconstruction of old variables"[3] and were boldly used in educating children about new Soviet values. We see this transformative creative spirit in Polien Iakovlev's animal tale in verse, *Ezh Bol'shevik* (*Hedgehog the Bolshevik*, 1925), in which a hedgehog organizes a victorious rebellion of the oppressed forest animals against their metaphorical tyrannical "tsar," the boar. Illustrated by Akim Ovanesov, the tale's cute and amicable bears, hares, foxes, and squirrels represent the subjugated classes that turn to the politically savvy and literate hedgehog-the-Bolshevik for protection and guidance. In Ovanesov's visual rendering, the hedgehog is outsized by most forest animals, but the narrative magnifies his political prowess and superiority in dealing with the autocratic boar. The hedgehog organizes the animals under the banner "Down with the Cruel Boar," and with a drumbeat produced by the hare wearing a *budenovka* (a pointed Red Army hat), he leads his united forest troop to the victorious campaign against the boar (fig. 6.1).

In the 1920s and early 1930s, books like Iakovlev's were indispensable for explaining revolutionary changes to children. Their goal was to teach the young – albeit in an entertaining manner – a range of unfamiliar concepts crucial to the creation of a new Soviet mythology, from the proletarian revolution to collectivism, internationalism, Leninism, socialism, class struggle, and industrialization, to name but a few. In numerous debates about the future of children's literature, authors, critics, and pedagogues focused on the issue of "translating communism to children"[4] in order to bring them up as "new people" and "builders of socialism."[5] Admittedly, among the most daring challenges faced by book authors and designers was how to educate millions of children – many of whom were unschooled – about nature, science, technology, and industrial progress in an accessible way and, in the process, to stimulate their interest in socialist construction. New illustrated books about science, technology, and natural phenomena had already begun to appear in the 1920s, but their publication reached its apogee during the tour-de-force unfolding of the first Five-Year Plan (1928–32). The popular "production book" that focused on "how things were made" and worshiped technology and the machine was particularly effective in projecting a vision of the future technocratic utopia.[6] Themes of gigantic socialist construction, fetishization of the machine, and harnessing nature for the benefit of humankind frequently carried direct political messages, but they simultaneously promised positive social and economic changes and captivated many young minds with their optimistic outlook.

Some of these books fascinated the world outside Soviet Russia and became especially popular in the United States, where progressive educators, just like their Soviet colleagues, were looking for ways to raise the new "modern child."[7] One book, *Rasskaz o velikom plane* (published in the USSR in 1930 and translated into English as *New Russia's*

6.1. Akim Ovanesov, cover of Polien Iakovlev, *Ezh Bol'shevik* (Rostov-Don: Burevestnik, 1925). The eponymous hedgehog leads his animal comrades to victory against a tyrannical boar.

Primer: The Story of the Five-Year Plan in 1931), by the science and technology writer Mikhail Il'in (1895–1953),[8] was almost immediately translated into many languages and described by the US National Education Association's journal as "more than significant" and "epochal." Even its sceptical reviewers found the book "mystical, romantic, and thrilling," and it remained a best-seller in the United States throughout 1931.[9]

Central to the primer was the depiction of the radical transformation of nature with the help of science and technology for the benefit of humankind. The industrial fantasy adopted in children's books clearly highlighted changing attitudes toward nature, which would henceforth be represented as subdued, disciplined, and rearranged according to human will. The robust "production book" actively celebrated the transformation of wild nature into rationally organized "culture," which, in a sense, fit into the Soviet leaders' agenda to steer their citizens from natural "spontaneity" to political "consciousness."

This chapter deals with early Soviet children's books that taught children new approaches to nature. I explore how the ideological and cultural currents of the day stimulated the visual aesthetics of these books and reflected the Soviet fixation on constructing a new, organized environment, or "second nature," as Maxim Gorky would put it. While the innovative pro-industrialization book produced gripping fantasy images of the desirable future, conventional nature writing continued to emphasize a binding relationship with the environment and the animal world. I also show that, although children's literature of the time may appear as environmentally hostile in its relentless glamorization of the machine and battling nature, it carried important messages of social progress and material prosperity. It taught young readers how scientific knowledge, rational thinking, and command of technology could empower them in standing up to the destructive forces of nature. The production book also encouraged the young to think how modern urban spaces could be created to take the place of old dirty roads and dilapidated huts. Overall, the educational purpose of these books, constructivist in spirit and style, was utilitarian and followed the general party line. In contrast to them, numerous nature-loving books continued to cultivate an affectionate and bonding relationship with the animal world. Notably, many prominent avant-garde artists (for example, Vladimir Lebedev, Dmitrii Bulanov, Vera Ermolaeva, El Lissitzky, and Vladimir Tatlin) illustrated both production books and books about playful animals, frequently bringing humans, machines, and animals together in a signature constructivist, experimental style that defined the aesthetics of early Soviet children's book culture. Ultimately, the multifaceted pictorial universe of the new children's book included both "nature" and "culture" and provided ground for raising the active Soviet child who would relentlessly reform nature but simultaneously treat it as a "speaking subject."[10]

"Second Nature" for a Better Future

As Perry Nodelman demonstrates in his study of picture books, images in children's books are signs that interpret reality and encourage children to take it for granted, adopting a certain point of view.[11] Since children, especially young children, form their ideas about the world through looking and seeing, the organization of the visual material in a picture inevitably has an impact on how they "perceive, read, and reinterpret their worlds through art."[12] Picture books are ideological spaces for shaping beliefs, promoting social practices, and teaching their audiences how to make connections between the image and the text. Nodelman writes, "We 'see' events ... and people as the narrative invites us to see them," thus making us take a "subject position" from within "the text's ideology."[13] Like many artifacts, picture books carry in them what Fredric Jameson calls "the ideology of form" – that is, "symbolic messages transmitted to us by the coexistence of various sign systems" that are themselves manifestations of political cultures.[14]

It was only a matter of time before images of "romanticized industrialization" would begin to form the core of Soviet culture and sweep through children's literature.[15] The party stressed the "increased need" for Soviet society to "possess the secrets of nature" and use them for the benefit of people.[16] Consequently, the "metaphorical violence" against nature resounded widely in children's books and abounded in words like "colonization" ("kolonizatsiia"), "transformation" ("preobrazovanie"), "cultivation" ("osvoenie"), "war" ("voina"), and "conquest" ("zavoevanie").[17] The new formulation of humankind as nature's master became another expression of the revolutionary spirit of the epoch. The production book was a natural candidate both for fulfilling the Soviet agenda of "Communist character-education" and spearheading the propaganda of industrialization for children.[18] It attracted those avant-garde illustrators who felt an aversion for the past and were eager to destroy it in order to construct the new world both in art and in life. The ideology of movement, change, speed, fragmentation, energy, war, death, the noise of machinery, and other symbols of destruction embraced by the international avant-garde since the birth of futurism promised political and aesthetic regeneration and nourished the imagination of innovative children's book authors and designers. The avant-gardists wanted to be a part of the big political picture, especially in its association with science and technology that promised the amelioration of human life.

There is little doubt that the avant-garde production book played a major role in creating the new Soviet way of seeing nature through verbal and visual narratives and that their new artistic forms, ideas, and themes penetrated into "far deeper levels of consciousness" than Soviet propaganda.[19] However, tempting as it may be to attribute the representation of nature in early Soviet picture books exclusively to the avant-garde aesthetic, it would be a mistake not to mention Maxim Gorky's central role in shaping the visual and verbal ideology in children's book culture. An ardent believer in science and technology and an enthusiastic supporter of "second nature" – the world acculturated by humankind – Gorky called upon children's authors and illustrators to develop the theme of "improving" and "improved" nature, a radically anthropocentric view that he, like many other Bolshevik dreamers, held at the time. For them, nature was dead matter, useful only if reordered and reorganized by people. But for Gorky specifically, nature was also synonymous with the countryside and the peasantry, whom he vehemently resented.[20]

Condemning the poetic "adulation" of "despotic" nature, Gorky appealed to Soviet writers to expose its "nasty tricks," such as "earthquakes, floods, hurricanes, droughts, and … other eruptions and storms of its blind forces." At the same time, he stressed the importance of celebrating the new Soviet people whose "will, intelligence, and imagination" made "second nature" possible.[21] Given Gorky's numerous writings on the subject, it is not difficult to see how he tried to compel authors to write about nature in a programmatic way. Particularly interesting is his article "O temakh" ("About Themes," 1933), in which he proposes the following plot outline for children's authors writing on the topic of nature: show its destructive power, proceed to describe humankind's war against its hostile essence, show how nature could serve humankind, and conclude with the celebration of Soviet labour achievements and victory over the elements.[22] Gorky's guidelines sent an unambiguous message: books about nature had to stay close to the party's industrialization program and become "important documents of the epoch."[23] As Douglas R. Weiner observes, Gorky's writing helped solidify "a new aesthetic and distinctive place for nature in the regime's symbology."[24] It is curious, however, that, despite his rigid formulation of the ideological tasks of children's literature, Gorky came down on both sides of the nature writing issue, pro-industrialization and pro-nature, and continued lending a hand to children's book creators of both persuasions.[25]

Gorky's "reformist" rhetoric on "second nature" nevertheless carried a creative seed that resonated with the artistic avant-garde's dream of re-modelling modern urban life with the help of new technology and architecture. Their own desire was to reshape public spaces beyond recognition by building massive communal residential housing with communal kitchens, cultural and educational centres, recreational areas, libraries, parks, and other constructed structures and spaces. The passive environment had to be actively reorganized for the benefit of people. These ideas were vividly articulated in the works of a leading theoretician and practitioner of constructivist architecture, Moisei Ginzburg. In his writing, he envisioned the obliteration of the border between the "architectural significance of the factory and residential house" and argued that modern urban planning should derive its "creative juice" from industrial construction.[26] He rejected the idea of architecture as an "aesthetic decoration of life" and believed that, rather than embellishing life, architects should "organize" it. It made sense to him that, during the period of industrial transition, "emotions of the aesthetic order" should be subordinated to the functional organization of space. Unsurprisingly, his ideas mesh with Gorky's statements about bypassing emotional attitudes to nature and replacing them with a more utilitarian one. The practical application of these ideas resulted in a functional, constructivist aesthetic of children's books dealing with the creation of "second nature."

The Production Book: Education for Modernity

From the late 1920s until the end of Stalinism, a great number of children's authors became involved in fulfilling the party's command to draw the young generation's attention to the agenda of industrialization.[27] Typically, their books featured a dynamic adventure plot unfolding against the background of gigantic socialist construction. Such period texts as *New Russia's Primer* (1930) and *Gory i liudi* (*Mountains and People*, 1932) by Mikhail Il'in; *Kara Bugaz* and *Kolkhida* by Konstantin Paustovsky; *Turksib* (1930) by Viktor Shklovsky; and *Tansyk* (1930) by Aleksei Kozhevnikov, adopted a "transformational" attitude toward nature. The great futurist poet Vladimir

Mayakovsky famously contributed his commanding voice to the campaign to wake up and overhaul dormant nature in his poem about Kuznetskstroi, one of the giant industrial construction sites in Siberia, written at the beginning of the first Five-Year Plan and at the end of his life:

<table>
<tr><td>

Here,
    explosions will roar
to chase away
    gangs of bears,
and the coal mines
    of the gigantic factory
        will blow up
            the depth
                of the earth.
Here,
    construction sites
      will grow
        like walls.
Sound your sirens,
        Steam!
We'll put Siberia

    on fire
      with sun-hot
        open-hearth
          furnaces.

</td><td>

Здесь
    взрывы закудахтают
в разгон
    медвежьих банд,
и взроет
    недра
      шахтою
стоугольный
    «Гигант».
Здесь
    встанут
      стройки
        стенами.
Гудками,
    пар,
      сипи.
Мы
    в сотню солнц
        мартенами
воспламеним
      Сибирь.[28]

</td></tr>
</table>

Commenting on children's books about the first Five-Year Plan, the artist Boris Grozevskii emphasized that "art, especially graphic art, is a strong and powerful weapon of class struggle," and publishers should pay more attention to their design standards.[29] The book market at the time was in fact saturated with illustrated books about industrialization for children of all ages.[30] But finding innovative visual codes to represent the great Soviet experiment in modernization was challenging. On the one hand, artists had to commit to the social prerogatives of the Bolshevik agenda; on the other, they had a penchant for an "infantilist aesthetic," an "escape into childhood, into play, into lighter and smaller forms, into the modeling of a world of 'make-believe.'"[31] New picture books found a solution to these seemingly irreconcilable issues and came to embody the very essence of the artistic avant-garde: "its enthusiastic impulse toward a de-psychologized technicism and its reductive impulse to the simplest of archaic structures."[32]

Il'in's heavily illustrated *New Russia's Primer* became "a literary paean to the First Five-Year Plan,"[33] educating a whole generation of young Soviet readers about the party's program of sweeping industrial development.[34] The primer's focus on "mammoth construction projects" and its depiction of "a gigantic battle with nature"[35] marked a tangible departure from pre-revolutionary standards of the romantic treatment of the environment. Together with his numerous other industrial epics,[36] Il'in's primer emanates a spirited rhetoric of battle for the creation of "second nature." It explains why modernization is necessary ("We build factories in order that there may be no poverty, no filth, no sickness, no unemployment, no exhausting labour"), progressive, and achievable, and correlates it with the party's goal to make life happy, "rational," and "just."[37] Casting aside the emotional contemplation of nature, he proposes a radically new way of looking at it: "If from a car window you see only wasteland, forests, and swamps, you see nothing. Wastelands are clay, sand, and stone. Forests are beams, rafters, staves, and ties. Peat swamps are electric current. Out of clay and sand we make bricks; out of clay and lime, cement; out of iron ore, steel. We must find raw materials."[38]

Combined with a new attitude towards labour and armed with machines, Soviets acquire unlimited possibilities in altering the environment for their benefit: "A great new power has appeared in Nature – the power of human labour. Not only the blind forces of Nature, but also the conscious, organized, planned labour of man now fashions rivers and lakes, plants forests, and transforms deserts, moderates and accelerates the flow of waters, creates new substances and new species of plants and animals."[39]

Abundant constructivist illustrations by Mikhail Razulevich (1904–1993) expertly reinforce Il'in's enthusiastic vision of Soviet modernity. Razulevich's striking cover design of the first edition of *New Russia's Primer* plays with scale and unambiguously privileges machines over humans (fig. 6.2). The cover composition featuring heavy industrial equipment leaves just a small chunk of space in the bottom right corner for a group of happy human faces that observe the machine world with awe and admiration. In the early years of industrialization, Razulevich's cover was subject to criticism for replacing real people by an agglomeration of dead things, and he decided to put the figures of two monumental male workers on the cover of the third (1931) and fourth (1933) editions, in compliance with the Stalinist new slogan "People make all the difference" (fig. 6.3).[40] But it is Razulevich's original book cover that sums up the main characteristics of what John McCannon calls a "five-year plan culture" – namely, its "tremendous preoccupation with the machine" and an apparent "antagonism towards nature and the elements."[41]

Razulevich's design for the book's interior is in tune with the constructivist organization of visual space.[42] Most of his images are repetitive and exclude humans and the natural world altogether. When people are included in the composition, they appear in positions subsidiary or complementary to the machines. The use of

6.2. Mikhail Razulevich's cover of the first edition of Mikhail Il'in, *Rasskaz o velikom plane* (Moscow & Leningrad: GIZ, 1930) privileges machines over humans.

photographs and photomontage, new techniques in book illustration pioneered by the constructivist photographer Gustav Klucis, was widespread in the 1920s and 1930s. In children's books, it was an effective form of educational propaganda because it emphasized the "objective" and "scientific" character of the narrated events.[43] Razulevich's photomontage in the primer advantageously enhanced the documentary character of Il'in's story. His rhythmically arranged photographs harmoniously, if not literally, blended with the text focused sharply on Soviet industrial achievement. Ultimately, the graphics of the primer confirmed the elements of the constructivist aesthetic: "the glorification . . . of the machine, of the diagram, the plan, of headlong forward motion," as well as "devaluation of simple, old human values"[44] (figs. 6.4 and 6.5).

A similar pictorial consciousness runs through another signature children's book of the time, Samuil Marshak's poem "Voina s Dneprom" ("The War against the Dnieper," 1931), illustrated by Georgii Bibikov. Marshak's poem initially presents the environment as "disorderly" and "chaotic," "almost as a consciously antisocialist force

6.3. Razulevich's cover for the third edition of Mikhail Il'in, *Rasskaz o velikom plane* (Moscow & Leningrad: GIZ, 1931) devotes more space to (male) workers.

that needs to be suppressed."[45] In its treatment of nature, this poem presents perhaps one of the most radical examples of teaching an aggressive attitude toward nature. Marshak's text destroys the emotional connection between people and nature when his Man-the-Conqueror, armed with technology, challenges the Dnieper. The poet anthropomorphizes the river but presents it as obstinate and capricious. He proceeds to threaten it:

Man said to the Dnieper:	Человек сказал Днепру:
I shall block you with a wall	– Я стеной тебя запру.
So that	Ты с вершины
You will fall from the heights	Будешь прыгать,
So that	Ты
You will	Машины
Move	Будешь
Machines	Двигать!
– "No," said the water,	– Нет,- ответила вода –
"Never and not for anything."	Ни за что и никогда!

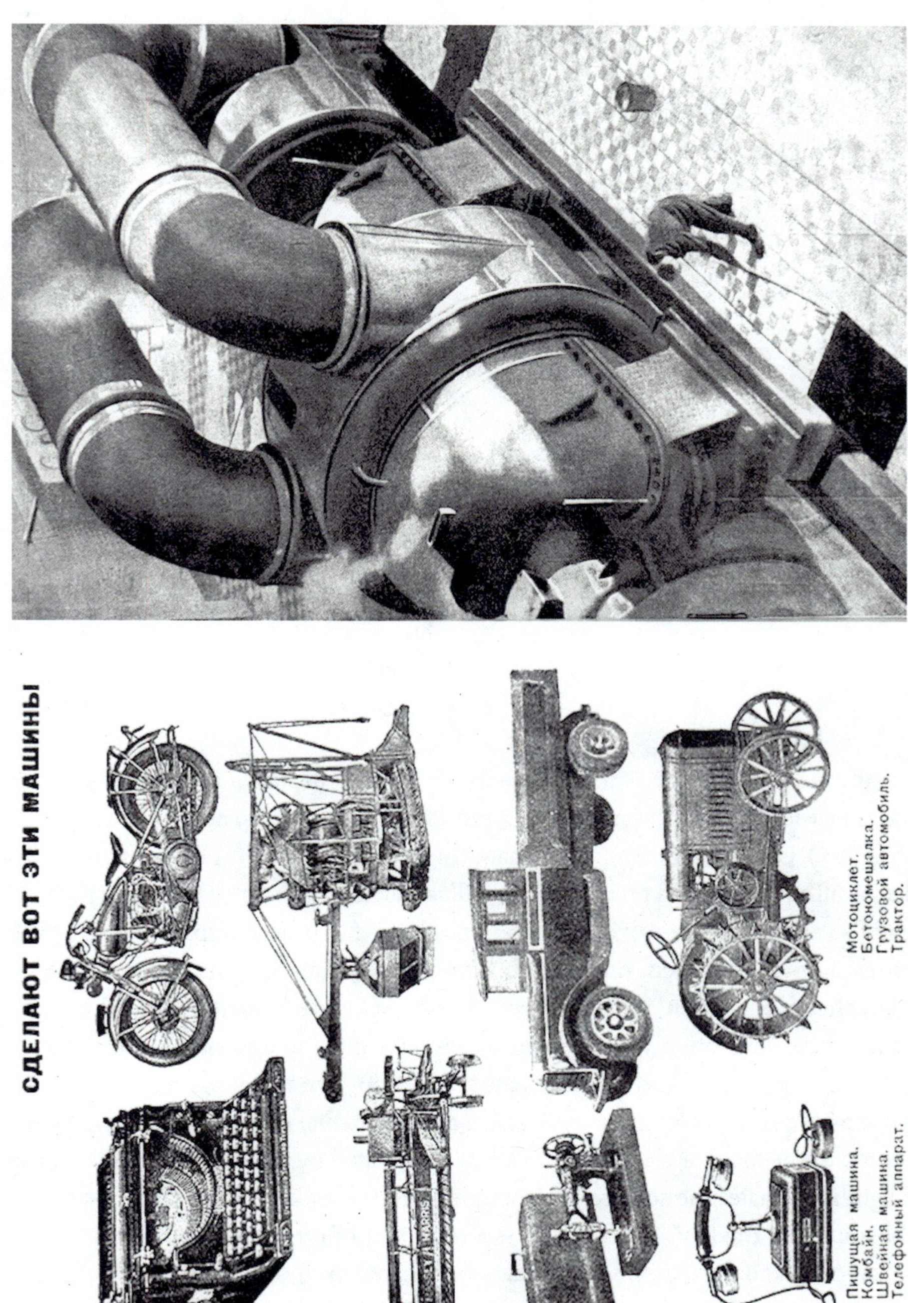

6.4. and 6.5. Mikhail Razulevich's illustrations for the third edition of Mikhail Il'in, *Rasskaz o velikom plane* (Moscow & Leningrad: GIZ, 1931).

When the stubborn and unruly river does not obey, it is forcefully silenced, punished, defeated, and finally ruled by humans. In the end, people profit from their actions:

Where there used to be reeds,	Где вчера качались лодки –
The steam engine is now running.	Заработали лебедки.
Where fish used to splash,	Где шумел речной тростник –
Dynamite is blowing up rocks.	Разъезжает паровик.
…	Где вчера плескались рыбы –
So that	Динамит взрывает глыбы.
The plough	…
Is moved	Чтобы
Along the black soil	Плуг
By electricity.	По чернозему
So that	Электричество
There is light	Вело.
In the street	Чтобы
And in homes	Улице
In the evening.	И дому
	Было
	Вечером
	Светло![46]

On the cover of the first edition of the book, Bibikov depicts a monumental image of a worker with a huge jackhammer in a position of readiness to attack the rebellious river (fig. 6.6). On the following pages, images of technology and of collectives of faceless workers – all equipped with powerful tools – illustrate the assault on nature, and pictures of dead fish and a multitude of construction machines fill the visual space (fig. 6.7). The gigantic scale of the depicted construction, dominated by cranes, trains, bridges, tractors, and other heavy equipment visually marginalizes the poetic text on the page. Ultimately, in the last three illustrations, Bibikov completely substitutes images of the Dnieper with an urbanist vision of a future without nature (fig. 6.8). The visual narrative concludes with the triumph of Soviet industrialization: a monumental constructivist-style building with a tower that pierces the evening sky, dominated by a massive dirigible whose floodlight illuminates the science-fictionesque scene. In looking at the last illustration, it is obvious that Bibikov's visual world is a reflection of the artistic spirit of the time: organization, standardization, schematization, dynamism, and a gigantic scale and size of new architectural structures reminiscent of Ginzburg's ideas about modern urban planning. Ginzburg thought that the new architectural style would present "a gigantic new world in which not a single achievement of modern genius will remain underused or uninvolved in the common creative stream." To him, "poetry and romanticism are

6.6. Georgii Bibikov's front cover for Samuil Marshak, *Voina s Dneprom* (Moscow: Molodaia gvardiia, 1931) features a worker ready to attack the unruly river with a jackhammer.

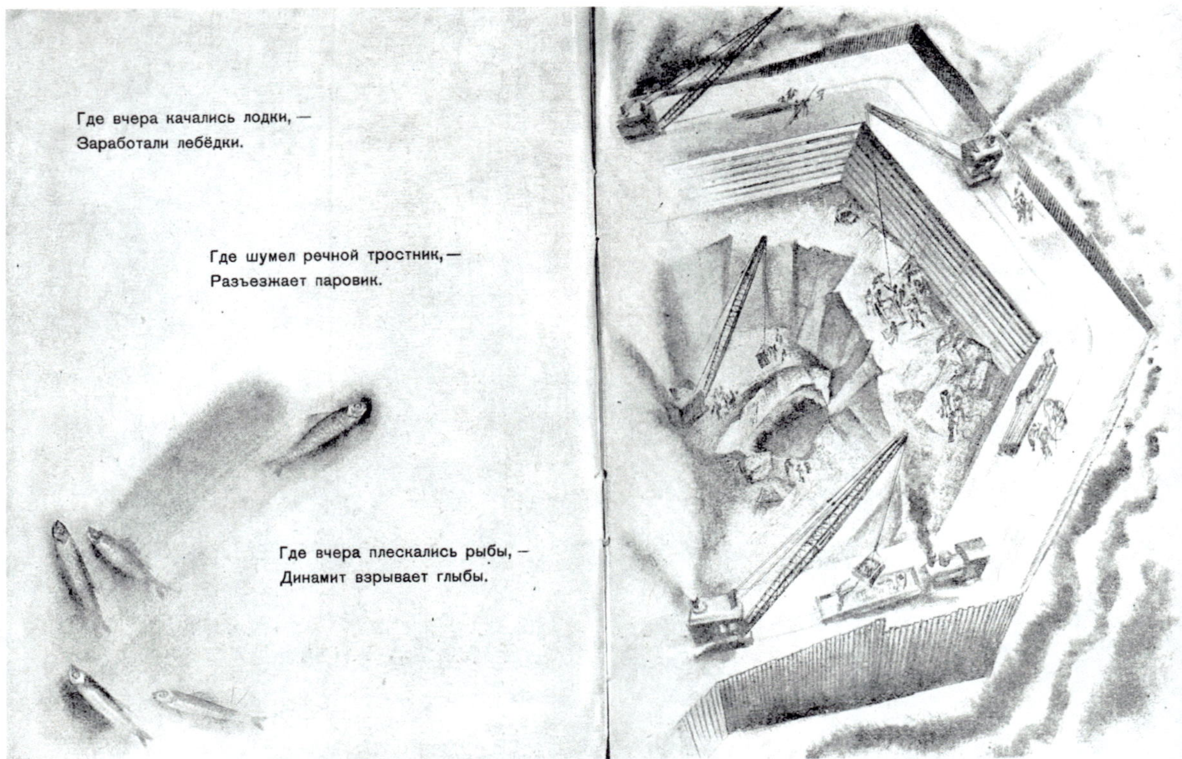

6.7. An illustration of Georgii Bibikov's in *Voina s Dneprom* depicts the result of technology conquering nature.

not there where fragrant hothouse flowers grow," but rather in the newly organized vivacious spirit of the streets and "monumental-dynamic architectural creations."[47]

A telling example of the new organization of space is the picture book *Park kul'tury i otdykha* (*Park of Culture and Leisure*, 1930), illustrated by Valerii Alfeevskii and Tat'iana Lebedeva (Mavrina). In contrast to their production picture book, *Na iakore* (*At Anchor*, 1931), dominated by huge ships, cranes, trains, and enormous port structures, *Park* is filled with pictures of highly structured public spaces in which people relax, play sports, read, eat, and stroll around. This new urban park is also a true place of culture (fig. 6.9).[48] One picture after another portrays the happy dynamic world of a future paradise that also includes nature: grass, trees, flowerbeds, an artificial pond, and a lake. In these pictures, nature is safe and functionally organized to provide people with comfort. The illustrators clearly savoured every detail in their imaginary park and painted them in bright and warm colours. The message of this and similar children's books was unambiguous: we need to improve the environment in order to enjoy a better life.

6.8. Georgii Bibikov's urbanist vision in *Voina s Dneprom*.

6.9. A beautiful place of recreation for new Soviet people, a park is also a place for enlightenment. This scene presents "Book Day" (written on the banner). The centre of the illustration is occupied by a pavilion with children's books, and the tower on the right has a logo of the State Publishing House (GIZ). Valerii Alfeevskii and Tat'iana Lebedeva, ill., *Park kul'tury i otdykha* (Moscow: Gosizdat, 1930).

Nature Back into Culture

While the production book establishes a visual plot that regulates and "organizes" nature and turns the new Soviet person into its operator, the animal book goes in the opposite direction. In early Soviet children's literature, the non-human creatures that populate the natural world are rarely touched by historical forces. The pictorial animal world moves, breathes, and entertains the child in a variety of visual styles and narrative scenarios. If the production book caters to reason and logic, the animal book, in contrast, appeals to the imagination and emotion. As we have seen earlier, the production book is a double-edged sword. On one hand, it educates the child about dealing with nature in such a way that would eventually lead to a better life for people. On the other hand, the utopia presented in it hinges on what Lucas Bessire describes as "apocalyptic futurism" – that is, on the destruction of the old way of life and temporality whereby the bond between people and nature is irrevocably severed.[49] Technology, as fascinating and powerful as it is, becomes "both vehicle and sign for the end of time"[50] and a separation between human and non-human worlds.

In the animal book, entirely different processes take place. Here, the pedagogical imagery trains the child's eye to see non-human creatures in the context of intercommunicability – not separation but unity, although perhaps with some distancing.[51] These books tell us that animals are our friends – that they are adorable and emotionally close to us and should be understood and treated with respect. Therefore, the animal book takes the reader into the world of "social relations –" that is, relations between humans and non-humans, and shrinks the gap between nature and culture that we see in the production book.[52] We see then that picture books about animals teach children to adopt a point of view that is profoundly "ecological" and emotional.

Although in the 1920s there were picture books that taught children Soviet homiletics and new cultural values, they were relatively few in the vein of Polien Iakovlev's *Hedgehog the Bolshevik*.[53] Most animal books fell into two categories: playful and naturalistic. The former group was particularly popular with avant-garde artists, as it offered a wide range of artistic possibilities. In 1922, Vladimir Lebedev captured the animated spirit of living nature in his *Slonenok* (*The Little Elephant*), based on a Rudyard Kipling story. It was an immediate success in the artistic world, and it soon became clear that his illustrations were "the manifesto of a new approach to children's book graphics."[54] Lebedev's animals were playful and mischievous and displayed elements of the avant-garde aesthetic (for example, one-dimensionality, schematization, "discarded details and connections," and unhinged composition) (fig. 6.10).[55] Arguably, no Russian artist before him had illustrated the animal world in so happy and topsy-turvy a manner. His influence on cutting-edge Soviet book illustration in the 1920s was immense,[56] but other talented artists also created

6.10. The playful animals in Vladimir Lebedev's illustrations in *Slonenok* displayed elements of the avant-garde aesthetic. Rudyard Kipling, *Slonenok* (*The Elephant's Child*), translated by Kornei Chukovsky (Petrograd: Gosudarstvennoe izdatel'stvo, 1922).

memorable images of remarkable animals for children, among them, Vladimir Konashevich, Vladimir Tatlin, Kirill Zdanevich, Lidia Popova, Dmitrii Bulanov, Evgenii Charushin, Iurii Pimenov, Teodor Pevzner, and Eduard Krimmer.

Generally, in the 1920s picture book animals had a wonderful life, "often expressing views at odds with rationalistic emphasis on the teleology of socialization."[57] Animals courted and married each other, talked on the phone, dressed up for hunting, played musical instruments and danced, and, on the whole, were disarmingly adorable.[58] Overall, Lebedev's animals were a significant contribution to children's book illustration, not only because they epitomized the experimental approach to training the child's eye in the new aesthetic, but also because they were among the first in early Soviet children's literature to appeal to the emotional world of the child. In his pictorial world, animals, despite their different shape from humans, act and play tricks like small children. They are plainly funny, entertaining, and joyful. In a predominantly peasant culture that was still barely literate, these books played a not insignificant role in the education of children's feelings.

Village children were unlikely to romanticize animals and, like their parents, treated them from a utilitarian perspective. For them, animals were either a source of food or means of transportation, guardians of the house or some other asset, but hardly frivolous, useless pets. Wild animals in particular did not inspire any attachment in village populations. In his 1925 summer travel diaries, Nikolay Punin recalls common attitudes to animals in provincial Russia:

> From my travels this summer I've gathered a general impression of provincial Russia. Most of all from conversations in the country (leaving out the local nuns), about wolves, and in the towns and cities, about mad dogs. Rabies, according to statistical evidence, has reached unprecedented proportions, and moreover occurs throughout Russia. The whole way people complained about the wolves and told of all kinds of terrible things … Of art – not a word, from no one, it doesn't exist.[59]

However, an artistic treatment of animal life appears in children's books that then begin slowly to reach the provinces. Going against the grain of the utilitarian treatment of animals, the art of Lebedev and other early Soviet illustrators, perhaps inadvertently, brought the "soul" and emotions of the animal closer to the child. Art thus played a role in acculturating and sensitizing the child to the natural world.[60] Unlike nature in the production book, animals were allowed to be playful and spontaneous, completely avoiding the general line of Soviet politics.

Yet playful animals defied the authority of conservative Soviet pedagogues, who became heavily involved in a heated discussion about the "correct" way to portray animals in children's books. In essence, the polemic – primarily in the pages of the short-lived but highly influential journal *Kniga detiam* (*Books for Children*, 1928–30) – focused on the pedagogical and ideological impact of anthropomorphism and animism on the child's mind. The proponents of anthropomorphic animals argued that these features were crucial for the development of the child's imagination and sense of humour, as well as their understanding of and interest in living nature.[61] Walking a fine line, even Anatoly Lunacharsky, the first Soviet people's commissar of education, spoke up in favour of anthropomorphism and animism.[62] Predictably, the main adversaries of playful animals in children's literature consisted of ideologically inclined literary critics and educators. They went as far as to claim that anthropomorphism and animism slowed down the child's cognitive processes and even caused a waste of nervous energy.[63] The powerful Nadezhda Krupskaia, Lenin's widow and the deputy minister of education at the time, straightforwardly dismissed playful animals in *Pravda*: "Animals acting like people are ridiculous."[64] Yet prosecuting picture books about living nature proved to be challenging, especially in the case of naturalistic literature (*prirodovedcheskaia literatura*), which educated the young reader about natural phenomena and their interconnectedness.

Love Thy Nature: The *Prirodovedy*

In the 1920s and 1930s, a sizeable group of nature writers (*prirodovedy*) continued the tradition of pre-revolutionary writing. Many of them, like Mikhail Prishvin, were already established before the revolution and had a background in natural sciences, but others, such as the writer-illustrator Evgenii Charushin and animal trainer Vladimir Durov, joined later. The worlds of their books took the readers away from Stalinist industrialization and taught a sensitive approach to nature. Numerous picture books by Vitalii Bianki and Charushin – who also illustrated Bianki's works – focused on the observation and understanding of nature and fostered a humanistic, "ecological" attitude. A keen observer of nature, Bianki was a "fresh breath of air" in children's literature about nature.[65]

Bianki was popular with different age groups: some of his stories were derived from fairy tales while others were "biographies" or adventures of animals and birds. Among the illustrators of Bianki's books were, besides Charushin, Nikolai Tyrsa and Petr Miturich, whose artistic sensibilities were pronouncedly modernist. In comparison with the schematic, depersonalized, and alienating depiction of the human world in the popular production book, the living world created by these illustrators was liberated and liberating.

In Bianki's *Pervaia okhota* (*First Hunt*, 1928), illustrated by Miturich and Vera Khlebnikova-Miturich, the main character, Puppy, performs his "rite of passage" in hunting and moves from one animal, bird, or insect to the next, trying to understand what they are. Bianki unobtrusively "psychologizes" the puppy's world through an omniscient narrator, representing the animal's inner thoughts. The visual images follow the narrative very closely, recording the puppy's facial expressions as he reacts to different creatures surrounding him. The attention to detail is extraordinary in both the verbal and visual texts, and, despite the illustrators' "primitivist" style, the natural world here appears in striking complexity. The puppy, in their interpretation, is not a terrible predator but a naïve metaphorical child exploring the world by making both observations and mistakes. Miturich and Khlebnikova were criticized for failing to create a realist image of an active and aggressive hunting dog by making his animal inquisitive and lovable (fig. 6.11).[66] Despite his outstanding contribution to naturalistic literature, Bianki, like Miturich, was considered not "sufficiently Soviet"[67] and was accused of "idealism, fantasy, and mysticism," as well as of "confusing children's understanding of nature and leading them away from reality."[68] Especially disturbing for the ideological critics was Bianki's occasionally "incorrect" negative image of humans who were portrayed as the "violators" of nature's harmony and as "thieves of its riches."[69]

Like Bianki's, Charushin's books avoid the "cold rationalism" of "transformational" literature of Il'in and educate the reader by "impacting their souls" and inciting in them a passionate and honest love of nature.[70] His stories are simple, but his animal characters are free from dry "scientific" depiction. In *Volchishko* (*Little Wolf*, 1931), the eponymous protagonist is caught by a man and brought to his home in a bag. In the course of the story, the wolf cub learns how to live with the man and the animals in his house (fig. 6.12)

6.11. One of Petr Miturich and Vera Khlebnikova-Miturich's illustrations for Vitalii Bianki, *Pervaia okhota* (Moscow: Molodaia gvardia, 1928). The illustrators were criticized for their unrealistic images of the young dog.

6.12. In this illustration from Evgenii Charushin's *Volchishko* (Moscow: Detizdat TsKVLKSM, 1938), a captured wolf cub becomes domesticated.

but eventually becomes lonely and runs away to the woods. The pictorial narrative shows how the initially timid and scared cub becomes secure and playful in his new home. Charushin's representation of the natural world in which people are not the master but a guest or friend made him the target of critical attacks. Although he depicts the characters in *Little Wolf* realistically, the story was labelled "harmful" for its "false notions of animal life" and "fairy-tale" mood.[71]

Conclusion: Educational Messages

The 1920s and 1930s were a time of modelling the new world, the new Soviet person, and the new culture. In the atmosphere of the restructuring of social and intellectual ecosystems, nature- and animal-friendly children's literature created a verbal and visual universe that bypassed the scientific utopianism of Gorky's vision of "improved" nature. While Soviet pedagogues treated whimsy and humour with distrust and suspicion, playful children's books created by avant-garde illustrators compensated for the stillness and dryness of the objectified human and natural world evidenced in production book. The naturalist book, on the other hand, imperceptibly taught children to establish a social relationship with nature. By treating nature as a different culture that one should understand and respect – not abuse or enslave according to human will – *prirodovedy* openly taught the ethics of "social relations"[72] with the living world. In essence, their ideological and ethical position, reinforced by skilful illustrations, supported the development of a child's "ecological identity" based on the conscientious interaction with "living and breathing" nature.[73]

While the avant-gardist production book aimed at inspiring the first Soviet generation of children to become active creators of the new world as workers, engineers, technical designers, and scientists, the message of authors of animal books to love and understand wild creatures was not lost on young readers. These authors and illustrators also participated in the publication of such Soviet periodicals as *V masterskoi prirody* (*In Nature's Workshop*, 1919–29), *Novyi Robinson* (*New Robinson*, initially called *Vorobei* [*The Sparrow*], 1923–5), and *Iunye naturalisty* (*Young Naturalists*, 1928–41), revered by the Soviet-wide Young Naturalist movement (*iunnaty*).[74] The art of these authors and illustrators most definitely resonated with the Young Naturalists, who conducted serious research and scientific observation of "undisturbed nature."[75] Characteristically, early Soviet picture books about nature and animals sent the young reader multiple and contradictory messages, reflecting the political complexity of the time. Thus, some of the Young Naturalists' leaders who promoted a careful treatment and study of nature adhered to the government doctrines of nature transformation, and consequently had "a great capacity to confuse the developing minds of older youths."[76] Even the most vocal popularizer of the "second nature" ideology, Gorky, seemed to be back-tracking from his position when he eulogized Prishvin's masterful prose for its "pantheism," "panpsychism," "geo-optimism," and a connection with "something ancient, oracular, and profanely beautiful."[77] In sum, picture books about nature educated the new Soviet child about the liberating power of science and technology in transforming nature for the sake of the people, but simultaneously emphasized that all wild creatures of the world had to be loved and respected. In these books, the utilitarian impulse thus met the emotional, as authors and illustrators celebrated both one and the other in a variety of representational artistic styles from different ideological perspectives.

NOTES

1 *Gor'kii i sovetskie pisateli*, 360.
2 Nikolajeva, *Aesthetic Approaches to Children's Literature*, 54.
3 Nikolajeva, *The Magic Code*, 116.
4 See Oushakine, "Translating Communism for Children."
5 Lunacharsky, Preface, 4; Khanin, "Bor'ba za detskogo pisatelia," 4.
6 For an in-depth discussion of the constructivist "production book" for children, see Steiner, *Stories for Little Comrades*, 111–68.
7 Mickenberg, "The New Generation," 129.
8 Mikhail Il'in's real name was Il'ia Iakovlevich Marshak. He was the younger brother of the celebrated children's book writer Samuil Marshak (1887–1964), whose work is discussed by Birgitte Beck Pristed in chapter 5.
9 Mickenberg, "The New Generation," 103.
10 In ecocriticism, the concept of nature as a "speaking subject" is essential for its liberation from humankind and the re-establishment of a connection between subject and object. For example, see Smith, "Dropping the Subject."
11 Nodelman initially developed his ideas on picture books in his seminal study, *Words about Pictures: The Narrative Art of Children's Picture Books*.
12 Albers, "Theorizing Visual Representation," 179. See also Berger, *Ways of Seeing*. On the interaction between the text and the visual image, see Nikolajeva, *Aesthetic Approaches to Children's Literature*, 223–9.
13 Nodelman, "Decoding the Images," 75. On ideology in picture books, see also Nikolajeva and Scott, *How Picturebooks Work*.
14 Jameson, *The Political Unconscious*, 98.
15 Bolotova, "The State, Geology and Nature," 103.
16 See, for example, Kovalev, Miasnikov, and Onufriev, eds., *Ocherk istorii russkoi sovetskoi literatury*.
17 Dobrenko, "Nadzirat'-nakazyvat'-nadzirat'," 671.
18 O'Dell, *Socialisation through Children's Literature*, 59.
19 Steiner, *Stories for Little Comrades*, 6.
20 On the formative sources of Gorky's anthropocentric views, see Agursky, "Velikii eretik." Also, Serguei Oushakine offers a stimulating discussion of Gorky's perspective on the industrial and technological transformation of nature and its connection with the creation of the new

socialist man, see Oushakine, "The Flexible and the Pliant." For the Russian-language version of the article, see Oushakine, "Pole boia na fone prirody."

21 Gorky, "O biblioteke poeta," 181. For more detailed analysis of Gorky's views on nature, see Dobrenko, *Politekonomiia sotsrealizma*. See also Gorky's own article, "O kul'ture" (1928).

22 Gorky, "O temakh," in *M. Gorky o detskoi literature*, 125.

23 Gorky, "Literaturu – detiam," 115.

24 Weiner, *Models of Nature*, 170.

25 Gorky emphasized the task of promoting nature and geography education, stressing the empirical studies of chemistry, biology, zoology, and indigenous cultures. See Gorky's article "Literaturu – detiam," 112–16.

26 Ginzburg, "Kharakternye cherty novogo stilia."

27 Lupanova, *Polveka*, 166.

28 Mayakovsky, "Rasskaz Khrenova o Kuznetskstroe i o liudiakh Kuznetska," 264. Mayakovsky's approach to nature is also well captured in his poem "Vladikavkaz-Tiflis" (1924), which contains the line "Breaking is not a shame in construction!" (*Dlia stroiki ne zhal' lomanii*).

29 Grozovskii, "Detskaia kniga o piatiletke," 3.

30 See, for example, Pavel Lopatin, *Piatiletka v deistvii*; Laptev, *Piatiletka*; A. Lopatin, *Tretii reshaiushii*; Kholodnyi, *Piatiletka*; Mislavskii, *Denprostroi*; Kirsanov, *Piatiletka*; Il'in, *Chto my stroim*.

31 Steiner, *Stories for Little Comrades*, 9. On the concept of "infantilist aesthetics," see Weld, *Voiceless Vanguard*.

32 Steiner, *Stories for Little Comrades*, 8–9.

33 McCannon, "Technological and Scientific Utopias," 161.

34 Between 1930 and 1936, six editions of *New Russia's Primer* were published, with circulation ranging from 50,000 to 100,000 copies.

35 McCannon, "Technological and Scientific Utopias," 159.

36 For instance, *New Russia's Primer.* (1930), *Kak chelovek stal velikanom* (*Working Giants, As Man Became Giant*, 1946), *Pokorenie prirody* (*The Subjugation of Nature*, 1950), and *Mountains and People: Stories of the Transformation of Nature* (1932), to name a few.

37 Il'in, *New Russia's Primer*, 16–17.

38 Ibid., 18.

39 Ibid., 143.

40 Karasik, *Udarnaia kniga sovetskoi detvory*, 128.

41 McCannon, "Technological and Scientific Utopias," 159.

42 For the use of photography and photomontage in children's books of 1920s and 1930s, see Karasik, *Udarnaia kniga sovetskoi detvory*.

43 Ibid., 4.

44 Steiner, *Stories for Little Comrades*, 175.

45 Weiner, *Models of Nature*, 169.

46 Marshak, *Voina s Dneprom*.

47 Ginzburg, "Kharakternye cherty novogo stilia."

48 In his book *Das sowjetische Jahrhundert: Archäologie einer Untergegangenen Welt*, Karl Schlögel emphasizes the important role of parks in the acculturation of people in early Soviet Russia. Gorky Park in Moscow was meant to be a "combine of happy life" (423), a space where 1930s migrants from villages into the city were given a chance to "escape their backwardness" (428) and where, "after the destruction of rural Russia and the great leap into the industrial age" (429), peasants became urban workers. With the consolidation of Soviet society in the 1950s and the shift from relentless social mobilization toward modest private

happiness (433), the Soviet park, with the model of Gorky Park, began to lose its central sociopolitical function.

49 Bessire, *Behold the Black Caiman*, 128–9. See also de Castro, "Exchanging Perspectives."

50 Bessire, *Behold the Black Caiman*, 128.

51 The notion of "intercommunicability" between humans and non-humans and their spiritual bond is discussed in de Castro, "Exchanging Perspectives," especially, 425–6.

52 "Social relations" between humans and non-humans presuppose a "spiritual unity" despite corporeal diversity, according to de Castro's study. See ibid., 465–6.

53 Husband, "'Correcting Nature's Mistakes,'" 303.

54 Steiner, *Stories for Little Comrades*, 42. Steiner discusses the innovative aspects of *The Little Elephant* on 42–6.

55 Ibid., 43.

56 Ibid., 51.

57 Kelly, *Children's World*, 82.

58 See, for example, Kornei Chukovsky, *Mukhina svad'ba* (*The Fly's Wedding*), illustrated by Vladimir Konashevich, 1924; Kornei Chukovsky, *Telefon* (*Telephone*), illustrated by Konstantin Rudakov, 1926; *Zaitchik* (*Little Bunny*), illustrated by Vera Ermolaeva, 1923; Kornei Chukovsky, *Svinki* (*Little Piggies*), illustrated by Konstantin Rudakov, 1929; and Natan Vengrov, *Myshata* (*Little Mice*), illustrated by Vera Ermolaeva, 1918.

59 Punin, *The Diaries, 1904–1953*, quoted in Rothenstein and Budashevskaya, *Inside the Rainbow*, 163.

60 Contemporary psychological research shows that children's books about animals in fact make young children attribute human-like characteristics to them. Animal books also affect the child's conceptual perception of animals. See Ganea et al., "Do Cavies Talk?"

61 Flerina, Kasatkina, and Pokrovskaia, "Tezisy ob antropomorfizme," 7.

62 Lunacharsky, "Puti detskoi knigi," 8.

63 For the discussion on animism and anthropomorphism in children's literature at the end of the 1920s, see the following sources: Kasatkina's comments in Romanenko, "Tezisy po voprosu ob antropomorfizme," 3; Prushitskaia, "Predely antropomorfizma v detskoj knizhke," 4; Molozhavyi, "Po voprosu o realizme," 7; Mikini, "Predel dopustimosti antropomorfizma"; and Lundberg, "O predelakh anthropomorfizma."

64 Krupskaya, "O 'Krokodile' K. Chukovskogo." This article was reprinted from *Pravda* 27 (1 February 1928).

65 Iakhontov, "Svezhaia struia v nashei zoolelletristike," 47.

66 Ibid.

67 Lupanova, *Polveka*, 160.

68 Kon, *Sovetskaia detskaia literatura*, 280.

69 Ibid., 282.

70 Chukovskaia, "Zerkalo, kotoroe ne otrazhaet."

71 Belakhova, "Pisatel' Charushin," 6.

72 De Castro describes "social relations" between "human species" and "nature," in which humans see the natural world as the "other" but try to find a more productive, holistic attitude toward it. See, for instance, de Castro, "Exchanging Perspectives." I thank Serguei Oushakine for this reference.

73 Thomashow, *Ecological Identity*, xiii.

74 Young Naturalist groups accepted schoolchildren from the fifth through the tenth grades. They were supervised by natural science teachers or professional scientists.

75 Weiner, *A Little Corner of Freedom*, 282.
76 Ibid., 283.
77 Maksim Gorky's letter to Mikhail Prishvin from Sorrento of 22 September 1926, in Gorky, *M. Gorky o detskoi literature*, 333–4.

BIBLIOGRAPHY

Agursky, M. "Velikii eretik (Gorky kak religioznyi myslitel')." *Voprosy filosofii* 8, no. 9 (1991): 54–74.

Albers, Peggy. "Theorizing Visual Representation in Children's Literature." *Journal of Literacy Research* 40, no. 2 (2008): 163–200.

Belakhova, M. "Pisatel' Charushin." *Detskaia literatura* 17 (1936): 2–7.

Berger, John. *Ways of Seeing*. New York: Penguin, 1972.

Bessire, Lucas. *Behold the Black Caiman: A Chronicle of Ayoreo Life*. Chicago: University of Chicago Press, 2014.

Bolotova, Alla. "The State, Geology and Nature in the USSR: The Experiences of Colonizing the Russian Far North." In *Understanding Russian Nature: Representations, Values and Concepts*, edited by Arja Rosenholm and Sari Autio-Sarasmo, 99–124. Helsinki: University of Helsinki, Aleksanteri Institut, 2005.

Chukovskaia, Lidiia. "Zerkalo, kotoroe ne otrazhaet: Zametki o iazyke kriticheskikh statei." *Novyi mir* 7 (1955). Chukfamily.Ru. http://www.chukfamily.ru/lidia/prosa-lidia/stati-prosa-lidia /zerkalo-kotoroe-ne-otrazhaet.

Dan'ko, E. "Zadachi khudozhestvennogo oformleniia detskoi knigi." In *Detskaia literatura. Kriticheskii sbornik*. Edited by A.V. Lunacharsky, 209–31. Moscow: Gosudarstvennoe izdatel'stvo khudozhestvennoi literatury, 1931.

de Castro, Viveiros Eduardo. "Exchanging Perspectives: The Transformation of Objects into Subjects in Amerindian Ontologies." *Common Knowledge* 10, no. 3 (Fall 2004): 463–84.

Dobrenko, Evgeny. "Nadzirat'-nakazyvat'-nadzirat': sotsrealizm kak pribavochnyi produkt nasiliia." *Revue des études slaves* 74, no. 4 (2001): 667–712.

Dobrenko, Evgeny. *Politekonomiia sotsrealizma*. Moscow: Novoe literaturnoe obozrenie, 2007.

Flerina, E., N. Kasatkina, and A. Pokrovskaia. "Tezisy ob antropomorfizme." *Kniga detiam* 2 (1928): 3–8.

Ganea, Patricia A., Caitlin F. Canfield, Kadria Simons-Ghafari, and Tommy Chou. "Do Cavies Talk? The Effect of Anthropomorphic Picture Books on Children's Knowledge about Animals." *Frontiers in Psychology* 5 (2014). https://www.ncbi.nlm.nih.gov/pmc/articles/PMC3989584/.

Ginzburg, Moisei. *Stil' i epokha. Problemy sovremennoi arkhitektury*. Moscow: Gosizdat, 1924.

Gor'kii i sovetskie pisateli: Neizdannaia perepiska. In *Literaturnoe nasledstvo*, vol. 70. Edited by I.S. Zil'bershtein and E.B. Tager. Moscow: Izdatel'stvo Akademiia nauk SSSR, 1963.

Gorky, M. "Literaturu – detiam." In *M. Gorky o detskoi literature: Stat'i, vyskazyvaniia, pis'ma*, 112–16. Edited by N.B. Medvedeva. Moscow: Detskaia literatura, 1968.

– "O biblioteke poeta." In *Sobranie sochinenii v tridtsati tomakh* Vol. 26. 176–85. Moscow: Gosizdat khudozhestvennoi literatury, 1953.

– "O kul'ture." *Kul'turnyi pokhod* (September–October 1928). Gorkiy-lit.ru. http://gorkiy-lit.ru /gorkiy/articles/article-124.htm.

Grozevskii, B.V. "Detskaia kniga o piatiletke. Oformlenie." *Kniga detiam* 5/6 (1930): 3–5.

Husband, William B. "'Correcting Nature's Mistakes': Transforming the Environment and Soviet Children's Literature, 1928–1941." *Environmental History* 11, no. 2 (2006): 300–18.

Iakhontov, A. "Svezhaia struia v nashei zoolelletristike." *Kniga detiam* 4/5 (1929): 47–52.

Il'in, M. *Chto my stroim*. Moscow: Gosudarstvennoe izdatel'stvo, 1930.

– *New Russia's Primer: The Story of the Five-Year Plan*. Translated by George Counts and Nucia Perlmutter Lodge. Boston: Houghton Mifflin, 1931.

Jameson, Fredric. *The Political Unconscious: Narrative as a Socially Symbolic Act*. Ithaca, NY: Cornell University Press, 1981.

Karasik, Mikhail. *Udarnaia kniga sovetskoi detvory. Fotoilliustratsiia i fotomontazh v knige dlia detei i iunoshestva 1920–1930kh godov*. Moscow: Kontakt-kul'tura, 2010.

Kelly, Catriona. *Children's World: Growing up in Russia, 1890–1991*. New Haven, CT: Yale University Press, 2007.

Khanin, D. "Bor'ba za detskogo pisatelia." *Kniga detiam* 1 (1930): 1–4.

Kholodnyi, Tikhon. *Piatiletka*. Illustrated by M. Mutsel'makher. Moscow: Krest'ianskaia gazeta, 1929.

Kirsanov, Semyon. *Piatiletka*. Illustrated by E. Ignatovich. Moscow: Gosizdat "Krasnyi proletarii," 1931.

Kon, Lidiia. *Sovetskaia detskaia literatura, 1917–1929*. Moscow: Gosudarstvennoe izdatel'stvo detskoi literatury, 1960.

Kovalev, V.A., A.S. Miasnikov, and N.M. Onufriev, eds. *Ocherk istorii russkoi sovetskoi literatury*. Part 2. Moscow: Akademiia nauk SSSR, 1955. OCR Biografia.Ru. http://www.biografia.ru/arhiv/ochlit02.html.

Krupskaya, N.K. "O 'Krokodile' K. Chukovskogo." *Kniga detiam* 2 (1928): 13–16.

Laptev, A. *Piatiletka*. Illustrated by A. Laptev. Moscow: Gosudarstvennoe izdatel'stvo, 1930.

Lopatin, A. *Tretii reshaiushii*. Illustrated by S. Boim and B. Sukhanov. Moscow: Molodaia gvardiia, 1931.

Lopatin, Pavel. *Piatiletka v deistvii*. Illustrated by Vladimir Golitsin. Moscow: Molodaia gvardiia, 1930.

Lunacharsky, A.V. Preface to *Detskaia literatura. Kriticheskii sbornik*. Edited by A.V. Lunacharsky. Moscow: Gosudarstvennoe izdatel'stvo detskoi literatury, 1931.

– "Puti detskoi knigi." *Kniga detiam* 1 (1930): 4–15.

Lundberg, G. "O predelakh anthropomorfizma kak literaturnogo priema v knigakh dlia detei." *Kniga detiam* 5/6 (1928): 3–5.

Lupanova, I.P. *Polveka. Sovetskaia detskaia literatura 1917–1967*. Moscow: Detskaia literatura, 1969.

Marshak, S. *Voina s Dneprom*. Moscow: Molodaia gvardiia, 1931.

Mayakovsky, Vladimir. "Rasskaz Khrenova o Kuznetskstroe i o liudiakh Kuznetska." In *Stikhi i poemy*. Moscow: Gosudarstvennoe izdatel'stvo detskoi literatury, 1960.

McCannon, John. "Technological and Scientific Utopias in Soviet Children's Literature, 1921–1932." *Journal of Popular Culture* 34, no. 4 (Spring 2001): 153–69.

Mickenberg, Julia. "The New Generation and the New Russia: Modern Childhood as Collective Fantasy." *American Quarterly* 62, no. 1 (March 2010): 103–34.

Mikini, E. "Predel dopustimosti antropomorfizma v detskoi knizhke." *Kniga detiam* 4 (1928): 3–6.

Mislavskii, Nikolai. *Denprostroi*. Illustrated by V. Lantsetti. Moscow: Gosizdat, 1930.

Molozhavyi, S. "Po voprosu o realizme v detskoi literature." *Kniga detiam* 4 (1928): 6–7.

Nikolajeva, Maria. *Aesthetic Approaches to Children's Literature: An Introduction*. Oxford: Scarecrow Press, 2005.

– *The Magic Code: The Use of Magical Patterns in Fantasy for Children*. Gothenburg, SW: Almqvist and Wiksell International, 1988.

Nikolajeva, Maria, and Carole Scott. *How Picturebooks Work*. New York: Garland Publishing, 2001.

Nodelman, Perry. "Decoding the Images: Illustration and Picture Book." In *Understanding Children's Literature*. Edited by Peter Hunt, 69–80. New York: Routledge, 1999.

– *Words about Pictures: The Narrative Art of Children's Picture Books*. Athens: University of Georgia Press, 1988.

O'Dell, Felicity Ann. *Socialisation through Children's Literature: The Soviet Example*. New York: Cambridge University Press, 1978.

Oushakine, Serguei. "The Flexible and the Pliant: Disturbed Organisms of Soviet Modernity." *Cultural Anthropology* 19, no. 3 (2004): 393–428.

– "Pole boia na fone prirody: Ot kakogo nasledstva my otkazalis." *Novoe literaturnoe obozrenie* 1 (2005): 263–98.

– "Translating Communism for Children: Fables and Posters of the Revolution." *Boundary 2* 43, no. 3 (2016): 159–219. https://doi.org/10.1215/01903659-3572478.

Prushitskaia, R. "Predely antropomorfizma v detskoi knizhke." *Kniga detiam* 3 (1928): 3–4.

Romanenko, A. "Tezisy po voprosu ob antropomorfizme i animizme v detskoi khudozhestvennoi literature." *Kniga detiam* 3 (1928): 3–4.

Rothenstein, Julian, and Olga Budashevskaya, eds. *Inside the Rainbow: Russian Children's Literature, 1920–1935. Beautiful Books, Terrible Times*. London: Redstone Press, 2013.

Rudova, Larissa. "Ekologicheskoe soznanie sovetskoi detskoi literatury 1930kh godov." In "Ubit' Charskuiu …": *Paradoksy sovetskoi literatury dlia detei (1920-e–1930-e gg.)*, edited by Marina Balina and V.Yu. Vyugin, 152–69. St. Petersburg: Aleteia, 2013.

Schlögel, Karl. *Das sowjetische Jahrhundert: Archäologie einer untergegangenen Welt*. Munich: C.H. Beck, 2018.

Smith, Eric Todd. "Dropping the Subject: Reflection on the Motives for an Ecological Criticism." In *Reading the Earth: New Directions in the Study of Literature and Environment*, edited by Michael P. Branch, Scott Slovic, and Daniel Patterson, 29–39. Moscow, ID: University of Idaho Press, 1998.

Steiner, Evgenii. *Stories for Little Comrades: Revolutionary Artists and the Making of Early Soviet Children's Books*. Seattle: University of Washington Press, 1999.

Thomashow, Mitchell. *Ecological Identity: Becoming a Reflective Environmentalist*. Cambridge, MA: MIT Press, 1995.

Weiner, Douglas R. *A Little Corner of Freedom: Russian Nature Protection from Stalin to Gorbachev*. Berkeley: University of California Press, 1999.

– *Models of Nature: Ecology, Conservation and Cultural Revolution in Soviet Russia*. Pittsburgh: University of Pittsburgh Press, 2000.

Weld, Sara Pankenier. *Voiceless Vanguard: The Infantilist Aesthetic of the Russian Avant-Garde*. Evanston, IL: Northwestern University Press, 2014.

chapter seven

AUTONOMY AND THE AUTOMATON: THE CHILD AS INSTRUMENT OF FUTURITY

SARA PANKENIER WELD

We are no more able to conceive of a politics without a fantasy of the future than we are able to conceive of a future without the figure of the Child.

Lee Edelman

In the chapter "The Future Is Kid Stuff" in his book *No Future: Queer Theory and the Death Drive*, Lee Edelman notes how "the Child" long has been upheld as an emblem of futurity.[1] Although Edelman critiques this view on the Child from the perspective of twenty-first-century queer theory, such thinking did reign without questioning at the beginning of the twentieth century. Indeed, "the pervasive invocation of the Child as the emblem of futurity's unquestioned value" that Edelman identifies proves fundamental to the propaganda, pedagogy, and art of the Soviet Union.[2] For example, two early Soviet picture books illustrated by artist Mikhail Tsekhanovskii – namely, *Sem' chudes* (*Seven Wonders*, 1926) by Samuil Marshak, and *Topotun i knizhka* (*Stomper and the Book*, 1926) by Il'ia Ionov – celebrate the technological achievements of the modern age and the future in terms of human and machine, as they strive to create automatons of the future by addressing an audience of children. If the child serves as an instrument of futurity for the fledgling Soviet state, then the early Soviet picture book serves as a primary tool to harness the capacity of the rising generation to build the future they envision.

If at first these picture books seek to shape children into ideal biomechanical inhabitants of a utopian technological future by celebrating new technologies and modern machines, then, under closer scrutiny, they also can be shown to question the limits of objectification, challenge boundaries between human and machine, and destabilize categories of "human" and "non-human" in ways that might be informed by and inform investigations of the post-social and the post-human in the present day. The treatment of the production of the human-machine in these books thus marks a remarkably early and highly illuminating investigation of subjects such as post-social object relations and post-human subjectivity, which continue to be debated today.

Technology, Mechanization, and Biomechanics

In *High Techne: Art and Technology from the Machine Aesthetic to the Posthuman*, R.L. Rutsky asserts that modernity defines itself through the issue of technology, whether utopian or dystopian.[3] Although technology, in his words, has "always been viewed in terms of an instrumental rationality,"

> in modernist art … a different *conception* of technology begins to emerge, a conception in which technology is no longer defined solely in terms of its instrumentality, but also in aesthetic terms. Indeed, aesthetic modernism can itself be defined by this relationship: by both the aestheticization of technology and the technologization of art. From the late nineteenth century on, then, aesthetic modernism becomes the privileged site for the conjunction of technology and art.[4]

It is precisely such a conjuction of technology and art, as well as an aestheticization of technology, that proves evident in these picture books, which celebrate and depict significant technological achievements of their day, and of the future, through innovative avant-garde imagery. Here technology is aestheticized, and new avant-garde approaches technologize art. This chapter investigates the aestheticized representation of technology and the production of the human-machine hybrid in picture books, books that themselves are intended as a sign of social advancement and as instruments for the realization of that utopian technological future through the use of the children who constitute their audience.

In its title, *Sem' chudes* (*Seven Wonders*), with text by Samuil Marshak and illustrations by Mikhail Tsekhanovskii, recalls the Seven Wonders of the Ancient World, but, in place of colossal monuments of ancient civilization, this book offers to Soviet children wonders of modern reality, including technological achievements such as trains, trams, and the telegraph (fig. 7.1). Similarly, Il'ia Ionov and Tsekhanovskii's *Stomper and the Book* displays the miraculous power of machines and a robot straight out of the future, as envisioned and realized futuristically by literature and art.[5] Rather than the colossal and singular architectural achievements of ancient civilizations, these books celebrate modern and multiple technologies of the Soviet era, which enhance the life of human beings as a collective. They also offer innovative explorations of new interactions between human and machine.

As Adam T. Smith observes in *The Political Machine*, "machines are efficacious not in isolation but in their encounters with us, in relation to our own forms of action."[6] He proceeds to ask, from a post-human perspective, "but how can we theorize the

7.1. Mikhail Tsekhanovskii's cover for Samuil Marshak, *Sem' chudes* (Leningrad: Raduga, 1926).

encounter of machines with human bodies that reserves some autonomy for both their, and our, unique ways of working in the world?"[7] The animation of technological objects in these two picture books partakes in an anthropomorphosis typical of early Soviet children's literature and children's literature in general, but it also reverses what Smith describes as a "transition from an 'infantile' presumption of things as participants in the world to the 'mature' modern mind inured to efficacy of objects."[8] If Smith warns that the "real danger of anthropomorphizing everything" is that it "leads back to anthropocentrism,"[9] then these books also stage intriguing post-social and post-human experiments, not only in ascribing agency to objects, but also in taking their perspective and entering into a kind of fusion of human and machine. Ultimately, they offer early explorations of complex post-social dynamics and perhaps even demonstrate, in Karin Knorr Cetina's terms, a "state of subjective fusion with the object of knowledge," making possible even the "sharing of a lifeworld."[10]

In celebrating modern Soviet technologies, these picture books continue in the thematic and aesthetic vein of Marshak's earlier collaboration with influential illustrator Vladimir Lebedev in *Vchera i segodnia* (*Yesterday and Today*, 1925). Its avant-garde illustrations visually contrast the technologies of the early twentieth century with outdated practices of the past. Offering evidence of this artistic and ideological lineage, three stamped imprints on the postcard on the cover of *Seven Wonders* reflect the titles of previous books by Marshak and Lebedev, including *Yesterday and Today*. Such picture books make the rhetorical assertion that modern Soviet reality, with its new technologies and human-machine aspirations, rivals the wonders of the ancient world and thereby places communism at the vanguard. As Charles Russell notes in *Poets, Prophets, Revolutionaries*, "the avant-garde wants to be more than a merely *modernist* art, one that reflects its contemporary society; rather it intends to be a *vanguard* art, in advance of, and the cause of, significant social change."[11] Early Soviet picture books thus unite, for a time, avant-garde aesthetics with communist ideology and instrumental approaches to achieving a utopian future. The further fact that these books address an audience of children displays the instrumentality of avant-garde art and picture books for children in particular. Through their propagandistic content, they seek to contribute to the shaping of the Soviet citizens of the future. Since children figure as emergent and not yet fully realized subjects, they prove a vulnerable and desirable target for such ideologically motivated efforts.

Under closer scrutiny, however, the ideologically charged and avant-garde celebration of modernity and the machine in these books also reveals, through details of text and image, how this propagandistic vision of the future challenges traditional models of the human form, the body, and individuality and instead offers visions of the mechanized human body. Such details bare the goal of Soviet ideology to socially engineer Soviet subjects of the future into a biomechanical ideal, such as envisioned by Aleksei Gastev in his work toward the scientific organization of labour (*nauchnaia organizatsiia truda*). Indeed, Gastev himself figured the present and future as youthful. For example, in "Vosstanie kul'tury" ("An Uprising of Culture," 1923), he writes that "a new youth burst into life. It came straight from the maw of revolution. In this new youth is the whole future of our USSR."[12] He also employs the discourse of youth and childhood to characterize the "power of revolution" as "the authentic child of the socialist uprising"[13] or to declare that "we are young."[14] In looking to the future, he sets "a course for active builders of life. If there aren't any, we must birth them."[15] Indeed, the child serves as an instrument for building that new socialist future in its ideal manifestation, while picture books in turn serve to "birth" them.

The ideal of that future included the application of Fredrick Winslow Taylor's principles to the "scientific organization of labor" through a mechanization of labouring bodies for maximal biomechanical efficiency. As Anindita Banerjee notes in *We Modern People*, "scientific socialism provided the frame for conceptualizing the proletarian state as a seamless collective of mechanized humans."[16] To achieve this, Gastev's Central Labour Institute also applied "Taylor's principles to the construction of the New Soviet Person."[17] In fact, as Banerjee notes, Gastev seeks to alter humanity itself: "As 'nothing but perfect machines whose technical progress is unlimited,' Gastev's imagined future was populated by barely identifiable humans who became indistinguishable from the instruments of their labor."[18] Such a biomechanical future envisions an assemblage of machines and humans working in perfect concert, an image worth keeping in mind in viewing Tsekhanovskii's illustrations depicting such scenes. In order to create this future and ideal worker, Gastev and others in various realms of Soviet life also attended to children and youth as the raw material out of which that future and a mechanized labour ideal might be produced.[19] Itself a wondrous new technology, the Soviet picture book for children thus becomes the instrument by which such a new citizen could be produced.

Theatre director Vsevolod Meyerhold applied similar biomechanical principles to theatre. In "Principles of Biomechanics," Mikhail Korenev reiterates Meyerhold's teachings: "The first principle of biomechanics: the body is a machine, the actor is the machinist."[20] Reflexologist Ivan Pavlov summed up Meyerhold's biomechanical principles similarly, when he offered the critique that Meyerhold "lowers everything to the level of portraying man as a mechanical engine,"[21] an image that also accords with avant-garde depictions of humans and the human-machine by Tsekhanovskii in *Seven Wonders* (see fig. 7.1). Yet something optimistic also emerges in the biomechanical vision, when Gastev proposes "that man does not need external mechanical prostheses to survive; the body itself is a machine that can develop its own armor or be utilized as a tool. Man's body contains within itself the ability to become a machine, and in so doing survive in the machine age."[22] Similarly, Meyerhold offers an optimistic vision of the child and its biomechanical perfection and futuristic perfectibility, as V.Es. describes in "The Actor of the Future and Biomechanics": "When we observe the movements of a child, we are enjoying his biomechanical ability. If we place this child in conditions where gymnastics and all types of sports are accessible and required, we will get a new man capable of any kind of work."[23] The new Soviet child thus serves to produce the new Soviet person. Whether set in the "factory" or the "schoolroom,"[24] these biomechanical approaches aim at the production of biomechanical machine-people and the optimized training of the new man, woman, and child. Technologically oriented Soviet picture books also work toward such a biomechanical ideal, but through the use of the mass-produced picture book.

Consider, for example, Lebedev's influential illustrations in *Yesterday and Today* and other works that render human forms easily reproducible, geometric, and machine-like and that forecast these similar and related developments in the early Soviet picture book. Yet Mikhail Tsekhanovskii takes this pedagogy of images to new heights in his treatment of human and machine in picture books that depict the wonders of the modern world and the technological achievements of the present day. In these books, the avant-garde love for modern technology and the machine merges with the instrumental focus on the future at the heart of Soviet communism and its propagandistic fixation on the child.

Modernity, Mechanics, and the Body

Samuil Marshak and Mikhail Tsekhanovskii's *Seven Wonders* celebrates seven largely technological achievements of the modern age for an audience of children. Noteworthy in the presentation of these seven wonders of modern technology is the almost complete absence of the human body. Particularly significant from the perspective of technology and art, and the human and machine assemblage,[25] however, is the sixth wonder, the typewriter, which represents new innovations in modern printing technology and does include representations of the human body. The images associated with the typewriter (fig. 7.2) explore print technology and the place of the individual human being in the age of mechanical reproduction. For these women, writing by machine purportedly becomes a joyful "game" ("igra"), while for "you," in contrast, it is "misery" ("gore").[26] This language marks the machine as out of reach and an object of desire that the reader is presumed to lack. The identical products of machine technology and printing are celebrated here: "All pages, as if one" ("Vse stranitsy, kak odna"). In contrast to distorted and uneven cursive handwriting using ink and a fountain pen, perfect typed or printed letters are unmarred by ink spots or smudges. As in *Yesterday and Today*, the advance represented by the typewriter over writing by hand is indicated by smudged ink on a notebook and the filthy traces of a fly.[27] The machine creates absolute perfection, while the human hand and organic life proves flawed. In this representation, the human body and other living things only mar the perfection of the machine-made.

Yet the accompanying illustrations also depict three women – or, rather, one woman reproduced in triplicate – in a technologically modern scene reminiscent of Lebedev's three old women using age-old technology to fetch water in his groundbreaking *Yesterday and Today*. The style of Tsekhanovskii's illustration recalls the flavour of newsprint, journalism, and advertising in the West in this period, as does the prominent Mercedes logo listed twice in Latin lettering. Here and on other pages in the book, visual citations recall contemporary newspapers, matchbox designs, tickets, stamps, and money, producing a collage-like effect through realia of the period. In this sense, one may consider Andreas Huyssen's observations about the pervasive influence of technology on the avant-garde: "The invasion of the very fabric of the art object by technology and what one may loosely call the technological imagination can best be

7.2. Mikhail Tsekhanovskii, typewriter illustrations, in *Sem' chudes*.

grasped in artistic practices such as collage, assemblage, montage and photomontage, forms which can not only be reproduced, but are in fact designed for mechanical reproducibility."[28] Like a collective of women working at Singer sewing machines, the typists and typewriters themselves look as if printed and replicated on newsprint.[29] The women exemplify human beings in service of the word but also of the machine and new printing technologies that would produce them. The thrice-replicated image here produces a Taylorized or optimized biomechanical assembly line, as advocated by Gastev. Interestingly, Tsekhanovskii's illustration achieves this by replicating a visual reference to Austrian-born Ernst Deutsch's famous poster used to promote the New Model 3 Mercedes typewriter. It features a woman in a long dress seated at a typewriter with an almost cigarette-like pen incongruously in her hand as she looks alluringly at the viewer with a tilted head and smile. Compared to Deutsch's model, however, Tsekhanovskii's typists seem more modest and less alluring, more troubled and less joyful, and their clothing and hair appear more constrained and less bold or stylish.

On the one hand, these human typists serve the machines, as if machines themselves. At the same time, they have themselves been mechanically reproduced, replicated, and printed, having been rendered as objects rather than subjects in the process, as their identical representation shows. Friedrich Kittler observes, "mechanical writing provides this 'advantage,' that is conceals the handwriting and thereby the character. The typewriter makes everyone look the same."[30] Tsekhanovskii illustrates that notion quite literally, where even the typists are typed, as it were. In truth, human beings hardly figure among the wonders of the modern world, for this book praises technology and the machine at the expense of the human. The individuated human has disappeared when the human and machine have blended into one single entity.

Indeed, the typist at her typewriter embodies a new assemblage of human and machine or, in this case, woman and machine, whose union Friedrich Kittler discusses in his chapter "Typewriter" in *Gramophone, Film, Typewriter*. One might recall Kittler's observation that, in fact, the English term "typewriter" ambiguously refers to the writing machine and to the female typist.[31] The Russian term *pishushchaia mashina* (writing machine), meanwhile, which, in *Seven Wonders*, is typed vertically beside the illustration of the typewriter above the typists, like the German *Schreibmaschine* advertised by Ernst Deutsch, blurs the boundaries of woman and machine, since both typist and machine are writing, and the "writing machine" in actuality is the assemblage of woman and machine. The unity of the woman-machine whole is underscored by its perfect replication in triplicate, which, paradoxically, reveals what constitutes a bipartite unit through the pattern of its repetition.

Accompanying these images, the two stanzas on the page both start with the same words, "Ladies are writing" ("Pishut baryshni"), while in the first stanza the personal pronoun "for them" ("dlia nikh") clearly refers to these typists. In the second, however, an ambiguity arises out of the pronoun, "To look at them is a pleasure" ("Pogliadet' na nikh priiatno"). Does it refer to these objectified women, who resemble mannequins or robotic humans? While "them" ostensibly refers to the pages, typed without any blemish, the ambiguity lingers when one reads, "All pages, as [if] one," where the subject "one" is feminine and singular. For indeed, all these women are themselves alike and as if one, since they too were mechanically reproduced and printed perfectly in triplicate upon a page, and woman and machine also blend into one entity.

Early twentieth-century anxiety about a new technological era finds famous reflection in Walter Benjamin's "The Work of Art in the Age of Mechanical Reproduction." There, Benjamin remarks that "the technique of reproduction detaches the reproduced object from the domain of tradition. By making many reproductions it substitutes a plurality of copies for a unique existence."[32] Benjamin also notes the new political portent and instrumentality of art, as authenticity disappears as a criterion and reproducibility becomes an element of design, as in the case of these printed women who themselves mechanically reproduce text, in contrast to the authenticity of the ink-stained notebook. Benjamin observes:

> To an ever greater degree the work of art reproduced becomes the work of art designed for reproducibility. From a photographic negative, for example, one can make any number of prints; to ask for the "authentic" print makes no sense. But the instant the criterion of authenticity ceases to be applicable to artistic production, the total function of art is reversed. Instead of being based on ritual, it begins to be based on another practice – politics. In the Soviet Union work itself is given a voice.[33]

The influence of Soviet politics and art on this thinking is clear, as Benjamin considers precisely the issues of technology and art that the politically engaged avant-garde bring to the fore, and as is shown by the depiction of the labours of women and machines.[34]

Producing the Human-Machine Hybrid

The age of mechanical reproduction and human capacity being augmented, and perhaps challenged, by new printing technology and real and imagined machines feature even more prominently in Il'ia Ionov's *Stomper and the Book*. Within the book, print technology and a humanoid robot reveal the anxieties, challenges, and paradoxes of the day as technology meets art on the pages of an avant-garde picture book for children. In fact, the book itself engages with history when its title page incongruously features the "authentic" old technologies of paintbrush, fountain pen, ink, and a compass. These offer a metatextual nod perhaps to the prehistory of the book, still initially sketched by hand, despite the fact that such technologies appear to be made obsolete by the celebration of the machine within the text. The complex relationships between human and machine, however, take centre stage in *Stomper and the Book*, where child and machine initially stand at odds, but then forge an alliance over the course of the book, even as the categories of human and machine blur and identity becomes mutational. Eventually readers witness how humans and children become more machine-like, even as the child hero – and readers along with him – learns to treat modern technologies with appropriate wonder.

Echoing the wonder toward technology shown in previous picture books, the cover of *Stomper and the Book* shows the book's protagonist, the boy Tolia, mesmerized by and reverent before the machine (fig. 7.3). The reader too, it seems to say, should deify the machine and show awe and respect for the product it produces, the book in the age of mechanical reproduction. The cover thus abundantly displays the

7.3. Mikhail Tsekhanovskii, cover for Il'ia Ionov, *Topotun i knizhka* (Moscow: Gosizdat, 1926).

avant-garde cult of the machine. As Andreas Huyssen remarks, "no other single factor has influenced the emergence of the new avant-garde art as much as technology, which not only fueled the artists' imagination (dynamism, machine cult, beauty of technics, constructivist and productivist attitudes), but penetrated to the core of the work itself."[35] In the cover illustration, Tolia, in a robotic pose, hypnotically turns a smooth and featureless face toward a complex printing machine, while his extended hand turns up in a praying posture, as if worshiping the machine. Around his neck, he wears a red kerchief, signalling his status as a Young Pioneer and his rightful and proper behaviour, as politically defined and circumscribed. Here is a child who is being trained according to proper protocol and is being socially engineered, as his perfected bodily biomechanics show, to be an ideal Soviet subject of the future.

The boy's robotic pose is very much to the point, for on the cover he is shown to behave in the proper way and as an example for emulation by child readers, who also are being shaped by this very book. By the story's end, the errant boy has indeed been made into someone who behaves "by the book." In this sense, one can understand why the cover cites the name of the robot Topotun (Stomper) while it depicts the boy Tolia. Tolia has become an automaton himself, as his biomechanical pose and reverent posture indicate. The boy and the robot, Tolia and Stomper, have become interchangeable. As signalled by the politically symbolic and revolutionary red, which itself echoes Orthodox associations of the holy icon, *Stomper and the Book* offers a transcendent passage into another sphere, but, in this case, the "spiritual" sphere of the machine. For out of a book emerges the humanoid robot Stomper, who conveys the boy Tolia into the world of machines and labour, where he is reborn.

The existence of the humanoid machine signals that this is the world of the future, where such an independently animated automaton can exist. For, by all appearances, Stomper is a "robot," to use the term first employed a few years before, in 1921, by Karel Čapek in his play *R.U.R.* (*Rossum's Universal Robots*). Čapek's play features "the manufacture of artificial people" or mechanical automatons who are built only to work on factory assembly lines, based on a belief that "the product of an engineer is technically at a higher pitch of perfection than a product of nature."[36] Their creator "rejected man and made the Robot"; but eventually the robots revolt against their masters.[37] Interestingly, according to Karel Čapek, the term "robot" itself was created by his brother Josef Čapek from the Czech *robota*, meaning servitude. As a robot or machine-man, Stomper speaks up for machines, objects, and inanimate things against those who mistreat them. He revolts on behalf of all machines to assist in re-engineering the human child Tolia, who did not properly respect the products of their labour.

In the opening scene of the book, Stomper "raised up his eyelashes" ("pripodnial svoi resnitsy") and looks back out of the book and at the boy.[38] In this initial scene, the inert object, or book, and a mere representation of a thing, the illustration of Stomper, take on life, as Stomper becomes an animate machine who can engage with a human child. This scene recalls Benjamin's notion of the aura, which can be considered the projection of a kind of living presence or spirit on the aesthetic object.[39] As Benjamin writes in "On Some Motifs in Baudelaire," "Experience of the aura thus rests on the transposition of a response common in human relationships to the relationship between the inanimate or natural object and man. The person we look at, or who feels he is being looked at, looks at us in return. To perceive the aura of an object we look at means to invest it with the ability to look at us in return."[40] Indeed, in this specular moment, by looking at the robot and interpreting part of its optical apparatus as eyelashes, the human being anthropomorphically ascribes humanity to the machine. Similarly, it is the child's imagination and animism that invests Stomper with the ability to raise its eyelashes to see. Initially, the human being invests the robot, or the illustration of a robot, with the ability "to look at us in return." Yet this early Soviet scenario of a boy and automaton also might be applied to contemporary debates on post-social studies, such as in Karin Knorr Cetina's analyses showing how humans do have social relations with objects in post-social knowledge societies.[41]

Through its aura, as R.L. Rutsky notes, "the image comes to be seen as 'animated' by an eternal, living spirit, by what Benjamin calls the 'breath of prehistory.'"[42] He adds that "Benjamin associates this 'prehistoric impulse to the past,' to the 'archaic symbolic world of mythology,' with 'memory, childhood, and dream.'"[43] In *Stomper and the Book*, childhood and dream animate the image, since the illustrations indicate that Stomper's animated state is book-ended by a flawed child looking into a book at the beginning and by a much-improved child seemingly awakening from a dreaming state at the end. The book with its visions of the future and of human and machine perfectibility thus appears to dwell in the realm of the child's imagination or dreams, where things take on a life of their own – and a futuristic technological utopia of machine-people is more easily realized. In its futuristic vision, and the shared lifeworld of human and machine its story offers, the book also offers a model of post-social object relations insofar as the book, an object itself, serves as a tool whereby the human enters into the perspective of objects and achieves intersubjectivity with hybrid entities straddling the traditional divide between human and machine, subject and object. Yet, from another perspective, the child depicted within this book is himself merely a representation, a biomechanical stand-in, and an automaton created by adults[44] as an instrument to produce a desired communist future; thus, this child is no less a robot or *robota* than Stomper.

In accordance with the book's aims and aspirations, the glimpse into the world of print technology that Tolia experiences with Stomper during the course of the book proves both informative and formative. Tolia learns about the printing process and gains a proper awe and respect for machines, print technology, and the printed book. Tolia, whose full name, Anatoly, means "sunrise," thus receives training from the pedagogy of images present in the book, as well as a secular Soviet insight into the value of and reverence for "The Book" as pedagogic object. At the same time, however, the dreamlike, or nightmarish, vision of a world of vast machines and diminutive labourers also offers a glimpse into a future where humans might serve as the *robota*, or servants/slaves, of the machines. The evident anxiety characterizing the first encounter of child and robot also colours such a view.

At the opening of the book, Stomper not only looks back at Tolia but also finds a voice. Stomper "angrily speaks" ("serdito govorit") to Tolia, thus displaying an utterly non-mechanical emotion aroused by post-social relations that animate him with human feelings. Like Čapek's mechanical men, Stomper revolts against this human, who would tear the pages of a book, and stands up for the object, thing, or book: "This children's book is a sorry sight!" ("Zhalok knigi detskoi vid!"). It is precisely Tolia's humanness, childishness, and boyishness that proves a problem, then. From the beginning, he is represented as "a naughty little thing" ("shalunishka")" and a "sloven" ("pachkun"), or someone who deviates from the expected norms of behaviour, and thereby a flawed specimen of humanity, although he is praised, perhaps redemptively, as "clever" ("umnyi"), giving him the potential for greater insight and, perhaps, enlightenment. In the first illustration in the book (fig. 7.4), two human hands with ten guiltily splayed fingers are labelled "Tolia's hands/fingers" ("Toliny ruki"), only these fingers and hands have fingertips and edges blackened with ink. This black ink marks Tolia's hands with an original sin from which he must be cleansed by reforming his ways and being reborn.

Жил был Толя шалунишка,
Умный был он, но пачкун.
Раз попалась Толе книжка,
В книжке видит: Топотун
Приподнял свои ресницы
И сердито говорит:
„Что ты треплешь все страницы?
Жалок книги детской вид!
Принесли ее опрятной,
Ни соринки на полях,

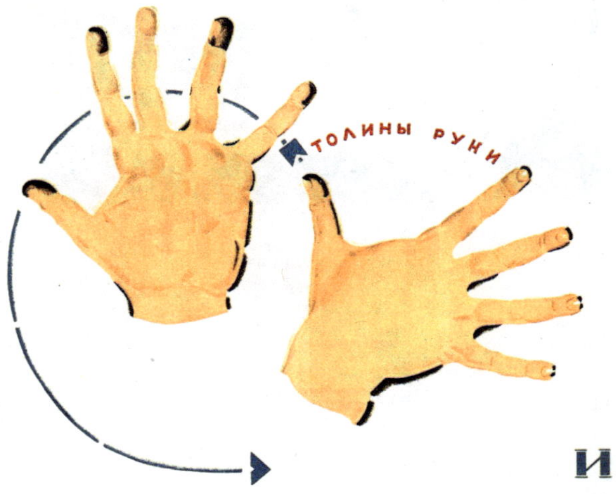

7.4. Tsekhanovskii's illustration of Tolia's ink-stained hands in *Topotun i knizhka*.

The next page (fig. 7.5) shows the damage wrought by the filthy and careless human hands of the naughty sloven, one might presume: a pile of torn pages from picture books of the period marred with spots of black ink and multiple flies, indicating the filth of organic life-forms. Among the torn sheets, two featured pages clearly come from Marshak and Lebedev's *Yesterday and Today,* which juxtaposes the wax candle and kerosene lamp of yesterday to electricity. Another clean white page features the shining pitcher and washing basin depicted on the dedication page of the picture book edition of Kornei Chukovsky's *Moidodyr* (*Wash'emclean,* 1923), illustrated by Iurii Annenkov, where a similarly slovenly child is reformed by objects that revolt against him. Thus does the book cite its sources through intertextual and intervisual references to the influential writers and illustrators to which it is indebted. Indeed, *Wash'emclean* offers a similar child-centred conversion narrative guided by an anthropomorphized object revolting against an insufficiently socialized subject, while *Yesterday and Today* sets up the same opposition between a dark past and a shining future.

If Tolia's careless and filthy flesh proves problematic, then the ink spots on his hands also more subtly refer back to the title page, which incongruously displays a

А теперь повсюду пятна,
Пятна даже на углах.
А недавно ни пылинки
Ни за что в ней не сыскать,
Было весело картинки
Друг за дружкой пробегать.
Вот пойдем, пострел, со мною,
Погляди с трудом каким
У машин порой дневною
Книжки делают другим".

7.5. Tsekhanovskii's illustration of mistreated books in *Topotun i knizhka*.

paintbrush, fountain pen, and ink. In addition to recalling the creator behind the book, these artistic tools, including the telltale black ink, now appear to relate to Tolia's own creative activities. In this sense, the ink on Tolia's hands, which mars the picture books he reads, offers signs of a diligent schoolboy or creative artist, if not the cleanest and most careful habits. This chaotic human creative impulse, a human kind of entropy, is being threatened, in a sense, in this book, where conformity, order, and clean, unmarred perfection prove more prized. Yet this value system also seems to threaten the faulty human body in some sense, and particularly the nonconforming one. In this sense, it could be that the problem with Tolia is that he likes his books too much, literally loving them to pieces, or that in his creative impulse he challenges the machines that more cleanly and perfectly print the pages of a book without the ink smudges of filthy human hands. For this book celebrates only "art in the age of mechanical reproduction" and shows that the flawed human body ought to be re-engineered to realize its Taylorist biomechanical potential instead of its old-fashioned creative aspirations.

An illustration dramatizing the confrontation between robot and boy (fig. 7.6) emphasizes the contrast of bared human flesh with the machine components of the robot. At first glance, Tolia appears in an extremely vulnerable pose, with a bare head

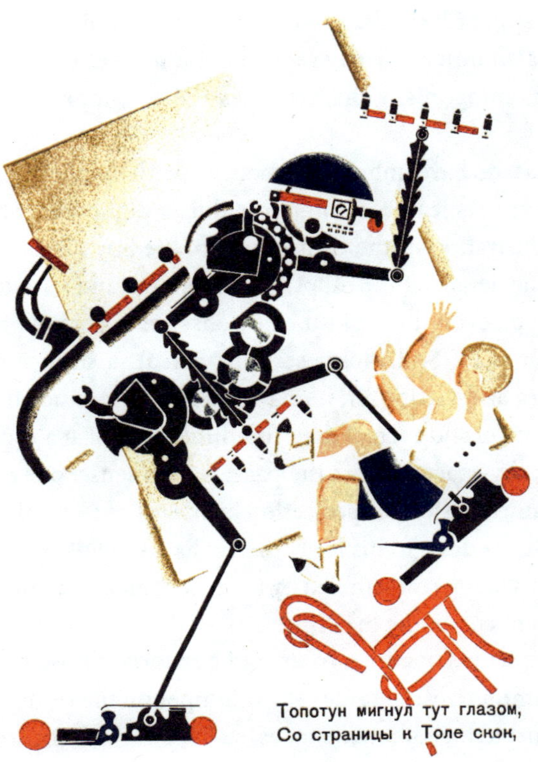

7.6. Tsekhanovskii's illustration of the confrontation between robot and boy in *Topotun i knizhka*.

and unshod feet and bent limbs fending off the threatening robot as his chair topples from beneath him. The dynamic composition thus captures Tolia suspended in air and full of kinetic energy, seemingly about to fall. In emerging out of the blank page faintly visible in a diagonal position behind him, the robot has taken on immense proportions and towers over the boy. One needle-like leg of the robot appears to impale the boy through his stomach, thus recalling the tripod Martians in H.G. Wells's *War of the Worlds*, which also inspired the similarly animate and angry machine Ophelia, who plays a role in Yuri Olesha's *Zavist'* (*Envy*, 1927).[45]

A mature awareness of perspective in the otherwise flattened and aperspectival composition registers the robot's leg as being behind the boy, while a naïve perspective processes an even greater threat. In either case, the illustration presents a threatening image dominated by the dynamic and mechanical form of the robot, Stomper. The boy is afraid, as revealed by the outstretched fingers of one hand, which involuntarily fend off attack or beg for mercy. Ironically, the mechanical shape of the machine-man in its basic structural components resembles the human skeleton reduced, for example, to circular geometry serving as joints for long and straight black limbs. Unlike Tolia's soft fleshy hands on the first page,

Stomper's hands appear like rakes, with short sharp points on each that, in their five-fold design, also unnecessarily replicate the human form. Here, at the beginning of the book, antagonism characterizes the relationship of Anatoly and the automaton.

Yet it is humans who have imbued the machine with human characteristics, created it in their own image, as it were. Stomper is thus a highly derivative machine-man. Tellingly, in the illustration of the confrontation, the boy's facial features do not appear at all, while the details of the robot's physiognomy and structure are rendered in precise detail. In fact, everything but the boy observes a perfect geometry that Tolia's faulty human flesh lacks. Still, closer scrutiny reveals a strange mirroring between the apparent victim and victimizer, human and machine, since their torsos are both diagonal and in parallel and each of their four limbs is bent at a roughly 90-degree angle and symmetrically spaced across the page. In this sense, one might consider how Gastev's biomechanical vision of "perfection by means of technology entails that man should regard violence done to his body merely as a kind of industrial reassembly."[46] Here a faulty child is being reassembled by the mechanical machine-man to be a more effective and efficient cog in the machine.

After this inauspicious opening, robot and boy forge a post-social alliance. When a now still more diminutive Tolia rides atop Stomper on the next page, even the boy is rendered largely through geometric shapes, such as curved portions of circles. From here on, the boy and the machines move in concert, with an ever-larger Stomper skating with the boy on his back and a blue biplane following behind. Tolia's arms, hands, and fingers, although fleshy and pink, again mimic the position of Stomper's rake-like arms, hands, and fingers. Although the child rides the machine-man, it is the child who is subordinated to the machine, rather than vice versa. This fact is underscored on the subsequent spread (fig. 7.7), when Tolia and Stomper encounter a miracle of modern machine technology. Both stand in awe before massive printing press machinery that dwarfs a number of apparently identical human labourers attending to the machines and carting away the products they produce. The first of four repetitive and rhythmic stanzas opens with the wondrous exclamation, "What a wonder / What a wonder" ("Chto za chudo, / Chto za chudo"), thus replicating the rhythmic sounds of a machine at work. The book thus gives voice, perhaps, to work itself, as Benjamin said.

On the lower left side of the spread, Tolia stands stunned and staring upward in a robotic and awkwardly biomechanical pose that expresses his evident awe, and again mirrors that of his machine-man mentor symmetrically opposite him. On the lower right side, Stomper also sits upright, with his head turned up and mouth open and his arms before him in a gesture of subservience or reverence. The printing machinery now speaks for itself through the rhythms embedded in a fast-moving trochaic tetrameter and replicate the sounds of machines at work, such as in the alliterative lines "Shum i shelest / Shum i shelest" ("Noise and rustling / Noise and rustling").

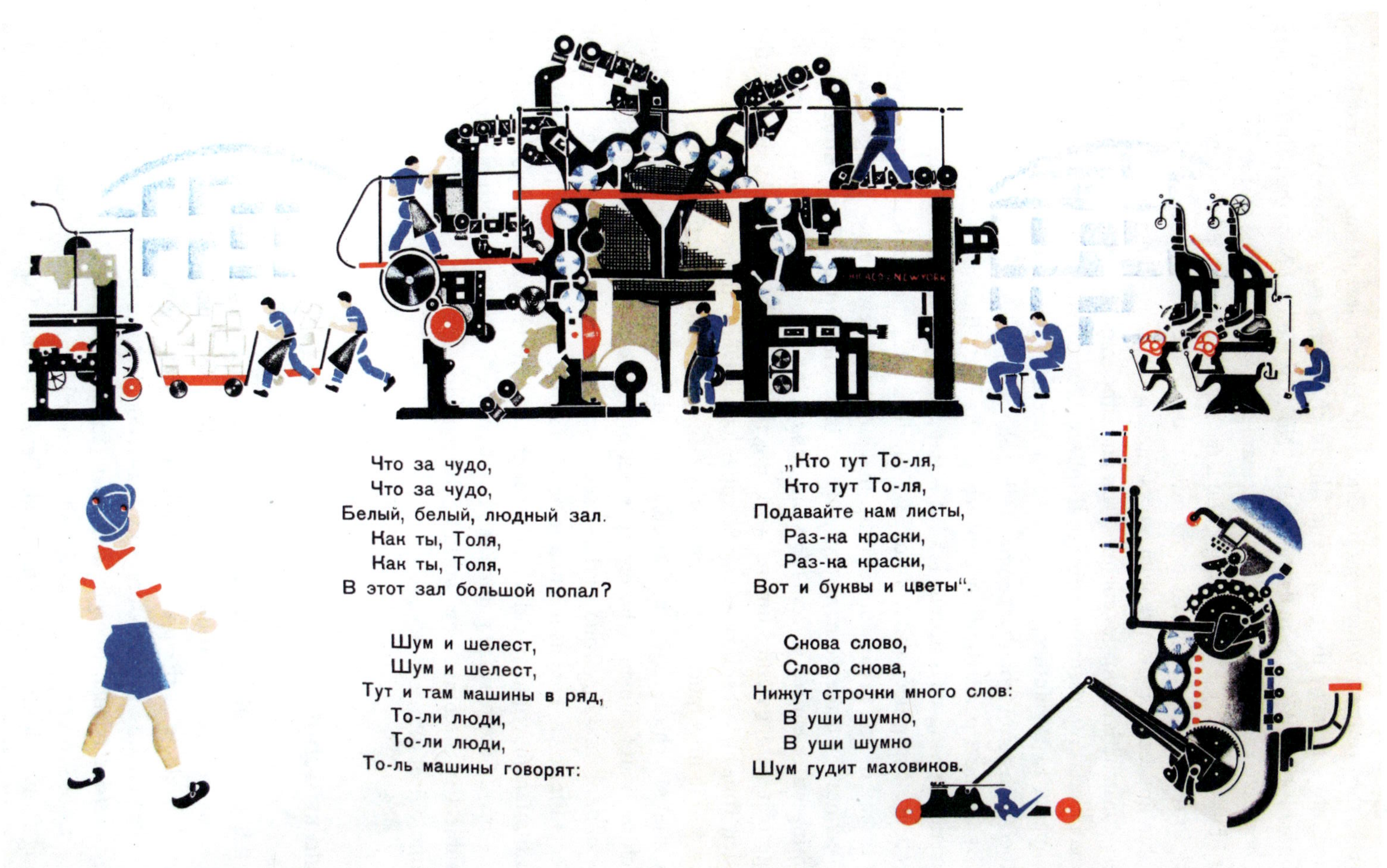

7.7. Tsekhanovskii's illustration of a printing press in *Topotun i knizhka*.

In this scene, in a formalist sense, the book bares its devices, as the book's readers witness the print technology that produced the book before them. The child Tolia is called into service by the people and "the machines in a row," who ask him to contribute his labour: "Apply to us the sheets, / Now the paints, / Now the paints, / There are both letters and colours" ("Podavaite nam listy, / Raz-ka kraski, / Raz-ka kraski, / Vot i bukvy i tsvety"). Interestingly, the large machine is labelled Chicago and New York in red Latin letters, perhaps to indicate the influence of American Taylorist assembly-line technology. Although represented in a flat, two-dimensional perspective, these constructivist images conjure print and lithograph technology of the day, with perfect circles representing cylindrical rollers through which sheets of paper rotate. Compared to the anthropomorphic robot Stomper, this machine is like a many-limbed monster or iron deity commanding all.

By the next page, the fully converted Tolia leads the way as he, Stomper, and four men driving carts heavily loaded with paper speed to the next location, where sheets are cut, glued, and bound. Like modern fates mechanically manipulating the thread of life, three women work machines that sew the books together. This trio echoes the three women at typewriters in *Seven Wonders,* or the three women fetching water earlier in *Yesterday and Today.* The scene displays how an assemblage of machines and humans work together to make books. Along with the reader, Tolia absorbs the message Stomper has delivered through the vision he has shown: "Oh how much and wonderfully / The people manufacture books!" ("Akh, kak mnogo i chudesno / Knizhki delaet narod!"). Through the anthropomorphic machine-man Stomper, who emerges out of the book to bring him into the factory of book-making, Tolia learns to see from the book's perspective and share an object's lifeworld. He has learned to appreciate the labours of machines, humans, and human-machine assemblages through the intervention of a hybridized machine-man. Stomper has guided the boy to achieve sympathy with object as well as subject in the brave new world of the machine and in the name of a utopian technological future.

Child as Robot

Yet this representation of the future also forecasts a dystopian and totalizing outcome. In another illustration (fig. 7.8), above four heavily burdened workers, printed products of the presses feature prominently. Instead of the picture books of Tsekhanovskii's predecessors, this illustration features the 1926 journal collection *Sovetskie rebiata: Sbornik dlia detei* (*Soviet Children: A Collection for Children*), whose cover was illustrated by Tsekhanovskii himself, alongside copies of the Young Pioneer journal *Novyi robinzon: Detskii zhurnal* (*New Robinson: Children's Journal*). The *Sovetskie rebiata* cover schematically represented here resembles in

7.8. Tsekhanovskii's illustration of reading material for children that has come off the printing press in *Topotun i knizhka*.

its basic composition the original cover by Tsekhanovskii. Both feature a Pioneer with a bugle, spade, and canteen on the left side of the middle section of the cover, while the words of the subtitle are superimposed upon a darker square, echoed in the simplified copy. "Sovetskie" is written in large letters across the top, while "rebiata" is written across the bottom. In the original, the child's skin and shirt are rendered in unprinted white, which emerges clearly in contrast to the red printed background. In Tsekhanovskii's reprinted book within a book, however, the colour scheme is changed from black and white on red to blue, red, and black on white. As a result, in this reproduction of a reproduction, the actual body of the child disappears. The child shown on this cover, as Evgenii Steiner notes,[47] has lost not only his face, hands, and individuality, but his entire body too. In the progression from "yesterday" to "today," and from human to machine, man, woman, and – now – child have lost their individuation and have become mass-produced or printed. In this respect, Tsekhanovskii surpasses even Vladimir Lebedev's radically reductivist approach to the human form.

In *Morozhenoe* (*Ice Cream*), Lebedev's proletarian children, despite wearing worker's garb and a red kerchief over a Pioneer uniform, remain individual. A degree of variation also persists in Lebedev's proletarian ice cream sellers and Tsekhanovskii's postmen in the early editions of *Pochta* (*The Mail*) or in the children he

7.9. Tsekhanovskii's illustration for L. Savel'ev (Leonid Lipavskii), *Pionerskii ustav* (*The Pioneer Charter*) (Leningrad: Gosizdat, 1926).

depicts later. But in this illustration in *Stomper and the Book* of a book within a book about books, Tsekhanovskii reduces the child to a bodiless uniform. This effectively represents the plight of the child in the age of mechanical reproduction and in the early Soviet period, as art and childhood have become ideological, politicized, and instrumentalized in the name of the future. Along with individuality and independent agency, the flawed flesh of the human child has been erased and replaced with a biomechanical ideal of almost pure geometry and abstraction.[48] In this image, as a result of avant-garde aesthetics and constructivist minimalism, as well as considerations of artistic technology and limitations of form due to mass reproduction and lithograph printing, Tsekhanovskii renders the child easily and infinitely reproducible. But the individual child and his authentic human flesh has been erased, to be replaced by a biomechanical ideal. Through its mechanical reproduction, it has lost its aura and, without face and eyes, the ability to look back in return.

For comparison, Tsekhanovskii's illustrations for *Pionerskii ustav* (*The Pioneer Charter*, 1926) by L. Savel'ev (pseudonym of Leonid Lipavskii) move in the same direction, making the body into a uniform and children into automatons. Part of the accompanying text reads in a robotic rhythm (fig. 7.9):

7.10. Tsekhanovskii's illustration of children reading in *Topotun i knizhka*.

We walk in row after row,	(Мы идем за рядом ряд,
A brigade of Young Leninists	Юных ленинцев отряд
…	…
Younger brother to the Komsomol,	Комсомольцу младший брат,
The pioneer steps into line.	Пионер вступает в ряд.
We go to relieve our predecessors.	Мы идем на смену смене.
We are led by comrade Lenin	Нас ведет товарищ Ленин)

Although Lenin's face is rendered in representative shaded detail, the faces and hands of six identical marching Pioneers lack detail.[49] As if washed clean of the filth of previous generations, they appear ready to march out of the right side of the page into a future for which they serve as a useful instrument and militarized brigade, no less. Their radical facelessness, different from that seen in Lebedev's work, echoes the facelessness evident in some of Kazimir Malevich's most radical depictions of the human form. Soviet children here metonymically become a collective of Pioneer uniforms, a collection of geometric shapes that are mass produced and mechanically printed. The human is no longer a person but has become an assemblage of objects. If the adult has become a cog in the wheel of the industrial machine or the communist enterprise, then the child clearly has also, if not even more so, as a slave, or *robota,* in servitude to the future. Children as a collective become a mechanically mass-produced series or set. Facial features and detail had already been lost in earlier depictions in *Stomper and the Book,* but in this detail of a book within the book, the flawed flesh of the human body, as conveyed by Tolia's filthy hands at the beginning of the book, has been cleansed to the point that it has been erased entirely. All that remains are the political trappings of the Young Pioneers, such as the red scarf, bugle, cap, and shorts. In contrast, the child initially threatened by the robot had not worn his Pioneer kerchief. Once Tolia grows to understand and respect the wonder of machines, however, he dutifully dons his red kerchief, following proper Pioneer form, while his body becomes increasingly geometric and robotic. In donning this uniform, however, the child or all "Soviet children" have become little more than a red kerchief, the symbol of the Pioneer youth organization, which promises a kind of Taylorism and optimized mass production of the new Soviet child and scales up for the collective the process aimed at the individual in *Stomper and the Book.*

Similarly, by the penultimate page of *Stomper and the Book,* four children with blank faces are deeply absorbed in the blank white pages of books (fig. 7.10). The text Tolia reads is laboriously spelled out below him to offer a propagandistic message for the child protagonist and children reading the book:

A book loves cleanliness,	Книга любит чистоту,
Cleanliness.	Чистоту.
Don't fold down the corners,	Уголки не загибай,
Don't get it dirty.	Не марай,
If you will read us,	Если будешь нас читать,
You will know a lot	Будешь много знать.

The image of children reading takes on a different cast, if what they read is mere pedagogy and propaganda such as this. The cleanliness being underscored here contrasts with the ink-stained creative fingers Tolia displayed at the beginning of the book. It also relates to brainwashing, the erasure of an older belief system, and the purging (*chistka*) of dissent and independent thought. Indeed, these picture books thus also display a future vision of the complete erasure of flawed human flesh in pursuit of a mechanized and easily reproducible ideal.

Conclusion

On the final page of *Stomper and the Book,* it is as if Tolia is reborn after the post-human visions he has seen. He discovers he is at home, while Stomper again exists within

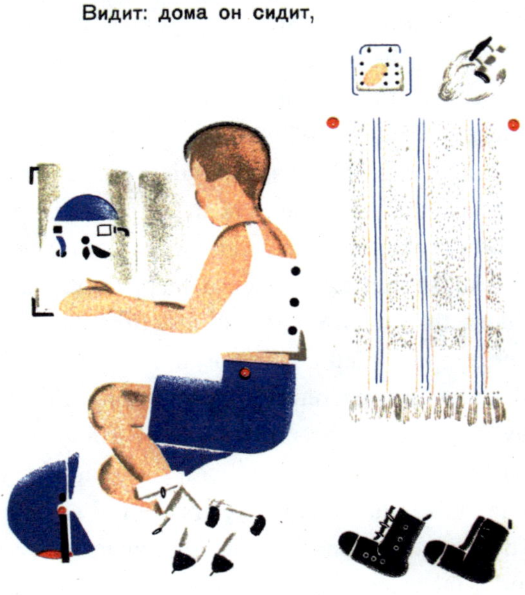

7.11 Tolia back home in Tsekanovskii's illustration for *Topotun i knizhka*.

the bounds of a book, although positioned so that his and Tolia's profiles mirror one another (fig. 7.11). Like *Alice's Adventures in Wonderland*, the story ends with this metatextual frame and an apparent awakening from a dream, as if every picture book is itself a kind of dream, whereby a post-social subject enters into a humanist art object as a portal into another perspective on the world, or shared lifeworld. In the accompanying illustration, Tolia appears in a position akin to the fetal position, lying without his outerwear, as if sleeping, among other objects assembled on this surface. Again, the boy appears vulnerable, but now no threat is apparent. Like an infant, Tolia awakens to a new life, one in which he has corrected his ways and been ideologically cleansed and converted, as his clean flesh and neatly ordered things show. It appears that Tolia has learned to serve machines, see them eye-to-eye, and treat their material products, and objects, with respect – thereby preparing him to one day work in concert with machines, like the labourers he saw. He now understands his own role in Soviet society. But in the process perhaps something else – the child's own subjectivity, creativity, and agency – has been erased.

Returning to the image on the cover, one observes that the robotic child displayed here is also the product of a Taylorist assembly line manufacturing process, and represents not just Tolia, but also the reader. This book, itself one of many, intends to purge the child of mistaken ways and transform children into effective biomechanical cogs in the wheel of a greater Soviet machine. Part of this social engineering of the child into an ideal Soviet citizen and instrument for the building of an imagined future involves not just making humans into machines and machines into people or machine-people. It also requires making the child into an automaton of adult aims and employing children as an instrument of futurity for the realization of a specific vision of that future. The child is being trained not to deviate from the authoritarian ideal. In that sense, the final, apparently cheerful words of the book sound more like a threat: "And cheerful Stomper/ Looks at him again" ("I veselyi Topotun/ Na nego opiat' gliadit"). That is, unless some sort of truce or understanding between human and machine, through the hybrid form of the machine-man represented by Stomper, has been established through the course of the book. For indeed, the categories of robot and *robota*, slaves and servants, machines and humans, appear far more fluid than it at first would appear, particularly within the covers of the book. In this sense, in this final image where a human being gazes at a machine, and a machine gazes at a human being, perhaps we witness the dawn of an emergent mutual and mutational understanding that blends the categories of subject and object, animate and inanimate, person and thing. Here one might recall Benjamin's words: "To perceive the aura of an object we look at means to invest it with the ability to look at us in return."[50] For here subject and object gaze at each other, having proven through their identity mutations and intersubjective relations that they are not so different from each other. In seeking compassion from subjects towards objects and displaying human emotions in the form of a machine that resembles a man, Stomper approaches Donna Haraway's concept of a cyborg and in some sense a post-human subjectivity.[51] For Stomper fluidly moves between the categories of inanimate and animate, representation and thing-in-itself through the means of the picture book. His subject position is not stable but mutational, and his hybrid subjectivity as machine-man has reassembled the boundaries between humans and machines.

Yet, paradoxically, something similar also might be said of the child, since the child's emergent subjectivity and political consciousness renders it, too, fluid and mutational. Although apparently a subject, the child may be treated as an object (like a pioneer kerchief) and in the process of being re-engineered is not necessarily allowed to be an agent or "to look at us in return." For example, *Stomper and the Book* castigates Tolia as a naughty child, sloven, or rascal in the beginning and end of the book as a result of exerting independent agency and creativity in ways that counter the ideology presented by the adult. So the child, too, emerges as both object and subject, and moves, in fact, from subjecthood towards objecthood during the course of the book. Insofar as the child represents an emergent subjectivity with the potential to become an active agent or instrument of the future, children are valuable, cultivated, and carefully inculcated. But, in so doing, adult ideologies construct the child as an object, an open book, an empty page, a blank face, or *tabula rasa*, available to be imprinted by the machinery of the state and through the children's books and propaganda it produces, as shown by images in the picture book itself. Early Soviet picture books, such as these books illustrated by Tsekhanovskii, thus construct a factory for the efficient production of the new and ideal Soviet person out of the rough raw material of real child readers, as paralleled by the politicized Young Pioneer youth organization also featured on its pages.

In short, for the avant-garde and for the early Soviet state, the child serves an instrument of futurity, to be employed in the service of the political machine. Childhood itself becomes a work of art, pedagogy, and politics, being re-engineered and reproduced mechanically by the picture book. And the child is the robot, or *robota*, of the man. As an instrument of futurity, the child is subjected to ideological imprinting through propagandistic presentations, such as of the technological wonders of a utopian future, that serve the ideological aims of adults and authorities in the present. If the flawed human body at times disappears entirely amid the celebration of technology, then before the aims of propaganda and pedagogy the real child too has been erased. An emergent subject has been made into an object. In fact, this ideal of the future, where human beings mechanically serve the machine of communist ideology, and a machine-man seems a possible ideal, would prove a fleeting dream. Indeed, it seems that behind the seemingly perfect work of art, which has been mechanically reproduced, there remains a pair of ink-stained human hands.

NOTES

1 Edelman, *No Future*, 11–12.
2 Ibid., 3–4.
3 Rutsky, *High Techne*, 73.
4 Ibid.
5 In this respect, one might compare these futuristic picture books to the visionary science fiction that Anindita Banerjee discusses as a model for modernity in Banerjee, *We Modern People*.
6 Smith, *The Political Machine*, 52.
7 Ibid.
8 Ibid., 40.
9 Ibid., 29.
10 Knorr Cetina, "Sociality with Objects," 18.
11 Quoted in Rutsky, *High Techne*, 75.
12 Gastev, *Vosstanie kul'tury*, 32.
13 Ibid., 55.
14 Ibid., 57.
15 Ibid., 36.

16 Banerjee, *We Modern People*, 87.
17 Gastev, *Kak nado rabotat'*, 164.
18 Banerjee, *We Modern People*, 153.
19 Ibid., 38.
20 Quoted in Law and Gordon, *Meyerhold, Eisenstein and Biomechanics*, 138.
21 Ibid., 57.
22 Vaingurt, *Wonderlands of the Avant-Garde*, 35.
23 Quoted in Law and Gordon, *Meyerhold, Eisenstein and Biomechanics*, 143.
24 Ibid., 38.
25 See Smith, "On Assemblages and Machines," in *The Political Machine*.
26 Notably, this instance marks the only case in the book where the second-person singular is used or the audience is addressed directly.
27 Relevant here is Friedrich Kittler's observation that "industrialization simultaneously nullified handwriting and hand-based work." Kittler, "Typewriter," in *Gramophone, Film, Typewriter*, 186–7.
28 Huyssen, *After the Great Divide*, 9.
29 In many senses, these women offer an updated vision of the women's sewing collectives envisioned in Chernyshevsky's *Chto delat'? (What Is to Be Done?)*.
30 Kittler, *Gramophone, Film, Typewriter*, 199.
31 Ibid., 183.
32 Benjamin, "Work of Art," 223.
33 Ibid. 226.
34 Miriam Hansen relates Benjamin's positive attitude toward technology to avant-garde aesthetics of the 1920s. See Hansen, "Benjamin, Cinema, and Experience," 181–2.
35 Huyssen, *After the Great Divide*, 9.
36 Čapek, *R.U.R.*, 3, 9.
37 Ibid.
38 The fact that the robot has eyelashes is absurd from a technical standpoint, since these body parts have an instrumental purpose, while in the robot they are purely ornamental and, it would seem, a nod to the human form.
39 Rutsky, *High Techne*, 26.
40 Benjamin, "On Some Motifs in Baudelaire," 190.
41 See Knorr Cetina, "Sociality with Objects."
42 Rutsky, *High Techne*, 185.
43 Ibid., 26.
44 See Rose, *Case of Peter Pan*.
45 Andrew Barratt notes that the scene (in Kavalerov's nightmare) where Ivan is impaled upon Ophelia's spike derives from the passage in *The War of the Worlds* where the trapped narrator watches the steel tentacle of a Martian machine searching for him. Barratt, *Yuri Olesha's "Envy,"* 35.
46 Vaingurt, *Wonderlands of the Avant-Garde*, 35.
47 Steiner, *Stories for Little Comrades*, 97.
48 In a certain sense, in this constructivist style, the child comprises pure Platonic shapes or forms. Indeed, the focus on the shaping of the child by beneficial influence, and the censoring of that which is deemed harmful, echoes Plato's educational ideal in *The Republic*, 401.
49 Steiner also notes the contrast in detail in the depiction of these faces. Steiner, *Stories for Little Comrades*.
50 Benjamin, "On Some Motifs in Baudelaire," 190.
51 Haraway, "A Cyborg Manifesto."

BIBLIOGRAPHY

Banerjee, Anindita. *We Modern People: Science Fiction and the Making of Russian Modernity.* Middleton, CT: Wesleyan University Press, 2012.

Barratt, Andrew. *Yuri Olesha's "Envy."* Birmingham, UK: University of Birmingham, 1981.

Benjamin, Walter. "On Some Motifs in Baudelaire." In *Illuminations: Essays and Reflections*, edited by Hannah Arendt, translated by Harry Zohn, 152–90. New York: Schocken Books, 1968.

– "The Work of Art in the Age of Mechanical Reproduction." In *Illuminations: Essays and Reflections*, edited by Hannah Arendt, translated by Harry Zohn, 217–51. New York: Schocken Books, 1968.

Čapek, Karel. "R.U.R. (Rossum's Universal Robots). A Play in Three Acts and an Epilogue." In *R.U.R. and the Insect Play* by Karel and Josef Čapek, translated by P. Selver. London: Oxford University Press, 1961.

Chukovsky, Kornei. *Moidodyr.* Illustrated by Iu. Annenkov. Petrograd: Raduga, 1923.

Edelman, Lee. *No Future: Queer Theory and the Death Drive.* Durham, NC: Duke University Press, 2004.

Gastev, Aleksei. *Kak nado rabotat': Prakticheskoe vvedenie v nauku organizatsii truda.* Moscow: Izdatel'stvo Ekonomika, 1966.

– *Vosstanie kul'tury.* Kharkiv: Molodoi rabochii, 1923.

Hansen, Miriam. "Benjamin, Cinema, and Experience: 'The Blue Flower in the Land of Technology.'" *New German Critique* 40 (1987): 179–224.

Haraway, Donna. "A Cyborg Manifesto: Science, Technology, and Socialist-Feminism in the Late Twentieth Century." In *Simians, Cyborgs and Women: The Reinvention of Nature*, 149–81. New York: Routledge, 1991.

Hellman, Ben. *Fairy Tales and True Stories: The History of Russian Literature for Children and Young People.* Leiden: Brill, 2013.

– "Samuil Marshak: Yesterday and Today." In *Russian Children's Literature and Culture*, edited by Marina Balina and Larissa Rudova, 217–39. New York: Routledge, 2008.

Huyssen, Andreas. *After the Great Divide. Modernism, Mass Culture, Postmodernism.* Bloomington: Indiana University Press, 1986.

Ionov, Il'ia. *Topotun i knizhka.* Illustrated by M. Tsekhanovskii. Leningrad: GIZ, 1926. http://pudl.princeton.edu/boundart.php?obj=76537411p.

Kittler, Friedrich A. "Typewriter." In *Gramophone, Film, Typewriter,* translated by Geoffrey Winthrop-Young and Michael Wutz, 183–263. Stanford, CA: Stanford University Press, 1999.

Knorr Cetina, Karin. "Sociality with Objects: Social Relations in Postsocial Knowledge Societies." *Theory, Culture, and Society* 14, no. 4 (1997): 1–30.

Kuznetsova, V., and E. Kuznetsov. *Tsekhanovskii.* Leningrad: Izdatel'stvo Khudozhnik RSFSR, 1973.

Law, Alma, and Mel Gordon. *Meyerhold, Eisenstein and Biomechanics: Actor Training in Revolutionary Russia.* London: McFarland, 1996.

Marshak, Samuil. *Bagazh.* Illustrated by Vladimir Lebedev. Leningrad: Raduga, 1926.

– *Morozhenoe.* Illustrated by Vladimir Lebedev. Leningrad: Raduga, 1925.

– *Pochta.* Illustrated by M. Tsekhanovskii. Leningrad: OGIZ, 1932.

– *Sem' chudes.* Illustrated by M. Tsekhanovskii. Leningrad: Raduga, 1926.

– *Stikhotvoreniia i poemy.* Edited by V.V. Smirnova and M.L. Gasparov. Leningrad: Sovetskii pisatel', 1973.

– *Vchera i segodnia.* Illustrated by Vladimir Lebedev. Leningrad: Raduga, 1925.

Olesha, Iu. *Zavist'. Tri tolstiaka. Rasskazy.* Moscow: Olimp, 1998.

Plato. *The Republic.* Translated by Francis MacDonald Cornford. Oxford: Oxford University Press, 1970.

Rose, Jacqueline. *The Case of Peter Pan, or The Impossibility of Children's Fiction.* Basingstoke, UK: Macmillan, 1984.

Russell, Charles. *Poets, Prophets, and Revolutionaries: The Literary Avant-Garde from Rimbaud to Postmodernism.* Oxford: Oxford University Press, 1985.

Rutsky, R.L. *High Techne: Art and Technology from the Machine Aesthetic to the Posthuman.* Minneapolis: University of Minnesota Press, 1999.

Savel'ev, L. (Leonid Lipavskii). *Pionerskii ustav.* Illustrated by M. Tsekhanovskii. Leningrad: Gosizdat, 1926.

Shklovsky, Viktor. "Iskusstvo kak priem." In *Gamburgskii schet. Stat'i-vospominaniia-esse. (1914–1933),* 58–72. Moscow: Sovetskii pisatel', 1990.

Smith, Adam T. *The Political Machine: Assembling Sovereignty in the Bronze Age Caucasus.* Princeton, NJ: Princeton University Press, 2015.

Sokol, Elena. *Russian Poetry for Children.* Knoxville: University of Tennessee Press, 1984.

Steiner, Evgenii. *Avangard i postroenie novogo cheloveka: Iskusstvo sovetskoi detskoi knigi 1920 godov.* Moscow: Novoe literaturnoe obozrenie, 2002.

– *Stories for Little Comrades: Revolutionary Artists and the Making of Early Soviet Children's Books.* Translated by Jane Ann Miller. Seattle: University of Washington Press, 1999.

Tsekhanovskii, Mikhail. *Sovetskie rebiata. Sbornik dlia detei. Maket oblozhki.* Illustrated by M. Tsekhanovskii. Moscow: Rossiiskii gosudarstvennii arkhiv literatury i iskusstva, 1925. http://www.rgali.ru/object/10996935.

Vaingurt, Julia. *Wonderlands of the Avant-Garde: Technology and the Arts in Russia of the 1920s.* Evanston, IL: Northwestern University Press, 2013.

Wells, H.G. *The War of the Worlds.* New York: Penguin, 2005.

Zavadskaia, E. "Tramvainoe teplo." *Detskaia literatura* 11 (1988): 54–6, 80–1.

chapter eight

SPELLS OF MATERIALIST MAGIC, OR SOVIET CHILDREN AND ELECTRIC POWER

KIRILL CHUNIKHIN

In 1924, authors Iakov Galitskii and Zinaida Valentinova and illustrator Vasilii Artem'ev issued the book *Skazka o mal'chike Pete, kotoryi nikogo ne boialsia na svete, nikomu klaniat'sia ne privyk, i kak emu v zabotakh i rabotakh pomog dobryi staryi Ded-Elektrik* (*The Tale of the Boy Petia, Who Wasn't Afraid of Anyone on Earth and Wasn't in the Habit of Bowing Down to Anyone, and about How Kindly Old Ded-Elektrik Helped Him in His Troubles and Work*). This fairy tale tells the story of Petia, a boy of working-class origins who refuses to serve Ivan Tsarevich and is thus imprisoned to await execution by being baked into a pie. One day in his dark cell, the boy combs his hair, causing sparks of static electricity to fall to the floor. These turn into small shining creatures called *svetiki* (lit., "little lights"). Taking pity on the boy, the *svetiki* suggest that Ded-Elektrik – literally "Grampa-the-Electrician" – might rescue him, and they teach Petia how to summon this potential intercessor, by flying a kite up into a storm cloud, where Ded dwells (fig. 8.1). At night, the boy is allowed to have a walk outside his cell. Petia follows the *svetiki*'s instructions and successfully contacts Ded-Elektrik, who descends as a fireball. First, he furnishes the boy's cell with an electric lamp and a telephone (so that he can talk to his parents); then, he powers a train that brings working-class people to the kingdom, who liberate the boy-prisoner and take power.

Apparently the first Soviet children's book to thematize electricity, *The Tale of the Boy Petia* used the language of children's stories to represent an essentially "adult" phenomenon central to early Soviet policy. Speaking at the Moscow provincial conference of the Russian Communist Party on 21 November 1920, Vladimir Lenin declared the seminal ideological formula: "Communism is Soviet power plus the electrification of the whole country."[1] Whereas Lenin's maxim effectively compressed the program of achieving communism into a single sentence, the six-hundred-page plan of the State Commission for the Electrification of Russia (GOELRO), issued in 1920,

8.1. Following the advice of the *svetiki,* Petia flies a kite, in order to contact Ded-Elektrik, who dwells in a storm cloud. Illustration by Vasilii Artem'ev, in Iakov Galitskii and Zinaida Valentinova, *Skazka o mal'chike Pete* (Moscow: Novaia Moskva, 1924), 43.

provided step-by-step instructions for electrification.[2] Arguing that the GOELRO plan was essentially a political program, Lenin proposed that it should be seen as the "second program of the Party."[3] Insofar as popularizing the electrification program throughout the Soviet state was considered crucial to its success, "all agitation and propagandistic organs, all party activities,"[4] were to be directed toward its advancement. Further, argued Lenin, electrification could not be carried out so long as Soviet people – the agents of the project – remained largely illiterate. In order to prepare people for their part in the electrification, various educational materials had to be issued.[5]

Along with adults, children were to be exposed to an "electric" education. The GOELRO plan would make little sense to them, but classes on electricity integrated into the school curriculum would prepare them for their future participation in the project.[6] Furthermore, books categorized as *nauchno-khudozhestvennaia* and *nauchno-tekhnicheskaia* literature (works focusing on science and technology) would introduce the basic concepts necessary for understanding electrification. However, such books, which typically relied heavily on verbal narrative, assumed some literacy on the reader's part.[7] Thus, while aimed at the majority of the Soviet population, the imperative of an "electric" education did not take pre- or semi-literate schoolchildren into account.

Nevertheless, it was inevitable that themes of electricity and electrification would find their way into books for preschool children. For one thing, it was hardly possible to depict the newly emerging communist society without depicting electrification, and the 1920s debates on children's literature acknowledged that introducing children to Soviet realities was a crucial goal. Electrification, moreover, ontologically linked as it was to communism and Soviet power, could help define just what the Soviets were actually building. As I will show, electricity in children's books was a highly emblematic topic, allowing the delivery of a variety of meanings of the Soviet project, including its cosmogony, ontology, and, to some extent, even its eschatology. Last, but not least, the widespread presence of the topic of electricity in children's books was due to the fact that, of the three elements of Lenin's formula (communism = Soviet power + electrification), the last was, perhaps, the most concrete, palpable, and amenable to visual representation within a book, even if doing had its complications.

This chapter demonstrates how authors of Soviet children's books elaborated unique representational schemes capable of advancing a complex technological reality within the world of children. In analysing books that deal with electricity, I approach them as essentially synthetic works of art, in which the visual and the verbal are subjected to a guiding organizing principle. Uncovering these principles helps explain the representational techniques used to produce the electricity imagery in question, explore how notions of electricity were constructed in a child's mind, and, ultimately, uncover unknown aspects of the Soviet history of modernity. In their introduction to *Energy Humanities*, Imre Szeman and Dominic Boyer claim that energy equals modernity.[8] However, the Soviet Union is largely absent from their analytic picture. This chapter helps fill that gap, exploring the ways in which the culture of socialist modernity devised a language of technology within the medium of the children's book.

The Challenge of the Electrification of Children's Books

The representation of electricity for pre- and semi-literate children was an ambitious task: Soviet children's books were to communicate a "scientific" phenomenon to an unprepared audience. Unable to explain electricity in terms of physics, authors had to come up with ways of making the subject palpable for and comprehensible to children. The target audience's greater receptiveness to the visual than the verbal significantly increased the role of the pedagogy of images; Soviet authors thus had to be especially innovative in establishing an "imagery of electricity." Depicting the socio-economic process of the electrification of the country was problematic as well: besides creating visual-verbal narratives adequately representing the course of this major project, authors had to keep updating these narratives in order to promptly showcase the latest achievements. Moreover, as electrification advanced, the need to teach children how to live in an electrified world was becoming more relevant.

The greatest challenge, however, was to adjust the nascent language of Soviet children's literature to the representation of electricity and electrification. In practice, in light of the ongoing debates on the legitimacy of the fairy tale as a genre, Soviet authors had to figure out, among other things, how to wed a fantastic narrative, essential to children's literature, to a "scientific" representation of electricity.[9] In pursuing edificatory goals, should books entirely "disenchant" electricity and represent it as a purely materialistic phenomenon? Or should books that dealt with electricity preserve some degree of magic so as to maintain their appeal for young children? The absence of clear literary precedent or guidelines, and, more generally, the reigning uncertainty about future directions of children's literature, led Soviet authors to experiment with the representation of electricity, to seek out an optimal proportion of fantasy and factual data for such books.

A first reading of the books analysed in this chapter suggests that the history of depicting electricity for children was one of gradual rationalization and disenchantment. Indeed, there seems to be a process by which technical, "scientific" representations replace electricity's "magic." However, while revealing this apparent disenchantment, I pay special attention to the magic that nevertheless remained in children's books. Such an approach allows us to detect the limits of electricity's rationalization, which was never complete. Despite constant attempts to rationalize electricity by representing it as a natural phenomenon, ostensibly materialist Soviet books nevertheless endowed electricity with magic and supernatural power: the power, that is, to act (affect and effect), to establish epochs and reconceptualize time, to transform space, and so on. Seeking an apt analytic frame to match the essentially ambiguous representation of electricity, I employ the term "materialist magic," which I illustrate throughout this chapter.[10] This term can help reveal the techniques and the limits of incorporating "wonders" into a children's literature that was supposed to avoid fairy-tale elements for the sake of "realist" representations. Analysing the shifting balance of magic and disenchantment of electricity in the 1920s and 1930s, I uncover, ultimately, how Soviet books represented electricity as an actant and modelled a specific relationship that children had with it.

The Magic of Electricity: Adapting the Fairy Tale

In chronological terms, the 1924 book about Petia was, technically, a product of the post-revolutionary period. However, the verbal-visual language its authors used to represent electricity relied heavily on pre-revolutionary aesthetics of children's literature. On the cover and title page, the lengthy title typical of fairy tales was designed in a stylized manner and accompanied with a vignette – features characteristic of pre-Soviet children's literature (fig. 8.2a–b). This title page is indicative of the authors' intention to adapt previous narratives to contemporary needs, to "modernize" the

8.2a–b. Cover and title page of Iakov Galitskii and Zinaida Valentinova, *Skazka o mal'chike Pete*. The verbal and visual language of this book, including its lengthy title, relied heavily on pre-revolutionary aesthetics of children's literature.

magic fairy tale with newly relevant Soviet content. Representing the conflict of the working class and the tsars in a fairytale mode, *The Tale of the Boy Petia* effectively frames a basic Soviet binary opposition in terms of good and evil. The "evil" pole includes not only allusions to the tsarist period, but also various elements of folklore and previous literary traditions (the minstrels known as *skomorokhi*, boyars, and so on), which are denounced in this updated fairy tale.

But while modernizing an old framework may have been propagandistically effective, the resulting book itself is hardly edifying. Making use of the fairy-tale scheme in this manner led inevitably to the representation of electricity as a magical power, which was fuelled, in particular, by the book's illustrations. The episode in which Petia "contacts" Ded-Elektrik is depicted as an essentially magical summoning ritual (fig. 8.1). Furthermore, upon Ded's descent from the heavens as a fireball, he turns into an anthropomorphized creature wearing a cowl made of lightning bolts. And the electricity brought by this intercessor (an almost literal *deus ex machina*) immediately improves the conditions of the boy's imprisonment (fig. 8.3). The figure of Ded works as a semantic and compositional centre of the image, the meaning of which he generates. Pointing at the lamp, Ded provokes the eye to look at it. The rays coming from the lamp lead the eye to further explore the space of the room and witness the light's impact on the environment – for instance, the scurrying away of a rat. Both the lamp and Ded in the picture radiate, which shows the essential unity of their "substance." The image represents electricity as a great power of magical origin, as it is derived from this seemingly omnipotent Ded. Instead of rationalizing electricity, then, the book mystifies it. Although at the end of the tale Ded advises that, in order to understand electricity, one must study, the book nevertheless depicts electricity as a form of sorcery.

In illustrating this episode of the installation of a ceiling light, Artem'ev relies heavily on precedents from European religious iconography. Ded's gesture (arm raised toward the light bulb) is reminiscent of a number of works of art, from Michelangelo's *The Creation of Adam* to Schnorr von Carolsfeld's *The Fourth Day of Creation* (fig. 8.4). A highly symbolic visual formula for European art, this gesture allowed the representation of a creation process while emphasizing the agency of the creator. Thus, in Artem'ev's illustration, a gesture normally used to represent supernatural events depicts, in a quasi-religious visual language, a major technological breakthrough of a secularized and would-be communist country. In effect "breathing life" into a lamp, Ded turns the installation of ceiling lights into a communist variant of the Genesis creation narrative: "Let there be light."

Further evidence of Artem'ev's intention to adapt previous visual formulae to contemporary needs is the engraving *Moses Showing the Ten Commandments* by Gustave Doré (fig. 8.5). Here, besides the emblematic gesture discussed above, one can find a compositional similitude with Artem'ev's illustration. Moses stands with his arm raised toward the sky, in which flashes a bolt of lightning; he holds the stone

8.3. Artem'ev's illustration of Ded-Elektrik installing an electric light in Petia's cell, in *Skazka o mal'chike Pete*, 42.

8.4. Julius Schnorr von Carolsfeld, *The Fourth Day of Creation*, woodcut from *The Bible in Pictures* (Leipzig: Georg Wigand, 1860), 4.

8.5. A comparison of Gustave Doré's engraving *Moses Showing the Ten Commandments* (1865) with Artem'ev's illustration in figure 8.3 provides evidence of the latter's intention to adapt earlier visual formulae in religious art for his own needs.

tablets, and light radiates from his head. In Artem'ev's illustration, the stone tablets have transformed into the arch of the door behind Ded-Elektrik, who carries a bag rather than tablets. Both Ded and Moses radiate light. In keeping with this example, several illustrations in the book constitute adaptations of existing works of art. As figure 8.6 shows, to represent electricity, Artem'ev has reworked Giorgione's famous *The Tempest* (ca. 1508), cropping its compositional scheme and emphasizing lightning with a zigzag sign.

It is an open question whether Artem'ev made use of religious iconography simply as a result of the influences arising from his own classical training as an artist. His adaptation was de facto a desacralization of religious imagery, its reappropriation for secular and profane topics. At the same time, his approach may have represented an attempt to deliver communism in a language potentially familiar to children. Notably, children in 1924 may still have been aware of such religious visual culture as icons. The artist's exploitation of religious visual imagery might thus have worked as a potentially appealing and effective representation. In such pictures, children would have seen familiar compositional schemes, depicting the advent of new "gods" like Ded-Elektrik.

8.6. In this illustration, Artem'ev has reworked the compositional scheme and lightning imagery of Giorgione's *The Tempest*. Iakov Galitskii and Zinaida Valentinova, *Skazka o mal'chike Pete*, 41.

But, most crucially, these new "communist gods" would have inherited their great "magical" power from the gods of the past. The significance of this newly obtained power was not limited to such utilities as electric light or telecommunication and transportation networks. Or, rather, the utility of electricity was far-reaching, acting as a liberating and revolutionary communist force: embodied within Ded-Elektrik, electricity allows the boy to escape and overthrow the tsarevich. After all, the revolution in this book succeeds only due to the specific connection between electricity and people.

Such representation of electricity as a direct contributor (alongside people) to revolution was not, in early Soviet culture, solely an appurtenance of fairy tales. For example, in 1925, Boris Arvatov, a theorist of proletarian art and culture, argued that relations between people and non-living things had to undergo a radical change.[11] The author saw capitalist society as marked by a major "gap" or "rupture" (*razryv*) between people and things, which were, in that system, basically passive objects of consumption.[12] It was up to proletarian culture to bridge this gap: once a firm cooperation between people and things was established, the latter would begin working as weapons and building-tools of socialism. The ultimate goal was to establish unique relations between people and non-living matter broadly defined, from objects to such productive forces of nature as electricity.[13] Arguably, *The Tale of the Boy Petia* introduced, in fairy-tale language, an example of the new type of relationship between people and natural forces envisioned by Arvatov. This relationship, as I will show, would evolve throughout the 1920s and into the 1930s.

This fairy tale shows that the conceptual frame of "active human–passive matter" is insufficient to understand the human/electricity relationship in Soviet children's literature. Such an anthropocentric perspective imputes a human exclusivity to the performance of agency, which was not the case for Soviet electricity imagery. From the inception of Soviet children's literature, electricity in books was an actant. The specific children/electricity relationship can be aptly described within the emerging philosophy of vital materialism. This "speculative onto-story" insists that agency is a capability shared by humans and non-humans alike.[14] Jane Bennett, the political theorist standing at the foundation of this philosophy, uses the term "assemblage," which recognizes that living and non-living objects establish vital horizontal human/non-human connections: in the fairy tale about Petia, it is precisely one such assemblage that makes the revolution possible.

In revealing the agentive force of electricity, the book makes use (even overuse) of magical fairy-tale elements, such as the electric sparks that magically transform into anthropomorphized *svetiki* to teach Petia how to summon Ded-Elektrik. In the mid-1920s, outright magic of this sort, inherited from the fairy-tale scheme, was already problematic: Soviet critics blamed the genre of the fairy tale for allegedly inculcating Soviet children with bourgeois consciousness. Consequently, the explicitly pre-tsarist "magical" representation in *The Tale of the Boy Petia* may have seemed a failure, so far as the elaboration of a new Soviet language for children's books was concerned: despite providing modern, relevant content, the authors and illustrator hardly fulfilled the goals of children's literature. Nevertheless, this may have been a useful failure: in this case, fairy-tale topoi enabled a testing of the limits of adapting pre-existing verbal and visual schemes for the representation of electricity. The book showed that communism could not be easily translated into children's language using fairy-tale and sacral visual imagery. The fairy tale would soon be replaced by new approaches to children's literature, in which electricity's "magic" would gradually give way to new modes of representation.

Coining the Idea of the Lamp

The 1925 book *Vchera i segodnia* (*Yesterday and Today*), written by Samuil Marshak and illustrated by Vladimir Lebedev, demonstrates a more revolutionary approach to children's books than that taken in the fairy tale of *The Tale of the Boy Petia*. In Marshak's book, objects of "yesterday" – a kerosene lamp, a quill, and so on – speak with objects of today, such as an electric lamp and typewriter.[15] Although the book still features certain "magic" phenomena (non-living things conversing with one another), this anthropomorphism emerges not within a fairy-tale framework but as a crucial element of the "productivist book" ("proizvodstvennaia knizhka"). As Boris Bukhshtab remarked, such an otherwise "criminal 'anthropomorphism'" was in this case acceptable, because here it provoked the reader's emotional connection to the objects depicted instead of serving the cause of "fairy-taleness" ("skazochnost'") per se.[16] Whereas the 1924 fairy tale about Petia depicted electricity as a significant power of magical origin, *Yesterday and Today* provides insights as to how an electric lamp actually works: the animated objects function to explain contemporary technological realities. For example, a conversation between a kerosene and an electric lamp reveals their similarities and differences in terms of design and maintenance. Thus, the authors use "magic" – that is, anthropomorphization – in order to partially disenchant electricity.

Lebedev's approach to illustrating Marshak's text marks a crucially innovative step in the project of explaining electricity to children; in order to make an electric lamp understandable, he depicts it not naturalistically but analytically. Unlike the kerosene lamp, the electric lamp is represented schematically (fig. 8.7): Lebedev's goal is to denote not a specific lamp, but the idea of an electric bulb as such. Omitting all minor details, the illustrator focuses on the lamp's major elements: glass bulb, tungsten filament, and cap. Stylistically, the image of the lamp becomes reminiscent of a "technical" visual language, adapted by Lebedev for children. Advancing the idea of the lamp and introducing the visual language of technology, Lebedev's illustration perfectly fulfils the goals of the pedagogy of images.

In educating children about electricity, Lebedev must have been cognizant of the specific needs of preschool readers: being more passive than active, they consequently rely more on the visual then the verbal.[17] To facilitate the reader's reception of the book's message, Lebedev seeks, in some of his illustrations, to establish a parallel visual narrative, one deriving from the "main" verbal text. In figure 8.7, one can see how such a visual narrative consists of a succession of heterogeneous signs: first, an electric bulb filled with candles, which allows the lamp's "power" to be visually measured; next, a working "radiating" lamp; then a question mark, expressing surprise at or non-understanding of the lamp; and finally, an exclamation sign marking the end of this visual utterance, and adding an extra degree of amusement or excitement to it. This visual utterance, albeit essentially stemming from the verbal text, is simultaneously autonomous enough to communicate the question about the nature of an electric lamp to preliterate children.

Fulfilling its pedagogic goal, the book provides an answer to the question of the working mechanics of an electric lamp. Lebedev's poster-like illustration (see fig. 8.7) not only succinctly summarizes Marshak's verbal exposition but also fully duplicates it as a visual narrative. Marshak's discourse conveys that the lamp shines bright because it is a relative of lightning. In figure 8.7, Lebedev depicts the lamp as connected to the zigzag symbol of a lightning bolt. Moreover, Lebedev attempts to visually represent the lamp as it speaks, situating it at the centre of the image, light radiating

8.7. Vladimir Lebedev's illustrations of various elements of an electric lamp evoke a "technical" visual language, adapted for children. Samuil Marshak, *Vchera i segodnia* (Leningrad: Raduga, 1925), 4–5.

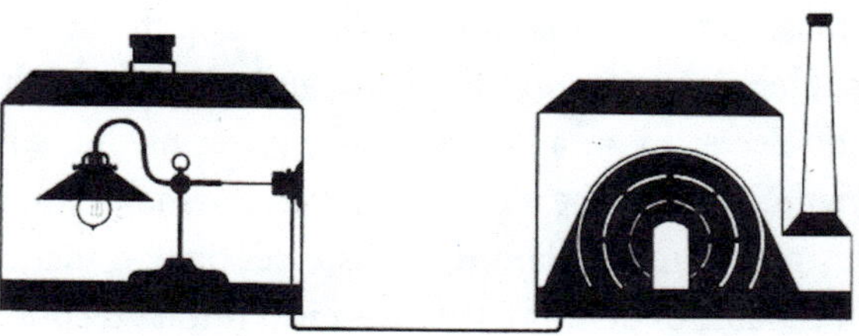

8.8. Lebedev illustrates the "secret" of electric light: electricity comes from a power station through wires. Marshak, *Vchera i segodnia*, 6.

from it along with its words. Finally, the "secret" of electric light is revealed (fig. 8.8): electricity comes from a power station through wires.

This synthesis of Marshak's words and Lebedev's pictures exposes readers to basic information regarding the structure and workings of an electric lamp. The book's meta-structure further serves to imprint the idea of the lamp in children's minds. Marshak and Lebedev, rather than trying to adapt pre-revolutionary forms, as in the case of the fairy tale about Petia, take advantage of a representational scheme that had emerged only recently. The structuring idea of *Yesterday and Today* – that is, is the binary opposition of "before and after" – determines the plot as well as Lebedev's individual approach to illustrations. Serguei Oushakine argues that the "before and after" template, one of the first in Soviet children's literature, arose in particular with Mayakovsky's 1918 book *Oktiabr' 1917–1918. Geroi i zhertvy Revoliutsii (October 1917–1918: Heroes and Victims of the Revolution).*[18] As seen in *Yesterday and Today*, such a frame proved productive, not only for the representation of complex social phenomena like revolution, but also for introducing technology and scientific concepts like electricity.

A major advantage of representation of this sort is that it supported the conceptualization of electricity by using existing background context and semantic blocks. In

Yesterday and Today, the electric lamp is counterposed to its predecessors the candle and the kerosene lamp. Exposed to these latter items in their daily life, children would be able to hypothesize a palpable notion of an electric lamp. For example, because candles were at the time used to measure the power of the lamp (the ratio of 50:1 is given in the book), the strikingness of the comparison itself brings home the great difference between these two illumination sources. Taking the upbringing of their pre- or semi-literate readers into account, then, the author and the illustrator elaborated a representation of electricity in a language and in terms that children would most likely be familiar with. Shaping the idea of the electric lamp in this way – in its generic relation to candles and kerosene lamps – was essentially a matter of establishing a binary opposition capable of defining the given invention's technological meaning.

This is not to say that *Yesterday and Today* represents the lamp as a completely rationalized technological device. Despite the rational explanation given of the lamp, electric light is nevertheless said to be "wondrous" or "miraculous" ("chudesnyi").[19] Is the *chudo* in question "merely" an amazing curiosity, or some unexplainable phenomenon or miracle? And does this *chudo* compromise or support the book's pedagogical mission of explaining electricity?

From its inception, the representation of electricity in children's books was marked by this coexistence of "science" and "wonders." For example, in *The Tale of the Boy Petia* Ded-Elektrik declares, "There are no wonders [or "miracles"; "chudes net"] in the whole wide world. The only wonder is science ["tol'ko v nauke est' chudo"]."[20] On one hand, this claim disenchants the world, advising Petia that there are no wonders (unexplainable phenomena) in it. On the other hand, the second sentence specifically defines science as a field of wonders. Such a contradictory representation of technology in Soviet books made electricity, among other things, a socialist technological "wonder/miracle," an example of materialist magic.[21]

Representing electricity as a wonder, Soviet authors exploited technology's affective potential, in a manner reminiscent of how, as Heike Behrend has observed, European colonizers of Africa "used the instruments actually intended for scientific research and documentation, especially the camera, to create 'wonders,' in order to astonish and terrify Africans."[22] Behrend further argues that this use of technology was twofold: first, displayed as wondrous objects, with an eye to introducing them [technological objects] as commodities in a circulation of desire; and second, as magical instruments to overpower the natives and furnish themselves with an aura of superhuman power."[23]

Behrend's conception is helpful in explaining the role of electricity in Soviet children's books. Soviet authors often depicted scenes of children's encounters with electric light as wondrous events, if not outright miracles, despite the materialist agenda of technological modernization specifically proclaimed as the mission of these books. As a result, electricity modernized and disenchanted the world but simultaneously revealed the great, almost enchanting power of the owners of this technology.

This great power was not explicitly divine or magical, but it was nevertheless virtually "supernatural," allowing the Soviet government, for example, to create a glass bulb, a kind of domesticized and safe lightning (see fig. 8.7).

The materialist wonder of the lamp, as espoused by Marshak and Lebedev, had a historical aspect: electricity worked as a reference point to constitute a new Soviet temporality. For example, the opposition of past (candles and kerosene lamps) and present (electric lamps) in *Yesterday and Today* was used to represent Soviet modernity, of which electricity was a crucial part. Books represented electrification as a major historical dividing line between tsarist Russia and the Soviet state. Accordingly, pre-revolutionary Russia was portrayed as a dark space, in contrast to a Soviet land illuminated by electric light.

The cover of Marshak and Lebedev's book (see fig. 15.1, page 468) visualizes the radical differences between past and present. It consists of two thematic blocks, the upper relating to "yesterday," and the lower to "today." The upper section depicts people of pre-Soviet Russia, who used kerosene lamps, had to get water from wells, and so on. The people of "today," by contrast, enjoy the

8.9. Lebedev depicts the redundant, dilapidated kerosene lamp of the past, replaced by the electric light associated with Soviet modernity. Samuil Marshak, *Vchera i segodnia*, 3.

advantages of electric light and indoor plumbing. The palette for each section shows the crucial role that *light* plays in defining Soviet modernity. The upper section is black-and-white, whereas the lower section is in colour. The blackness of "yesterday" constitutes an absence of light. In this crude visual opposition, Lebedev represents electric light as a major criterion in defining the differences between the two historical periods.

As the book goes on, the role of electric light for Soviet modernity is further revealed in the conflict between objects of the past (kerosene lamps, candles) and the electric lamp. The book opens with a kerosene lamp complaining of not being used anymore: she has been put in a corner, thus losing (most importantly from a conceptual standpoint) her formerly central position on the table (fig 8.9). Given the table's status as a home's communal gathering-place, this relegation also indicates that the kerosene lamp has lost her major function. Henceforth, it would be up to the electric lamp to illuminate the room, inviting people to gather round by making them visible. Lebedev visually emphasizes the loss of status of the kerosene lamp and candle: they are depicted as dilapidated, ready to fall apart. Ultimately, on a "domestic level," this episode represents the story of advancing Soviet modernity, about to dramatically change the country's way of life.

In addition to constructing the idea of the lamp from children's existing conceptual material, then, Marshak and Lebedev also explain electricity historically. The lamp is thus afforded both a synchronic and a diachronic meaning. Historicizing the lamp enables a partial solution to a key sticking point in the depiction of electricity in children's books: how to reveal the genesis of electricity without reference (as in *The Tale of the Boy Petia*) to magic or magic-seeming entities. In a sense, Marshak and Lebedev debunk the wonder of electric light by inscribing the lamp in a historical context, endowing it with a genealogy: this device is the next step in the evolution of lamps, after the candle and the kerosene lamp. Most significantly, because the authors link the emergence of the electric lamp to the advent of a new sociohistorical formation, historicizing the lamp meets the ideological needs of historical materialism. However, in Soviet children's literature, the electric light was not only the prerequisite of the revolution (as in *The Tale of the Boy Petia*) or its result (as in *Yesterday and Today*). After its emergence and domestication, electricity itself became a *base* that affected the *superstructure*.[24] Integrated into the Soviet environment, electricity immediately launched a series of consequent materialist wonders, triggering the country's thoroughgoing transformation into a proper socialist space.

Socialist Alchemy

Conquering domestic space, electric light radically transformed it. Books like *Egor-Monter* (*Egor the Electrician*, 1928) by Nikolai Smirnov and *Elektromonter* (*The Electrician*, 1931) by Boris Ural'skii depicted how electric light enabled a new spatiality (figs. 8.10 and 8.11). Both books feature a scene with a child sitting at a table, reading a book under an electric lamp. This visual topos symbolized that, within the electrification in the Soviet Union, a new space for children – a learning space – had emerged. Electricity transformed previously dark domestic space into a studying environment. Consequently, electric light provided by the Soviet government was symbolically linked to enlightenment ("prosveshchenie").

While establishing this new domestic learning-space for children to inhabit, electric light also created a new time in which to live. As Aleksandr Deineka's illustration for the cover of *The Electrician* makes clear, electric light enables one to study at any time: the darkness beyond the window is no longer any hindrance. Electric light thus signified independence from the natural flow of time. It allowed one, moreover, to make use of the dark hours that had previously gone to waste. As a result, the time to actively *live* within the twenty-four-hour clock-frame increased – a thought occasionally made explicit in Soviet children's books.[25] Considering the interdependent

„Должно быть, это Егор электричество в деревню проводит“,— смекнул.

Стал Егор с тех пор электричества бояться пуще собак. Даже слова этого выговорить без страха не мог. К реке не ходил. Все думал, закинешь удочку в воду, а оттуда искра вместо рыбы. Убьет еще.

Только один раз, уже осенью, сидит он в избе. Вдруг дверь открылась и входит в комнату незнакомый человек с проволокой. Егор испугался, думал это за ним пришли. Спрятался под стол. А человек у отца спрашивает:

— Где вам тут электрическую лампочку вешать?
Егорка из-под стола высунулся и говорит:

14

— Не надо нам лампочки. Я это электричество знаю. Оно, как из ружья, палит. Еще кур перебьет.

— Ничего не палит,—сказал человек.— Это оно в дураков палит, которые провода соединяют. А умным оно работать помогает.

Повесил лампочку над самым столом.

И под этой лампочкой Егор всю зиму букварь читал по вечерам. И уж светло было... С коптилкой не сравнишь!

15

8.10. Galina and Ol'ga Chichagova, illustration of a child reading using electric light, in Nikolai Smirnov, *Egor-Monter* (Moscow: GIZ, 1928),15.

8.11. Aleksandr Deineka's cover illustration for Boris Ural'skii, *Elektromonter* (Moscow: OGIZ-Molodaia gvardia, 1931).

spatiotemporal aspects of the topos of a child reading under a lamp, one can conclude that Soviet books represented electric light as capable of creating a new Soviet chronotope.

Macro space in the Soviet Union likewise underwent major transformations. In her article on cinema, electrification, and the transformation of Soviet space, Emma Widdis argues that the GOELRO plan contributed significantly to establishing Soviet mental mapping.[26] Among other things, electrical networks made it possible to organize relations between centre and periphery. Electricity in children's books worked in a similar manner: electrical networks put diverse elements of the country together in a single, electrically driven socialist entity. For example, *The Electrician* depicts power stations as centres spreading electricity through wires in multiple directions: "To houses, to the factory / To the south, to the east" ("V doma, na zavod, / na iug, na vostok"). In organizing this distribution of energy, power stations centralized the country, integrating its far-flung parts into a whole. Electrical networks spread from power plants to reach non-electrified territories, immediately transforming them into socialist lands. Books effectively communicated the significance of the changes brought by electrification. For example, a spread from the book *Dneprostroi* – about the Soviet enterprise that constructed the Dnieper Hydroelectric Station – showcases scenes of industry, transportation, and medical developments that owe their new existence to electricity (fig. 8.12). Implying that such things were hardly to be found prior to the revolution, the book depicts Soviet electrification as a radical, widely consequential transformation.

Significantly, electricity was not just a subject of transformation, but also an object of conversion. Books like *Dneprostroi* and Vladimir Voinov's *80 000 loshadei* (*80,000 Horses*, 1925) focused on both the effects of electrification and the techniques of electricity generation. As for the latter, Soviet authors favoured hydropower as the signature Soviet method essential to the GOELRO plan. Depicting how hydropower emerged via the conversion of a natural resource into electricity, these authors underscored that such a method required no human labour except that of the constructing of a dam. It was water, not people, that produced electricity. Emphasizing the agency of water, Soviet children's books made great use of the anthropomorphization of rivers, despite this being a theoretically "harmful" fairy-tale element. Anthropomorphization was thus decidedly not an outdated rhetorical device (at least, not in this case), but rather the precise expression of a contemporary type of socialist production that occurs when nature converts its energy from water to electricity according to human design and under human control.

Simultaneously, the anthropomorphization of rivers made for an accessible explanation of the nature of electricity. Avoiding explicit magic, books featuring personified rivers made it possible to explain the power of electricity indirectly, with reference to the power of the river – terms quite likely to be in a child's capacity to envision. Depicting rivers as wild, powerful currents to be tamed, Soviet books played

8.12. An illustration by Vera Lantsetti showcases various developments that would have been impossible without electricity. Nikolai Mislavskii, *Dneprostroi*, 2nd ed (Moscow: GIZ, 1930), 6–7.

up their unruly mightiness so as to show children the scale of the power converted from water into electricity.[27] Representation of this sort made a compelling homage to Soviet labour: depicting Soviet people struggling with rivers, books heroized the builders of communism. All told, the hydropower topic in children's books was extremely effective, in propagandistic and explanatory terms alike.

To sum up, Soviet children's books depicted the major process of energy generation and utilization as a kind of Soviet alchemy. Electricity (a power obtained from, in effect, converting water into energy) instantiated the old dream of the philosopher's stone that turned base metals into gold; electricity transmuted space into *Soviet* space. It could thus be supposed that books on hydropower, rather than depicting a mere technological process of obtaining energy from rivers, ultimately showcased how river-derived electricity could advance communism. The making of communism from water was the materialist magic of Lenin, the grand alchemist, who had inspired Soviet electrification and who orchestrated (after 1924, in spirit) its conversions and transformations.

The books on electricity discussed so far espoused the idea of this energy as a virtually supernatural power that signified the advent of a new historical period, and created a new, Soviet chronotope. In depicting the production of electricity from water, books carefully followed Lenin's motto about the crucial role electrification played in the establishment of communism. Soviet power over electricity enabled the colonization of non-Soviet spaces by transforming them into communist ones. The spell of materialist magic cast by lamps was, thus, not only affective but also effective.

Although such books provided some basic facts on electricity, what they provided was still far from a complete rationalization. The nature of electricity remained mysterious for children, who, should they have been keen to learn more, would be told that they would have to study. Indeed, children's untutored, unaccompanied forays into the world of electricity could prove traumatic. In the 1928 book *Egor the Electrician*, for example, a boy excited to learn that electricity can power the cinema, trains, and so on undertakes to electrify his own family's house. But the attempt causes a regional blackout, and Egor develops a fear of electricity. This book, and others, served as a sort of "Danger! High Voltage!" sign for children – they were to *keep out* of the electrified world, which was a far from natural environment.

Montage of New Ecology

In the 1930s, the Soviet Union celebrated a major success with respect to its electrification, as the GOELRO plan had been over-fulfilled already by 1931. Soviet children's books responded to this new reality accordingly, with new representations of electricity. Whereas earlier books like *80,000 Horses* and certain others had depicted electrification as an ongoing process that would radically alter life in the Soviet Union, books in the 1930s began to represent electrification as a partially accomplished goal. The electrified world was, for that matter, already a natural environment for Soviet children. For example, the 1930 book *The Electrician*, authored by Ural'skii and illustrated by Deineka, having begun with an episode of the electrification of a room, goes on to depict electricity as something entirely habitual and deeply integrated in daily life.

The visual imagery Deineka developed for this book greatly advances the representation of the electrified world. As already observed, the cover shows a boy reading a book under an electric lamp (see fig. 8.11). Notably, whereas the 1928 *Egor the Electrician* had concluded similarly, Deineka's depiction here constitutes the opening episode. The shift of this scene within the book is indicative of the transformation that had occurred in the representation of the electrification in children's literature: from now on, stories would not *lead to* electrification, but would take place, rather, in an already electrified environment.

Electric light, so effectively depicted on the cover of *The Electrician*, is palpable throughout the book. In order to achieve this, Deineka overturns formerly dominant representations of electric light; instead of visualizing it graphically – as radiating lines – he provides a painterly representation using the colour yellow.[28] Filling the surface with yellow and contrasting it with the blue window, the artist manages to effectively illuminate the room. The cover thus programs yellow as the colour associated with the source of electric light. Relying heavily on yellow and its derivatives throughout the book, Deineka manages to sustain this visual sense of the presence of electric light during the whole act of reading. The illustration on the back cover depicts

8.13. Aleksandr Deineka's illustration for the back cover of *Elektromonter* shows electricity as part of the natural (here, rural) environment and also depicts electrification as an already accomplished task – domestically as well as socially.

electricity as part of not only the domestic or urban environment but also the natural environment (fig. 8.13). Here one can see electric wires traversing a rural space. Birds sit on them, and a cow grazes among the poles holding them up. The industrial objects are thus integrated into the rural environment, not in conflict with it; they look organic and natural in this landscape. The date in the corner of this illustration further contributes to the representation of the electrification of rural areas as something already achieved. The book's first and last images, then, cumulatively depict an already achieved electrification on both the micro (domestic) and macro (rural) levels. They are idyllic in the sense of showcasing peaceful and harmonious environments, where everything is in order.

For that reason, perhaps, the cover images features no electrician, the book's eponymous hero: while everything is running smoothly, there is no need for one. As the book shows later, an electrician comes only when something needs to be repaired. In the world of this book, electrical malfunctions are represented as unusual situations that cause children to behave unusually. Thus, a broken doorbell not only slows down the pace of one's activities, but also underscores the tedium of life in a non-electric (as opposed to electrified) world:

Our life has become very dull,
it must be said,
and everyone has to knock on the door.
Has to knock for a very long time,
to be bored for a very long time,
to wait until
the doorbell is fixed.[29]

Representing electrical malfunctions not as solely technical but also as existential problems, this book extends the responsibilities of an electrician far beyond the mere repair of wires. An electrician maintains all things electric in order to sustain the natural flow of life within the electrified world. Once electricity stops reaching a certain space, be it a door in a home or a cinema, life malfunctions within that space. A socialist location that is de-electrified, moreover, virtually ceases to be Soviet, because it has been excluded from the all-encompassing electrical networks. The children in this book are perplexed, almost immobilized, upon finding themselves in such a non-space and experiencing how habitual scenarios of life in the electrified world can go wrong. For example, when the power goes out at the cinema, the children hesitate whether to stay or leave; only the arrival of an electrician resolves this uncertainty. Thus, the actual function of an electrician is to restore both the electric flow and the flow of life within the electrified world. An electrician – an *elektromonter* – montages the malfunctioning reality back into a proper socialist entity. Arriving at a malfunctioning space, he restores it to Soviet spacetime, heals the holistic nature of the Soviet ecology.

Easily solving whatever technical problems may occur, the electrician is clearly recognizable in this book. The reader is repeatedly given a description of his appearance ("he wears a leather jacket / and big boots") and a precise inventory of his instruments ("in his bag he has a file, / a screwdriver, pliers, / a gimlet, screws, / and wires, / a radio headset, / and still more wires").[30] However, none of the electricians in the book have any individual features that might distinguish them from one another. They are de-individualized, seeming almost like identical androids. Such a representation occurs because Deineka hardly sought to create an image of a particular electrician (a person whose job it is to be an electrician), but rather to establish a recognizable visual type of electricians as such.[31] Advancing a clear image of an electrician, and emphasizing his importance to everyday life, this book romanticized, even heroized, the profession, and helped propagandize it as a career choice: readers must have been impressed by this image of a virtual superman possessed of the arcane knowledge required to sustain a happy life in the electrified world.

Such a representation of the electrician demonstrates the significant shift that electricity imagery had undergone in the course of the 1920s. Unlike in the 1924 fairy tale of Petya, electricity here is not a magical power created by magical creatures like Ded-Elektrik, but rather a commodity held in common by the whole nation, existing in and of itself and requiring professional maintenance. But the process of rationalization nevertheless remains incomplete: electricity still preserves the features of a wonder, with the electrician holding exclusive access to "electrical knowledge." Transferring this knowledge to children would call for the elaboration of new modes of representation.

The Pedagogy of Troubleshooting: The Lamp as a Deconstruction Toy

In 1936–7, two books – *V strane Dzin'-Dzin'* (*In the Country of Ding-Ding*) and *Puteshestvie po elektrolampe* (*A Journey through an Electric Lamp*), respectively – marked a new stage of depicting electricity for children in the Soviet Union. In these books, children were, at last, not told to "keep out" of electricity: on the contrary, they were shown how to handle it, encouraged even to "try this at home." Although books for adolescents had already provided some tips on working with electricity,[32] these two volumes stand out due to their unique verbal-visual language, which had the potential to engage children with no or very basic literacy.

In these books, what children were to wonder at was not electricity per se, but an electrical malfunction, a rupture in what was now the normal order of things. The two books feature similar plots, the premise of each being a mechanical glitch. *In the Country of Ding-Ding* begins with a doorbell that stops working. The book represents a doorbell as an entirely natural device for children: they are very experienced in using it, having already mastered its semiotics ("one ring is cheerful, two is thoughtful, three is angry"). The doorbell glitch in this case keeps the children from entering their own flat, and they are consequently unable to begin doing their homework. In *A Journey through an Electric Lamp*, the breakdown is more dramatic: children find themselves alone in the dark when their father's desk lamp stops working. The malfunctions in the books, thus, paralyse children's activities.

Emulating situations liable to occur in an electrified world, these books further introduce scenarios of solving technical problems. In order to restore order, the children do not (as in *The Electrician*) call an adult specialist, but instead imagine themselves turned small enough to explore electric circuits. Journeying thus through the wires and mechanisms of doorbells and table lamps, the child adventurers uncover how electric devices work (with young Soviet readers following them in this pursuit). Travelling from one component of a device to another, the children analyse each, testing whether it is in order. Thus, in a playful mode, these books actually work as troubleshooting manuals, depicting a series of practical steps to diagnose a possible technical problem.[33]

The visual plays a crucial role in this pedagogy of troubleshooting. In order to illustrate children's adventures, Mikhail Makhalov, in *Journey through an Electric Lamp*, uses photomontage, combining various aspects of reality within a series of convincing photo-"documentary" images. For example, the cover image (fig. 8.14) projects the

8.14. Mikhail Makhalov, cover illustration for Nikolai Bulatov and Petr Lopatin, *Puteshestvie po elektrolampe* (Moscow: Detizdat, 1937). The photomontage combines the macro level (a map) and micro level (a lamp) to evoke different aspects of electricity.

story as a typical one for the country: a map on the macro level and a lamp on the micro level show different perspectives on electricity within a single compound image.

This image sets a credible frame in which the events occur. The authors do not insist that they portray a fantastic world; indeed, the book stipulates that the children do not *become* small, but only *imagine* they are small. By representing children's adventures as imaginary, rather than explicitly fantastic, the authors manage to partially conceal the magic essential for stories about shape-shifting. However, magic is nevertheless present in the book, which is neither surprising nor in violation of the "rules" for children's books: from 1934 on, as Marina Balina has shown, Soviet children's literature began to roll back its previous rejection of the fairy tale.[34]

Most notably, this masked magic in *A Journey through an Electric Lamp* in no way conflicts with the book's educational agenda; quite the contrary – it advances this agenda. In his illustrations for the book, Makhalov combines photographs of miniaturized children with those of objects (wires, lamps, and so on). Having carefully retouched the children's images, the artist represents their adventures as naturalistically as possible. Due to the contrast between the sizes of the children and the devices they explore, representation of the latter emerges as extremely palpable, even hyper-realistic. When combined with montage, such a close-up enables objects to be depicted with considerable visual and technological accuracy. For example, one illustration (on page 12) features a multi-view projection consisting of a front elevation and a cross-section. Within this picture, the reader is faced with both a formal representation of the device (as it is typically seen) and a structural one (as it is organized). Furthermore, on the next page, the viewpoint zooms in on the lamp socket, making the device's design comprehensible (from a scheme executed in an entirely technical language). Thus, has Makhalov represented an everyday object – a lamp – in its mechanical complexity, defamiliarizing it. Having broken the "automatic perception" (to echo Shklovsky) of this typical object as a commodity, he offers instead a clear technological dimension, which becomes, in this book, the actual space of children's adventures.

Such a representational scheme was also the case for *In the Country of Ding-Ding*. However, compared to that book about a doorbell, *A Journey through an Electric Lamp* goes further in exposing children to technological realities. Besides the adventurous verbal-visual storyline, it includes an additional scientific narrative: separate schemes and verbal sections introduce basic facts about electricity. Whenever the storyline leads the children to a new component, the book provides supplemental reference material related to the given technology. For example, in the illustration in figure 8.15, the children are shown inside the lamp, which a large hand is attempting to turn on. The next page does not add anything to the narrative, but supplies a brief, footnote-like explanation of what a switch is. Such pages do not affect the storyline but function like intervals in the adventure, pauses in which certain basic facts are introduced. The children thus traverse not only the physical lamp, but also this parallel narrative; movement from one page to the next is also a movement from one knowledge-domain to another.

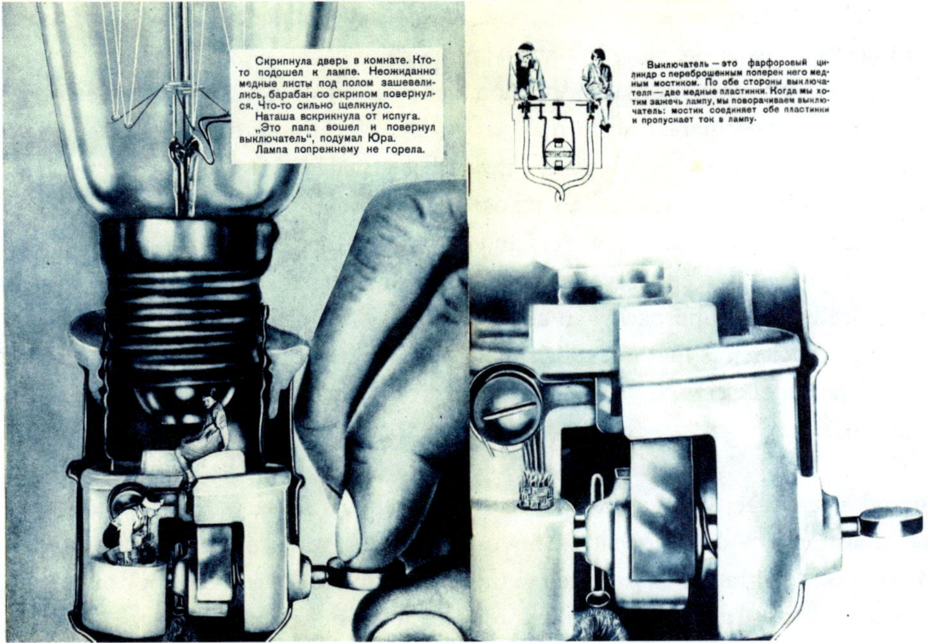

8.15. Makhalov's illustration depicting children travelling through the wires and mechanisms of a lamp, uncovering how the device works, in *Puteshestvie po elektrolampe*, 14–15.

In this book, then, electricity is not just an established symbol of "enlightenment" but also a symbolic *space* in which learning takes place. This "electric education" of children in *A Journey through an Electric Lamp* is achieved in a unique manner: via the deconstruction of a lamp within a verbal-visual narrative. Episodes of the book represent the lamp as a set of details, affording the child reader an unprecedentedly nuanced understanding of this device's design. In order to appeal to children, this deconstruction is executed in a "play" mode: the children in the book explore parts of the lamp physically, with its various components subjected to their haptic contact – that is, children play with the lamp. Their interaction with it has been, from the first, a *game*, as is stated quite plainly on the book's final page: "The journey is over. Now there is light, now they can take up a new game [*prinimat'sia za novuiu igru*]."[35] The lamp in this journey is thus a deconstruction toy allowing children to construct an understanding of the lamp's design and maintenance.

Ultimately, this book represents the successful adaptation of a troubleshooting manual for children. An unprecedentedly accurate and informative guide on the handling of electric devices, *A Journey through an Electric Lamp* may be considered a highlight of Soviet representations of electricity, as it utterly demystified the lamp as a technological device. Thus, in the late 1930s, years after the inception of electrification, and notwithstanding the debates on the legitimacy of the fairy tale, Soviet children's literature managed to elaborate a language adequate to the task of representing electricity, by keeping an optimal proportion of fantasy and technical data.

On its way to this optimal proportion, the imagery of electricity and electrification underwent dramatic transformations. As electrification progressed in the Soviet Union, authors updated and perfected the verbal-visual languages they used to depict electricity for children. In order to expose pre- and semi-literate readers to contemporary technological realities, writers and illustrators adapted pre-revolutionary narratives, exploited nascent "revolutionary" representational schemes, and developed authentically Soviet approaches to children's books. Whereas the initial representation of electricity was that of explicit magic, subsequent books disenchanted it. The rationalization of electricity was achieved in diverse manners, from representing the lamp "analytically" in *Yesterday and Today* to deconstructing it in *A Journey through an Electric Lamp*. Nevertheless, despite the continuous disenchantment, electricity worked as an affective and effective power, and always preserved some measure of materialist magic – a magic that did not fundamentally compromise the rationality of Soviet books, but rather contributed to the efficacy of the Soviet pedagogy of images.

Ironically, it is "magic" that makes possible the most "scientific" narrative on electricity discussed here, in *A Journey through an Electric Lamp*. Subjecting children to a wondrous metamorphosis, the authors situate them, not in a fairy-tale world, but in a technological environment governed by strict scientific laws. Thus does magic contribute to the book's practical-pedagogical agenda. Providing a technological perspective on the lamp, this book disenchants electricity, in a sense bearing out Ded-Elektrik's proclamation that "there are no wonders in the whole wide world." In doing so, however, the book also affirms Ded's further claim that "the only wonder is science." Even as it admirably advances the Soviet materialist project of rationalizing electricity, this book demonstrates that technology can still operate beyond any rational understanding.

Electrical Thing-Power, or Pure Materialist Magic

Crucially, even as they explore the electric circuit, the children Natasha and Iura in *A Journey through an Electric Lamp* do not end up actually fixing the lamp; rather, the lamp works as an actant and *repairs itself*:

> Natasha suddenly screamed in fright again. Iura looked up and froze in horror. The base of the light bulb was rotating and slowly sliding down … The light bulb was moving down … The light bulb had almost pushed Natasha to the porcelain floor, to the copper plate … – Natasha! Watch out! Something sparkled, there was a smell of burning, and … the lamp started to shine with an even and bright light.[36]

How can components move by themselves in the supposedly "scientific" world of electricity? After this act of self-repair on the lamp's part, Natasha proposes a hypothesis to explain the original malfunction: someone must have slightly rotated the light bulb, partially unscrewing it; electrical contact having been lost, it stopped working. She further suggests that, during their adventure, the light bulb was retightened (*dovernuli*), such that it was now back in order. But who could have possibly manipulated the lamp?

The logic of the text gives no clue as to any human agent. Natasha and Iura could hardly have unscrewed the light bulb, or else they would not have had to search for the cause of the malfunction (unless they had forgotten they had done this). Moreover, they would not be physically able to rotate the bulb and to observe this procedure simultaneously. The third and final human character in the book – the father – interferes in the storyline by checking the lamp's switch (see fig. 8.15). The text clearly registers this action of his, but we have no indication that it was he who had been rotating the bulb. As for explaining the bulb's movements from the point of view of common sense – this is likewise problematic. Of course, we could hypothesize that someone entered the room in order to, first, loosen the bulb to make the lamp stop working, then retighten it; but what would be the motivation for this? Was it a prank? Ruling out the possibility of human agency, and considering the passage quoted above, one may conclude that the light bulb rotated itself, thus operating as an actant. Even in this most "scientific" and nearly magic-free book, then, the agency of electricity is explicitly present, specifically in the wilful actions of a lamp.

How to account for the lamp's inherently alogical, ascientific behaviour in this otherwise rational environment? Is this yet another case of materialist magic? We could address these questions with recourse to the philosophy of vital materialism. In approaching the efficacy of non-living matter, Bennett introduces the term "thing-power": "the curious ability of inanimate things to animate, to act, to produce effects dramatic and subtle."[37] If applied to Soviet children's books, this term helps clarify the essential agency of electricity, the representation of which did not necessarily require magical elements like anthropomorphism. To the contrary, the very trend of disenchantment – the removal of magical elements – contributed to the disclosure of the thing-power of electricity.[38] In a way, the thing-power of electricity is a kind of magic without magic, a purely materialist magic.[39]

But if this book depicts a strictly scientific environment where both children and electricity operate as actants, how might we define the relationship between them? *A Journey through an Electric Lamp* establishes a strong connection between children and electricity: they have formed a new type of ecology – a children/electric assemblage, in which these components mutually affect one another.[40] Clearly, children can affect the electric lamp: they can use it, explore it, and, theoretically, repair it. But electricity can likewise affect the children: malfunctioning as if by its own will, the lamp defines the children's activities. The light bulb's sporadic rotations wholly paralysed the children's life, prompting them to leave the darkness by traversing a dangerous, potentially traumatic electric circuit.

Such mutual determinism of children and technology, so evident in 1937, logically stems from the evolution of the imagery of electricity. In the course of being rationalized throughout the 1920s and 1930s, electricity was ever more integrated into life, ultimately becoming a part of the natural environment and, perhaps, becoming *nature* as such. During this evolution of electricity imagery, as I have shown, children's agency vis-à-vis electricity, and the agency of electricity itself, expanded significantly. In Soviet books, children transformed from passive observers of electrification into active users (operators) capable of dealing with major technical malfunctions. As for electricity, initially a great trouble-saver, it could also become a troublemaker: in *A Journey through an Electric Lamp*, the lamp blackout is referred to as *konets sveta* (lit. "the end of the light" or "end of the world"), presenting a quasi-apocalyptic scenario caused by electricity. These diverse capabilities of electricity reveal the grand scale of the myth of electricity as represented in children's books. Electricity had played a key role in the creation of the country, was central to its development, and maintained its vitality. Thus, the Soviet myth of electricity introduced aspects of Soviet ontology, cosmogony, and eschatology to Soviet children.

Finally, what motivated such an explicit focus on the agency of electricity? Perhaps due to the authors' artistic intuition, Soviet books, willy-nilly, proved highly attentive to carefully interpreting Lenin's maxim that "communism is Soviet power plus the electrification of the whole country." This formula implies that electricity is an actant in building communism: its significance to the project is on a par with that of Soviet power (an assemblage of people, resources, and institutions). Thus, Lenin had envisioned electricity as an agentive force and as an actant, and Soviet books managed to provide a perfect translation of this reality into children's language.

NOTES

I am grateful to Serguei Oushakine and Marina Balina, who initiated and undertook this publication project. I very much appreciate Yuri Leving's support, as well as the feedback of participants of the *Pedagogy of Images* symposium. Aleksei Kozhevnikov has provided insightful comments on this article. I would also like to thank the editors for their efforts in making my argument clearer.

1 Lenin, "Moskovskaia gubernskaia konferentsiia RKP(b)," 30.
2 GOELRO is the Russian acronym for the State Commission for the Electrification of Russia (Gosudarstvennaia komissiia po elektrifikatsii Rossii). The first edition of the GOELRO plan from 1920 comprised nine parts comprehensively covering electrification-related issues in each region of the country. For the first part of the plan, see *Plan elektrifikatsii RSFSR*.
3 Lenin, "Doklad Vserossiiskogo tsentral'nogo ispolnitel'nogo komiteta" (22 December), 157, 161.
4 Lenin, "Moskovskaia gubernskaia konferentsiia RKP(b)," 32.
5 Lenin, "Proekt rezoliutsii po dokladu ob elektrifikatsii" (ca. 21–9 December 1920), 196.
6 Ibid.
7 For example, Il'in, *Solntse na stole*.
8 Szeman and Boyer, "Introduction: On the Energy Humanities," 1–14.
9 On attacks on and apologias for the fairy tale in the 1920s–30s, see Balina, "Introduction for Part II: Fairy Tales of Socialist Realism," 105–8.
10 This chapter does not discuss electrification as a social phenomenon of Soviet society, where, perhaps, it also functioned as a form of magic. Such analysis would require special

anthropological research. For that reason, I am consciously ignoring the extremely complex debates on the issue of magic, focusing instead solely on how the discourse on/of children's literature approached magic (*volshebstvo*).

11 Arvatov, "Byt i kul'tura veshchi."

12 Ibid., 77–9.

13 Ibid., 81–2.

14 Bennett, *Vibrant Matter*, 3–4.

15 For more discussion of this cover, see the chapter by Alexey Golubev in this volume.

16 Bukhshtab, "Stikhi dlia detei," 117.

17 Gerchuk, *Khudozhestvennaia struktura knigi*, 77.

18 Oushakine, "Translating Communism for Children," 181–4.

19 "As from me / There pours a wondrous light / Because I am a relative / Of the heavenly lightning!" ("Mezhdu tem kak ot menia / L'etsia svet chudesnyi / Potomu chto ia rodnia / Molnii nebesnoi!"). Marshak, *Vchera i segodnia*, 5.

20 Galitskii and Valentinova, *Skazka o mal'chike Pete*, 70.

21 More broadly, technology in early Soviet children's literature was often conceptualized precisely as a technological wonder; see, for example, Marshak, *Sem' chudes*.

22 Behrend, "Photo Magic," 132.

23 Ibid.

24 As Arvatov puts it, "technology is not only an engine, but also a social-material form within which this engine exists" ("Byt i kul'tura veshchi," 75).

25 This idea occurs, for instance, in Andreev, *Dva brata*.

26 Widdis, "'Strana s novym krovoobrashcheniem'."

27 This was indeed the case for such grand rivers as the Dnieper. However, even when portraying comparatively minor rivers such as the Volkhov, Soviet authors did not hesitate to exaggerate its "might": "The Volkhov hurls its waters and ... ferocious as a devil, whips its foam unto the heavens" (ibid., 5).

28 Deineka, of course, hardly invented the use of yellow to signify electric light (the colour occurs in the 1928 *Egor the Electrician* [see fig. 8.10]); but he is notable for having put it to maximum use.

29 Ural'skii, *Elektromonter*, 5.

30 Ibid., 1, 3, 9, 11.

31 The dehumanized electricians function here as "non-human actors," to borrow a term of Bruno Latour. In his article on the "sociology of a door-closer," Latour (writing as Jim Johnson) argues that "humans are not necessarily figurative; for instance you are not allowed to take the highway policeman as an individual chum. He/she is the representative of authority ... [of] the administrative *machinery*" ("Mixing Humans and Nonhumans Together," 306; emphasis in original).

32 For example, Litvinov, *Elektrifikatsiia*.

33 In the 1936 book, the children manage to fix the doorbell, but the lamp in the 1937 work presents a far more complicated scenario, as discussed in the concluding section of this chapter.

34 Balina, "Introduction," 105–8.

35 Bulatov and Lopatin, *Puteshestvie po elektrolampe*, 25.

36 Ibid., 16.

37 Bennett, *Vibrant Matter*, 6.

38 Bennett's approach to things is, moreover, particularly suitable for analysing the world of childhood: adults, she argues, have lost the ability to see the thing-power: "*Thing-power* perhaps has the rhetorical advantage of calling to mind a childhood sense of the world as filled with all sorts of animate beings, some human, some not, some organic, some not" (ibid., 22).

39 An accidental malfunction having nothing to do with human agency was also the case in *The Electrician*: "Out of the blue [*ni s togo ni s sego*] / The doorbell broke" (3). In the most literal sense, this unaccountability reflects the children's point of view (they do not know how or why the doorbell broke); but at the same time, it exemplifies the thing-power.

40 For a discussion of the interdependence of human and nonhuman actants, see Bennett, *Vibrant Matters*, 21, 365.

BIBLIOGRAPHY

Andreev, Mikhail. *Dva brata*. Illustrated by Vladimir Tvardovskii. Moscow: Raduga, 1925.

Arvatov, Boris. "Byt i kul'tura veshchi. (K postanovke voprosa)." In *Al'manakh proletkul'ta: Kult'tura i byt. Organizatsiia byta. Iskusstvo i proizvodstvo. Kritika i bibliografiia. Proletkul'ty na mestakh*, 75–82. Moscow: n.p., 1925.

Balina, Marina. "Introduction for Part II: Fairy Tales of Socialist Realism." In *Politicizing Magic: An Anthology of Russian and Soviet Fairy Tales*, edited by Marina Balina, Helena Goscilo, and Mark Lipovetsky, 105–21. Evanston, IL: Northwestern University Press, 2005.

Behrend, Heike. "Photo Magic: Photographs in Practices of Healing and Harming in East Africa." *Journal of Religion in Africa* 33, no. 2 (2003): 129–45.

Bennett, Jane. *Vibrant Matter: A Political Ecology of Things*. Durham, NC: Duke University Press, 2010.

Bukhshtab, Boris. "Stikhi dlia detei." In *Detskaia literatura: Kriticheskii sbornik*, edited by Anatolii Lunacharsky, 103–30. Moscow-Leningrad: Gosudarstvennoe izdatel'stvo khudozhestvennoi literatury, 1931.

Bulatov, Nikolai, and Pavel Lopatin. *Puteshestvie po elektrolampe*. Illustrated by Mikhail Makhalov. Moscow: Detizdat, 1937.

Bulatov, Nikolai, Lev Kassil', and Pavel Lopatin. *V strane Dzin'-Dzin'*. Illustrated by Mikhail Makhalov. Moscow: Izdatel'stvo detskoi literatury, 1936.

Galitskii, Iakov, and Zinaida Valentinova. *Skazka o mal'chike Pete, kotoryi nikogo ne boialsia na svete, ni komu klaniat'sia ne privyk, i kak emu v zabotakh i rabotakh pomog dobryi staryi Ded-Elektrik*. Illustrated by Vasilii Artem'ev. Moscow: Novaia Moskva, 1924.

Gerchuk, Iurii. *Khudozhestvennaia struktura knigi*. Moscow: RIP-Kholding, 2014.

Il'in, Mikhail. *Solntse na stole*. Moscow: Izdatel'stvo detskoi literatury, 1935.

Johnson, Jim. "Mixing Humans and Nonhumans Together: The Sociology of a Door-Closer." *Social Problems* 35, no. 3 (1988): 298–310. www.nyu.edu/projects/nissenbaum/papers"/Latour_Mixing.pdf.

Lenin, V.I. "Doklad Vserossiiskogo tsentral'nogo ispolnitel'nogo komiteta." In Lenin, *Polnoe sobranie sochinenii*, 128–91.

– "Moskovskaia gubernskaia konferentsiia RKP (b.), 20–22 Noiabria 1920. Nashe vnutrennee i vneshnee polozhenie i zadachi partii. Rech' 21 Noiabria." In Lenin, *Polnoe sobranie sochinenii*, 17–38.

– *Polnoe sobranie sochinenii* 42. Moscow: Izdatel'stvo politicheskoi literatury, 1970.

– "Proekt rezoliutsii po dokladu ob elektrifikatsii." In Lenin, *Polnoe sobranie sochinenii*, 196–7.

Litvinov, Pavel. *Elektrifikatsiia*. Illustrated by Lev Smekhov. Moscow: Molodaia gvardiia, 1930.

Marshak, Samuil. *Sem' chudes*. Illustrated by Mikhail Tsekhanovskii. Leningrad-Moscow: Raduga, 1926.

– *Vchera i segodnia*. Illustrated by Vladimir Lebedev. Leningrad-Moscow: Raduga, 1925.

Mislavskii, Nikolai. *Dneprostroi.* Illustrated by Vera Lantsetti. 2nd ed. Moscow: Gosudarstvennoe izdatel'stvo, 1930.

Oushakine, Serguei. "Translating Communism for Children: Fables and Posters of the Revolution." *Boundary* 243, no. 3 (2016): 181–4. https://read.dukeupress.edu/boundary-2/article/43/3/159 /56169/Translating-Communism-for-Children-Fables-and.

Plan elektrifikatsii RSFSR. Vvedenie k dokladu 8-mu S"ezdu Sovetov Gosudarstvennoi komissii po elektrifikatsii Rossii. Moscow: Gosudarstvennoe tekhnicheskoe izdatel'stvo, 1920.

Smirnov, Nikolai. *Egor-Monter.* Illustrated by Galina Chichagova and Ol'ga Chichagova. Moscow: Gosudarstvennoe izdatel'stvo, 1928.

Szeman, Imre, and Dominic Boyer. "Introduction: On the Energy Humanities." In *Energy Humanities: An Anthology*, edited by Imre Szeman and Dominic Boyer, 1–13. Baltimore: Johns Hopkins University Press, 2017.

Ural'skii, Boris. *Elektromonter.* Illustrated by Aleksandr Deineka. Moscow-Leningrad: Gosudarstvennoe izdatel'stvo, 1930.

Voinov, Vladimir. *80 000 loshadei.* Illustrated by Boris Pokrovskii. Leningrad: Gosudarstvennoe izdatel'stvo, 1925.

Widdis, Emma. "'Strana s novym krovoobrashcheniem': Kino, eletrifikatsiia i transformatsiia sovetskogo prostranstva." In *Sovetskaia vlast' i media*, edited by Sabine Hänsgen and Hans Günther, 450–63. St. Petersburg: Akademicheskii proekt, 2005.

"DO IT ALL YOURSELF!" TEACHING TECHNOLOGICAL CREATIVITY DURING SOVIET INDUSTRIALIZATION

MARIA LITOVSKAYA

> Real life provides an endlessly rich, multidimensional, and increasingly complex material for shaping all the facets of a child's organism. This material – when used without distortion, simplification, or fabrication – steadily organizes the child's experience, providing an orientation for navigating through natural and social phenomena. At the same time, it enhances the child's plasticity and creative capabilities, all the while leading him toward reality, and not away from it.
>
> *Stepan Molozhavyi*, On Realism in Children's Literature

By the late 1920s, the Soviet People's Commissariat of Enlightenment (Narkompros) succeeded in creating a new network of periodicals: aimed at adolescents, these publications were to advance the ideology of the state.[1] Refracting Soviet pedagogical discourse, new magazines and newspapers provided their audience with the basics of "political literacy," shaping the political and social identity of a new generation of Soviet people. These periodicals envisioned their adolescent readers as fundamentally curious beings, keen to observe the world's events and to understand how that world operated. The new periodicals were meant to satisfy this curiosity, but they also taught young readers how to structure their experiences (including visual perception) through the lens of the interests of the Soviet state.

This chapter examines one of these publications – the magazine *Delai vse sam* (*Do It All Yourself*; *DIAY*), which was published in 1928–31 in Sverdlovsk (the former and current Ekaterinburg), one of the centres of Soviet industrialization (fig. 9.1). I will outline the reasons for *DIAY*'s creation against the backdrop of historical events in general and the history of Soviet pedagogy in particular, and then trace the transformation of the journal's strategies and tactics over time. I will approach the magazine as an example of a variegated (or, to use a term employed in contemporary Russian studies,

---

Chapter translated by Lev Nikulin

9.1. *Delai vse sam*, a magazine for Young Techies was launched in 1928 in Sverdlovsk. *Delai vse sam*, no. 3 (1930).

kreolizovannyi [creolized]) text – that is, a text in which verbal and non-verbal components act as organic parts of a whole composition, creating complementary relations with one another.[2] Taken together, the verbal and the pictorial propose, translate, and support certain methods of seeing, depicting, and understanding the world.[3]

Who Were the Young Techies and Why Did They Need Their Own Magazine?

The late 1920s and early 1930s constitute a period when the revolutionary utopia went through a rapid "grounding": the concreteness of the Five-Year Plans, with their clearly defined chronological boundaries, translated utopia into the language of routine socialist construction. Anatoly Lunacharsky, people's commissar of enlightenment, wrote in 1929:

We have no need to fear the word "utilitarianism" [*utilitarnost'*]. Let the bourgeoisie measure "usefulness" by its petty scale. But for us, every use, even the smallest, is in the end connected with the greatest utility: the building of socialism in its grandest scope. For us, being useful by no means denotes being denigrated from the height of a great ideology to lowly service in the name of grey, everyday, petty concerns. On the contrary: for us, to be useful is to be plugged into the life of society in one of its most beautiful moments, the most decisive in the history of mankind.[4]

This period promised attractive opportunities for young people, who were well aware that the plants and factories everywhere sprouting up amid Soviet industrialization would require not unskilled labourers, but engineers, technicians, and trained workers – imaginative innovators and creative specialists. During this time, pedagogy underwent a major shift: the idea of education through entertainment was replaced by the idea of education through the inclusion of students in the fulfilment of concrete, governmentally important (yet age-appropriate) tasks. These tasks varied, depending on the young person's age, place of residence, and education level. But the overarching principle remained: educators strove to direct the activity of adolescents toward constructive, technological goals.

The republishing of the articles and books of Aleksei Gastev, a poet and the head of the Soviet Institute for the Scientific Organization of Labour, was helpful in this regard. Already in 1921, Gastev had formulated the principles of "industrial pedagogy" aimed at developing in schoolchildren not only effective labour skills but also a particular system of assumptions and expectations – in Gastev's terminology, a "labour orientation" ("trudovaia ustanovka"). Aspiring to make cultural education "more operative, more vital [*zhiznennoe*]," he emphasized in his works that building socialism would be impossible without "organizing communities that unite management and initiative. The new, active culture that we need so much can only emerge on the foundation of this unity." Correspondingly, in Gastev's view, the new literature for adolescents should follow the same path, focusing on the plans and achievements of socialist construction:

> Of course, a dry official report on victories in the expansion of a trade-fair in Nizhny Novgorod, or a memo on the extreme difficulties encountered by an expedition to Svalbard, or the narrative of a captain whose ship had completed a risky journey through the Kara Sea, would all do so much more than the most thrilling book by Mayne Reid or the pedagogical methods employed in our schools today.[5]

For the leaders of Soviet pedagogy and education, young people's coming of age was firmly linked with their direct involvement in carrying out the program for the economic development of the Soviet Union. As the young country underwent constant and rapid change, its coevals were expected to become full participants in these changes – anticipating their life in the world being built by their elders.

Such key theoreticians and practitioners of Soviet education as Mariia Krupenina, Stanislav Shatskii, and Boris Ignat'ev strove to replace the idea of conflict between rebellious adolescents and conservative adults (which naturally existed in families and schools) with the idea of the two generations partnering in socially beneficial labour. Carrying out this cooperation would call for input not only from the government, but also from adolescents themselves. The state assumed the responsibility of outlining the long-term economic and political tasks for the young generation, and of providing young people with opportunities for professional education and development.[6] In turn, in order to participate competently in the life of the country, adolescents were expected to understand the content of the ongoing changes, including the USSR's economic policies.

In order to effectively transform schoolchildren into the workers, technicians, and engineers of tomorrow, the Soviet state initiated a special movement organized around Stations of Young Technicians (*Stantsii iunykh tekhnikov*). There schoolchildren were encouraged to test and develop their technological creativity (*tekhnicheskoe tvorchestvo*) by building working models of radio receivers, power plants, cars, and even flying vehicles. Along with modelling and construction, the stations' activities also included discussions about the development of technology in the world and the economic development of the USSR.[7] The schoolchildren who took part in the work of these stations came to be known as "Young Technicians" or "Young Techies" (*iuntekhi*).

The Youth Central Technical Station (YCTS) was established at an assembly of the Young Techies on 12 October 1926, marking the beginning of an organizational wave: technical stations were set up in such large regional centres of the country as Nizhny Novgorod and Sverdlovsk. In 1928, the movement received official support. A resolution of the Central Committee of the Communist Party of 25 June 1928, "On the status and immediate goals of the pioneer movement," stated that

> building on children's interest in labour, they should be taught how to work together, how to develop the skill of organizing their labour, and how to work according to a set plan (preparing preliminary calculations and diagrams, taking care of instruments, materials, etc.). Such education should be carried out on a large scale – through the extensive development of various clubs of young technicians, amateur radio operators, chemists, or electro-technicians.[8]

In 1930, increased support from the state resulted in a decision to transition children's technical stations to government funding. This change had a major impact. In 1931, there were 150 Young Techies' stations in operation throughout the country. By 1934, there were 647 stations in the Russian Federation alone.[9] The funding, however, remained rather minimal, and shortages of materials necessary for the Techies' creative activities were ongoing. This was apparently one of the considerations inducing the stations to expand their curriculum: along with developing pupils' technical imagination and engineering skills, the stations also sought to integrate young people into the process of collective production. Students were asked to manufacture such useful products as teaching aids for local schools or basic equipment for workers' locker rooms in nearby factories. For these projects, students (working without compensation) frequently recycled such materials as empty cans, wrapping paper, or broken kitchenware.

The intersection of political, economic, and pragmatic interests of the rapidly developing country produced an educational byproduct: the Young Techies' stations served as a crucial platform that facilitated the younger generation's preparation for socially useful labour. Periodicals were supposed to provide additional help, effectively functioning as technical manuals and as "textbooks" in political economy and economic geography. Also, they were supposed to be a source of inspiration.

The first publication directly aimed at the Techies was the magazine *Znanie – sila* (*Knowledge Is Power*). Produced by Young Guard publishing house (Molodaia gvardiia) publishing house in Moscow, the first issue of the magazine appeared in January 1926.[10] Originally conceived as a monthly "popular science and adventure" ("nauchno-populiarnyi i prikliuchencheskii") magazine for young adults, in 1928 it became the flagship publication of the Young Technicians.

Another magazine, *Delai vse sam* (*Do It All Yourself*), was based not in the country's capital but in the city of Sverdlovsk, the administrative centre of the newly created Ural region (*oblast'*), which was supposed to be crucial for the industrial development envisioned in the first Five-Year Plan.[11] Put out by the Ural Regional Executive Committee as a supplement to the regional youth newspaper *Vskhody kommuny* (*Sprouts of the Commune*), *DIAY* was intended for participants of the "technology and invention clubs."[12] Distributed across the Ural region, the magazine's print run reached up to 10,000 copies – a substantial number for a publication of this status. The magazine, however, was short-lived: it was terminated in 1931. (By contrast, Moscow's *Znanie – sila/Knowledge is Power* is still going.) Meant to shape the world view of the adolescent reader as an active builder of socialism, *DIAY* represented a fascinating pedagogical and artistic phenomenon of the period. In the magazine, "dry," informative stories were often run alongside poetry or short fiction. Keeping in mind the limited literacy skills of its reader, the magazine accompanied textual materials with multiple diagrams, blueprints, photographs, and other information-laden visuals.

How Should the Young Techies Occupy Themselves?

The title *Do It All Yourself* encapsulated three major points of Soviet educational doctrine of the 1920s: the magazine encouraged the adolescent reader to *be active*; it offered *the whole country* as a stage for their activity; and it suggested some measure of (supervised) *autonomy*. Two key aims were spelled out in the inaugural issue. The first represented a modest solution to an organizational problem: "With the publication of *Do It All Yourself*, the makeshift activity of the technology and invention clubs will be replaced by activity naturally anchored by a plan."[13] The second, more ambitious, goal concerned education in general: "We and only we have the great task at hand: to finish building the grand edifice of socialism on the solid foundation laid down by our fathers under the leadership of the Communist Party."[14]

The semantic tension between the concrete, "down-to-earth" activity of the Young Techies and such grandiose conceptions of their significance for the building of socialism conditioned the content of this periodical's every issue. The tone was set in the inaugural number by a clumsy but energetic poem in which the independent technological creativity of the Techies was paired with the grand goals of the Five-Year Plan:

The Young Techie is handy!	У юнтеха руки ловки!
Do you see the dust clouds over there?	Видишь, как клубится пыль?
That's Sashka – from wreckage	Это Сашка из обломков
He constructed an automobile!	Смастерил автомобиль!
Kolka is no slouch, either;	Колька тож умом не беден,
Though he's small in size,	Ростом хоть и невелик,
From a can he made	У него из банки сделан
A first-class steam engine!	Первоклассный паровик!
Let's get together, the whole crowd.	Соберемтесь всей гурьбою,
Keep out, laziness and rudeness!	Лень и дерзость, к нам не лезь!
We always carry with us	Мы всегда несем с собой
The wonderful slogan – DIAY.	Славный лозунг – ДВС.
We'll hum like a swarm of bees,	Загудим пчелиным роем,
We'll build project after project	Мы придем за строем строй
And we – the youth – will build	И мы – юные – построим
A worldwide Magnitostroi![15]	Мировой Магнитострой!

The scope and orientation of *DIAY* reflected the dominant approach toward the Soviet adolescent of the time: the Techies' ages (ten to fifteen) meant that they had been raised under Soviet power and that their Soviet beliefs were (in general) already well-formed. The Techies thus required no explanation for the necessity of collective labour in building a historically unprecedented socialist country. They – again, due to their age – were competitive. In order to channel adolescent energy in a productive direction (so the argument went), it was sufficient to map out for young people the goals of their practical activity and provide them with instructions, specifying how these goals could be achieved. Early issues of the magazine offered the Young Techies difficult but solvable problems: to improve conditions for workers in factories; to create teaching aids for schools; or to introduce, in their own families, new methods of managing a household. Following its overall program, the magazine also outlined directions and possible solutions.

Significantly, all the written texts used in *DIAY* – from short stories to commentaries and thematic columns – were motivated by the same concern: to demonstrate the nation-wide significance of the activity that, while appearing trivial, could significantly improve the everyday lives of ordinary people through a tacit but inescapable link to technology. For example, issue no. 5 in 1930 contained a short story about how two young brothers living in a rural settlement spent their school holidays. As described from the perspective of the adults around them, they are far from typical children on vacation: "Together with the local children, they were reading some sort of books, diligently sketching something on paper, debating and trying to convince one another of something. And a few days later, with serious looks, they carried a parcel with the strange address 'Children's Technical Station' to the post office."[16] At one point, defying their parents and tradition, the brothers refuse to go to church, devoting their time instead to making a real improvement in the family's everyday life by constructing an electric flytrap: "A three-sided log with wire wrapped around it hung down from the ceiling. The log was covered in jam taken from the pie their mother had baked that morning. Under the log, a large lid from a tin can was supported by crossed strands of twine; every minute, flies fell into it." Amazed by this feat of engineering, the father still grumbles at his sons' refusal to go to Sunday services, "but in this grumbling there was no anger. Just the opposite: it hid surprise and a certain amount of pride in his lads."[17] With reason had they stood their ground.

The flytrap – a product of the new lifestyle of the younger members of the family – becomes an element of the healthy everyday life of the older members. It changes the life of the family as a "social unit" and reorders relationships within it. The new has conquered the old; at the same time, this intervention of technology in everyday life has created the possibility of parental respect for children's input.

Characteristically, one of the magazine's preceding issues had already published a diagram of this flytrap, as well as instructions for making it.[18] The story and the illustration complemented one another: the editors were pointedly directing the reader's attention back toward the diagram, which may otherwise have been ignored. The reader was thus able not only to imagine the flytrap but to visualize it in detail. Moreover, readers could even build it, if they so chose, in the months between the two issues. And the story's conclusion affirmed the worthwhileness of attempts to implement technological ideas from the magazine: the effort, assured *DIAY*, would be rewarded, or at least respected.

The authors of *DIAY* tried to translate abstract appeals from governmental organs into concrete technological directives, and to teach their readers to do the same. For instance, following the call by the Central Committee of the Young Communist League (Komsomol) to improve the quality of school instruction, the magazine observed that education in the natural sciences was hindered by a lack of adequate technical equipment:

> Few schools have quality equipment for the chemistry and physics classroom, yet we know that any theory must be tested by experiments. It's true, our classrooms improve with every year, but certainly the pace of this improvement could be increased, and this is exactly the area where the Young Techies could offer their help.
>
> Young Technicians of the Ural region! Let us help our schools. Let us show how we can work in the areas of physics and chemistry. Let us test our skills by practice.
>
> The Techies have an important role to play in equipping classrooms. Young Techies of the Ural region! The classrooms await your work![19]

The reader was then invited to follow the call to arms with concrete projects. Such invitations were invariably accompanied in *DIAY* with illustrations, usually a diagram or blueprint of a useful object a Techie could produce. For example, the same issue included a set of diagrams showing how to repurpose a metal tomato sauce can as a coal oven, a container, or other simple devices useful in conducting science experiments in the classroom. The illustration offers only one solution to the problem outlined in the text, while nudging the reader to explore other possibilities for creative recycling and invention that might yield new devices.

In every issue, the magazine offered a variation of the same rhetorical move from the general to the specific, and then to the technological. Using multiple scales, *DIAY* taught young readers to keep the overall (ideological) goals in mind, using them to organize their practical activity and everyday life, and, at the same time, to imbue their private, concrete technical activity with a larger social significance. The magazine consistently translated the grandiose idea of building socialism into concrete proposals, enabling the ordinary school-aged reader to easily join the process of constructing a new society. As a result, the ideal reader envisioned by *DIAY* emerges as a genuine guide to the new life: confidently and efficiently, the Young Techies "clue in" their out-of-touch parents, improving the everyday life of their family (and school) in accordance with socialist ideals.

DIAY also subtly trained its readers to understand their place in society through its typography and layout. Like most periodicals of its time, the magazine followed a predictable, if not rigid, compositional structure in displaying its materials. Columns were placed according to a strict and inviolable hierarchy of authors. Each issue opened with a lead article by the editors, who represented the voice of the state and the source of collective reason. Just as predictably, issues usually concluded with letters from readers, whose ideological reliability was, of course, far less certain.

The lead editorial not only communicated the will of the government, but also translated its slogans into specific tasks for young citizens. At this level, there was no room for the independence of the adolescent reader: authorized by adults, the editorial would explain how things stood in the Soviet Union. Drawing the adolescent's attention to the central problems of the so-called "current moment" ("tekush-chii moment"), the editorial would specify how, for instance, the electrification and radiofication of the country would bring the bright future closer.

Such technological innovations were also meant to improve the daily life of every individual, and it is on this level of concrete technological knowledge that readers' labour-saving suggestions and technological improvements were welcomed by the magazine. Students were invited (even strongly encouraged) to take part in solving these problems by, for example, constructing a wall lamp that could be used by their family, or building (with the help of a diagram) a radio set for the workers' breakroom in the nearest factory.

Picturing the Everyday for the Young Techies

In the creolized discourse of *DIAY*, images were as central as text, and the editors were persistent in their attempts to supplement general statements with pictorial narratives. The omnipotence of technology, routinely proclaimed by the magazine, had to manifest itself in the organization of its own, creolized, structure as well. From the first issue, the magazine strove to be an *illustrated* one. However, a lack of resources of the sort available to other publications for children significantly restrained the magazine's ambitions and pushed its authors to make the most out of the least. Colour appeared in *DIAY* only on the covers; inside, the magazine was done in black and white (figs. 9.2 and 9.3). Quality photographs were impossible to reproduce; as a workaround, the layout artists resorted to ink drawings, capitalizing on the graphic power of outlines and clichéd images. Visual interest was maintained via inventive typography and layout, as well as combinations of different fonts.

There was no skilled artist on the magazine's staff, but, despite this, the design of the first page of the first issue (see figure 9.3) evinces a strong desire to produce the impression of an energetic and modern publication through the deployment of images of moving vehicles and active children, the gear-like ornament in the top part of the page, and the curly characters of the heading "Young Techies." This playful "making do" with limited graphic resources did not last long: within a short period, the magazine switched to a more common model of adult publications, using differently scaled fonts as the main tool for creating a sense of dynamism on the page.

Figurative illustrations began to take on the role of a *DIAY* logo. Several issues of the magazine presented, in the top left corner of the first page, a profile drawing of a boy in front of an abstractly rendered symbol of technological progress – be it a truck, airplane, train, or camera. In other cases, factographic images of technological mechanisms and devices were called upon to substantiate the content of articles. Issue six of *DIAY* is exemplary in this respect (fig. 9.4). Announcing its overall theme at the top

9.2. "Mechanize Everyday Life!" The cover of *Delai vse sam*, no. 6 (1929).

of the first page as "The Everyday" ("Bytovoi"), the magazine follows it up with the slogan-statement "The Young Techie is an active fighter for the new everyday [*novyi byt*]." The table of contents appearing on the same page develops this theme and slogan further. The editorial column on the right declares:

The old daily life [*byt*] holds millions of our mothers and sisters in the clutches of the kitchen and the washbasin, keeping them far from the building of socialism. Thousands of minor household chores prevent them from learning literacy and hold them back from collective labour. It is the duty of the Young Techie pioneer to help the Party and Komsomol in the hard task of liberating women from the captivity of the old way of life. Every Techie can (with some ingenuity) use technical innovations to release his mother from several hours of drudgery every day, freeing her to spend those hours on education and collective labour.[20]

The editorial is prefaced with an excerpt from the Young Pioneers' code: "The pioneer prepares to become a selfless fighter against poverty and oppression, and for socialism!" Visually, the article is broken up by a quote in cursive, with the source

9.3. *Delai vse sam*, no. 1 (1928): 2.

№ 6

СОДЕРЖАНИЕ

ЕЖЕМЕСЯЧНЫЙ

детский журнал по технике
приложение к газете
„Всходы Коммуны“.

БЫТОВОЙ

Юнтех—активный борец за новый быт.

„Пионер готовится стать самоотверженным борцом против нищеты и гнета, за социализм.

(Закон юных пионеров).

Растет и перестраивается наша страна.

На смену древней русской „дубинушке" идет точная и сильная машина.

Рабочий — социалистическим соревнованием, крестьянин—коллективизацией добивают остатки старого, изнурительного и непродуктивного ручного труда, труда в одиночку.

Но итти вперед надо сомкнутым строем, не должно быть отстающих.

Старый быт цепкими лапами кухни и корыта держит миллионы наших матерей и сестер вдали от социалистической стройки.

Тысячи мелких домашних забот, не дают им научиться грамоте, мешают участвовать в общественной работе.

Обязанность пионера-юнтеха помочь партии и комсомолу в трудном деле раскрепощения женщин из плена старого быта.

„По проводам нашей ребячей энергии, мы должны передать ток на кухню, туда, где по-старинке трудятся матери и сестры".

(Из наказа Всесоюзного пионерского слета).

Каждый юнтех пораскинув умом может техническими улучшениями хозяйства освободить мать на несколько часов в день для учебы и для общественной работы.

В наших городах летом душно и пыльно, мало деревьев, мало зелени, которая очищала бы воздух.

Задача юнтехов познакомиться с пятилеткой городского строительства, достаточное ли место там уделено зеленой площади, и самим подумать над планами городских садов и бульваров.

Каждый дом страдает от мелких, но прожорливых вредителей: крыс, тараканов, клопов, мух; этим хищникам давно об'явлена война, юнтех должен ускорить победу над ними, совершенствуя и механизируя борьбу, помня, что решающее значение в войне даже с мелким врагом, имеет совершенство техники орудий борьбы.

Приближается лето, время пожаров. Юнтех должен приложить все усилия к тому, чтобы изгнать красного петуха из наших деревень и городов. Введение противопожарных мер, устройство предохранителей от пожаров, все это стоит в задачах юнтехов.

Помни и выполняй пункты пионерского слета по борьбе со старым бытом.

---

indicated in bold: "'We must use the wires of our young power to send electricity to the kitchen, where our mothers and sisters are confined as in old times' (*Directives of the All-Union Pioneer Rally*)." This somewhat unintelligible statement performs a justificatory function, legitimizing the message of the editorial by reference to a higher authority (the Pioneer organization).

A page outlines the issue's general theme and concrete tasks, delineating each in indented bulleted points: devise a plan for green spaces in the city; free up one's mother for political education; declare war on household insects; strengthen fire safety. Then, the magazine proceeds to depict the ideal future as envisioned through the prism of contemporary ideological priorities. In 1929, the dominant model of socialist city planning was still based on the idea of the commune, and the magazine closely hews to this ideological doxa:

> The education of the new generation will be given great attention in the new city. Thirty preschool facilities will be erected. Kindergartens and boarding schools will be created. All children younger than sixteen will live and grow together, as one collective. Schools will simultaneously be laboratories and workrooms, and will contain gardens as well. From a young age, children will grow up as active participants in collective building.[21]

As the materials in this issue emphasize, this new city of the socialist future is not just a plan: it is already being built in the vicinity of the reader, who may simply go out onto the street and verify the truth of the magazine's description: "Instead of the old Ekaterinburg with its small, musty houses ... instead of the bourgeois dream (a house with three rooms and a kitchen), huge buildings are being erected – not yet quite communes, but very close to them."[22] The construction of one of these buildings – the "Boarding house of employees of the GPU [the State Political Directorate]" – is described in detail, supported by a photomontage of heavily retouched images of facades unusual for Sverdlovsk (fig. 9.5). No architectural blueprints of the house are provided, and the reader must trust the writer's tempting description:

> Architecturally, the building is very simple. Yet inside, it is equipped with all amenities. We walked through washrooms, gymnasiums, a reading room, a special room for photographic work, rooms for enthusiasts of electricity, chemistry, physics, chess, and music. There are special rooms dedicated to individual activities, where one can prepare for work or simply study. Everything is set up so that every person can rest after work in a cultured way, spending their free time usefully for themselves and others.[23]

This passage seeks to captivate the imagination of the Young Techie reader with the possibilities of a new socialist way of life, to be made possible in part through

9.5. Photomontage of building facades, *Delai vse sam*, no. 6 (1929): 9.

this same reader's personal effort and involvement. In your free time, the magazine suggests, you can contribute to the "liberation of women" ("raskreposhchenie zhenshchin"), toward which end, thematic columns like "Make This Yourself" ("Delai sam") and "Practical Trifles" ("Prakticheskie melochi") supply helpful blueprints for a vegetable peeler, a water heater, a stand for an iron, a self-closing gate, and other practical devices designed to ease housework.

Grownup Models for Young Techies

Among the illustrated materials of *DIAY*, a special place was held by technical blueprints (*skhemy*). Every issue featured numerous images, accompanied by detailed descriptions of how to turn the diagrams into real (and useful) objects (fig. 9.6). Very few responses from Techies to these diagrams were published in the magazine, but, from those that were, it is clear that technical blueprints and diagrams were the type of item readers valued most. From the standpoint of these respondents, *DIAY* was especially useful when aiming not at imaginary Young Techies, but at real ones, whose technological creativity the magazine would fuel with practical advice. As one of these "real" Young Techies was quoted in the column "Readers of *DIAY*": "The printing, paper, and in general the technical side of the magazine are superb. *The pictures are clear and distinct. DIAY is a must for all kids interested in technology.*"[24]

The explanation for this heightened interest in technical diagrams, voiced by other *detkory* (children's correspondents) as well, lies in these young people's self-perception not as children who had to be entertained with colourful and/or funny pictures, but as conscious, pragmatic participants of socialist construction. Indeed, for such readers, the lack of bright colours and amusing pictures may even have been a plus, confirming as it did their sense of involvement in the serious task of creating truly useful objects. Expecting from the magazine clear diagrams and useful advice instead of striking visual experiments, *DIAY*'s readers were not playing at work: they were earnestly preparing for their future occupation.

Of course, this was an attitude the magazine carefully cultivated. In this regard it would be useful to compare *DIAY* with *Ezh* (*The Hedgehog*), another major youth magazine (fig. 9.7). On *DIAY*, a solitary Young Techie, dressed in work clothes, carries diagrams and smiles at something out of view (fig. 9.8). Standing next to a radio tower and a self-propelling vehicle, he looks provocative, even challenging, in comparison to the colourfully rendered tight-knit group of children shown on the cover of *Ezh* working on posters. The latter children are hardly distinguishable from their pre-revolutionary counterparts, while the appearance of the Young Techie points to an essential difference: he is a conduit of new ideas – he knows how to draw diagrams, how to manufacture objects (according to those diagrams), and how, ultimately, to hasten the coming of the future. Depicted this way, new Soviet childhood is endowed with a

КОПИЛКА ДОСТИЖЕНИЙ

ЭЛЕКТРИЧЕСКИЙ СИГНАЛИЗАТОР ОТ ВОРОВ

Электрический сигнализатор от воров это вещь очень простая, которую может сделать каждый мальчик и девочка.

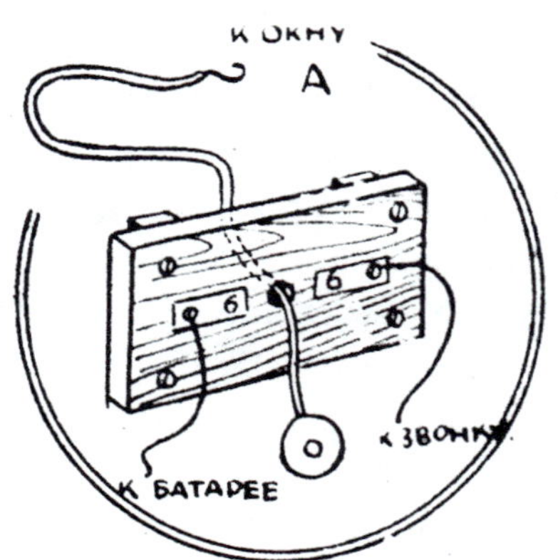

Воры могут проникнуть в комнату двумя путями: через окна или через двери. Следовательно нужно, чтобы при открывании двери или окна звонок звонил, т. е. чтобы замыкало цепь. Такой сигнализатор я и описываю.

Устроен он следующим образом. На деревянную дощечку прикрепляются две медные пластинки. В доске между пластинками делают отверстие. В это отверстие должен свободно проходить шнурок на одном конце которого, прикрепляется медная шайба, а другой конец прикрепляется к окну или двери так, что вор при открывании окна или двери потянет шнурок и доведет шайбу до соприкосновения с пластинками (рис. А) и звонок зазвонит, т. е. шайба замкнет цепь. Схема этой проводки показана на рис. Б.

В настоящее время воры ухитряются прежде чем начать свою операцию,

перерезать провода и звонок обречен на молчание. Но мы юнтехи, оказались хитрее их. Мы придумали устроить такую штуку, что когда вор перережет провода — звонок звонит.

Для этого нужно иметь две батареи. Положительный полюс первой батареи соединен с началом обмотки электромагнита звонка. Конец обмотки через замкнутый известитель идет к отрицательному полюсу второй батареи. Шайба извеcтителя соединена с дверями, так что при открывании их она освобождается и размыкает цепь, шнур. В этом случае делается тонкая нить, так чтобы она легко рвалась и размыкала цепь.

Цепь включения батарей и извеcтителя показана на рис. Б.

Н. Криножин.

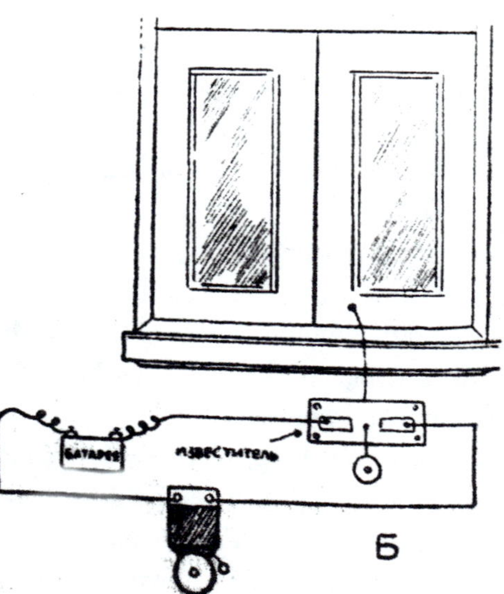

9.6. "A Bank of Achievements." Instructions and diagrams for making an electric thief-protection alarm at home. *Delai vse sam*, no. 4 (1929): 30.

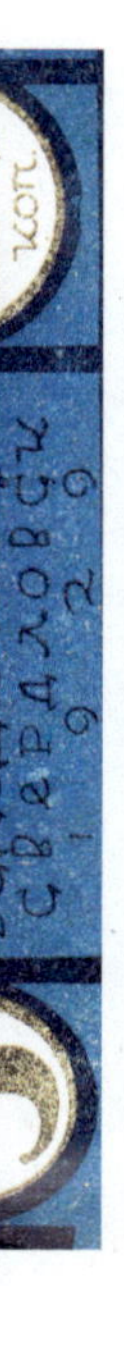

9.8. A Young Techie on the cover of *Delai vse sam*, no. 3 (1928).

9.7. Illustration by Irina Sunderland on the cover of *Ezh*, no. 9 (1928).

9.9. Cover of the first issue of *Delai vse sam*, no. 1 (1928).

new value in relation to the traditions of preceding epochs, a value that is revolutionary in the full sense of the word. The Young Techie's solitariness is not a sign of abandonment or social marginalization; it evinces, rather, his fundamental independence.

The cover of the very first issue of *DIAY* (fig. 9.9) might appear a bit gloomy, but it underscores this unexpected revolutionary character. The foundations of society were changing dramatically and irreversibly, contrary to the world's expectations. As a generation, Soviet adolescents were to shatter former boundaries in relations between adults and children. They were barging into an ossified world to assume the role, not of pupils, but of comrades, ready to share in the adult task of reordering the world. This readiness to acknowledge the equality of adolescents and adults also implied a certain degree of knowledge and responsibility for what was happening in the country. Thus did *DIAY* confront its readers with dispatches from "industrial front-lines" without simplifying their technical prose, although accompanying them with clarifications (fig. 9.10).

For more experienced readers, *DIAY* offered schematic maps, blueprints, and photographs of industrial projects in the Ural region (fig. 9.11). Through these images, the magazine provided Young Techies with a skeleton version of current economic

9.10. "The Main Indicators of the First Five-Year Plan in the Urals," in *Delai vse sam* no. 1 (1928): 3–4.

9.11. "The Project Magnitstroi" – the Magnitogorsk construction site. *Delai vse sam*, no. 6 (1929): 18.

processes, teaching them how to discern a structured and clear blueprint behind the chaotic appearance of everyday activities. By learning to distil the "code" as the essence of the activity, the reader, however, also learned how to fit the multiplicity of facts and processes into this ready-made scheme.

The text abounded with schematics and diagrams – a form of creolization that, at first glance, performed the purely pragmatic function of familiarizing Young Techies with the principles of operation and instructions for creating a specific device. But at the same time, this approach harboured secondary symbolic significance: it bore witness to adult conversations with technologically literate young people, who were to see not just the diagram but the essence of any phenomenon: from the construction of a door lock to the Magnitostroi industrial project, and to the development of industry during the first Five-Year Plan in general.

The editors' fascination with diagrams, graphics, and other schematic images was not limited to ideological training; it had a pedagogical purpose as well. Images were supposed to communicate collective knowledge and rationalize established goals; they took the Five-Year Plan, the whole upheaval it represented for the region, and made it proportionate to the young reader, observable and graspable.

Diagrams focalized and clustered socialist construction, identifying visible centres and nodes. The fact that these centres were changing all the time (reflecting the emphasis of the moment – be it industry, agriculture, construction, or something else) only simplified the task of orientation. The world emerged as divisible into fragments, but the development of each of these was subordinate to the overall direction, guided by the idea of socialism. In fact, when taken as a whole, these diagrams presented the young reader with a compound blueprint of the future, accompanied by commentaries that clarified its ideological import. Defined by adults, the plan of the future was communicated to schoolchildren as a structured (diagramed) combination of key industrial goals and political aims. Given that the state (supposedly) knew what it was doing, adolescents were not asked for their input. Instead, they were informed about the details of industrial development in the country as a whole and in the region in particular, and – importantly – invited to help carry out these plans.

From Young Techies to Agitators

Taking the Young Techies seriously had another important aspect: along with adults, they were held responsible for victories *and* defeats in the "building of socialism." The first editorial column of *DIAY* already set the stern tone for interacting with the reader: "We have had many successes, but even more failures."[25] Not shying away from the adolescents' daily experience – cramped living conditions, drunkenness, delinquency, and other social problems and flaws – for a while *DIAY* offered only one, seemingly universal, solution: it advised the Young Techies to improve the everyday life of adults by introducing minor technological innovations.

The evolution of the political situation in the USSR in the 1930s, however, influenced the understanding of what a Young Techie could do. This change triggered a corresponding shift in the content and visual design of *DIAY*. Beginning in 1930, every issue of *DIAY* included some share of negative information regarding impediments to industrialization:

> Industry in the Ural region fulfilled 67.5% of its quotas in the first quarter. The Ural region failed to provide the country with cast iron, copper, and ore worth seventy million rubles; it fell short of providing builders with 200,000 barrels of cement ... What causes such a shameful under-fulfilment of the plan? There is only one answer. We have failed to truly "master production, its technology, and its financial-economic aspect" (Stalin).[26]

The magazine's shift in tone was most likely linked to a major political event in Soviet history in 1928–30: the defeat of the "right-wing opposition," associated first and foremost with the figure of Nikolai Bukharin. In addition, in August 1930, polytechnic educators convened in Moscow at their first all-Russian congress to discuss structural changes. Following the direction of the reforms adopted at the congress, all urban schools were linked to local factories, while village schools were all associated with respective collective farms (*kolkhozes* or *sovkhozes*) or machine tractor stations. Another major decision directed primary schools to create special workrooms for their pupils; high schools had to set up laboratories and workshops directly connected to industrial production.[27]

Suddenly, the Young Techies evolved into agents of dramatic changes in "adult" production. As *DIAY* put it in 1931:

Pioneers and schoolchildren have found the best way of learning production techniques by establishing sponsorship [*shefstvo*] of thousands of shop-floor machines and devices. Entrusted to the Pioneers, the electric furnace of the Verkh-Isetsk metallurgical factory (VIZ) fulfilled 190% of its target. On the occasion of this victory, the Pioneers posed the following questions to their comrades who sponsor machines and devices in the Ural region: "To what extent have the workers mastered the machines you sponsor? Did the machines and devices work ceaselessly round the clock in the service of socialism?" The Pioneers and schoolchildren must immediately respond to the call of the kids from VIZ. They must check on the work of their wards. They must see to it that the workers assigned to the machines, as well as the machines themselves, outperform their targets by 150–200%.[28]

This transformation of the reading audience into acting vigilantes created a conflict the magazine could not survive. The initial task of the periodical was to validate and popularize technological creativity by assigning it a national significance. Simultaneously, the magazine taught readers the basics of visual literacy: how to discern the future behind a diagram, how to transform a diagram into a material object. Originally, the Techies emerged as objects of pedagogical care; their independence was limited to low-level (albeit occasionally complex) technical interventions and projects. Yet by 1931, their role had undergone a radical shift: the Techies were Pioneers charged with overseeing their "wards" – the devices by which workers fulfilled production plans (fig. 9.12). The adolescents were given a fundamentally new mission: "Along with members of the Komsomol, read the speeches of comrade Stalin to every worker, to your mother and father. Tell them how to 'face technology!' Recruit workers and your parents into the Stalin technology brigades, and make sure that shock workers [*udarniki*] take on concrete responsibilities in mastering technology. Get workers involved in production technology study groups!"[29] Young Techies were now supposed to be production inspectors, worker organizers, propagandists of governmental decisions, and embodiments of the new political equality between adults and children. In this picture of the world, the pedagogical function of *DIAY* was rendered obsolete. Instead, the magazine was expected to turn itself into a version of *Sputnik agitatora* (*The Agitator's Companion*), a source of propaganda materials to be disseminated to the masses by skilful propagandists.[30]

The radical change of the content and function of *DIAY* was reflected also on the formal level. Figurative illustrations and practical blueprints were replaced by blurry photographs and fragmentary maps. The abstract move of overlaying a ready-made scheme onto real phenomena became literal: as seen in figure 9.13, a fuzzy photograph

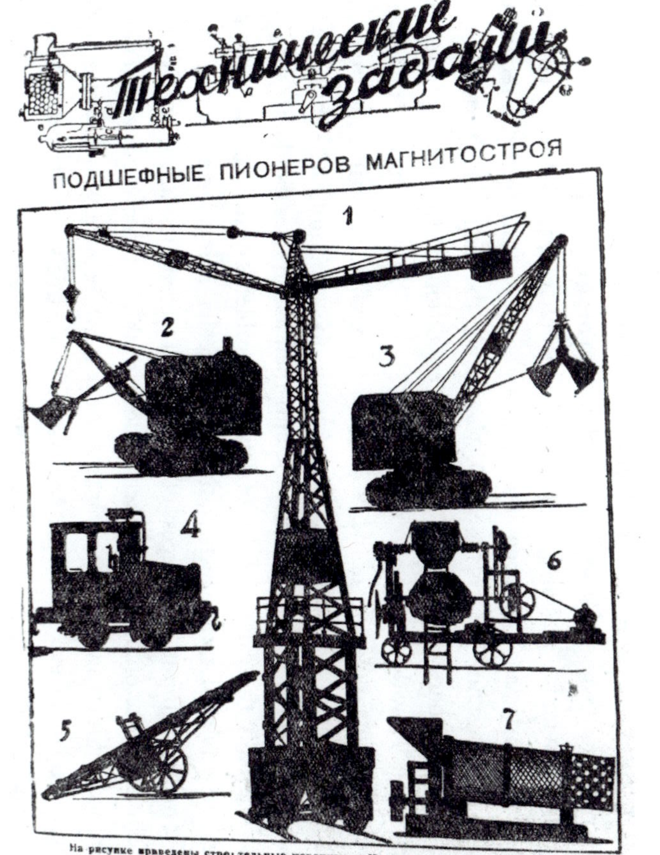

9.12. "Technical Tasks: Things to Be Taken Care of by the Pioneers of the Magnitstroi." *Delai vse sam*, no. 6 (1931): 12.

9.13. A diagram of the growth of national income in the USSR, England, and the United States. *Delai vse sam*, no. 16 (1930): 1–2.

(a montage of construction objects) is superimposed with the white lines of a graph showing the rate of development in large industrial countries (the USSR, the United States, and Great Britain): real life and diagrams become fused.

Under the new visual regime, photos of cheerful Young Techies and diagrams of radio receivers, iron stands, and futuristic aero-sleighs gave way to photographic depictions of factory floors and machines; static images of students from vocational schools (fig. 9.14); and schoolchildren working in a real factory, creating mockups of dirigibles (fig. 9.15), or building complex factory devices (fig. 9.16). At the same time, the creative typesetting techniques characteristic of the magazine's first issues were replaced with a dense and monotonous layout. The original creolized organization of *DIAY*, actively merging visual and textual components, seemed to lose its purpose: the magazine's visual design had come into conflict with its written components.

As the critical level of the materials steadily increased, the visual language of the magazine moved in the opposite direction: an invariably lethargic layout was amplified by blurry, unfocused, and static photographs. This downgrading of the visual could be read semiotically: by the early 1930s, there was no need to rely on the technique of creolization in order to bring new Soviet man (and woman) into the fold of official knowledge. All the government's pronouncements were equally important, and if some statements were meant to carry more weight, their significance would be communicated through repetition in quotations and headlines.

From the beginning, there was a certain tension between the pictorial and textual materials featured in *DIAY*. Graphs, diagrams, and clear, distinct pictures depicted a Soviet life that was dynamic yet planned, and oriented toward the future. The "protagonists" of this vision were the confident and energetic Young Techies and the wise scientists of the past whom the Techies would have to measure up against. This vision of a dynamic Soviet life was also built around a peculiar constellation of amazing ideas that demonstrated "what people have thought up" (as the title of a recurring column in the magazine put it) (fig. 9.17). Meanwhile, the magazine's textual materials described the hard realities of Soviet living conditions at the outset of the first Five-Year Plan: "How does the worker live today? He is still almost entirely under the power of the drunken old way of life. Vodka, cards, cursing, and grime are frequent guests in the family of the worker."[31] Characteristically, a column highlighting technological "achievements" listed an "electric anti-theft alarm" as a candidate for production. Originally, these descriptions of flaws and problems were meant to stimulate the practical activity of Young Techies; they symbolically delineated areas that could benefit from Techie input. The success of creolization techniques during the first two years of the existence of *DIAY* had much to do with the fact that negative phenomena remained "hidden away" in the *words* of the text, while positive ones were made visibly appealing to the eye, in *images*. As a result, within this scopic strategy, the negative appeared as fragmentary, while the positive seemed dominant, at least visually. For example, the article "What We Are Building in the Urals" ("Chto my stroim na

Urale") describes product short-ages and outdated factories.[32] But the visual narrative sends a different message: the schematic map of new construction, photographs of finished plants, the symbolic representation of the materials to be produced in future factories, the figure of the metalworker, the depiction of a burning electric lamp, and even the bolded text of key words pointing out flaws, are used to communicate the dynamic nature of the life flowing beyond the magazine's pages (fig. 9.18).

This device of "hiding" the negative in the text and "accentu-

9.14. A "fabzavuchitsia" – a female student at a factory vocational school. *Delai vse sam*, nos. 2–3 (1931).

ating the positive" through images was maintained in the magazine until the end of its existence. It was the balance of the two that underwent a radical change: with the transformation of the magazine's outlook, the textual and the negative became more salient. Staged photographs of Young Techies and vocational school pupils, unfocused images and vague captions, low-contrast diagrams, unbroken text – all this conveys the impression of disarray and, simultaneously, of a dull predictability of the narrative. For example, a column about Ivan Polzunov (1728–1766), the Russian pioneer of the steam engine, is capped with a comparison of the treatment of workers in Russia under serfdom and under the Soviets – of course, to the benefit of the period of the first Five-Year Plan:

> Workers' inventions are being taken up and popularized. Inventors are given the opportunity to study and the time to develop their ideas. The Soviet Union helps them and encourages them. There are many worker-inventors in the factories of the Soviet Union – the unknown heroes of everyday labour who save the country millions of rubles. The Young Techies must follow their work and try to emulate them. They must try to work and to invent for the benefit of the building of socialism.[33]

The article's text is illustrated with a blurry photograph of a factory machine accompanied by an equally vague caption: "This machine was perfected by comrade Ivanov, a worker of the Ufalei factory. The machine cuts metal-facing time by a factor of four."[34] There is no attempt to encourage the reader to find out what sort of a machine this is and how precisely it has been improved; the magazine's new design has no more room for diagrams or blueprints. The ideology of curiosity and technological creativity has

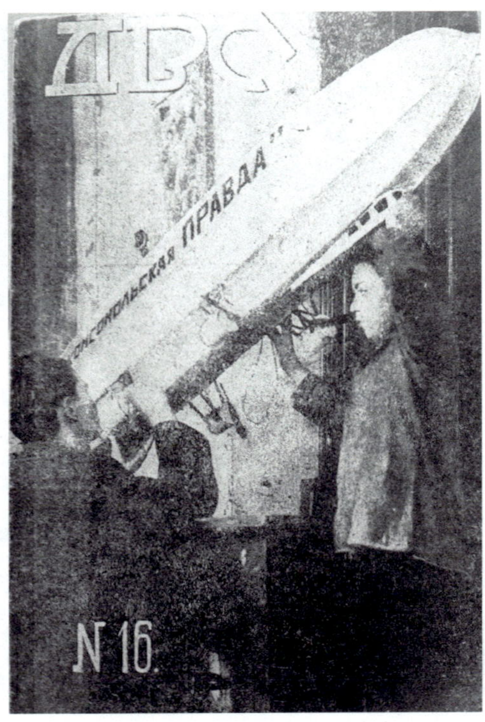

9.15. "The Young Techies' Dirigible." Cover of *Delai vse sam*, no. 16 (1930).

9.16. Cover of *Delai vse sam*, nos. 14–15 (1930).

До чего люди додумались

Велосипед—лодка

Недавно два германских изобретателя Альберт Кут и Герман Буан построили своей конструкции велосипед, который может быть быстро перео орудован в лодку. Лодка вмещает 3-х человек и развивает скорость до 17 километров в час.

При испытании машина показала блестящие результаты. Изобретателями было проехано 3.000 километров по суше и озерам без всяких препятствий.

Такой системы велосипед получит широкое применение для путешествий.

Переносная электростанция

В современном строительстве все больше и больше применяются разнообразные машины приводимые в действие электрической энергией.

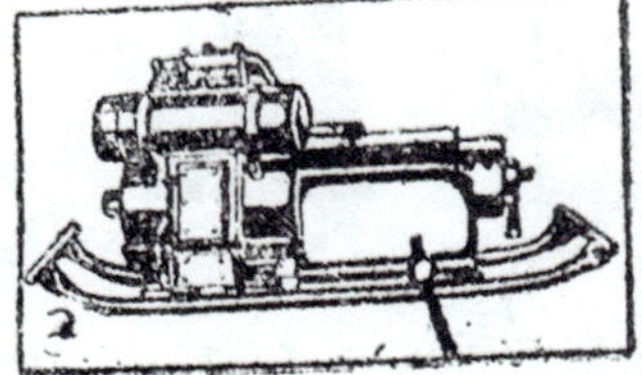

Между тем подводка электрической энергии к месту стройки бывает не всегда

возможна и употребление электрического оборудования сокращающего на много время стройки, становится невозможным.

Недавно американская фирма Вестингауз выпустила переносную электрическую станцию.

Станция состоит из одноцилиндрового бензино-мотора, соединенного гибким сцеплением с динамо-машиной. Вырабатываемая энергия подается к месту потребления обычными проводами.

Применение таких электростанций дает экономию.

Воздушный корабль

Величайший в мире пассажирский самолет Дорнье совершил полет через Атлантический океан из Европы в Америку, имея на борту 82 человека.

Самолет движется силою 12 мощных авиационных двигателей, расположенных над 48 метровым крылом аэроплана. Приведенные в действие моторы развивают

силу, равную 7.200 лошадиных сил, и несут самолет со скоростью 240 километров в час. Поднявшись на аэроплане до Х, как его зовут немцы, можно пролететь с полной нагрузкой 3.2 0 километров, не возобновляя запасов бензина

За машинами воздушного корабля наблюдает 12 человек, а в его удобных просторных каютах помещаются 70 пассажиров.

9.17. "What People Have Thought Up": a portable power-station. *Delai vse sam*, nos. 14–15 (1930).

9.18. Detail of the spread for "What We Are Building in the Urals." *Delai vse sam,* no. 4 (1929): 16–17.

been shunted aside in favour of an ideology emphasizing the subjection of adolescent activity to the will of the state.[35]

The growing disconnect between the magazine's original intent and its later incarnation resulted in a dramatic transformation. The periodical that had formerly encouraged each individual reader (at least grammatically, with a singular imperative) to do it all yourself ceased to exist. It was replaced with a new publication: *Tekhnika – smene* (*Technology for the Shift,* 1931–41). The grammar of the new title retained an (implied) imperative – let shift workers and those who will replace them be supplied with technology. Yet, in the new version, the addressee is depersonalized: "shift" can be read not only as a collective subject (a working shift of professionals who master technology, understanding it and knowing how to use it), but also as a passive recipient of knowledge and skills transmitted from above.

Conclusion

Delai vse sam was produced by a team with limited artistic talent and material resources, but it did have ambitious educators interested in finding new ways of influencing a particular group of adolescents. While their means of visual expression were limited, the editors nonetheless relied on the active deployment of visual language to advance their pedagogical agenda. Any illustrated magazine may be seen as a variegated or creolized text that intertwines various methods of seeing and depicting. The combination of letters and pictures within the page-space of *DIAY* allows us to discern the subject position from which the young reader was encouraged to perceive the world. The adolescent reader found in *DIAY* a picture of the world in which slogans defined semantics while diagrams provided structure. Blending visually distinct schemes with party slogans (embedded in the editorials), the magazine accomplished its main pedagogical task: to inculcate in the Soviet adolescent an interest in independent technological creativity for the benefit of the industrial goals of the state.

DIAY did not whitewash the present: young readers were told directly of the imperfect, contradictory nature of the USSR's socio-economic condition. Moreover, the task of the Young Techie reader was precisely to overcome these difficulties and solve the problems – on the way toward a distinctly formulated socialist goal. Social flaws, in other words, were not ignored, but put in perspective. Striving toward the future and guided by the Five-Year Plan, the Young Techie was taught to develop a project-oriented manner of thinking. The trick was to transform a problem identified by the latest political directive into a concrete local task. Operationalized this way, the task was then structured with the help of technological instructions and diagrams provided by adults. Finally, newly invented machines and devices were called upon to change the situation and resolve social issues.

With the help of multiple diagrams, the reader was trained to identify the internal skeleton ("diagram") of an object or process. The reader learned, moreover, how to perform a reverse engineering, by imaging an object that grows out of a model. Accompanied by detailed technical instructions and success stories, this schematic- and diagram-based education significantly changed the status of the Young Techies, turning them into coequal partners of adult workers and engineers.

As I have suggested, this educational model was not limited to technological experiments alone; economic and political education was conducted in the same way. Provided with ready-to-use templates, the adolescent reader was taught to correlate them with economic descriptions or political statements. Numerous diagrams, illustrations, and photographs helped the reader build a vocabulary of concepts *and* a readily available stock of images of Soviet industrialization that needed no further explanation. The depiction of a factory, a power line, a hydroelectric dam, or an industrial construction site functioned as factographic evidence and as an index, simultaneously providing a pictorial confirmation and graphic scheme of the country's development. The images in the magazine also acted as a source of inspiration: the portrayal of Young Techies with their projects and innovations invited other readers to join the club and find their own place in the "grownup life of production." At the same time, the constant transformation of the socialist state, its permanently unfinished nature, promised the young reader an opportunity to take part in development plans designed by the state.

This openness to adolescent input, however, was short-lived. Following party directives, the editors of *DIAY* gradually "evolved" the Young Techie movement, taking it to its logical conclusion. The student learning how to turn diagrams and blueprints into useful flatirons and radio receivers morphed into an overseer of backward adults, exhorting them to recognize the importance of Soviet slogans (and, to be sure, of diagrams and blueprints). It was no longer thought necessary to stimulate technological creativity in young readers. Instead, these innovators became the state's taskmasters.

When read today, *DIAY* produces an unexpected effect. For a propaganda periodical, it gave a surprisingly truthful picture of "real life" in the USSR at the outset of industrialization. The magazine featured schemes of inspiring plans alongside descriptions of limited material possibilities. It combined images of cheerful Young Techies with the statue-like stillness of photographed adolescents, offsetting the clarity of instructive and tested technical diagrams with blurry photographic representations of "our achievements."

NOTES

1 See Alekseeva, *Sovetskie detskie zhurnaly*; Kolesova, *Detskie zhurnaly Sovetskoi Rossii*; Kholmov, *Stanovlenie sovetskoi zhurnalistiki dlia detei.*

2 See Anisimova, *Lingvistika teksta i mezhkul'turnaia kommunikatsiia*; Bernatskaia, "K probleme 'kreolizatsii' teksta"; Sorokin and Tarasov, "Kreolizovannye teksty i kommunikativnaia funktsiia."

3 See Voroshilova, *Politicheskii kreolizovannyi tekst*; Korda, "Lokativnost' kak osnova organizatsii kreolizovannogo zhurnalistskogo teksta."

4 Lunacharsky, "Sotsialisticheskoe stroitel'stvo i iskusstvo," 1.

5 Gastev, *Kak nado rabotat'.*

6 See Arnautov, "Razvitie sistemy sovetskogo srednego obrazovaniia"; Veikshan and Rives, *Sovetskaia proizvodstvenno-trudovaia shkola.*

7 Bulatov, "Tekhnicheskie znaniia – molodezhi."

8 "O sostoianii i blizhaishikh zadachakh pionerdvizheniia," 36.

9 See Gorskii, *Tekhnicheskoe iskusstvo iunykh konstruktorov*; Naumov, "Sozdanie sistemy detskikh tekhnicheskikh stantsii"; and Iartsev, "Stanovlenie i razvitie sistemy detskogo tekhnicheskogo tvorchestva," 17.

10 This publishing house was organized under the Central Committee of the All-Russian Komsomol in 1922; it was to produce books and periodicals aimed at the adolescent and young-adult age cohorts.

11 The Ural region was created from the Ekaterinburg, Perm, Tiumen, and Cheliabinsk provinces by the All-Russian Central Executive Committee on 3 November 1923, only to be disbanded on 17 January 1934. Both the formation and dissolution of this administrative unit were motivated by the Soviet leadership's drive for effective control over the territory.

12 Besides the publications intended specifically for them, the Young Techies were also fond of "adult" popular-science publications, especially *Radio liubitel'* (*Radio Enthusiast*, 1924–30; from 1930–41, *Radio front* [*The Radio Front*]).

13 *Delai vse sam*, no. 1 (1928): 1, 2.

14 Ibid., 2.

15 A. Bykov, "Iuntekhi." Ibid., 1. Magnitostroi (Magnetic Construction Site) was a major industrial project of the first Five-Year Plan in the Ural region.

16 *Delai vse sam*, no. 5 (1930): 8.

17 Ibid.

18 *Delai vse sam*, no. 6 (1929): 11.

19 *Delai vse sam*, no. 5 (1930): 13.

20 *Delai vse sam*, no. 6 (1929): 1.

21 Ibid., 4.

22 *Delai vse sam*, no. 6 (1929): 9.

23 Ibid., 2.

24 *Delai vse sam*, no. 2 (1929), inside cover; my emphasis.

25 *Delai vse sam*, no. 1 (1928): 1.

26 Delai vse sam, nos. 4–5 (1931): 1

27 See Arnautov, "Razvitie sistemy sovetskogo srednego obrazovaniia."

28 *Delai vse sam*, nos. 4–5 (1931): 1. VIZ (the Russian acronym for Verkh-Isetsk plant) refers to the metallurgical works in the city of Sverdlovsk; its refurbishing was part of the program of industrialization.

29 *Delai vse sam*, nos. 2–3 (1931): 3–4. The exhortation to "face technology" appeared in the article by Stalin "O zadachakh khoziaistvennikov," *Pravda*, no. 35 (1931).

30 This Soviet magazine, first published in 1925, gave party activists practical advice on how best to communicate Soviet policy (domestic and foreign), as well as the USSR's position in the world, to the average citizen.

31 *Delai vse sam*, nos. 2–3 (1931): 3

32 *Delai vse sam*, no. 17 (1929): 32.

33 *Delai vse sam*, no. 5 (1930): 18.

34 Ibid.

35 See Litovskaia, "Regional'nyi zhurnal dlia detei v kontekste sovetskoi periodiki."

BIBLIOGRAPHY

Alekseeva, M.I. *Sovetskie detskie zhurnaly 20-kh godov.* Moscow: Izdatel'stvo MGU, 1982.

Anisimova, E.E. *Lingvistika teksta i mezhkul'turnaia kommunikatsiia (na materiale kreolizovannykh tekstov).* Moscow: Academia, 2003.

Arnautov, N.B. "Razvitie sistemy sovetskogo srednego obrazovaniia v 1920–1930e gody." *Vestnik NGU. Seriia "Pedagogika"* 11, no. 1 (2010): 111–18.

Bernatskaia A.A. "K probleme 'kreolizatsii' teksta: istoriia i sovremennoe sostoianie." *Rechevoe obshchenie: Spetsializirovannyi vestnik*, no. 3 (2000): 104–10.

Bulatov, N.P. "Tekhnicheskie znaniia – molodezhi." *Nasha rabota (zhurnal moskovskogo komiteta RKSM)*, no. 1 (1922): 2–4.

Gastev, A.K. *Kak nado rabotat'.* Moscow: Izdatel'stvo VTsSPS, 1927. http://litlife.club /br/?b=274107&p=32

Gorskii, V.A. *Tekhnicheskoe iskusstvo iunykh konstruktorov.* Moscow: DOSAAF, 1980.

Iartsev, N.N. "Stanovlenie i razvitie sistemy detskogo tekhnicheskogo tvorchestva v usloviiakh dopolnitel'nogo obrazovaniia (na primere Samarskoi oblasti)." PhD diss., Ulyanovsk State Pedagogical University, 2006.

Kholmov, M.I. *Stanovlenie sovetskoi zhurnalistiki dlia detei.* Leningrad: Izdatel'stvo LGU, 1983.

Kolesova, L.N. *Detskie zhurnaly Sovetskoi Rossii 1917–1977.* Petrozavodsk: Petrozavodskii gosudarstvennyi universitet, 1993.

Korda, O.A. "Lokativnost' kak osnova organizatsii kreolizovannogo zhurnalistskogo teksta (na primere publikatsii zhurnala 'Russkii reporter')." *Problemy istorii, filologii, kul'tury*, no. 1 (2012): 343–52.

Litovskaia M.A. "Regional'nyi zhurnal dlia detei v kontekste sovetskoi periodiki 1920–1930-kh gg.: dinamika ideologicheskikh prioritetov." In *"Ubit' Charskuiu ...": paradoksy sovetskoi literatury dlia detei (1920-e–1930-e gg.)*, edited by M. R. Balina and V. Iu. V'iugin, 110–34. St. Petersburg: Aleteiia, 2013.

Lunacharsky, A.V. "Sotsialisticheskoe stroitel'stvo i iskusstvo." *Izvestiia TsIK SSSR i VTsIK*, no. 259 (1929): 1.

Molozhavyi, S. "Po voprosu o realizme v detskoi literature." *Kniga detiam*, no. 4 (1928): 6–7.

Naumov, A.V. "Sozdanie sistemy detskikh tekhnicheskikh stantsii v 1920–30-kh gg. na territorii sovremennoi Nizhegorodskoi oblasti." *Otechestvennaia i zarubezhnaia pedagogika*, no. 6 (2016): 30–6.

"O sostoianii i blizhaishikh zadachakh pionerdvizheniia: Postanovlenie Tsentral'nogo Komiteta VKP(b) ot 25 maia 1928 g." In *Direktivy i dokumenty po voprosam pionerskogo dvizheniia*, edited by V.S. Khanchin, 36–40. Moscow: Izdatel'stvo Akademii pedagogicheskikh nauk.

Sorokin, Iu. A., and E.F. Tarasov. "Kreolizovannye teksty i kommunikativnaia funktsiia." In *Optimizatsiia rechevogo vozdeistviia*, edited by R. G. Kotov, 180–6. Moscow: Nauka, 1990.

Veikshan, V., and S. Rives. *Sovetskoe proizvodstvenno-trudovaia shkola: pedagogicheskaia khrestomatiia*. Vol. 1. 3rd ed. Edited by A.G. Kalashnikov. Moscow: Rabotnik prosveshcheniia, 1925.

Voroshilova, M.B. *Politicheskii kreolizovannyi tekst: kliuchi k prochteniiu*. Ekaterinburg: Ural'skii gosudarstvennyi pedagogicheskii institut, 2013.

chapter ten

THE CAMEL AND THE CABOOSE: VIKTOR SHKLOVSKY'S *TURKSIB* AND THE PEDAGOGY OF UNEVEN DEVELOPMENT

MICHAEL KUNICHIKA

"I saw this camel myself and told Turin about it," Viktor Shklovsky writes in *Turksib* (1930), a work on the Turkestan-Siberia Railroad ostensibly intended for an audience of children and published in tandem with the release of an eponymous film directed by Viktor Turin.[1] "Everyone enjoyed the camel," Shklovsky went on. "I see it in all the journals." Versions of this image of the camel standing near rails (fig. 10.1) appeared throughout Soviet media of the time, such as a collage in the journal *Nastoiashchee* (*Now*), where one sees a camel, train, and boy, whose smiling face suggests a sense of the encounter between the old and the new as joyful and welcome (fig. 10.2).

For Shklovsky, however, the juxtaposition between the camel and rails indicated a fundamental conflict. "The camel smells the rails," he observed in the caption: "He probably doesn't entirely enjoy the smell of rails. It smells of competition." These lines encapsulate much of what animates both Shklovsky's book and Turin's film – namely the task of representing the modernization of Central Asia and how that process thereby created numerous emblems of uneven development. Both works seize upon such emblems, where one finds conjoined the signs of time past, time present, and time future. Along with the camel and the rails, which juxtapose forms of mobility and the transport of goods by caravans to trains, the work also juxtaposes various forms of life, from nomadism to proletarianism. It highlights the benefits that will allegedly accrue to Kazakhstan and Turkestan, and the vast regions of Siberia, once these regions are integrated into a planned economy and the vestiges of the past are overcome. Before that can happen, the work describes, for example, the various natural obstacles facing the construction of the railroad – desert sands, impassable mountains and lakes, the intense summer heat and winter cold. While valorizing modernization, the book is also quasi-ethnographic, focusing on how the inhabitants of these regions have adapted to its conditions, albeit through assuming that they live stultified lives subject to the privations of an untamed nature and a desolate geography.

10.1. Vera Lantsetti and Mikhail Seregin's illustration of a camel and rails, in Viktor Shklovsky, *Turksib.* 2nd ed. (Leningrad: GIZ, 1930), 14.

The book does all this while also disclosing a whole host of formal discontinuities, which we can discern in its structure and themes. The book's graphic designers, Vera Lantsetti and Mikhail Seregin, place images on each page that are set alongside the passages in which Shklovsky makes his case for the promise of Turksib. Each image is supplied with a caption by Shklovsky. The images, which included both drawings and photographs, do not generally correspond to the passages on the page; frequently, they anticipate themes and figures discussed at another point in the book, or they narrate their own stories of modernization, rail construction, and Central Asian life. Indeed, this non-correspondence between the images and the passages on a given page make the relationship between the two seem fairly helter-skelter, and also work toward creating various parallel narratives a reader can follow. The structure means that the images are not subordinated to Shklovsky's narrative, or vice versa. Neither is primary, and both lend the work an overall formal dynamism. Considered together, the images and Shklovsky's text disclose the various techniques of instructing a readership – indeed, a child readership – not only on the challenges of uneven development in Central Asia, but also on the modes by which one should understand a world being increasingly given over to image production and the particular mental states this novel relationship of images and texts sought to create.

With its complex formal structure and its modernizing theme, Shklovsky's book and Turin's film both typify much of the cultural production of the late 1920s. They grapple with the problem of uneven development, while also finding it aesthetically productive – even though, to be sure, the narrative arcs of both works looks forward to a time when modernization has synchronized time, space, and thereby human life. In this regard, the camel is just one example of how both works track various "shocks of the old" – those surprising forms of endurance and persistence, such as the apogee of horsepower during the First World War, which possessed their greatest utility when one might have thought them obsolete.[2] Such forms belonged to the ongoing conundrum of uneven development, a problem for politics as much as for art: while the age of trains and automobiles is poised to replace the age of nomadism and caravans, they compete with each other for the attention of readers and viewers, and for aesthetic use by writers. As Shklovsky indicates, the past can still be enjoyed (if only as part of the exotica of a Central Asian bestiary), perhaps even accommodated – no

10.2. A. Nikulin, montage from *Turksib. Nastoiashchee*, Nov.–Dec. 1930.

small conundrum for a work seeking to educate a child who is expected to enjoy a caboose more than a camel.

Such instabilities of readerly interest – another arena for the competition between the old and the new – are only one of the curiosities generated by the book. Another is what age group Shklovsky imagines for it. His *Turksib* lacks the visual resplendence of other children's books from the period: its colours are drab, and the images are documentary and ethnographic in their theme and form. The work starts with the promise that it will narrate an adventure tale of things – to be sure, a venerable plot for children's literature – but with new content. That plot, however, disintegrates as the work touches on various subjects, such as agriculture, the economic integration of the constituent republics, the topography and geology of Central Asia – such topics were perhaps not entirely the most common, or thrilling, for a child. There are also stray anecdotes about a ficus brought to the desert (with no accompanying image, so a child reader would have to know what a ficus is). Child readers are also treated to an extended discussion of the competition between flax and cotton production, which they likely did not sense serves as Shklovsky's personal allegory of writing after modernism.

Where other period children's books certainly deploy the forms and devices associated with the modernist tendencies – as other chapters in this volume well attest – Shklovsky's might be considered a subset of that phenomenon: a children's book written by a Russian formalist, who is well aware of the devices of children's books but who also seeks to marshal them back into the service of documentary reportage. We might imagine an adolescent reader, one who needs edification on modernization, but also another reader attuned to the basic transformations of Shklovsky's prose efforts in the 1920s and his rapprochement with documentary realism over the course of that decade.

Such a reading is an attempt to grapple with the different facets of the work, which disjoint its narrative structure and widen the scale of its various tonalities. Indeed, the work at times seems like a deformation of a children's book, or a classic concatenation of Shklovskian devices, each one belonging to a particular kind of narrative (a travelogue, a pedagogy on uneven development and economic production, an ethnography of the Kazakhs, a production novel, and so on), each seeming to vie with one another, and none assuming control over the structure of the book. It has no dominant theme other than its subject of rail construction. In their discordance, these pieces of the narratives seem no more and no less than devices, the recognition of them as stock resources one could use in cobbling together a children's book.[3]

Full of such shards of narratological possibilities and of recognizable forms, *Turksib* stakes its claim on an audience of children (at least adolescents) at a transitional moment of literary modernism, its devices and resources repurposed for documentary. These features, in turn, can be approached from multiple angles. *Turksib* presents an adventure tale of common things (*obyknovennye veshchi*), but it also zoomorphizes machines in an effort to create what it calls a "portraiture of things," a genre in which objects acquire countenances and enter into affective relationships with their viewers. *Turksib* couples these features within an ethnographic project, and thus – much like the project of the railroad itself – the book marks the convergence of these formal issues and the broad political project of modernizing ethnicities.

Caravans and the Shock of the Old

As with much of the period's cultural production, *Turksib* grapples with problems of development as part of a generalized "crisis of time" when, to borrow from François Hartog, the relationship between past, present, and future can no longer be perceived as "self-evident."[4] The rail project of Turksib was to function as something of a developmental time-machine, eradicating the whole problem of unevenness by promising that Central Asians could leap over various historical stages in becoming proletarian.[5] Such developmental leaps were only one of the many temporal schemes one finds in Shklovsky's *Turksib*. As a documentary project, the work remains largely committed to depicting various conjunctures of past and present, even while making proleptic gestures toward the promised beneficence of the railroad. We find that sentiment expressed in such comments as "in many places machines work instead of people" and "the automobiles outpace bulls and camels."[6] For the most part, however, *Turksib* is thoroughly a work about transition – indeed, is fascinated by it – even though Shklovsky affirms that the past will ultimately be superseded.

While the Turksib railroad exemplified the projects of the Five-Year Plans, this developmental focus on the Central Asians pointed to several distinctive features of the project. First, among the large-scale *novostroiki* of the period, the project was one of the few to grapple with ethnicity – namely, how to turn ethnic Kazakhs, many of whom were nomadic herders, into proletarians. As Mathew Payne has observed, Turksib "did not represent the conquest of nature as grandly as the Dnepr Dam nor showcase the assimilation of modern technology like Magnitogorsk, but it did come to embody the regime's commitment to ethnic modernity."[7] In that regard, the project interwove the historiographies of socialist modernization and the nationalities question. This dimension of the project encourages us to also consider how Shklovsky's *Turksib* grappled with the question of ethnicity and ethnography as a subject of a children's book, and, moreover, as a matter of its own formal features.

One particularly charged example of this relationship comes in the book's very form, as it depicts the project of modernizing ethnic Kazakhs. In this case, the reader finds Kazakhs standing in front of a *yurt*, seemingly enraptured as they watch an automobile (fig. 10.3). Shklovsky's caption informs readers that locals refer to automobiles as *shaitan-arba* or "the devil's cart" ("chortova telega"). So many perspectives are on offer at this moment: the Kazakhs on the automobile; Shklovsky's on the Kazakhs; the reader's, instructed by Shklovsky, on the entire scene. The scene, too, incorporates ethnographic elements, since one knows from the caption that the Kazakhs associate the automobile with the diabolic and this information provides a glimpse, however brief, into their lifeworlds. The sequence also indicates an overarching modernizing ethos, since we know that the automobile belongs to the prospecting party, which not only enters the space of the *aul*, or village, but also defines a particularly modern relationship to space (i.e., prospecting as a form of rationalizing space). That relationship is presumably distinct from that of the Kazakh nomads, who, as Shklovsky tells his readers earlier in *Turksib*, traverse space in broad circles.[8] The scene thereby juxtaposes the Kazakh *aul* with the modernity of the prospecting party, while also gesturing toward a future in which the space of the nomads, too, will become rationalized and regimented by the rail and car.[9]

When we view these images today, what might stand out for us is how a reader of the time may have been asked to consider the ways in which the media of photography and of the book both participate in the process of modernization. We will see below, in fact, how this sequence presents a complex case in which forms of visuality commonly ascribed to modernism and modernity have to also take into account questions of ethnicity (in a similar way that Turksib itself marked a confrontation between modernization and ethnicity). This aspect of the book marks the modernization of the mind reading these images, while the train undertakes to modernize

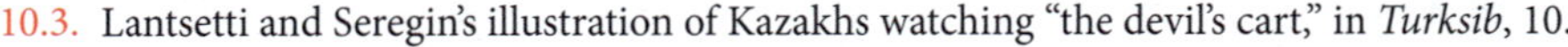

10.3. Lantsetti and Seregin's illustration of Kazakhs watching "the devil's cart," in *Turksib*, 10.

Central Asian peoples and space. Together, in other words, the two media are hardly just recording and reporting the encounter with the car to a readership of children far beyond Central Asia; they work together to form a circuit of communication that asks the child reader to understand not only what they are seeing but also how the images work together, or at least to be taught how to comprehend them.

We can consider more closely, for example, the images in figures 10.3 and 10.4. The first depicts Kazakh children looking (as a kind of ethnic mirror for the book's own reader). Even though the object of their gaze isn't pictured, the caption tells us what they are allegedly looking at. Since the image on the next page depicts the prospecting automobile (fig. 10.4), one assumes they are indeed looking at the prospecting party, given the classic mental connections central to the montage structures of juxtaposition. Placing the images together implies a grammar of relations, adumbrated by Shklovsky's text.

The grammar structuring how these images relate to one another differentiates the book from other ethnographic modes employed in children's books. Consider, for example, Efim Khiger's *Narody SSSR* (*Peoples of the USSR*, 1926) (fig. 10.5) and his *Narody Azii* (*Peoples of Asia*, 1926), where a child would have found an array of ethnic types. This format, however richly illustrated, operates with a form of ethnography that provides a taxonomy of racial diversity, perhaps even spectacularizes it and sets these *types* in relation to an ordered structure of display.[10] While this structure, as scholars such as Francine Hirsch would remind us, are hardly less complex than the kinds of images we find in *Turksib*, the rudimentary linking of image to image in a taxonomy does not generate the relationship between the images we find in *Turksib*. The images in the book are almost cinematic, the cropping and combining of various images furnish the reader with classic cases of the Kuleshov effect, with its emphasis

10.4. Lantsetti and Seregin, illustration of a prospecting car, in *Turksib*, 11.

on generating meaning by placing two images in sequential order than would otherwise be present in a single image. For example, as noted above, there is nothing in the photo of the children watching that indicates what they are looking at; it's only through juxtaposition that we're made to think they are watching the prospecting car. Thoroughly fungible, the image is essentially about looking and about affirming that the objects of modernity, in their novelty, are worth looking at. In that form, these photos operate in service of an ethnographic gaze that renders the Kazaks backwards in their act of looking, even though the book holds out the possibility of their future transformation from their present state, which the book considers them to be woefully benighted – they think the car's diabolical! In this regard, such moments reveal how *Turksib* operates via modern media to inculcate in a reader an understanding of the logic of image relations and the ethnographic organization of the world.

Such structures of juxtaposition have been central to the pre-eminent modernist forms of montage and collage. They have also underpinned various accounts of ethnographic practice. As Katerina Clark elaborates, "whichever way the paradigmatic gesture is defined – collage, montage, breaking or confusing the frame, and so on – it involves placement or juxtaposition with the aim of confounding borders and hierarchies. One has to place the like against the unlike in order to 'see' anew."[11] Shklovsky's text offers us another function of juxtaposition, which, as we saw above, is edification – how, that is, to see something as a modernized person would.

In anthropological thought, by extension, at least since the 1970s and 1980s, figures such as George Marcus and James Clifford have singled out one particular moment in the development of ethnography and anthropology during the twentieth century as an alternative point of origin for the social sciences: that moment occurred

10.5. Efim Khiger, image of peoples on the cover of *Narody SSSR* (Leningrad: Raduga, 1926).

in and following 1925, centred in Paris at the Institute of Ethnology and a decade later the Collège de Sociologie. It marked, in Clifford's view, a stunning interweaving of surrealism (understood as both an aesthetic movement and general world view) and ethnography. In his essay "On Ethnographic Surrealism" (1988), Clifford argues:

> The surrealist elements of modern ethnography tend to go unacknowledged by a science that sees itself engaged in the reduction of incongruities rather than, simultaneously, in their production. But is not every ethnographer something of a surrealist, a reinventor and reshuffler of realities? Ethnography, the science of cultural jeopardy, presupposed a constant willingness to be surprised, to unmake interpretive syntheses, and to value – when it comes – the unclassified, unsought other … Ethnography cut with surrealism emerges as the theory and practice of juxtaposition.[12]

Juxtapositions, insofar as they produce the incongruous, also place into jeopardy the hierarchies they compare. A central juxtaposition of *Turksib*, for example, is the camel and the rails, which Shklovsky believed indicated a sense of competition between the old and the new. But the juxtaposition could also be understood as a competition for the child reader's attention. If the rail was eventually supposed to render the camel outmoded, why, as Shklovsky suggest, do people enjoy the latter? Why did it appear in so many journals of the time, just as it did in the *Turksib* film? What we see here is how much the past, when juxtaposed with the future, in fact acquired greater legibility and aesthetic charge. The juxtaposition of the two confers upon the old something radically more aesthetically "enjoyable," now that it can be perceived in a juxtaposition with the future that would annul it.

To press further about the image: is it, as Shklovsky understood it, always about competition? We see one alternative in the collage of the camel, train, and a Central Asian youth that A. Nikulin made for the journal *Nastoiashchee* (see fig. 10.2). His montage does not emphatically evince the ideology of modernization in the way that Shklovsky's *Turksib* does, though both rely upon juxtaposition to highlight the varieties of developmental modes in Central Asia. Instead, Nikulin presents uneven development with a jovial Central Asian face, which could just as well indicate a process not of competition but of gradualism, perhaps even the accommodation of the multiple times present in the region.

How, then, might we consider how times past, present, and future work in these texts in relation to these other categories of juxtaposition, modernism, and theories of ethnography? Here, we might call upon a moment from the early 1920s, when we find forms of ethnography emerging that did not rest upon structures of juxtaposition, but rather on interweaving and transformation. Waldemar Borogaz, writing in the introduction to a collection of sketches published as *Revoliutsiia v derevne* (*Revolution in the Countryside*), called for a "new ethnography" that aspired to capture the "interweaving" of past and present, even the "transformation" of one into the other:

The new ethnography equally studies both the past and the modern. For the creation of culture never ceases. And for the new ethnography, ancient Russia, folklore, magic, and the new Soviet Russia, the communist party, equally present an object of study, a natural-scientific ethnography phenomenon. The old transforms into the new, the old interweaves with the new into completely unbroken, unexpected combinations. And to approach the study of this new *byt* [or "daily life"] with old, prepared cliché is impossible and absurd.[13]

This view – which, to my mind, represents a remarkable attempt to reconcile ethnography and history and to ally ethnography with the tracking of cultural change rather than the description of stasis – encourages us to also attend to the multiple temporal signatures that crop in *Turksib* that do not easily fit with the idea of juxtaposition of, or a competition between, the old and new.[14]

The camel and the railroad – a master trope for the work – should not blind us to the various ways that the work tracks multiple temporal relationships. Indeed, we find the work disclosing temporal combinations that reveal the "interweaving" of old and new, as Borogaz understood it. Some of these are ethnographic moments: for example, the "worker-Kazakhs" (fig. 10.6) who continue to wear traditional Kazakh hats, or *malakhai* (one of several times Shklovsky informs his readers of native words for such things as "canals" ["akai"]), alongside "konservy" ("goggles").[15] This new type, "the worker-Kazakh," the figure produced by the modernization effort, stands in opposition to the other ethnographic types we see throughout the work, in particular those of the nomads, who are made to seem obdurately stalled in their backwardness.

Perhaps even more significant, the reader glimpses how modernization occurs fitfully in Central Asia and how the past is not only accommodated but also still relied upon in constructing the present. Shklovsky tells his reader that the camels themselves bring rations and building supplies to the construction, evidenced also in the illustration of the excavator bucket (fig. 10.7). Modernization, in other words, is built on the support structure of the past forms it promises to supersede. (That irony acquires a profoundly grim cast in Solzhenitsyn's *Arkhipelag Gulag* [*The Gulag Archipelago*], when he remarks on how the construction of the White–Baltic Sea Canal was essentially accomplished with stone-age equipment.[16]) For his part, Shklovsky was informing his readership of an actual feature of the construction of Turksib. We know from Payne another facet of this story on how the construction project relied upon camel power, as it were. The incomplete construction of the railroad in 1924 meant that some 1400 kilometres remained unbuilt, and that "transport between the two railheads relied on inefficient and grindingly slow camel caravans that took up to seventy days."[17] To use a camel caravan to link two sections of rail is something of a remarkable image. The persistence of the old regime, to borrow from Arno Mayer, could thereby be seen to come in multiple forms: the previous regime of mobility symbolized by the camel caravan was integrated into that of the industrial

10.6. Lantsetti and Seregin, Kazakh proletarians, in *Turksib*, 19.

10.7. Lantsetti and Seregin, "Portrait of the bucket," in *Turksib*, 17.

age. What *Turksib* thereby allows us to see is how modernization emerges in disconnected zones, only slowly integrated, rather than as some rational extension from a central point. In this light, the supreme trope of competition between past and present again gives way to ideas of accommodation and transition, indicating the reliance (however begrudging) upon, rather than annulment of, the past.

The year before *Turksib* was published, Shklovsky had touched on similar themes in his *Tekhnika pisatel'skogo remesla* (*Technique of Writing Craft*). In that book, he offered as his "central piece of advice is to write about modernity, to write about definite things, about definite events."[18] Shklovsky partially followed his own advice in *Turksib*; he was, after all, writing about the modernization project and its necessity. But the modernity he described was one consisting of multiple times that were competing with, or accommodating one another.

Shklovsky's vision of modernity in *Turksib*, in fact, seems perversely interested in tracking how modernization falters. For all their purported power, the machines described in *Turksib* seem poorly equipped to function in their new environment. As Shklovsky notes in the section "Paravoz v vode" ("Train in Water"), during the construction a train came under "siege" by water, which disrupted the movement of goods.[19] Shklovsky's description of the construction of Turksib does not present some facile story about the domination of nature, but rather it seems vastly more invested in revealing the obdurate resistance of nature. This is all the more notable because Shklovsky traces how vestigial forms are present not only in the Kazakhs, but also in city dwellers, who come to work in the desert, but whose *byt* is profoundly out of sync with it. He recounts, for example, the story of a ficus plant:

> I once saw such a ficus in the desert.
>
> A worker had been sent in the advanced detachment to the construction. He had brought his wife with him, and his wife had brought the ficus with her – she'd never imagined what a desert was. Imagine, lying there is desert, sand, grass blowing about in wisps upon a hill, and in the middle of the desert stood two chairs and a pot with a ficus.
>
> To build the road, it's necessary to refuse the ficus and every habit of urban life.[20]

No more caravans, with their outmoded forms of mobility; no more ficuses, with their hold on desires for habituated urban life: the pedagogy typified by this passage instructs the reader into the necessary restructuring of daily life. What is difficult to discern, again, is what this anecdote of the abandoned ficus is doing in these pages. While it may stretch our sense of what kinds of narratives may be typical of a children's book, it does seem to invoke its stylistic tropes (imagine yourself!) only to offer a perhaps atypical object to the adolescent imagination (a ficus in the desert!). In effect, the *byt* of urban life (those, for example, that might surround the metropolitan reader of the work) is transformed and defamiliarized, slipping here into the accidentally exotic.

A Portraiture of Things

What the train and the ficus also indicate was that Shklovsky was following through not only on his advice to write about modernity but also definite things. In *Turksib*, two other images – one depicting an excavator bucket and the other a cotton bloom (figs. 10.7 and 10.8) – bring together various themes within them. In his comment on

А вот портрет цвета хлопчатника. Посмотрите, какой он нежный и какой красивый. Когда у нас будет много хлопчатника, то будет и много материи; для этого нужно не только увеличивать количество обработанной земли, но и изменить способ обработки, выбирать самые лучшие семена для посева.

10.8. Lantsetti and Seregin, "Portrait of the cotton bloom," *Turksib*, 32.

the two photographs, Shklovsky instructs his reader not only to look upon the two objects but also to relate to them in a particular way, instructing the reader to find the bucket sympathetic and the blossom tender. The genre into which Shklovsky encoded these images was a *portraiture* of things, which certainly marks one of the most curious forms of object relations elaborated in *Turksib* and one where the volume seems to grapple with the story of objects so often elaborated in children's books.

This portraiture of things comes alongside the other image forms in the work, and their respective *generic* associations. The images in *Turksib* are drawings (*risunki*) and photographs and include a map of Turksib that comes at the end of the work and that finally grounds the reader in cartographic space. The modes of these images are often determined by their subject matter, from the ethnographic to the industrial photo, from the picturesque and the landscape photos. On one level, each image possesses a particular pedagogical function, set in tandem with other functions: they provide details on the processes of construction, the kinds of machines used, the reaction of locals to the process, and the rationale for the construction.

The portraits, however, suggest an aesthetic and empathetic relationship to the objects depicted, one that seeks to encourage an affective orientation of the reader to the mechanisms and products of constructing the railroad. The "portrait of the bucket" (fig. 10.7), for example, presents no mere industrial thing: it possesses a countenance, and a sympathetic one at that. Shklovsky apparently wants to construct it as an "object of affection," a move typifying children's literature and its affective regimentation of technophilia. When planes, trains, automobiles, and excavators become attractive – indeed, not just attractive but anthropomorphically sympathetic – is difficult to say. Yet, one of the curious features of the particular anthropomorphizing trope here is that it seems actually at variance with the depiction of the excavator bucket, as though Shklovsky is forcing it to become an object of affection, when we had also learned that it has "iron jaws on steel necks."[21] Perhaps all the figurative action Shklovsky expends upon the excavator, from the initial anthropomorphism that ascribes it a countenance to the zoomorphisms that ascribe it a body, transfers the competition between the camel and the rails into the realm of machines: the excavator is figuratively invested with the form and affective associations formerly ascribed to camels.

Along with considering these devices in relation to the genre of the work as a children's book, we can also see how Shklovsky shares a view toward matter that we find throughout modernism internationally. In Jeffrey Schnapp's words, "modern materials emerge as autonomous forces within an overarching modernist prosopoeia. Beyond even their symbolic import, they become protagonists and heroes endowed with powers of agency and moral value, capable of sharing in the particular and universal attributes of human subjects and/or of serving as prosthetic extensions of humanity."[22] In this light, we might note how Shklovsky does not only want his readers to look upon the images, he also wants them to relate to these objects with forms of affect he deems proper to them. Sympathy and tenderness, on the one hand; aesthetic appreciation on the other. But the heightened focus on the bucket itself seems to deform the commonplace status of objects and animals in children's books. A classic device of children's literature, the animation of material, seems here to purposefully misfire: Shklovsky deforms the device at the very moment he invokes it in order to give his text some purchase on being a children's book written by a Russian formalist.

Let me turn here to the portrait of the cotton bloom that concludes *Turksib* (see fig. 10.8). The image and caption bring to a close the various themes of irrigation, the increased production of material, and the opposition between cash crops and grains (one of the central problems of Central Asian and Siberian agriculture that Turksib was supposed to ameliorate).[23] The image thereby bookends the work in multiple ways, since it also returns to the theme that opens the work – namely, Shklovsky's brief lesson on the political economy of things: "What a grand journey these things make to be collected on our table in the morning. The most far-flung traveller is tea: it has arrived from China. White bread is somewhere from the Northern Caucasus. Butter is from Vologda."[24] Shklovsky follows a track familiar to figures such as Dziga Vertov, who had furnished in his film *Kino-glaz* (1924) extensive lessons training his viewership in political economy by focusing on how things are made. In *Turksib*, Shklovsky takes up this basic question of "everyday things," to touch on both the political and narrative economies contained within them: "If we were to tell the history of each thing, then so much time would pass that we would sit at the table for morning tea, and breakfast, and lunch, and dinner."[25] Its narrative concerns with telling an adventure of things and the tone of this opening indicate the work's orientation toward children's literature: while it gestures toward this orientation, it does not maintain it throughout the work.

A thing can disclose a story, but not all stories can be told. The narrative expenditure each thing would involve dwarfs the amount of time one could possibly devote to it. Still, Shklovsky does continue in the narrative to opt to tell his reader a story about tablecloths, which forms the metonymic relationship that motivates the progression from one section to the next. One reads in a caption, for example, a focus on the materiality of the tablecloth that serves as a reflection upon the status of the book as a whole. His reference to it as "like paper" ("bumazhnye") extends the concept of the narrative economy of things and gives the work a connecting theme he will elaborate on over the course of the book. Such a device would have operated differently in Shklovsky's other works: for the sake of comparison, such appeals to materiality as in *Tret'ia fabrika* (*Third Factory*, 1926) drop away here, since the tablecloth's status as paper (just as the book's own) is subordinated to a travel narrative about matter and the movement of things.[26] Modernist devices, in effect, are now at the service of children marveling at the book they hold in their hands.

Shklovsky elevates the drama surrounding the entire question of the tablecloth in the subsequent section, which he entitles "Who, whom? Flax or Cotton?" ("Kto kogo – len ili khlopok?"). Shklovsky's reference to Lenin's famous formula "kto-kogo?" ("who will vanquish whom?") makes the two crops into another pair of competitors that Shklovsky traces in the work. Where the first pair, the camel and the train, marks both a developmental competitor and a sign of Shklovsky's competition with Turin (that is, it was both a sign of uneven development and invested with metapoetic value), flax carries with it a similar duality: it is central to *Turksib*'s narrative and pedagogical purpose, but it is no less central to Shklovsky's own repertoire of writerly images. He had signaled his particular affection for flax in *Third Factory*, where he associated it and its production with both writing and modernity, in particular identifying flax with writers and artists he admires for resisting adhering to norms and as a figure for more complex forms of modernist narrative.[27] In *Turksib*, Shklovsky traces flax production back to Egypt and explains the difficulty of its production in comparison with that of cotton, but ultimately concludes that "flax, cotton, and fur are all necessary for life." All of this seems in keeping with the thematic demand of unpacking the origins of things, but it also discloses a central sign of Shklovsky's own literary career. The presence of flax calls attention to how various devices are pressed into service in an adventure tale and the various ways that Shklovsky marries modernist devices to elaborating a travel narrative form. Such are the ways in which this formalist children's book encodes multiple devices and histories into its pages; they, too, were undergoing transition in the hands of a writer who was himself transitioning between multiple modes of writing and addressing different kinds of audiences.

Vizhu: The Modernist Autopsy

There is a curious feature of Shklovsky's comment about seeing a camel and telling Turin. He notes how the camel had become a significant object in its own right, making the rounds of various journals. Why does he feel the need to note that he had seen the image in other venues? Perhaps he was simply trying to take credit for the discovery of the camel – and thus of the conjunction of the camel and the rails – rather than allowing it to be ascribed to Turin (as the montage by Nikulin does [see fig. 10.2]). Perhaps his comment was also meant to testify to the sheer fact of something having been seen. *Turksib* is full of passages where Shklovsky insists to his reader that he's seen something and on how to see: as we have noted above, he describes what is visible in particular images; he instructs his readers on how to feel about what they see; and he coordinates various gazes, intersecting around different signs of modernization.

In this section, I want to take up how this testifying to seeing things oneself belongs to a topos related to two particular forms, the modernist poem of travel and silent Russian film in the 1920s. What might this volume's focus on a "pedagogy of images" tell us about the cultural production of modernity in the 1920s, for which this topos links up with a particular view of history and historical experience that is grounded in acts of seeing. In the context of the 1920s, there is perhaps no greater assertion of this topos than in Dziga Vertov's *Shestaia chast' mira* (*One Sixth of the World*), a work that in fact opens with the proclamation "I see" (fig. 10.9). With Vertov, this statement is no ordinary proclamation of seeing, which we can register in the graphic intensity of the intertitle that Aleksandr Rodchenko designed for the film. For the opening moments of the film, all that is clear is where this act of seeing is located – it is "In the land of Capital" – and the date, 1926. Neither the speaker of the statement nor the direct object of the verb is yet made clear. And so, for a few moments, the act of seeing is the primary matter to which the audience is asked to attend – of seeing in its intransitive mode ("I see"), rather than transitive form ("I see what"). It's as though, in proclaiming this act of seeing, whoever speaks also proclaims their own coming into being, grounding their existence through the act of sight itself. At the very least, it announces that what would seem so ordinary a verb – *videt'*, to see – is anything but ordinary in the context of cinema.

In *One Sixth*, several curiosities emerge from this point. It is not Vertov who speaks here, but rather the *kino-glaz*, or cine-eye, that curious apparatus whose twin capacities of recording and speaking ensure its place among the highest ranks of

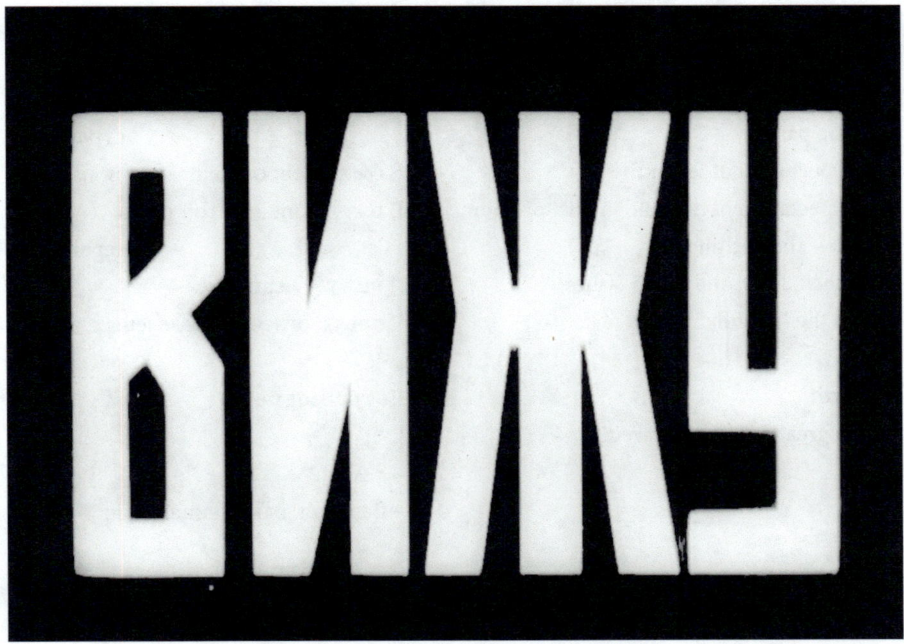

10.9. Still from Dziga Vertov's *Shestaia chast' mira* (1926).

modernism's great avatars of vision. Indeed, although the *kino-glaz* had spoken in Vertov's earlier manifestos, it had not yet done so in film. Even when it appeared as the central subject of his earlier film *Kino-glaz* (1924), Vertov still treated the camera as though it were a third-person character. But in *One Sixth*, it served as the central agent of both sight and speech. Shortly following the proclamation of sight, the *kino-glaz* then enumerates what falls within its vast purview:

> In the land of Capital
> I see
> the golden chain of Capital
> the foxtrot
> the machines
> and you
> I see you

While such a statement is one of the famously idiosyncratic features of Vertov's film, he was not alone in Soviet Russia to deploy this topos of "I see." Indeed, it seems that proletarian poets had quickly picked up the topos of *vizhu* followed by a catalogue of sites, in order to chart their experience of the present day. Mikhail Gerasimov, in *Electropoema*, begins his eponymous poem by announcing:

<table>
<tr><td>

– Earth
Here I've come to you
I see, you entirely damp with
Spring passion,
In expectation of fecundity
In expectation of the golden dust of grain.
I see — the flashing
Of black, fiery, and green lashes
Unto the horizon.
[…]
– Earth
– Oh great one, my beloved!

</td><td>

– Земля
Вот я пришел к тебе
Я вижу, ты вся преешь весенней
           страстью,
В ожидании оплодотворения,
В ожидании золотой пыли
           зерен.
Я вижу – мерцание
Черных, огненных и зеленых
           ресниц
До горизонта.
[…]
– Земля,
– Великая, влюбленная моя![28]

</td></tr>
</table>

Gerasimov then goes on to intersperse the *poema* with a range of other sites he witnesses. What unites both Vertov and Gerasimov in their use of this topos was a common source: Walt Whitman, whose poem "Salut au Monde," in particular, furnished a powerful model for writers, artists, and film-makers to articulate their experience of viewing a vast array of peoples, geographical locations, and nations; it enabled a form for cataloguing, indeed revelling in visual experience.[29]

Together with this cluster of works, we might consider a work thematically close to those we are considering here – Blaise Cendrars, also a devoté of Whitman, and his *La Prose du Transsibérien et de la petite Jehanne de France* (1913). The work allows us to consider further what these proclamations of seeing could mean for the account of vision and locomotion at play in *Turksib*. Consider, for example, the following lines from Cendrars:

<table>
<tr><td>

J'ai vu
J'ai vu les trains silencieux les trains
    noirs qui revenaient de l'extrême
    orient et qui passaient en fantômes
Et mon oeil, comme le fanal d'arrière,
    court encore derrière ces trains.
A Talga 100.000 blessés agonisaient
    faute de soins
J'ai visité les hopitaux de Krasnoiarsk
Et a Khilok nous avons croisé un long
    convoi de soldats fous
J'ai vu dans les lazarets des plaies
    béantes des blessures qui saignaient
    à pleines orgues

</td><td>

I saw
I saw the silent trains the black trains
    returning from the Far East and
    going by like phantoms.
And my eyes, like tail lights, are
    still trailing along behind those
    trains
At Talga 100,000 wounded were dying
    with no help coming
I went to the hospitals at Kranoyarsk
And at Khilok we met a long convoy
    of soldiers gone insane
I saw in quarantine gaping sores and
    wounds with blood gushing out

</td></tr>
</table>

<table>
<tr><td valign="top">

[...]
Et j'ai vu
J'ai vu des trains de 60 locomotives
    qui s'enfuyaient à toute vapeur
    pourchassées par les Horizons en
    rut et des bandes de corbeaux qui
    s'envolaient déseperément après
Disparaître
Dans la direction de Port-Arthur

</td><td valign="top">

And the amputated limbs danced
    around or flew up in the raw air
[...]
And I saw
I saw trains with 60 locomotives
    streaking away chased by hot hori-
    zons and desperate crows
Disappearing
In the direction of Port Arthur.[30]

</td></tr>
</table>

These lines, with all their "I have seen's" reminded poetry critic Marjorie Perloff of Rimbaud and Walt Whitman: she observes how Cendrar's poem "sounds at first rather like Walt Whitman: the long free verse line ... But the voice we hear is curiously unlike Whitman's oracular, rapturous 'I.'"[31] On one level, what calls our attention is the topos itself; on another, it's the generic situation in which it is located, the *modernist poem of travel*. Cendrars and Vertov form two parallel branches of a genealogy that reaches back to Whitman, in whom they both likely found this topos of "I see" or "I saw." They not only share this common source but also a similar geography of the Russian hinterland and of the East. And, moreover, they share the endeavour to link the topos to a catalogue of their own times, their own modernity, through the modernist poem of travel.

In the case of Vertov, the modernist poem of travel is more specifically called the *kino-probegi* (film races), which consummately manifest his aesthetic values by turning radical juxtapositions in space and time into a pre-eminent sign of the cinema's power to reorganize time, space, and ultimately the mind of the spectator. Vertov affixes the mobility of cinema to new forms of locomotion, from airplanes to motorcycles, steam ships, motorcars, and railroads. Locomotion was no less central to Cendrars, but for him these modes of travel threaten to upheave human measures of time and space. It was why John dos Passos christened him "the Homer of the Transsiberian" in a review that appeared in 1926, just as Vertov's own take on these spaces of the Soviet hinterland and Far East made its way to the screen.[32]

What is it about this particular modernist lineage that emphasizes cataloguing the basic fact of things having been seen or being in the very process of being seen? And might the syntactic form of "I see," which we find Vertov adopts from Whitman, and "I have seen," which we find in Rimbaud and Cendrars, tell us something more than a change in tense? "I see" or "I have seen" form a travelling topos in which we find interwoven various strands of modern poetry and film. All of these "I see's" or "I have seen's" are significant topoi, even though they might seem commonplaces that verge of clichés, so dead they hardly warrant any attention. On the other hand, their very repetition suggests that Cendrars and Vertov, among others, foreground the pronouncement in order to restore to the act of sight some particular value in relation to the experience of modernity.[33]

Beyond their affiliation with all those ocular metaphors belonging to the standard account of the ocularcentrism, whether of modernism locally or Western thought generally, the topos possesses a particular function in historical writing and the historicity claimed by modernity. François Hartog notes, in his *Mirror of Herodotus*, that, as early as the Greek historian, we see the topos of "I saw" taking form as an "autopsy," which is "the guarantor of what is said": this "first form of history, the one Hegel calls 'original history,' is organized around an 'I have seen' and, from the point of view of what is said, that 'I have seen' lends credibility to [a] statement insofar as I saw what I have seen. Through my discourse I render visible what is invisible (for you)."[34] Hartog use of "autopsy" in the sense of personal observation (French: *autopsie*; Greek: *autos* + *optos* [seen]) was intimately bound up with the rhetorical tradition of *enargeia* in Greek, and *demonstratio* in Latin, both of which rhetorically aspired to bring images to the mind's eye of auditors. As Carlo Ginzburg remarks, "*demonstratio* designated the orator's gesture that indicated an invisible object, rendering it almost palpable – *enarges* – to the listener, thanks to an almost magical power of the words themselves. Similarly, the historian succeeded in communicating to his readers his own experience – direct, as a witness, or indirect placing an invisible reality before their eyes. *Enargeia* was a means to communicate the *autopsia* – in other words, immediate vision – by virtue of style."[35]

In this light, Hartog's conception of "autopsy" charts a significant shift in the very status of "autopsy" in relation to modernity, in as much as it comes to describe a particular world in which events are already taken as *historical* through and through, and, as such, they require, indeed, demand, a spectator. He cites Pierre Nora: "History is never without its reporter-spectator and its spectator-reporter; it is seen as it happens and this 'voyeurism' gives the current event its own specificity in relation to history and its already historical smell. Autopsy it may be, but autopsy of a different kind – constructed autopsy."[36] Hartog had already speculated that this form of autopsy leads toward spectacularization, and a switch from history to journalism. Finding an apt remark by Jorge Luis Borges, who ties together history and the cinema, Hartog writes:

> Since that day (Valmy) historical days have abounded and one of the tasks facing governments (particularly in Italy, Germany, and Russia) has been to fabricate or simulate them, relying heavily upon preliminary propaganda and persistent publicity. Such days, reflecting the influence of Cecil B. de Mille, have less to do with history than with journalism. I have sometimes suspected that history, real history, is more modest and that its essential dates may sometimes remain secret for many years.[37]

With Vertov, one cannot help but be caught up in such a form of the autopsy that Hartog describes. But it is an autopsy of a different order; it rests upon a deictic "I" transformed into a community of viewers whose acts of seeing serve as the guarantee of a historical. To enter Vertov's cinema is to be made to sense, indeed to articulate – "I see …" – the historicity of the present.

It is in this context that I think we can consider parallel moments we find in Turin and Shklovsky, in order to see how the pedagogy of images functions in their works. Along with the sequence in the book, there is a brief section in the film when Turin depicts a range of Kazak nomads coming to see the construction and the train. The sequence begins as an ethnography, revealing their way of life and customs. The premise of the sequence is that the Kazakhs come "from the farthest corners" in order "to see" ("videt'") the construction. The verb could perhaps be unmarked, but what is notable is that the nomads come to Turksib not to sell goods or to trade: they come only to see. And in that moment, they are rendered subject-viewers of modernization, the audience of construction placed on screen for the audience of the film to watch and to scrutinize.

We should also note here that the vertb *videt'* is invoked as part of the broader issue of a form of Soviet spectacle in which the five-year projects are at once object, and agent of history and modernity. They are no less than time warps too: the fact that the nomad Kazakhs race on horseback to see the spectacle of Turksib should remind us that the film is negotiating ideas of uneven development while pointing to a time when socialism would facilitate the leap from nomadism into proletarianism, with a significant bypassing of the historical stages in between. This potential of cinema to effect modernization is a commonplace in the historiography of cinema and modernity, indeed from the historiography of visuality generally. In Franco Cassetti's words, "through the elaboration of its gazes, the cinema furnishes the bordering frame within which the age makes itself knowable – and bearable – to its subjects and spectators."[38] *Videt'*, in this regard, operates under the sign of a visuality in the book and the film in which vision and visuality are the quintessential signs of Soviet modernity, affirming a link to the essential circuit between spectacle and media events. *Turksib*, as a construction project, film, and children's book, was a total media event for all ages to enjoy and by which to be edified about the (sometimes fitful) nature of modernization.

NOTES

1 Shklovsky, *Turksib*, 14.

2 Edgerton, *The Shock of the Old*, 33.

3 My discussion of the historiography of modernism and the function of artistic devices relies on T.J. Clark's analysis of the status of the device and challenge to mimetic realism in *Farewell to an Idea*, 180. Where Clark's work tracks the status of devices in the transition from realism to modernism, an examination of the inversion (modernism to realism) can be found in Fore, *Realism after Modernism*. The status of ethnography in *Turksib* could serve as a point of comparison with the philosophical anthropology central to Fore's account, as it operates in a context of the transition from modernist back to documentary realism.

4 Hartog, *Regimes of Historicity*, 16.

5 Turar Ryskulo, the Kazakh representative to Sovnarkom, subscribed to this view of radical developmental leaps when he argued that "Leninism affirms the view that under the leadership

of the laboring proletariat backward nations may be led to socialism without having to endure a long process of capitalist development." Cited in Payne, *Stalin's Railroad*, 19.

6   Shklovsky, *Turksib*, 23, 30.

7   Payne, *Stalin's Railroad*, 1–2.

8   In describing this view on modernization, Shklovsky invokes a period trope reported in other travelogues throughout Soviet Russia, where locals (of any ethnic origin) encounter the representative machines of modernity, from planes and trains to automobiles. Shklovsky, *Turksib*, 7. Boris Pil'niak, for example, had reported an encounter with natives in the hinterland in 1926, in his "Rossiia v polete," in which they ask about the plane he arrives in: "we are often asked: have you flown here for good or ill?" Pil'niak, *Rossiia v polete*, 28.

9   In part, this seems to track with the shift in the status of the *aul* that Payne reports, from "a romantic embodiment of folk ways" into "an embarrassing relic of primitivism." Payne, *Stalin's Railroad,* 20.

10   Khiger, *Narody SSSR*; Khiger, *Narody Azii*. The cataloguing entry in the collection of the Houghton Library at Harvard University is uncertain about the date.

11   Clark, *Farewell to an Idea*, 34.

12   Clifford, "On Ethnographic Surrealism," 174.

13   Borogaz, *Revoliutsiia v derevne*, 5.

14   Borogaz offers a form of ethnography untroubled by later divisions between such categories as history and ethnography, the latter putatively unable to account for change. See also Furet and Le Goff, "Histoire et ethnologie." Notably, both works take their point of departure from the status of decolonization and ethnography, a process that, *mutatis mutandis*, could also be seen in relation to Soviet nationalities policy and modernization. For more on Le Goff and Furet and the ramifications of decolonization on ethnography, see Ginzburg, "Microhistory," in *Threads and Traces*, 198–200.

15   Borogaz, *Revoliutsiia v derevne*, 19.

16   As Solzhenitsyn trenchantly observed in *The Gulag Archipelago*: "The Country required the canal so urgently and in such haste that it could not even find any wheelbarrow wheels for the project! It would have been too difficult an order for Leningrad factories. No, it would be unjust, most unjust, unfair to compare this most savage construction project of the twentieth century, this continental canal build 'with wheelbarrow and pick,' with the Egyptian pyramids; after all, the pyramids were build with *contemporary* technology!! And we used the technology of forty centuries earlier" (91).

17   Payne, *Stalin's Railroad*, 18.

18   Shklovsky, *Tekhnika pisatel'skogo remesla*, 33.

19   Ibid., 19

20   Ibid., 22.

21   Shklovsky, *Turksib*, 29.

22   Schnapp, "The Fabric of Modern Times," 192.

23   Payne, *Stalin's Railroad*, 17.

24   Shklovsky, *Turksib*, 2.

25   Ibid.

26   Another angle of approach, this time from the history of children's books, might be to consider how so many children's works make special appeals to touch. As Walter Benjamin has observed, "in children's books, even children's hands were catered to as much as their minds or their imaginations," and he described the various things children's books included to make a story tactilely appealing: "trap doors, moveable strips, pull outs, etc." Benjamin, "The World of Children's Books," 437.

27 As Grits remarks, "the complexity with which the metaphor is elaborated … comes from post-poning the explanation of its primary sense, from playing with its solution, from developing in considerable detail the allegorical set." Grits, "The Work of Viktor Shklovsky," 101.

28 Gerasimov, *Elektropoema*.

29 For more on this relationship of Vertov and Whitman, see my "Ecstasy of Breadth."

30 Cendrars, "La Prose du Transsibérien et de la Petite Jehanne de France," in *Du Monde Entier*, 27.

31 Perloff, *The Futurist Moment*, 16.

32 Dos Passos, "Homer of the Transsiberian," 222, cited in Vigneras, "Blaise Cendrars," 311. For more on Cendrars's influence on Dos Passos, see Dow, "Jon Dos Passos." Dos Passos's views on Cendrars and the theme of travel were formed largely on the basis of the works that appeared together in 1919 in *Du Monde Entier* ("La Prose du Transsibérien et de La Petite Jehanne de France," [1913], 43–80; "Les Pâques à New York" [1913], 11–38; "Le Panama, ou les aventures de mes sept oncles" [1918], 85–124).

33 Rosalind Krauss observes that, "of course, modernism's visual model had significantly transformed those of earlier times. This is true whether we think of the Middle Age's preaching model, in which vision, seen as the most vivid and precise of the senses was to be the conduit through which religious matter could most directly and most enduringly affect the soul; or whether we take an empiricist model, with painting transcribing that mosaic of sensation through which reality announces itself to a perceiving subject. Modernism trans-mutes these models according to its own, altered sense of the task of visuality. To exclude the domain of knowledge, both moral and scientific, to rewrite the visual in the realm of a reflexive relation to the modality of the vision rather than to its contents, to savour in and for itself qualities like *immediacy, vibrancy, simultaneity, effulgence* and to experience these as qualities without objects – the intransitive verbs of vision, as it were – all of this is to enter what in quite another mood we might describe as the modernist fetishization of sight." Krauss, "Antivision," 147. Further, "Contained in the visual metaphor – the ground-ing of art in the fundamental properties of vision – is the commitment to productiveness and to mastery, to the acquisitiveness and accomplishment of sight, to its usefulness, its prowess, its determined busy-ness. Miming this productivity was – for the psychology of the 1920s – the very project that initiated man into the act of art, where representation is, simply, a way of appropriating things." Krauss, "Antivision," 149. For a different account of visibility, see Banfield, *Phantom Table*, which shares the "visual model" of modernism, but does not commit to the centrality of the subject to the account of modernism as does Krauss in these lines, and per force seeks to return modernist visuality precisely to the domain of knowledge.

34 Hartog, *Mirror of Herodotus*, 267.

35 Ginzburg, "Description and Citation," in *Threads and Traces*, 9–10.

36 Hartog, *Mirror of Herodotus*, 266–7.

37 Ibid., 267.

38 Cassetti, *Eye of the Century*, 6.

BIBLIOGRAPHY

Banfield, Ann. *The Phantom Table: Woolf, Fry, Russell and the Epistemology of Modernism*. Cambridge: Cambridge University Press, 2000.

Benjamin, Walter. "The World of Children's Books." *Selected Writings*: Vol. 1: *1913–1929*. Cambridge: Harvard University Press, 1996.

Bogoraz, Waldemar, ed. *Revoliutsiia v derevne: Ocherki.* Leningrad: Krasnaia Nov', 1924.

Cassetti, Franco. *Eye of the Century: Film, Experience, Modernity.* New York: Columbia University Press, 2008.

Cendrars, Blaise. *Du Monde Entier.* Paris: Éditions de la Nouvelle revue française, 1919.

Clark, T.J. *Farewell to an Idea: Episodes in the History of Modernism.* New Haven, CT: Yale University Press, 1999.

Clifford, James. "On Ethnographic Surrealism." In *The Predicament of Culture*, 117–51. Cambridge, MA: Harvard University Press, 1988.

Dos Passos, John. "Homer of the Transsiberian." *Saturday Review of Literature*, 16 October 1926.

Dow, William. "John Dos Passos, Blaise Cendrars, and the 'Other' Modernism." *Twentieth Century Literature* 42, no. 2 (1996): 396–415.

Edgerton, David. *The Shock of the Old: Technology and Global History since 1900.* Oxford: Oxford University Press, 2007.

Fore, Devin. *Realism after Modernism: The Rehumanization of Art and Literature.* Cambridge: MIT Press, 2012.

Furet, Fraçois and Jacques Le Goff. "Histoire et ethnologie." In *Méthodologie de l'histoire et des sciences humaines.* Vol. 2. *Mélange en l'honneur de Fernand Braudel*, 105–25. Toulouse: Éditions Privat, 1973.

Gerasimov, Mikhail. *Elektropoema.* Moscow: Izdatel'stvo pisatelei Kuznitsa, 1923.

Ginzburg, Carlo. *Threads and Traces: True False Fictive.* Translated by Anne C. Tedeschi and John Tedeschi. Berkeley: University of California Press, 2012.

Grits, Fyodor S. "The Work of Viktor Shklovsky: An Analysis of *Third Factory*." In Viktor Shklovsky, *Third Factory.* Ann Arbor, MI: Ardis, 1977.

Hanzen-Love, Aage. *Russkii formalizm: Metodologicheskaia rekonstruktsiia razvittia na osnove printsipa ostraneniia.* Translated by S.A. Romashko. Moscow: Iazyki russkoi kul'tury, 2000.

Hartog, François. *Mirror of Herodotus: The Representation of the Other in the Writing of History.* Translated by Janet Lloyd. Berkeley: University of California Press, 2009.

– *Regimes of Historicity.* Translated by Saskia Brown. New York: Columbia University Press, 2015.

Khiger, Efim. *Narody Azii.* N.p.: Raduga, 1926.

Khiger, Efim. *Narody SSSR.* N.p.: Raduga, 1926.

Krauss, Rosalind. "Antivision." *October* 36 (1986): 147–54.

Kunichika, Michael. "Ecstasy of Breadth: The Odic and Whitmanesque in Vertov's 'One Sixth of the World'." *Studies in Russian and Soviet Cinema* 6, no. 1 (2012): 53–74.

Payne, Matthew. *Stalin's Railroad: Turksib and the Building of Socialism.* Pittsburgh: University of Pittsburgh Press, 2001.

Perloff, Marjorie. *The Futurist Moment: Avant-Garde, Avant Guerre, and the Language of Rupture.* Chicago: University of Chicago Press, 1986.

Pil'niak, Boris. *Rossiia v polete.* Moscow: Moskovskii rabochii, 1926.

Schnapp, Jeffrey. "The Fabric of Modern Times." *Critical Inquiry* 24, no. 1 (Autumn 1997): 191–245.

Shklovsky, Viktor. *Tekhnika pisatel'skogo remesla.* Moscow: Molodaia gvardiia, 1930.

– *Tret'ia fabrika.* 1926. Letchworth, UK: Prideaux Press, 1978.

– *Turksib.* 2nd ed. Leningrad: Gosudarstvennoe izdatel'stvo, 1930.

Solzhenitsyn, Aleksandr. *The Gulag Archipelago, 1918–56. An Experiment in Literary Investigation.* Vol. 2 Translated by Thomas P. Whitney. New York: Harper & Row, 2007.

Vigneras, L.A. "Blaise Cendrars." *French Review* 14, no. 4 (1941): 311–18.

chapter eleven

AEROPLANE, AEROBOAT, AEROSLEIGH: PROPELLING EVERYWHERE IN SOVIET TRANSPORTATION

KATHERINE M.H. REISCHL

In 1923, in the avant-garde journal *G: Material for Elemental Form-Creation*, El Lissitzky describes the course of human progress founded on mechanical propulsion:

1st State

The human being walks, takes steps. The movement is discontinuous, from point to point, the whole sole has to touch the earth …

2nd State

The first invention is – the wheel. Discontinuous walking transforms into continuous rolling: the wheel touches the earth at a single point …

3rd State

The second invention – the screw, the propeller. Continuous rolling transforms into continuous gliding.[1]

While Lissitzky imagines this foundation for a new mobile architecture, his abstractions project a vision in which energy is "liberated" to form a new system of movement, leaving behind the human body for machines that might no longer be grounded by "an imitation of the human hand."[2] Lissitkzy's utopian *vezdekhodnost'* (go-everywhere-ness) – built on the foundations of the propeller's continuous gliding – sees only the expansive exhilaration of technological advancement, not its limitations.[3] The propeller becomes the material manifestation of hypermobility.

More generally speaking, an analysis of any kind of "mobility" presupposes a system of limitations that allows for predictability, repetition, and structured discourse.[4] Roads structure travel in a predetermined direction; its users travel a road according to a set of particular laws.[5] The Soviet vehicle – from plane to train to aerosleigh – was no exception. As its mechanical body was literally shaped by its production within Soviet space, so too was its image on new tracks and roads, on the ground and within the sphere of Soviet imaging. But, not unlike Lissitzky's unbounded view of propulsion, Soviet transportation was also imagined in print and text as both a kinetic object of liberation *and* a prosthetic helpmate in its participation in the ideologically charged public sphere. Such a synthesis rendered a world infinitely and powerfully traversable in a system of not just (auto)mobility, but even of *vezdekhodnost'* – a hypermobility that found its most expansive reach in the mobile form of the children's book. By flying, riding, and gliding along the roads of the children's book, on routes more or less travelled, this chapter explores the mobility systems organized by the limitations and imaginative potential of Soviet transportation. In illustrations from children's books from the early Soviet period, including constructivist illustration and photographic reportage, *vezdekhodnost'* takes on a meta-character as representations are transformed and transferred from adult and children's media, structuring readers as students, passengers, and drivers in a variety of novel Soviet modes of transportation. These transnational and transmedial rides in novel vehicles, including the hydroplane and aerosleigh, reveal both the seemingly infinite kinetic potential of the vehicle as apparatus, as well as those demarcating boulevards of Soviet ideology, propelling both child and adult along the roads of the imagined ideal and the real.

Poster to Book and Back Again

In the adventurous early years of Soviet children's books, stories and aesthetics were shaped by the austere and revolutionary design of the constructivists. Inspired by the revolution and the utopian dreams of technology and design, their aesthetic embraced a new bold typography and graphic illustration.[6] This transformative epiphany is on display in the Chichagova sisters' poster "Daesh' novuiu detskuiu knigu" (In with the new children's book, fig. 11.1). This iconographically constructed poster is divided into unequal sections. On the left, the "forms of the old *knizhki-skazki*" (little fairy-tale books) – including a freewheeling demon, Baba Yaga, and Kornei Chukovsky's crocodile – are thrown down and out with the single posterized cry, "doloi …" (down with …).[7] Taking over two-thirds of the total poster, the right heralds the new: "In with the new children's book!" The oversized Lenin in the centre oversees the icons of Soviet youth and production below, as the reader reads along a vertical axis: "victory [over] nature." The viewer is equally invited to render a mobile *smychka* (union) along the many horizons, textual and figural: labour and technology link to the factory, riding soldiers and airplanes soar across victory.[8] The modes of transportation and activity, potentially ready to move in any prescribed direction, contrast with the almost uniform downward slope of the fairy-tale creatures in the left panel.[9] Here the viewer can still intuit the relationship between the old and new by reading across: old *skazka* (fairy-tale) heroes are transported and transformed, grounding model flights of fancy on (mini) Soviet planes. But the most essential ideological grounding also creates the

11.1. Anna Gelina and Ol'ga and Galina Chichagova, "Daesh' novuiu detskuiu knigu," (ca. 1928).

"ground" on which this activity occurs: the proclamations of "New Children's Every-day Life" ("Novyi detskii byt") and the ideological frame in text: "The new book will help cultivate a new generation" ("Novaia kniga pomozhet vospitat' novuiu smenu"). This dictate is wrought and uttered by the proclamation of Lenin's icon; it becomes a road on which the new generation might travel.

The Chichagova sisters were themselves artistically cultivated as students of Aleksandr Rodchenko at the Higher Arts and Technical Studios in Moscow (VKhUTEMAS). Together they produced roughly twenty books for children, many of which were in collaboration with author Nikolai Grigorievich Smirnov, at a moment when the picture book shared clear visual sensibilities with the poster.[10] A self-identified constructivist, Ol'ga Chichagova also made her own small con-tribution to the textual framing of the constructivist movement in the journal *Korabl'* (*The Ship*) in 1923. Her mini-manifesto captures the oft-quoted tenets of constructivist art: "The task of constructivism is the organization of constructiv-ist everyday life (*byt*) through the creation of the constructivist man ... We – the constructivists – must strive to enter into all areas of human culture, and, having destroyed the old bourgeois principles from the inside, organize new forms of being through the education of the new constructivist person."[11] Art organizes life, and, in so doing, actively shapes and educates the new Soviet subject. From the typography to the iconography of the Chichagovas' poster, this manifesto is mobilized in action in word, image, and organization: the embrace of the constructed world (*tekhnika*) and rejection of the old fairy tales.[12]

Notably, however, the fairy-tale icons remain intact; while marginalized, they are still given a prescribed space in their pictorial form. In a sense, their presence poster-izes Nadezhda Krupskaia's contemporaneous writings on children's literature. While she rejects the reliance on fairy-tale for its mysticism and religiosity, she acknowl-edges that its form and content gave children a "great deal" ("ochen' mnogoe") in its imaginative potential, thereby "expanding children's horizons."[13] At its most generous accounting, the fairy-tale captures truths pertaining directly to life, to relationships between people, and to reality (*real'naia deistvitel'nost'*).[14] The task before the new Soviet children's literature becomes a reformulation of content: communist content. Such a turn does not mean subjecting the child to the stilted program of the party, to boring accounts of party congresses, but rather providing "living images" ("zhivye obrazy") that form the young reader's communist consciousness.[15] Returning to the poster, this relationship is even more fully evident within the "revolutionary" right half. The young Pioneer not only observes the model vocations of the Soviet adult (the Red Army soldiers, pilot, mechanic, driver), he too is made into an active agent: trumpeting, farming, ploughing, and propagandizing. Here is a constructivist render-ing the icon's *zhitie* (saint's life) structure, an old form rendered anew.

And how better to inform, in Krupskaia's formulation, a child's "material out-look" ("materialisticheskoe mirovozzrenie") than with those material objects that

11.2a. Ol'ga and Galina Chichagova, cover for Nikolai Smirnov's *Put' na sever* (Moscow: Novaia Moskva, 1924).

themselves have a kind of "living image": the vehicle's *vezdekhodnost'*.[16] One iconic mode of Soviet transportation omitted from the Chichagovas' poster is the train. The train is by no means a new icon of modernity in Russian literature for children. In fact, the iconography of the train can be easily mapped onto a teleology of socialist progress from a symbol of exploitation to one of post-revolutionary progress.[17] Enter the Smirnov/Chichagovas' collaboration *Put' na sever* (*Way to the North*, 1924), the "story of how the Murmansk railway was constructed." The peculiar shape and orientation of this snowplough train on the book's cover clearly echoes the photographic figure opening Lissitzky and Ilya Ehrenburg's short-lived, constructivist journal *Veshch'/Objet/Gegenstand* (*Object*, Berlin, 1922) (figs. 11.2a–b). The snowplough train on the first page of *Veshch'* operates according to a unique opening logic. Here, the photographic excerpt is an interlocutor in a strategically formed material dialogue, declaring that the train will "push out the old." The train's juxtaposition with the suprematist forms on the right (black square and circle) serves to aestheticize the vehicle, inviting the reader to consider it as a constructivist object and, by extension, to make a viewer see a mechanistic utility in Kazimir Malevich's black square and circle. So too does the train itself structure the page, as the diagonal line of the snowplough

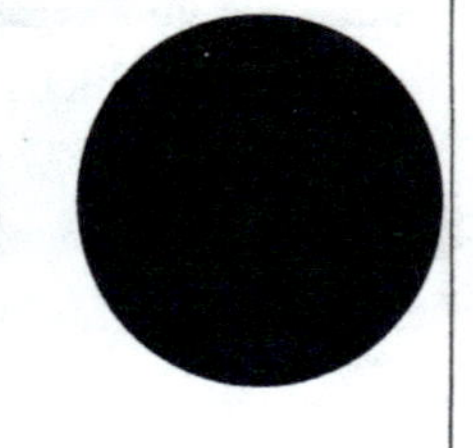

11.2b. First page of El Lissitzky and Ilya Ehrenburg's *Veshch'/Objet/Gegenstand,* no. 3 (1922).

aligns with the title of the magazine. The packed fullness of the composition and the orientation of the objects emphasize the "thingness" of the journal's title, while the bold type across the central horizontal axis illuminates the constructivist relationship between object (like the plough) and the aesthetic space of the journal, labelled "art and the public sphere" ("iskusstvo i obshchestvennost").[18]

The adaptation of the train to the cover of the children's book is governed by different aesthetic laws. No longer a photographic rendering, the primary shapes of the front triangular plough are exaggerated; however generalized in the loss of photographic indexicality, the train is distinctly recognizable as "train," with its upright smokestack. Moreover, its *put'* (way) is rendered literally – as the train track that had been obscured in the photograph in *Veshch'*. In the wood-block simplification on the Chichagovas' cover, functionality is foregrounded as the snowplough clears the "way to the north." This visualized instrumentation also reveals a paradoxical relationship in these two examples: the photographically reproduced image is viewed in terms of its form (constructivist aestheticization), not its original function; the block print's dynamism is channelled in service of its subject's primary function (train-plough).

The wood-block print illustrations accompanying *Put' na sever* further serve to illustrate the work and industry of constructing the railway, and, in this more staid function, they have a landscape orientation that contrasts that of the constructivist "objects" of *Veshch'*. As the story moves thematically through the construction of the railway – harbour, forest, excavators and dynamite, bridges – the book is read almost entirely on a horizontal, progressive grounding, metonymically laying the tracks on the ground from page to page. In borrowing from original object to constructivist object to children's book illustration, the forms of constructivism remain an organizing element visually, although they no longer carry with them a revolutionary visual dynamism. Rather, in this exercise, *vezdekhodnost'* is channelled in a single directionality wherein no obstacles could possibly stand in the way of progress to the north.

Propelling Old and New

The figure of Charlie Chaplin provides another point of entry in the exploration of mobility in the early Soviet imaginary with a body at its centre, from modernist journal to the children's book. As one of the most popular cultural figures of the 1910s and 1920s, with both cinema audiences and modern artists alike, Chaplin became a mobile character reformulated by the vision and hand of the constructivists in and around modern transportation.[19] Chaplin-as-illustration ("drawn" from film) appeared increasingly in the early 1920s in avant-garde journals, including in the pages of *Veshch'* and *Kino-fot* (*Film-photo*).[20] Varvara Stepanova's "propeller-Chaplins," featured in *Kino-fot* in 1922 (particularly issue no. 3), punctuate short articles by Aleksandr

Rodchenko lauding Chaplin-as-Charlot: this persona was the model of instantaneity (*on momentalen*) and of the "new man," and it was claimed in the language of revolution, contemporary life, and communism. In these illustrations, Chaplin begins as the "man on the propeller," with arrows denoting the potential directions of motion. The next print shows Chaplin in motion, while the final image depicts him either in the act of stopping or starting the plane's propeller. Although the subject is not moving forward (no destination is expected), the diagonal signals the potential for motion, but without direction; the airplane too is strikingly absent except in the last image, leaving the reader with only the bodily potential of Chaplin's figure – fused with the propeller – making this figure the icon of maximal dynamism and mobility, and, in light of Rodchenko's text, the model of contemporary instantaneity. Thus, the link between technology, modernity, and Chaplin's form is achieved visually through the plane's propeller – transforming Chaplin into another illustrated embodiment of an infinitely circular *vezdekhodnost'* – in its most literal interpretation.[21]

This fusion of body and propelled mobility informs design beyond the pages of the children's book and the journal. After reaching to the skies with his dynamic Monument to the Third International, Vladimir Tatlin crafted model gliders, his *Letatlin* (1929–31) and his stylized, but more practically, grounded sleds made of repurposed bicycle frames.[22] Like almost all of Tatlin's designs, these "vehicles" were imbued with revolutionary potential to transform the way in which bodies move through space in the fusion of the organic (body) with the mechanical (apparatus). However, even in this reach "up" toward revolutionary design, the *Letatlin* is perhaps rather like the transformation of the *skazka*, a much more universal impulse to reformulate the old. Tatlin's design clearly evokes the Icarus myth and da Vinci's Renaissance designs for single-man flight. Moreover, its early display in the Italian Hall of the State Arts Museum in Moscow places the design floating above representations of classical art.[23] In a room of copies, one might well wonder if the transformation of the iconography of old could be considered complete.

As Tatlin's designs and Stepanova's drawings transform bodies by bringing them into a closer fusion with the apparatuses of mobility, it is in the Chichagovas' children's book where Chaplin is returned to a more traditional role as passenger (fig. 11.3). In *Puteshestvie Charli* (*Charlie's Travels*, 1924), the constructivist Charlie travels around the world on various modes of transportation (airplane, hot air balloon, hydroplane, rickshaw, car).[24] However, the "happy American" appears as a recognizable figure only twice: at the opening of the book, standing before the globe, and later at the doors of a tram as he arrives back home. In large part, the figures of transportation come to act as heroes that organize movement through their respective spaces – that is, determining mobility as they dominate and animate the sky, land, and sea. Thus alternating between aerial and land-based modes of transport – animated by Chaplin's happy figure – the airplane flies to Moscow and the train traverses Russia's expanse. A sharp break, typographically and ideologically speaking, comes at the end:

11.3. Galina and Ol'ga Chichagova, page from Nikolai Smirnov, *Puteshestvie Charli* (Moscow: Gosizdat, 1924).

Charlie Chaplin recedes and his telegram (spread across five pages) reads: "I – Charlie Chaplin – having most recently and safely travelled all over the world – THANK: THE SAILORS, PILOTS, DRIVERS, RICKSHAWS and the others for driving me. I SEND MY REGARDS TO THE WORKERS OF ALL COUNTRIES! Charlie Chaplin. America. The movie-screen."[25] As Chaplin disappears entirely from figurative representation, the reader sees his proclamation accompanied by images of those workers he thanks. Undoubtedly this declaration contains the echoes of the ever-present call to unite the proletarian workers of the world. While Chaplin-the-happy-American exists outside the ideological framework of the Soviet state, his transformation is enacted via constructivist mobility (his ability to go anywhere), first activated in the pages of *Kino-fot*. *Vezdekhodnost'* reforms this hybrid Chaplin to impart the bold communist greeting: a constructivist blessing of recognition to the world proletariat.[26]

The sleek traversal of transportation forms across media and imagination is further pronounced in the look of Soviet-branded modes of propelled transport: the airplane, the *glisser* (hydroplane), and aerosleigh. Each of these propelled modes of transportation plays at *vezdekhodnost'* in the pages of the children's book both as transportation and as carriers of ideology. However, the vast difference between the systems of automobility in the Soviet Union and those in the West bears noting. The key claims to luxury and individualism that characterize Western automobility as embodied in the American car play no part in the Soviet car's "most celebrated attribute." As Lewis Siegelbaum has shown, the key to the Soviet car's imaging "lay not in [its] intrinsic design or performance, still less in the physical mobility, privacy, and freedom [it] afforded, but rather in the assembly-line technology associated with [its] production."[27] But the cases of the Soviet airplane, *glisser*, and aerosleigh present something still different. Most centrally, the metonymic power embodied in these modes of transport was decidedly collective, focusing not on production, and still less on the human role in the "assemblage" of automobility, but rather on an inclusive, mobile, and ever-ready image of propulsion.

In large part, the airplane in production books for children is represented as the already embodied Soviet product, that carrier, representative, and creator of vertical power in its traversal of the sky. As M. Il'in's far-reaching *Rasskaz o velikom plane* (*New Russia's Primer: The Story of the Five-Year Plan*, 1930) claims with respect this flexible and far-reaching system of aerial *vezdekhodnost'*:

> By 1932 we shall have 138 air-lines, 110,000 kilometers of air-ways. This is six times as much as we have at present. It will then be possible to fly from Moscow to Vladivostock and Tashkent, from Novosibirsk to Berlin. Tens of air-lines will go over the forests of Siberia, over the mountains of the Caucasus. In 1932, 12,000 passengers, 3500 tons of mail, and 2500 tons of freight will be transported by air. But the airplane will not be engaged in transport only. It is not merely a carrier and postman, it is also a huntsman, a photographer, an agronomist.
>
> Airplanes will serve the fur industry in Siberia by discovering seal rookeries set as black spots against the white snow. They will destroy injurious parasites by spraying crops and forests with chemicals. They will aid in the constructing of railways by photographing the earth from above.[28]

Il'in's presentation frames the airplane as part of an ever-expanding system as well as agent in all essential activities of the rapidly industrializing nation in the frame of the ideological rhetoric of the Five-Year Plan: postman, hunter, photographer, agronomist. In its ascent, the plane can efficiently transport precious goods across great distances, while representing in itself a way to conquer land through the parallel production of instantaneous topographic maps.[29] So too is the airplane a weapon, striking out against the enemies of agricultural production (parasites), and a hunter, identifying the sites where the untapped riches of the far reaches of the USSR might lie. In total, the body of the plane contains within itself a powerful system of mobility.

While in Il'in's representation the Soviet plane is but one piece of production within the Great Plan, a smaller book, Ida Stuchinskaia's *Kryl'ia Sovetov* (*Soviet Wings*,

1930), designed by P. Suvorov and illustrated with photographs, makes the Soviet plane its hero. The plane flies across the diagonal of the cover, likely circling for a landing; we, viewers, might look up to admire its speed (fig. 11.4a). From the start, the text relates the plane to the buzz it caused in the media, speaking directly to the mobility of the message: "They write in the papers: The Soviet engineer has come up with an unusual airplane – a strong, fast, three-engine plane. It will fly twelve people. The airplane was built in Moscow and named 'Soviet Wings.'"[30] This opening signals the book's hybrid composition between reportage and innovate typographical design. The photographs read almost exclusively on a horizontal plane, unlike the dynamic capture of the cover, while the text is often structured in a ladder layout and varied in size to signal the height of the plane or excitement of the awestruck reader, visually reminiscent of the innovative typography of the futurists and constructivists (see the example in figure 11.4b).[31] This book, in following the flight of the "Soviet Wings" to Berlin to meet adoring crowds abroad, clearly and legibly builds (and builds) to its final underscored message. It boldly reads: "The English, German, and French know now what great, strong planes there are in the USSR. *Warring with the country of the Soviets will not be easy.*"[32] In the final photograph, the plane rests on the Moscow aerodrome runway, rising powerfully over a great mass of the Soviet proletariat. Resting on its evidence – photographs and laddered text – the "Soviet Wings" are ready to spring up into action.

Kryl'ia Sovetov is remarkable not only in its representation of the airplane's powerful mobility, but also in the fitting combination of mobile vehicle and mobile medium. As Mikhail Karasik observes, photography is itself both the most economic and "most mobile" ("samaia mobil'naia") illustration for Soviet children's books.[33] It appears only natural that the striking appearances of the hydroplane and the aerosleigh would also be depicted through photographic illustration in Soviet children's books. The (almost) infinitely mobile quality of the hydroplane is suggested in the title of *Lodka-vezdekhodka* (*The Boat That Goes Everywhere*, 1933) by Lev Kassil'. The photographically illustrated book enlivens the already wondrous machine, which rushes at the reader from the front cover. However, much like the presentation in Stuchinskaia's *Kryl'ia Sovetov*, the hydroplane comes to be tamed by the rhetorical structure of the book and the dynamic – but staid – presentations of the photographs inside.

Lodka-vezdekhodka shares another common trope with *Kryl'ia Sovetov* – that is, the image of the awe-struck child before the miraculous machine. In *Kryl'ia Sovetov*, the moment of rapturous wonder appears like an echo of Stepanova's Propeller-Chaplin. In the former, a French shepherd boy in enthusiastic perusal of the plane climbs not into the pilot's seat but onto the propeller itself (fig. 11.4b). The French boy serves as a naive other and, through a very short intervention in the text (stating that he is from the nearby town of Nevers), as a vehicle himself to pinpoint the location of the plane. But in *Lodka-vezdekhodka*, the child's body serves a more central function in the rhetorical exploration of rapture, providing the proxy for the Soviet child-reader.

● Вышли все из самолета. Сразу промокли насквозь: дождь лил.

Темно, вокруг ни домов, ни людей.

Куда попали — не знали.

Зажгли фонарик, стали моторы осматривать.

И увидели: сломался маленький, совсем маленький винтик.

Живо починили.

А куда лететь дальше — не знали.

И решили заночевать в поле, в самолете.

Утром подошел к самолету пастух,
рассказал, что недалеко деревня и город. А город французский—НЕВЕР.

11.4b. Petr Suvorov, illustration for Ida Stuchinskaia, *Kryl'ia Sovetov.*

11.4a. Petr Suvorov, cover design for Ida Stuchinskaia, *Kryl'ia Sovetov*
(Moscow: GIZ, 1930).

11.5. Evgenii Nekrasov, illustration for Lev Kassil', *Lodka-vezdekhodka* (Moscow: OGIZ, 1933).

A group of children, with their back to the camera, look "down" on the hydroplane pictured beneath them on the page (fig. 11.5). That picture poses the child-reader's questions: Just what is this wondrous and intrepid machine? What is its secret?

As is intimated by the foregrounded engine in figure 11.5, the answer lies not in the wonders of magic but in the technology of construction. The flat-bottomed boat looks, from the water, "like an airplane with its wings cut off."[34] Yet the propulsion of the engine allows the lithe boat to fly across the water, even when the shallowness of a small river would make it impassible for an ordinary barge. The textual structure of *Lodka-vezdekhodka* repeats along these lines. A later *zagadka* (puzzle) reads along the bottom of another page: "What boat goes just so: not in the water, not on it, not under it? … It is the boat-that-goes-everywhere, the on-the-water runner."[35] As typefaces shift, growing and shrinking alongside a variety of photographic illustrations, the text also moves between such puzzles and the more straightforward ideological inscription of the objects within that system of hydroplane mobility, explaining that the Soviet Union needs "the boat-that-goes-everywhere, on-the-water runners" due to the land's particular geographic challenges.[36] The list of goods for transport and variety of vocations reads as though from Il'in's *Rasskaz o velikom plane*: the hydroplane can transport newspapers, letters and other mail, and journals to the distant kolkhozes; a sanitary hydroplane can transport both doctor and mobile pharmacy to far reaches; a fire-fighting hydroplane could arrive faster than any other mode of transportation with water at hand.[37] Thus, the hydroplane becomes part of a tripartite list of the most essential linkages of Soviet *vezdekhodnost'* of the title: sky and airplane; land and train; water and hydroplane.

The novelty of the hydroplane comes to serve as metonym for Sovietness, not unlike the figure of the Chichagovas' constructivist Charlie. While Charlie needed many vehicles to "go everywhere," the airplane and hydroplane provide an all-in-one substitution. Moreover, as a vessel, the hydroplane, rather than the body (Charlie), also necessarily carries more weight, both literally and metaphorically. The final words and image (fig. 11.6) create the most dynamic visual effect in the book:

Old bourgeois countries are like rusty ships. They are sluggish. They are deeply rooted in the old world. They are in the shallows. The Young Soviet country looks like the mighty hydroplane. It sets itself against the old currents. It is not afraid of enemy opposition. It outperforms all countries, and races through all obstacles to a new life.
So it goes on the hydroplane.

The hydroplane –
This is the speed
This is the pace
This is a step into the future.[38]

And this very "step into the future" is rendered mimetically: by opening the foldout page, the young reader can virtually race along the water in the vessel of a glimmering Soviet future. This page-based movement, material and imagined, is the mobility of that very future.

Aerosleighs

Perhaps the most ubiquitous form of novel transportation innovation was the Soviet *aerosani* (aerosleigh). The propeller-driven sleigh was not an exclusively Soviet (or Russian) phenomenon, but it was embraced, produced, and fully branded by Soviet-Russian power in the pages of the children's book, in popular and elite journals, and in film. Designated as military sleighs, aerosleighs first appeared on the front in the First World War and were used in even greater numbers during the Second World War, proving an efficient vehicle for reconnaissance and raids. The powerful sleigh was particularly suited to Russia's challenging northern clime and facilitated the Soviet Union's aspirations for Arctic colonization and exploration.[39] Unlike the airplane, whose power was also vested in travel across Soviet borders, aerosleighs were relegated largely to northern Russian landscapes, and the Arctic (claimed by the USSR in part as its own new frontier). However, much like Charlie's rides from American film to Soviet press, the aerosleigh's novel appeal made it a ready-made object for the American transportation imaginary. While at once speaking to collaboration between the two allies in the midst of the Second World War and continuing

11.6. Last pages by Evgenii Nekrasov for Lev Kassil' *Lodka-vezdekhodka.*

the pre-war competition for technological advancement, a 1943 issue of *Science and Mechanics* utilizes aerosleigh development and military success to forge a new path between America and the USSR:

> During the recent victorious winter offensive against the Nazis, the Russian army used sleds driven with airplane propellers to convey fighting men, arms, ammunition and supplies across the snow-covered, frozen, and windswept steppes … As far back as 1924, Russia obtained plans and specifications for the original "air sleighs" from Chester B. Wing, civic leader, pioneer automobile dealer, aviator, and former mayor of St. Ignace, Upper Peninsula, Michigan … From his aerosleds the Russians developed their present battle sleds.[40]

In addition to the highly localized geographic pinpoint in St. Ignace in the short text, a small accompanying photograph purports to show the tests and improvements by a Russian pilot in Michigan. Carrying such ideologically charged baggage, it is unsurprising that aerosleighs were of popular interest from the late 1920s through the end of the Second World War. Featured on the covers of journals such as *Znanie – sila* (*Knowledge Is Power*) for children (fig. 11.7) and *Za rulem* (*At the Wheel*) for adults, aerosleighs were marked by their Soviet origin of production at Tsentral'nyi aerogidrodinamicheskii institute (TsAGI, Central Aerohydrodynamic Institute), their reproducibility for model enthusiasts, and their mobility in highly publicized runs across Soviet Russia.[41] Their agency was celebrated following their role as a reconnaissance vehicle in the coverage of the real-life rescue efforts of the Cheliuskin expedition (1933–4), fictionalized in the film *Semero smelykh* (*The Brave Seven*, dir. Sergei Gerasimov, 1936). In each of these iterations, the aerosleigh embodied its own novel symbolic order in systems of *vezdekhodnost'*. As a mobilized vehicle for war and reconnaissance, its main function was to *create* a way for wherever it might go (no snowplough necessary), in defiance of nature and enemy opposition, to carry its goods, drivers, and soldiers to the field of victory.

Outside this military imaginary, one encounter with the aerosleigh harkens back to Stepanova's Chaplin-Propeller-Man. As with the hydroplane, the propeller is the sleigh's defining feature; it is the technological force that transforms an ordinary sleigh into a powerful vehicle. This sum of parts is rendered into the abstract propeller form in the first issue of the journal *30 dnei (30 Days)* in 1928, cutting through the serenity of a stylized birch forest (fig. 11.8). While *30 dnei* is, strictly speaking, not a journal for children or youth, the appearance of a simple and accessible poem by Aleksandr Zharov might easily speak to a young reader. Zharov contributed no small part to literary youth culture, including slogans and short poems for posters throughout the 1950s and 1960s, and, most notably, he lent his pen to the composition of the Pioneers' anthem. In this dynamic presentation in *30 dnei*, his "Aerosleigh" is superimposed onto an uncredited design. The words emerge from the propeller

11.7. Aerosleigh on the cover of *Znanie-sila*, no. 23 (1931).

of the aerosleigh itself, with the arc of the poem's title structured by that propeller's circular motion.[42] As the propeller visually breaks the ornamental trees, so too does the sled of the poem:

Into that forest,	(В тот лес,
where the swallow and brook	где рулады и трели
trilled and wove roulades (music) –	плели соловей и ручей, –
today bursts the propeller	сегодня ворвался пропеллер
of the wonderful	диковинных,
miracle-sleigh.	чудо-саней).[43]

As the propeller cuts through the bucolic scene, the miraculous sleigh transforms the poet's encounter with the Russian forest: "our Russian winter / I felt / as never before" ("я нашу российскую зиму / почувствовал, / как никогда").][44] In the final lines, the distant jingling of bells ("eseninskii zvon bubentsov" ["Eseninskii jingle of bells"]) evokes the romantic imagination of old. However, this aural experience is rendered strange by the break and rush of the aerosleigh's propeller. The propeller is

11.8.　Aleksandr Zharov, "Aerosani," *30 dnei*, no. 1 (1928): 81. Illustrator unknown.

11.9. Cover for Sergei Tret'iakov and Boris Gromov, *Polnym skol'zom* (Moscow: Molodaia gvardiia, 1930).

the site of power and propulsion, propelling not only its passengers but also the poetic word into new forms of novel mobility.

For several prominent photojournalists, the power of the aerosleigh proved an irresistible subject, which they felt compelled to tackle for young readers. In 1930, Sergei Tret'iakov, in collaboration with *Izvestiia* correspondent Boris Gromov, covered the test runs of the new NAMI (Nauchnyi avto-motornyi institute / Scientific Auto-Motor Institute) and TsAGI models of aerosleighs.[45] Their *Polnym skol'zom* (*Full Glide*, 1930) is aimed at a more advanced young reader than the picture book, with extensive text lightly illustrated by journalistic photographs (fig. 11.9).[46] The trope of forward progress propels the work. Tret'iakov and Gromov follow the triumphs and dangers of the test run as the correspondents ride along the aerosleigh "pilots," revelling in the rush of movement and the danger of travelling at top speeds. Much like Zharov's poem, the text and images describe speeding by bucolic scenes, including sluggish horses and Moscow's old churches. Even a Russian literary past is added to complete a "long" picture of continuous automobility, as the aerosleigh makes a pilgrimage to the house where the nineteenth-century poet Nekrasov was

11.10. Sergei Tret'iakov, "The House Where the Poet Nekrasov Was Born." From Sergei Tret'iakov and Boris Gromov, *Polnym skol'zom*.

born, a juxtaposition of the old and new that makes each appear anachronistic: one a vision of the future, the other a house representing the old (fig. 11.10). Further, this inscription of the Russian literary past into the long look of *aerosani-vezdekhodnost'* makes Gogol a technological prophet. As Tret'iakov writes: "It turns out that Gogol, describing the monstrously exaggerated troika in *Dead Souls*, quite accurately described the ordinary aerosleigh."[47] Not unlike Chichikova's troika in the novel, the aerosleigh approaches the fantastic, described repeatedly in Tret'iakov's account as something almost ineffable for the lay observers (perhaps as incredible as Chichikov's own proposals had seemed to his interlocutors): What is it? How does it fly? In the almost poetic description of Tret'iakov, he answers, "Supported by wings on the air, the airplane glides over the strata of the atmosphere. Supported by skis on snow, the aerosleigh glides over the strata of snow's icy crust."[48]

The visual ode to the aerosleigh comes in full force in picture-book form with the illustrated *Aerosani* (*Aerosleigh*, 1931) by photojournalist Roman Karmen. Much like the structure of *Kryl'ia Sovetov*, the final destination of the aerosleigh's run is the Moscow aerodrome. Like airplanes in Il'in's *Rasskaz o velikom plane* and *Lodka-vezdekhodka* by Kassil', the aerosleigh is tasked here with the functional roles of transporter and scout. After an epic "test" run from the site of production in Leningrad to the centre of (aerial) power in Moscow, the aerosleigh would be ready to scout the riches of the forests, precious metals in the earth, and fur in the north, and would serve in the essential transport of mail, newspapers, and other information. Along the route to Moscow (through forests and small towns), the aerosleigh once again comes face-to-face with the "old." In the hierarchy illustrated in the book (fig. 11.11), the aerosleigh occupies the top (new) position, propeller spinning as an already-defined path extends from its fellow sled ahead. Below, the horse-drawn sled lags behind, with a path stretching into an interminable distance. Such a clear-cut dichotomy between the old and new – legible for the literate adult and visible for the not-yet-literate child – was easily posterized and even miniaturized as a postcard.[49] Thus, even while repeating much of the same thematic points of Tret'iakov and Gromov's earlier *Polnym skol'zom*, Karmen's picture book is far more successful as a visual narrative.

The aerosleigh's victory over metaphorical aerospace as enacted in its run to the aerodrome in Karmen's *Aerosani* is a key to that vehicle's unique embodiment of *vezdekhodnost'* in Soviet media. For the technological enthusiasts Karmen and Tret'iakov, such an incarnation might be achieved not by the camera still alone, but through the dynamic motion of cinema. However, the very conditions that the aerosleigh was designed to overcome, including extreme cold, foiled many attempts by the kino-chroniclers to gain useable footage of a thrilling ride in the novel vehicle. As Karmen wrote in 1931 in *Kino-gazeta*: "To date we have no film about *aerosani*. Even the shortest of such films would show the enormous role the Soviet metal snowmobile [*snegokhod*] plays on the front of the struggle with impassible roads, in the national economy, and in defence of the country."[50] Just a few years later, the 1936 film *Semero smelykh* (*The Brave Seven*, dir. Sergei Gerasimov), while laying no claims to the objectivity of journalistic or documentary capture, achieved what the kino-chroniclers could not in the "cockpit" of the aerosleigh. In a key turning point in the film, the titular brave seven are stranded on their Arctic expedition. While their airplane is buried in heavy snow (grounded on two fronts), the aerosleigh easily traverses its obstacles in the Arctic landscape. The camerawork featuring the heroic aerosleigh, which was shot while riding along in the vehicle itself, was a high point of the film for at least one American reviewer, who noted that the "photography taken under difficult, outdoor conditions, has a rugged distinction" – despite the film's heavy-handed ideological content.[51] In conquering aerospace on the snow and the territory of the North in the Soviet imaginary, the filmic capture of the *vezdekhodnost'* of the aerosleigh enabled a remarkable international triumph of Stalinist artistic cinema, gliding at full speed (*polnym skol'zom*).

However, Karmen's earlier *Aerosani* is visually structured to overcome those roadblocks faced by documentary capture for his child readers at home. His book reads like a film, often displaying the "subjective camera" perspective wherein the point of view of the character – in this case, the pilot – and viewer coincide (fig. 11.12).[52] We might again speculate as to the success this book might have for a young reader,

11.11. "Novoe/Staroe" ("New/Old"). From Roman Karmen's *Aerosani* (Moscow: OGIZ, Molodaia gvardia, 1931).

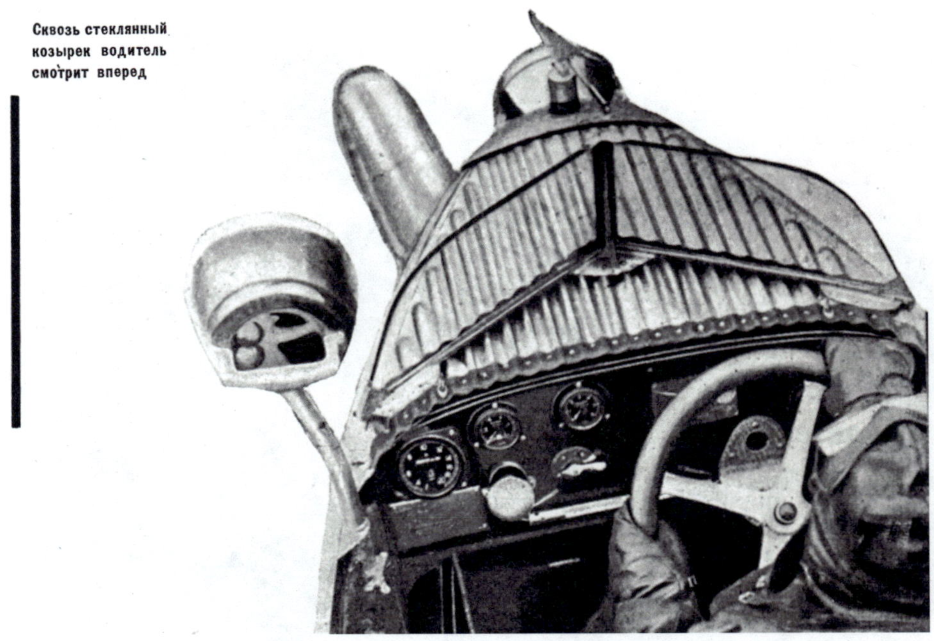

11.12. *Polnym skol'zom* (*Full Glide*). From Roman Karmen, *Aerosani* (Moscow: OGIZ, Molodaia gvardia, 1931).

offering a virtual ride long before the child could become pilot or the oft-offered role of mechanic. If we view the splayed book so both its front and back photomontaged covers are visible, the aerosleigh's unfolded *vezdekhodnost'* models the creation of its own image and that of its author (fig. 11.13). On the book's front cover, the enormous head of the pilot looms over the run of the aerosleigh; on the back, the photograph of the man with the movie camera (Karmen) seems to take his place. The identity of the man on the cover could be a pilot featured in the book, but, almost as easily, his leather cap and goggles could be those worn by Karmen on the back cover. The picture on the back cover also clearly marks Karmen-the-photographer's transformation into Karmen-the-film-maker. Karmen had just begun to work as a kino-chronicler, and it appears that he had hoped to use the captivating dynamism of the vehicle's *vezdekhodnost'* to forward not only a body in motion but his career's "step into the future," fusing the link between autobiography and automobility.[53] Here the cameraman and pilot are fused into one, and, by proxy, children reading the book might imagine themselves to be the photographer/camera operator as they play the role of pilot in *Aerosani* (fig. 11.14). Both author-photographer and child enter into the system of *vezdekhonost'* as active agents with the potential reach of universal mobility. The novel aerosleigh, captured and reanimated by its likely mobilized ally – the cinematically orchestrated children's book – provides the thrill of the living image, grounded in a decidedly Soviet imagination.

11.13. Front and back covers of Roman Karmen's *Aerosani*.

11.14. Final image in Roman Karmen's *Aerosani*.

A Conclusion via the Kabakovian Imagination

A 1972 illustration from *Murzilka* by Il'ia Kabakov evinces the transformation of the aerosleigh. In a short feature, "Begom po sugrobam" ("In a Run over the Snowdrifts") the aerosleigh glides without its requisite skis, thereby becoming a hybrid of the aeroboat and aerosleigh – a hydrofoil – as it traverses the water as well as snow (fig. 11.15). Here the aerosleigh, in losing much of its technological specificity, is now capable of a greater degree of mobility, traversing all seasons in a pastel future land. Rather than juxtaposing the aesthetic of past (Nekrasov's house in Tret'iakov or the horse-drawn sleigh in Karmen), here the fairy-tale land of Ivan Bilibin meets the future city of an industrial, Soviet imagination. And while Kabakov's illustrations are known to stray from technological exactitude, these miniaturized forms also preclude any virtual ride offered by the photographic illustrations of an earlier age. Aerosleighs are but one of many representatives of transportation on snow, propelling Soviet citizens toward an emerging "future city" but wrought in a language that no longer concerns itself with the abandonment of "old." Gone too is the thrill of technology, either in its "austere spirit" embodied by the constructivists or its all-powerful and outsized propeller. Is this one potential outcome for the final evolution of this Soviet fairy tale? Certainly, the kinetic apparatus no longer defines the aesthetic of the children's illustration; rather, in a Kabakovian pastiche, the incursion of *skazka* makes the new into something that looks and moves impossibly like the magic of old. Therein we might

11.15. Il'ia Kabakov, illustrations for Anatolii Lel'evr, "Begom po sugrobam," *Murzilka,* no. 4 (1972): 17.

see the embodiment of Adorno's glib summation of the fate of all social utopias: "The leap into the future, clean over the conditions of the present, lands in the past."[54] Or, perhaps, more positively rendered as a synthesis of *vezdekhodnost'*, the hybrid vehicle offers the child's imagination the mobility to move not just everywhere in space, but also everywhere in time – from past to future and back again.

While the horizons of the child might be ever expanding, shaped by imagined, virtual, and real travels through the pages of the children's book, so too do they come to be defined by a definite number of set paths laid by systems of Soviet mobility. Each meeting point of space, time, and technology potentially opens onto new trajectories, defined in part by the mode of travel from land to sky and back again. At key points, like filling stations, these paths intersect with the dominant lines of adult cultural productions – arts journals, photography, film – creating points of substitution, borrowing, adaptation, and translation. It is in this supra-land of Soviet *vezdekhodnost'* that we might set out to conquer, not with a magic carpet of old, but with something potentially more powerful: the ever-hybridized mobile propellers of Soviet iconography and ideology into a limited future.

NOTES

1 Lissitzky, "Wheel – Propeller and What Will Follow," 106. First published in 1923, the journal *G: Material zur Elementaren Gestaltung (G: Materials for Elemental Form-Creation)* was a platform for the works of the European avant-garde, edited by Hans Richter. Lissitzky was also on the editorial board for the journal's first issues.

2 Ibid., 106.

3 A heavy-handed translation of *vezdekhodnost'* might be "go everywhere-ness."

4 Urry, *Mobilities*, 13. The "mobility turn" in Western scholarship, informed largely by social science, considers travel, transport, and communication as organizational factors inextricably tied to economic and social forms. It considers mobilities as social ordering, and as "processes of flow" (Urry, *Mobilities*, 6). See also *The Routledge Handbook of Mobilities*.

5 For Urry, automobility "captures a double sense, both of the humanist self as in the notion of autobiography, and of objects or machines that possess a capacity for movement, as in automatic ..." This decidedly American (or Ford-ified) notion of automobility locates the automobile driver as part of the assemblage of a whole "culture of mobility," which is focused on the individual's emancipation from dependence on the public sphere, from systems of "public mobility" (Urry, "The 'System' of Automobility," 25).

6 Gerchuk, *Sovetskaia knizhnaia grafika*, 23.

7 The All-Russian Congress for Pre-School Education purged folktales from children's reading in 1924. The rhetorical "final word" was given by Esfir Ianovskaia in her *Nuzhna li skazka proletarskomu rebenku?* (1925), stating in no uncertain terms that fairy tales were detrimental to building a child's class consciousness. While Chukovsky's *Crocodile* was attacked as early as 1920 for its unsound anthropomorphism, Krupskaia renewed the attack in *Pravda* in 1928. Her final summation calls it "bourgeois muck" (*buzhuaznaia mut'*). Krupskaia, "O 'Krokodile,'" 5; see also Hellman, *Fairy Tales and True Stories*, 355–8.

8 The term "smychka" refers to the "union" of the city and the country, which was a Soviet policy and social movement from the 1920s until the mid-1930s to bring together the urban proletariat and the agrarian peasant both culturally and politically.

9 Vladimir Favorskii also writes about the vertical and horizontal principles of artistic construction. See "O grafike kak ob osnove knizhnogo iskusstva," in *V.A. Favorskii*, 316–19.

10 Gerchuk notes that constructivist books have an affinity with the poster form. See Gerchuk, *Sovetskaia knizhnaia grafika*, 24. The *proizvodstvennaia knizhka* is discussed by Nikolai Chuzhak in "Khudozhestvennaia detskaia kniga," 30. See also Oushakine, "Translating Communism for Children." Nikolai Smirnov was only ever given tertiary credit in the trio's books, speaking to the primacy of the graphic design.

11 Chichagova, "Konstruktivizm," *Korabl'*, 7.

12 Gerchuk also describes their aesthetic as "consciously chang[ing] the ... drawing with charts and diagrams, not so much even as a visual aid, but to get closer ... to the native language of machinery itself" (Gerchuk, *Sovetskaia knizhnaia grafika*, 24).

13 Krupskaia, cited in Kon, *Sovetskaia detskaia literatura*, 72–3.

14 Kon, *Sovetskaia detskaia literatura*, 74.

15 Ibid. Gorky's introduction to *1001 Nights* (1929) famously speaks to similar points about the importance of the flights of imagination that would take on a new technological form in later eras, a kind of reorientation for the traditional fairy tale, including the substitution of the flying carpet for the image of the airplane. Gorky, "O skazkakh," 86.

16 Krupskaia, "Detskaia kniga," 2.

17 Some highlights include Nikolai Nekrasov's *Zheleznaia doroga* (1864) and Nikolai Grigor'ev's *Bronepoezd Gandzia* (1924). The train's appearance as icon of the expansion of Soviet railway campaigns was central in the imaging of the Turksib project, connecting Moscow, Siberia, and beyond (propagandized and aestheticized in film, text, and illustration). See Kunichika's contribution to this volume. Mikhail Il'in's *Rasskaz o velikom plane* (1930), to be discussed later in this chapter, also devotes many pages to the new train lines that will connect Moscow to Siberia ("Kak priblizit' Sibir' v Moskve?" 142–4; "Novye puti," 144–5). The notion of identification with the illustrated object in children's books, specifically that of a child with a steam engine, is the starting point for Vladimir Favorskii's discussion of the

"realism" of children's drawings and spatial imaginations in 1935. See Favorskii, *V.A. Favor-skii*, 459–63.

18 Oushakine's analysis of Lissitzky's own suprematist children's book, *Pro dva kvadrata* (1922), could easily apply in this case: "Elementary means, elementary building blocks, could create a highly dynamic environment that activates readers' creative potential … Through his imaginative typography and topography of the book space, Lissitzky encouraged the reader to oscillate constantly between the image and the word, between an abstract idea and a concrete form, between a picture and a real object." Oushakine, "Translating Communism for Children," 195. For more on the journal *Veshch'*, see also Reischl, "Вещь/Objet/Gegenstand."

19 As Yuri Tsivian has shown, these "Charlots" are riddled with false readings and mistranslations of Chaplin-from-cinema. We can add Fernand Leger's illustrations to this list – creating the drawn Chaplin for Dadist Iwan Goll's *Die Chaplinade* (*The Chapliniad: A Film Poem*). His drawings were known in Russia by 1922, but without Goll's text. See Tsivian, "Charlie Chaplin and His Shadows," 75.

20 The illustrations are by both Leger and Varvara Stepanova. They are also included in Ilya Ehrenburg's *A vse-taki ona vertitsia* (1922). Tsivian includes his own translation of Ehrenburg's Chaplin introduction: "Charlot is one of us: he is new, he is left-wing, he is a FUTURIST … Charlot does not rely on inspiration; he is not an intuitive comedian, but a meticulous CONSTRUCTOR whose movements are based on schemata as rigorous as those of a medieval juggler" (Tsivian, "Charlie Chaplin and His Shadows," 75).

21 Yuri Tsivian shows that this gag (Chaplin is attempting to jump start the plane, the plane starts, Chaplin is caught spinning on the propeller) is not from a Chaplin film at all. A mistake in a Moscow review in *The Spectacle* is to blame. This film with the man on the propeller is likely a film featuring one of Chaplin's imitators (Tsivian, "Charlie Chaplin and His Shadows," 78). The propeller structure also forms the backdrop for one of Klucis and Sen'kin's photomontages, *Deti i Lenin* (1924).

22 Tatlin's sled designs are featured in the article "Khudozhnik."

23 A copy of Michelangelo's *David* is visible in period photographs.

24 Evgenii Steiner characterizes Chaplin's presence as "livening up" the book. Steiner, *Stories for Little Comrades*, 196. However, there is more at stake in Chaplin's appearance and disappearance here. The exchange between adult and children's media is also apparent in the visual intertext, as *Kino-fot* is visible on the *Gazetnyi kiosk* in Chichagovas and Smirnov, *Detiam o gazete*, 16.

25 Smirnov, *Puteshestvie Charli*.

26 Similar visual and ideological themes are echoed when Chaplin is substituted for a more likely and appropriate human hero: the Pioneer. Boris Uralskii's *Polet na slet*, illustrated by Vera Lantsetti (1931), is just one such example. The plane brings the representative Pioneers to the mass meeting (*slet*), but it is primarily through the drive, initiative, and vision of the Pioneer (rather than the assumed power of the plane) that it is made possible.

27 Siegelbaum, *Cars for Comrades*, 2–3. The visual impact and celebration of automobile production is also captured in Ignatovich and Rodchenko's photo series for the journal *Daesh'* in 1929.

28 The translation is from George Counts and Nucia Perlmutter's translation of Il'in as *New Russia's Primer: The Story of the Five-Year Plan*, 138–9; the original Russian is from Il'in, *Rasskaz o velikom plane*, 147.

29 The aerial photograph included in *Bol'shevistskii slet* is evidence of the transformation from single plots of cultivated lands with individual owners: now, when we look down from the plane, we should see one master, the *kolkhoz*. *Bol'shevistskii slet*, 10. And we should keep in mind that, in just a few years, with the onset of the Second World War, the airplane will again be instrumental in military campaigns, aerial assaults, and information reconnaissance.

30 Stuchinskaia, *Kryl'ia Sovetov*, 2.

31 For example, in the first pages, when the plane reaches dizzying heights it is presented graphically by shrinking text [*VYSHE i vyshe*]. Ibid., 6.

32 Ibid., 16 (emphasis – originally in bold – in original).

33 This book, like *Polnym skol'zom*, *Lodka-vezdekhoda*, and *Aerosani* to be discussed later in this chapter, is an example of the adaptation of the ubiquitous *photo-ocherk* (short documentary sketch) in production with both GIZ and Molodaia gvardiia. See also Karasik, "Fotograficheskii proekt v detskoi knige," 347–50.

34 Kassil', *Lodka-vezdekhodka*, 12.

35 Ibid., 11.

36 Ibid., 12.

37 Ibid., 12–14.

38 Ibid., 34–5.

39 For example, the *aerosani* makes a prominent appearance in a special Arctic issue of *SSSR na Stroike* (*USSR in Construction*) in 1933.

40 "Russian Army Uses an AEROSLED," 49. The January 1937 *Popular Mechanics Magazine* also features aerosleighs on its cover and includes a longer article, focusing on leisure sledding. There is no mention of the Soviet innovation.

41 For example, see the covers of *Za rulem*, no. 4 (1928) and no. 9 (1929), photographs by Arkadii Shaikhet; see also the cover of *Znanie-sila*, no. 23 (1931).

42 This poem is included in nearly every volume of collected works by Zharov. See, for example, his collection *Strana iunosti*.

43 Zharov, "Aerosani," 31.

44 Ibid.

45 Boris Gromov would also be aboard the famed Cheliuskin expedition in 1933–4. The role of the *aerosani* in the rescue operation became part of the children's imaginary in books like Boris Zhitkov's *Pomoshch' idet* (1948). The cover of the 1948 edition features the *aerosani* most prominently among the vehicles rushing to aid. On Gromov, see also McCannon, *Red Arctic*, 119.

46 TsAGI manufacture is the better known of the two, and its presentation in the book sets the stage for the inscription of the aforementioned transportation marvels into the body of the aerosleigh: the hydroplane *(glisser)* and the "Kryl'ia Sovetov" airplane. Gromov and Tret'iakov, *Polnym skol'zom*, 6–7.

47 Ibid., 16.

48 "Опершись крыльями о воздух, скользит по пластам атмосферы аэроплан. Опершись лыжами о снег, скользят по пластам наста аэросани." Ibid., 5.

49 This image in particular of Karmen's *aerosani* circulated in postcard format.

50 Karmen, "Pobediteli snezhnykh ravnii," 7

51 B.R.C., "At the Cameo," *New York Times*, 15 June 1936.

52 Nikolajeva and Scott, *How Picturebooks Work*, 125.

53 On this connection between automobility and autobiography, see Urry, "The 'System' of Automobility," 25. Tret'iakov too used the *aerosani*'s image, although to a lesser degree, in at least one overview of his author-photographer oeuvre. In his two-page contribution to the children's journal *Pioner*, titled, "Where I Have Been with My Camera" (1934), he includes a small feature on *aerosani* among exemplary images of his work with the proletariat abroad and in kolkhozes at home. Tret'iakov, "Gde ia byl s fotoapparatom," 10–11. For more on Tret'iakov and the image of *aerosani* in his biography as an author-photographer, see Reischl, "'Where I Have Been'…"

54 Adorno, "Messages in a Bottle," 43.

BIBLIOGRAPHY

Adorno, Theodor. "Messages in a Bottle." In *Mapping Ideology*, edited by Slavoj Zizek, 34–44. London: Verso, 2012.

Bol'shevistskii slet: 16 s'ezd VKP(b). Moscow: Gosudarstvennoe izdatel'stvo, 1930.

Chichagova, G., O. Chichagova, and N. Smirnov. *Detiam o gazete*. Moscow: Gosizdat, 1926.

– *Dlia chego krasnaia armiia*. Moscow: Molodaia gvardiia, 1927.

– *Puteshestvie Charli*. Moscow: Gosizdat, 1924.

– *Put' na sever*. Moscow: Movaia Moskva, 1924.

Chichagova, Ol'ga. "Konstruktivizm," *Korabl'*, nos. 1–2 (1923): 7–8.

Chuzhak, Nikolai. "Khudozhestvennaia detskaia kniga." *Sovetskoe iskusstvo*, no. 6 (1926): 27–32.

Favorskii, V.A. *V.A. Favorskii: Literaturno-teoreticheskoe nasledie*. Moscow: Sovetskii khudozhnik, 1988.

Gerchuk, Iurii. *Sovetskaia knizhnaia grafika*. Moscow: Znanie, 1986.

Gorky, Maksim. "O skazkakh." *Sobranie sochinenii v 30 t.* Vol. 25: 86. Moscow: GIXhL, 1953.

Gromov, B., and S. Tret'iakov. *Polnym skol'zom*. Moscow: Molodaia gvardiia, 1930.

Hellman, Ben. *Fairy Tales and True Stories: The History of Russian Literature for Children and Young People (1574–2010)*. Leiden: Brill, 2013.

Il'in, M. *New Russia's Primer: The Story of the Five-Year Plan*. Translated by George Counts and Nucia Perlmutter. Boston: Houghton Mifflin, 1931.

– *Rasskaz o velikom plane*. Moscow: Gosizdat, 1930.

Karasik, Mikhail. "Fotograficheskii proekt v detskoi knige." In *"Ubit' Charskuiu ...": Paradoksy sovetskoi literatury dlya detei (1920-e–1930-e gg.)*, edited by Marina Balina and V.Yu, 330–50. Vyugin. St. Petersburg: Aleteia, 2013.

Karmen, Roman. *Aerosani*. Moscow: Molodaia gvardiia, 1931.

– "Pobediteli snezhnykh ravnii." *Kino-gazeta*, nos. 12/13 (1931). Rossiiskii gosudarstvennii arkhiv literatury i iskusstva (RGALI), Roman Karmen, f. 2829, op. 1 ed. 116, p. 6.

Kassil', Lev. *Lodka-vezdekhodka*. Moscow: Ogiz, 1933.

Kon, Lidiia. *Sovetskaia detskaia literatura, 1917–1929*. Moscow: Gosudarstvennoe izdatel'stvo detskoi literatury, 1960.

Krupskaia, Nadezhda. "Detskaia kniga – mogushchestvennoe orudie sotsial'isticheskogo vospitaniia." *Pravda*, 3 Feb. 1931.

– "O 'Krokodile' K. Chukovskogo." *Pravda*, 1 Feb. 1928.

Lissitzky, El. "Wheel – Propeller and What Will Follow." In *G: An Avant-Garde Journal of Art, Architecture, Design, and Film, 1923–1926*, edited by Detlef Mertins and Michael W. Jennings, and translated by Steven Lindberg with Margareta Ingrid Christian, 106. Los Angeles: Getty Publications, 2010.

McCannon, John. *Red Arctic: Polar Exploration and the Myth of the North in the Soviet Union, 1932–1939*. Oxford: Oxford University Press, 1998.

Nikolajeva, Maria, and Carole Scott. *How Picturebooks Work*. New York: Garland Publishing, 2001.

Oushakine, Serguei. "Translating Communism for Children: Fables and Posters of the Revolution." *Boundary* 243, no. 3 (2016): 159–219. https://doi.org/10.1215/01903659-3572478.

Reischl, Katherine M.H. "*Вещь/Objet/Gegenstand* on the International Stage," *Journal of Modern Periodical Studies* 8, no. 2 (2017): 134–56.

– "'Where I Have Been with My Camera': Sergei Tret'iakov and Developing Operativity." *Russian Literature* 103–5 (2019): 119–43.

Routledge Handbook of Mobilities, ed. Peter Adey, et al. Abingdon: Routledge, 2013.

"Russian Army Uses an AEROSLED Pioneered in Michigan Snows." *Science and Mechanics*, Spring 1943.

Siegelbaum, Lewis. *Cars for Comrades.* Ithaca, NY: Cornell University Press, 2008.

Steiner, Evgenii. *Stories for Little Comrades: Revolutionary Artists and the Making of Early Soviet Children's Books.* Seattle: University of Washington Press, 1999.

Stuchinskaia, Ida. *Kryl'ia Sovetov.* Moscow: GIZ, 1930.

Tatlin, Vladimir. "Khudozhnik: Organizator byta." *Rabis*, no. 48 (1929): 4–5.

Tret'iakov, Sergei. "Gde ia byl s fotoapparatom." *Pioner*, nos. 5/6 (1934).

Tsivian, Yuri. "Charlie Chaplin and His Shadows: On Laws of Fortuity in Art." *Critical Inquiry*, no. 3 (Spring 2014): 71–84.

Uralskii, Boris. *Polet na slet.* Illustrated by Vera Lantsetti. Moscow: Gosudarstvennoe izdatel'stvo, 1930.

Urry, John. *Mobilities.* Cambridge: Polity Press, 2007.

– "The 'System' of Automobility." *Theory, Culture and Society* 21, nos. 4/5 (2004): 25–39.

Zharov, Aleksandr. "Aerosani." *30 dnei*, no. 1 (1928): 81.

– *Strana iunosti, 1921–1968.* Moscow: Gos. izd-vo "Khudozh. lit-ra," 1968.

III.1. A spread from Aleksandr Deineka's picture book *Parad Krasnoi Armii* (*The Red Army Parade*) (Moscow: Ogiz, 1930).

POWER

Part III concludes this exploration of primers in Soviet modernity by focusing on the crucial issue of power. Insofar as the country's transformation was fundamentally rooted in the forceful consolidation of resources, institutions, and people, power was central to Soviet modernity. The institutional aspects of this powerful urge to modernize are relatively well known; the contributions to this section focus instead on the ways power and institutions of power transformed less tangible entities such as time, identity, and labour.

Kevin M.F. Platt's chapter examines representations of temporality in spatial forms. Five-Year Plans offered a new way of thinking about chronology: moving forward *in time* was usually envisioned as moving *in space*. Also, and crucially, this movement had to be objectified – in the form of new construction sites, new objects, and new frontiers. Time had to be mapped and materialized. A different aspect of the Soviet preoccupation with time – or, rather, timelessness – is examined in the chapter by Daniil Leiderman and Marina Sokolovskaia. Focusing on the images of Lenin's death in Soviet children's books, the authors demonstrate how the deceased Lenin emerged in a dual capacity: as both a corpse and a symbol of immortality – that is, as a sign of trauma and a promise of its healing.

Stephen M. Norris investigates a less morbid but no less ubiquitous aspect of Soviet life: the Red Army. He argues that Soviet-era children's book illustrators encouraged children to engage in "ocular play" and to learn how to "see in Soviet" by using the figure of the Red Army soldier as a basic ocular model. In his chapter, Alexey Golubev studies another crucial aspect of the new Soviet ocular regime: labour. Peasants and workers – the two dominant classes in the USSR – quickly eclipsed fairy-tale princes and princesses to take the central position in children's literature. Golubev reveals the specifics of visual representations of these new classes by foregrounding images of the working body. Concrete and realistic, such images were instrumental in transforming the initial goal: representations of class were gradually displaced by visual signs of professional belonging.

Thomas Keenan's chapter offers one more unexpected reversal, by exposing the secret core of Soviet modernity – its *Amerikanizm*. Abstracted from its original capitalist expression and deployed for communist needs, pictures of American modernity were presented in children's literature as a materialist replacement for fairy-tale magic and fantasy: enchanting, enticing, and frightening at the same time.

chapter twelve

SPATIALIZING REVOLUTIONARY TEMPORALITY: FROM MONTAGE AND DYNAMISM TO MAP AND PLAN

KEVIN M.F. PLATT

Seeing the Revolution

Boris Shikhman's 1926 children's book in verse, *Kak chetvero zheleznodorozhnykh rebiat sozdali pionerskii otriad* (*How Four Railroad Kids Created a Pioneer Troop*), is framed by two images – the first and last of the fourteen simple, monochrome representational line drawings by V.G. Bekhteev that illustrate the book.[1] The first – the frontispiece (fig. 12.1) – shows a village street with the figures of several children in the middle of the dusty roadway engaged in a match of "gorodki," a Russian game in which a bat is thrown in order to destroy an assembly of wooden rods. At the conclusion of the book, a larger full-page illustration (fig. 12.2) shows ranks of children marching in the same street from precisely the same point of view. They are led by three boys – one beating on a drum, one blowing a horn, and one carrying a tattered flag. The book's story bridges this transformation in the life of the village children: from rural disorder, a game founded on a metaphor of destruction, and alienated, detached figures to a disciplined mass of bodies moving in unison, mobilized for the construction of a new society.

Yet despite the reorganization of the village visibly wrought in Bekhteev's illustrations, this book exemplifies the difficulty of representing revolutionary social transformation in the mid-1920s. Although the story culminates in the ordering of young bodies, it is not clear exactly what they are mobilized to achieve, in the midst of a dusty, unchanged rural scene. At the most fundamental level, these two images, separated by twenty-six pages, present a spatial analogue for change over time. Their juxtaposition functions like that of film shots, joined by montage; we might cite Sergei Eisenstein's explanation of the dialectical function of such a montage: "The incongruence in contour of the first picture – already impressed on the mind – with the subsequently perceived second picture engenders, in conflict, the feeling of motion."[2]

12.1. Vladimir G. Bekhteev, frontispiece showing the disorder and inert state of Russian village
life, from Boris Shikhman, *Kak chetvero zheleznodorozhnykh rebiat sozdali pionerskii otriad.*
(Moscow: Molodaia gvardiia, 1926), 7.

Or we could think about representation of time in more allegorical manner, as
it is represented in the parade: the implied motion of the marchers and the direction of their gazes signifies their movement into the future. Yet the book shows the
reader no image of this future. If the existing images are locked in the dialectical
tension of montage, the synthetic moment lies beyond the covers of the book. In
terms of rendering time as space, the future may only be imagined as the location
toward which the children are marching or as an illustration on a page yet to be
drawn.

Shikhman's narrative, too, may be seen as an effort to educate young readers about
revolutionary social and political development by spatializing temporality. For, in
order to transform the village – to advance it in history – the four children must
first complete a journey. At the start of the book, its eponymous protagonists face a
dilemma. Although they are motivated to work for the common good, to organize a
Pioneer troop, "having cast off old customs" ("brosiv starye manery"), the other children in their remote village of railroad workers are politically inert. And, in addition
to facing the resistance of the "unconscious folk" ("nesoznatel'nyi narod"), the protagonists are stymied by their own lack of knowledge:

12.2. Vladimir G. Bekhteev, final illustration showing revolutionary mobilization of village children, from *Kak chetvero zheleznodorozhnykh rebiat sozdali pionerskii otriad*, 31.

In order to create the troops, the units	Чтоб создать отряды, звенья,
All the same one needs some know-how	Все же надобно уменье.
Without instructions, without a charter	Без инструкций, без устава,
We are no troop, but just a throng.	Не отрад мы, — а орава.[3]

When the four activist children turn to their parents for help, they are shushed:

The stoker just waved them away	Кочегар лишь отмахнулся,
The engineer he cracked a smile	Инженер—тот улыбнулся
And pronounced it shameful for Vania	И сказал, что стыдно Ване
To waste his time on such nonsense.	Заниматься пустяками.[4]

In response to their stagnant environment, the would-be Pioneers decide to set off for the "Red Capital" ("Krasnaia stolitsa") to acquire the direction they lack. At night, they take a railway handcar and depart for Moscow. The intrepid travellers face terrible weather and exhaustion and finally nearly run head-on into a train. Returned to the village by the train workers, they are not scolded, but rather are treated as heroes. Moved by the children's revolutionary passion, the adults of the village decide to write to the Komsomol for guidance. As the epilogue explains, a month later, the parade of the final illustration takes place.

Like Bekhteev's illustrations, this plot presents a spatial allegory of revolutionary temporality. The genre of Shikhman's book is that of the quest story in a landscape in which the components of the time horizon have been geographically distributed, in a form of "uneven development," between a progressive centre, the locus of the future and of revolutionary consciousness, and a backwards periphery, mired in the past and physically sundered from that centre.[5] Yet although the children do eventually receive "instructions" and a "charter" that allow them to organize their Pioneer troop, they never reach the goal of their quest, the "Red Capital." The periphery remains disjointed from the centre, and the past from the future. The spatio-temporal disconnect of the book may be recognized as an instantiation of the dialectic of elementality – disordered and undirected rebellious action – and revolutionary consciousness – future-oriented and disciplined – that is so familiar from the cultural production and political thought of this era.[6] The jarring plot twist whereby dangerous insubordination is rewarded expresses a different challenge: how is one both to valorize revolutionary activism against authority and to instil social cohesion among the young? This poorly mediated gap between past rebellion and present discipline, which might be called a temporal double vision or "modal incoherence," represents in condensed form one of the challenges of revolutionary history throughout Soviet public culture of 1920s, which sought to both enshrine the revolutionary enthusiasm and iconoclasm of past events and to channel them into construction of a new society.

The representation of a politically significant conception of temporality was among the fundamental tasks faced in the Soviet effort to create a new children's literature, a process that, as Serguei Oushakine has observed, involved "translation of the revolution's logic, content, and promise into a new book form and into a new language."[7] Of course, any narrative may be viewed as a representation of time, and each modern ideology relates to history in its own manner.[8] Yet a *sui generis* conception of temporality was a uniquely important aspect of Soviet political culture, predicated as it was on radical transformations that were to lead to an unprecedented form of future social life. Both the success of the Soviet undertaking and the legitimacy of the regime depended on inculcating a sense of revolutionary temporality among the population. Shikhman's book demonstrates the utility of spatialization as one strategy to "translate" revolutionary temporality into visual and comprehensible form for children. It also demonstrates the difficulties that beset renderings of Soviet time as picture-book space. The absence of concrete images of the future society, the "uneven development" and lack of integration of the landscape, and the modal incoherence of its plot are indicative of hurdles faced by early Soviet authors and artists in representing revolutionary temporality.

The term "modal incoherence," is here inspired by Katerina Clark's seminal work on socialist realism, which describes a different rift in the temporal structure of literary representation: not between the iconoclastic revolutionary past and the socially disciplined present, but between the novelistic time of the realist plot, focused on the present, and the epic or "great" time of the coming communist society that was available to a revolutionary vision that could "see the future."[9] In the present chapter, my account arcs forward through a series of examples of spatialized representations of time from the 1920s and early 1930s, concentrating on representations of two moments of intensified and intentional historical transformation – the October Revolution and the Five-Year-Plan. As will be seen, the two variants of modal incoherence might be seen as successive stages in a genealogy of Soviet temporality. By the early 1930s, Soviet children's books had brought the future into view in picture books that, in distinction from Shikhman's book, tied Soviet geography together and lay it before young readers as a completely integrated and transparent spatial analogue of socialist time. The spatially coherent and visible picture of temporal processes was most fully realized in books representing the Five-Year-Plan itself. Yet as we shall see, as Soviet time was becoming more integral and visible – resolving the first instance of modal incoherence – it also lost both revolutionary dynamism and its very grasp on children's lived reality in encountering the second.

Revolution, Time, and Space

Reflections of early Soviet specialists and commentators on Soviet children's literature regularly include in lists of centrally important topics "the revolution" and discuss the "revolutionary book." These seemingly transparent terms were, however, extraordinarily slippery. As a topic for children's literature, "revolution" could refer to "revolutionary events" – historical subjects to be studied and known (including not only the October Revolution, but also the 1905 Revolution and more remote events of a revolutionary character). Yet, quite commonly, "revolution" was used in a more abstract sense – to refer to the reified essence of the experience of time and politics born with the October Revolution, yet pretending to universality, representative of the movement of history itself during this era of social transformation. This usage of "revolution" signalled the expectation of still greater social transformation to come not only in the USSR but across the globe itself in the form of world revolution. As, for instance, German communist leader Ernst Thälmann proclaimed from the front page of *Pravda* in the same year that Shikhman's book was published, "socialist development is progressing and the forces of the revolution are growing."[10] Soviet public and political discourse of the 1920s was suffused with this abstract application of the term "revolution."[11] Furthermore, as is attested by scholarly studies of the era, the historicization of the October Revolution in early Soviet culture as a whole was an ongoing project that passed through a number of stages in its development over the course of the first decades of the Soviet project.[12] As a reflection of the capaciousness and mobility of the concept of "revolution," many commentators recognized that the question of its proper representation for children presented no little difficulty. As one participant in a 1928 research project sponsored by the People's Commissariat of Enlightenment (Narkompros) explained:

> The goals of revolutionary upbringing cannot be limited simply to development of this feeling of instinctive belonging to the revolutionary milieu – this still purely reactive revolutionary sensibility. To the contrary, the stronger the development of this revolutionary instinct ..., the more urgent becomes the necessity of giving form to this elemental sensibility ... Before revolutionary literature stands the task of investing a definite ideational content into this nearly intangible revolutionary feeling in order to show the child the revolution not only in its everyday static form, but also as a complete process, in all its dramatic quality, in the unfolding of its inspiring and uplifting goals.[13]

For children's authors, the problem was to show the revolution simultaneously as facts of social life, as achieved historical events, and as a conception of ongoing, dynamic, and future-oriented historical becoming.

As a starting point in categorizing variant concepts of temporality during the first decade after the October Revolution, we may turn to Susan Buck-Morss's description of two phenomenological stances that she identifies in early Soviet public life, which, in her view, correspond to the positions regarding politics and temporality associated with the cultural avant-garde, on the one hand, and the political vanguard of the Communist Party, on the other. Buck-Morss's analysis is schematic, but for this reason can serve as a launching pad for a more historically nuanced account of the diversity of ways that early Soviet children were interpellated into revolutionary temporality. The avant-garde, as Buck-Morss explains, was committed to a "lived temporality of interruption, estrangement, arrest" that aimed to "inspire imagination in a way that sets reality in question" and to "open up time for alternative visions."[14] In contrast, the "armed vanguard 'submits' to a conception of time that, so long as it remains victorious, legitimates its own rule." This is a conception of history based on a "'plan' that locks in future meaning," as a result of which "time's indeterminacy and openness is colonized."[15] Buck-Morss conceives of the early Soviet era as a battle between these two conceptions of temporality, a battle that the avant-garde lost, so that, by the end of the 1920s, "art was no longer to inspire imagination in a way that set reality into question but, rather, to stage affirmative representations of reality that encouraged an uncritical acceptance of the party's monopolistic right to control the direction of social transformation."[16]

Buck-Morss's categories are helpful, but not without certain correctives. Rather than conceiving these two conceptions of revolutionary temporality as the properties of warring camps – as though avant-garde artists were the only actors capable of imagining the future as alternative visions in flux, as though every Bolshevik were wedded to a mechanistic and predetermined comprehension of social transformation, or as though each individual work or artist condenses one or the other of these opposed categories – let us instead take these categories as representative of poles of temporal experience in the 1920s per se, as heuristic markers between which temporality was experienced and expressed in far greater variety and complexity. As will become apparent, illustrated literature for children does not, in fact, neatly fall into a coherent chronological sequence in which easily identifiable principles follow one another in distinctive waves or face off in a clear-cut contest. Rather, across the messy terrain of the unevenly regulated cultural life of the early Soviet era, the accumulated forms of representation of temporality in children's literature present a palimpsest of conceptions that grew more complex over time. As is evident from Shikhman's and Bekhteev's book, individual works are best seen as more or less successful attempts to mediate between diverse temporal modalities, rather than as instantiations of ideal types.

A children's storybook of 1929 features a peasant lad, Misha, who sees a parade on a trip to the city with his father, who explains that "The workers are celebrating the revolution" ("Revoliutsiiu rabochie prazdnuiut"). Upon his return, he explains to his friends that he "saw the revolution in the city" ("Ia revoliutsiiu v gorode videl"). "And what was it like?" ("Kakaia ona?"), ask his friends. He answers, "They were carrying twelve flags with various tassels and big horns were playing music" ("Dvenadtsat' flagov nesli s raznymi kistiami i muzyka igrala v bol'shie truby").[17] This story by A. Neverov is an allegory for the question facing illustrators of Soviet children's literature: how indeed was revolution, in all its complexity, to be envisioned for the young? Yet this question was itself an instance of a larger problem that had occupied avant-garde culture since the turn of the century: the representation of time in visual art. In a tradition that may be traced back to G.E. Lessing's *Laocoon* (1766), classical aesthetic theory held the literary and the visual arts as distinct, in that the former could represent temporal processes while the latter merely presented static instants in time.

Modernists across Europe mounted a range of challenges to this principle, from cubist multiperspectivalism, in which, according to Carl Einstein's contemporary account, "temporal notions of movement are transformed into a static simultaneity in which the primordial elements of contrasting movement are condensed," to the Italian futurist obsession with speed and dynamism, which was most commonly expressed in paintings that relied on blur or multiple superimposed images of a single object to communicate movement, such as Giacomo Balla's *Dog on a Leash* (1912).[18]

12.3. Russian avant-garde experiment in the visual representation of time in painting: Kazimir Malevich, *Tochil'shchik* (*The Knife Grinder*, 1912).

Russian avant-gardists, too, took up the project of eliding the barrier between what Lessing had called the "arts of space" and the "arts of time" – we may take, for example, the decomposed stages of action in Kazimir Malevich's 1912 painting *The Knife Grinder* (fig. 12.3) or multiple examples from avant-garde bookmaking that sought by typographical means to present poetic texts in perceptual collapse into simultaneity.[19] The example and the theory of film was undoubtedly imbricated in the experiments of cubists, futurists, and many others at the intersection of visuality and temporality, so much so that Pavle Levi has recently proposed the category "cinema by other means" to describe the broadly modernist phenomena of cinematic experimentation without the film apparatus in the age of film's challenge to static representation.[20]

Which returns us to Eisenstein's conceptions of montage, introduced above. Filmic montage, in its various forms, was both analogous to and exemplary for prominent solutions to the representation of time in children's literature – those solutions most capable of communicating a dynamic conception of revolutionary temporality. Yet, as we will see below, the authors and illustrators of early Soviet children's literature adapted the conceptual and technical arsenal of the avant-garde in varying manner, ultimately leading to spatialized representations of temporality that flattened the openness of the avant-garde future into a "colonization" of the future by plan and determinacy and departed from the most radical potentials of avant-garde artistic practices.

Temporality as Matrix

Among the earliest spatialized representations of revolutionary time in Soviet children's picture books is the 1918 collaboration between Vladimir Mayakovsky and prominent avant-garde artists Kseniia L. Boguslavskaia, Vladimir I. Kozlinskii, Sergei N. Makletsov, and Ivan A. Puni, *Oktiabr' 1917–1918. Geroi i zhertvy revoliutsii* (*October 1917–1918: Heroes and Victims of the Revolution*). In both its textual and graphic representations, this book, intended to be read aloud to preliterate children or beginning readers, shows revolutionary temporality not so much as a historical event but rather as an agonistic conflict and a rupture in the temporal flow, unfolding in the present. Yet it should also be noted that this work shows no actual violent conflict in its illustrations, and instead, as in classic montage theory, breaks down components of action into contrasting, juxtaposed elements. It offers two series of social types, first representing "heroes" of revolutionary culture in nine full-page illustrations, and then its "victims" in nine more. The fact that the representatives of the future precede those of the past is perhaps the most obvious indication of the orientation of this work on a moment of simultaneity rather than a representation of temporal flow. References to actualities of conflict are restricted to Mayakovsky's chastushka-like couplets and quatrains that accompany each illustration, but they are most forcefully communicated in the cut between the pages. In effect, the book is a proto-image of Eisenstein's conception of the "montage of attractions" that he would formulate in subsequent years as a formal method for delivering a "shock" to the viewer's psyche – a representation that shows events in their unfolding, not as "an idea composed of separate shots stuck together," but rather as "an idea that derives from the collision of two shots that are independent of one another."[21] Dynamic revolutionary temporality emerges not as a presentation of an ordered sequence of temporal states but in the gap between opposed images representative of past and future.

Like all of the figures depicted in the book, the unsigned illustration of the "automobilist" (fig. 12.4) stands alone in a full-page portrait, opposite a blank page and so commanding full attention – his arms crossed in a commanding pose. Mayakovsky's quatrain explains that:

If the White soldier trembles like a leaf	Если белогвардеец задрожит, как лист,
And packs of them scatter, howling,	И кучи его рассыпятся воя,
It's because the automobilist is coming	Это едет автомобилист
In his armoured car.	Машиной броневою[22]

12.4. "The automobilist," a figure of futurity, presented in futurist stylistic idiom, from Vladimir Mayakovsky, *Oktiabr' 1917–1918. Geroi i zhertvy revoliutsii* (Petrograd: Otdel izobrazitel'nykh iskusstv Kommissariata narodnogo prosveshcheniia, 1918), 15.

In contrast, the well-fed figure of the "priest" (fig. 12.5) – also an unsigned illustration – stands with hands crossed over his ample belly and a smug expression.[23] The accompanying quatrain explains:

Crimson flags unfurled	Развевались флаги ало
Across Mother Russia	По России-Матушке,
The priests were hit hardest of all –	Больше всех попам попало
The little Father and little Mother.	Матушке и батюшке.[24]

Revolution is presented via opposed principles, the collision of which is communicated in a formal, rather than a representational solution. Time has been rendered as a matrix of opposed cells across which revolutionary process and temporal transformation are distributed.

Heroes and Victims of the Revolution communicates the distinction between the revolutionary order and the bourgeois world of the past by consistent stylistic choices

12.5. "The priest," a figure of the past presented in the form of a time-worn leftist caricature, from *Oktiabr' 1917–1918. Geroi i zhertvy revoliutsii*, 31.

and uses of the page (beyond the pronounced stylistic distinctions between the four illustrators). The "heroes" are presented, even in cubist abstraction, as coherent portraits with regular, although idealized, human proportions, while the "victims" appear as caricatures drawing on the traditions of leftist satirical drawing. The work reserves the most avant-garde styles – founded on the communication of dynamism by means of a graphic deconstruction of figures, spaces, and objects – for the heroes, as is most emphatically expressed in the "automobilist," surrounded by decomposed elements of motor cars, ready to speed off the page. The other revolutionary figures are presented in uncluttered spaces – open horizons of action – while the bourgeois are hemmed in, caught in busy, enclosed environments that trap them in the social spaces of the past, as with the priest, surrounded by church domes and crosses.[25]

This demarcation of battle lines drawn between human actors locked in agonistic confrontation, distributed in juxtaposed cells, communicates the sense of ongoing conflict we may associate with the immediate post-revolutionary years, when this book was created. Yet undeniably, revolutionary temporality as a compression of opposed horizons of expectation around the present was an important modality up through the 1930s and beyond. Understandably, the principles of graphic and conceptual organization inaugurated in *Heroes and Victims of the Revolution* were echoed in other children's illustrated books in the course of the decade that, however, drew battle lines between past and future in a different manner, reflecting the changing conjunctures of Soviet public culture. Although the central condensation points of opposed temporal vectors in *Heroes and Victims of the Revolution* are the human figures, each is accompanied by representative objects, like the attributes of saints: a rifle and a banner for the Red Army soldier, and a samovar, Victrola, cuckoo clock, and sack of flour for the kulak. This opposition between a mobile human figure and one trapped in a bourgeois interior anticipates the reconceptualization of early Soviet culture as a battle for a new everyday life (*za novyi byt*) that was to come to the fore in the early 1920s. It was just such a conflict over the everyday that was adopted as the organizing principle of one of the most well-known conceptual heirs of *Heroes and Victims of the Revolution*, the 1925 collaboration between Samuil Marshak and Vladimir Lebedev, *Vchera i segodnia* (*Yesterday and Today*).[26]

This work is organized around contrasts between categorically opposed objects of everyday life that palpably represent the transformation of the social world wrought by the Soviet era, in this case presented as a series of oppositions in temporal order. Like other well-known examples of children's literature of this era, Marshak and Lebedev tell their story from the point of view of the objects themselves, which are anthropomorphized into active agents of social transformation.[27] The animation of objects is not as pronounced in *Yesterday and Today* as in the works examined by Oushakine and Balina in the introduction to this volume (no animated washstands chasing after dirty children here), yet Lebedev's illustrations do grant objects a central role in revolutionary social transformations. On successive pages, Marshak and Lebedev tell the story of the replacement of the gas lantern and stearin candle by the electric light bulb, and of yoke and buckets for hauling water by plumbing and running water. Everyone who has written with a pen and ink knows the challenges and frustrations of cursive, blotches, and splatter. Marshak and Lebedev offer their young readers the salvific alternative of the typewriter – a writing implement in keeping with the mechanized aesthetic of industrial futurity. Lebedev's illustration of an abandoned, empty inkwell and pen, on a page disfigured by blots and splotches (and also what appear to be caricature doodles of the old-fashioned clerks who could wield such outdated writing tools) (figs. 12.6) is complemented by an italic typeface, repellent, perhaps, to school children tormented by calligraphy exercises. In contrast, the following page presents the neat and precise image of a typewriter (fig. 12.7), with text in a typeface to match, in a geometric array that graphically rips language and poetry apart (so much so that the order of reading becomes a matter of equivocation). Curiously, whereas Marshak's quatrains on pen and ink animate the voice of the objects themselves, when it comes to the typewriter the text adopts the point of view of the child, amazed at the miracle of technology:

12.6. Vladimir Lebedev, illustration showing outdated writing implements, from *Vchera i segodnia,* by Samuil Marshak (Leningrad: Raduga, 1925), 8.

The machine abruptly breaks apart	Вдруг разъедется машина –
Half goes shooting to the right	Едет вправо половина…
What is happening? And why?	Что такое? Почему?
What a strange confounding sight!	Ничего я не пойму![28]

Yet perhaps this shift from familiar to distanced viewpoints, as well as the sheer awe induced by the workings of the typewriter, reveal the aspirational nature of the book's representation of social change. Although the title of the book claims the various progressive objects as representations of "today," for many – perhaps for a majority of young Russian readers of 1925 – electricity in the home and indoor plumbing could only be anticipated in the future. In reality, pen and ink would remain standard writing implements in Soviet life well into the late Soviet era. Nevertheless, Marshak's and Lebedev's book is aptly titled, for it remains at base a representation of revolutionary temporality as a scene of conflict between opposed social and political principles in the here and now.

The 1930 book *Nashi vragi i druz'ia* (*Our Enemies and Friends*), by Nikolai V. Studenetskii, with illustrations by Aminadav M. Kanevskii, who was to go on to a long

Запятые,   Вдруг разъедется машина—

Точки,   Едет вправо половина...

Строчки

Бьют кривые   Что такое? Почему?

Молоточки.   Ничего я не пойму!

12.7. Lebedev's illustration showing a modern typewriter (an Underwood), from *Vchera i segodnia*, 9.

career of children's book illustration in the Stalinist era, demonstrates the continued relevance of the model of formal composition inaugurated by Mayakovsky and his collaborators a decade earlier, yet also some shifts in its deployment that reflect changing Soviet conceptualizations of space and time.[29] Studenetskii's and Kanevskii's work relies on the same principle of personification of political conflict in opposed human figures as found in *Heroes and Victims of the Revolution*, yet it projects the matrix of contrasting characters onto the international scene, drawing its lines of battle between the Soviet workers' state and the capitalist West. Like the heroized "worker," "telegraph operator," and so on of the earlier work, Kanevskii draws his Soviet soldiers, Pioneers, and oppressed peasants and workers of the world as regularly proportioned and attractive figures, in contrast to bloated and repulsive imperialists and capitalists (figs. 12.8 and 12.9).

Yet this book also sharply departs from earlier uses of montage principles to represent the dynamic temporality of revolutionary conflict in the present. Oushakine has described the recycling of standard representational devices in Soviet children's literature and the growing schematism of these devices, including those discussed

12.8. Aminadav M. Kanevskii, illustration showing a warmongering capitalist and a general, external threats to socialist society, from *Nashi vragi i druz'ia*, by Nikolai V. Studenetskii (Moscow: Krestianskaia gazeta, 1930), 6.

here, as a "posterization" of Soviet political culture.[30] *Our Enemies and Friends* undoubtedly presents a posterization of the principles of its predecessors. It is emblematic of the changed Soviet public address to children that, although the years of the Five-Year Plan were not devoid of social violence, this book does not dwell on internal enemies of the Soviet state. Whereas *Heroes and Victims of the Revolution* presented young readers with images of figures who were in those years of civil war engaged in ongoing military conflict, *Our Enemies and Friends* entirely elides the kulaks and bourgeois, who were rapidly being "liquidated" in 1930. Instead, reflecting the rise to dominance in the late 1920s of the doctrine of "socialism in one country," the line between opposed camps is now inscribed into geography as the border of the USSR, which defends an apparently homogeneous territory of futurity from the archaic social forces that threaten it from without.[31] If, in the earlier works, the formal principle of montage communicated the "idea" of temporal conflict through a spatial formal construction, *Our Enemies and Friends* literalizes the spatialization of conflict as geography, distributing it across a global landscape in which opposed temporal principles are flattened into simultaneity, while Soviet space is integrated into a coherent whole. Conflict is distanced from the here and now of Soviet children, lifted from formal principle into actuality, in a story of coherent territories in ideological conflict.

12.9. Kanevskii's illustration showing Red Army soldiers and Pioneers, representative figures of socialist modernity, from *Nashi vragi i druz'ia*, 9.

As we will see below, this movement reflects a broader trend toward the projection of temporality onto geographical space in the late 1920s and 1930s.

Cinematic Geography

By the mid-1920s, with the end of the civil war and the death of Lenin, the October Revolution had moved into the middle distance of past events and gradually had become the subject of more properly historical children's literature. In early Soviet public discourse as a whole, the historicization of 1917 reached a turning point with the 1927 celebration of October, for which the state and its cultural agents invested enormous energy in documentation and codification of revolutionary history. The late 1920s also saw the arrival on the scene of a new generation of children's authors and artists, many of whom, straddling in their professional lives the worlds of avant-garde culture and children's literature, adapted other solutions to the representation of revolutionary temporality from the realm of visual art and cinema. In this regard, the works of Leonid Savel'ev, and in particular his 1930 children's book *Chasy i karta Oktiabria* (*The Clock and Map of October*), with illustrations by Georgii Petrov, demonstrate the intersection of revolutionary temporality with geographic spatialization.

"Savel'ev" was the professional pseudonym of Leonid Lipavskii, a central figure in the Oberiu-Chinari group of avant-garde poets, artists, and "homegrown philosophers" who were affiliated at the end of the 1920s and the start of the 1930s with the Leningrad division of the state Children's Publishing House (Detgiz), led by Marshak. Members of the group employed by Marshak's organization included Daniil Kharms, Alisa Poret, Nikolai Zabolotsky and others (see Goscilo's chapter in this volume for more detail). Of these, Savel'ev was perhaps the most institutionally invested, working from the late 1920s onwards as an author and editor on dozens of projects. His books for children include a series of works devoted to revolutionary history: *Okhota na tsaria* (*The Hunt for the Tsar*, 1929), telling the history of the drive to assassinate Alexander II by the People's Will underground terrorist organization in the 1880s; *Nemye svideteli* (*Mute Witnesses*, 1930), recounting the history of revolution in Russia organized around the spaces and edifices of the city, the "witnesses" of events; and *Shturm Zimnego* (*The Storm of the Winter Palace*, 1938). *The Clock and Map of October* is among the most successful of his works – republished in 1931 and rediscovered in the late Soviet period, when it was republished several times more.[32]

The title of *The Clock and Map of October* frankly announces a focus on the relationship between revolutionary space and time. Less overtly, it also references Savel'ev's interest in the adaptation of film techniques for children's literature, for the work is a response to Eisenstein's influential 1928 film *October*, codirected with Grigorii Aleksandrov, a chronicle of the revolutionary year originally commissioned for its tenth anniversary. In the film, maps, on which the Military Revolutionary Committee mark out the progress of the uprising, which are shown in intercutting shots with Bolshevik forces carrying out their missions as they take control of the city, are a repeated element of the film's conceptual montage (see sequences at 49:58, 1:09:53).[33] Clocks are another – shown in various forms throughout the film and culminating in the extraordinary closing sequence of spinning, speeding clock faces from around the world that communicates the revolution's triumph over time and space (starting at 1:54:07). Savel'ev and Petrov adapted these two figures of Eisenstein's film as the structural foundation of their book.

The Clock and Map of October is organized in a chronology beginning at 3:00am on the night of 24 October 1917 and ending at 6:00am on the morning of 26 October, when the Congress of Soviets officially claimed power and "the Revolution triumphed" (19). A list of events is described in terse prose that resembles a film script, each entry initiated by a place name. Along the left margin, each event is accompanied by a clock face showing the time; along the right, by a tiny line-drawing. These drawings are themselves reproduced as iconic signs, looming far larger than to scale, inscribed on three two-page maps – the first two marked "24 October" and "25 October" and showing all of central Petrograd, the last also marked "25 October," but showing only the immediate locale of the Winter Palace (fig. 12.10). Not all of the events in Savel'ev's chronology correspond precisely to scenes in Eisenstein and Aleksandrov's film, yet a

12.10. Georgii Petrov, illustration "mapping" events of 25 October 1917, from *Chasy i karta Oktiabria*, by Leonid Savel'ev (pseud.) (Leningrad: Detgiz, 1931), 16–17.

great many of them do – to the degree that Savel'ev frequently borrows *October*'s intertitles and Petrov's drawings reproduce its shots. As an example, we may take a shot (51:44) of sailors from the battleship *Aurora* taking control of the Nikolaevskii Bridge that Petrov mimics for the entry announcing that all bridges are under Bolshevik control (fig. 12.11), or Savel'ev's report that, when the Cossacks were ordered by phone to mobilize in defence of the palace, they "answered 'We're saddling our horses' and decided to stay in the barracks" ("otvetili 'sedlaem konei' i reshili ostat'sia v kazarmakh," 13), closely following a scene from the film (53:00) and precisely echoing its intertitle.

A striking comparison may be drawn between *The Clock and Map of October* and the 1929 picture book by Alisa Poret, *Kak pobedila revoliutsiia* (*How the Revolution Triumphed*), with unattributed text by Nikolai Zabolotsky. As Yuri Leving explains in a detailed analysis in chapter 2 in the present volume, that book also quotes extensively from Eisenstein and Aleksandrov's film. Like Savel'ev, Poret and Zabolotsky were members of the Oberiu-Chinari circle, and, considering the similarity of the projects, their respective books were undoubtedly created in parallel and in conversation. Strikingly, both works experiment with the projection of multiple "shots" in a single image, representing distinct moments in a developing event, and, in so doing, realizing the conceptual collision of distinct temporal moments central to Eisenstein's conception of montage. Yet the books are very different in their effects. Poret's, as Leving explains, bursts both space and chronological sequence asunder, in one of the fullest expressions of Buck-Morss's avant-garde revolutionary temporality in all early Soviet children's literature. In contrast, Savel'ev's version, by cutting the chain of events into discrete and seemingly interchangeable elements and bringing them into simultaneity on a map, instead elides the tension and historical potential of the revolutionary moment – the "eventness" of the revolution. It is almost as if, in adapting *October*'s representation of the 1917 uprising, Savel'ev and Petrov deliberately subverted the directors' core project, driving toward "a simple presentation or demonstration of events" rather than "a tendentious selection of, and comparison between, events, free from narrowly plot-related plans."[34] The charged metaphorical images of Eisenstein and Aleksandrov's montage sequences are literalized, becoming nothing more than … clocks and maps. Taken on their own, Savelev's chronological entries are a dull register of happenings. The chief interest for young readers of this book lies not in the tension of the revolutionary rupture in time but rather in play with the book as an object, a matrix of correspondences between map and chronology that projects time across space, allowing for a mastery of history as completed, predictable, and predetermined.

Mapping Time

Savel'ev's chronology in *The Clock and Map of October* is prefaced by a single page offering a more traditional narrative account of how Lenin foresaw and prepared

12.11. Georgii Petrov's micro-illustration of Bolshevik forces seizing control of Petrograd's bridges from *Chasy i karta Oktiabria* (1931), 13, and the shot of sailors taking control of the Nikolaevskii Brige from Sergei Eisenstein's *October* (1928).

the October uprising, repeating twice that "Lenin gave the plan" ("Lenin dal plan"), confirming the book's projection of the events of October as law-governed and predictable. In 1930, "plan" was linked in public discourse most emphatically with the Five-Year Plan, of course – and let us note that, in Russian, a secondary meaning of "plan" is "map." For Savel'ev and his colleagues at Litizdat, however, the implicit linkage of the book to the present was in need of additional emphasis: in the 1931 edition of *The Clock and Map of October*, featuring more involved drawings by the prominent illustrator Nikolai Lapshin, a narrative epilogue was added that brought the story up to the present, affirming that now, as in 1917, "a battle is raging" ("idet boi"), but victory is assured: "We know what we have to do. We have a clock and a map. Our map is the map of the Five-Year-Plan. Our clock is the Industrial Economic Plan" ("My znaem, chto nam delat'. U nas est' chasy i karta. Nasha karta – karta piatiletki. Nashi chasy – promfinplan").[35] The epilogue was accompanied by a new map of the USSR as a whole, strewn with the factories, oil rigs, and power stations projected in the Five-Year Plan and protected at its borders by artillery and battleships.

This addition to Savel'ev's book communicates the shifting institutional priorities of Soviet children's literature at the start of the 1930s. As T. Trifonov, one of the authors of a collection of essays on children's literature assembled by the Leningrad section of the Union of Soviet Writers in 1930, under the editorship of Anatoly Lunacharsky announced: "Books about the revolutionary past turn out to be significantly better than books about the revolutionary present. Regardless of the importance and significance of the history of revolutionary struggle, this fact seems to us to be sadly symptomatic: it points to the departure of a significant part of children's authors 'into history,' to their insufficient connection with contemporaneity."[36] In a separate contribution to the same volume, Trifonov joined with the entire collective of authors to call for new efforts in the production of children's literature in response to the new conjuncture of the "period of reconstruction," which brought with it completely new topics for children's literature: "the Five-Year Plan of socialist construction, socialist competition, shock labour, the collectivization of agriculture."[37] Children's literature of the day was in fact rapidly turning to these new challenges and, in the process, built on the spatializing principles pioneered by Savel'ev and Petrov to transform presentations of historical process to children, in step with the transformed sensibility characteristic of the Great Break – the Stalin "revolution" that was so deeply unlike its predecessor, precisely in its projections of a concrete and tangible horizon of futurity.

The same year that he published *The Clock and Map of October*, Savel'ev produced *Chto my stroim* (*What We Are Building*), with drawings by the talented illustrator of children's books about technology Vladimir A. Tambi. The work begins by deploying the montage principle of contrasting representations of opposed epochs familiar from the works examined at the start of this chapter.[38] Its first two pages feature full-page illustrations showing "how they worked back then" ("kak rabotali prezhde") and "how they work now" ("kak rabotaiut teper'"). The first shows a curvilinear landscape featuring a seaside factory that belches dirty smoke near fields that are being mowed by hand and a little village, complete with church. A ship with sails glides across a sea. The second shows a modern Soviet factory; rectilinear canals, fields, and docks; steamships; and fields being mowed by combines. The rest of the book, however, abandons the principle of contrasting temporal cells, leaving it in the past, as it were, and focuses all energy on describing further idealized Soviet spaces and phenomena. *What We Are Building* is a description of what is to be built in the course of the Five-Year Plan and offers readers in accessible yet technically precise pictures and words the central objects of the Soviet drive for industrialization and collectivization: hydroelectric stations, blast furnaces, combines, railroads, the Red Army, and so on. Between pages of illustrations and explanations, Savel'ev and Tambi offer space for readers' notes, with prompts that encourage children not only to study and remember the book's lessons but to record their own participation – for example, "How our school participates in socialist competition" ("Kak nasha shkola uchastvuet v sotssorevnovanii"). A full page is devoted to captioned pictures of the heroes of socialist construction (no victims are to be found here), as well as a line where the child is to inscribe "who I will be" ("kem ia budu"). The work ends with a map of the USSR that shows the locations of major projects of the Five-Year Plan, yet which is accompanied by a prompt to find out about others and inscribe them. If economic development is currently "uneven" in this map, the reader, together with the state, may envision the process of transformation that will institute homogeneous space and time across Soviet geography, which is now coherent and interlinked, rather than decomposed and disunited, as it had been in Shikhman's *How Four Railroad Kids Created a Pioneer Troop*, with which we began. The spatialization of revolutionary temporality has now been extended into a future that completely overshadows the present and past, a future that has become visible and predictable and the construction of which enlists the energies of the child-reader.

Another work from this same year presents one of the most striking examples of the new solidity and presence of the Soviet future brought by the Five-Year Plan. *Five-Year Plan* (*Piatiletka*), written and illustrated by Aleksei M. Laptev in 1930, dramatizes in its first pages the miracle of visualization that it sets out to perform for young readers:

The artist Laptev came into Gosizdat and asked the editor:
    – "Have you seen the Five-Year Plan?"
    – "What do you mean?" said the editor, who didn't get it.
    – "Have you seen the Five-Year Plan?" repeated the artist.
    – "What a question!" said the editor. "To see the construction of the Five-Year Plan, you'd have to travel over the whole country! Can you do such a thing sitting in Moscow?"
    – "You can," said Laptev.

– "Now that's interesting!" exclaimed the editor. "In the Five-Year Plan we are building new factories, plants and hydroelectric stations. We're organizing thousands of collective farms and printing millions of books. Who is going to show me that?"

– "I am," said the artist. And he put this book on the editor's table and said, "Look!"[39]

As Laptev's meta-story makes clear, the Five-Year Plan was revolutionary, not only
in what it would accomplish, but in the manner that it rendered the future suddenly
close and known for Soviet men, women, and children. Here, the force of art and
the political authority of Moscow can make the vision of the whole and of the future
tangible and present for young readers. Laptev's book is a lovely and inventive thing.
Utilizing maps, facts, and figures, it tells the story of the Five-Year Plan in terms of the
radical transformations it will make in the economic realities of the Soviet Union –
that is to say, it tells the story of the future. It solves the problem of the potential dryness of its statistics and facts and figures through engaging and bright illustrations
that create overlapping systems of line, colour, and perspective, and through a fold-
out technology that allows the reader to actively transform the economic situations of
the past into those of the future. Each of the book's ten fold-out pages is, in this sense,
a window into a concrete, shared future that the country as a whole is to bring into being, and that readers can create for themselves in the book (figs. 12.12 and 12.13). As
a spatialized representation of temporality, Laptev's book presents an image of time as
geographical integration and chronological synchronization.

Books such as these presented young readers with completely tangible images of
futurity associated with the monumental projects of the era. For instance, N. Shifrin's
Oktiabriatskaia (*Oktiabriata Book*, 1930) combines rhythmic children's verse with line
and colour drawings similar in their dynamism to those of Poret's *How the Revolution
Triumphed*, yet aimed at a dynamic engagement with socialist construction rather
than at a narration of past revolutionary dynamism. M. Gurevicha and A. Igumovna's
Kuznetsstroi: sotsialisticheskii gigant (*Kuznetsstroi: Socialist Giant*, 1932) contains inspiring images of the enormous scale and grandeur of the Kuznets steel plant, as well
as a narrative concerning heroic shock workers and Komsomol members, punctuated
by discussion of their antireligious campaigns. Konstantin Piskunov's *Komsomol'skoe
plemia* (*The Komsomol Tribe*, 1931) presents a seamless historical trajectory that leads
from the participation of youth in strikes and revolutionary organization in the tsarist era to the place of the young in the events of the 1905 Revolution, the October
Revolution, and the founding of the Komsomol, right up to the role of the Komsomol
in the Five-Year Plan. Piskunov's work links up scenes of revolutionary action in the
past with those of the Five-Year Plan in the present, ending with the proclamation that
"We are ready for future battles for a worldwide October!" ("My gotovy k budushchim
bitvam za mirovoi Oktiabr'!").

This new wave of children's literature in the years of the Five-Year Plan represents
a sea-change in conceptualizations of temporality – the rise to the fore in children's

12.12. Folded page from writer and illustrator Aleksei Laptev's interactive, foldout storybook, allowing young readers to "realize" the future results of the Five-Year Plan. *Piatiletka* (Moscow: Gosizdat, 1930), 11 (folded).

literature of what Buck-Morss calls "vanguard" temporality, the "'plan' that locks in future meaning," as a result of which "time's indeterminacy and openness is colonized."[40] Certainly, these books mark a major shift in their visions of the shape of the future. In place of the open horizons of revolutionary action, oriented toward the break with the past – the revolutionary rupture between montage cells – yet remarkably uncommitted with regard to programs, policies, and conceptualizations of the future, these later works present a world in which the contours of the future are clearly demarcated, graphable, and mappable, predictably arising from past revolutionary history. Furthermore, the

12.13. Unfolded page from Laptev's *Piatiletka*, 11.

range of these books, which of course participate in a broader visual culture of the Five-Year Plan, offers remarkably consistent and unified images of Soviet futurity. Huge factories tower in heroic profile. Electrical or other infrastructural networks stretching into the distance or hydroelectric dams are presented in sublime aerial views that command and control huge swathes of landscape, often with airplanes shown in the distance to rationalize the technology of vision instantiated in the image. Collectivized agriculture is shown in images of groups of tractors, progressing in staggered ranks across expansive fields. In contrast with earlier images of a socialist present as the mobilization of ordered human bodies in tension with an unchanged human environment, as in the conclusion of Shikhman's *How Four Railroad Kids Created a Pioneer Troop*, the human figure, still ordered in labour or a triumphant march, shrinks to tiny dimensions, dwarfed by the reality of the looming grandeur of an industrialized and collectivized future.

Yet for all of the concreteness of these images of futurity, it must also be said that they remained, for many young readers, merely images. The first two pages of Lipavskii and Tambi's *What We Are Building* claim to depict "how they worked back then" and "how they work now," yet, for the vast majority of Soviet children, these illustrations in fact presented "how we work now" and "how we may someday work in the future." Despite the triumph of the completion of the first Five-Year Plan ahead of schedule, for many readers socialist industry and agriculture as depicted in these works would always remain visions of a deferred future. With this disorienting double vision, *What We Are Building*, Laptev's *Five-Year Plan*, and many other picture books like them echoed the temporal indeterminacies of a new era of revolutionary temporality. In the words of Clark:

> The future, as represented in the official version of history – History – functioned in rhetoric as another Great Time – a time when life would be qualitatively different from present-day reality ... There was an absolute cut-off between actual historical reality and the "reality" of these official Great Times ... The meaning of all present-day reality was derived from its relationship with these mythic times.[41]

Rather than viewing these works, then, as an utter rejection of the revolutionary dynamism apparent in Soviet children's visual culture of the 1920s, the socialist realist modal incoherence of the early 1930s and later may be taken as a displacement of that of the earlier era, or its sublimation in works that, perhaps despite the best intentions of authors and artists, presented readers with ever new spatiotemporal figures of the problematic gap between revolutionary dynamism and grand plans for and maps of future achievements.

NOTES

1 Shikhman, *Kak chetvero zheleznodorozhnykh rebiat*. Vladimir Georgievich Bekhteev (1878–1971) was a significant avant-garde illustrator – a collaborator of Vassilii Kandinskii in the founding of the Neue Künstlervereinigung München in 1909 who was also associated with Der Blaue Reiter group. In the early Soviet period, he illustrated a number of children's books and Russian literary classics.
2 Eisenstein, "Dialectic Approach to Film Form," 50.
3 Shikhman, *Kak chetvero zheleznodorozhnykh rebiat*, 14.
4 Ibid., 15.
5 For a fuller exploration of "uneven development" in the geographical imagination of socialist modernity, see Michael Kunichika's contribution to the present volume.
6 On the consciousness-elementality dialectic, see Wolfe, *Revolution and Reality*, 135–58; Clark, *The Soviet Novel*, 19–24; Platt, *History in a Grotesque Key*, 26–30.
7 Oushakine, "Translating Communism for Children," 173.
8 As Karl Mannheim observed, all ideologies may be categorized by their orientation toward history. See Mannheim, *Ideology and Utopia*.
9 Clark, *The Soviet Novel*, 36–45, 142. Clark's terms are derived from Bakhtin, "Epic and Novel."

10 The example was taken nearly at random to represent the ubiquity of this idea in the 1920s. Tel'man, "VII Rasshirennyi plenum IKKI," 1.

11 See Flerina, "Opytno-issledovatel'skaia rabota po doshkol'noi knige," 5; Lilina, *Detskaia khudozhestvennaia literatura*, 61, 66; Trifonov, "Revoliutsionnaia detskaia kniga," 22–42, esp. 28–36.

12 Platt, *History in a Grotesque Key*, 130–44; Corney, *Telling October*; Rosenstone, "*October* as History."

13 Margolina, "Revoliutsionnaia literatura dlia detei," 57. The problem of representation of the revolution in children's literature as a historical and social process was recognized by Bolshevik propagandists from the first post-revolutionary years. See Kon, *Sovetskaia detskaia literatura*, 30.

14 Buck-Morss, *Dreamworld and Catastrophe*, 62–3.

15 Ibid., 67.

16 Ibid., 62.

17 Neverov, *Revoliutsiia*. The book features illustrations by Aleksei F. Pakhomov, a young protégé of legendary children's book illustrator Vladimir Lebedev (see below). For additional discussion of this and other of Neverov works, see Oushakine, "Translating Communism."

18 Einstein, "Notes on Cubism," 166.

19 For a discussion of Malevich's *Knife Grinder* and its relation to Italian futurist predecessors, see Milner, *Kazimir Malevich*, 57–8. On futurist books, see Janecek, *The Look of Russian Literature*, 19–25. For aesthetic and philosophical overviews of the problem of temporality in visual representation, see Gombrich, "Moment and Movement in Art" and le Poidevin, *The Images of Time*.

20 Levi, "Cinema by Other Means."

21 Eisenstein, "Dramaturgy of Film Form," 26.

22 Mayakovskii, *Oktiabr' 1917–1918. Geroi i zhertvy revoliutsii*, 15 (without numeration).

23 Both the automobilist and the priest are likely the work of either Puni or Boguslavskaia – Makletsov and Kozlinskii appear to have signed their contributions to the book. In style, too, the unsigned illustrations are more daring, avant-gardist compositions, incorporating elements of cubism and a freer style of representation than Kozlinskii's and especially Makletsov's signed illustrations.

24 Mayakovskii, *Oktiabr' 1917–1918. Geroi i zhertvy revoliutsii*.

25 These principles are also evident in the treatment of women in the book. The two female "heroes" are the "Seamstress" (*Shveia*) and "Washerwoman" (*Priachka*), both of whom the text exhorts rather than lionizes, and both of whom are presented in enclosed, claustrophobic spaces. Despite the efforts of the authors to include representatives of both genders among the positive figures, it seems that they could not bring themselves to view women as being as heroic as men.

26 On "new everyday life," see Fitzpatrick, *The Cultural Front*, esp. 1–15, 65–90; Neumann, "Revolutionizing Mind and Soul?"; Reznik, "Byt ili ne byt."

27 As Boris Gasparov observed in a seminal article, such a conception of animate objects as agents of social change may be traced from pre-revolutionary futurist circles to post-revolutionary children's literature. See Gasparov, "Moi do dyr." On Vladimir Lebedev's book illustrations in relation to avant-garde aesthetics, see Weld, "The Square as Regal Infant."

28 Marshak, *Vchera i segodnia*, 8.

29 Studenetskii, *Nashi vragi i druz'ia*.

30 Oushakine, "Translating Communism."

31 For an overview of the rise of the doctrine, see Van Ree, "Socialism in One Country."

32 *Mute Witnesses* has no substantive connection, apart from its title, to Evgenii Baur's 1914 film of the same name. All of Savel'ev's works were originally published in Leningrad by Detgiz. Later editions of *The Clock and Map of October* include three editions by the same publisher in

1969, 1970, and 1977 with new illustrations by Nikolai Liamin, and a 1980 edition published in Frunze by Mektep Press with illustrations by D. Cherikchiev. The discussion and page numbers below reference the first edition, of 1930. On Savel'ev's career as a children's author, see Shchekotov, "Marshrutom mysli i talanta."

33 All time codes refer to Eisenstein and Aleksandrov, *Oktiabr'*.

34 Eisenstein, "The Montage of Film Attractions," 36.

35 Savel'ev, *Chasy i karta Oktiabria*, 16–17.

36 Trifonov, "Revoliutsionnaia detskaia kniga," 31.

37 Ketlinskaia et al., "Detskaia literatura v rekonstruktivnyi period," 10.

38 Savel'ev and Tambi, *Chto my stroim*.

39 Laptev, *Piatiletka*, 1 (without numeration).

40 Buck-Morss, *Dreamworld and Catastrophe*, 62–3.

41 Clark, *The Soviet Novel*, 40.

BIBLIOGRAPHY

Bakhtin, Mikhail. "Epic and Novel." In *The Dialogic Imagination*, edited and introduction by M. Holquist, 3–40. Austin: University of Texas Press, 1981.

Buck-Morss, Susan. *Dreamworld and Catastrophe: The Passing of Mass Utopia in East and West.* Cambridge, MA: MIT Press, 2000.

Clark, Katerina. *The Soviet Novel: History as Ritual.* 2nd ed. Chicago: University of Chicago Press, 1985.

Corney, Frederick C. *Telling October: Memory and the Making of the Bolshevik Revolution.* Ithaca, NY: Cornell University Press, 2004.

Einstein, Carl. "Notes on Cubism." Translated and introduced by Charles W. Haxthausen. *October* 107 (2004): 158–68.

Eisenstein, Sergei. "A Dialectic Approach to Film Form." In *Film Form: Essays in Film Theory, and The Film Sense*, edited and translated by Jay Leyda, 45–63. Cleveland, OH: Meridan Books, 1957.

– "The Dramaturgy of Film Form." In *Film Theory and Criticism: Introductory Readings*, edited by Leo Braudy and Marshall Cohen, 6th ed., 23–40. Oxford: Oxford University Press, 2004.

– "The Montage of Film Attractions." In *The Eisenstein Reader*, edited by Richard Taylor and William Powell, 35–59. London: BFI Publishing, 1998.

Eisenstein, Sergei, and Grigorii Aleksandrov, *Oktiabr'*. DVD. Mosfilm. Moscow: Ruscico, 2010.

Fitzpatrick, Sheila. *The Cultural Front: Power and Culture in Revolutionary Russia.* Ithaca, NY: Cornell University Press, 1992.

Flerina, E.A. "Opytno-issledovatel'skaia rabota po doshkol'noi knige." In *Kakaia knizhka nuzhna doshkol'niku: sbornik*, edited by E.A. Flerina and E. Iu. Shabad, 5–15. Moscow: Gosudarstvennoe izdatel'stvo, 1928.

Gasparov, Boris. "Moi do dyr." *Novoe literaturnoe obozrenie*, no. 1 (1992): 304–19.

Gombrich, E.H. "Moment and Movement in Art." *Journal of the Warburg and Courtauld Institutes* 27 (1964): 293–306.

Janecek, Gerald. *The Look of Russian Literature: Avant-Garde Visual Experiments, 1900–1930.* Princeton, NJ: Princeton University Press, 1984.

Ketlinskaia, V., P. Chagin, T. Trifonov, K. Vysokovskii, and M. Dubianskaia. "Detskaia literatura v rekonstruktivnyi period." In *Detskaia literatura: kriticheskii sbornik*, edited by A. Lunacharsky, 9–12. Moscow: Gosudarstvennoe izdatel'stvo khudozhestvennoi literatury, 1931.

Kon, Lidiia. *Sovetskaia detskaia literatura, 1917–1927: Ocherk istorii russkoi detskoi literatury.* Moscow: Gosudarstvennoe izdatel'stvo detskoi literatury, 1960.

Laptev, A. *Piatiletka.* Moscow: Gosudarstvennoe izdatel'stvo, 1930.

Lenin, Vladimir I. "Doklad vserossiiskogo tsentral'nogo ispolnitel'nogo komiteta." *Polnoe sobranie sochinenii v 55 tomakh,* 5th ed. Vol. 42. Moscow: Izdatel'stvo politicheskoi literatury, 1970.

Le Poidevin, Robin. *The Images of Time: An Essay on Temporal Representation.* Oxford: Oxford University Press, 2007.

Levi, Pavle. "Cinema by Other Means." *October* 131 (2010): 51–68.

Lilina, Z.I. *Detskaia khudozhestvennaia literatura posle Oktiabr'skoi revoliutsii.* Kiev: Izdatel'stvo "Kul'tura" Gostresta "Kiev-pechat'," 1929.

Mannheim, Karl. *Ideology and Utopia: An Introduction to the Sociology of Knowledge.* Translated by Louis Wirth and Edward Shills. New York: Harcourt, Brace, 1955.

Margolina, S. "Revoliutsionnaia literatura dlia detei doshkol'nogo vozrasta." In *Kakaia knizhka nuzhna doshkol'niku,* edited by E. Flerina and E. Shabad, 50–63. Moscow: Gosudarstvennoe izdatel'stvo, 1928.

Marshak, Samuil. *Vchera i segodnia.* Illustrated by Vladimir Lebedev. Leningrad: Raduga, 1925.

Mayakovskii, V. *Oktiabr' 1917–1918. Geroi i zhertvy revoliutsii.* Petrograd: Otdel izobrazitel'nykh isskustv kommisariata narodnogo prosveshcheniia, 1918.

Milner, John. *Kazimir Malevich and the Art of Geometry.* New Haven, CT: Yale University Press, 1996.

Neumann, Matthias. "Revolutionizing Mind and Soul? Soviet Youth and Cultural Campaigns during the New Economic Policy (1921–8)." *Social History* 33, no. 3 (2008): 243–67.

Neverov, A. *Revoliutsiia: Rasskazy.* Moscow: Gosudarstvennoe izdatel'stvo, 1930.

Oushakine, Serguei. "Translating Communism for Children: Fables and Posters of the Revolution." *Boundary* 243, no. 3 (2016): 159–219. https://doi.org/10.1215/01903659-3572478.

Platt, Kevin M.F. *History in a Grotesque Key: Russian Literature and the Idea of Revolution.* Stanford, CA: Stanford University Press, 1997.

Reznik, Aleksandr. "Byt ili ne byt? Lev Trotskii, politika i kul'tura v 1920-e gody." *Neprikosnovennyi zapas,* no. 90 (2013): 88–106.

Rosenstone, Robert. "*October* as History." *Rethinking History: The Journal of Theory and Practice* 5, no. 1 (2001): 255–74.

Savel'ev, L. *Chasy i karta Oktiabria.* Leningrad: Detgiz, 1931.

Savel'ev, L., and V. Tambi. *Chto my stroim. Tetrad' s kartinkami.* Leningrad: Detgiz, 1930.

Shchekotov, Iu. "Marshrutom mysli i talanta." *Detskaia literatura* 3 (1985): 23–7.

Shikhman, Boris. *Kak chetvero zheleznodorozhnykh rebiat sozdali pionerskii otriad.* Illustrated by V.G. Bekhteev. Moscow: Molodaia gvardiia, 1926.

Studenetskii, N. *Nashi vragi i druz'ia.* Moscow: Izdatel'stvo "Krest'ianskaia gazeta," 1930.

Tel'man, Ernst. "VII Rasshirennyi plenum IKKI. Vnutripartiinye voprosy VKP(b). Preniia po dokadu tov. Stalina, Rech' tov. Tel'mana." *Pravda,* 18 December 1926.

Trifonov, T. "Revoliutsionnaia detskaia kniga." In *Detskaia literatura: Kriticheskii sbornik,* edited by A. Lunacharsky, 22–42. Moscow: Gosudarstvennoe izdatel'stvo khudozhestvennoi literatury, 1931.

Van Ree, Erik. "Socialism in One Country: A Reassessment." *Studies in East European Thought* 50, no. 2 (1998): 77–117.

Weld, Sara Pankenier. "The Square as Regal Infant: The Avant-garde Infantile in Early Soviet Picturebooks." In *Children's Literature and the Avant-Garde,* edited by Elina Druker and Bettina Kümmerling-Meibauer, 113–26. Amsterdam: John Benjamins, 2015.

Wolfe, Bertram D. *Revolution and Reality: Essays on the Origin and Fate of the Soviet System.* Chapel Hill: University of North Carolina Press, 1981.

chapter thirteen

"POOR, POOR IL'ICH": VISUALIZING LENIN'S DEATH FOR CHILDREN

DANIIL LEIDERMAN AND MARINA SOKOLOVSKAIA

Another boy, a little younger, came home from kindergarten crying. "What's wrong?" his mother pressed him. "Did someone upset you?" "I am afraid of Lenin," said the boy in a quivering whisper. "What?" said his mother, now equally scared. "Galina Nikolaeva said that Lenin is dead, but also alive, and that he really loves children."

Lev Rubinshtein, "In Your Mausoleum"

Lenin's death on 21 January 1924 proved to be a major upheaval in the public and private lives of Soviet citizens. In the wake of the civil war, with no precedent for the legitimate transfer of power in the post-revolutionary era, the death of the first Soviet leader could not but trouble the public. The trauma of Lenin's demise had to be forged into a unifying public event, precisely because the public's reaction was both diverse and intense. On 24 January, a special report on the Ural region issued by the Joint State Political Directorate (the Soviet secret police organization between 1923 and 1934, usually known as OGPU) already had documented a broad range of reactions, including lamentation, anger, sadness, disorientation, and optimism in the region. The record describes public reactions through short, concrete anecdotes and quotes: "He died at the wrong time … The time is such that the authority of a living, even if insane, LENIN is direly needed ... The intelligentsia and anti-Soviet elements are agitated. What is going to happen? Will there be repressions?"[1] Some organizing discourse was sorely needed to quell fears and organize public affect.

The party appropriated the dead Lenin, depriving him of the right to be a private individual after his demise. Instead, taking the place of the "collective" – body, history, desire – he condensed and represented for the masses the full spectrum of their feelings – first and foremost, the mourning and the loss associated with the era of the civil war and "war communism." This is why contemporaneous representations of the dead Lenin alternate between private being and political leadership. As the leader of a global revolutionary project, Lenin could not die, even if he died as a discrete being. In death, Lenin no longer belonged to himself, as every portrait and image superseded his actual body and private history. This was most pronounced in children's stories, where the effort to make the national tragedy pedagogical produced an unintentionally broad and occasionally ghoulish discourse of images and practices around Lenin's death and corpse.

Soviet children's books were both a rapidly expanding medium and a means to "wrestle children's literature from their enemies."[2] However, a unified position on what qualified as proper Soviet children's literature and what did not emerged only by the mid-1930s.[3] As a result, in the period of prolific publication occurring throughout the 1920s, Soviet children's literature was a palimpsest of heterogeneous materials ranging from more conventional animal and fairy tales to ideological works, like Nikolai Smirnov's *Dlia chego Krasnaia armiia* (*What the Red Army Is For*, 1927), that explained to children the new political reality and sought to integrate them as Soviet subjects.

Lenin's death shaped a genre of its own, ordering the plots of numerous children's books of the 1920s as the seminal event at their centre. For party authorities, the intensity of public feeling surrounding Lenin's death proved a particular challenge, and thus early children's books about his death were explicitly intended as an instrument for overcoming the trauma that society had collectively endured. Books from this time sought to explicate the leader's death as a political event. Such efforts were often at odds with the personal intensity of grief. A book titled *Leninu. 21 ianvaria 1924* (*For Lenin, January 21st, 1924*) collected a record of offerings: hundreds of wreaths from the various Soviet nations are photographed and documented, their inscriptions noted and translated into Russian (fig. 13.1). Metallic palm leaves, porcelain and paper flowers, ribbons, portraits of Lenin in various media, and other decorative offerings form a peculiar garden of death. The laying of wreaths performs and ritualizes the loyalty of the mourners and affirms both the power and authority embodied in the corpse and the revolution as the vibrant, strategic continuation of that power. Children and children's collectives also participated in the ceremonial offering of funerary wreaths for the occasion. From a contemporary vantage point, the children's active involvement in these morbid ceremonies may appear as the result of the new authorities' excessive efforts to propagandize youth. However, such efforts made the mistake of treating children as a blank, if bereaved, slate for positive pedagogical messages, rather than as the co-creators of a separate discourse, as innocent as it was morbid, as proper as it was surreal, and as informed by scary fairy tales and by parables of the new social order. Even after Stalin's death, children's books on the subject focused on other scenes and focal points, occluding the significance of the immediate experience of death's physical presence in children's books after the revolution. The intensity of the sight of Lenin's dead body was unprecedented for children's literature in the 1920s. This intensity changes in later texts, instead focusing on the solemn experience of seeing the dead Lenin displayed in the mausoleum, rather than

**ОСИРОТЕВШИЕ ДЕТИ
ПЕРЕЯСЛАВСКОЙ-ПОЛТАВСКОЙ
ДЕТКОММУНЫ им. ЛЕНИНА.**

ТЫ УМЕР, НО ЖИВЕШЬ
И ВЕЧНО БУДЕШЬ ЖИТЬ
В СЕРДЦАХ ТВОИХ ПИТОМЦЕВ.
СПИ ВЕЧНЫМ СНОМ,
НАШ ДОРОГОЙ ОТЕЦ.

Венок из ветвей живой ели с еловыми шиш-
ками, перевитый черной лентой.

(Размер 50×60 см.).

ОТ ДЕТЕЙ ПУШКИНСКОЙ ШКОЛЫ.

[Станция Пушкино, Северных жел. дор.].

ДОРОГОМУ ДЯДЕ
ИЛЬИЧУ.

Венок из металлических посеребренных паль-
мовых листьев. Внизу его прикреплено несколько
фарфоровых красных цветов гвоздики, лилии и
посеребренных листьев розы. Вокруг венка об-
вязана красная кумачевая лента.

(Размер 40 × 50 см.).

13.1. Examples of funeral wreaths for Lenin presented by grieving children. The top caption indicates, "the wreath was made from spruce brunches, with a black funeral band threaded through it." It was presented by "orphaned children from the Pereiaslavl'–Poltavskii Children Commune named after Lenin, who also wrote: 'You died, but you are alive, and you would be always alive in the hearts of your offspring (pitomtsev). Rest in peace, our dear father.'" *Leninu. 21 ianvaria 1924* (Moscow: GOZNAK, 1924).

overcoming the fact of his death. By 1927, Lenin increasingly appears as a portrait within the home, as a domesticated corpse, rather than as an acutely traumatic one.

Death was a familiar sight throughout Soviet history; especially for the numerous homeless or displaced children who survived the revolution and civil war. Sometimes death was a personal trauma, sometimes a meaningful memorial, sometimes a lurid spectacle. Lenin's death was not exceptional because it introduced children to the existence of death; it was exceptional because it was not like the deaths that they were already used to. Unlike the anonymous and nationally insignificant deaths of strangers in the street, or even of the children's own relatives, after Lenin's death, his face proliferated alongside assertions of his immortality. His death was collectively shared and collectively mourned in spectacles whose significance was conveyed directly to children. Here was a death that actually mattered, that called for mourning. At the same time, the impact of Lenin's death was articulated through the trope of familiarity, as a number of children's books directly relate his visage to that of a dead relative. Lenin embodied a shared death, and therefore his representations sought to unify and resolve the trauma of the civil war by converting it into the foundation of a new home.

Lenin's death not only unified public sentiment but also provoked the publication of numerous texts written by both the professional literati and enthusiastic amateurs in an effort to find meaning in his loss.[4] The two main motifs of these texts are the assertion that, although Lenin the man is dead, Lenin the leader of the world proletariat continues to live in the party and the people, and through the stated goal that Lenin's memory be preserved for posterity in the consciousness of the masses. Thus, in his article "Il'ich – Lenin," the activist and journalist Lev Sosnovskii writes:

> Yes, Lenin lives and will continue to live. We will make sure of it, as long as we have the strength. The first thing we will do in Russia, instead of building granite and marble monuments (there will be a time for them yet), is ensure that every hut and worker's hovel has a free little book on the life and works of Lenin. Such a book will be compiled by Lenin's closest students, written simply and clearly, printed on good paper in large font, equipped with a portrait and released in every language … This book will be distributed through schoolchildren, for it is the rare family that doesn't have a child in school. The second thing we will do is release a second, more detailed book about Lenin's life and works to distribute freely to every educational employee in our nation, as a guide to teaching Leninism in schools. Lenin will penetrate into corners where few have heard of him, and will win millions of minds and hearts with the work of communism.[5]

Children play a crucial role in this pedagogical project, as the front line of Lenin's invasion of the domestic. The public square and the monument are insufficient, the home must be conquered, and through children's books, children's pedagogy, and children themselves, Lenin will penetrate all corners of Soviet society. The emerging

Lenin embodies a clear, authoritative ideal, but one entrusted to the children's own patchwork and contradictory discourse.

The Children's Lenin

There are numerous records of children's experiences of Lenin's death.[6] Books on Lenin were one of the primary instruments in the development of his cult, especially when it came to media meant for children. In the 1920s, one of the most significant recurring plots of children's books on Lenin revolved around recording children's reactions to Lenin's demise and illustrating appropriate acts of grieving. Many writers tried to use this premise to affirm the simplicity and purity of the mutually invested relationship between Lenin and children. As Anatoly Lunacharsky wrote, Lenin's favourite things "are children and kittens."[7] However, this recurring premise conflicted with records of the children's reactions, which often disagreed with the overarching positive message. One such record of a child's reaction to Lenin's death from the days of mourning says: "Now his body has died, but his work lives on. We shouldn't be afraid without Il'ich." While this seemingly reinforces the intended positive pedagogical message, it also complicates it by mentioning the child's fear.[8] Another, spoken in the context of a mock funeral with one of the kindergarteners playing the part of Lenin, while the others circle the table as representatives of the public, asks "Our Lenin died; did yours die too?" This perplexing question opens an abyss between the intended pedagogical discourse on Lenin and the message that the children had received.[9]

There are other records indicating the intense emotional investment specific to children in this context, such as a child's drawing subtitled "All the adults have left, and only children remain around the grave."[10] Even this image should give us pause, suggesting that the children's grief exceeds the intensity of adult grief by an inexplicable margin. Where have the adults gone? Who is responsible for the children left behind? Is it the adults who lack a purity of feeling, or does the children's reaction represent an unmanageable excess?

Pavel Dorokhov's *Kak Petun'ka ezdil k Il'ichu* (*How Petun'ka Rode to See Il'ich*) was released three times, in 1925, 1927, and 1929, in different editions.[11] A film came before the first edition, as one of the very first Soviet children's movies, popularizing Petun'ka's story.[12] Dorokhov's text for children about Lenin's death is not just a literary narrative: it also relies on illustrations to construct its meaning. Neither the New Moscow edition of 1925 nor the Moscow Worker edition of 1927 indicates the names of the artists. However, the 1929 edition is illustrated by Petr Aliakrinskii (1892–1961), an acknowledged master of book illustration. The changing illustrations in each edition highlight a shift in the overall representation of the narrative, emphasizing different aspects of the plot of Petun'ka's encounter with Lenin, which remains consistent.

Petun'ka's father leaves him at an orphanage to save them both from starvation; in an evident substitution for his own father, Petun'ka constantly thinks about Lenin, conversing with his portrait. One cold winter morning, Petun'ka learns that Lenin has died and that every Soviet citizen, including children, may attend his funeral for a farewell. Petun'ka sneaks out at night, fleeing the orphanage and joining some homeless children at a railroad station, and heads to Moscow in a coal-bearing train. Along the way, he enters the stream of people heading to see Lenin. After twice visiting the House of the Unions, where Lenin's corpse lies, he decides to return home. Dorokhov recounts an adventure of socialization: the hero is unchanged psychologically, but, through a ritualistic act, Petun'ka acquires a proper understanding of death, not as a source of horror but as a shared social experience, allowing him to reintegrate into his new society, the Soviet orphanage.

The child-reader here receives a text that represents the civil war, hunger, the abandonment of children by their parents, homelessness, vagrancy, risk, bravery, solidarity, heroism, and death as obvious, necessary, and clearly explicable parts of life. Death appears to Petun'ka and the reader three times. The first encounter takes place when Lenin's portrait reminds the child of his late grandfather Nazar; the man in the portrait looks familiar, if not familial, and similarly dead. Death next appears when Petun'ka is placed in the orphanage and ruminates about the fate of his family and the proximity of death, while also dreaming of civil war heroism, in which the fantasy of the heroic act defers and escapes death indefinitely. Finally, the impact of Lenin's death prompts the protagonist to action. The books advocate a clear trajectory: the child is to leave the childhood home to find a new, adult home in Soviet society, through an engagement with death represented by Lenin, his corpse, and his portrait.

The scenes chosen for illustration in the different editions of Dorokhov's book mostly overlap. Thus, we see the same episodes of the protagonist gazing into Lenin's portrait or the long line of people waiting by the House of the Soviets amidst a mournful and grandiose urban landscape. Conversely, the protagonist has various adventures, which remain consistently invisible to the reader. Adventures like travelling in a coal wagon with other homeless children, or eating sausage for the very first time, have no accompanying illustration. At the same time, the different editions emphasize and represent very different images of the same event, altering their meaning in significant ways.

The covers of the first two editions both depict the line of people waiting in front of the House of the Soviets. Despite portraying the same scene, the 1925 and 1927 covers differ in their visual representation of the event. In the 1925 cover illustration (fig. 13.2), the crowds are made up of disparate bodies united into streams of dynamic energy snaking their way into the House of the Unions. They are placed alongside two narrow buildings, which ambiguously resemble a train rushing into the House of the Soviets. This visual ambiguity unifies the protagonist's train journey with the waiting throng as similar vectors of intense movement drawn toward Lenin's body. The letters

13.2. Cover of the 1925 edition of Pavel Dorokhov, *Kak Petun'ka ezdil k Il'ichu* (Moscow: Novaia Moskva, 1925), showing snaking crowds of mourners approaching Lenin's mausoleum.

in which the title is rendered emphasize the energy running through the scene. The House of the Soviets itself seems to be drawing in chaotic forces, transmuting them into an intense light that illuminates the whole square, while the combination of the building and the train (or wall) forms a bulwark between the public in the foreground and an encroaching darkness apparent in the background. The intense whiteness of the square is legible both as snow around the throngs and as light in the reflection on the windows. This cover describes the event of Lenin's death as both a turbulent gathering and a tense coiling of massive social energies into an explosive dynamism, while the brightness that bathes the scene in front of the House of Soviets wards off the darkness beyond.

In the 1927 cover (fig. 13.3), the line of mourners becomes static and anonymous, with the unitary crush of bodies broken only by the intimate scene of three men gathering around the fire in the foreground. This scene only emphasizes the monumental distance between these men and the House of the Soviets, which looms cyclopean in the background. The area around Lenin is designated in black, and is the most real and detailed part of the image, while the crush of bodies and the earth itself alternate as vague silhouettes in red and white. Once again, there is the sense of intense light throughout the scene, separating the colours into binary contrasts of red and white; once again, this light seems to penetrate the whole scene, with only the House of the Soviets in clear focus, followed by the campfire, which is still more of a silhouette than a visible object. Compared to the 1925 edition, the crowd is much less energetic, the line so static that it is possible and even necessary to build a campfire, while the House of the Soviets is larger and more intimidating. If the 1925 cover represented uncontrollable social energies coming together in the common purpose of mourning Lenin and warding off darkness, the 1927 cover represents the enormous distance and difficulty of reaching him, and darkness hangs like a solid block above the whole scene, creating a sharp contrast with the glowing roof of the House of the Soviets.

Aliakrinskii's cover for the 1929 edition (fig. 13.4) completely changes the scene, making it so that the audience no longer has to reach Lenin – because he was in their home all along. Instead of the line of people, there are only a boy and a girl, kneeling in an ill-defined but domestic space while lifting an improbably large and, if the scale is to be trusted, impossibly heavy portrait of Lenin. If the 1925 and 1927 covers emphasized the distance between the child reader and Lenin – in the first case, apparent as a coiling of social energies embodied in the crowds, and, in the second, as the static and burdensome obstacle of a looming iceberg – here Lenin is not distant at all. He is present immediately within the home, if somehow askew from the children in both his lack of colour and the misdirection of his gaze, past both the children and the reader. Here he is found as a massive portrait improbably lost in darkness and discovered by the children, and there is no explanation for why the children are clutching such a heavy portrait while kneeling – all descriptions within the story place it on the orphanage wall. However, the contrast between intense light and malevolent darkness

13.3. Cover of the 1927 edition of Pavel Dorokhov's *Kak Petun'ka ezdil k Il'ichu* (Moscow: Moskovskii rabochii, 1927), showing snaking crowds of mourners approaching Lenin's mausoleum.

13.4. Petr Aliakrinskii, cover art for the 1929 edition of Pavel Dorokhov's *Kak Petun'ka ezdil k Il'ichu* (Moscow: GIZ, 1929), showing two children lifting and admiring Lenin's portrait.

present in both other covers also remains here, as the children cast stark but hazy shadows indicating the presence of a bright light behind them, while the portrait's shadow is a dense and black. The light creates the impression that the children are rescuing the portrait from a cellar masquerading as the portrait's shadow.

The covers accentuate moments when the protagonist exits his world and enters the breadth of history. Lenin's death is integral to such scenes. By 1929, though, it was necessary to emphasize the return home, where Lenin would already be waiting to be discovered. Within the narrative, Petun'ka's repeated communion with Lenin's portrait becomes another boundary between private life and historical narratives, collapsing the two each time the portrait "speaks" with the boy: "suddenly it seemed to Petun'ka that Il'ich's round lips trembled in a gentle smile, his left, squinting eye winking wryly."[13] Presumably, children reading the book would gaze at the portrait, learn of Lenin's death, and get the chance to say their farewells to the beloved leader along with Petun'ka. By depicting children together with the portrait on the cover of the 1929 edition, and concluding the book with an image of a boy holding a sled and waving good-bye to the reader, Aliakrinskii represents history as a private and identifiable episode. However, his cover visualizes a converse motif, representing the modes of engagement with Lenin's portrait – gazing, conversation, identification – as universal responses shaped by history. Aliakrinskii transforms the brief episode of Petun'ka's conversation with the portrait into the story's central image: the act of gazing both anticipates the drama of the death and Petun'ka's journey, and concludes it upon his return. Petun'ka's act of gazing and identification expands to include readers, with Lenin's portraits enabling them to parallel and repeat Petun'ka's personal relationship with Lenin, but not necessarily with Lenin's corpse. This expansion makes Petun'ka's quest more accessible to the reader. Instead of travelling from Lenin's portrait in the orphanage to Lenin's corpse, and then back to Lenin's portrait and his true home in Soviet society, the reader is encouraged by the cover's change of emphasis to journey from Lenin's portrait at home to Lenin's portrait at home, omitting the corpse entirely.

Yet, even at the end of the 1970s, children's games would still include Lenin's corpse in irreverent adventures: "We had a legend that the body in the Mausoleum is a fake, while the real Lenin was smuggled out and buried somewhere in the Urals. When we were six to eight years old, we would dig around for the grave in our playground courtyard."[14] These children, seeking Lenin's "real" corpse, lived among a proliferation of his images in a textually mediated reality. Conversely, children of the 1920s possessed fewer opportunities to see Lenin's image, instead relying on the accounts of eyewitnesses and first-hand encounters to form powerful and immediate visual impressions fixated on Lenin as a corporeal body.

The visceral fixation on Lenin's corpse in 1920s children's narratives also changed, as death in the Soviet state became less of a public spectacle, shifting to the occlusion of the camp and prison. If children of the revolution related to Lenin's death through their own memories of corpses, children of the 1970s would encounter these books as ready sources of delightfully morbid imagery, divorced from the immediate experiences of Lenin's contemporaries.

Silhouettes

The 1925 edition of Dorokhov's book represented the experience of Lenin and Lenin's body as a source of intense magnetism, as evidenced by the cover, where streams of energy, embodied in the throngs of people, the train or wall, and the letters of the title hurtling toward the Palace of the Soviets, form a bulwark against a looming darkness. The central feature of the illustration in the 1925 edition persists and is even accentuated in the 1927 edition: both utilize silhouettes to great effect, shaping them through intense contrasts of light and dark.

In the 1925 edition, silhouettes are deployed for a variety of reasons. In the two-page image shown in figure 13.5), silhouettes serve to distinguish between the specific and defined bodies of the negative characters, such as the priest, on the one hand, and the generic unity of the positive Soviet crowd in front of the Palace of the Soviets on the other. In the image depicting Lenin lying in state (fig. 13.6), the silhouettes distinguish between Lenin's individuated and recognizable face and the anonymous unity of the assembled public. In both cases, silhouettes set up a unity of flesh, joining disparate bodies together and offering purposefully indefinite bodies for the reader to occupy: the Red Army soldier presented as a silhouette in the foreground explicitly invites the reader to inhabit his vantage point. The indistinctness of the silhouette offered to the reader as a surrogate body relies on strong contrasts. The iteration of solid blacks and whites produces alternating points of focus and indistinctness. In the image of Lenin's body, there are clear points of focus: Lenin's face and the children surrounding him are vividly lit up. The rest of the scene seems to fall into silhouette because of the intensity of the light bathing the focal points.

The use of silhouettes to link visual experience and social unity appears throughout Soviet children's books of the 1920s. For instance, in Piotr Zamoiskii's children's book *V derevne* (*In the Village*), illustrated by Vitalii Vermel', the opening short story "Lampa" (The Lamp) describes the boy Mot'ka, who, despite his parents' pleas, has become addicted to cigarettes. Neither threats nor persuasion motivate Mot'ka; however, the arrival of "a man with a big lamp" in the village drastically changes the situation. The arriving projectionist delivers a lecture on the dangers of smoking, using his projector (the "big lamp") to show the "terrifying lungs" of a smoker. The sight deeply unnerves Mot'ka: "His heart was pounding. He even started sweating."[15]

In the illustration accompanies the story (fig. 13.7), we see the silhouettes of spectators at the lecture, raising their hands to respond to the lecturer's questions. We see the lecturer's dramatic gesture pointing at the "terrifying" lungs on the slide. Vermel' emphasizes the piercing light of the shining slide, penetrating the gloom of

13.5. Silhouette of a snaking crowd of mourners below, with villainous characters above, in the 1925 edition of *Kak Petun'ka ezdil k Il'ichu*, 40–1.

13.6. Illustration of Lenin lying in state, in the 1925 edition of *Kak Petun'ka ezdil k Il'ichu*, 35.

13.7. Vitalii Vermel', illustration in silhouette of a young boy learning about the dangers of smoking, from Piotr Zamoiskii, "Lampa" in *V derevne* (Moscow: GIZ, 1925), 11.

the viewing hall, and he organizes his composition around the contrast between the dynamic gesture of the speaker, the light, and the static and receptive crowd of viewers. But what do they see, and what do we see?

In the depicted circle of light, we see two bent ovals in a faint shaky line, two ephemeral little clouds, hardly a spectacle capable of evoking terror. The substitution of an indistinct phantasm for the terrible immediacy of bodily imagery, or of the body highlighted with a blinding light bulb for the visceral sight itself, is a crucial and specific factor of this era's visuality, intended to moderate traumatic experiences of death on a social scale. Whether discussing Lenin or lung cancer, this visuality substitutes the spectacle of visceral death with its ultimate, intended meaning and leaves the spectacle itself to the imagination.

However, within this visuality, in *How Petun'ka Rode to See Il'ich*, the hidden, imagined spectacle of Lenin's bodily death is shown to be vividly and luridly intense. The sight of Lenin's corpse is represented as both blinding light and swallowing darkness, but, in both cases, the intensity of the visual experience overwhelms the intended message. For example, Petun'ka twice finds his way into the House of the Soviets, twice appearing before Lenin's coffin. The first time he "wanted to gaze at the face, but his eyes, cloudy with tears, could see nothing but a big, bright spot."[16] The second time, the hero thinks he sees Lenin smiling at him. The reader is confronted with the process of looking closely, but not seeing, experiencing much the same lack through a notable absence of illustrations. We also do not get to see Lenin's glowing visage; however, this absence conforms to the loss of vision experienced by the protagonist in his grief. Perhaps this blurring of the line between blindness and overwhelming sight informs some of the intense contrasts between light and darkness on each edition's cover.

Within the narrative and the images offered to us, we are like the protagonist, for, like him, we cannot and do not actually see Lenin. As a result, we too become vulnerable to Petun'ka's visions of a living Lenin smiling through his corpse. The protagonist's eyes take a while to adjust to the peculiar optics of seeing Lenin, forcing him to return to the coffin for conclusive evidence of Lenin's demise, only to find the ghoulish smile instead. Can this smile be depicted or illustrated as Petun'ka experienced it: as a repressed trauma made lucid, but also uncanny through repetition? Could such an illustration communicate Petun'ka's experience of sight, blindness, and revelation, his act of peering past the boundaries of life and death, without turning into surrealism or magical realism? The silhouettes and sharp contrasts of the illustrations emulate the blinding revelatory power of Petun'ka's vision, much like the lit-up silhouette of the lungs that so traumatized Mot'ka. The images both express and mitigate the visceral materiality of the exposed body, because they represent a physical desire, a present memory of violence, and an uncontrollable wave of public feeling that needs to be contained in a cohesive discourse. The silhouette is a way of discussing the body in public, specifically Lenin's body, with a sustained visual and emotional intensity, but without confronting the corpses of memory and the carcass of the leader. The silhouette in this book alleviates the trauma of Lenin's death by decorporealizing his body into a public unity, but the trauma nevertheless remains, resurfacing unpredictably. This is why, by the end of the 1920s, an opposite tendency in the representation of Lenin begins to dominate, and it is associated with Lenin's portrait rather than his silhouette.

The Corpse and the Portrait

If readers of the early 1920s could engage with Lenin as a symbolic, distant figure, readers of the mid- and late 1920s could access excerpts of Lenin's autopsy and other explicit descriptions of Lenin's body accompanying the accounts of his preservation and mummification. A deeply visceral discourse around Lenin's actual exhibited corpse gripped the public's imaginary. This discourse primed their visual expectations, making them associate the cultural impact of Lenin's death with his body, represented through a series of corporeal substitutions – from the actual mummy to the detailed descriptions of Lenin's corpus. This was not solely an effort to transform the traumatic bodily experience that Lenin's death encapsulated into a culturally mediated narrative. Lenin's image derived a portion of its power from the immediacy of the memory embodied and stabilized through the exhibition of Lenin's mummy, not only from the original's status as a "leader," "father," or "grandfather." This contact could even be imaginary, but its traces, acquired through first-hand accounts, films, or literary texts, were remembered as immediate and embodied.

Kuznetsov's 1925 book *Lenin i krest'ianstvo* (*Lenin and the Peasantry*) embeds a jarringly physical image in a pastoral idyll. The illustrated cover depicts a peasant embracing an enormous haystack in a field of titanic clovers, a veritable Garden of Eden. In this promised kingdom of plenty, Lenin's portrait appears above, in an insert that separates his space from the peasant and his field. Lenin smiles and gazes at the peasant, both removed from the scene and in obvious continuity with it – in reality, he is elsewhere, but he is able to see the peasant in his promised land. The insert with Lenin connects black-and-white reality and the peasant's colourful world while leaving Lenin invisible and omniscient, as though he were haunting the peasant or looking at him from the vantage point of God. The barrier between the realistic black-and-white portrait and the colorful drawing is vivid: Lenin emerges from the heart of an authentic reality, hinting at both the authenticity of the text and its unreality, as well as at his own trans-temporal, visionary omnipresence. The cover brings together the Edenic illustration and the real Lenin to signify their eternal unity. At the same time, the opening text is unnervingly physiological: "Vladimir Il'ich's blood vessels (or veins through which the blood runs) have long since started hardening." This visceral opening is the preface to several politically educational texts, whose claim to authority is affirmed by their proximity to Lenin's flesh. Lenin's portrait on the cover directs the reader into the interior of his veins, as a material documentary signifier of the future reality of the unreal, fairy-tale image of the peasant's idyll. This "document" reifies Lenin's corpus into a paradoxical and deeply perverse relationship with reality. Even the supposedly clarifying statement "veins through which the blood runs" does not properly clarify, as the (presumably young) reader learns the textbook definition of "blood vessels" but not the significance of Lenin's hardening veins to the subject matter at hand. Lenin's veins unnerve an adult reader instead of evidencing the reality of the unreal, idealized farmland. In a child reader, they more likely evoke pity for Lenin's complicated illness and curiosity at the grotesquely physical detail.

Anna Grinberg's 1929 *Rasskazy o smerti Lenina* (*Stories of Lenin's Death*) for young children includes passages recounting Lenin's demise as a drama of bodily disintegration. "Suddenly his arm and leg lost feeling, … suddenly he lost his tongue … Ten doctors opened his body. Everything was healthy, firm, strong. Only the brain was in ruins."[17] While the tone of Grinberg's passage tries to approximate a medical discourse, it involuntarily comes to resemble mythic or fairy-tale narration, with ten doctors performing a mysterious ritual. Many other children's stories fixate on Lenin's corpse, and all the surrounding emotions, through jarring, surreal, and morbid imagery. In such stories, the pedagogical intention is to present "Uncle Lenin" as the leader of the nation, chief of the proletariat, and provider of daily bread, but also as a private individual who has a mother and a wife, who lives in a world of familiar objects and routines. Yet here, dismembered by ten doctors, he also appears as an individual with a broken brain, whose hardening veins in an otherwise healthy body mean something indeterminate for society – in short, an interesting monster from a scary story.

In texts from 1924, ceremonies of saying farewell to Lenin's body appear to be key events in the lives of children in orphanages and kindergartens, and also a major motif of children's games and drawings. Such drawings often fixate on the visual imagery surrounding the corpse (flags, Lenin's suit) alongside accounts of lamenting adults, their tears and spoken farewells. Adult texts surrounding Lenin's death represent the leader as a symbolic figure who points the way into the future. Conversely, children's texts preserve Lenin as a private, visceral body: children prefer to look at Lenin's corpse rather than to follow his gaze into the future.

The difference between these two optical discourses around Lenin – between adult allegories of Lenin as a symbol of future progress and children's narratives of Lenin as a familiar and physical (if undead) presence – is resolved only through a shared engagement, direct or recounted, with his portrait. This engagement unifies all three discourses – Lenin as the great leader, Lenin as the simple man, and Lenin as Koshchei the Deathless – in a single, ritualized act of communion through the act of gazing. The portrait reassembles Lenin's corpse, enthroning it within the home. The portrait restores the dismembered Lenin to a bodily unity.

In the 1925 edition of *How Petun'ka Rode to See Il'ich*, the first image inside the book represents a silhouette of a girl and a boy near Lenin's portrait (fig. 13.8), surrounded by signs of domestic comfort. However, the passage in the text where Lenin

13.8. Illustration showing two children in domestic comfort admiring Lenin's portrait, in the 1925 edition of *Kak Petun'ka ezdil k Il'ichu*, 3.

winks at Petun'ka transforms this domesticity. Lenin is meant to beckon the children into the outside world, into engaged and responsible adulthood, from his privileged and authoritative position in the home. Instead, however, the text makes Lenin into a vivid corpse who is both dead and immortal, and currently resides in a discomfortingly familiar portrait. In the image, Lenin doubles the boy as a fellow silhouette, indicating a unity of purpose that is noticed by the girl, whose gesture suggests apprehension or surprise. Such silhouettes in early Soviet children's books create both sharp contrasts and unitary bodies to stabilize and channel the outpouring of grief over the death of the leader. Portraits sought to harness these desires and return them home, both literally and symbolically.

In 1924, kindergarteners played "Lenin's funeral," transforming the fact of his death, and the raw immediacy of his corpse, into a ludic engagement.[18] Their gazes were turned to Lenin's body first and to portraits of him second, shifting from one to the other, if not in reality, then in the course of reading books on his death. As Lenin's death became more distant, by the late 1920s, the portrait was increasingly substituted for direct physiological and haptic links to the corpse, forging a continuity between body and portrait. A visitor to the mausoleum in 1956 recalls, "We entered. Lenin and Stalin strongly resembled portraits. When I grew up and started to understand, I realized they were made up to resemble their portraits. Their bodies are intangible, as though vacating. There was the feeling that they had laid themselves down there straight from their portraits."[19]

The inseparability of the body and the portrait consolidates by the 1930s, when numerous texts begin to manipulate the reader's attention and gaze, instead of testifying to the documentary reality of the immediate experience of Lenin's death. Such texts are no longer eyewitness accounts, but are explicitly fictions, and Lenin's physical presence, so common in narratives of the 1920s, is absent from their plots and metaphors, substituted by a consolidated hybrid of body and portrait. The repetition and proliferation of Lenin's body, both as corpse and as portrait, becomes a crucial component of his identity in the public imaginary. If the silhouette haunts the early children's books as Lenin's shade, there to restrain the raw experience of his corpse, the portrait restores Lenin's body and spirit into a corporeal unity within the home.

This shift informs the powerful desire to possess Lenin's portrait that is evident in children's narratives. One account of a child's recollection of the line to the House of the Soviets reads, "Vendors of little portraits of Lenin walk along with the crowd. The crowd is silent. Everyone wants to have one, to show the others that you too are bearing the weight of the loss."[20] Children cut portraits of Lenin out of newspapers or ask for them as presents, and assemble Lenin corners with them. In Dorokhov's story, the children of the orphanage decorate Lenin's portrait on the wall with a wreath they themselves made, which they hang underneath a slogan that reads "Dear Lenin, we love you and are sorry for you!" The portrait on the wall comes to represent grief: in the 1925 edition, a boy decorates a wall with an arrangement around a funerary portrait of Lenin (fig. 13.9) while, in the 1927 edition (fig. 13.10), children are depicted weeping together by its side. These images reproduce children's mourning as immediate and corporeal, but somewhat uninterested in the social project that is supposed to embody Lenin for futurity and posterity. Notably, if in the 1925 edition both Lenin and the child appear as dense black silhouettes whose intensity is not matched by the rest of the scene (for instance, the other pictures and slogan appear as defined objects), in the 1927 edition, both the children and Lenin portrait have defined faces, clothes, and shading.

In Pavel Ial'tsev's play *K Leninu* (*To Lenin*, 1925), the eleven-year-old Grishut'ka runs away from home to say good bye to Il'ich. The play's publication didn't include a single image, but a portrait is central to the lives of the protagonists. Before deciding to run away to see Lenin, Grishut'ka examines Lenin's portrait along with his sister Katiushka in their family hut. Katiushka asks, "What do you think, does the real Lenin look like that?" Grishut'ka responds, "If they draw him looking like this, then this is what he looks like."[21] In Dorokhov's books, the orphans Petun'ka and Katiusha compare Lenin's forehead with the forehead of their "late grandfather Nazar"; Grishut'ka and his sister compare Lenin's bald head with "grandfather Efim's" pate. To all these children, Lenin's portrait looks like someone familiar, someone close to them and embedded in their daily lives, but, most importantly, someone dead. Familiar, and even dear, but dead.

Grishut'ka explicitly wants to say farewell, while Petun'ka motivations are described a bit differently. In the latter's story, the children listen to their teacher's tales of Lenin, examine illustrations in the newspaper, and enquire if everyone is allowed to

13.9. Illustration showing child assembling a ceremonial wall display for Lenin, in the 1925 edition of *Kak Petun'ka ezdil k Il'ichu*, 11.

bear witness to his body. They "envied those children they could see in the newspaper pictures," envied their immediate access to Lenin's desirable corpse.[22] Their desire pushed them toward flight, leading the protagonists to leave their home, suffer various difficulties (including the risk of being captured by a train conductor or Red Army soldier) and deprivations (having to ride in a coal-car, forgo food, stand in line in the freezing cold). Lenin's actual body represents something acutely traumatic and desirable, and Lenin's portrait seeks to harness both this trauma and desire.

The 1929 edition of *Petun'ka*, whose cover reconfigures the encounter with the portrait as the central scene, represents Lenin's portrait as a literal opening to the outside, where the act of gazing at the portrait pushes the protagonist outward, into the greater world, channelling the trauma of Lenin's passing into a useful pedagogical project. The portrait encourages the children to transform their tragedies (in the plural, as this generation certainly suffered more than just Lenin's death) into a positive social project. It is no coincidence that Aliakrinskii's first illustration for Dorokhov's book after the cover shows children facing Lenin's portrait adjacent to a globe: he evokes Lenin to charge children with responsibility for the future of the world. Their journey is a crucial part of this charge, depicting a troubled and unhappy world that gradually transforms in later books, such as those by Ivan Molchanov and Sergei Kostin, into an Edenic urban landscape of realized socialism.

In all cases, the children are charged to return home eventually. However, the moment of return virtually never appears in these books. For instance, Dorokhov's illustrators depict a boy, bread, a coffin, even some evil bourgeois, but never a home. These signifiers range from ambivalently neutral to directly confrontational but are never

13.10. Illustration showing children crying and mourning Lenin through a ceremonial wall display, in the 1927 edition of *Kak Petun'ka ezdil k Il'ichu*, 13.

necessarily domestic. The only real signifier of domesticity remains the portrait itself, still in its original position on the wall, where it once prompted the child protagonists to seek Lenin, and where it will receive their return into the home and Soviet society.

In Ivan Molchanov's 1927 *Kol'ka and Lenin,* the protagonist similarly dreams of meeting Lenin while gazing at his portrait in anticipation. Just when Kol'ka and his father travel to Moscow to meet him, Lenin dies, and Kol'ka daydreams of meeting the leader and speaking with him. This imagined conversation is illustrated with an image of railroad lines and a train depot (fig. 13.11). The artist does not make the meeting visible, offering instead an image of displacement and travel, of universal homelessness and energetic movement. Lenin's portrait and corpse remains fixed, invisible but central points that both come to coincide with the child's home.

Lenin's Homecoming

In the official discourse aimed at children, Lenin acquires a new grave in the home, where children can lament his passing and return him to life. This domesticity relies

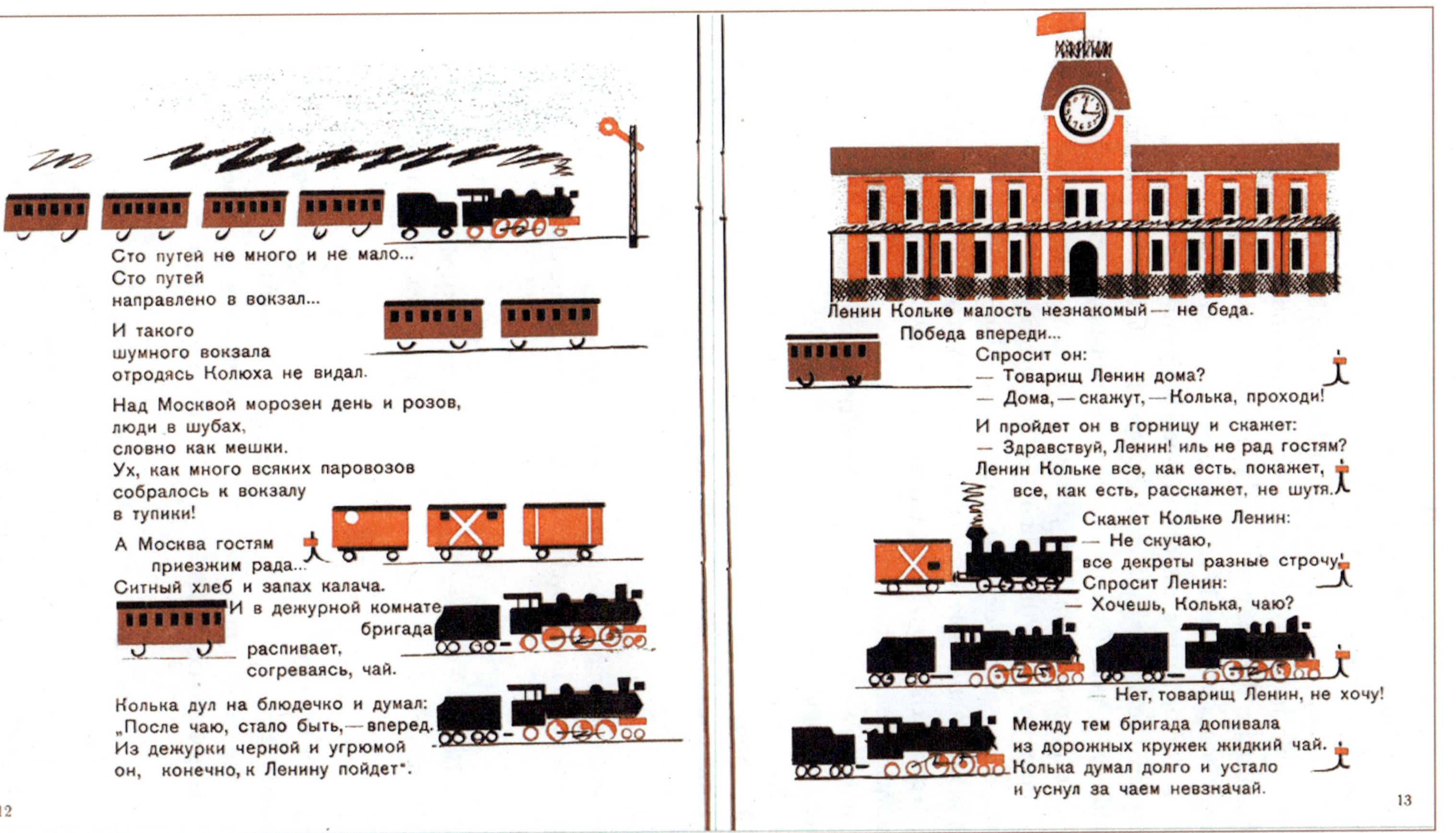

13.11. S. Kostin, illustration showing railroads and a train depot in dynamic movement through the text, in Ivan Molchanov, *Kol'ka i Lenin* (Moscow: GIZ, 1927), 12–13.

on the imagining of Lenin's non-death as embodied in his portrait. Children's trips to Ulyanovsk to Lenin's home relied on the corporeal familiarity of Lenin, depicting him through mundane domesticity rather than heroic futurity. Depictions of Lenin's life from the 1920s emphasize the simplicity and poverty of his home. Lenin's proletarian poverty has little in the way of impactful visual expression in such early accounts – a lack of home rather than the presence of a poor one. Characteristically, in the majority of children's books from the 1920s, Lenin seemingly lacks a home, even in the sense of the eternal domicile. For instance, in Dorokhov's story, the teacher describes how "Il'ich appeared before the children as though alive. He hid from foes, built a tent in a field and lived there."[23] Quite unlike the homeless Lenin hiding in his tent, the children of the orphanage, given up by parents unable to house or feed them, lived well, gathered under the comforting light of the "dark-green lamp," and enjoyed pies with tea from a copper teapot, depicted in the 1925 edition in an illustration where the children sit around the table with tea, listening to the tale.[24] The comforting domesticity protects the children from the terrors of death and history, presumably suffered by the homeless Lenin in his tent.

Lenin's homelessness (except as a portrait) and corporeal suffering were both calculated to prompt a heroic or pedagogical discourse but were distorted by the children's discourse into a pitiful but positive image of a vulnerable and dead Lenin looking for a home. Instead, inverting the uncanny, here an authoritative discourse of political power and violence was denatured into a sympathetic tale of a scary but loveable *vurdalak*, the traditional Slavic vampire: a walking corpse that haunts the homes of the people it loved most in life.

Anna Grinberg offers the following poem composed by children as a particularly startling example of Lenin's lovable homelessness and vulnerability in the eyes of the children:

You died, Il'ich!	Ты умер, Ильич!
And you are all alone now,	И ты остался совсем один,
Poor, poor Il'ich!	Бедный, бедный Ильич!
You were nice,	Ты был хороший,
I will give you my room	Я отдам тебе мою комнату,
And I love you.	И я тебя люблю.
You will be in the world again,	Ты опять будешь на свете,
And we are going to touch you.	И мы будем тебя трогать.[25]

In order to reach Lenin, children had to leave their home, become adults in the dangerous outside world, and find a new home in Lenin's image and mission for the future. The intended pedagogical content of the books about Lenin's death was to point children outwards, into Soviet reality, as a space that they had to brave, if not conquer, just as Lenin did in his tent and as Petun'ka did in his quest. However, the outcome is rather different. As the poem shows, children imagine Lenin as a sympathetic, displaced, and lonely wandering corpse that must be welcomed into the home and offered the children's room, in an impractical gesture more appropriate for an imaginary friend than a national leader. The final line, "and we are going to touch you," again exhibits the peculiarity of Lenin's visceral presence in the children's imaginary.

For Freud, the uncanny is the familiar and domestic made distressing and discomforting through the interrelated processes of repression and repetition. In children's narratives of Lenin's death, we see the inversion of the uncanny: instead of something domestic becoming terrifying or uncomfortable, a monumental, authoritarian power appears as the embodiment of death but is made familiar and domesticated through children's repetitive play with images of Lenin, alive and dead.

Since the late 1920s, Lenin exists in Soviet children's literature primarily as a kindly undead monster crawling from his grave to visit those who love him most, a monster who may be in the mythic Kremlin or buried in the playground sandbox, just waiting to be found, dug up, and brought home, alive once more. The peculiar image voiced by a child in one work – "all the adults have left, and only children remain around the grave" – is meant to sound reverential but instead sounds disturbingly ludic, especially when read in conjunction with lines such as "we are going to touch you." Lenin becomes a sad and lonely corpse to be pitied, invited inside, and lovingly poked. His portrait, the sole permissible object of possessive ownership, a sign of loyalty and an assertion of adulthood, also becomes the bearer of inverted uncanny energies within the home. When coming alive to wink or smile, as is depicted in children's literature, the portrait becomes an automaton that crosses the line between life and death, a symbol of Lenin's blood and flesh as much as of his vision and mission, codified through expectations gleaned from fairy tales and horror stories – a symbol productively misunderstood and recontextualized into an appropriate project for strange games. Children often play at funerals, but rarely for national leaders or with the expectation that the dead will come shuffling back into their homes, looking just like their beloved portraits. Lenin becomes a double for the home, welcoming children into the dread and creeping horror of Soviet adulthood.

NOTES

1 *PP OGPU po Uralu* #1, 24 January 1924, 60. TSOOSO, f.4, pp.2; dok. 61 (Gosudrastvennye informatsionnye svodki oblastnogo otdela OGPU), p. 60.

2 "In 1921, at the end of the civil war, the book industry hit its lowest level ever, delivering to the market only 33 book titles for children ... In 1926 there were already 936 titles." Oushakine, "Translating Communism for Children," 165.

3 Ibid., 178.

4 See Tumarkin, *Lenin Lives!*, 134–64.

5 Sosnovskii, "Il'ich – Lenin," 54.

6 Lin, *Deti i Lenin* (1924) and *Lenin i deti* (1925); Sats, *Deti o Lenine*. These books all had similar contents: poems, recollections, children's essays and eavesdropped conversations, drawings and their titles, all consolidated into a faltering and jubilant speech about the significance of Lenin in the lives of Soviet children.

7 Lunacharsky, *Vladimir Il'ich Lenin*, 9.

8 Grinberg, *Il'ich*, 7.

9 Orlova, *Deti-doshkol'niki o Lenine*, 20.

10 Ibid., 56.

11 Pavel Dorokhov (1886–1942) perished in the Great Terror, and his books ended up in the "special depository" ("spetskhran") for politically problematic books.

12 In her lectures collected in *The Birth of Film for Children*, K.K. Paramonova writes that the film *How Petun'ka Rode to See Lenin* was shown consistently in theatres over the course of several years and that the documentary scenes of Lenin's funeral contained in it were enthusiastically received by the public.

13 Dorokhov, *Kak Petun'ka ezdil k Il'ichu* (1925), 10.

14 Recollection recorded by Marina Sokolovskaya in Yekaterinburg, 2012.

15 Zamoiskii, *V derevne*, 11.

16 Dorokhov, *Kak Petun'ka ezdil k Il'ichu* (1925), 37.

17 Grinberg, *Rasskazy o smerti Lenina*, 5–7.

18 See Prokof'eva, *Deti-doshkol'niki o Lenine*.

19 Interview recorded by Marina Sokolovskaya in Perm in 2014.

20 Grinberg, *Il'ich*, 29–30.

21 Ial'tsev, *K Leninu*, 13.

22 Dorokhov, *Kak Petun'ka ezdil k Il'ichu* (1929), 12.

23 Ibid., 11.

24 Ibid., 16–17.

25 Grinberg, *Il'ich*, 47–8.

BIBLIOGRAPHY

Dorokhov, Pavel. *Kak Petun'ka ezdil k Il'ichu*. Moscow: Novaia Moskva, 1925.

– *Kak Petun'ka ezdil k Il'ichu*. Moscow: GIZ, 1927.

– *Kak Petun'ka ezdil k Il'ichu*. Moscow: GIZ, 1929.

Grinberg, Anna, ed. *Il'ich: Detskie rasskazy i stikhi o Vladimire Il'iche Lenine*. Moscow: Novaia Moskva, 1924.

– *Rasskazy o smerti Lenina*. Photo collages by Sergei Sen'kin. Moscow: GIZ, 1929.

Ial'tsev, P. *K Leninu! Detskaia teatral'naia p'esa v trekh kartinkakh*. Moscow: GIZ, 1925.

Kuznetsov, I. *Lenin i krest'ianstvo*. Moscow: GIZ, 1925.

Leninu. 21 ianvaria 1924. Moscow: Tipografiia fabriki "Goznak," 1924.

Lilina, Zlata, ed. *Velikii uchitel'. Leninskaia khrestomatiia*. Illustrated by school children from the 4th Experimental MONO School. Leningrad: Gosudarstvennoe izdatel'stvo, 1924.

Lin, Il'ia, ed. *Deti i Lenin*. Photomontages by Gustav Klucis and Sergei Sen'kin. Moscow: Molodaia gvardiia, 1924.

–, ed. *Lenin i deti*. Photomontages by Gustav Klucis and Sergei Sen'kin. Moscow: Molodaia gvardiia, 1925.

Lunacharsky, A. *Vladimir Il'ich Lenin*. Leningrad: GIZ, 1924.

Orlova, Rebeka, ed. *Deti-doshkol'niki o Lenine*. Moscow: GIZ, 1924; reprinted St. Petersburg: Krasnyi matros, 2007.

Oushakine, Serguei. "Translating Communism for Children: Fables and Posters of the Revolution." *Boundary* 243, no. 3 (2016): 159–219. https://doi.org/10.1215/01903659-3572478.

Paramonova, K.K. *Rozhdenie fil'ma dlia detei (Nekotorye voprosy istorii det. kinematografa 1918-1925 gg.)* Moscow: N.P., 1962.

Rubinshtein, Lev. 2006. "V Mavzolei tvoiu." *Stengazeta*, 19 October 2006. http://stengazeta.net/?p=10002186.

Sats, Natal'ia, ed. *Deti o Lenine.* Moscow: Novaia Moskva, 1925.

Sosnovskii, L. "Il'ich-Lenin." *V dni skorbi. 21 ianvaria–27 ianvaria 1924 g.* Moscow: Moskovskii rabochii, 1925.

Tumarkin, Nina. *Lenin Lives! The Lenin Cult in Soviet Russia.* Cambridge, MA: Harvard University Press, 1983.

U velikoy mogily. Moscow: Krasnaia zvezda, 1924.

Zamoiskii, P. *V derevne. Rasskazy dlia detei.* Illustrated by V. Vermel'. Moscow: GIZ, 1925.

chapter fourteen

YOUNG SOLDIERS AT PLAY: THE RED ARMY SOLDIER AS ICON

STEPHEN M. NORRIS

Conscious of the way images could be used as weapons in the battle to create communism, Soviet-era children's book illustrators attempted to fashion a particular visual pathway for young people to "see Soviet." One important means to accomplish this aim was through repetition: again and again (and again), Soviet children were encouraged to engage in what might be called "ocular play." This game consisted of having fun through seeing but, in doing so, also accomplishing the greater aim of building a better society. One icon in this game was the Red Army soldier, who served as a model for how to become Soviet. Looking at books about the Red Army allowed Soviet children to imagine themselves taking part in the serious fun of building socialism, guarding the socialist motherland, and transforming themselves into socialist subjects.

Story I: Two Boys at Play

Ivan and Stepan live in the countryside. One day a Red Army detachment arrives and marches through the town, singing a jaunty tune. The two boys stop playing and watch. Ivan asks Stepan, "Why do we need a Red Army?" Stepan suggests "So that they can sing songs" (fig. 14.1). Nikolai Smirnov's 1927 children's book *Dlia chego krasnaia armiia* (*What the Red Army Is For*) opens with this scene. The vignette serves as a way to draw young readers into a lesson about what the Red Army means for Soviet society. Through the observant, questioning eyes of Stepan and Ivan, young readers learn about the Red Army's activities. They soon understand that their initial view of the Red Army as all fun and games (or songs and singing) is a little off the mark. The next pages of the story establish a pattern that will be followed throughout: the two boys are separated by the text from the more dominant image of Red Army soldiers.

14.1. In this image, Ivan and Stepan stare at a column of marching soldiers. When Ivan asks what the Red Army is needed for, Stepan suggests it's so they can sing songs. Galina and Ol'ga Chichagova's illustration invites the viewer to take Ivan and Stepan's viewpoint. Illustration from Nikolai Smirnov, *Dlia chego Krasnaia armiia* (Moscow: Molodaia gvardia, 1927), 3.

We do not see the boys' faces; rather, the viewer is encouraged to read the story through their eyes. Galina and Ol'ga Chichagova depict the two boys rather simply, each one wearing the clothes and caps that identify them as lower class and thus the "right" class for the lesson offered on these pages. Emblazoned in red is the word "Pekhota" (infantry), providing one of the story's pedagogical aspects: the youngest readers are meant to learn the word and to associate it with the accompanying picture of a dozen Red Army soldiers marching in two rows toward the reader. More detailed text that tells the story of Ivan and Stepan allows more advanced readers a chance to delve more fully into their experiences, thus making this book a combination picture narrative and illustrated book.[1]

What do Ivan and Stepan see? The members of the detachment wear the recognizable peaked cap, or *budenovka*, of a Red Army soldier and are visually represented as a purposeful collective. Some of the soldiers do not have facial features; instead, they are depicted as embodying the iron discipline required of all defenders of the Soviet

Union. Our eyes, like Ivan's and Stepan's, are drawn to the red star on top of the caps of the soldiers, the red rifles slung over their shoulders, and the red word "infantry."

As Ivan and Stepan continue to follow the soldiers, they see them in trenches, crouched down, and readying their rifles for defence. Ivan and Stepan note that the Red Army soldiers are no longer singing. They may now, the two boys wonder, be playing hide-and-seek. The two boys go on to receive other lessons on how soldiers fly airplanes, work with telephones, fire a howitzer, ride in the cavalry, drive motorcycles, fight in tanks, dispense gas while wearing masks, shine floodlights to protect the country from infiltration, and ultimately stand guard. The two ask questions of each other, drawing the young reader into the story. When they hear a cannon's roar, they initially hide in the bushes before they realize it's just the Red Army properly loading and firing it. Throughout their adventure, the two boys still believe that Red Army work is fun, full of games that they can mimic (and, by extension, the young reader can engage in the same imaginary play). Their lessons are accompanied by repetitive visual packaging: the soldiers retain their basic shape, their uniformity, their peaked caps, their red stars, their red rifles.

Smirnov's story and the Chichagovas' illustrations narrate the role the Red Army plays in defending the Soviet motherland but also makes army work appear to be exciting: young readers can see with Ivan and Stepan that being in the army means holding guns, flying planes, riding horses and motorcycles, and defusing bombs. The story concludes with a Red Army commander encouraging the boys to learn that the Red Army exists for them and that they too can aspire to be part of it. His back is to us while the boys face us: the lesson has been learned, the image suggests, and now the boys are ready to learn from the officer and to take that knowledge back home (fig. 14.2).

The young Soviet reader can now look directly at the two boys and see himself in their faces (the book was aimed primarily at young boys). As the commander explains, the actual Red Army is not really a game, for soldiers must defend the country, its workers, and its peasants. At home, however, and for the time being, the boys can play at soldiers. They conscript some friends, dress in the same red peasant shirts, grab wooden rifles, and march in the disciplined, uniform fashion they have just observed. After observing the Red Army in action, the book concludes that "when they [Ivan and Stepan] played Red Army, they knew what the Red Army was needed for and how it worked."[2]

What the Red Army Is For, like so many other children's books from the time that focus on patriotism and defence of the Soviet motherland as essential values for young children to embrace, casts Ivan and Stepan as symbolic models for readers to follow. They are not so much representations of actual Soviet children as they are imagined ideals. In this role, the two boys invite their peers to ask the same questions, have the same patriotic fun, and learn the same lessons that they do. By the end, the Red Army commander becomes the adult who intones the didactic message to Ivan and Stepan. Play at soldier, he instructs, but remember that the Red Army is protecting you.

ЧАСОВОЙ

Стоит красноармеец с ружьем, по сторонам зорко смотрит. Увидал ребят, закричал громким голосом:

— Стой! Кто такие?

Молчат ребята: больно испугались.

Наконец, Степан расхрабрился:

— Мы-то простые ребята из деревни Чижовки, — говорит, — а вот ты чего здесь стоишь?

— Для того стою, - отвечает красноармеец, — чтоб никого не пропускать.

Да как засвистит в свисток! Прибежал тут еще красноармеец.

— Шагайте, — говорит, — к командиру! И повел ребят куда-то по дороге. Шепчет Степка Ивану:

— Пропали наши головушки! Лишит нас красный командир жизни. Не уйдешь, значит, никуда от Красной армии! Все она видит и днем и ночью.

КРАСНЫЙ КОМАНДИР

Привел красноармеец ребят к красному командиру, тот посмотрел на них строго и спрашивает:

— Вы тут чего, ребята, шатаетесь? У нас ученье происходит, маневры, а вы тут по дорогам бегаете! А если конница вас затопчет, или броневик задавит, или газ задушит, или пуля зацепит, — кто отвечать будет? Кто вы такие и что вам здесь понадобилось?

Отвечает Иван:

— Мы — ребята из деревни Чижовки. Хотели узнать, для чего Красная армия нужна.

— Ну, что ж, узнали?

— Узнать-то узнали, да не все поняли. Не то для того она, чтобы песни петь, не то в догонялки да в прятки играть. Не то в масках ходить, не то из пушек палить. Не то в темноте ребят искать и их вперед не пускать.

Засмеялся красный командир и говорит:

— Правильно вы поняли, ребята, да не совсем. Не для того Красная армия, чтобы ребят не пускать, а для того, чтоб трудящийся народ–рабочих да крестьян в обиду не давать. Все для этого она должна и видеть, и знать, и всюду поспевать.

Не в прятки мы играем, а страну от неприятеля обороняем. Маски надеваем — себя от газов защищаем. Учимся мы по врагу из пушек метко палить и на него в атаку ходить. А вот как победим всех наших противников, тогда с песнями по домам разойдемся. Поняли?

— Как не понять, — отвечают ребята. — Только вот в чем вопрос: чего же неприятель не идет, раз все к его приходу готово?

— Потому и не идет, ребята, что все готово. Ступайте теперь домой да кланяйтесь от меня деревне.

14.2. On the left, a solitary Red Army soldier stands ready to defend his country. To the right, the company commander instructs Ivan and Stepan that they should carry their new knowledge about the Red Army with them as they grow up. Galina and Ol'ga Chichagova, illustration from *Dlia chego Krasnaia armiia*.

A School for Socialism: Invented Traditions and Ocular Play in Early Soviet Culture

To interpret Smirnov's book and the illustrations by the Chichagovas, it might be best to reconstruct the Soviet "period eye." Using the concept pioneered by Michael Baxandall in his study of fifteenth-century Italian painting,[3] let's recreate the mental equipment an average Soviet citizen, particularly a Soviet child, would have brought to looking at and reading Smirnov and the Chichagovas' book. As we will see, the purpose of the book was to engage in what might be termed "ocular play" and, through it, to engage in the process of "seeing Soviet."

What the Red Army Is For provides a window through which to view the symbolic child of early Soviet culture: the book and its illustrations construct images of Soviet children as imagined by adults. While this project is significant for understanding the visual and rhetorical power of "the child" in early Soviet culture, it does not provide us with clues about the actual lived experience of Soviet children. Instead, books such as *What the Red Army Is For* demonstrate how the symbolic child remained at the centre of moral, political, and educational debates in the USSR.[4] Soviet children's books that featured the Red Army employed the symbolic child in hopes of creating active, engaged citizens who would model their behaviour on the depictions within. To do so, books such as Smirnov's drew on symbols, images, and ideas aimed at Soviet adults and made them accessible to children. Below I will try to fashion the "period eye" of early Soviet culture: the distinctive habits, visual clues, language, and styles of that time and place, focusing on those related to the Red Army.

Visual perception begins when an object reflects a pattern of light on or to the eye. This light is then refracted as it passes through the cornea. It then travels through the pupil and is further refracted by the lens. The cornea and lens act together as a compound lens to project an inverted image onto the back of the eye, the retina. This screen-like part of the eye contains the photoreceptor cells and opsins that in turn carry the image, light, and colour to the brain for processing, called visual phototransduction. We may also call this, using the Harvard scientist David Hubel's terms, "the visual pathway."[5] Once the journey has been completed, the art historian Michael Baxandall has argued, the "human equipment for visual perception ceases to be uniform."[6] The brain interprets the data sent down the visual pathway and does so through what Baxandall terms "experience" or "one's cognitive style."[7] Much of this style is culturally produced, informed by the society that has influenced the viewer's experience. As Baxandall puts it: "A society develops its distinctive skills and habits, which have a visual aspect, since the visual sense is the main organ of experience, and these visual skills and habits become part of the medium of the painter [Baxandall exclusively focused on oil paintings]: correspondingly, a pictorial style gives access to the visual skills and habits and, through these, to the distinctive social experience."[8] Only when we can understand the visual style of a time and place, or employ the "period eye," can we "read" a visual text well.

In the case of Soviet visual culture, officials and artists worked to create specific skills and habits viewers would acquire and use to interpret images. They did so by establishing a series of visual invented traditions, repeated again and again as a means to establish the proper way to "see Soviet." Perhaps none of these visual traditions was more recognizable than the Red Army soldier wearing a *budenovka* and greatcoat with red insignia, standing guard over the socialist motherland. This image was the one captured in Smirnov and the Chichagovas' book and employed to help Soviet children also acquire a Soviet way of seeing.

Eric Hobsbawm famously described invented traditions as "a set of practices, normally governed by overtly or tacitly accepted rules and of a ritual or symbolic nature, which seek to inculcate certain values and norms of behavior by repetition, which automatically implies continuity with the past." As he notes, "the peculiarity of 'invented' traditions is that the continuity with it [*sic*] is largely factitious," for "they are responses to novel situations which take the form of reference to old situations, or which establish their own past by quasi-obligatory repetition."[9] The Soviet state invented a host of traditions that correspond to the latter part of Hobsbawm's schema;[10] the Red Army, particularly its evolution under the reforms associated with Mikhail Frunze in 1924 and 1925, also brought pre-revolutionary ideas about nationhood, patriotism, and masculinity into Soviet culture. The army, as depicted visually and textually, became viewed as a school for socialism, a virtual classroom of sorts that could teach Soviet citizens and Soviet children the proper values, behaviours, and new traditions that would help them become Soviet.

Tracing the evolution of this tradition through the pages of *Pravda* is an instructive way to grasp how the Red Army came to be depicted as a school for socialism and how the Red Army soldier became a symbol of defence of the motherland. The paper served as a primary site for establishing the Soviet period eye and, with it, the dominant textual and visual symbols of the Red Army man from which Smirnov, the Chichagovas, and other children's authors and illustrators drew. *Pravda*, Jeffrey Brooks has written, was "the center of the [Soviet] informational system, and it was more influential and more closely scrutinized by the authorities and concerned citizens than any other publication."[11] Caricatures published on its pages formed part of the paper's "interactive sphere," an innovative part of *Pravda* that aimed to draw more readers (and viewers, in this case) by making them part of the story (or image), in turn helping them to become Soviet.

On 23 February 1918, *Pravda* printed an article that laid out the organization of the new Red Army, noting that its primary function was to "defend the socialist fatherland [*zashchita sotsialisticheskogo otechestva*]."[12] The newspaper openly called on "proletarians" and "soldiers" to join the Red ranks of the "Soviet Socialist Army" in order to protect their revolution.[13] Just four years later, the paper began to celebrate Red Army Day on 23 February. The 1922 edition was devoted entirely to the Red Army and its significance. The articles all attempted to establish the "newness" of the Red Army and how it served as a representative symbol of the Soviet experiment itself. Lev Trotsky's lead article noted that the Red Army was roughly the same age of the Soviet Republic and declared the fifth year of both to be one for "education."[14] With the civil war now won, the article suggested, the Red Army could serve as a model for creating the new system and its new citizens. It should, in short, become a classroom that could offer instruction both to its soldiers and to all citizens on how to become Soviet. Other articles were entitled "The Red Army and Its Tasks," "The Old and New Army," and "The Red Cavalry," highlighting the basic points Trotsky made. The special issue also published a poem by Ivan Filipchenko entitled "The Red Army," which implored soldiers to guard the borders against the state's enemies and praised the Red Army of workers and peasants before imploring them to now "turn swords into ploughshares."

The 1922 issue established certain notions that would continue to resonate for years: the Red Army had been "born" alongside the revolution, its soldiers were the true embodiments of the state's goals, the Red Army man was himself "new" and would remain vigilant in protecting the Soviet state. The Soviet Union, as a 1923 article put it, was founded on the blood of Red Army heroes, and its continued survival depended on honouring this foundation.[15] The major change introduced in the latter part of the 1920s was for *Pravda* to celebrate Red Army Day with a visual image on its front page. Dmitrii Moor's 1925 cartoon, "Long Live the Red Army, the Defender of Workers' Rights!", employs the image of the Red Army soldier he had popularized in his posters – Moor did much to create the period eye in early Soviet culture, repeatedly casting Red Army soldiers in his civil war prints.[16] A larger-than-life soldier wearing his *budenovka* and greatcoat stands at the border between the Soviet Republic, which now bears the advanced technological culture the revolution has brought, and Europe, which is surrounded by top-hatted capitalists united in their exploitation of workers. Red Army Day had already generated the textual template that could be applied again and again; now it had a visual equivalent. The following year, Viktor Deni's "Vsegda na strazhe" ("Always on Guard") would employ this visual trope: in this version, the Red Army soldier wears his recognizable garb and protects a factory and a farm (fig. 14.3).[17]

This, then, was the cultural ready-made created and employed by Smirnov and the Chichagovas.[18] In a very short time, Soviet officials and cultural figures fashioned a repetitive invented tradition associated with the Red Army and its representative soldier. The institution itself served as a school for socialism, a site for inculcating the values of the Soviet system and for stressing the need to defend the Soviet Union from its enemies and to protect the growth of socialism within its borders.

14.3. By the time *What the Red Army Is For* appeared in 1927, the Red Army soldier standing guard while wearing a *budenovka* had become a recognizable icon in Soviet visual culture. Viktor Deni's front-page cartoon for *Pravda* on Red Army Day is one of numerous examples from the 1920s that featured this figure. "Vsegda na-strazhe," *Pravda*, 23 February 1926, 1.

Moor, Deni, and other artists created the visual shorthand for these ideas: the tall, serious, focused soldier wearing his *budenovka* and his greatcoat festooned with the insignia of the Red Army while standing guard helps use the visual "in order to summon a new reality into being," as Valerie Kivelson and Joan Neuberger have proposed.[19] In this sense, the experience of seeing could have a transformative effect: looking at Red Army soldiers standing guard across the vast Soviet motherland established a new parameter of the possible.[20] Soviet citizens and Soviet children, by looking at the numerous representations of this soldier, could imagine themselves in his shoes, protecting socialism. The repetitiveness of Red Army soldiers standing guard speaks to the nature of both this early Soviet invented tradition and of the early Soviet "period eye": throughout the 1920s, the image was seemingly everywhere, establishing itself as a distinctive aspect of that time and place. The repetitive nature of the Chichagovas' images built on this new tradition: in their work, the repeated use of the red star, red rifle, and red words drew the eye to the familiar object of the Red Army soldier.

At the same time, the style of the Red Army soldier in *What the Red Army Is For* had a particular, mid-1920s flavour to it. Nikolai Smirnov and the Chichagovas had teamed up before and had established themselves, as Alla Rosenfeld has written, as pioneers in "the development of [the] scientific and technical genre of children's books."[21] Inspired by the work of Aleksandr Rodchenko, their teacher at the Higher Art and Technical Workshops in Moscow (VKhUTEMAS), the Chichagovas substituted compass and ruler for brush and pen.[22] Their illustrations were "usually drawn as a generalized flat silhouette that exaggerates its peculiarities," often employing contrasting colours.[23] In books such as their 1926 *Detiam o gazete* (*For Children about the Newspaper*), Smirnov and the Chichagovas depicted items, from newspapers to teapots and telephones, as emotionally affective objects that would help define socialism itself.[24] Their work in *What the Red Army Is For* fits into this pattern, for the text and illustrations clearly bear the stamp of their previous work. In a sense, the illustrations of Red Army soldiers and their activities marry the constructivist approach with the ready-made Red Army soldier created by Moor and Deni.

Children's books such as *What the Red Army Is For* introduced what might be called "ocular play." For a child, seeing Soviet could be associated with viewing the Red Army soldier, with his recognizable cap and red star, and connecting him to various roles that were fun to play at but ultimately serious activities. The two boys repeatedly exclaim in the text of the book: encouraged by Ivan to look at the awesomeness of a tank, for example, Stepan cries, "yes, it's unbeatable!"[25] Moor's and Deni's Red Army soldiers were meant to be viewed seriously, mostly by adult eyes. The Chichagovas' soldiers, by contrast, looked the same but were meant to be gazed at through the eyes of children: they were meant to be seen as fun. Soviet children's literature thus attempted to build a very specific architecture of the visual cortex that Soviet children would use to interpret images.[26] In the case of playing at being a soldier, Smirnov and the Chichagovas were creating a schema that attempted to unite perception and affect. Young readers would see what it was like to be a soldier, learn to associate the Red Army man with defending the socialist motherland, and be encouraged to play these roles until they grew old enough to join the Red Army. In a sense, the all-too-familiar Red Army soldier, born in civil war posters, recast in Bolshevik media outlets, and then recast again in children's books such as this one, ensured that a Soviet visual cortex would immediate recognize this familiar figure and process this visual information as a source of ocular play and a visual pathway to creating socialism. *What the Red Army Is For* was, to use the words of the Soviet psychologist Lev Vygotsky, creating the imagined situation that would teach a child to guide his behaviour "not only by immediate perception of objects or by the situation immediately affecting him but also by the *meaning* of this situation."[27] For boys, playing at soldier was enough. In doing so, they acted out the desires the state wanted for them (Ivan and Stepan, of course, are idealized children). The next step would come when they became young adults and could transform themselves into real soldiers.

Iconic Interlude: The Budenovka *and* Bogatyri

The Red Army soldier, as conveyed above, functioned as an icon in the new world imagined by the Bolsheviks and their artists. Coincidentally, but also suggestively, at the very time that Smirnov was writing his book and the Chichagovas were illustrating it, Sergei Bulgakov was writing about icons and their significance within Russian Orthodoxy. His essay "The Name of God," written in the 1920s, argues that a holy icon "is not just a picture, a human artifact, a photograph; it is also a bearer of God's power and a holy hieroglyph of the Name of God." Icons are not empty symbols, he wrote, for they invoke the divine. Part of icons' power, Bulgakov argued in a 1931 follow-up essay, "The Icon and Its Veneration," resides in the frequency with which they are "the objects of our contemplation." The more people "gaze upon these icons," he stated, the more people will be "motivated to remember" their content and to venerate them.[28] The Red Army soldier functioned similarly in early Soviet culture. His repeated appearance turned him into a new, secular icon. Artists who drew these soldiers for the purposes of propagandizing Soviet values did so in the hopes that children would gaze at the soldier again and again, contemplate him, and venerate him.

Making new secular icons required adapting old ones. The task also necessitated the creation of visually recognizable figures with recognizable features. The Red Army soldier's *budenovka*, complete with a red star on its front, became his most recognizable visual symbol. Dmitrii Moor's posters from 1919 onward – particularly his famous 1920 design "Ty zapisalsia dobrovol'tsem?" ("Have You Volunteered?") (fig. 14.4) – helped popularize the cap as a quintessential sartorial image of the new soldier and the way he defended the Soviet experiment. By 1922, *Pravda* articles would employ the term to refer to the stereotypical Red Army soldier.[29] The hat therefore became part of the period eye created under the new Soviet system, the visual shorthand of the "new" army and its newly forged peasants and workers. As the above analysis indicates, it also served as a focal point for ocular play among Soviet youth.

The *budenovka* first appeared in 1918 or 1919, when the Revolutionary Military Committee approved it as the official headgear and then officially introduced it to the army (fig. 14.5). The construction of the invented tradition associated with the Red Army and its soldiers helped associate the peaked hat with the Red Army: the name *budenovka* speaks to this process, for it received its nickname when it was popularized by Semen Budennyi and his cavalrymen. However, the hat was new neither in its provenance nor in its symbolic significance. There is some evidence that the "new" headgear of the Red Army had first been designed in 1915 to be worn

14.4. Dmitrii Moor, the well-known poster artist who had drawn tsarist patriotic images featuring Cossack heroes, adapted his previous work in his famous civil war poster "Ty zapisalsia dobrovol'tsem?" ("Have You Volunteered?") (1920). It became iconic in its own right, helping to spread the image of a Red Army defender wearing the newly designed *budenovka*.

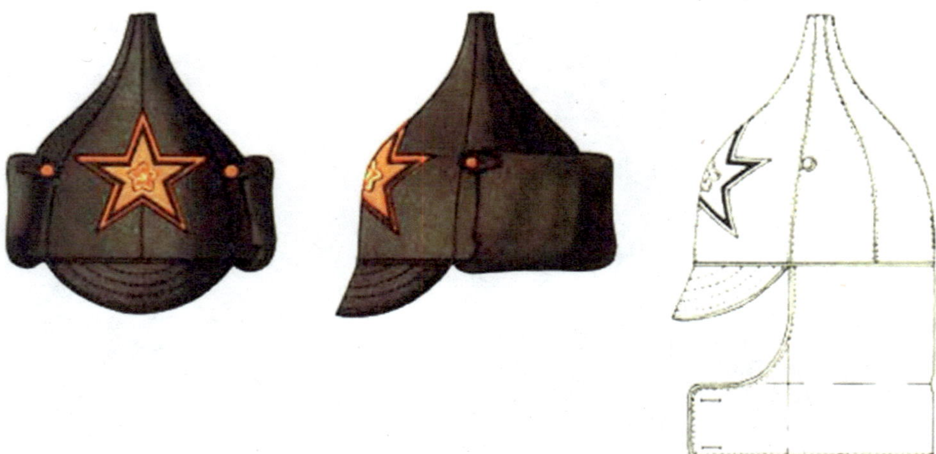

14.5. The original 1918/19 design for the *budenovka*. This most recognizable symbol of the Red Army soldier was designed by the famous artist Viktor Vasnetsov and modelled after the medieval helmets worn by *bogatyri*, heroic knights who defended their motherland.

by victorious Russian soldiers when they paraded through Berlin and Constantinople. When the early victory in the Great War failed to materialize, the design sat on the shelf, revived in 1918 for another war. The cap was indisputably the brainchild of Viktor Vasnetsov, the Russian painter, who called it the *"bogatyrka"* and who designed it to resemble the helmets worn by medieval knights he helped make famous in his paintings. Vasnetsov wanted Imperial Russian troops, and later Red Army soldiers, to be inspired by the patriotism of the mythic Russian *bogatyr*.[30] In this sense, what came to be known as the *budenovka* embodied a pre-1917 masculine, patriotic culture associated not just with the knights in Vasnetsov's paintings but also the countless popular images, stories, and other sources about larger-than-life peasants defending the motherland.[31]

The image of the Red Army soldier wearing his peaked cap therefore helped to transfer pre-revolutionary notions about masculinity and patriotism across 1917. The soldier captured in Dmitrii Moor's posters and cartoons, the same soldier who appeared in Smirnov and the Chichagovas' book, was a revision of Koz'ma Kriuchkov, the Cossack hero of 1914, and other *bogatyri* who had graced *lubki* and lithographs for over a century. Kriuchkov, as well as the Cossacks who appeared in 1812 caricatures or the Cossacks who had appeared in *lubki* from the Crimean War, were also lauded for their valour in defending their homeland.[32]

In this way, holy icons of Russian nationhood such as the *bogatyr* and the soldier defending his motherland could be fused to make Soviet icons and their headgear.

14.6. Viktor Vasnetsov, *Bogatyri* (1898). Vasnetsov's famous painting featured three mythic medieval knights, including Ilia Muromets (centre), permanently poised to defend their homeland. The painting served as an important vehicle to spread notions of the heroism, courage, and strength associated with the *bogatyr* to early twentieth-century viewers. The artist would adapt the helmet into his design for the *budenovka*, transferring the *bogatyr*'s attributes to the Red Army soldier who wore it.

Vasnetsov's plan worked: through countless posters, cartoons, photographs, films, and other visual sources, the *budenovka* became a vital part of Soviet culture and a Soviet way of seeing. Putting the cap on your head also meant becoming Soviet.

Story II: A Soviet Metamorphosis

Vania is a young farm boy called up for military service. While his elderly parents stand beside their hut, looking rather glum, Vania sets off to join Semen Budennyi's cavalry. Using rhythmic, short, rhyming verses, Evgenii Redin and Valerian Shcheglov's 1928 book, *Krasnoarmeets Vaniushka* (*Red Army Soldier Vania*) narrates Vania's journey. His metamorphosis might be best understood as the next step in Ivan and Stepan's lives recounted in the first story above: once they got a little older and desired to stop playing soldier, they would have to take Vania's journey.

Employing a visual style reminiscent of civil war–era ROSTA windows – large displays of the propaganda posters produced by the Russian Telegraph Agency – Shcheglov's illustrations tell Vania's tale. We first meet him wearing a brown coat over a bright red *kosovorotka* (a Russian peasant shirt) and patterned blue pants. He is clutching a pot in one hand and a rucksack in the other. While he is not smiling, his face is young, optimistic, and hopeful: our eyes are drawn to Vania through his bright red shirt. By contrast, his mother and father slouch in front of their *izba* (peasant hut). Visually, Shcheglov is contrasting the old with the new: Vania, the larger, more hopeful figure, is about to become part of the new Soviet collective. His parents, stuck in their ways, their traditional clothes, and their traditional home, are left behind. Before Vania can become more modern, and therefore more Soviet, he has to change his appearance and his mentality. On the next page, we see him working on the former. A cheery, well-coiffed barber cuts off Vania's unruly locks. Although the young man looks glum, he is beginning his transformation into a Red Army man (figs. 14.7 and 14.8).

Vania's path takes him away from the backward village and toward Bolshevik consciousness. Along the way, he learns to adopt the sort of "culturedness" ("kul'turnost'") the state stressed as a means to become more "Soviet." Vania receives a haircut "from ear to ear" so that he looks more modern, more civilized, and better prepared to defend his motherland. He learns to eat healthy *shchi* with his spoon, to keep his horse (and, one assumes, himself) clean. He becomes literate, learning the alphabet, hones his skills on horseback, keeps his body physically fit through gymnastics, and goes to the club in order to read the newspapers and listen to the gramophone.

Most importantly, Vania changes his clothes. After the haircut, he gives up his peasant clothes for a Red Army uniform, complete with *budenovka* and red star. Vania has become Soviet, and allowed the reader of the book to witness his transformation,

14.7. and 14.8. Evgenii Redin and Valerian Shcheglov's *Red Army Soldier Vania* picks up where *Dlia chego Krasnaia armiia* left off, as its protagonist leaves his peasant home to join the Red Army. As its first two illustrations show, Vania's parents and the life he led with them are out of date; he must transform himself in order to be a true soldier. This process begins with cutting his hair. *Kransoarmeets Vaniushka* (Leningrad: Raduga, 1928), 2–3.

to identify with it because of the familiar garb. His change therefore represents another example of the Soviet visual cortex at work, another example of engaging in ocular play. In the first two pages, Vania's face is determined, anxious; by the third, when we see him for the first time in his Red Army attire, he is smiling. For the remainder of the book, he maintains a cheery outlook: he is focused while training, grinning while learning and listening. Vania's facial expressions, combined with his uniform, generate a positive affective range for the young reader to identify with him. Clothes (and peaked cap), it seems, can make the Soviet man and, with it, the young Soviet viewer (figs. 14.9–14.11). After following this trajectory, Vania is commissioned as a Red Army soldier by none other than Budennyi himself (identified as "the commander"). Vania is wearing his red shirt again, but this time he has his *budenovka* on as its namesake shakes his hand. By the end, Vania has become the Red Army man referred to in the title.

14.9.–14.11. A Soviet Metamorphoses: Vania has become cultured and, as a result, has "become Soviet." He has trained his body and studied to improve his mind. He has also donned the Red Army uniform and *budenovka*. In the last illustration, the cap's namesake, Semen Budennyi, congratulates Vania as he completes his journey. *Kransoarmeets Vaniushka*, 4–5, 10.

Becoming Cultured

Red Army Soldier Vania reads like a checklist of the revolutionary values the historian David Hoffmann has identified as key to the early Soviet experiment.[33] As Hoffmann has written, the New Soviet Person the revolution aimed to create was meant to be clean, sober, efficient, and prepared to sacrifice his or her individual interests for the good of the collective. This Soviet civilizing process stressed a number of values for citizens to embrace, including "cultured" dress and decorum. Vania, representing an idealized young man about to become an adult, moves from the old way of life to the new. He becomes Soviet by transforming his body and his mind, by embracing the values of the new system. He does so, as Redin and Shcheglov emphasize, by aspiring to be like Budennyi and to take part in the larger collective, here represented by the Red Army. By capturing these Soviet values visually, Redin and Shcheglov (and the other artists mentioned above) helped to turn the Red Army soldier into both a mediator and an embodiment of Soviet culture. The soldier is not a simple, stock figure, but an object that helps readers learn about themselves and their world. Similarly, the soldier perfectly embodies the attributes of that time and place. In performing this dual role, the Red Army soldier helped to translate socialist values for readers and transform children into the ideal Soviet subject.[34]

Shcheglov, who would go on to enjoy an illustrious career as a book illustrator, had gone through a metamorphosis similar to the one he depicted. He joined the Red Army in 1920 at the age of nineteen and continued the artistic studies he had begun in his native Kaulga while working as a soldier. He plied his trade in the army's poster division, learning how, in the words of his Soviet biographer, to "help the soldiers understand more clearly their purpose in liberating their country."[35] From the beginning, his work helped define "the fighting spirit of the Red Army soldier."[36] After he left the army, he went to Leningrad and retrained as a Soviet artist, initially as a pedagogic-formalist (*pedagogi-formalisty*) who wanted to combine subjectivism and formalism.[37] His Soviet biography would make much of his Red Army career and his "birth" as a Soviet subject in the civil war: in a sense, Shcheglov's biography was fit into the one he sketched in *Red Army Soldier Vania*, one of his first works after demobilization. Shcheglov would return again and again to the Red Army soldier as a quintessential symbol of the Soviet state and its values, even while adapting his style to meet the demands of socialist realism.

Red Army Soldier Vania represents the first stage in the metamorphosis all young Soviet men, including Shcheglov, must go through. In this example, however, young readers and viewers are being drawn into this process through another example of ocular play: Vania's journey is meant to be instructive, but also fun. Vania, like other young Soviet men, must prepare for the future by abandoning his biological family and joining the new, rational, literate, clean, healthy, Soviet one. Vania may have played being a soldier while a child, but now it is time to make the next step and enter the real "school of socialism." Young readers might look at Vania's metamorphosis and again engage in ocular play, seeing his gymnastics, sword fighting, and horseback riding as worthy of emulating, but the message of Shcheglov's illustrations is more serious. Ivan and Stepan could go back home and play soldier in *What the Red Army Is For*, but Vania is in his new home, the Red Army, and must leave childhood play behind.

Vania's metamorphosis, while aimed as an instructive example for young people, also presents a visual narrative of the Frunze reforms and how they aimed to transform soldiers. Under the reforms, the army attempted to build a new soldier and use him as a model for Soviet citizens to follow. In 1924, Frunze, Andrei Bubnov, Kliment Voroshilov, and Mikhail Tukhachevskii travelled around the country to persuade civilians that they too needed to embrace military values in order to defend the socialist experiment. Frunze called this initiative "the militarization of the civilian populace" and declared that "we cannot prepare the country for defense if we rely solely on our military resources."[38] Schools became a primary site for the institution of this project; the Soviet nation would benefit, as Frunze would declare, from "cultured, literate, and politically educated soldier-citizens."[39]

The result, as Mark Von Hagen concludes in his study of the Red Army, was that "by the end of the 1920s the Red Army was a fundamentally different institution from the units of Red Guards and former imperial soldiers improvised in 1917."[40] The army had been professionalized and made into a model institution; it became "a school for socialism" in "sociopolitical training and cadre formation."[41] Its function in this regard was to build the state's institutional structure and shape the political culture of Soviet socialism. One final lesson taught in this school was that the Soviet state was surrounded by hostile capitalist powers that wanted to defeat the socialist experiment; therefore, the USSR had to militarize society to defend it.

Redin and Shcheglov's book therefore spread the "lessons" of the Frunze reforms to Soviet children, even if this tutorial was a little more fun. Ivan and Stepan in *What the Red Army Is For* represented the symbolic child as a preteen; Vania was the boy who had once played soldier now grown up. Shcheglov, the illustrator, had taken part in the biographical trajectory the Frunze reforms asked all citizens to undertake; *Red Army Soldier Vania* could act as a textbook from which others could learn.

Conclusion: The Soviet Childscape

Soviet children playing soldier, and thus becoming "Soviet," illustrates one part of the symbolic Soviet child created in 1920s children's books. This symbolic child in turn formed a part of what might be called the "Soviet childscape." According to the archaeologist and anthropologist Clive Gamble, a "childscape" is the "material project of growing children." "Childscapes," he writes, are "composed of emotionally charged arrays, including material culture ... These arrays are learned as related categories and used as an individual authors their own emerging networks and identity." The childscape, he concludes, "is where our identity is created and its metaphorical basis established through references to emotional, material, and symbolic resources."[42]

What the Red Army Is For and *Red Army Soldier Vania* serve as two examples of how the Soviet childscape was formed and how it sought to grow its children into vigilant, playful, cultured, militarized men ready to fight for the socialist motherland. The part of the Soviet childscape cultivated in these books replanted pre-revolutionary notions of heroism and masculinity: boys could engage in ocular play by seeing the fun of being a soldier and could begin to transform themselves into Soviet men by learning to be like Vanya, but girls remained absent from this project.[43] The books, along with other visual and textual examples invoking the Red Army soldier with his *budenovka*, attempted to produce an affective response among young readers through "seeing and doing" and by "making war fun."[44]

Although the real Soviet child and how he might have reacted to these books will always remain elusive, the Soviet childscape centred on modelling young soldiers was one created for the generation born after 1917. This generation, it turned out, would be the one conscripted to fight in the Great Patriotic War. Raised on notions of playing at soldier and transforming oneself through the school of Red Army socialism, the generation raised within this Soviet childscape would experience the real violence of war between 1941 and 1945.

NOTES

1 According to the typologies explored in Nikolajeva and Scott, *How Picturebooks Work*, 6.
2 Smirnov, Chichagova, and Chichagova, *Dlia chego Krasnaia armiia*, 16.
3 Baxandall, *Painting and Experience*. Baxandall's second chapter is entitled "The Period Eye."
4 Here I draw from Albarrán, *Seen and Heard in Mexico*, 3–4.
5 See Hubel, *Eye, Brain, and Vision*. For the updated version, see http://hubel.med.harvard.edu/index.html.
6 Baxandall, *Painting and Experience*, 29.
7 Ibid., 29–30.
8 Ibid., 152.
9 Hobsbawm, "Introduction," 1, 2.
10 See, for example, Frederick Corney's study of the storming of the Winter Palace and how the Soviet state established traditions around it in *Telling October*.
11 Brooks, *Thank You, Comrade Stalin!* xix.
12 "Organizatsiia Krasnoi Armii," 2.
13 Ibid., 3.
14 Trotsky, "Piatyi god – god ucheby," 1.
15 "Prikaz Revoliutsionnogo Voennogo," 1.
16 See White, *The Bolshevik Poster*.
17 See also Deni's 1927 cartoon in Deni, "9 Years," 1.
18 I borrow the phrase "cultural ready-made" from Goscilo, "Slotting War Narratives."

19 Kivelson and Neuberger, "Seeing into Being," 6.

20 Ibid., 4.

21 Rosenfeld, "Figuration versus Abstraction," 180. Smirnov was a playwright who also authored popular novels, including his 1930 *Jack Vosmerkin: The American*, about a Russian peasant boy who grew up in America but returned to Soviet Russia.

22 Rosenfeld, "Figuration versus Abstraction," 180.

23 Ibid.

24 For more on this topic, see Kiaer, *Imagine No Possessions*.

25 Smirnov, Chichagova, and Chichagova, *Dlia chego krasnaia armiia*, 10.

26 I am again drawing on David Hubel's work.

27 Vygotsky, "Igra i ee rol'" (my emphasis).

28 Both essays appear in Bulgakov, *Icons in Name of God*. The first quote comes from 125–6, the second from 1.

29 "Krasnaia armiia," 3.

30 See Oltarzhevskii, "'Bogatyrka', stavshaia budenovkoi."

31 This is a topic I explore in my book. See Norris, *A War of Images*.

32 See Petrone, "Family, Masculinity, and Heroism."

33 Hoffmann, *Stalinist Values*. See also Kelly, *Children's World*. Kelly writes that, by the mid-1920s, "the regime was committed to a view of society as a rational, politically literate, hygienically aware, 'cultured' collective, and education was expected to teach rational collectivism from the beginning" (67).

34 Here I am drawing on Jordanova, *The Look of the Past*.

35 Gankina, *Valerian Vasil'evich Shcheglov*, 6.

36 Ibid.

37 Ibid., 7.

38 Von Hagen, *Soldiers in the Proletarian Dictatorship*, 240.

39 Ibid., 241. Frunze, *Na novykh putiakh*.

40 Von Hagen, *Soldiers in the Proletarian Dictatorship*, 326.

41 Ibid., 343.

42 Gamble, *Origins and Revolutions*, 228, 229

43 These connections have been explored in Petrone, "Masculinity and Heroism." The masculinization of early Soviet society as an imaginary construction that took place on the page is the subject of Eliot Borenstein's book *Men without Women*.

44 Robert Bird, ed., *Adventures in the Soviet Imaginary*, 27.

BIBLIOGRAPHY

Albarrán, Elena Jackson. *Seen and Heard in Mexico: Children and Revolutionary Cultural Nationalism*. Lincoln: University of Nebraska Press, 2014.

Baxandall, Michael. *Painting and Experience in Fifteenth-Century Italy*. 2nd ed. Oxford: Oxford University Press, 1988.

Bird, Robert, ed. *Adventures in the Soviet Imaginary: Children's Books and Graphic Art*. Chicago: University of Chicago Library, 2011.

Borenstein, Eliot. *Men without Women: Masculinity and Revolution in Russian Fiction, 1917–1929*. Durham, NC: Duke University Press, 2000.

Brooks, Jeffrey. *Thank You, Comrade Stalin! Soviet Public Culture from Revolution to Cold War*. Princeton, NJ: Princeton University Press, 2000.

Bulgakov, Sergius. *Icons in the Name of God*. Translated by Boris Jakim. Grand Rapids, MI: Eerdmans, 2012.

Corney, Frederick. *Telling October: Memory and the Making of the Bolshevik Revolution*. Ithaca, NY: Cornell University Press, 2004.

Deni, Viktor. "9 Years: Our Guard." *Pravda*, 23 February 1927.

Frunze, Mikhail. *Na novykh putiakh: Stat'i i doklady*. Moscow: Voen. vest. 1925.

Gamble, Clive. *Origins and Revolutions: Human Identity in Earliest Prehistory*. Cambridge: Cambridge University Press, 2007.

Gankina, E. *Valerian Vasil'evich Shcheglov*. Moscow: Sovetskii khudozhnik, 1954.

Goscilo, Helena. "Slotting War Narratives into Culture's Ready-Made." In *Fighting Words and Images: Representing War across the Disciplines*, edited by Elena Baraban, Stephan Jaeger, and Adam Muller, 132–60. Toronto: University of Toronto Press, 2012.

Hobsbawm, Eric. "Introduction: The Invention of Tradition." Introduction to *The Invention of Tradition*, edited by Hobsbawm Ranger and Terence Ranger, 1–14. Cambridge: Cambridge University Press, 1983.

Hoffmann, David. *Stalinist Values: The Cultural Norms of Soviet Modernity, 1917–1941*. Ithaca, NY: Cornell University Press, 2003.

Hubel, David. *Eye, Brain, and Vision*. New York: Scientific Library of America, 1995.

Jordanova, Ludmilla. *The Look of the Past: Visual and Material Evidence in Historical Practice*. Cambridge: Cambridge University Press, 2012.

Kelly, Catriona. *Children's World: Growing Up in Russia, 1890–1991*. New Haven, CT: Yale University Press, 2007.

Kiaer, Christina. *Imagine No Possessions: The Socialist Objects of Russian Constructivism*. Cambridge, MA: MIT Press, 2005.

Kivelson, Valerie, and Joan Neuberger. "Seeing into Being: An Introduction." In *Picturing Russia: Explorations in Visual Culture*, edited by Valerie Kivelson and Joan Neuberger, 1–11. New Haven, CT: Yale University Press, 2010.

"Krasnaia armiia." *Pravda*, 23 March 1922.

Nikolajeva, Maria, and Carole Scott. *How Picturebooks Work*. New York: Garland, 2001.

Norris, Stephen N. *A War of Images: Russian Popular Prints, Wartime Culture, and National Identity, 1812–1945*. DeKalb: Northern Illinois University Press, 2006.

Oltarzhevskii, Georgii. "'Bogatyrka', stavshaia budenovkoi." *Lenta.ru*, 31 January 2015. http://lenta .ru/articles/2015/01/31/budenovka/.

"Organizatsiia Krasnoi Armii." *Pravda*, 23 February 1918.

Petrone, Karen. "Family, Masculinity, and Heroism in Russian Posters of the First World War." In *Borderlines: Genders and Identities in War and Peace, 1880–1930*, edited by Billie Melman, 95–120. London: Routledge, 1998.

– "Masculinity and Heroism in Imperial and Soviet Military-Patriotic Cultures." In *Russian Masculinities in History and Culture*, edited by Barbara Evans Clements, Rebecca Friedman, and Dan Healey, 172–93. Houndsmills, UK: Palgrave, 2002.

"Prikaz Revoliutsionnogo Voennogo Soveta Respubliki k 5-letiiu Krasnoi armii." *Pravda*, 23 February 1923.

Rosenfeld, Alla. "Figuration versus Abstraction in Soviet Illustrated Children's Books, 1920–1930." In *Defining Russian Graphic Arts, 1898–1934: From Diaghilev to Stalin*, edited by Alla Rosenfeld, 166–98. New Brunswick, NJ: Rutgers University Press, 1999.

Shcheglov, V. *Krasnoarmeets Vaniushka*. Moscow: Raduga, 1928.

Smirnov, Nikolai, Galina Chichagova, and Ol'ga Chichagova. *Dlia chego krasnaia armiia*. Moscow: Molodaia gvardiia, 1927.

Trotsky, Lev. "Piatyi god – god ucheby." *Pravda*, 23 February 1922.

Von Hagen, Mark. *Soldiers in the Proletarian Dictatorship: The Red Army and the Soviet Socialist State, 1917–1930*. Ithaca, NY: Cornell University Press, 1990.

Vygotsky, Lev. "Igra i ee rol' v psikhicheskom razvitii rebenka." (1931). *Soviet Psychology* 5, no. 3 (1967): 62–76.

White, Stephen. *The Bolshevik Poster*. New Haven, CT: Yale University Press, 1988.

chapter fifteen

THE WORKING BODY AND ITS PROSTHESES: IMAGINING CLASS FOR SOVIET CHILDREN

ALEXEY GOLUBEV

Does such a book exist that would show children the world – not a toy world as used to be shown in times gone by, but the real world that is fighting and restructuring itself; the world, not stopped, but at full speed?

Samuil Marshak, "On the Background and Legacy of Children's Literature"

Three dark, old, and hunched figures trudge atop the cover of Samuil Marshak's 1925 book *Vchera i segodnia* (*Yesterday and Today*), illustrated by Vladimir Lebedev (fig. 15.1). A woman with a kerosene lamp, a water-carrier with a shoulder pole, and a clerk with a pen and inkpot barely cope with their cumbersome accoutrements. "Yesterday," reads the title in black above their heads. "Today," reads the title in bold red beneath three other figures depicted on the cover's bottom half. They are an electrician, a plumber, and a typist, three bright young people proudly carrying the tools of their trade: electric wires and lamps, pipes and faucets, and a typewriter. The general idea behind this contrast is conveyed both in Lebedev's illustrations and Marshak's poetry. In the past ("yesterday"), people's relationship with material objects, with things, was oppressive, exploitative. The same relationship "today" is one of friendship and harmony.

The juxtaposition in Lebedev's image is not only about the different politics of pre-Soviet and Soviet *things* (i.e., the dichotomy of obsolescence and archaism versus modernity and progress). It also contains a meta-descriptive element, commenting on the genre of children's literature itself. Pre-1917 children's book illustrations, informed by a sentimental understanding of childhood, had avoided depicting working bodies in their interaction with the means of production. The dramatis personae of imperial children's literature could be heroic, romantic, melancholic, or poetic; but they were rarely described or depicted as labouring bodies.[1] The figures in the upper part of Lebedev's picture, those belonging to yesterday, reflect this melancholic pre-revolutionary approach to the representation of labour for children. The crooked,

15.1. Vladimir Lebedev, cover of Samuil Marshak, *Vchera i segodnia* (Leningrad: Raduga, 1925).

shadowy silhouettes seem to repel the viewers' gaze, inducing it to turn instead to the bright red figures below – a movement further intensified by the top-to-bottom logic of reading the page of a book. Unlike earlier books, the politics of early Soviet literature rendered children's books *just the place* for representations of the labouring body. The Soviet leadership's Marxist ideology created a political demand for labour as a central theme of new Soviet literature and art. Soviet authors and illustrators of children's books responded to this demand by creating a wide range of texts and images that sought to glorify labour and the labouring body. Lebedev's image here reflects this paradigm shift. It is not only material objects, things, that have changed between "yesterday" and "today," but also human bodies. In the past, exploitation distorted them; the emancipation of labour has dignified them. Shut away from the gaze of young readers in pre-revolutionary children's literature, working bodies came to be prominently featured in order to perform class and citizenship for Soviet children.

This chapter examines early Soviet children's book illustrations of the working body as attempts to introduce class and citizenship in the visual literacy of the child reader. In developing this argument, I would prefer to leave aside the framework that treats Soviet children's book illustrations as just another form of Soviet propaganda, serving – whether the artists in question consciously willed this or not – to indoctrinate children in communist ideology.[2] Ideological conditions of early Soviet Russia undoubtedly influenced artistic production, but primarily in the sense of making artists attentive to themes and objects that pre-revolutionary children's literature had kept far from young eyes.[3] Labour – and the labouring body – was one of these themes, all the more important as labour was the foundation of official Soviet morality and, consequently, of Soviet education. As Vladimir Lenin declared at the Third All-Russian Congress of the Russian Young Communist League in October 1920, "Communist morality is … the basis of communist training, education, and teaching. That is the reply to the question of how communism should be learnt."[4] This political demand fell on fertile ground, as Soviet artists were keen to create new cultural forms that would eradicate bourgeois culture, keep it from reproducing in the norms and values of Soviet citizens, and instead inculcate the spirit of social emancipation and equality.[5]

The emergence of labour and class in Soviet children's book illustration was thus part of a fundamental cultural paradigm shift: the replacement of late imperial culture with a new proletarian one. In these conditions, Soviet illustrators had to experiment with new forms in order to understand, organize, and represent the visual experience that was part of everyday reality but that had never been "translated for children."[6] Their experiments went in two major directions. One focused on the aesthetics of class by representing Soviet labouring bodies in typical positions and situations. In a way, this approach represented an essentialist understanding of class as a relatively fixed set of characteristics to be described in illustrations. The other approach was part of the early Soviet avant-garde, and as such aspired to invent and propose new ways of seeing the social. Those avant-garde artists who experimented with children's books used modernist techniques of fragmentation and montage to explore the anatomy of class: its physical condition, its intimate interaction with tools and products, and its inclusion in broader technical systems and networks.

Among the best-known artists to take the aestheticist position in illustrated children's books was Boris Kustodiev (1878–1927), who, long before the October Revolution, had made his fame with portraits and scenes of provincial Russian life.[7] He was associated with the World of Art (Mir iskusstva) artistic group, whose founder, Sergei Diaghilev, established a journal of the same name with the explicit agenda of promoting an aestheticist approach to art.[8] Unlike many other members of the World of Art, who fled Russia after October 1917, Kustodiev embraced the revolution, pursuing a successful career as a book illustrator, including for children's books for the publishers Brokgauz-Efron, Raduga, and Gosizdat. His interest in carnivalesque aspects of Russia's ancien régime translated into illustrations for such books as Lidiia Lesnaia's

Dzhimmi Dzhoi v gosti k pioneram (*Jimmy Joy Visits the Pioneers*, 1925) and Nadezhda Pavlovich's *Bol'shevik Tom* (*Tom the Bolshevik*, 1925), which borrowed their garish colours and simple graphics from the *lubok* (coloured woodcut or lithographic prints that were extremely popular in early twentieth-century Russia).

At the same time, Kustodiev illustrated several works that explicitly dealt with the new class hierarchy in Russia. His colouring books *Trud* (*Labour*, 1925) and *Sel'skii trud* (*Rural Labour*, 1925) personified and glorified some of the most typical professions of the Russian proletariat and peasantry, respectively. Masons, shoemakers, carpenters, and so on are depicted in both books in the midst of the working process, with tools of their trade and products of their labour, and usually against the backdrop of a stylized urban or rural landscape (fig. 15.2). Using a sketchy drawing technique (dictated by the purpose of these illustrations – to be coloured in), Kustodiev shows people working in harmony with their immediate material environment. In these representations, labour seems more a *natural* than a social phenomenon: figures of workers are organically integrated into the landscape, producing an "aesthetic unity," as one Soviet-era scholar of early Soviet children's books characterized this approach.[9]

Kustodiev also turned to the theme of class and labour in his illustrations for Anna Pokrovskaia's biography of Vladimir Lenin, published by Gosizdat in 1925.[10] Here, as in his earlier illustrations for Maxim Gorky's works, the material led him to engage more explicitly with the theme of class struggle. The book introduced its young readers to a basic ontology of classes as they had existed in imperial Russia: peasants, workers, landowners, and industrialists. The narrative begins with the exploitation of the working classes by elites under the old regime, which Kustodiev illustrates with genre scenes contrasting everyday life in poor and wealthy families, as well as with scenes of police violence against workers and peasants. The book then discusses the origins of the revolution in the growth of the working class in St. Petersburg, a thesis followed by industrial scenes of factories and workshops. In this visual definition of the proletariat, sooty workers toil before the undying flames of open hearths, taming and shaping hot metal in a gigantic facility that simultaneously dwarves its denizens and transforms them, through their engagement in its shared activity, into members of the proletariat. The working class is defined through a quintessentially proletarian activity – steelmaking – a synecdoche that, in the early Soviet cultural context, acted as a powerful symbol to describe the envisioned transition from a decadent, flesh-and-bone bourgeois society to the communist utopia of steel and machines.[11]

In order to depict class for children, Kustodiev turned to the device of typecasting or typicalization, depicting situations, figures, faces, and body postures that could be interpreted and perceived as typical for a certain class. His peasants, for instance, have beards and homemade clothing and tools; his workers are shown in brown and blue coveralls, either amid the work process or the revolutionary struggle; and his bourgeoisie engage in virtually nothing but the leisurely enjoyment of their wealth. This

15.2. Boris Kustodiev, "The Carpenter," in Boris Kustodiev and Mikhail Pavlov, *Sel'skii trud* (Leningrad: Brokgauz-Efron, 1925), 3.

approach was rooted in the portrait art of the late imperial period and was quite characteristic for Kustodiev himself, both before and after the revolution.[12] Moreover, as Victoria Bonnell has shown in her study of the early Soviet poster, during this period the search for *tipazh* – an artistic representation of a certain social group that would capture its most typical features – was an important aspect of Soviet art in general.[13]

It was not only Kustodiev, of course, whose art essentialized class through its typical representatives. Numerous books published in the 1920s featured imagery apparently inspired by the *lubok*, with its folk stylization through the use of unnaturally bright colours and simplistic techniques. The publisher Raduga, in particular, brought out several children's books illustrated in this style, including *Zhelezo* (*Iron*) by M. Froman (pen name of Mikhail Frakman), illustrated by Mikhail Fogt (1926) and *Len* (*Flax*) by Mikhail Andreev, illustrated by Nina Fogt (1926). *Iron* includes three poems about the professions of blacksmith, miner, and foundry worker, whom the illustrations capture at their most intense moments of labour: the blacksmith with raised hammer and shoeing a horse; the miner with raised pickaxe and navigating tunnels with a cart of coal; the foundry man taming the flames of an open hearth and melting iron (fig. 15.3).

15.3. Mikhail Fogt's illustration of a foundry man, in M. Frakman and M. Fogt, *Zhelezo* (Leningrad: Raduga, 1926), 9.

Using isometric perspectives, Mikhail Fogt (a graduate of the Leningrad Higher Art and Technical Institute who subsequently worked as a professional topographer) depicted a monumental industrial world of production operated by robust, well-built men who performed class and masculinity through demanding physical labour. The aesthetic moment of these illustrations lay in the mastery and control that working-class men exercised over this grand material world. This aesthetic moment naturalized labour as a heroic, Promethean phenomenon, as the reiteration of the Soviet man's power over technological systems, large and small. This symbolic operation is particularly evident in Mikhail Fogt's image above, where the composition is created by the gaze of the foundry man as he surveys a workshop animated and transformed by his labour.

Flax, illustrated by Nina Fogt, while more lyrical and poetic, takes a similar approach to the visualization of class for children. Nina Fogt graduated from the School of Technical Drawing of Baron Alexander von Stieglitz, and her work as a children's book illustrator drew extensively on her experience in applied design. This is particularly evident in *Flax*, where her drawing technique imitates linen needlework: lines resemble stitches, there are many embroidery patterns, and the colour scheme is dominated by white, red, and blue. This drawing technique is especially conducive to the representation of peasant labour as a festival (after all, embroidery was more typical of festive as opposed to casual dress), another form of its naturalization.[14] As such, labour in *Flax* becomes a spectacle, a transformation stimulated by the figures of female peasants who perform their class and gender by singing and dancing as they work. Moreover, their labour is manual, and all labour operations represented in the book are domestic, artisanal, and synchronized with the agricultural cycle, while the end products are consumed within the household, never reaching the market. In the latter half of the 1920s, the Soviet government was striving to mechanize agricultural labour and increase the commodity exchange between urban and rural markets, but Nina Fogt's representation of rural labour hinted at its archaic, pre-socialist character (fig. 15.4).

The aestheticization of class in Soviet children's literature was a tendency that followed the principles introduced by the World of Art at the turn of the twentieth century. As described by Soviet art critic Vsevolod Petrov, "the defining aesthetic principles of *World of Art* [were] stylization, retrospectivism, and interpretation of the real world as spectacle."[15] As a result, class in this artistic tradition was visualized in a series of stylized and clichéd images – a steelworker before an open hearth, or peasant girls – that referred not so much to actual labour processes as to earlier cultural traditions and stereotypes. More importantly, this aesthetic approach implied strong symbolic connections between class and gender, as well as between class and age.

Scenes of industrial labour in children's book were populated by male figures, as, for example, in Vladimir Mayakovsky's *Kem byt'?* (*What Should I Be [When I Grow Up]?*), illustrated by Nisson Shifrin (1929), in which the male protagonist assumes the professional roles of engineer, driver, carpenter, lathe operator, and architect. Similarly, in Samuil Marshak's *Voina s Dneprom* (*The War with the Dnieper*, 1928), illustrated by Georgii Bibikov, the grandeur of industrialization is glaringly masculine, as young and middle-aged male bodies strain to build Europe's largest (at the time) hydroelectric power plant. Boris Kustodiev's *Rural Labour*, for its part, emphasizes elderliness in its stylization of male peasants (see fig. 15.2). Depicting industrialization as the domain of the male and the modern, and agriculture as that of the female and archaic, Soviet children's literature displaced class onto gender and age, using highly visible and recognizable patterns of social distinction (male/female, young/old) to represent class divisions that, as theorized by Marxists, were far more abstract.

The Soviet avant-garde, meanwhile, with its quite particular politics of art, suggested its own ways of visualizing class for young readers. In one of his early texts, a key figure of the Soviet avant-garde, the film director Sergei Eisenstein, formulated – as if responding to Vsevolod Petrov's definition of the World of Art cited above – a new approach to cinema and the performing arts: "The way of completely freeing

15.4. Nina Fogt's illustration of girls in a flax field, in M. Andreev and N. Fogt, *Len* (Leningrad: Raduga, 1926), 2.

the theatre from the weight of 'illusionary imitativeness' and 'representationality,' which up until now has been definitive, inevitable and solely possible, is through a transition to montage of 'workable artifices.'"[16] Extrapolated to children's literature, the methods promoted in Soviet culture by Eisenstein and other avant-gardists were diametrically opposite to the aestheticism of Boris Kustodiev, Nina Fogt, and many other illustrators. The stylized representations of workers and peasants in illustrated books of the latter would fall, in Eisenstein's gloss, under the category of "illusionary imitativeness," while their tendency to merge people, tools, products, and landscape into spectacle for young audiences would fit the concept of "representationality" (the original Russian term *predstavliaemost'* alludes to performance and spectacle) (see, e.g., fig. 15.3). To these representational techniques that did not so much *describe* class as construct and *ascribe* it,[17] avant-garde illustrators counterposed techniques that explored entanglements of classed bodies, machines, and industrial networks. Their project was, in a way, about the anatomy of classes, which included not only the working body but also its prostheses: tools and machines.

In 1923, Aleksei Gastev, a Soviet pioneer of scientific management, published the book *Iunost', idi!* (*Youth, Go!*), meant to popularize scientific management for Soviet teenagers. The book had three illustrators: Iosif Shpinel' (who produced most of the collages), Ol'ga Deineko, and A. Makeeva. As in his other works, Gastev in *Youth, Go!* interprets the October Revolution as a unique historical opportunity to restructure society by modelling the organization of labour according to the workings of machinery itself. Richard Stites describes Gastev's conception of socialist labour as one of "revolutionary utopias" – "sparkling and kinetic vision of a vast continent unified by steel, electricity, and asphalt, of bright and throbbing machinery glinting in the sunlight as it labored to refashion a world, and of workers trained by industrial metronomes into something resembling a huge and elegant corps de ballet tending that machinery and deriving its graceful precision from it was a romantic dream."[18]

Gastev, indeed, was deeply interested in exploring the liminal states between the human and the machine. The network of bodily and mechanic locomotion, with one blending into the other, is one of the central themes of his books. The illustrations of *Youth, Go!* reflect this fragmented understanding of the working body. The book, addressed to young-adult enthusiasts of communist construction, encourages them to scrupulously examine how their bodies move and work, to *train* their bodies to be "working machines," master both primitive tools and the most advanced equipment, and transform the backward vastness of Soviet Russia. "Form youth teams of mechanics and go across Russia, go to its untouched spaces, go and *bring culture to the virgin land* … Become the children of the march and the camp. Good young feet, vigilant eyes, trained hands, organized head, a few tools, a notepad, reference books, a limited sum of money."[19] To illustrate Gastev's ideas, Iosif Shpinel' created a series of sketches in the suprematist and constructivist styles that accentuated this approach to the "education of the body as a working machine"[20] (fig. 15.5).

Shpinel's artistic education took place in one of the prominent centres of Soviet avant-garde art and architecture: from 1921 to 1926, he studied in the architecture department of the Higher Art and Technical Workshops in Moscow (VKhUTEMAS). Later he worked as a set designer with such prominent film directors as Aleksandr Dovzhenko (*The Arsenal*, 1929, and *Ivan*, 1932), Mikhail Romm (*Boule de Suif*, 1934), and Sergei Eisenstein (*Alexander Nevskyi*, 1938, and *Ivan the Terrible*, 1944–6).

His illustrations for *Youth, Go!* convey an image of the body reduced to a number of basic geometric shapes – circles, triangles, rectangles; a body devoid of symmetry and naturalness, and instead resembling a mannequin with limbs suspended on spherical joints and body parts freely detachable one from another. And yet this was the representative of the new working class – "the class that led a revolt … worthy of the name 'revolution,'" and that "had charted out its hopes for a century ahead" ("otmerivshii svoi nadezhdy na stoletie vpered").[21] In order to fulfil these hopes, its young members had to mobilize their mental selves and to restructure their bodies, so that the bodies as wholes and their separate organs could work in harmony with machines. Montage, a technique popularized not only by Eisenstein but also, in its photographic version, by Aleksandr Rodchenko, was a perfect fit to convey this

15.5. Iosif Shpinel', "Precise reconnaissance, alertness," in Aleksei Gastev, *Iunost', idi!* (Moscow: VTSSPS, 1923), 13.

message on the visual level. Shpinel's montages challenged the aestheticist approach to the visualization of the working class, offering for young eyes a new form of social imagination that dismantled the human, removing it from the centre of social life and placing it on the same visual level with machines. In *Youth, Go!*, the anatomy of the human hand is followed by the anatomy of an axe, insofar as both are part of a single whole: the new socialist working class (fig. 15.6).

Photomontage, with its explicit challenge to the holistic understanding of the body, became an important method in Soviet children's books that thematized new class formation and class struggle. A key text in this category was *Petiash* (1920), written by Viktor Gornyi (pen name of Viktor Savin) and illustrated by Gustavs Klucis, one of the earliest proponents and popularizers of photomontage in Soviet Russia. *Petiash* is the story of a Pioneer and student of a Moscow factory trade school, Petia (Petiash) Travin, who has come back to his home village for summer vacation. To show Petiash's rootedness in the new, industrial class culture of post-revolutionary Russia, Klucis superimposes the boy's figure over a workshop with his fellow factory-school students, which, in turn, is positioned against the background of enormous

15.6. Iosif Shpinel', "Victory is still ahead." In Aleksei Gastev, *Iunost', idi!*, 33.

and complex machinery (fig. 15.7). The montage creates the impression of an intricate connection between the boys and the machines: the huge factory wheels are set in motion by the labour of young workers, who, in turn, acquire their working-class identity through their work at the factory. In the book's logic, this connection empowers the new working-class generation: as if responding to Gastev's call to "bring culture" to the backward vastness of Russia through his industrial experience, Petiash overcomes the apathy of peasants in his home village, children and adults alike; confronts surviving representatives of the exploiting classes; organizes a Pioneer squad; stages a propaganda show; and eventually leads the villagers in their fatal vengeance on local class enemies.

This approach to the visualization of class was dominant in Soviet productivist children's books throughout the 1920s and early 1930s. If machines and industrial devices loomed large (even huge) on their pages, the purpose was not to dwarf people and reduce their importance, but rather to empower them in their struggle to transform backward, uncultured, apathetic, and sometimes openly resistant Russia into a vibrant socialist society. Il'ia Ionov's *Topotun i knizhka* (*Stomper and the Book*, 1926), illustrated by Mikhail Tsekhanovskii, for example, features a huge anthropomorphic robot,

15.7. Gustav Klucis, "[Petiash] calls himself a *fabzaichik*," (a diminutive term for a student of a factory trade school). In Viktor Gornyi and Gustav Klucis, *Petiash* (Moscow: Novaia Moskva, 1920), 7.

Stomper, that jumps out of a book page upon discovering that the protagonist, a naughty boy named Tolia, regularly damages his books. Stomper takes Tolia to a factory and shows him the entire book production process in order to educate the boy and transform him into a cultured person. Quite peculiarly, the workers at the book factory have no distinct faces; only the contours of their heads are visible, with Tsekhanovskii moreover using the same colour patterns for them as for their equipment – de-emphasizing human figures in his illustrations and putting them on a par with machines and tools. This technique was quite typical for the productivist genre of Soviet illustrated children's literature. For example, it was employed by the sisters Galina and Ol'ga Chichagova in Nikolai Smirnov's *Detiam o gazete* (*For Children about the Newspaper*, 1924) (fig. 15.8), and by Nikolai Troshin and Ol'ga Deineko in their co-authored and co-illustrated books *Kak khlopok sitsem stal* (*How the Cotton Became Chintz*, 1929), *Khlebozavod No. 3* (*Bread Factory No. 3*, 1930), and *Tysiachu plat'ev v den'* (*A Thousand Dresses a Day*, 1931). Sometimes, as in Aleksandr Samokhvalov's *Vodolaznaia baza* (*The Diving Base*, 1928), people and their tools blend into one another, producing perfect cyborgs capable of working in extreme conditions (in this case, underwater).

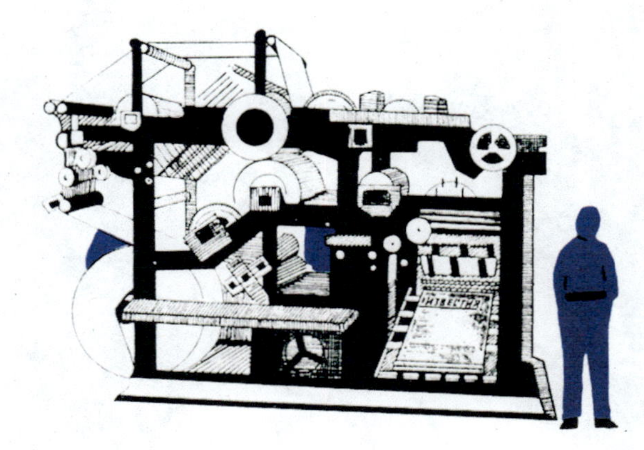

15.8. Galina Chichagova, "Rotary machine," in Nikolai Smirnov, Galina and Ol'ga Chichagova, *Detiam o gazete* (Moscow and Petrograd: Gosizdat, 1924), 13.

In recent decades, scholars including Boris Groys, Mikhail Heller, and Evgenii Steiner have interpreted these de-individualization techniques of the Soviet avant-garde as evidence of an unholy alliance between artists and the Soviet authorities, with the former furnishing the latter with symbolic and cultural tools to fully subjugate the population, strip it of free will, and reduce it to "cogs in a machine."[22] The search for a rigid ideological scheme behind Soviet children's literature leads Steiner, in particular, to claim that "the Constructivists ended up … completely eliminating the body from their maximalist project."[23] But here Steiner appears to take the holistic conception of the human body as a default norm and disregard its politics, as a result mistaking the *hybrid* body of the Soviet productivist book for the body's *lack*. This approach seems unwarranted, as Soviet children's book illustrators never interpreted the fusion of bodies and machines as a goal in itself. Quite the contrary, the mechanization of the working body was a means of its empowerment: even in Gastev's *Youth, Go!*, for all its imagery of fragmented, asymmetric bodies and emphasis on human-machine assemblages, the model working-class body, as seen in one of Ol'ga Deineko's illustrations for the book (fig. 15.9), turns out to gain strength and momentum from machines, but not blend into them.

15.9. Ol'ga Deineko, "The greatness of movement," in Aleksei Gastev, *Iunost', idi!* (Moscow: VTSSPS, 1923), 31.

Like the illustrators discussed above who took an aestheticist approach to children's literature, constructivist artists could not represent class per se or through such innate characteristics as its values or morals; their particular choice was to portray it through assemblages of working bodies and machines. To a certain degree, this approach negated the difference between proletariat and peasantry: in its didactic pathos, the productivist children's book represented socialist labour in an idealized form: how it *ought to be*, once young readers have mastered cutting-edge technologies and labour methods. Provided with modern agricultural equipment, peasants are shown successfully transformed into a rural proletariat, as in Ia. Miller and P. Basmanov's *Maslozavod* (*The Creamery*, 1931) and A. Mogilevskii's *Lovetskii kolkhoz* (*The Fishing Kolkhoz*, 1931). This politics of representation conceived the working body as a mechanized one, objectifying class through technologically advanced means of production, most importantly machines – the prostheses of the Soviet labouring body.

At the beginning of the 1930s, these two approaches to the representation of class in children's book illustration began to converge in a style that combined the didactic pathos of the constructivist book with narrative aspects (a story within a picture) and aesthetic values associated with the World of Art and its post-revolutionary successors. In 1933, this shift was addressed by Samuil Marshak – at the time, an editor of the Leningrad publishing house Detgiz – in a lengthy editorial in *Izvestiia* on the current state of Russian-language children's literature. For Soviet children, complains Marshak in the piece, "the whole world is populated by a posterish [*plakatnyi*] bourgeoisie and similarly posterish proletariat"; the main task of Soviet children's literature for the decade to come, he argues, should be to go beyond this simplified representation. "Does such a book exist," he asks in the editorial's opening, "that would show children the world – not a toy world as used to be shown in times gone by, but the real world that is fighting and restructuring itself; the world, not stopped, but at full speed?"[24]

Marshak's statement should be placed in the context of a fundamental paradigm shift in Soviet literature. It was made in the wake of the All-Union Communist Party Central Committee's 1932 resolution "On the Reconstruction of Literary and Artistic Organizations," and during preparations for the First Congress of Soviet Writers, which would establish socialist realism as the official theory and method of Soviet literature. One of the basic postulates of socialist realism was the perceived national unity of the Soviet Union, which downplayed the role of class. As historians of the interwar Soviet Union have shown, the 1930s were the period when class gradually lost its importance as the fundamental category of Soviet citizenship, a process culminating in the 1936 Constitution of the Soviet Union, which ended the practice of political disenfranchisement on the basis of class origin.[25] Marshak's reference to "posterish" representations of classes in earlier books for children – some of which he himself had produced in cooperation with the prominent illustrator Vladimir Lebedev, like the book *Yesterday and Today* mentioned in the beginning of this article – signalled a changed politics of literature. The new pedagogy of children's book illustration was no longer about how to teach children to recognize class divisions and class struggle in a proletarian state; the working body of socialism now had to undergo a transformation from a *classed* body into a *national* one. In his article, as well as in the plenary speech he delivered at the First Congress of Soviet Writers, Marshak offered, as a model of the new Soviet children's literature, *Rasskaz o velikom plane* (*The Story of the Great Plan*, 1930; published in the United States in 1931 as *New Russia's Primer: The Story of the Five-Year Plan*), written by Mikhail Il'in (pen name of his brother Il'ia Marshak) and illustrated by Mikhail Razulevich. The book describes the goals set by the first Five-Year Plan for the Soviet nation. As Lidiia Chukovskaia, Marshak's fellow editor at Detgiz, would later describe in her memoir: "The protagonist of *The Story of the Great Plan* … is a generalized image of the Soviet people. It tells of the heroic labour of the people. Its political message is the advantage of a planned, socialist economy over the chaos of a capitalist economy."[26]

The book presented its young readers with idealized imagery of socialist labour, in which machines ease the stress of toil required by people, and thus blur the traditional division of labour:

> The Five-Year Plan is one of the first great battles in the war [i.e., the war to conquer the vast Soviet territory for the Soviet people, to make it the people's own]. We must burrow into the earth, break rocks, dig mines, construct houses. We must take from the earth, lift, and transport millions of tons of ore, of coal, of peat, of building materials. But are we to do all of this with our hands? With shovel, spade, and pick? No, other weapons are needed here. We must have a shovel which can raise a wagonload of earth at once. We must have a pick which can break huge boulders into bits. But even if we should make such a shovel or such a pick, who would wield it? Obviously giant workmen are needed. But are there such giant workmen? There are. There is a giant excavator. It has only one arm, but this arm is twenty meters in length.... In the little cabin at the base of the arm sits one man, a mechanic, with seven electrical motors. For each movement of the excavator there is a special motor like a special muscle.[27]

The photographs and collages by the book's illustrator, Mikhail Razulevich, create a spectacle of people and machines working in unison. But unlike in the constructivist book, with its attentiveness to the human/machine interaction, here their assemblages are products of economic planning – of abstractions, that is, of Soviet ideology. Il'in is quite clear as to the goals that "the great plan" sets for people and machines: they are to transform the national space into a socialist landscape. Consequently, Razulevich represents the labouring body of socialism as a Soviet – rather than classed or gendered – body. His illustrations blur the borders between various social categories: male and female, young and old, peasant and proletarian. When the second edition of *The Story of the Great Plan* was published in 1931, the cover illustration featured two miners in work clothes, Davy lamps in their hands, shot from below, in an apparent allusion to the photography of Aleksandr Rodchenko. One of the figures seems to be a middle-aged man, but as to the other, it is much harder to identify the gender; of such clues as body shape or gender-specific clothing or hairstyle, the illustration offers nothing. In a similar way, it is impossible to say if the people we see in a photo of students at a tractor-operator course are peasants or workers. The utilitarian clothing and universal mechanization of labour in Razulevich's illustrations problematize class and gender distinctions (see figs. 6.2–6.6 in Larissa Rudova's chapter in this book). This approach can be observed in many other children's books of the early 1930s, such as *Kuznetskstroi: sotsialisticheskii gigant* (*The Kuznetskii Metallurgy Plant: A Socialist Giant*, 1932), written by Mikhail Gurevich and illustrated by Andrei Igumnov (fig. 15.10) or *Kolkhoznaia vesna* (*Collective Farm Spring*, 1931) written by Zoia Aleksandrova and illustrated by Aleksei Laptev (fig. 15.11).

15.10. Andrei Igumnov, "A Komsomol casting shop," a spread from *Kuznetskstroi: sotsialisticheskii gigant*, by Mikhail Gurevich (Moscow: OGIZ, 1932), 11.

15.11. Aleksei Laptev, "Kolkhoz," illustration from Zoia Aleksandrova, *Kolkhoznaia vesna* (Moscow: OGIZ, 1931), 4.

This vision of the triumphant mechanization of labour, the gradual disappearance of social distinctions, and the emergence of a single Soviet nation were apparently a product of recent historical changes. The introduction of the first Five-Year Plan and a militant de-kulakization campaign had dealt a final blow to remaining market relations in the Soviet economy. At the level of official rhetoric, social tensions could no longer be explained as a product of labour exploitation and class struggle, phenomena ostensibly overcome. Instead, as is well documented in studies of Stalinist literature, these tensions were now explained as a product of foreign intriguing and interference: no longer a class struggle, but rather an assault on the national body.[28]

It is thus unsurprising that in 1933 Marshak should refer to the children's literature of the preceding decade as portraying a "posterish" dichotomy of classes. The "real world" as it was then "restructuring itself" had no more use for visualization of the working body as a classed body, and the aesthetic forms that Soviet children's book illustrators had experimented with during the 1920s were now obsolete. Throughout the 1930s, Soviet children's book illustration increasingly interpreted labouring bodies of workers and peasants as parts of the Soviet national body. Leonid Savel'ev's exercise book *Chto my stroim* (*What We Are Building*, 1930), illustrated by Vladimir Tambi and published as a supplement to a work of the same title by Mikhail Il'in, visualized this logic in one of its illustrations, a page showing the various occupations that would be involved in the first Five-Year Plan. Each of the twenty-three figures representing these typical occupations is accompanied by the tools of their trade; taken all together, they form a spectacle of socialist labour – so far from class struggle, this is more like a pageant of professions. In the Soviet cultural logic of the 1930s, building a socialist society no longer required a grand strategy of class struggle, and authors and illustrators of Soviet children's literature instead focused on the tactics of socialist construction through professional labour. As a consequence, beginning in the 1930s, Soviet children's literature saw a sharp uptick in illustrated books about various occupations, whereas class became an increasingly obsolete concept in the Soviet visual vocabulary.

NOTES

1 Sergei Tret'iakov made this observation in regards to prerevolutionary Russian literature of the imperial age ("The Biography of the Object," 59–60). See also Sviridov, "Bol'she khoroshikh knig dlia detei," 23–4.

2 See Steiner, *Stories for Little Comrades*, 3–11.

3 Oushakine, "Translating Communism for Children," 165–70.

4 Lenin, "The Tasks of the Youth Leagues," 295.

5 See, for instance, Kiaer, *Imagine No Possessions*.

6 Oushakine, "Translating Communism for Children."

7 For more discussion of Kustodiev's art and biography see Helena Goscilo's essay in this volume.

8 Kennedy, "The *World of Art* and Other Turn-of-the-Century Russian Art Journals."
9 Kuznetsova, "U istokov sovetskoi detskoi knigi," 71. The author here uses the phrase "aesthetic unity" specifically to characterize the work performed by former World of Art members for the publisher Raduga.
10 Kravchenko (ed.), *Detiam o Lenine*. Pokrovskaia's name was not mentioned in the book; on her authorship, see Arzamastseva, "Podvizhniki detskogo chteniia," 19.
11 See Hellebust, *Flesh to Metal*; and Clark, *The Soviet Novel*, 93–113.
12 Milotvorskaia, "Boris Mikhailovich Kustodiev," 209. One of Kustodiev's printed albums was titled *Rus: Russian Types* (Kustodiev and Zamiatin, *Rus': Russkie tipy*).
13 Bonnell, *Iconography of Power*, 38, 104–5.
14 Gordeeva, *Russkaia narodnaia odezhda*, 5.
15 Petrov, *Mir Iskusstva*, 31.
16 Eisenstein, "Montage of Attractions," 79.
17 For a discussion of how the Soviet authorities and intellectuals projected Marxist class categories onto the Soviet population, see Fitzpatrick, "Ascribing Class."
18 Stites, *Revolutionary Dreams*, 155.
19 Gastev, *Iunost', idi!*, 27 (emphasis in original).
20 Ibid., 25.
21 Ibid., 5.
22 Groys, *The Total Art of Stalinism*, 14–32; Heller, *Cogs in the Wheel*, 259–61.
23 Steiner, *Stories for Little Comrades*, 97.
24 Marshak, "O nasledstve i nasledstvennosti v detskoi literature," 280, 283.
25 Fitzpatrick, "Ascribing Class"; Alexopoulos, *Stalin's Outcasts*.
26 Chukovskaia, *V laboratorii redaktora*, 276.
27 Il'in, *New Russia's Primer. The Story of the Five-Year Plan*, 28–30.
28 For a detailed account of this transformation, see Clark, *Moscow: The Fourth Rome*.

BIBLIOGRAPHY

Alexopoulos, Golfo. *Stalin's Outcasts: Aliens, Citizens, and the Soviet State, 1926–1936*. Ithaca, NY: Cornell University Press, 2003.
Arzamastseva, Irina. "Podvizhniki detskogo chteniia." *Detskiie chteniia* 1, no. 1 (2012): 12–42.
Bonnell, Victoria. *Iconography of Power: Soviet Political Posters under Lenin and Stalin*. Berkeley: University of California Press, 1998.
Chukovskaia, Lidiia. *V laboratorii redaktora*. Moscow: Iskusstvo, 1960.
Clark, Katerina. *Moscow: The Fourth Rome*. Cambridge, MA: Harvard University Press, 2011.
– *The Soviet Novel: History as Ritual*. Bloomington: Indiana University Press, 2000.
Eisenstein, Sergei. "Montage of Attractions: For 'Enough Stupidity in Every Wiseman.'" Translated by Daniel Gerould. *Drama Review* 18, no. 1 (1974): 77–84.
Fitzpatrick, Sheila. "Ascribing Class: The Construction of Social Identity in Soviet Russia." *Journal of Modern History* 65, no. 4 (1993): 745–70.
Gastev, Aleksei. *Iunost', idi!* Moscow: VTsSPS, 1923.
Gordeeva, Valentina. *Russkaia narodnaia odezhda*. Moscow: Izobrazitel'noe iskusstvo, 1974.
Groys, Boris. *The Total Art of Stalinism: Avant-Garde, Aesthetic Dictatorship, and Beyond*. Translated by Charles Rougle. Princeton, NJ: Princeton University Press, 1992.
Hellebust, Rolf. *Flesh to Metal: Soviet Literature and the Alchemy of Revolution*. Ithaca, NY: Cornell University Press, 2003.

Heller, Mikhail. *Cogs in the Wheel: The Formation of Soviet Man.* New York: Knopf, 1988.

Il'in, Mikhail. *New Russia's Primer. The Story of the Five-Year Plan.* Translated by George S. Counts and Nucia P. Lodge. Boston: Houghton Mifflin, 1931.

Kennedy, Janet. "The *World of Art* and Other Turn-of-the-Century Russian Art Journals." In *Defining Russian Graphic Arts: From Diaghilev to Stalin, 1898–1934,* edited by Alla Rosenfeld, 63–78. New Brunswick, NJ: Rutgers University Press and the Jane Voorhees Zimmerli Art Museum, 1999.

Kiaer, Christina. *Imagine No Possessions: The Socialist Objects of Russian Constructivism.* Cambridge, MA: MIT Press, 2005.

Kravchenko, Anna, ed. *Detiam o Lenine.* Moscow, Leningrad: Gosizdat, 1925.

Kustodiev, B.M., and E.I. Zamiatin, *Rus': Russkie tipy.* Petrograd: Akvilon, 1923.

Kuznetsova, G. "U istokov sovetskoi detskoi knigi." *Detskaia literatura,* no. 7 (1976): 70–3.

Lenin, Vladimir. "The Tasks of the Youth Leagues." In *Collected Works* by Vladimir Lenin, 31: 283–99. Moscow: Progress Publishers, 1977.

Marshak, Samuil. "O nasledstve i nasledstvennosti v detskoi literature." In *Sobranie sochinenii* by Samuil Marshak, 7: 279–311. Moscow: Khudozhestvennaia literatura, 1971.

– *Vchera i segodnia.* Illustrated by Vladimir Lebedev. Leningrad: Raduga, 1925.

Milotvorskaia, M.B. "Boris Mikhailovich Kustodiev." In *Ocherki po istorii russkogo portreta kontsa XIX–nachala XX veka,* edited by N.G. Mashkovtsev and N.I. Sokolova, 195–220. Moscow: Iskusstvo, 1964.

Oushakine, Serguei. "Translating Communism for Children: Fables and Posters of the Revolution." *Boundary 2* 43, no. 3 (2016): 159–219.

Petrov, Vsevolod. *Mir Iskusstva.* Leningrad: Izobrazitel'noe iskusstvo, 1975.

Steiner, Evgenii. *Stories for Little Comrades: Revolutionary Artists and the Making of Early Soviet Children's Books.* Translated by Jane Ann Miller. Seattle: University of Washington Press, 1999.

Stites, Richard. *Revolutionary Dreams: Utopian Vision and Experimental Life in the Russian Revolution.* New York: Oxford University Press, 1989.

Sviridov, N.V. "Bol'she khoroshikh knig dlia detei." *Detskaia literatura* (1971): 8–25.

Tret'iakov, Sergei. "The Biography of the Object." Translated by Devin Fore. *October,* no. 118 (2006): 57–62.

chapter sixteen

AMERIKANIZM: THE BRAVE NEW NEW WORLD OF SOVIET CIVILIZATION

THOMAS KEENAN

A peculiarity of the educative project of early Soviet children's books was that its objective was not to help young readers assimilate into an established societal world, but to exhort them to participate in the construction of a new civilization. Soviet children's books of the interwar period found themselves in the position of having to represent the abstraction of an aspirational world – the society their young readers were charged with building. Their function vis-à-vis the world they were representing was, in this sense, more prescriptive than descriptive, and this task called for some repertoire of established models and legible visual vocabularies to represent what was still in essence an imaginary category.

In these books' representation of the contemporary world at large and the new Soviet civilization's place in that world, that new civilization emerges as the immediate successor of another: American civilization. Soviet illustrated publications for children and youth from the 1920s and 1930s persistently imply, via a variety of techniques, a direct line of succession to the fledgling Soviet civilization from contemporary American modernity. There are, on the one hand, numerous depictions of choreographed mass production, industrial farming and grand engineering projects, which the historian of the early Soviet period will recognize as derivative of Taylorism and Fordism and other American engineering and agricultural innovations. Beyond these, though, within the visual language of early Soviet juvenile literature, images of the still aspirational reality of a Soviet civilization are frequently assembled from elements otherwise seen in – and only in – representations of contemporary American modernity. This iconography appears to represent a kind of visual-narrative translation for a juvenile audience of an important element of early Soviet ideological discourse – the concept of "Americanism" and of the new Soviet civilization as a "new America."

Early Soviet ideologues spoke frequently of "Americanism" as an elemental force that produced the engineering marvels of American industrial and urban modernity, a force distinct from the capitalist corruptions associated with these initial manifestations, and one that could, and indeed must, be deployed cleanly, free of any contaminating capitalist residue, to build the new Soviet civilization. Looking at more than twenty publications produced between 1918 and 1931, we see repeated efforts to communicate to a juvenile readership the notion that contemporary American industrial and urban modernity is the model for the Soviet project on the threshold of realization, and that this model, whose original capitalist expression was perverted by the injustices of that now superseded ideology, can be safely redeployed in the construction of the new socialist civilization.

In a few instances, this idea is presented at the narrative level or by way of verbal cues. Beyond these, though, there is a broader visual system observed across at least twenty-four publications from the first two decades of the Soviet era that presents young Soviet readers with strikingly similar pictures of two distinct realities: the actual reality of American modernity and the aspirational reality of a Soviet modernity project those readers were exhorted to realize. This visual system draws subtle distinctions between the American and Soviet images. It directs the viewer to perceive, in the former, manifestations of the productive surging force of modernity encumbered by the capitalist environment, and, in the latter, that same force achieving its purer, more perfect expression. Thus is the young Soviet reader encouraged to see the pictures of American modernity as correctible or perfectible within the Soviet project.

Taken cumulatively, the narrative and graphic devices discussed here betray a particular instructive agenda. They look to be parts of a larger design to excite enthusiasm for the engineering feats of American modernity, while at the same time cultivating an antipathy towards the competitive individualism and social disaggregation of American capitalist society. These narratives and images seem devised to encourage their juvenile readership to believe that the thrilling secular miracles of American modernity can be had without the perverse injustices of capitalism, and that indeed this modernity will ultimately achieve its culmination in a new socialist world pure of those corruptions – in that same environment of ideological rectitude and collectivist justice where Soviet children will grow into happy, sublimely fulfilled exponents of a humanity remade through socialist enlightenment. These publications subtly implant the idea that the future of this thrilling modernity belongs to Soviet socialism, and that their young readers have brighter futures as constituents of the righteous Soviet totality than does their cohort in the fragmented decadence of contemporary America.

Amerikanizm

The word *Amerikanizm* had widespread currency through the 1920s as a neologism denoting the innovative, organizational, and productive force of America, which

Nikolai Bukharin in a 1923 speech identified as the element that had somehow to be combined with Marxist doctrine in order to propel the new Soviet state toward its destiny.[1] The term and the concept, however, were fraught with anxiety for early Soviet ideologues, an anxiety stemming from a conflicted and ambivalent relationship to the American phenomenon. Four years after the revolution, the Soviet state was forced by practical exigencies to tolerate private enterprise, at least provisionally. This was happening at the same time as the United States – the world's second youngest major state and the one closest behind the infant Soviet state on the sociopolitical and socio-economic evolutionary ladder, per Marxist doctrine – was experiencing a massive economic boom and leading the world in technological and engineering innovations. Indeed, one of the many inevitable compromises of the early Soviet period was the mass importation of technology from the United States. Marxism posited capitalism as an ineluctable phase of passage between feudalism and socialism, and, from this perspective, as a fuller and purer embodiment of free-market capitalism than any other contemporary polity, the United States was further evolved than European nations,[2] most of which were still at least nominally ruled by monarchs in the early twentieth century. It was only by virtue of a sort of Russian populist exceptionalism conceived by figures such as Herzen and Bakunin, conceded by Marx and seized upon by Lenin, that the Bolshevik Revolution had been able to bypass the capitalism phase and give immediate rise to a socialist state on the territory of an autocratic monarchy. Early Soviet Russia thus had a closer kinship with the United States than with Europe, and the fact that the United States was a relatively young state engendered by a violent revolution against a monarchic European power contributed to this sense of affinity.

Because the Bolshevik Revolution had bypassed the capitalist-industrial phase of socio-economic and sociopolitical evolution, adoption of the industrial and technological innovations produced by American capitalism was indispensable for the viability of the new Soviet state. At the same time, the Soviets could not afford to slacken their ideological vigilance and lose sight of the fact that, in the wake of its own revolution in the name of freedom, America had reverted to a socio-economic system based on exploitation and an unequal distribution of labour and wealth. Any emulation of the American experiment by the Soviet state had to be ideologically pure, an imperative made all the more urgent by the provisional restoration of private enterprise under the New Economic Policy.

In response to this predicament, it became something of an article of early Soviet doctrine that the force responsible for the technological and engineering feats of American modernity was ideologically neutral, entirely distinct from the market forces and competitive individualism of capitalism. In the early post-revolutionary years, Soviet ideologues and intellectual and cultural figures – among them Lenin, Stalin, Trotsky, Bukharin, Karl Radek, and Aleksei Gastev – conceptualized the energy and audacity responsible for America's massive productivity and breakneck innovations in architecture and engineering as an elemental force that was not itself the product of the capitalist system, a force that was per se devoid of ideology and could be channelled to drive the same processes in the new socialist state.[3] In the years when cosmopolitanism was still the order of the day, Lenin, Bukharin and later Stalin spoke of this force, using the neologisms *Amerikanizm* and *Amerikanizatsiia*, as vitally necessary to bring about the rapid modernization and industrialization critical for the survival of the fledgling Soviet civilization.[4] Ideologues cautioned that the Soviet state had to assimilate the products of American innovation in an ideologically pure way and that the exploitative injustice of American capitalism must in no way be allowed to contaminate Soviet industrial processes, but most of the discourse on *Amerikanizm* was predicated on the belief that this was possible. It was posited as an ideologically and politically neutral charge that could be safely deployed in the building of Soviet civilization. The American Revolution and American capitalism, with their subversion of rigid longstanding social hierarchies and their increased social mobility, had unleashed a great constructive energy. The Bolshevik Revolution was the next (and final) logical phase in this process, and the Soviet state was destined to be the site of a new manifestation of this energy, rechannelled and vastly magnified. The phrase "American Russians" ("Amerikanskie russkie") was coined to denote the new exponents of this force among the Soviet population, and the Soviet Union was referred to by numerous official and unofficial figures as New Proletarian America.[5] There was a general sense that the torch of *Amerikanizm* – the juggernaut momentum of modernization – was passing from capitalist America to the new Soviet state. Indeed, massive immigration of American workers to the Soviet Union was enthusiastically anticipated and encouraged,[6] the rationale being that, since the segment of the population most responsible for America's productivity and innovation was also the segment least able to enjoy their fruits, the most energetic and productive Americans would be eager to move to a new society where they would work to improve the lives of all people, themselves included, rather than to enrich parasitic capitalist proprietors.

Soviet luminaries roundly celebrated the novel and audacious urban landscape of American cities, characterized by such fantastic feats of contemporary engineering as skyscrapers, elevated railroads, and widespread electrification. Skyscrapers, which continued to grow higher in New York and Chicago since they first appeared in the 1880s, were a marvel of contemporary engineering and still a distinctly American phenomenon in the 1920s. Skyscraper architecture had produced a built environment in these American metropolises that was entirely unlike anything seen before. For the infant Soviet state, with its ambition to transform reality through the force of the people's will, these massive towering structures, which exponentially altered the scale of the urban environment, and in general the utterly new landscape that American industry and engineering had willed into existence, were tremendously impressive and compelling achievements.[7] America's defining pioneering advances in aviation, industrialized farming, and mass production were likewise admired and taken as models for the new Soviet world under construction.

A fascination with American modernity manifested itself in the arts as well. There is the application of Taylorism in the theatrical work of Meyerhold, and other manifestations of *Amerikanizm* in the work of Lev Kuleshov, Vadim Shershenevich, and Sergei Tret'iakov.[8] Renderings of the modern American metropolitan cityscape crowded with skyscrapers adorn numerous Soviet book jackets in the 1920s. American themes are prominent, if not dominant, in the popular music of the NEP era. Perhaps most famously in the realm of artistic culture, the poets Sergei Esenin and Vladimir Mayakovsky travelled to America in the 1920s and produced work in a variety of genres in which they presented fundamentally ambivalent attitudes toward America, combining expressions of rapturous admiration for the dazzling wonders of the novel American urban environment with those of alarm and dismay at American social injustices and a perceived spiritual or cultural bankruptcy.[9]

In terms of the early Soviet view of the wider world and modernity, an interesting global map of the evolution of modern architecture emerges on the pages of the late 1920s/early 1930s journal *Sovremennaia arkhitektura* (*Contemporary Architecture*). The architecture of the Old World – the European centres – is criticized as suffering from a pompous faux-Roman grandiosity and a disorderly "eclecticism."[10] In the New World – the American metropolises of New York and Chicago – a new architecture, presented as a kind of elemental force, has erupted, sending towers of unprecedented heights skyward. Capitalism's cult of individualism, however, perverts this force on the site of its initial emergence. Extraneous ornamentalist flourishes all too often mar the astonishingly bold outsize structures produced by America's ultra-modern engineering and design achievements. This journal depicts America's ultra-modern architecture as susceptible to infection by European eclecticism and faux-Roman imperial pretensions because of its drive toward the aggrandizement of individual champions of industry and commerce. Again, such critiques advance a conception of the modernity itself as an elemental force that is ideologically neutral, that is not itself the product of the capitalist individualist drives characteristic of the site of its original manifestation, that is not inextricable from capitalist ideologies and processes. Numerous articles express the notion that this force can be freed from the perverting influences of capitalism and achieve its supreme expression in the new Soviet civilization. They also argue that, while it is critical that American architects and engineers be enlisted as technical consultants in Soviet building projects, it is just as essential that those consultants be overseen by Soviet directors capable of ensuring the ideological purity of the resulting structures.

That the pre-industrial Soviet metropolises of Moscow and Petrograd/Leningrad had to be radically transformed – both in order to accommodate the mass migration there from the countryside and for them to become the representative capitals of a new Soviet civilization – was an imperative unanimously recognized among the post-revolutionary élite. The model for the new Soviet city and in particular the question of whether to adopt and how to adapt the urban model of the twentieth-century

American metropolis were matters of some debate, a debate that filtered down into contemporary juvenile literature. In the mid-1920s on the pages of the youth magazine *Smena* (*The Shift*), different models of the "city of the future" are discussed. Some pieces present the "skyscraper city" as an oppressive inhuman landscape born of the will of profiteers to maximize real-estate income, a landscape where the proletariat are warehoused in dark crowded towers. Others enthusiastically embrace it as the perfect model for the socialist metropolis, "a . . . victory of humanity over the skies."[11] In general, the subject of American metropolitan urbanism is widely photographically and pictorially represented, and its suitability as a model for the Soviet civilization project widely discussed, in the periodical literature for young readers through the first decade and a half of the post-revolutionary era. Around this same time, Trotsky published his pamphlet "O novom byte" ("On the New Daily Life"), where, in sections titled "Collectivism and Americanism," "What Is Americanism?", and "What Should We Take from the Americans?", he discusses American metropolitan skyscraper urbanism as a model that is, with minor modifications, ideally suited for the Soviet communal living project.[12]

Amerikanizm in Early Soviet Juvenile Literature

Arguably, all the early Soviet period's so-called production books and the books depicting industrial farming, railroads, aeronautics, and other feats of modern engineering implicitly reference, to some extent, the United States of America, inasmuch as, historically, we know that Soviet ambitions in these areas were informed by contemporary American achievements (fig. 16.1). The Five-Year Plan books, logically, in some measure represent efforts to compete with America, then the world's most advanced country in terms of engineering, technology, and mass production, and to enlist the products of American capitalist ultra-modernity in the righteous project of building a socialist utopia (figs. 16.2 and 16.3).

This is made more explicit in some cases than in others. Some texts mention America by name. Others stick to the more generic "capitalists." In the latter cases, however, America is unquestionably the primary referent as the world's most industrially and technologically advanced power at the time. Moreover, for anything published in 1930 or afterwards, America would also have the crucial significance of the site of the stock market crash of 1929 – the catastrophe that seemed to expose and punish the perversions and injustices of capitalism and to portend an impending ultimate collapse of that system. The borrowing of American technology and even of American expertise is often openly declared but always presented as a transfer of technology and knowledge from succeeded to successor – the migration of the force of modernity from a decadent civilization to an ascendant new civilization where that force will achieve its apotheosis.[13] These texts tend to emphasize the imperative to ensure

16.1. A rendering of the early twentieth-century American metropolis à la New York or Chicago by Boris Kustodiev in Lidia V. Lesnaia, *Dzhimmi Dzhoi v gosti k pioneram* (Leningrad: GIZ, 1920).

16.2. A hypothetical Soviet city of the future dominated by skyscrapers, radio towers, and elevated railroads, from Aleksei Laptev, *Piatiletka* (Moscow: GIZ, 1930).

16.3. Vladimir Akhmet'ev's depiction of a future Soviet Moscow crowded by skyscrapers, from Nina Saksonskaia, *Pesn' o dirizhable* (Moscow: OGIZ-Molodaia gvardia, 1931).

the new civilization's ideological purity and to guard vigilantly against infection by the capitalist perversions that attend manifestations of engineering and technological ultra-modernity in America.

There are a few instances in which this imperative is addressed at the level of the narrative. In these examples, the introduction of American engineering novelties into the environment of the fledgling Soviet civilization is initially disruptive, gives rise to perverse capitalist impulses (envy, greed, or arrogance), and requires ideologically corrective interventions. In *Dom i domishko* (*Home and Hovel*), from 1930, the introduction of an American element, the skyscraper, occasions a number of conflicts which ultimately achieve a collectivist resolution. Righteous but unenlightened figures of the aging disenfranchised Russian worker (Grandma and Grandpa) have an irrational attachment to the familiar structure of their dilapidated wooden hovel, and experience a kind of awed terror at the towering alien structure of the skyscraper. The more enlightened figure of the Soviet child recognizes the promise of collectivism and social progress inherent in the new structure and reassures the reader that there is a place in the new collective home for *babushka* and *dedushka*.[14] Another conflict arises when the sight of the skyscraper arouses a proprietary impulse in an onlooker who wants to own the building. The child exposes the perversion of this individualistic possessive drive and instructs the reader on how to read the new structure: as a product of a mass collective effort, built for mass collective benefit, a structure built for the builders.[15]

Elsewhere these conflicts are played out in a world of anthropomorphized objects. In *Spor mezhdu domami* (*Buildings' Quarrel*), from 1925, the introduction of towering many-storeyed buildings into the early Soviet context brings with it a divisive individualism and a jockeying for pride of place among the buildings themselves. Visually patent derivatives of contemporary Soviet representations of American metropolitan structures, the buildings are depicted as requiring re-education to the collectivist ethos in order to understand that, in the new Soviet civilization, progress is not driven by competition and the promise of individual glory. In *Kak primus zakhotel fordom sdelat'sia* (*How the Primus Stove Came to Want to Be a Ford*) from 1927, the introduction of the state-of-the-art American automobile excites envy in another gas-fuelled machine – the primus stove. Awed by the power and speed of the Ford, it develops a fantasy of becoming one itself, as well as a disdain for its own much more humble function as a kitchen appliance. In the primus stove's musings, Ford is paired in a rhyme with "proud" or "haughty" ("eslib ia byl 'Fordom' / Byl by ia uzhasno gordym"; "If I were a 'Ford'/ I would be terribly proud"). The stove entertains aggressive and self-aggrandizing fantasizes about using the great power and speed of the Ford to scatter everyone and everything in its path and leave them in its dust. Ultimately, both the primus stove and the towering buildings are re-educated and made to understand the principle of distributed effort and distributed benefit – the notion that rewards and honour come not as benefits commensurate with the individual's efforts and contributions, but as equal participation in the benefits and glory of collective achievement. In a meeting with Kalinin, the primus stove is made to understand that the seemingly modest function it serves as a kitchen appliance is essential to the collective effort of the new socialist civilization, and that it therefore participates in the glory of that civilization as much as the speedy and imposing new American machines. The arrogant towers in *Spor mezhdu domami* are finally humbled and bow deeply before the small structure of the elementary school, which, they come to understand, provides the foundational learning on which the towers themselves rest. In the end, the primus stove and the towering buildings come to accept an order where there can be no pride of place, where all constituents of the civilization are equally valuable and equally beneficiary, and glory is produced by all for all.

More broadly, Soviet illustrated juvenile literature from this period presents a conflicted and ambivalent posture vis-à-vis American modernity in visual configurations that recur across numerous publications illustrated by different artists. The division of American modernity into ideologically neutral productive elements and extraneous capitalist vices, the transfer of the productive elements to the new environment of the nascent Soviet civilization, and the ideologically pure expression of those elements in the realization of the Soviet project are implicitly communicated in images where the recurrence and variation of visual vocabularies establish pictures of an actual American reality and an aspirational Soviet reality as versions of one another. In this versioning, the Soviet pictures resemble a correction, in various senses, of the American ones: new ideal versions of the American pictures, where the constituent elements have been subsumed and harmonized under an overarching order, and the fragmentation and cacophony of the American pictures have been resolved in new pictures of a total, universally beneficent integration.

One encounters the occasional image of the American countryside in children's books of this period, usually connected with representations of high-speed locomotives. A vast, largely rural territory with great distances between urban centres was, of course, another aspect of the affinity between the new Soviet polity and the United States, and the development of railroads was the principal measure addressing the imperative to preserve cohesion of the far-flung geopolitical entity. Indeed, America's singularly advanced railway system and locomotive engineering were technologies the Soviets were working expeditiously to assimilate.

The abstraction "Americanism," however, tends more often to be synecdochically represented by images of twentieth-century American metropolitan urbanism. In Aleksei Gastev's book *Iunost' idi!* (*Youth, Go!*) from 1923 and Iurii Gralitsa's book *Detskii internatsional* (*Children's International*) from 1926, we see a kind of emblematic complex instantiated in condensed images that appear to represent America in configurations of cubic skyscrapers with rows of rectangular windows, ironwork of bridges or cranes, and a car or car wheel. The two vectors of the American phenomenon as represented in these synecdochic icons are gravity-defying altitude (skyscraper architecture) and horizontal speed (automotive machines). In the textual accompaniment to the visual iconography in *Youth, Go!* – "We'll take the tempest of the USSR Revolution and infuse the pace of American life" – we see a reference to a more conceptual speed, the "speed of life" or "pace of life" in America, as though life itself somehow moved faster there. Gastev's proposition here, once again, seems to imply that this force is politically or ideologically neutral, that the force itself is not the product of capitalism and not inextricable from the original capitalist site of its manifestation, that it can be safely transferred to Soviet life (fig. 16.4). In *Children's International*, two juxtaposed floating renderings – one of a Ford and one of a cluster of skyscrapers and an ironwork bridge representing New York City – are captioned by verse text emphasizing, on the one hand, the speed of the automobile and the exhilarating spectacle of the soaring structures and, on the other, the exploitative inequities of American capitalism (fig. 16.5).[16]

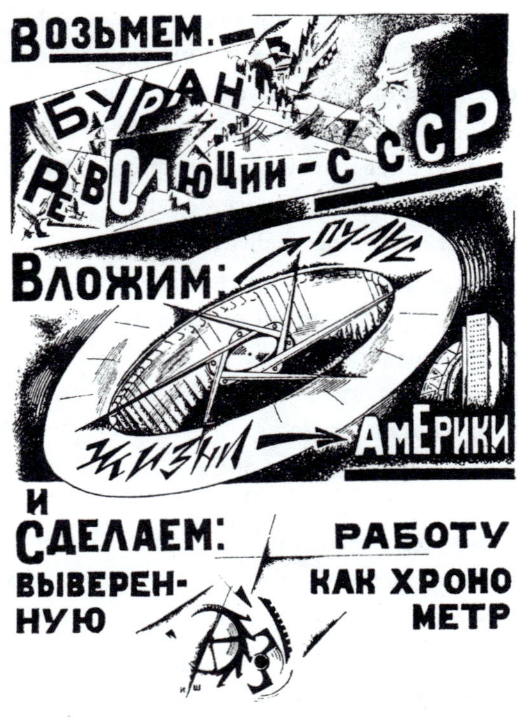

16.4. A composite image by Iosif Shpinel' with text that reads "We'll take the tempest of the USSR Revolution, infuse the pace of American life and produce work as precise as a chronometer." From Asleksei Gastev, *Iunost', idi!* (Moscow: VTSSPS, 1923).

Elsewhere these emblems are expanded into pictures extending across the implicit virtual three-dimensional grid of perspectival two-dimensional representation. These full-scale representations of American metropolitan cityscapes appear in several Soviet juvenile publications from the 1920s and 30s.[17] They are dominated by skyscrapers, which form the vertical axis and set the grand scale of the depicted space. In several cases, these distinctly American marvels of contemporary engineering are presented in apparently haphazard clusters. Motley agglomerations of towers of varying heights and shapes, multiple peaks and height variation at irregular intervals seem to represent the eclecticism and divisive egotism condemned on the pages of *Sovremennaia arkhitektura* and *Smena*. The ultimate effect of these compositions is that of an imposing but disordered crowding of idiosyncratic individual structures in the absence of any greater overarching structure or design. In some illustrations, towers featuring curved or jagged lines disrupt the rectilinearity and quasi-uniformity of elongated rectangular boxes with grids of rectangular windows.[18] In others, the disposition of rectangular-box towers creates curved or irregular lines.[19] Overall, the disordered ensembles

„Форд" в поля бросает глянец,
по дороге вьется пыль,
завернул американец,
осадив автомобиль.
— Здравствуйте, родные братцы!

Хоть внушают вам восторг
небоскребы и Нью-Йорк,
но нетрудно разобраться,
что, как прочие рабочие,
за работой дни и ночи мы
тянем каторжный свой срок!

16.5. Georgii Echeistov, an illustration for Iurii Gralitsa, *Detskii internatsional* (Moscow: GIZ, 1926).

of skyscrapers in these depictions of contemporary American metropolitan urbanism deviate from or disrupt the rectilinearity and order of the implicit three-dimensional grid of the perspectival two-dimensional illustrations (fig. 16.6).

The visual clutter of the skyscrapers on the vertical axis is compounded on the horizontal axis by the paths of moving machines and the movements and sightlines of human figures. In the visual-verbal icons from *Youth, Go!* and *Children's International*, the vertical axis of the towering architectonic structures combines with the horizontal axis of the speeding automobile. These more fully elaborated pictures of American modernity feature three categories of ultra-modern high-velocity machine: cars, trains, and airplanes. The speedy horizontal motion of these machines introduces a visual cacophony on the horizontal axis that echoes the disunity of the skylines. The paths of vehicles are meandering and/or intersect with the courses of other vehicles or pedestrians, setting up tangled networks of potential blockages and collision courses that thwart the order of the pictures' implicit three-dimensional grids. In Boris Kustodiev's illustration from *Dzhimmi Dzhoi v gosti k pioneram* (*Jimmy Joy Visits the Pioneers*, 1925), two elevated railroads intersect at an acute angle (see fig. 16.1). Cars

5

Везет нас поезд
      целый день,
то лес,
      то город мимо.
И
мимо ихних деревень
летим
      с хвостом из дыма.

6

Качает пароход вода.
Лебедка тянет лапу—
      подняла лапой чемодан,
      а мы идем по трапу.
      Пароход полный,
      а кругом волны,
      высоки и солоны.
      Волны злятся—
            горы вод
      смыть грозятся пароход.
      Ветер,
         бурей не маши нам,—
быстро движет нас машина:
под кормой крутя винтом,
погоняет этот дом.
Доехали до берега—
      тут и Америка.

16.6. (this page and opposite) A drawing by David Shterenberg of New York harbour and the skyscrapers and elevated trains of Manhattan, from Vladimir Mayakovsky, *V. Maiakovskii – Detiam* (Moscow: OGIZ-Molodaia gvardia, 1931).

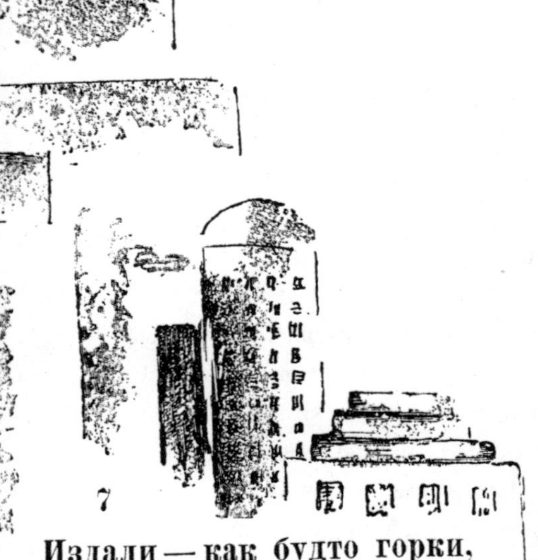

7

Издали — как будто горки,
ближе — будто
горы тыщей, —
        вот какие
в Нью-Йорке
стоэтажные домища.
Все дни народ снует вокруг
с поспешностью блошиною,
не тратят зря —
            ни ног, ни рук,
        а все творят машиною.
Как санки
        по снегу
            без пыли
скользят горой покатою,
так здесь
скользят
        автомобили,
и в них
сидят богатые.

speed in a curved arc that crosses directly in front of the path of a tram on a curved track. Six airplanes appear to meander aimlessly in the sky above without any clear direction. The sightlines and paths of the foregrounded human figures likewise intersect, showing those figures to be at cross purposes. Similarly, in David Shterenberg's Manhattan landscape from Vladimir Mayakovsky's *Detiam* (*For Children*), there is no order or direction to the cars at the bottom of the page (see fig. 16.6). The miniscule human figures too are scattered and follow disparate intersecting paths. Miniaturized against the enormous scale of the buildings, they are drawn as looking either down or straight ahead and appear as alienated from the gargantuan built environment as they are from each other.

This vertical polarization is a device used in several depictions of American cityscapes to separate a productive modernizing force from capitalist vices that corrupt the expressions of that force in contemporary America. In *Grishkiny puteshestviia: Amerika* (*Grishka's Travels: America*), verse text accompanying an image of lower Manhattan crowded with skyscrapers juxtaposes the awesome height of the towers with a flattening oppressiveness on the ground (see note 16). In Shterenberg's drawing from Mayakovsky's *For Children*, the pedestrian figures are so tiny against the height of the Manhattan skyscrapers that they are almost not recognizable as human. An earthbound or down-weighed quality is frequently an implied property of greedy oppressors and cowed masses, while human figures representing carriers of the productive energy of Americanism, generally children or workers, are endowed with a kind of levity. In *Zheleznye puteshestvenniki* (*Iron Travellers*, 1931), drawings of an imposing Manhattan skyline are juxtaposed with insurgent workers with upstretched arms. The cover of the eighth issue of *Pioner* (*Pioneer*) in 1933 (fig. 16.7) foregrounds heavyset, jowly American policemen snarling at a crowd of lean youth marching under upheld red "May 1st" banners, which extend as high in the visual field of the image, as do the rectangular skyscrapers in the background.

Polarization of elements of a thrilling vigorous and transformative modernity (up) and a slothful decadent parasitism (down) can be observed in illustrations by Boris Kustodiev for two parallel American-Soviet succession narratives from 1925. In these books – *Bol'shevik Tom* (*Tom the Bolshevik*), with text by Nadezhda Pavlovich, and *Jimmy Joy Visits the Pioneers*, with text by Lidiia Lesnaia – illustrations featuring heavy, decrepit idle wealthy American adults and strong insurgent young protagonists visually plot vertical trajectories in stories about American boys getting out from under their oppressive, indolent guardians and realizing their dreams of escaping America to join the Pioneers in Leningrad. In *Tom the Bolshevik*, a reworking of the Tom Sawyer story, the illustrations show the lean young hero rising above reclining and/or declining figures of an obese aunt and crumbling American patriarchs to meet his destiny in the land of the Bolsheviks. In *Jimmy Joy*, upward momentum is a defining property of Jimmy, who is always shown, often through contrivances of perspective, either located in or climbing toward the uppermost part of the picture. Jimmy's

16.7. May Day march, cover of *Pioner*, no. 8 (1933).

youthful buoyancy is, again, in some images contrasted against the inert weight of an aging American oppressor class.

The illustration from *Jimmy Joy* in figure 16.1 establishes a visual connection between the levity of the young male protagonist, on his way to join the Pioneers, and the vertical momentum of American modernity as manifested in the new American metropolitan built environment. Against a background of lofty skyscrapers jutting into the sky, soaring airplanes, and stilted railroads high above the ground, a car conveying Jimmy's father, a wealthy capitalist identified by the satirical topoi of the top hat and monocle, is weighted down in the foreground by the burdensome encumbrances of immoderate wealth. The backdrop for this image is full of exhilarating upward momentum and gravity-defying marvels of contemporary engineering. Heavy, powerful locomotives glide high above the ground on elevated railroads, sending plumes of white and black smoke skyward. Skyscrapers shooting into the sky crowd the centre of the upper half of the picture. Airplanes – in 1925 an American novelty allowing humans to triumph over gravity – fill the surrounding airspace. While ostensibly part of the foregrounded ensemble of Americans, the child protagonist is separated from them by the image's vertical polarization. He is elevated well above the figures of American adults, and alone seems drawn into the upward sweep of the American urban landscape that makes up the image's background. Balanced precariously on its lower right corner, the suitcase in which he is stowed seems almost to float on top of the car, and the angle that frames his face (the angle formed by the lower-left, upper-left, and upper-right corners of the suitcase) points almost straight up, resembling a kind of upward arrow. A representative of the newest generation of Americans, Jimmy seems to partake of the power that willed the new towering American urban reality into existence and gave human beings the power of flight, while the American adults are represented as heavy, earthbound, laden down with the ill-gotten spoils of capitalist exploitation.

A migration of the force responsible for American modernity to the more just Soviet project, presented in *Tom the Bolshevik* and *Jimmy Joy* through the narrative conceit of the American juvenile hero who escapes to the land of the Bolsheviks, also manifests itself in many publications of this period in the visual language of their illustrations. Images by different artists from numerous publications demonstrate a variety of strategies for depicting an aspirational Soviet civilization that is both strikingly reminiscent of representations of the contemporary American metropolis, and an expression of an ethos radically antithetical to that of American capitalism. These images reinflect the landscape of American metropolitan urbanism to produce something that looks very much like a socialist New York or Chicago, with the energy and engineering marvels that typify those ultra-modern urban environments somehow harmonized under an overarching collectivist justice.

In some of these illustrations, this same vertical polarization, used in American cityscapes to separate elements representing corrupt decadence from those representing a vigorous modernity, is used to distinguish between elements belonging to the

16.8. Crowd carrying red banners. The banner in the foreground reads "We are the builders of a new life." Cover of *Smena*, no. 1 (1924).

pre- and post-revolutionary realities in Russia. The cover image on the very first issue of the youth magazine *Smena* shows a crowd passing under an archway carrying red banners (fig. 16.8). The banner in the foreground reads "We are the builders of a new life." The archway, which represents the implied "old life," is a ponderous piece of architecture assembled from large pieces of heavy stone. The artist represents its succumbing to gravity in crumbly ragged details, the broken arch and stone ruins piled on the ground. This foregrounded archway serves as a kind of proscenium for the "new life" beyond it in the background. The new life is represented in towering skyscraper structures, elevated roadways raised high above the ground on slender ironwork, and airplanes and a rigid airship hovering in the sky. The weight and decrepitude of the earthbound old life is juxtaposed with the new life's levity and vigour, which soars into the sky or floats above the ground. The tallest structure of the cityscape of the "new life" flies a red banner, doubling a red banner held up by the highest-placed member of the marching crowd.

A similar vertical polarization informs the visual and verbal representation of the old versus the new in the book *Home and Hovel*. In this illustrated narrative, the word *dom* (building, house, or home) denotes a new Soviet residential structure, the many-storeyed steel, stone, and glass tower pushing into the sky, while *domishko*, a pejorative diminutive form of *dom* – refers to a low and fragile wooden structure slowly giving in to gravity.[20] An illustration on the book's back cover shows the rickety two-storey *domishko* sinking toward the ground, while a scaffolded structure for the *dom* ascends in the background. Higher still than this structure is an airplane hovering in the sky.

In *Buildings' Quarrel* and *How the Primus Stove Came to Want to Be a Ford*, Soviet assimilation of the products of American modernity is played out on the narrative level, which depicts overweening objects being subordinated to a larger collectivist order and ultimately coming to see the justice of this. Elsewhere the idea of the Soviet project rechannelling the force of American modernity and modifying and harmonizing the products of American modernity within the new collectivist civilization is communicated primarily through visual means. Perhaps the crudest device is the application of socialist verbal labels to towering structures unmistakably derivative of American skyscraper architecture (or representations thereof in early Soviet graphic arts). In *Buildings' Quarrel*, for example, a towering many-storied building of somewhat fanciful design, including a circular socket at the top to accommodate a large clock, is labelled with banners that read "Main co-op" and "Everything for everyone" (fig. 16.9). One of Aleksei Laptev's illustrations for his 1930 book *Five-Year Plan* also demonstrates this tactic (see fig. 16.2). Renderings of towering structures essentially indistinguishable from early Soviet illustrations of American skyscrapers bear signs reading "Gazeta Pravda redaktsiia" (*Pravda* editorial office), "Institut im. Lenina" (Lenin Institute), and "Zavod VTUZ" (Polytechnic Institute). Moreover, networks of power lines and banners displaying Five-Year Plan slogans connect the towers and impart a sense of cohesion and universal participation in a totalizing project to an image that otherwise looks very much like the composition of randomly crowded individualized towers and elevated railroads seen in Kustodiev's American landscape in *Jimmy Joy*. In *Home and Hovel*, verbal text that distinguishes the cityscape in the illustrations from its capitalist forebears achieves an ideological reinflection of the skyscraper structure. The verse text, which describes these towering structures as a kind of secular miracle,[21] declares that they are not for sale, that they cannot be bought or sold because they were built for the same workers whose collective effort produced them.[22]

Elsewhere in renderings of an aspirational Soviet civilization that resemble ideologically corrected American metropolises, more subtle formal and compositional properties communicate the subordination of the elements of this ultra-modern built environment to a single unifying inspiring principle. In some instances, this is achieved through a greater uniformity of towering structures – most often rectilinear hexahedrons with grids of rectangular windows – and/or greater regularity in their disposition (fig. 16.12).[23] In others, multitudes of smokestacks and radio towers on

16.9. Nikolai Kupreianov's illustration of a Soviet co-op modelled on the American skyscraper department store. The vertical signs tell us that this store has "everything for everyone." From Nikolai Agnivtsev, *Spor mezhdu domami* (Ryazan: Druz'ia detei, 1925).

16.10. Skyscrapers in the background of the Shukhov tower in an illustration by Evgeniia Abramova in Elizaveta Tarakhovskaia, *Radio-brigada* (Moscow: GIZ, 1930).

Soviet skylines place a decisive emphasis on technology, production, and industry, in contrast to the emphasis on consumption or aesthetic grandiosity in similar American metropolitan landscapes (figs. 16.10 and 16.13).[24] In several of these illustrations, the ironwork of cranes or towers of scaffolding dominate the modern metropolitan Soviet skylines.[25]

This composition has the effect both of accentuating the process of building these ambitious structures and the enormous coordinated collective effort this construction requires, and of allowing the illustrator to suggest a not yet unveiled Soviet expression of the massive innovative vigour that produced the ultra-modern American metropolises. Thus do some artists postpone representation of a yet to be realized Soviet project of a new, vibrant, speedy, and soaring Americanoid metropolis entirely free of the vices and perversions of capitalism. The accent on construction in these images (the prominence of cranes and scaffolding) also has the effect of implying upward motion, whereas, in the pictures of American cityscapes, clusters of towering structures have the static, ossified aspect of a civilization that has achieved its peak and begun to decline (figs. 16.11 and 16.14).

Several representations of the construction of this new Soviet urbanism, in addition to foregrounding the mass-coordinated effort of the building process, emphasize the collectivism and uniformity of the civilization for which these structures are being produced (fig. 16.14). Behind scaffolding and other construction apparatuses emerge hive-like structures of grids of identical rectangular windows repeated ad infinitum on towering rectangular structures as a synecdoche or emblem of a new Soviet urbanism under construction, a wider, more total picture of which is not yet in evidence.[26] In a subset of images, such as in Mikhail Gurevich's *Kuznetskstroi sotsialisticheskii gigant* (*Kuznetsk Metallurgy Plant: Socialist Giant*, 1932), ensembles of massive tower-like factory structures seem to stand in for the skyscraper cityscapes and to provide the vertical axis and grand scale for a grid that includes ordered horizontal rows of vehicular and pedestrian motion (fig. 16.15). The greater rectilinearity and regularity in the form and arrangement of the towering skyscraper-like structures in these images of a Soviet civilization (with respect to their counterparts in early Soviet representations of the contemporary American metropolis) is thus reinforced on the horizontal axes of the imaginary three-dimensional space of the images; a consistent rectilinearity – seemingly a spatial expression of an ideological rectitude – is evident in the paths of moving machines and people. The tangled disorder of multitudes of vehicles and pedestrians, each pursuing their own individual ends and cutting their own arbitrary paths through the space of the picture, is corrected in pictures of a new Americanoid Soviet urbanism. Here automobiles and airplanes travel in formation or in tandem, or along straight paths, and this imparts a purposefulness to their motion.[27] The acute-angle criss-crossing of railroads observed in American urban landscapes such as Kustodiev's from *Dzhimmi Dzhoi* is corrected into a right-angle grid in analogous Soviet metropolitan landscapes, such as Laptev's in *Five-Year Plan*. In general, the flow of traffic, like the towering structures that dominate the landscapes, reinforces rather than deviates from the implicit three-dimensional grid of the represented space. A total cubic structure emerges, one whose grid of straight channels geometrically corrects or rectifies the multitudinous mess of individual machines and pedestrians in the American cityscapes. A sense of total participation and individual fulfilment and self-realization within a totalizing order is expressed through the human figures in these images as well. These tend to be rendered as grouped identical figures forming larger repeated complexes, or minimally differentiated figures engaged in some common enterprise.[28] In some images, the repetition of composite figures (composed of groupings of human figures or combinations of human figures and machines) echoes the patterning of the grids of rectangular skyscraper widows, which often extend beyond the visual field, implying potentially infinite replication. When the sightlines of human figures in these pictures are traceable, they tend to share a common focus, enthusiasm for which is sometimes expressed by upstretched arms.

16.11. (this page and opposite) Unknown artist, from Agniia Barto, *Dom i domishko* (Moscow: Rabochaia Moskva, 1930).

Кто это на улице
встал столбом?
Стоит на дом любуется:
— ВОТ ЭТО ДОМ!

Дом из камня высечен.
Уступы — этажи.
— Вот, берите тысячи,
я хочу тут жить!

16.12. S. Kostin's illustration of a child's dream city, composed of the elements of the contemporary American urban metropolis: skyscrapers with grids of windows, high-speed automobiles and locomotives, and airplanes. In Ivan Molchanov, *Kol'ka i Lenin: rasskaz dlia detei* (Moscow: GIZ, 1924).

16.13 Efim Khiger, design for Nikolai Tikhonov, *Sami* (Leningrad: GIZ, 1924).

16.14. Tatiana Zvonareva's illustration of a Soviet city under construction shows a landscape of rising skyscrapers with grids of rectangular windows. In Nina Saksonskaia, *Mamin most* (Moscow: OGIZ-Molodaia gvardia, 1933).

16.15. Andrei Igumnov, illustrations for Mikhail Gurevich, *Kuznetskstroi: sozialisticheskii gigant* (Moscow: OGIZ, 1932).

Lucy Sprague Mitchell and the Juvenile Literature of 1920s American Metropolitan Urbanism

Another aspect of early Soviet interest in contemporary American modernity was an attentiveness to developments in early childhood education and children's books coming out of left-leaning circles in the United States, and in particular out of New York. The figure of greatest note here is Lucy Sprague Mitchell, an advocate of early childhood education reform who in 1916 was one of the founding members of the New York–based Bureau of Educational Experiments. Sprague Mitchell criticized the traditions of fairy tales and folkloric, fantastic narratives in children's literature. She found that they perpetuated unfortunate and irrational patriarchal models of social organization and behaviour, and actually hindered children's cognitive and psychological development.

She counterposed her own novel genre of children's narrative, the "here and now story," and in 1921 published her *Here and Now Story Book*.[29] The book contains a lengthy introduction in which Sprague Mitchell expounds her idea that children's literature should cultivate cognitive faculties and foster psychological development by helping children to understand and achieve agency in their actual environment. For her audience, that environment is early twentieth-century American modernity, primarily the ultra-modern environment of New York City in the 1920s. The book features stories such as "The Subway Car," "Boris Takes a Walk and Finds Many Different Kinds of Trains," "Boris Walks Every Way in New York," "Automobile Song," and "The Sky Scraper."[30] Sprague Mitchell was extensively translated and published in the Soviet Union. Sixteen Soviet editions of her work were issued between 1924 and 1930, including a 1925 translation of her *Here and Now Story Book*. Individual editions of the stories "Boris Walks Every Way in New York" ("Kak Boria gulial po N'iu–Iorku"), and two separate editions of "Sky Scraper" ("Neboskreb") were also published in 1927 (fig. 16.16). It is easy to see the parallels, or "isomorphism," to use the language of the scholar Evgenii Steiner,[31] between Sprague Mitchell's here-and-now philosophy and early Soviet ideas about the educative potential of children's literature, whether or not direct influence is proposed. It should be noted, though, that Steiner and Julie Mickenberg do indicate that Sprague Mitchell enjoyed large print runs in the Soviet Union and was read and referenced by practitioners of and commentators on the new Soviet children's literature.[32]

Early Soviet books, much like the American books of Sprague Mitchell, use the secular miracles of early twentieth-century industry and engineering to excite young readers' curiosity and imagination. This implicit coincidence between Soviet and American children's literature in this period makes sense, given the existential reality of America's singular industrial advancement and the early Soviet predicament. But what seems most interesting in the period up until the mid 1930s is a much more explicit referentiality to American cities in these books' images, a surprising consistency

16.16. Konstantin Vialov, an illustration from the second Soviet monographic edition of Lucy Sprague Mitchell's story "The Sky Scraper," in *Neboskreb* (Moscow & Leningrad: Gosudarstvennoe izdatel'stvo, 1930).

between the visual vocabulary used to represent Soviet and American modernity in early Soviet children's books and the necessary shift in representational modality moving from the American books to their early Soviet analogues.

The assertively indicative mode of Sprague Mitchell's "here and now" books becomes a subjunctive or imperative mode in the early Soviet ones. Sprague Mitchell's books are in a sense aimed at defamiliarizing the realia of their young readers' environment and inspiring appreciation for their ultra-modern urban world of 1920s New York City. Exposition of the astounding feats of science and engineering that produced familiar features of the American urban child's landscape was meant to replace the fiction of magic as a catalyst for excitement, curiosity, and imaginative creativity. A visual vocabulary strikingly similar to that used both in American and Soviet publications to represent the contemporary ultra-modern urbanism of the American metropolis is applied, often with very little modification, in the representation of an entirely aspirational reality: the new Soviet modernity that the juvenile reader is exhorted to build. The word "miracle" (*chudo*) is used to characterize the construction of skyscrapers in *Dom i domishko*[33] and a larger dream-vision cityscape in *Kol'ka i Lenin* (1927),[34] the illustrations for which feature towering buildings with grids of rectangular windows, airplanes, and speeding cars and trains. Unlike in Sprague Mitchell's American books, in the books for Soviet children this visual vocabulary of modernity is constituted from representations of phenomena unlike anything their readership has ever seen. In some cases, this is diegetically motivated, in that images of purely imaginary Soviet landscapes crowded with towering structures appear as dream visions of children imagining the Soviet capitals. This is the case in *Kol'ka i Lenin* and *Sami* from 1924.[35] Elsewhere, however, similar compositions of towering structures, soaring aircraft, and speeding automobiles are used casually to represent a Soviet modernity still to be built. Far from defamiliarizing elements of the Soviet child-reader's existential environment, these visual vocabularies would have been unrelatable to the environment of their target readership, even in Moscow and St. Petersburg. Used in the indicative mode in Soviet books depicting contemporary American metropolitan urbanism, these images would have represented for their young Soviet beholders a remote reality of almost total alterity. The Soviet modernity these visual vocabularies are engaged to represent in other contexts is an entirely aspirational one.

The representations of a Soviet civilization considered here manifest an interesting aspect of the Soviet project's conception of its place in the world and in history in the 1920s and 30s. Adopting a philosophy of children's literature very similar to that proposed by Lucy Sprague Mitchell and New York's Bureau of Educational Experiments, to whatever extent they were or were not directly influenced by it, these early Soviet children's books rely heavily on the iconography of American metropolitan urbanism in their presentation of an exhilarating modernity to take the place of the alluring magic and fantasy of fairy tales as a stimulus for curiosity and imagination. In a broad sample of books and images, the same visual vocabulary used to represent one category of imaginary reality, a remote objective reality of which the reader has had no direct experience, is used to represent an imaginary reality of another category, the aspirational reality of a yet to be built Soviet modernity. The ambivalence inherent in Soviet *Amerikanizm* manifests through a variety of visual and narrative devices. The tension between admiration for the industrial and engineering feats of American modernity and abhorrence of its socio-economic injustices is rendered in vertically polarized images: heavy decrepit capitalist oppressors against backdrops of lofty exhilarating landscapes of skyscrapers, aircraft, and elevated railroads, and insurgent children and workers against those same backgrounds. Anxieties about the Soviet emulation of American modernity and the potential compromise of ideological purity are staged in a variety of scenarios where division and discord occasioned by American importations achieve an ideologically correct resolution, in which people and objects experience epiphanies and achieve consciousness of their own place and function in the harmonious whole of the socialist civilization. These visual and narrative efforts to represent an aspirational Soviet modernity to their juvenile audience stand as particular manifestations of anxieties, in the era of the New Economic Policy and the first Five-Year Plan, about the backwardness of Russia and its dependence on the products of American capitalist modernity, and about the Soviet promise that collectivist socialist forces could produce a modernity that would match and then surpass America's.

NOTES

1 Rogger, "Amerikanizm and the Economic Development of Russia," 384.

2 Ball, *Imagining America*, 24.

3 Ibid., 23–33.

4 Ibid., 30–3.

5 Ibid., 26, 32. It is interesting to note that "Novaia Amerika" is the title of a 1913 poem by Alexander Blok about a future industrialized Russia. In 1921, Mayakovsky wrote these verses for an electrification campaign poster: "Just you wait, bourgeois! There will be New York in Tetiushi! There will be paradise in Shuy!" See Hasty and Fusso, *America through Russian Eyes*, 12; Rogger, "Amerikanizm and the Economic Development of Russia," 390.

6 Sawyer, "Shedding the White and Blue," 66.

7 A fixation with towering structures is seen in constructivist projects such as Tatlin's plans for the Monument to the Third International, in the later neoclassical plans for the unrealized Palace of the Soviets (designed to surpass the Empire State Building, then the world's tallest structure), and in the *vysotki* that would be built in Moscow in the 1940s and 1950s.

8 Ball, *Imagining America*, 37.

9 Hasty and Fusso, *America through Russian Eyes*, 12–13.

10 Ginzburg, "Mezhdunarodnyi front sovremennoi arkhitektury," 41–6.

11 Lopatin, "Gorod neboskrebov i gorod-sad," 31–2; Globa-Mikhailenko, "Pishcha budushchego," 20–1.

12 Trotsky, *O zadachakh derevenskoi molodezhi*, 15–19.

13 For some representative examples, see Mislavskii, *Dneprostroi*, 14–20; Laptev, *Piatiletka*; Levidov, "Beda i vina odnogo amerikantsa," 16–17.

14 Barto, *Dom i domishko*, 9.

15 Ibid., 8–9.

16 "Форд в поля бросает глянец, / по дороге вьется пыль, / завернул американец, / осадив автомобиль. / — Здравствуйте, родные братцы! / Хоть внушают вам восторг / небоскребы и Нью-Йорк, / но нетрудно разобраться, / что, как прочие раобчие, / за работой дни и ночи мы / тянем каторжный свой срок." ("The Ford casts its gleam into the fields / dust swirls along the road / an American has swerved up, / having hit the breaks on his automobile. / Greetings, my brothers! / While well you may be filled with awe/ for skyscrapers and New York, / it's not hard to see, / that, like all other workers, / our work that continues

day and night / is the never-ending sentence we serve"). Here "vostorg" (awe or amazement) is the lynchpin rhyme linking "N'iu-Iork" and "katorzhnyi svoi srok" (hard-labour sentence), used here as a trope to characterize the exploitation of workers. In another book from the early 1920s, the *N'iu–Iork*/*vostorg* rhyme pair emphasizing the rapture excited by the sight of the ultra-modern American metropolis is immediately qualified by language of oppression, as the young protagonist is nearly "flattened" by the automobiles in New York City: "Кто не взглянет на Нью-Йорк, / От него придет в восторг. / Облака боятся, чтобы / Не задеть за небоскребы, / А внизу — автомобили / Гришку чуть не раздавили." ("Anyone who sees New York, / Is bound to be amazed. / The very clouds are afraid / To catch themselves on the skyscrapers, / But down below the automobiles / Nearly flattened Grisha") Gralitsa, *Detskii internatsional*, 24; Krandievskaya, *Amerika*.

17 For a representative sample, see Ivanter, *Zheleznye puteshestvenniki*; Krandevskaya, *Amerika*; Lesnaia, *Dzhimmi Dzhoi*; Mayakovsky, *V. Maiakovskii – Detiam*; Mitchell, *Neboskreb*; Shvarts, *Kino-zagadki*; Simonov, *Puteshestvie Charli*.

18 See figures 16.1 and 16.6 and also Ivanter, *Zheleznye puteshestvenniki*, 3; Shvarts, *Kino-zagadki*; Simonov, *Puteshestvie Charli*, 6.

19 Ivanter, *Zheleznye puteshestvenniki*, 4.

20 "Во двор пришли рабочие, / осмотрели, оглядели: / – Дом стоит еле-еле! / Потолок на кухне – / того гляди – рухнет" ("The workers entered the yard, / 'round they looked, they looked all around: / – The house is barely standing! / The ceiling in the kitchen / Might come crashing down at any moment"). Barto, *Dom i domishko*, 2.

21 "Стройся, / стройся, НОВЫЙ ДОМ! / Высокий, / высоченный! / Каменные стены! / Смотрит бабка, / смотрит дед. / — То ли верить, / то ли нет. / С каждым часом, / с каждым днем / вырастает НОВЫЙ / ДОМ. Он оделся / в леса, / он высоко / поднялся …/ ЧУДЕСА!" ("Rise, / rise, NEW HOME! / Tall, / towering! / Stone walls! / Grandma looks, / grandpa looks. / "Do we believe our eyes, / or not?" / With every hour / every day / rises / the NEW / HOME. It is clad / in scaffolding, / it has risen / tall… / MIRACLES!"). Ibid., 6.

22 "Кто это на улице / встал столбом? / Стоит на дом любуется: — ВОТ ЭТО ДОМ! / Дом из камня высечен. / Уступы — этажи. / — Вот, берите тысячи, / я хочу тут жить! / — Ступай себе, / дружища, / куда глядят / глаза, / Не купишь / дом - / за тыщи / его купить / нельзя! / Для нас, / для наших братьев -/ для тех, / кто силу тратит, / построен / этот/ ДОМ" ("Who's that there on the street / stopped dead in his tracks? / He stands amazed by the building: 'NOW THAT'S A HOME! / A building carved out of stone. / Not mountain ledges, but floors!' / 'Please, take my thousands, / I want to live here!' / 'Move along, / chum, / beat it! / You won't buy / this buliding / with your thousands / it can't / be bought! / For us, / for our brothers / for those / who work, for us / this / home/ was built'"). Ibid., 8–9.

23 See figures 16.10–16.12. See also Zilov, *Gorodskaia ulitsa*; Molchanov, *Kol'ka i Lenin*, 5; Saksonskaia, *Mamin most*; Mayakovsky, *Miud*, 10; Emden, *Pesnia o mame*; Neverov, *Revoliutsiia, rasskazy*, 4.

24 See figures 16.3, 16.10, and 16.13. See also Zilov, *Gorodskaia ulitsa*; Emden, *Pesnia o mame*.

25 See figure 16.14. See also Levidov, "Beda i vina odnogo amerikantsa," 16; Kapulin, "Brigadir moego serdtsa," 22–3; Mayakovsky, *Kem byt'*, 7; Gastev, *Iunost' idi!*, 42; Mayakovsky, *Miud*, 10; Barto, *Dom i domishko*, 5–6.

26 See figures 16.12 and 16.14. See also Meksin, *Stroika*, 5, 7; Meksin, *Stroika: odinnadtsat' pesenok*, 6–7.

27 See figures 16.2, 16.9, and 16.12. See also Zilov, *Gorodskaia ulitsa*.

28 Kapulin, "Brigadir moego serdtsa," 23; Saksonskaia, *Mamin most*; Meksin, *Stroika*, 5, 7; Meksin, *Stroika: odinnadtsat' pesenok*, 6–7.

29 Mitchell, *Here and Now Story Book.*
30 Interestingly, the "Boris" stories follow a young immigrant Russian boy living in New York
    City as he explores the marvels of his new ultra-modern urban environment. In these stories,
    Russia is presented as an entirely rural, almost idyllic, country. Boris's provenance from such
    a place motivates a sort of wide-eyed astonishment at everything he encounters in New York:
    skyscrapers, elevated trains, subways, cars, electric lights. This, in turn, serves as a device to
    create a fresh perspective on and stimulate curiosity about these features of New York's urban
    landscape in juvenile readers for whom they would have been far more familiar sights.
31 Steiner, "Mirror Images," 208.
32 Ibid., 209; Mickenberg, "The New Generation," 113.
33 See the verse in note 21 above.
34 Molchanov, *Kol'ka i Lenin,* 4.
35 Tikhonov, *Sami,* 5.

BIBLIOGRAPHY

Avgnitsev, Nikolai. *Kak primus zakhotel fordom sdelat'sia.* 2nd ed. Leningrad: Raduga, 1927.
– *Spor mezhdu domami.* Ryazan: Druz'ia detei, 1925.
Ball, Allan M. *Imagining America. Influence and Images in Twentieth-Century Russia.* Lanham,
    MD: Rowman & Littlefield, 2003.
Barto, Agniia. *Dom i domishko.* Moscow: Rabochaia Moskva, 1930.
Emden, Esfir'. *Pesnia o mame.* Moscow: Gosudarstvennoe izdatel'stvo, 1930.
Gastev, Aleksei. *Iunost' idi!* Moscow: VTsSPS, 1923.
Ginzburg, Moisei. "Mezhdunarodnyi front sovremennoi arkhitektury." *Sovremennaia arkhitektura,*
    no. 2 (1926): 4–46.
Globa-Mikhailenko, N. "Pishcha budushchego," *Smena,* no. 18 (1925): 20–1.
Gralitsa, Iurii. *Detskii internatsional.* Moscow: Gosudarstvennoe izdatel'stvo, 1926.
Gurevich, Mikhail. *Kuznetskstroi: Sotsialisticheskii gigant.* Moscow: OGIZ; Gosudarstvennoe
    antireligioznoe izdatel'stvo, 1932.
Hasty, Olga Peters, and Susanne Fusso, eds. *America through Russian Eyes, 1874–1926.* New Haven,
    CT: Yale University Press, 1988.
Ivanter, Ben'iamin. *Zheleznye puteshestvenniki.* Moscow: Gosudarstvennoe izdatel'stvo, 1931.
Kapulin, Vladimir. "Brigadir moego serdtsa." *Smena,* no. 36 (1930): 22–3.
Krandievskaia, Natal'ia. *Amerika.* Vol. 1 of *Grishkiny puteshestvia: Veselye priklyucheniya v 6
    tomakh.* Illustrated by Ye. Kuttser. Berlin: Izdanie detskoi biblioteki "Nakanune," 1923.
Laptev, Aleksei. *Piatiletka: risunki i maket.* Moscow: Gosudarstvennoe izdatel'stvo, 1930.
Lesnaia, Lidiia. *Dzhimmi Dzhoi v gosti k pioneram: Skazka.* Leningrad: GIZ, 1925.
Levidov, Mikhail. "Beda i vina odnogo amerikantsa." *Smena* nos. 23/24 (1930): 16–17.
Lopatin, P.I. "Gorod neboskrebov i gorod-sad." *Smena,* no. 10 (1924): 31–2.
Mayakovsky, Vladimir. *Kem byt'.* Moscow: OGIZ, Molodaia gvardiia, 1932.
– *Miud.* Moscow: Gosudarstvennoe izdatel'stvo, 1930.
– *V. Maiakovskii – Detiam.* Moscow: OGIZ, Molodaia gvardiia, 1931.
Meksin, Iakov. *Stroika.* Moscow: GIZ, 1930.
– *Stroika: odinnadtsat' pesenok.* Moscow: Gosudarstvennoe izdatel'stvo, 1926.
Mickenberg, Julia. "The New Generation and the New Russia: Modern Childhood as Collective
    Fantasy." *American Quarterly* 62, no. 1 (March 2010): 113.

Mislavskii, Nikolai. *Dneprostroi*. Illustrated by Vera Lantsetti. 2nd ed. Moscow: Gosudarstvennoe izdatel'stvo, 1930.

Mitchell, Lucy Sprague. *Here and Now Story Book, Two- to Seven-Year-Olds*. New York: E.P. Dutton, 1921.

– *Neboskreb*. Moscow: Gosudarstvennoe izdatel'stvo, 1930.

Molchanov, Ivan. *Kol'ka i Lenin: rasskaz dlia detei*. Moscow: Gosudarstvennoe izdatel'stvo, 1927.

Neverov, Aleksandr. *Revoliutsiia, rasskazy*. Moscow: GIZ, 1930.

Pavlovich, Nadezhda. *Bol'shevik Tom*. Leningrad: Borkgauz-Efron, 1925.

Rogger, Hans. "Amerikanizm and the Economic Development of Russia." *Comparative Studies in Society and History* 23, no. 3 (1981): 382–420. https://doi.org/10.1017/S0010417500013426.

Saksonskaia, Nina. *Mamin most*. Moscow: OGIZ, Molodaia gvardiia, 1933.

Sawyer, Benjamin J. "Shedding the White and Blue: American Migration and Soviet Dreams in the Era of the New Economic Policy." *Ab Imperio* 1 (2013): 65–84.

Shvarts, Evgenii. *Kino-zagadki*. Leningrad: Gosudarstvennoe izdatel'stvo, 1930.

Simonov, Nikolai. *Puteshestvie Charli*. Moscow: Gosizdat, 1924.

Steiner, Evgenii. "Mirror Images: On Soviet-Western Reflections in Children's Books of the 1920s and 1930s." In *Children's Literature and the Avant-Garde*, edited by Elina Drucker and Bettina Kümmerling-Meibauer, 189–216. Philadelphia: John Benjamins, 2015.

Tikhonov, Nikolai. *Sami*. Leningrad: Gosudarstvennoe izdatel'stvo, 1924.

Trotsky, Lev. *O zadachakh derevenskoi molodezhi i O novom byte*. Moscow: Novaia Moskva, 1924.

Zilov, Lev. *Gorodskaia ulitsa*. 2nd ed. Moscow: G.F. Mirimanov, 1929.

ILLUSTRATION CREDITS

Introduction. Fig. 0.1: Reproduced courtesy of the Cotsen Children's Library, Department of Rare Books and Special Collections, Princeton University Library; Fig. 0.2: Public domain; Fig. 0.3: Reproduced courtesy of the Cotsen Children's Library, Department of Rare Books and Special Collections, Princeton University Library; Figs. 0.4–0.18: Public domain; Figs. 0.19–0.21: Reproduced courtesy of the Cotsen Children's Library, Department of Rare Books and Special Collections, Princeton University Library; Figs. 0.22–0.25: Public domain.

Part I. Fig. I.1: Reproduced courtesy of the Cotsen Children's Library, Department of Rare Books and Special Collections, Princeton University.

Chapter 1. Fig. 1.1: Reproduced courtesy of the Cotsen Children's Library, Department of Rare Books and Special Collections, Princeton University Library; Fig. 1.2: University of Southern California, USC Digital Library; Figs. 1.3–1.13: Reproduced courtesy of the Cotsen Children's Library, Department of Rare Books and Special Collections, Princeton University Library; Fig. 1.14: Public domain; Fig. 1.15: Reproduced courtesy of the Cotsen Children's Library, Department of Rare Books and Special Collections, Princeton University Library.

Chapter 2. Fig. 2.1: Alisa Poret, family; Fig. 2.2: Collection of the State Museum of Arts named after A. Kasteev, Republic of Kazakhstan; Figs. 2.3–2.4: *October*, Dir. S. Eisenstein (Sovkino, USSR, 1927); Fig. 2.5: Alisa Poret, family; Fig. 2.6: *The Birth of a Nation*, Dir. D.W. Griffith (Epoch Producing Co., David W. Griffith Corp., USA, 1915); Figs. 2.7–2.9: Alisa Poret, family; Fig. 2.10: *Strike*, Dir. S. Eisenstein (Proletkul't, USSR, 1925); Fig. 2.11: Alisa Poret, family; Figs. 2.12–2.14: *White Eagle*, Dir. I. Protazanov (Mezhrabpomfilm, USSR, 1928); Fig. 2.15: Alisa Poret, family; Figs. 2.16–2.17: *Strike*, Dir. S. Eisenstein (Proletkul't, USSR, 1925); Fig. 2.18: Public domain; Fig. 2.19: Alisa Poret, family; Fig. 2.20: Satz, Autograph: NE 86 (Beethoven-Haus Bonn); Fig. 2.21: *Arsenal*, Dir. A. Dovzhenko (Odesskaia kinofabrika, USSR, 1929); Fig. 2.22: *Battleship Potemkin*, Dir. S. Eisenstein (Mosfilm, USSR, 1925); Figs. 2.23–2.24: Alisa Poret, family; Fig. 2.25: Collection of A. Esipovich-Roginskaya (St. Petersburg), used with the owner's permission; Fig. 2.26: Alisa Poret, family; Fig. 2.27: Wikimedia, public domain; Fig. 2.28: Alisa Poret, family; Fig. 2.29: From the catalogue Chekhab-Abudaya, Mounia. *Hajj – The Journey through Art: Exhibition Album* (Milan: Skira, 2013); Fig. 2.30: Alisa Poret, family; Fig. 2.31: *Arsenal*, Dir. A. Dovzhenko (Odesskaia kinofabrika, USSR, 1929); Fig. 2.32: *Strike*, Dir. S. Eisenstein (Proletkul't, USSR, 1925);

526   Illustration Credits

Fig. 2.33: *October*, Dir. S. Eisenstein (Sovkino, USSR, 1927); Figs. 2.34–2.35: Alisa Poret, family; Fig. 2.36: *October*, Dir. S. Eisenstein (Sovkino, USSR, 1927).

Chapter 3. Fig. 3.1: Russian State Library, Moscow. Reproduced with permission of the estate of Arkadii Shaikhet; Figs. 3.2–3.5: Russian State Library, Moscow; Fig. 3.6: Film frame enlargement courtesy of Barbara Würm; Figs. 3.7–3.11: Russian State Library, Moscow.

Chapter 4. Figs. 4.1–4.6: Public domain; Figs. 4.7–4.8: Archive of A. Rodchenko and V. Stepanova, Moscow, courtesy of Aleksandr Lavrentiev; Fig. 4.9: Reproduced courtesy of the Cotsen Children's Library, Department of Rare Books and Special Collections, Princeton University Library; Fig. 4.10: Archive of A. Rodchenko and V. Stepanova, Moscow, courtesy of Aleksandr Lavrentiev; Fig. 4.11: Public domain.

Chapter 5. Figs. 5.1–5.4: Reproduced courtesy of the Cotsen Children's Library, Department of Rare Books and Special Collections, Princeton University Library; Fig. 5.5: Danish Pedagogical University Library, Emdrup; Fig. 5.6: Reproduced courtesy of Russian State Children's Library; Figs. 5.7–5.8: Reproduced courtesy of the Cotsen Children's Library, Department of Rare Books and Special Collections, Princeton University Library; Fig. 5.9: Danish Pedagogical University Library, Emdrup, public domain; Fig. 5.10: Reproduced courtesy of the Cotsen Children's Library, Department of Rare Books and Special Collections, Princeton University Library.

Part II. Fig. II.1: Reproduced courtesy of the Cotsen Children's Library, Department of Rare Books and Special Collections, Princeton University Library.

Chapter 6. Fig. 6.1: Courtesy of the National Library of Russia; Figs. 6.2–6.8: Reproduced courtesy of the Cotsen Children's Library, Department of Rare Books and Special Collections, Princeton University Library; Fig. 6.9: Courtesy of the Russian State Electronic Children's Library, Moscow; Figs. 6.10–6.11: Reproduced courtesy of the Cotsen Children's Library, Department of Rare Books and Special Collections, Princeton University Library; Fig. 6.12: Reproduced courtesy of the National Library of Russia.

Chapter 7. Figs. 7.1–7.8 and figs. 7.10–7.12: Reproduced courtesy of the Cotsen Children's Library, Department of Rare Books and Special Collections, Princeton University Library; Fig. 7.9: Courtesy of the National Library of Russia.

Chapter 8. Figs. 8.1–8.3: Courtesy of the National Library of Russia; Figs. 8.4–8.5: Public domain; Fig. 8.6: Courtesy of the National Library of Russia; Figs. 8.7–8.15: Reproduced courtesy of the Cotsen Children's Library, Department of Rare Books and Special Collections, Princeton University Library.

Chapter 9. Figs. 9.1–9.6: Reproduced courtesy of the Belinskii Regional Library, Ekaterinburg; Fig. 9.7: Courtesy of the National Library of Russia; Figs. 9.8–9.18: Reproduced courtesy of the Belinskii Regional Library, Ekaterinburg.

Chapter 10. Fig. 10.1: Reproduced courtesy of the Cotsen Children's Library, Department of Rare Books and Special Collections, Princeton University Library; Fig. 10.2: Public Domain; Figs. 10.3–10.4: Reproduced courtesy of the Cotsen Children's Library, Department of Special Collections, Princeton University Library; Fig. 10.5: Public domain; Figs. 10.6–10.8: Reproduced courtesy of the Cotsen Children's Library, Department of Special Collections, Princeton University Library; Fig. 10.9: Public domain.

Chapter 11. Fig. 11.1: Reproduced courtesy of the Cotsen Children's Library, Department of Rare Books and Special Collections, Princeton University Library; Fig. 11.2: Blue Mountain Project, Princeton University Library; Figs. 11.3–11.6: Reproduced courtesy of the Cotsen Children's Library, Department of Rare Books and Special Collections, Princeton University Library; Figs. 11.7–11.10: The Russian State Library, Moscow; Figs. 11.11–11.14: Reproduced courtesy of the Cotsen Children's Library, Department of Rare Books and Special Collections, Princeton University Library; Fig. 11.15: Copyright 2019 Artists Rights Society (ARS), New York.

Part III. Fig. III.1: Reproduced courtesy of the Cotsen Children's Library, Department of Rare Books and Special Collections, Princeton University Library.

Chapter 12. Figs. 12.1–12.2: Reproduced courtesy of the Cotsen Children's Library, Department of Special Collections, Princeton University Library; Fig. 12.3: Yale University Art Museum, public domain; Fig. 12.4: Reproduced courtesy of the Cotsen Children's Library, Department of Special Collections, Princeton University Library; Figs. 12.5–12.9: Reproduced courtesy of the Cotsen Children's Library, Department of Special Collections, Princeton University Library; Fig. 12.10: Harvard's Houghton Library Collection, no release required by library policy, copyright expired; Fig. 12.11: Public domain; Figs. 12.12–12.13: Reproduced courtesy of the Cotsen Children's Library, Department of Special Collections, Princeton University Library.

Chapter 13. Fig. 13.1: Public domain; Figs. 13.2–13.3: Reproduced courtesy of the Cotsen Children's Library, Department of Special Collections, Princeton University Library; Fig. 13.4: Reproduced courtesy of Russian State Children's Library; Figs. 13.5–13.6: Reproduced courtesy of the Cotsen Children's Library, Department of Special Collections, Princeton University Library; Fig. 13.7: Russian State Children's Library, open access; Figs. 13.8–13.11: Reproduced courtesy of the Cotsen Children's Library, Department of Special Collections, Princeton University Library.

Chapter 14. Figs. 14.1–14.2: Reproduced courtesy of the Cotsen Children's Library, Department of Special Collections, Princeton University Library; Fig. 14.3: Public domain; Figs. 14.4–14.6: Public domain; Figs. 14.7–14.8: Reproduced courtesy of the Cotsen Children's Library, Department of Special Collections, Princeton University Library; Figs. 14.9–14.11: Reproduced courtesy of Russian State Children's Library.

Chapter 15. Figs. 15.1–15.3: Reproduced courtesy of the Cotsen Children's Library, Department of Special Collections, Princeton University Library; Fig. 15.4: Public domain; Figs. 15.5–15.11: Reproduced courtesy of the Cotsen Children's Library, Department of Special Collections, Princeton University Library.

Chapter 16. Figs. 16.1–16.7: Reproduced courtesy of the Cotsen Children's Library, Department of Special Collections, Princeton University Library; Fig. 16.8: Public domain; Figs. 16.9–16.16: Reproduced courtesy of the Cotsen Children's Library, Department of Special Collections, Princeton University Library.

CONTRIBUTORS

Marina Balina is Isaac Funk Professor and Professor of Russian Studies Emerita at Illinois Wesleyan University. The focus of her scholarship is on historical and theoretical aspects of twentieth-century Russian children's literature. She is editor or co-editor of eleven volumes, including *Endquote: SotsArt Literature and Soviet Empire Style* (2000); *Politicizing Magic: Russian and Soviet Fairy Tales* (2005); *Russian Children's Literature and Culture* (2008); *Petrified Utopia: Happiness Soviet Style* (2009); *Constructing Childhood: Literature, History, Anthropology* (2011); *Cambridge Companion of the 20th Century Russian Literature* (2011); *To Kill Charskaia: Politics and Aesthetics in Soviet Children's Literature of the 1920s and 1930s* (2014); and *Hans Christian Andersen and Russia* (2020). Together with Larissa Rudova, she is a founding member of the international research group ChEEER (Childhood in Eastern Europe, Eurasia, and Russia), affiliated with ASEEES. The group unites scholars dedicated to the study and promotion of children's literature of the former Eastern Bloc.

Aleksandar Bošković is a lecturer in Bosnian/Croatian/Serbian in the Department of Slavic Languages and Literatures at Columbia University. His research interests include Russian and East Central European avant-garde literature and visual culture, Yugoslav and post-Yugoslav literature and cinema, and literary theory. He has published essays on issues of digital mnemonics, Yugonostalgia and cultural memory, avant-garde photobooks, Serbian poetry and post-Yugoslav fiction, Künstlerroman, and the theory of possible worlds. He is the author of *The Poetic Humor in Vasko Popa's Oeuvre* (2008) and the exhibition catalogue *Temporary Monument: Photomontages for Mayakovsky's poem "To the Workers of Kursk" by Yuri Rozhkov* (The Harriman Institute, 2015). He is currently working on several projects, including an anthology of Yugoslav Zenithist publications from the 1920s (with Steven Teref) and a monograph on early Soviet cinépoetry.

Kirill Chunikhin is a senior lecturer at the Higher School of Economics, St. Petersburg, Russia, with a PhD from Jacobs University, Bremen. Currently, he is working on his first monograph, provisionally entitled *Shared Images of the Cold War: American Art in the Soviet Union*. This book will explore how American art became subject to competing policies of representation both in the Soviet Union and the United States during the late 1940s to the mid-1960s. Chunikhin has been awarded multiple fellowships, including a Terra Foundation Predoctoral Fellowship at the Smithsonian American Art Museum and a Pontica Magna Fellowship at the New Europe College in Bucharest. His research interests include American-Soviet cultural contacts, Soviet children's literature, and the history of Soviet materiality. His most recent project on the Soviet fate of Cubism is forthcoming in *The Russian Review*.

Alexey Golubev is an assistant professor of Russian history and digital humanities at the University of Houston. During the academic year of 2020–1, he is serving as the Joy Foundation Fellow at the Radcliffe Institute for Advanced Study, Harvard University. His most recent book, *The Things of Life: Materiality in Late Soviet Russia* (2020), is a social and cultural history of material objects and spaces during the late socialist era. His first book, co-authored with Irina Takala, *The Search for a Socialist El: Finnish Immigration from the United States and Canada* in the 1930s (2014), addressed the circulation of ideas, objects, and people within the global socialist movement during the Great Depression. His work has appeared in such academic journals as *Kritika: Explorations in Russian and Eurasian History*, *The Soviet and Post-Soviet Review*, *Ab Imperio*, *Rethinking Marxism*, *Cahiers du monde russe*, *Canadian Slavonic Papers*, and *Novoe literaturnoe obozrenie*.

Helena Goscilo, a professor of Slavic at Ohio State University, has written extensively on gender and culture, with an emphasis on the contemporary period, though her publications encompass analyses of culture from the eighteenth to the twenty-first century, with topics ranging across art, music, film, folklore, graphics, literature, gender politics, and celebrity studies. She recently has academized her passion for all modes of visual expression, with a current focus on film, graphics, and art. She has authored or edited more than twenty volumes and journal issues, including *TNT: The Explosive World of Tatyana Tolstaya's Fiction* (1996); *Dehexing Sex* (1996); *Russian Culture of the 1990s* (2000; ed.); *Preserving Petersburg: History, Memory, Nostalgia* (2008; co-ed. with Stephen Norris); *Cinepaternity: Fathers and Sons in Soviet and Post-Soviet Film* (2010; co-ed. with Yana Hashamova); *Reflections and Refractions: The Mirror in Russian Culture* (2010; ed.), *Putin as Celebrity and Cultural Icon* (2012; ed.); *Fade from Red: Screening the Cold War Ex-enemy, 1990–2005* (2014; co-authored with Margaret Goscilo); and *Russian Aviation, Space Flight, and Visual Culture* (2017; co-ed. with Vlad Strukov). Her current monographs are *Graphic Ideology: The Soviet Poster from Stalin to Yeltsin* and a study of current Polish female directors, tentatively titled *Film's Feisty Femmes*. The volume *Burning Questions, Cool Lens: Polish Film Today*, co-written with Beth Holmgren, is scheduled for publication in 2021.

Thomas Keenan is Slavic, East European, and Eurasian studies librarian at Princeton University, where he oversees the development of one North America's largest research collections for the study of Eastern Europe and the territories of the Former Soviet Union. He holds a PhD in Slavic Languages and Literatures (Yale). At Princeton, one of Thomas's principal foci is the development of the library's collections in Russian visual culture. This includes collaboration with curator Andrea Immel on the expansion of the Cotsen Children's Library's holdings in early Soviet illustrated literature for children. He is current chair of the European Studies Section of the Association of College and Research Libraries and serves on the Steering Committee of Princeton's Slavic Digital Humanities Working Group, and is actively involved in efforts to use contemporary digital information technologies to transmit the riches of Slavic, East European, and Eurasian collections in different media. His current book project is an examination of the productivity of the generic matrix of Dante Alighieri's *Divine Comedy* in Russian literature of the nineteenth and twentieth centuries.

Michael Kunichika is an associate professor in the Russian Department at Amherst College and a contributing faculty member of the Film and Media Studies Department. His book *"Our Native Antiquity": Archaeology and Aesthetics in the Culture of Russian Modernism* (2015) received an honourable mention for the ASEEES Wayne S. Vucinich Book Prize. Kunichika's research focuses primary on Russian and Soviet modernism, critical theory, and cinema studies, particularly of the silent period. He is currently working on two books: the first considers anti-imperialist aesthetics in the cinema and cultural criticism of the 1920s; the second examines prehistory in late socialism as it emerged as an object of study in such disciplines as archaeology, art history, and semiotics. Along with these studies, his published or forthcoming work includes articles in *Ab Imperio, Studies in Russian and Soviet Cinema,* and *RES: Anthropology and Aesthetics.*

Daniil Leiderman teaches art history in the Department of Visualization at Texas A&M University. In 2016, he defended his PhD dissertation, entitled "Moscow Conceptualism and 'Shimmering': Authority, Anarchism, and Space," at Princeton University. His dissertation investigated the Moscow conceptualists, a circle of experimental artists and writers that emerged in Moscow's unofficial artistic scene in the early 1970s in the context of nonconformism, tracing their development of the critical strategy called "shimmering" and its relationship to contemporary post-Soviet and post-Crimean artistic resistance. Most recently, he has been working on the representation of Eastern Europe and Russia in contemporary video games and related media.

Yuri Leving is University Research Professor in the Department of Russian Studies, Dalhousie University. He was an Alexander von Humboldt Senior Research Fellow at Heidelberg University and a research fellow at the American Academy in Rome and at the Aleksanteri Institute in Helsinki. Leving is the author of seven monographs and editor of six volumes of articles, including *Poetry in a Dead Loop (Mandelstam and Aviation)* (2021); *Joseph Brodsky in Rome* in three volumes (2020); *A Revolution of the Visible (2018); Marketing Literature and Posthumous Legacies* (2013); *Lolita: The Story of a Cover Girl – Vladimir Nabokov's Novel in Art and Design* (2013); and *Anatomy of a Short Story* (2012). He has published over a hundred scholarly articles on various aspects of Russian and comparative literature. He served as a commentator on the first authorized Russian edition of *The Collected Works of Vladimir Nabokov* in five volumes, and was the curator for the exhibition "Nabokov's Lolita: 1955–2005" in Washington, DC, which celebrated the fiftieth anniversary of the publication of *Lolita*. He is the founding editor of the *Nabokov Online Journal.* The American Association of Teachers of Slavic and East European Languages (AATSEEL) named him the 2017 recipient of the award for Outstanding Contribution to Scholarship.

Maria Litovskaya is a senior researcher at the Institute of History and Archeology of the Ural Division of the Russian Academy of Sciences and a professor at the Ural Federal University (Ekaterinburg, Russia). She is co-editor of the academic journal *Detskie chtenia* (Children's Reading), which focuses on the history of the genre. She has authored or co-authored several books on Soviet and post-Soviet literature, as well as about 150 essays on Russian culture of the twentieth and the twenty-first centuries.

Stephen M. Norris is Walter E. Havighurst Professor of Russian History and director of the Havighurst Center for Russian and Post-Soviet Studies at Miami University in Ohio. His scholarship focuses on Russian visual history, nationhood, propaganda, film, and popular images. He is the author of *A War of Images: Russian Popular Prints, Wartime Culture, and National Identity, 1812–1945* (2006) and *Blockbuster History in the New Russia: Movies, Memory, Patriotism* (2008), both of which discuss Russian cultural history. He is the editor or co-editor of five more books on Russian history and culture, including *Russia's People of Empire: Life Stories from Eurasia, 1500 to the Present* (2012, with Willard Sunderland) and *The City in Russian Culture* (2018, with Pavel Lyssakov). He is currently writing a biography of the Soviet political caricaturist Boris Efimov.

Serguei Alex. Oushakine is a professor of anthropology and Slavic languages and literatures at Princeton University. His research interests include studies of such early Soviet intellectual and aesthetic movements as Formalism and Constructivism; he is also interested in exploring post-Soviet development in newly independent states through the lens of postcolonial theory. He has published on nostalgia, affect, memory, and trauma. He authored the award-winning book *The Patriotism of Despair: Nation, War, and Loss in Russia* (2009), and has edited or co-edited multiple books as well as issues of journals. His latest book, *A Medium for the Masses: Photomontage and the Optical Turn in Early Soviet Russia,* was published in 2020 by the Garage Museum of Contemporary Art in Moscow.

Kevin M.F. Platt is Edmund J. and Louise W. Kahn Term Professor in the Humanities and Professor of Russian and East European studies at the University of Pennsylvania. He works on representations of Russian history, Russian historiography, history and memory in Russia, Russian lyric poetry, and global post-Soviet Russian cultures. He is the author of *Terror and Greatness: Ivan and Peter as Russian Myths* (2011) and *History in a Grotesque Key: Russian Literature and the Idea of Revolution* (1997), the co-editor (with David Brandenberger) of *Epic Revisionism: Russian History and Literature as Stalinist Propaganda* (2006), and the editor of *Global Russian Cultures* (2019). He has also edited and contributed translations to a number of books of Russian poetry in English translation, most recently *F Letter: New Russian Feminist Poetry* (2020). His current projects include a study of contemporary Russian culture in Latvia titled *Near Abroad* and an investigation of twentieth-century global cultural exchange.

Birgitte Beck Pristed is an associate professor in Russian studies at the Department of Global Studies, Aarhus University, Denmark. She holds a PhD from the Johannes-Gutenberg-University of Mainz, Germany. She is author of an illustrated monograph on contemporary Russian book design and print culture, *The New Russian Book: A Graphic Cultural History* (2017). Her main research areas are print and media history, and visual and material cultures of the Soviet and post-Soviet eras, with a second strand in Russian children's culture. Her current research project focuses on the media history of Soviet paper. Pristed was previously a Danish teacher at the Maxim Gorky Literary Institute in Moscow and a curator in the Workers' Museum in Copenhagen.

Katherine M.H. Reischl is an assistant professor in Slavic languages and literatures at Princeton University. Her research interests lie primarily at the intersections of literature, art, and culture in twentieth-century Russia, with particular attention to questions of authorship and problems of mediation. She has published on Soviet children's book illustration and photography, and is the author of the monograph, *Photographic Literacy: Cameras in the Hands of Russian Authors* (2018). She is the co-project lead on a large-scale digital humanities project at Princeton University, "Playing Soviet: The Visual Language of Early Soviet Children's Books."

Larissa Rudova is Yale B. and Lucille D. Griffith Professor in Modern Languages and Professor of German and Russian at Pomona College, Claremont, California. She is the author of two monographs on Boris Pasternak, *Pasternak's Short Fiction and the Cultural Vanguard* (1994) and *Understanding Boris Pasternak* (1997). She has co-edited a volume of scholarly articles, *Russian Children's Literature and Culture* (2008), as well as three thematic clusters on children's and young adult literature and culture for *Slavic and East European Studies Journal*, *The Russian Review*, and *Filoteknos: Anthropology of Childhood*. Together with Marina Balina, she is a founding member of the international research group, ChEEER (Childhood in Eastern Europe, Eurasia, and Russia), affiliated with ASEEES. Her numerous articles have been published in American, Canadian, European, and Russian journals and scholarly volumes. Her research interests include modern Russian literature and popular culture; cinema studies; gender studies; children's and young adult literature; Russian material culture; fashion studies; and representations of childhood. She is currently co-editing and contributing to a volume of scholarly articles, *Childhood in/as History and Story*.

Marina Sokolovskaia teaches courses on the arts of the twentieth century and on contemporary art life in Ekaterinburg at Ural Federal University. She was chief librarian at Sverdlovsk Regional Library and exhibition curator at the Metenkov's House Museum of Photography. Since 2016, she has been the head of the Exhibitions Department at the Boris Yeltsin Museum, collaborating with art galleries and museums in Ekaterinburg, Perm, and Chelyabinsk. Her main research interests include Soviet culture, children's drawing, the history of the book in the twentieth century, visual arts of the twentieth century, and museum studies.

Sara Pankenier Weld is an associate professor of Russian and comparative literature at the University of California, Santa Barbara, where she specializes in interdisciplinary research on childhood in Russian literature, art, film, and theory, as well as in comparative perspective. She is the author of *Voiceless Vanguard: The Infantilist Aesthetic of the Russian Avant-Garde*, an interdisciplinary study of avant-garde literature, art, and theory (2014), which received the International Research Society for Children's Literature Book Award (IRSCL) in 2015. She also published a chapter on the avant-garde infantile in the volume *Children's Literature and the Avant-Garde*, edited by Elina Druker and Bettina Kümmerling-Meibauer. Her most recent book, *An Ecology of the Russian Avant-Garde Picturebook* (2018), offers recontextualizing word and image analysis of early Soviet picture books in the context of censorship. Other publications related to childhood, infancy, children's literature, and picture books include articles and book chapters on works by various Russian authors and illustrators. Her research interests include Russian literature, comparative literature, and Scandinavian literature; avant-garde literature, art, and theory; childhood and modernism; word and image; and children's literature and picture books.

Erika Wolf is Professor and Dean of Faculty in the School of Advanced Studies at the University of Tyumen (Russia). She is an art historian with particular interest in modernism and modernity, propaganda, cross-cultural representation, illustrated magazines, and Soviet visual culture, especially the history and criticism of photography. She has received fellowships from the Fulbright Foundation, the International Research Exchange Board, the Center for Advanced Studies of the Visual Arts, the Kennan Institute, and the Harriman Institute. She has contributed to exhibition projects at international art museums, including the Reina Sofia in Madrid and the Art Institute of Chicago. In 2012, she made extensive contributions to the Reina Sofia publication *The Worker Photography Movement (1926–1939): Essays and Documents*. She works closely with *the Ne boltai! Collection*, a private archive of twentieth-century political art. She has completed two books that draw extensively from this collection: *Koretsky: The Soviet Photo Poster* (2012) and *Aleksandr Zhitomirsky: Photomontage as a Weapon of World War II and the Cold War* (2016).

INDEX

STUDIES IN BOOK AND PRINT CULTURE

General Editor: Leslie Howsam

Janice Cavell, *Tracing the Connected Narrative: Arctic Exploration in British Print Culture, 1818–1860*

Elspeth Jajdelska, *Silent Reading and the Birth of the Narrator*

Martyn Lyons, *Reading Culture and Writing Practices in Nineteenth-Century France*

Robert A. Davidson, *Jazz Age Barcelona*

Gail Edwards and Judith Saltman, *Picturing Canada: A History of Canadian Children's Illustrated Books and Publishing*

Miranda Remnek, ed., *The Space of the Book: Print Culture in the Russian Social Imagination*

Adam Reed, *Literature and Agency in English Fiction Reading: A Study of the Henry Williamson Society*

Bonnie Mak, *How the Page Matters*

Eli MacLaren, *Dominion and Agency: Copyright and the Structuring of the Canadian Book Trade, 1867–1918*

Ruth Panofsky, *The Literary Legacy of the Macmillan Company of Canada: Making Books and Mapping Culture*

Archie L. Dick, *The Hidden History of South Africa's Book and Reading Cultures*

Darcy Cullen, ed., *Editors, Scholars, and the Social Text*

James J. Connolly, Patrick Collier, Frank Felsenstein, Kenneth R. Hall, and Robert Hall, eds, *Print Culture Histories Beyond the Metropolis*

Kristine Kowalchuk, *Preserving on Paper: Seventeenth-Century Englishwomen's Receipt Books*

Ian Hesketh, *Victorian Jesus: J.R. Seeley, Religion, and the Cultural Significance of Anonymity*

Kirsten MacLeod, *American Little Magazines of the Fin de Siècle: Art, Protest, and Cultural Transformation*

Emily Francomano, *The Prison of Love: Romance, Translation and the Book in the Sixteenth Century*

Kirk Melnikoff, *Elizabethan Publishing and the Makings of Literary Culture*

Amy Bliss Marshall, *Magazines and the Making of Mass Culture in Japan*

Scott McLaren, *Pulpit, Press, and Politics: Methodists and the Market for Books in Upper Canada*

Ruth Panofsky, *Toronto Trailblazers: Women in Canadian Publishing*

Martyn Lyons, *The Typewriter Century: A Cultural History of Writing Practices*

Marina Balina and Serguei Alex. Oushakine, eds, *The Pedagogy of Images: Depicting Communism for Children*